FOUNDATION PRESS

Pension and Employee Benefit Statutes and Regulations

SELECTED SECTIONS

2012

By

DAVID A. PRATT
Professor of Law
Albany Law School

FOUNDATION PRESS
2012
THOMSON REUTERS™

1 New York Plaza, 34th Floor
New York, NY 10004
Phone Toll Free 1–877–888–1330
Fax 646–424–5201
foundation–press.com

ISBN 978–1–59941–971–8

Mat #41126965

To Nick, Sarah and Sam, with much love

ACKNOWLEDGMENTS

Thanks to Bruce Wolk, who prepared the 2010 and earlier editions of this book; to Theresa Colbert, for her expert legal assistance; and to Ariele Doolittle, for her superb research assistance.

Table of Contents

INTERNAL REVENUE CODE OF 1986

EMPLOYEE RETIREMENT INCOME SECURITY ACT OF 1974

AGE DISCRIMINATION IN EMPLOYMENT ACT OF 1967

AMERICANS WITH DISABILITIES ACT OF 1990

ERISA REORGANIZATION PLAN

TREASURY REGULATIONS

AGE DISCRIMINATION REGULATIONS

ERISA REGULATIONS

INTERNAL REVENUE CODE OF 1986

§ 25B. Elective deferrals and IRA contributions by certain individuals.

(a) Allowance of credit—In the case of an eligible individual, there shall be allowed as a credit against the tax imposed by this subtitle for the taxable year an amount equal to the applicable percentage of so much of the qualified retirement savings contributions of the eligible individual for the taxable year as do not exceed $2,000.

(b) Applicable percentage—For purposes of this section—

(1) Joint returns—In the case of a joint return, the applicable percentage is—

(A) if the adjusted gross income of the taxpayer is not over $30,000, 50 percent,

(B) if the adjusted gross income of the taxpayer is over $30,000 but not over $32,500, 20 percent,

(C) if the adjusted gross income of the taxpayer is over $32,500 but not over $50,000, 10 percent, and

(D) if the adjusted gross income of the taxpayer is over $50,000, zero percent.

(2) Other returns—In the case of—

(A) a head of household, the applicable percentage shall be determined under paragraph (1) except that such paragraph shall be applied by substituting for each dollar amount therein (as adjusted under paragraph (3)) a dollar amount equal to 75 percent of such dollar amount, and

(B) any taxpayer not described in paragraph (1) or subparagraph (A), the applicable percentage shall be determined under paragraph (1) except that such paragraph shall be applied by substituting for each dollar amount therein (as adjusted under paragraph (3)) a dollar amount equal to 50 percent of such dollar amount.

(3) Inflation adjustment—In the case of any taxable year beginning in a calendar year after 2006, each of the dollar amounts in paragraph (1) shall be increased by an amount equal to—

(A) such dollar amount, multiplied by

(B) the cost-of-living adjustment determined under section 1(f)(3) for the calendar year in which the taxable year begins, determined by substituting "calendar year 2005" for "calendar year 1992" in subparagraph (B) thereof.

Any increase determined under the preceding sentence shall be rounded to the nearest multiple of $500.

(c) Eligible individual—For purposes of this section—

(1) In general—The term "eligible individual" means any individual if such individual has attained the age of 18 as of the close of the taxable year.

(2) Dependents and full-time students not eligible—The term "eligible individual" shall not include—

(A) any individual with respect to whom a deduction under section 151 is allowed to another taxpayer for a taxable year beginning in the calendar year in which such individual's taxable year begins, and

(B) any individual who is a student (as defined in section 152(f)(2)).

(d) Qualified retirement savings contributions—For purposes of this section—

(1) In general—The term "qualified retirement savings contributions" means, with respect to any taxable year, the sum of—

(A) the amount of the qualified retirement contributions (as defined in section 219(e)) made by the eligible individual,

(B) the amount of—

(i) any elective deferrals (as defined in section 402(g)(3)) of such individual, and

(ii) any elective deferral of compensation by such individual under an eligible deferred compensation plan (as defined in section 457(b)) of an eligible employer described in section 457(e)(1)(A), and

(C) the amount of voluntary employee contributions by such individual to any qualified retirement plan (as defined in section 4974(c)).

(2) Reduction for certain distributions—

(A) In general—The qualified retirement savings contributions determined under paragraph (1) shall be reduced (but not below zero) by the aggregate distributions received by the individual during the testing period from any entity of a type to which contributions under paragraph (1) may be made. The preceding sentence shall not apply to the portion of any distribution which is not includible in gross income by reason of a trustee-to-trustee transfer or a rollover distribution.

(B) Testing period—For purposes of subparagraph (A), the testing period, with respect to a taxable year, is the period which includes—

(i) such taxable year,

(ii) the 2 preceding taxable years, and

(iii) the period after such taxable year and before the due date (including extensions) for filing the return of tax for such taxable year.

(C) Excepted distributions—There shall not be taken into account under subparagraph (A)—

(i) any distribution referred to in section 72(p), 401(k)(8), 401(m)(6), 402(g)(2), 404(k), or 408(d)(4), and

(ii) any distribution to which section 408A(d)(3) applies.

(D) Treatment of distributions received by spouse of individual—For purposes of determining distributions received by an individual under subparagraph (A) for any taxable year, any distribution received by the spouse of such individual shall be treated as received by such individual if such individual and spouse file a joint return for such taxable year and for the taxable year during which the spouse receives the distribution.

(e) Adjusted gross income—For purposes of this section, adjusted gross income shall be determined without regard to sections 911, 931, and 933.

(f) Investment in the contract—Notwithstanding any other provision of law, a qualified retirement savings contribution shall not fail to be included in determining the investment in the contract for purposes of section 72 by reason of the credit under this section.

(g) Limitation based on amount of tax—The credit allowed under subsection (a) for the taxable year shall not exceed the excess of—

(1) the sum of the regular tax liability (as defined in section 26(b)) plus the tax imposed by section 55, over

(2) the sum of the credits allowable under this subpart (other than this section and sections 25A(i), 25D, 30, 30B, and 30D) and section 27 for the taxable year.

§ 45E. Small employer pension plan startup costs.

(a) General rule—For purposes of section 38, in the case of an eligible employer, the small employer pension plan startup cost credit determined under this section for any taxable year is an amount equal to 50 percent of the qualified startup costs paid or incurred by the taxpayer during the taxable year.

(b) Dollar limitation—The amount of the credit determined under this section for any taxable year shall not exceed—

(1) $500 for the first credit year and each of the 2 taxable years immediately following the first credit year, and

(2) zero for any other taxable year.

(c) Eligible employer—For purposes of this section—

(1) In general—The term "eligible employer" has the meaning given such term by section 408(p)(2)(C)(i).

(2) Requirement for new qualified employer plans—Such term shall not include an employer if, during the 3-taxable year period immediately preceding the 1st taxable year for which the credit under this section is otherwise allowable for a qualified employer plan of the employer, the employer or any member of any controlled group including the employer (or any predecessor of either) established or maintained a qualified employer plan with respect to which contributions were made, or benefits were accrued, for substantially the same employees as are in the qualified employer plan.

(d) Other definitions—For purposes of this section—

(1) Qualified startup costs—

(A) In general—The term "qualified startup costs" means any ordinary and necessary expenses of an eligible employer which are paid or incurred in connection with—

(i) the establishment or administration of an eligible employer plan, or

(ii) the retirement-related education of employees with respect to such plan.

(B) Plan must have at least 1 participant—Such term shall not include any expense in connection with a plan that does not have at least 1 employee eligible to participate who is not a highly compensated employee.

(2) Eligible employer plan—The term "eligible employer plan" means a qualified employer plan within the meaning of section 4972(d).

(3) First credit year—The term "first credit year" means—

(A) the taxable year which includes the date that the eligible employer plan to which such costs relate becomes effective, or

(B) at the election of the eligible employer, the taxable year preceding the taxable year referred to in subparagraph (A).

(e) Special rules—For purposes of this section—

(1) Aggregation rules—All persons treated as a single employer under subsection (a) or (b) of section 52, or subsection (m) or (o) of section 414, shall be treated as one person. All eligible employer plans shall be treated as 1 eligible employer plan.

(2) Disallowance of deduction—No deduction shall be allowed for that portion of the qualified startup costs paid or incurred for the taxable year which is equal to the credit determined under subsection (a).

(3) Election not to claim credit—This section shall not apply to a taxpayer for any taxable year if such taxpayer elects to have this section not apply for such taxable year.

§ 72. Annuities; certain proceeds of endowment and life insurance contracts.

(a) General rule for annuities—(a) General rules for annuities [applicable to amounts received in taxable years beginning on or after January 1, 2011].

(1) **Income inclusion**. Except as otherwise provided in this chapter, gross income includes any amount received as an annuity (whether for a period certain or during one or more lives) under an annuity, endowment, or life insurance contract.

(2) **Partial annuitization**. If any amount is received as an annuity for a period of 10 years or more or during one or more lives under any portion of an annuity, endowment, or life insurance contract—

(A) such portion shall be treated as a separate contract for purposes of this section,

(B) for purposes of applying subsections (b), (c), and (e), the investment in the contract shall be allocated pro rata between each portion of the contract from which amounts are received as an annuity and the portion of the contract from which amounts are not received as an annuity, and

(C) a separate annuity starting date under subsection (c)(4) shall be determined with respect to each portion of the contract from which amounts are received as an annuity.

(b) Exclusion ratio—

(1) In general—Gross income does not include that part of any amount received as an annuity under an annuity, endowment, or life insurance contract which bears the same ratio to such amount as the investment in the contract (as of the annuity starting date) bears to the expected return under the contract (as of such date).

(2) Exclusion limited to investment—The portion of any amount received as an annuity which is excluded from gross income under paragraph (1) shall not exceed the unrecovered investment in the contract immediately before the receipt of such amount.

(3) Deduction where annuity payments cease before entire investment recovered—

(A) In general—If—

(i) after the annuity starting date, payments as an annuity under the contract cease by reason of the death of an annuitant, and

(ii) as of the date of such cessation, there is unrecovered investment in the contract,

the amount of such unrecovered investment (in excess of any amount specified in subsection (e)(5) which was not included in gross income) shall be allowed as a deduction to the annuitant for his last taxable year.

(B) Payments to other persons—In the case of any contract which provides for payments meeting the requirements of subparagraphs (B) and (C) of subsection (c)(2), the deduction under subparagraph (A) shall be allowed to the person entitled to such payments for the taxable year in which such payments are received.

(C) Net operating loss deductions provided—For purposes of section 172, a deduction allowed under this paragraph shall be treated as if it were attributable to a trade or business of the taxpayer.

(4) Unrecovered investment—For purposes of this subsection, the unrecovered investment in the contract as of any date is—

(A) the investment in the contract (determined without regard to subsection (c)(2)) as of the annuity starting date, reduced by

(B) the aggregate amount received under the contract on or after such annuity starting date and before the date as of which the determination is being made, to the extent such amount was excludable from gross income under this subtitle.

(c) Definitions—

(1) Investment in the contract—For purposes of subsection (b), the investment in the contract as of the annuity starting date is—

(A) the aggregate amount of premiums or other consideration paid for the contract, minus

(B) the aggregate amount received under the contract before such date, to the extent that such amount was excludable from gross income under this subtitle or prior income tax laws.

(2) Adjustment in investment where there is refund feature—If—

(A) the expected return under the contract depends in whole or in part on the life expectancy of one or more individuals;

(B) the contract provides for payments to be made to a beneficiary (or to the estate of an annuitant) on or after the death of the annuitant or annuitants; and

(C) such payments are in the nature of a refund of the consideration paid, then the value (computed without discount for interest) of such payments on the annuity starting date shall be subtracted from the amount determined under paragraph (1). Such value shall be computed in accordance with actuarial tables prescribed by the Secretary. For purposes of this paragraph and of subsection (e)(2)(A), the term "refund of the consideration paid" includes amounts payable after the death of an annuitant by reason of a provision in the contract for a life annuity with minimum period of payments certain, but (if part of the consideration was contributed by an employer) does not include that part of any payment to a beneficiary (or to the estate of the annuitant) which is not attributable to the consideration paid by the employee for the contract as determined under paragraph (1)(A).

(3) Expected return—For purposes of subsection (b), the expected return under the contract shall be determined as follows:

(A) Life expectancy—If the expected return under the contract, for the period on and after the annuity starting date, depends in whole or in part on the life expectancy of one or more individuals, the expected return shall be computed with reference to actuarial tables prescribed by the Secretary.

(B) Installment payments—If subparagraph (A) does not apply, the expected return is the aggregate of the amounts receivable under the contract as an annuity.

(4) Annuity starting date—For purposes of this section, the annuity starting date in the case of any contract is the first day of the first period for which an amount is received as an annuity under the contract; except that if such date was before January 1, 1954, then the annuity starting date is January 1, 1954.

(d) Special rules for qualified employer retirement plans—

(1) Simplified method of taxing annuity payments—

(A) In general—In the case of any amount received as an annuity under a qualified employer retirement plan—

(i) subsection (b) shall not apply, and

(ii) the investment in the contract shall be recovered as provided in this paragraph.

(B) Method of recovering investment in contract—

(i) In general—Gross income shall not include so much of any monthly annuity payment under a qualified employer retirement plan as does not exceed the amount obtained by dividing—

(I) the investment in the contract (as of the annuity starting date), by

(II) the number of anticipated payments determined under the table contained in clause (iii) (or, in the case of a contract to which subsection (c)(3)(B) applies, the number of monthly annuity payments under such contract).

(ii) Certain rules made applicable—Rules similar to the rules of paragraphs (2) and (3) of subsection (b) shall apply for purposes of this paragraph.

(iii) Number of anticipated payments—If the annuity is payable over the life of a single individual, the number of anticipated payments shall be determined as follows:

If the age of the annuitant on the annuity starting date is:	*The number of anticipated payments is:*
Not more than 55	360
More than 55 but not more than 60	310
More than 60 but not more than 65	260
More than 65 but not more than 70	210
More than 70	160

(iv) Number of anticipated payments where more than one life—If the annuity is payable over the lives of more than 1 individual, the number of anticipated payments shall be determined as follows:

If the combined ages of annuitants are:	*The number is:*
Not more than 110	410
More than 110 but not more than 120	360
More than 120 but not more than 130	310
More than 130 but not more than 140	260
More than 140	210

(C) Adjustment for refund feature not applicable—For purposes of this paragraph, investment in the contract shall be determined under subsection (c)(1) without regard to subsection (c)(2).

(D) Special rule where lump sum paid in connection with commencement of annuity payments—If, in connection with the commencement of annuity payments under any qualified employer retirement plan, the taxpayer receives a lump-sum payment—

(i) such payment shall be taxable under subsection (e) as if received before the annuity starting date, and

(ii) the investment in the contract for purposes of this paragraph shall be determined as if such payment had been so received.

(E) Exception—This paragraph shall not apply in any case where the primary annuitant has attained age 75 on the annuity starting date unless there are fewer than 5 years of guaranteed payments under the annuity.

(F) Adjustment where annuity payments not on monthly basis—In any case where the annuity payments are not made on a monthly basis, appropriate adjustments in the application of this paragraph shall be made to take into account the period on the basis of which such payments are made.

(G) Qualified employer retirement plan—For purposes of this paragraph, the term "qualified employer retirement plan" means any plan or contract described in paragraph (1), (2), or (3) of section 4974(c).

(2) Treatment of employee contributions under defined contribution plans—For purposes of this section, employee contributions (and any income allocable thereto) under a defined contribution plan may be treated as a separate contract.

(e) Amounts not received as annuities—

(1) Application of subsection—

(A) In general—This subsection shall apply to any amount which—

(i) is received under an annuity, endowment, or life insurance contract, and

(ii) is not received as an annuity, if no provision of this subtitle (other than this subsection) applies with respect to such amount.

(B) Dividends—For purposes of this section, any amount received which is in the nature of a dividend or similar distribution shall be treated as an amount not received as an annuity.

(2) General rule—Any amount to which this subsection applies—

(A) if received on or after the annuity starting date, shall be included in gross income, or 72(e)(2)(B) if received before the annuity starting date—

(i) shall be included in gross income to the extent allocable to income on the contract, and

(ii) shall not be included in gross income to the extent allocable to the investment in the contract.

(3) Allocation of amounts to income and investment—For purposes of paragraph (2)(B)—

(A) Allocation to income—Any amount to which this subsection applies shall be treated as allocable to income on the contract to the extent that such amount does not exceed the excess (if any) of—

(i) the cash value of the contract (determined without regard to any surrender charge) immediately before the amount is received, over

(ii) the investment in the contract at such time.

(B) Allocation to investment—Any amount to which this subsection applies shall be treated as allocable to investment in the contract to the extent that such amount is not allocated to income under subparagraph (A).

* * *

(5) Retention of existing rules in certain cases—

(A) In general—In any case to which this paragraph applies—

(i) paragraphs (2)(B) and (4)(A) shall not apply, and

(ii) if paragraph (2)(A) does not apply, the amount shall be included in gross income, but only to the extent it exceeds the investment in the contract.

* * *

(D) Contracts under qualified plans—Except as provided in paragraph (8), this paragraph shall apply to any amount received—

(i) from a trust described in section 401(a) which is exempt from tax under section 501(a),

(ii) from a contract—

(I) purchased by a trust described in clause (i),

(II) purchased as part of a plan described in section 403(a),

(III) described in section 403(b), or

(IV) provided for employees of a life insurance company under a plan described in section 818(a)(3), or

(iii) from an individual retirement account or an individual retirement annuity.

Any dividend described in section 404(k) which is received by a participant or beneficiary shall, for purposes of this subparagraph, be treated as paid under a separate contract to which clause (ii)(I) applies.

* * *

(6) Investment in the contract—For purposes of this subsection, the investment in the contract as of any date is—

(A) the aggregate amount of premiums or other consideration paid for the contract before such date, minus

(B) the aggregate amount received under the contract before such date, to the extent that such amount was excludable from gross income under this subtitle or prior income tax laws.

(7) [Repealed]

(8) Extension of paragraph (2)(b) to qualified plans—

(A) In general—Notwithstanding any other provision of this subsection, in the case of any amount received before the annuity starting date from a trust or contract described in paragraph (5)(D), paragraph (2)(B) shall apply to such amounts.

(B) Allocation of amount received—For purposes of paragraph (2)(B), the amount allocated to the investment in the contract shall be the portion of the amount described in subparagraph (A) which bears the same ratio to such amount as the investment in the contract bears to the account balance. The determination under the preceding sentence shall be made as of the time of the distribution or at such other time as the Secretary may prescribe.

(C) Treatment of forfeitable rights—If an employee does not have a nonforfeitable right to any amount under any trust or contract to which subparagraph (A) applies, such amount shall not be treated as part of the account balance.

(D) Investment in the contract before 1987—In the case of a plan which on May 5, 1986, permitted withdrawal of any employee contributions before separation from service, subparagraph (A) shall apply only to the extent that amounts received before the annuity starting date (when increased by amounts previously received under the contract after December 31, 1986) exceed the investment in the contract as of December 31, 1986.

* * *

(f) Special rules for computing employees' contributions—In computing, for purposes of subsection (c)(1)(A), the aggregate amount of premiums or other consideration paid for the contract, and for purposes of subsection (e)(6), the aggregate premiums or other consideration paid, amounts contributed by the employer shall be included, but only to the extent that—

(1) such amounts were includible in the gross income of the employee under this subtitle or prior income tax laws; or

(2) if such amounts had been paid directly to the employee at the time they were contributed, they would not have been includible in the gross income of the employee under the law applicable at the time of such contribution.

* * *

(m) Special rules applicable to employee annuities and distributions under employee plans—

(1) [Repealed]

(2) Computation of consideration paid by the employee—In computing—

(A) the aggregate amount of premiums or other consideration paid for the contract for purposes of subsection (c)(1)(A) (relating to the investment in the contract), and

(B) the aggregate premiums or other consideration paid for purposes of subsection (e)(6) (relating to certain amounts not received as an annuity),

any amount allowed as a deduction with respect to the contract under section 404 which was paid while the employee was an employee within the meaning of section 401(c)(1) shall be treated as consideration contributed by the employer, and there shall not be taken into account any portion of the premiums or other consideration for the contract paid while the employee was an owner-employee which is properly allocable (as determined under regulations prescribed by the Secretary) to the cost of life, accident, health, or other insurance.

(3) Life insurance contracts—

(A) This paragraph shall apply to any life insurance contract—

(i) purchased as a part of a plan described in section 403(a), or

(ii) purchased by a trust described in section 401(a) which is exempt from tax under section 501(a) if the proceeds of such contract are payable directly or indirectly to a participant in such trust or to a beneficiary of such participant.

(B) Any contribution to a plan described in subparagraph (A)(i) or a trust described in subparagraph (A)(ii) which is allowed as a deduction under section 404, and any income of a trust described in subparagraph (A)(ii), which is determined in accordance with regulations prescribed by the Secretary to have been applied to purchase the life insurance protection under a contract described in subparagraph (A), is includible in the gross income of the participant for the taxable year when so applied.

(C) In the case of the death of an individual insured under a contract described in subparagraph (A), an amount equal to the cash surrender value of the contract immediately before the death of the insured shall be treated as a payment under such plan or a distribution by such trust, and the excess of the amount payable by reason of the death of the insured over such cash surrender value shall not be includible in gross income under this section and shall be treated as provided in section 101.

* * *

(10) Determination of investment in the contract in the case of qualified domestic relations orders—Under regulations prescribed by the Secretary, in the case of a distribution or payment made to an alternate payee who is the spouse or former spouse of the participant pursuant to a qualified domestic relations order (as defined in section 414(p)), the investment in the contract as of the date prescribed in such regulations shall be allocated on a pro rata basis between the present value of such distribution or payment and the present value of all other benefits payable with respect to the participant to which such order relates.

* * *

(p) Loans treated as distributions—For purposes of this section—

(1) Treatment as distributions—

(A) Loans—If during any taxable year a participant or beneficiary receives (directly or indirectly) any amount as a loan from a qualified employer plan, such amount shall be treated as having been received by such individual as a distribution under such plan.

(B) Assignments or pledges—If during any taxable year a participant or beneficiary assigns (or agrees to assign) or pledges (or agrees to pledge) any portion of his interest in a qualified employer plan, such portion shall be treated as having been received by such individual as a loan from such plan.

(2) Exception for certain loans—

(A) General rule—Paragraph (1) shall not apply to any loan to the extent that such loan (when added to the outstanding balance of all other loans from such plan whether made on, before, or after August 13, 1982), does not exceed the lesser of—

(i) $50,000, reduced by the excess (if any) of—

(I) the highest outstanding balance of loans from the plan during the 1-year period ending on the day before the date on which such loan was made, over

(II) the outstanding balance of loans from the plan on the date on which such loan was made, or

(ii) the greater of (I) one-half of the present value of the nonforfeitable accrued benefit of the employee under the plan, or (II) $10,000.

For purposes of clause (ii), the present value of the nonforfeitable accrued benefit shall be determined without regard to any accumulated deductible employee contributions (as defined in subsection (o)(5)(B)).

(B) Requirement that loan be repayable within 5 years—

(i) In general—Subparagraph (A) shall not apply to any loan unless such loan, by its terms, is required to be repaid within 5 years.

(ii) Exception for home loans—Clause (i) shall not apply to any loan used to acquire any dwelling unit which within a reasonable time is to be used (determined at the time the loan is made) as the principal residence of the participant.

(C) Requirement of level amortization—Except as provided in regulations, this paragraph shall not apply to any loan unless substantially level amortization of such loan (with payments not less frequently than quarterly) is required over the term of the loan.

(D) Related employers and related plans—For purposes of this paragraph—

(i) the rules of subsections (b), (c), and (m) of section 414 shall apply, and

(ii) all plans of an employer (determined after the application of such subsections) shall be treated as 1 plan.

(3) Denial of interest deductions in certain cases—

(A) In general—No deduction otherwise allowable under this chapter shall be allowed under this chapter for any interest paid or accrued on any loan to which paragraph (1) does not apply by reason of paragraph (2) during the period described in subparagraph (B).

(B) Period to which subparagraph (a) applies—For purposes of subparagraph (A), the period described in this subparagraph is the period—

(i) on or after the 1st day on which the individual to whom the loan is made is a key employee (as defined in section 416(i)), or

(ii) such loan is secured by amounts attributable to elective deferrals described in subparagraph (A) or (C) of section 402(g)(3).

(4) Qualified employer plan, etc—For purposes of this subsection—

(A) Qualified employer plan—

(i) In general—The term "qualified employer plan" means—

(I) a plan described in section 401(a) which includes a trust exempt from tax under section 501(a),

(II) an annuity plan described in section 403(a), and

(III) a plan under which amounts are contributed by an individual's employer for an annuity contract described in section 403(b).

(ii) Special rule—The term "qualified employer plan" shall include any plan which was (or was determined to be) a qualified employer plan or a government plan.

(B) Government plan—The term "government plan" means any plan, whether or not qualified, established and maintained for its employees by the United States, by a State or political subdivision thereof, or by an agency or instrumentality of any of the foregoing.

* * *

(t) 10-percent additional tax on early distributions from qualified retirement plans—

(1) Imposition of additional tax—If any taxpayer receives any amount from a qualified retirement plan (as defined in section 4974(c)), the taxpayer's tax under this chapter for the taxable year in which such amount is received shall be increased by an amount equal to 10 percent of the portion of such amount which is includible in gross income.

(2) Subsection not to apply to certain distributions—Except as provided in paragraphs (3) and (4), paragraph (1) shall not apply to any of the following distributions:

(A) In general—Distributions which are—

(i) made on or after the date on which the employee attains age 59½,

(ii) made to a beneficiary (or to the estate of the employee) on or after the death of the employee,

(iii) attributable to the employee's being disabled within the meaning of subsection (m)(7),

(iv) part of a series of substantially equal periodic payments (not less frequently than annually) made for the life (or life expectancy) of the employee or the joint lives (or joint life expectancies) of such employee and his designated beneficiary,

(v) made to an employee after separation from service after attainment of age 55,

(vi) dividends paid with respect to stock of a corporation which are described in section 404(k), or

(vii) made on account of a levy under section 6331 on the qualified retirement plan.

(B) Medical expenses—Distributions made to the employee (other than distributions described in subparagraph (A), (C) or (D)) to the extent such distributions do not exceed the amount allowable as a deduction under section 213 to the employee for amounts paid during the taxable year for medical care (determined without regard to whether the employee itemizes deductions for such taxable year).

(C) Payments to alternate payees pursuant to qualified domestic relations orders—Any distribution to an alternate payee pursuant to a qualified domestic relations order (within the meaning of section 414(p)(1)).

(D) Distributions to unemployed individuals for health insurance premiums—

(i) In general—Distributions from an individual retirement plan to an individual after separation from employment—

(I) if such individual has received unemployment compensation for 12 consecutive weeks under any Federal or State unemployment compensation law by reason of such separation,

(II) if such distributions are made during any taxable year during which such unemployment compensation is paid or the succeeding taxable year, and

(III) to the extent such distributions do not exceed the amount paid during the taxable year for insurance described in section 213(d)(1)(D) with respect to the individual and the individual's spouse and dependents (as defined in section 152, determined without regard to subsections (b)(1), (b)(2), and (d)(1)(B) thereof).

(ii) Distributions after reemployment—Clause (i) shall not apply to any distribution made after the individual has been employed for at least 60 days after the separation from employment to which clause (i) applies.

(iii) Self-employed individuals—To the extent provided in regulations, a self-employed individual shall be treated as meeting the requirements of clause (i)(I) if, under Federal or State law, the individual would have received unemployment compensation but for the fact the individual was self-employed.

(E) Distributions from individual retirement plans for higher education expenses—Distributions to an individual from an individual retirement plan to the extent such distributions do not exceed the qualified higher education expenses (as defined in paragraph (7)) of the taxpayer for the taxable year. Distributions shall not be taken into account under the preceding sentence if such distributions are described in subparagraph (A), (C), or (D) or to the extent paragraph (1) does not apply to such distributions by reason of subparagraph (B).

(F) Distributions from certain plans for first home purchases—Distributions to an individual from an individual retirement plan which are qualified first-time homebuyer distributions (as defined in paragraph (8)). Distributions shall not be taken into account under the preceding sentence if such distributions are described in subparagraph (A), (C), (D), or (E) or to the extent paragraph (1) does not apply to such distributions by reason of subparagraph (B).

(G) Distributions from retirement plans to individuals called to active duty—

(i) In general—Any qualified reservist distribution.

(ii) Amount distributed may be repaid—Any individual who receives a qualified reservist distribution may, at any time during the 2-year period beginning on the day after the end of the active duty period, make one or more contributions to an individual retirement plan of such individual in an aggregate amount not to exceed the amount of such distribution. The dollar limitations otherwise applicable to contributions to individual retirement plans shall not apply to any contribution made pursuant to the preceding sentence. No deduction shall be allowed for any contribution pursuant to this clause.

(iii) Qualified reservist distribution—For purposes of this subparagraph, the term "qualified reservist distribution" means any distribution to an individual if—

(I) such distribution is from an individual retirement plan, or from amounts attributable to employer contributions made pursuant to elective deferrals described in subparagraph (A) or (C) of section 402(g)(3) or section 501(c)(18)(D)(iii),

(II) such individual was (by reason of being a member of a reserve component (as defined in section 101 of title 37, United States Code)) ordered or called to active duty for a period in excess of 179 days or for an indefinite period, and

(III) such distribution is made during the period beginning on the date of such order or call and ending at the close of the active duty period.

(iv) Application of subparagraph—This subparagraph applies to individuals ordered or called to active duty after September 11, 2001. In no event shall the 2-year period referred to in clause (ii) end on or before the date which is 2 years after the date of the enactment of this subparagraph.

(3) Limitations—

(A) Certain exceptions not to apply to individual retirement plans—Subparagraphs (A)(v) and (C) of paragraph (2) shall not apply to distributions from an individual retirement plan.

(B) Periodic payments under qualified plans must begin after separation—Paragraph (2)(A)(iv) shall not apply to any amount paid from a trust described in section 401(a) which is exempt from tax under section 501(a) or from a contract described in section 72(e)(5)(D)(ii) unless the series of payments begins after the employee separates from service.

(4) Change in substantially equal payments—

(A) In general—If—

(i) paragraph (1) does not apply to a distribution by reason of paragraph (2)(A)(iv), and

(ii) the series of payments under such paragraph are subsequently modified (other than by reason of death or disability)—

(I) before the close of the 5-year period beginning with the date of the first payment and after the employee attains age 59½, or

(II) before the employee attains age 59½, the taxpayer's tax for the 1st taxable year in which such modification occurs shall be increased by an amount, determined under regulations, equal to the tax which (but for paragraph (2)(A)(iv)) would have been imposed, plus interest for the deferral period.

(B) Deferral period—For purposes of this paragraph, the term "deferral period" means the period beginning with the taxable year in which (without regard to paragraph (2)(A)(iv)) the distribution would have been includible in gross income and ending with the taxable year in which the modification described in subparagraph (A) occurs.

(5) Employee—For purposes of this subsection, the term "employee" includes any participant, and in the case of an individual retirement plan, the individual for whose benefit such plan was established.

(6) Special rules for simple retirement accounts—In the case of any amount received from a simple retirement account (within the meaning of section 408(p)) during the 2-year period beginning on the date such individual first participated in any qualified salary reduction arrangement maintained by the individual's employer under section 408(p)(2), paragraph (1) shall be applied by substituting "25 percent" for "10 percent".

(7) Qualified higher education expenses—For purposes of paragraph (2)(E)—

(A) In general—The term "qualified higher education expenses" means qualified higher education expenses (as defined in section 529(e)(3)) for education furnished to—

(i) the taxpayer,

(ii) the taxpayer's spouse, or

(iii) any child (as defined in section 152(f)(1)) or grandchild of the taxpayer or the taxpayer's spouse,

at an eligible educational institution (as defined in section 529(e)(5)).

(B) Coordination with other benefits—The amount of qualified higher education expenses for any taxable year shall be reduced as provided in section 25A(g)(2).

(8) Qualified first-time homebuyer distributions—For purposes of paragraph (2)(F)—

(A) In general—The term "qualified first-time homebuyer distribution" means any payment or distribution received by an individual to the extent such payment or distribution is used by the individual before the close of the 120th day after the day on which such payment or distribution is received to pay qualified acquisition costs with respect to a principal residence of a first-time homebuyer who is such individual, the spouse of such individual, or any child, grandchild, or ancestor of such individual or the individual's spouse.

(B) Lifetime dollar limitation—The aggregate amount of payments or distributions received by an individual which may be treated as qualified first-time homebuyer distributions for any taxable year shall not exceed the excess (if any) of—

(i) $10,000, over

(ii) the aggregate amounts treated as qualified first-time homebuyer distributions with respect to such individual for all prior taxable years.

(C) Qualified acquisition costs—For purposes of this paragraph, the term "qualified acquisition costs" means the costs of acquiring, constructing, or reconstructing a residence. Such term includes any usual or reasonable settlement, financing, or other closing costs.

(D) First-time homebuyer; other definitions—For purposes of this paragraph—

(i) First-time homebuyer—The term "first-time homebuyer" means any individual if—

(I) such individual (and if married, such individual's spouse) had no present ownership interest in a principal residence during the 2-year period ending on the date of acquisition of the principal residence to which this paragraph applies, and

(II) subsection (h) or (k) of section 1034 (as in effect on the day before the date of the enactment of this paragraph) did not suspend the running of any period of time specified in section 1034 (as so in effect) with respect to such individual on the day before the date the distribution is applied pursuant to subparagraph (A).

(ii) Principal residence—The term "principal residence" has the same meaning as when used in section 121.

(iii) Date of acquisition—The term "date of acquisition" means the date—

(I) on which a binding contract to acquire the principal residence to which subparagraph (A) applies is entered into, or

(II) on which construction or reconstruction of such a principal residence is commenced.

(E) Special rule where delay in acquisition—If any distribution from any individual retirement plan fails to meet the requirements of subparagraph (A) solely by reason of a delay or cancellation of the purchase or construction of the residence, the amount of the distribution may be contributed to an individual retirement plan as provided in section 408(d)(3)(A)(i) (determined by substituting "120th day" for "60th day" in such section), except that—

(i) section 408(d)(3)(B) shall not be applied to such contribution, and

(ii) such amount shall not be taken into account in determining whether section 408(d)(3)(B) applies to any other amount.

(9) Special rule for rollovers to section 457 plans—For purposes of this subsection, a distribution from an eligible deferred compensation plan (as defined in section 457(b)) of an eligible employer described in section 457(e)(1)(A) shall be treated as a distribution from a qualified retirement plan described in 4974(c)(1) to the extent that such distribution is attributable to an amount transferred to an eligible deferred compensation plan from a qualified retirement plan (as defined in section 4974(c)).

(10) Distributions to qualified public safety employees in governmental plans—

(A) In general—In the case of a distribution to a qualified public safety employee from a governmental plan (within the meaning of section 414(d)) which is a defined benefit plan, paragraph (2)(A)(v) shall be applied by substituting "age 50" for "age 55".

(B) Qualified public safety employee—For purposes of this paragraph, the term "qualified public safety employee" means any employee of a State or political subdivision of a State who provides police protection, firefighting services, or emergency medical services for any area within the jurisdiction of such State or political subdivision.

* * *

§ 83. Property transferred in connection with performance of services.

(a) General rule—If, in connection with the performance of services, property is transferred to any person other than the person for whom such services are performed, the excess of—

(1) the fair market value of such property (determined without regard to any restriction other than a restriction which by its terms will never lapse) at the first time the rights of the person having the beneficial interest in such property are transferable or are not subject to a substantial risk of forfeiture, whichever occurs earlier, over

(2) the amount (if any) paid for such property,

shall be included in the gross income of the person who performed such services in the first taxable year in which the rights of the person having the beneficial interest in such property are transferable or are not subject to a substantial risk of forfeiture, whichever is applicable. The preceding sentence shall not apply if such person sells or otherwise disposes of such property in an arm's length transaction before his rights in such property become transferable or not subject to a substantial risk of forfeiture.

(b) Election to include in gross income in year of transfer—

(1) In general—Any person who performs services in connection with which property is transferred to any person may elect to include in his gross income, for the taxable year in which such property is transferred, the excess of—

(A) the fair market value of such property at the time of transfer (determined without regard to any restriction other than a restriction which by its terms will never lapse), over

(B) the amount (if any) paid for such property. If such election is made, subsection (a) shall not apply with respect to the transfer of such property, and if such property is subsequently forfeited, no deduction shall be allowed in respect of such forfeiture.

(2) Election—An election under paragraph (1) with respect to any transfer of property shall be made in such manner as the Secretary prescribes and shall be made not later than 30 days after the date of such transfer. Such election may not be revoked except with the consent of the Secretary.

(c) Special rules—For purposes of this section—

(1) Substantial risk of forfeiture—The rights of a person in property are subject to a substantial risk of forfeiture if such person's rights to full enjoyment of such property are conditioned upon the future performance of substantial services by any individual.

(2) Transferability of property—The rights of a person in property are transferable only if the rights in such property of any transferee are not subject to a substantial risk of forfeiture.

(3) Sales which may give rise to suit under section 16(b) of the securities exchange act of 1934—So long as the sale of property at a profit could subject a person to suit under section 16(b) of the Securities Exchange Act of 1934, such person's rights in such property are—

(A) subject to a substantial risk of forfeiture, and

(B) not transferable.

(d) Certain restrictions which will never lapse—

(1) Valuation—In the case of property subject to a restriction which by its terms will never lapse, and which allows the transferee to sell such property only at a price determined under a formula, the price so determined shall be deemed to be the fair market value of the property unless established to the contrary by the Secretary, and the burden of proof shall be on the Secretary with respect to such value.

(2) Cancellation—If, in the case of property subject to a restriction which by its terms will never lapse, the restriction is cancelled, then, unless the taxpayer establishes—

(A) that such cancellation was not compensatory, and

(B) that the person, if any, who would be allowed a deduction if the cancellation were treated as compensatory, will treat the transaction as not compensatory, as evidenced in such manner as the Secretary shall prescribe by regulations,

the excess of the fair market value of the property (computed without regard to the restrictions) at the time of cancellation over the sum of—

(C) the fair market value of such property (computed by taking the restriction into account) immediately before the cancellation, and

(D) the amount, if any, paid for the cancellation,

shall be treated as compensation for the taxable year in which such cancellation occurs.

(e) Applicability of section—This section shall not apply to—

(1) a transaction to which section 421 applies,

(2) a transfer to or from a trust described in section 401(a) or a transfer under an annuity plan which meets the requirements of section 404(a)(2),

(3) the transfer of an option without a readily ascertainable fair market value,

(4) the transfer of property pursuant to the exercise of an option with a readily ascertainable fair market value at the date of grant, or

(5) group-term life insurance to which section 79 applies.

(f) Holding period—In determining the period for which the taxpayer has held property to which subsection (a) applies, there shall be included only the period beginning at the first time his rights in such property are transferable or are not subject to a substantial risk of forfeiture, whichever occurs earlier.

(g) Certain exchanges—If property to which subsection (a) applies is exchanged for property subject to restrictions and conditions substantially similar to those to which the property given in such exchange was subject, and if section 354, 355, 356, or 1036 (or so much of section 1031 as relates to section 1036) applied to such exchange, or if such exchange was pursuant to the exercise of a conversion privilege—

(1) such exchange shall be disregarded for purposes of subsection (a), and

(2) the property received shall be treated as property to which subsection (a) applies.

(h) Deduction by employer—In the case of a transfer of property to which this section applies or a cancellation of a restriction described in subsection (d), there shall be allowed as a deduction under section 162, to the person for whom were performed the services in connection with which such property was transferred, an amount equal to the amount included under subsection (a), (b), or (d)(2) in the gross income of the person who performed such services. Such deduction shall be allowed for the taxable year of such person in which or with which ends the taxable year in which such amount is included in the gross income of the person who performed such services.

§ 86. Social security and tier 1 railroad retirement benefits.

(a) In general—

(1) In general—Except as provided in paragraph (2), gross income for the taxable year of any taxpayer described in subsection (b) (notwithstanding section 207 of the Social Security Act) includes social security benefits in an amount equal to the lesser of—

(A) one-half of the social security benefits received during the taxable year, or

(B) one-half of the excess described in subsection (b)(1).

(2) Additional amount—In the case of a taxpayer with respect to whom the amount determined under subsection (b)(1)(A) exceeds the adjusted base amount, the amount included in gross income under this section shall be equal to the lesser of—

(A) the sum of—

(i) 85 percent of such excess, plus

(ii) the lesser of the amount determined under paragraph (1) or an amount equal to one-half of the difference between the adjusted base amount and the base amount of the taxpayer, or

(B) 85 percent of the social security benefits received during the taxable year.

(b) Taxpayers to whom subsection (a) applies—

(1) In general—A taxpayer is described in this subsection if—

(A) the sum of—

(i) the modified adjusted gross income of the taxpayer for the taxable year, plus

(ii) one-half of the social security benefits received during the taxable year, exceeds

(B) the base amount.

(2) Modified adjusted gross income—For purposes of this subsection, the term "modified adjusted gross income" means adjusted gross income—

(A) determined without regard to this section and sections 135, 137, 199, 221, 222, 911, 931, and 933, and

(B) increased by the amount of interest received or accrued by the taxpayer during the taxable year which is exempt from tax.

(c) Base amount and adjusted base amount—For purposes of this section—

(1) Base amount—The term "base amount" means—

(A) except as otherwise provided in this paragraph, $25,000,

(B) $32,000 in the case of a joint return, and

(C) zero in the case of a taxpayer who—

(i) is married as of the close of the taxable year (within the meaning of section 7703) but does not file a joint return for such year, and

(ii) does not live apart from his spouse at all times during the taxable year.

(2) Adjusted base amount—The term "adjusted base amount" means—

(A) except as otherwise provided in this paragraph, $34,000,

(B) $44,000 in the case of a joint return, and

(C) zero in the case of a taxpayer described in paragraph (1)(C).

(d) Social security benefit—

(1) In general—For purposes of this section, the term "social security benefit" means any amount received by the taxpayer by reason of entitlement to—

(A) a monthly benefit under title II of the Social Security Act, or

(B) a tier 1 railroad retirement benefit.

* * *

§ 125. Cafeteria plans.

(a) In general—Except as provided in subsection (b), no amount shall be included in the gross income of a participant in a cafeteria plan solely because, under the plan, the participant may choose among the benefits of the plan.

(b) Exception for highly compensated participants and key employees—

(1) Highly compensated participants—In the case of a highly compensated participant, subsection (a) shall not apply to any benefit attributable to a plan year for which the plan discriminates in favor of—

(A) highly compensated individuals as to eligibility to participate, or

(B) highly compensated participants as to contributions and benefits.

(2) Key employees—In the case of a key employee (within the meaning of section 416(i)(1)), subsection (a) shall not apply to any benefit attributable to a plan for which the statutory nontaxable benefits provided to key employees exceed 25 percent of the aggregate of such benefits provided for all employees under the plan. For purposes of the preceding sentence, statutory nontaxable benefits shall be determined without regard to the second sentence of subsection (f).

(3) Year of inclusion—For purposes of determining the taxable year of inclusion, any benefit described in paragraph (1) or (2) shall be treated as received or accrued in the taxable year of the participant or key employee in which the plan year ends.

(c) Discrimination as to benefits or contributions—For purposes of subparagraph (B) of subsection (b)(1), a cafeteria plan does not discriminate where qualified benefits and total benefits (or employer contributions allocable to statutory nontaxable benefits and employer contributions for total benefits) do not discriminate in favor of highly compensated participants.

(d) Cafeteria plan defined—For purposes of this section—

(1) In general—The term "cafeteria plan" means a written plan under which—

(A) all participants are employees, and

(B) the participants may choose among 2 or more benefits consisting of cash and qualified benefits.

(2) Deferred compensation plans excluded—

(A) In general—The term "cafeteria plan" does not include any plan which provides for deferred compensation.

(B) Exception for cash and deferred arrangements—Subparagraph (A) shall not apply to a profit-sharing or stock bonus plan or rural cooperative plan (within the meaning of section 401(k)(7)) which includes a qualified cash or deferred arrangement (as defined in section 401(k)(2)) to the extent of amounts which a covered employee may elect to have the employer pay as contributions to a trust under such plan on behalf of the employee.

(C) Exception for certain plans maintained by educational institutions—Subparagraph (A) shall not apply to a plan maintained by an educational organization described in section 170(b)(1)(A)(ii) to the extent of amounts which a covered employee may elect to have the employer pay as contributions for post-retirement group life insurance if—

(i) all contributions for such insurance must be made before retirement, and

(ii) such life insurance does not have a cash surrender value at any time.

For purposes of section 79, any life insurance described in the preceding sentence shall be treated as group-term life insurance.

(D) Exception for health savings accounts—Subparagraph (A) shall not apply to a plan to the extent of amounts which a covered employee may elect to have the employer pay as contributions to a health savings account established on behalf of the employee.

(e) Highly compensated participant and individual defined—For purposes of this section—

(1) Highly compensated participant—The term "highly compensated participant" means a participant who is—

(A) an officer,

(B) a shareholder owning more than 5 percent of the voting power or value of all classes of stock of the employer,

(C) highly compensated, or

(D) a spouse or dependent (within the meaning of section 152, determined without regard to subsections (b)(1), (b)(2), and (d)(1)(B) thereof) of an individual described in subparagraph (A), (B), or (C).

(2) Highly compensated individual—The term "highly compensated individual" means an individual who is described in subparagraphs (A), (B), (C), or (D) of paragraph (1).

(f) Qualified benefits defined—For purposes of this section, the term "qualified benefit" means any benefit which, with the application of subsection (a), is not includible in the gross income of the employee by reason of an express provision of this chapter (other than section 106(b), 117, 127, or 132). Such term includes any group term life insurance which is includible in gross income only because it exceeds the dollar limitation of section 79 and such term includes any other benefit permitted under regulations. Such term shall not include any product which is advertised, marketed, or offered as long-term care insurance.

***

(j) **Simple cafeteria plans for small businesses** [applicable to years beginning after December 31, 2010].

(1) In general. An eligible employer maintaining a simple cafeteria plan with respect to which the requirements of this subsection are met for any year shall be treated as meeting any applicable nondiscrimination requirement during such year.

* * *

§ 219. Retirement savings.

(a) Allowance of deduction—In the case of an individual, there shall be allowed as a deduction an amount equal to the qualified retirement contributions of the individual for the taxable year.

(b) Maximum amount of deduction—

(1) In general—The amount allowable as a deduction under subsection (a) to any individual for any taxable year shall not exceed the lesser of—

(A) the deductible amount, or

(B) an amount equal to the compensation includible in the individual's gross income for such taxable year.

(2) Special rule for employer contributions under simplified employee pensions—This section shall not apply with respect to an employer contribution to a simplified employee pension.

* * *

(4) Special rule for simple retirement accounts—This section shall not apply with respect to any amount contributed to a simple retirement account established under section 408(p).

(5) Deductible amount—For purposes of paragraph (1)(A)—

(A) In general—The deductible amount shall be determined in accordance with the following table:

For taxable years beginning in:	*The deductible amount is:*
* * *	
2008 and thereafter	$5,000

(B) Catch-up contributions for individuals 50 or older—

(i) In general—In the case of an individual who has attained the age of 50 before the close of the taxable year, the deductible amount for such taxable year shall be increased by the applicable amount.

(ii) Applicable amount—For purposes of clause (i), the applicable amount shall be the amount determined in accordance with the following table:

For taxable years beginning in:	*The applicable amount is:*
2006 and thereafter	$1,000

(C) Catchup contributions for certain individuals—

(i) In general—In the case of an applicable individual who elects to make a qualified retirement contribution in addition to the deductible amount determined under subparagraph (A)—

(I) the deductible amount for any taxable year shall be increased by an amount equal to 3 times the applicable amount determined under subparagraph (B) for such taxable year, and

(II) subparagraph (B) shall not apply.

(ii) Applicable individual—For purposes of this subparagraph, the term "applicable individual" means, with respect to any taxable year, any individual who was a qualified participant in a qualified cash or deferred arrangement (as defined in section 401(k)) of an employer described in clause (iii) under which the employer matched at least 50 percent of the employee's contributions to such arrangement with stock of such employer.

(iii) Employer described—An employer is described in this clause if, in any taxable year preceding the taxable year described in clause (ii)—

(I) such employer (or any controlling corporation of such employer) was a debtor in a case under title 11 of the United States Code, or similar Federal or State law, and

(II) such employer (or any other person) was subject to an indictment or conviction resulting from business transactions related to such case.

(iv) Qualified participant—For purposes of clause (ii), the term "qualified participant" means any applicable individual who was a participant in the cash or deferred arrangement described in such clause on the date that is 6 months before the filing of the case described in clause (iii).

(v) Termination—This subparagraph shall not apply to taxable years beginning after December 31, 2009.

(D) Cost-of-living adjustment—

(i) In general—In the case of any taxable year beginning in a calendar year after 2008, the $5,000 amount under subparagraph (A) shall be increased by an amount equal to—

(I) such dollar amount, multiplied by

(II) the cost-of-living adjustment determined under section 1(f)(3) for the calendar year in which the taxable year begins, determined by substituting "calendar year 2007" for "calendar year 1992" in subparagraph (B) thereof.

(ii) Rounding rules—If any amount after adjustment under clause (i) is not a multiple of $500, such amount shall be rounded to the next lower multiple of $500.

(c) Special rules for certain married individuals—

(1) In general—In the case of an individual to whom this paragraph applies for the taxable year, the limitation of paragraph (1) of subsection (b) shall be equal to the lesser of—

(A) the dollar amount in effect under subsection (b)(1)(A) for the taxable year, or

(B) the sum of—

(i) the compensation includible in such individual's gross income for the taxable year, plus

(ii) the compensation includible in the gross income of such individual's spouse for the taxable year reduced by—

(I) the amount allowed as a deduction under subsection (a) to such spouse for such taxable year,

(II) the amount of any designated nondeductible contribution (as defined in section 408(o)) on behalf of such spouse for such taxable year, and

(III) the amount of any contribution on behalf of such spouse to a Roth IRA under section 408A for such taxable year.

(2) Individuals to whom paragraph (1) applies—Paragraph (1) shall apply to any individual if—

(A) such individual files a joint return for the taxable year, and

(B) the amount of compensation (if any) includible in such individual's gross income for the taxable year is less than the compensation includible in the gross income of such individual's spouse for the taxable year.

(d) Other limitations and restrictions—

(1) Beneficiary must be under age 70½—No deduction shall be allowed under this section with respect to any qualified retirement contribution for the benefit of an individual if such individual has attained age 70½ before the close of such individual's taxable year for which the contribution was made.

(2) Recontributed amounts—No deduction shall be allowed under this section with respect to a rollover contribution described in section 402(c), 403(a)(4), 403(b)(8), 408(d)(3), or 457(e)(16).

(3) Amounts contributed under endowment contract—In the case of an endowment contract described in section 408(b), no deduction shall be allowed under this section for that portion of the amounts paid under the contract for the taxable year which is properly allocable, under regulations prescribed by the Secretary, to the cost of life insurance.

(4) Denial of deduction for amount contributed to inherited annuities or accounts—No deduction shall be allowed under this section with respect to any amount paid to an inherited individual retirement account or individual retirement annuity (within the meaning of section 408(d)(3)(C)(ii)).

(e) Qualified retirement contribution—For purposes of this section, the term "qualified retirement contribution" means—

(1) any amount paid in cash for the taxable year by or on behalf of an individual to an individual retirement plan for such individual's benefit, and

(2) any amount contributed on behalf of any individual to a plan described in section 501(c)(18).

(f) Other definitions and special rules—

(1) Compensation—For purposes of this section, the term "compensation" includes earned income (as defined in section 401(c)(2)). The term "compensation" does not include any amount received as a pension or annuity and does not include any amount received as deferred compensation. The term "compensation" shall include any amount includible in the individual's gross income under section 71 with respect to a divorce or separation instrument described in subparagraph (A) of section 71(b)(2). For purposes of this paragraph, section 401(c)(2) shall be applied as if the term trade or business for purposes of section 1402 included service described in subsection (c)(6). The term compensation includes any differential wage payment (as defined in section 3401(h)(2))

(2) Married individuals—The maximum deduction under subsection (b) shall be computed separately for each individual, and this section shall be applied without regard to any community property laws.

(3) Time when contributions deemed made—For purposes of this section, a taxpayer shall be deemed to have made a contribution to an individual retirement plan on the last day of the preceding taxable year if the contribution is made on account of such taxable year and is made not later than the time prescribed by law for filing the return for such taxable year (not including extensions thereof).

(4) Reports—The Secretary shall prescribe regulations which prescribe the time and the manner in which reports to the Secretary and plan participants shall be made by the plan administrator of a qualified employer or government plan receiving qualified voluntary employee contributions.

(5) Employer payments—For purposes of this title, any amount paid by an employer to an individual retirement plan shall be treated as payment of compensation to the employee (other than a self-employed individual who is an employee within the meaning of section 401(c)(1)) includible in his gross income in the taxable year for which the amount was contributed, whether or not a deduction for such payment is allowable under this section to the employee.

(6) Excess contributions treated as contribution made during subsequent year for which there is an unused limitation—

(A) In general—If for the taxable year the maximum amount allowable as a deduction under this section for contributions to an individual retirement plan exceeds the amount contributed, then the taxpayer shall be treated as having made an additional contribution for the taxable year in an amount equal to the lesser of—

(i) the amount of such excess, or

(ii) the amount of the excess contributions for such taxable year (determined under section 4973(b)(2) without regard to subparagraph (C) thereof).

(B) Amount contributed—For purposes of this paragraph, the amount contributed—

(i) shall be determined without regard to this paragraph, and

(ii) shall not include any rollover contribution.

(C) Special rule where excess deduction was allowed for closed year—Proper reduction shall be made in the amount allowable as a deduction by reason of this paragraph for any amount allowed as a deduction under this section for a prior taxable year for which the period for assessing deficiency has expired if the amount so allowed exceeds the amount which should have been allowed for such prior taxable year.

(7) Special rule for compensation earned by members of the armed forces for service in a combat zone—For purposes of subsections (b)(1)(B) and (c), the amount of compensation includible in an individual's gross income shall be determined without regard to section 112.

(8) Election not to deduct contributions—For election not to deduct contributions to individual retirement plans, see section 408(o)(2)(B)(ii).

(g) Limitation on deduction for active participants in certain pension plans—

(1) In general—If (for any part of any plan year ending with or within a taxable year) an individual or the individual's spouse is an active participant, each of the dollar limitations contained in subsections (b)(1)(A) and (c)(1)(A) for such taxable year shall be reduced (but not below zero) by the amount determined under paragraph (2).

(2) Amount of reduction—

(A) In general—The amount determined under this paragraph with respect to any dollar limitation shall be the amount which bears the same ratio to such limitation as—

(i) the excess of—

(I) the taxpayer's adjusted gross income for such taxable year, over

(II) the applicable dollar amount, bears to

(ii) $10,000 ($20,000 in the case of a joint return for a taxable year beginning after December 31, 2006).

(B) No reduction below $200 until complete phase-out—No dollar limitation shall be reduced below $200 under paragraph (1) unless (without regard to this subparagraph) such limitation is reduced to zero.

(C) Rounding—Any amount determined under this paragraph which is not a multiple of $10 shall be rounded to the next lowest $10.

(3) Adjusted gross income; applicable dollar amount—For purposes of this subsection—

(A) Adjusted gross income—Adjusted gross income of any taxpayer shall be determined—

(i) after application of sections 86 and 469, and

(ii) without regard to sections 135, 137, 221, 222, and 911 or the deduction allowable under this section.

(B) Applicable dollar amount—The term "applicable dollar amount" means the following:

(i) In the case of a taxpayer filing a joint return:

For taxable years beginning in:	*The applicable dollar amount is:*
* * *	
2007 and thereafter	$80,000

(ii) In the case of any other taxpayer (other than a married individual filing a separate return):

For taxable years beginning in:	*The applicable dollar amount is:*
* * *	
2005 and thereafter	$50,000

(iii) In the case of a married individual filing a separate return, zero.

(4) Special rule for married individuals filing separately and living apart—A husband and wife who—

(A) file separate returns for any taxable year, and

(B) live apart at all times during such taxable year, shall not be treated as married individuals for purposes of this subsection.

(5) Active participant—For purposes of this subsection, the term "active participant" means, with respect to any plan year, an individual—

(A) who is an active participant in—

(i) a plan described in section 401(a) which includes a trust exempt from tax under section 501(a),

(ii) an annuity plan described in section 403(a),

(iii) a plan established for its employees by the United States, by a State or political subdivision thereof, or by an agency or instrumentality of any of the foregoing,

(iv) an annuity contract described in section 403(b),

(v) a simplified employee pension (within the meaning of section 408(k)), or

(vi) any simple retirement account (within the meaning of section 408(p)), or

(B) who makes deductible contributions to a trust described in section 501(c)(18).

The determination of whether an individual is an active participant shall be made without regard to whether or not such individual's rights under a plan, trust, or contract are nonforfeitable. An eligible deferred compensation plan (within the meaning of section 457(b)) shall not be treated as a plan described in subparagraph (A)(iii).

* * *

(7) Special rule for spouses who are not active participants—If this subsection applies to an individual for any taxable year solely because their spouse is an active participant, then, in applying this subsection to the individual (but not their spouse)—

(A) the applicable dollar amount under paragraph (3)(B)(i) shall be $150,000; and

(B) the amount applicable under paragraph (2)(A)(ii) shall be $10,000.

(8) Inflation adjustment—In the case of any taxable year beginning in a calendar year after 2006, the dollar amount in the last row of the table contained in paragraph (3)(B)(i), the dollar amount in the last row of the table contained in paragraph (3)(B)(ii), and the dollar amount contained in paragraph (7)(A), shall each be increased by an amount equal to—

(A) such dollar amount, multiplied by

(B) the cost-of-living adjustment determined under section 1(f)(3) for the calendar year in which the taxable year begins, determined by substituting "calendar year 2005" for "calendar year 1992" in subparagraph (B) thereof.

Any increase determined under the preceding sentence shall be rounded to the nearest multiple of $1,000.

* * *

§ 223. Health savings accounts.

(a) Deduction allowed—In the case of an individual who is an eligible individual for any month during the taxable year, there shall be allowed as a deduction for the taxable year an amount equal to the aggregate amount paid in cash during such taxable year by or on behalf of such individual to a health savings account of such individual.

(b) Limitations—

(1) In general—The amount allowable as a deduction under subsection (a) to an individual for the taxable year shall not exceed the sum of the monthly limitations for months during such taxable year that the individual is an eligible individual.

(2) Monthly limitation—The monthly limitation for any month is 1/12 of—

(A) in the case of an eligible individual who has self-only coverage under a high deductible health plan as of the first day of such month, $2,250.

(B) in the case of an eligible individual who has family coverage under a high deductible health plan as of the first day of such month, $4,500.

(3) Additional contributions for individuals 55 or older—

(A) In general—In the case of an individual who has attained age 55 before the close of the taxable year, the applicable limitation under subparagraphs (A) and (B) of paragraph (2) shall be increased by the additional contribution amount.

(B) Additional contribution amount—For purposes of this section, the additional contribution amount is the amount determined in accordance with the following table:

For taxable years beginning in:	*The additional contribution amount is:*
* * *	
2009 and thereafter	*$1,000*

(4) Coordination with other contributions—The limitation which would (but for this paragraph) apply under this subsection to an individual for any taxable year shall be reduced (but not below zero) by the sum of—

(A) the aggregate amount paid for such taxable year to Archer MSAs of such individual,

(B) the aggregate amount contributed to health savings accounts of such individual which is excludable from the taxpayer's gross income for such taxable year under section 106(d) (and such amount shall not be allowed as a deduction under subsection (a)), and

(C) the aggregate amount contributed to health savings accounts of such individual for such taxable year under section 408(d)(9) (and such amount shall not be allowed as a deduction under subsection (a)).

Subparagraph (A) shall not apply with respect to any individual to whom paragraph (5) applies.

(5) Special rule for married individuals—In the case of individuals who are married to each other, if either spouse has family coverage—

(A) both spouses shall be treated as having only such family coverage (and if such spouses each have family coverage under different plans, as having the family coverage with the lowest annual deductible), and

(B) the limitation under paragraph (1) (after the application of subparagraph (A) and without regard to any additional contribution amount under paragraph (3))—

(i) shall be reduced by the aggregate amount paid to Archer MSAs of such spouses for the taxable year, and

(ii) after such reduction, shall be divided equally between them unless they agree on a different division.

(6) Denial of deduction to dependents—No deduction shall be allowed under this section to any individual with respect to whom a deduction under section 151 is allowable to another taxpayer for a taxable year beginning in the calendar year in which such individual's taxable year begins.

(7) Medicare eligible individuals—The limitation under this subsection for any month with respect to an individual shall be zero for the first month such individual is entitled to benefits under title XVIII of the Social Security Act and for each month thereafter.

(c) Definitions and special rules—For purposes of this section—

(1) Eligible individual—

(A) In general—The term "eligible individual" means, with respect to any month, any individual if—

(i) such individual is covered under a high deductible health plan as of the 1st day of such month, and

(ii) such individual is not, while covered under a high deductible health plan, covered under any health plan—

(I) which is not a high deductible health plan, and

(II) which provides coverage for any benefit which is covered under the high deductible health plan.

(B) Certain coverage disregarded—Subparagraph (A)(ii) shall be applied without regard to—

(i) coverage for any benefit provided by permitted insurance,

(ii) coverage (whether through insurance or otherwise) for accidents, disability, dental care, vision care, or long-term care, and

(iii) for taxable years beginning after December 31, 2006, coverage under a health flexible spending arrangement during any period immediately following the end of a plan year of such arrangement during which unused benefits or contributions remaining at the end of such plan year may be paid or reimbursed to plan participants for qualified benefit expenses incurred during such period if—

(I) the balance in such arrangement at the end of such plan year is zero, or

(II) the individual is making a qualified HSA distribution (as defined in section 106(e)) in an amount equal to the remaining balance in such arrangement as of the end of such plan year, in accordance with rules prescribed by the Secretary.

(2) High deductible health plan—

(A) In general—The term "high deductible health plan" means a health plan—

(i) which has an annual deductible which is not less than—

(I) $1,000 for self-only coverage, and

(II) twice the dollar amount in subclause (I) for family coverage, and

(ii) the sum of the annual deductible and the other annual out-of-pocket expenses required to be paid under the plan (other than for premiums) for covered benefits does not exceed—

(I) $5,000 for self-only coverage, and

(II) twice the dollar amount in subclause (I) for family coverage.

(B) Exclusion of certain plans—Such term does not include a health plan if substantially all of its coverage is coverage described in paragraph (1)(B).

(C) Safe harbor for absence of preventive care deductible—A plan shall not fail to be treated as a high deductible health plan by reason of failing to have a deductible for preventive care (within the meaning of section 1871 of the Social Security Act, except as otherwise provided by the Secretary).

(D) Special rules for network plans—In the case of a plan using a network of providers—

(i) Annual out-of-pocket limitation—Such plan shall not fail to be treated as a high deductible health plan by reason of having an out-of-pocket limitation for services provided outside of such network which exceeds the applicable limitation under subparagraph (A)(ii).

(ii) Annual deductible—Such plan's annual deductible for services provided outside of such network shall not be taken into account for purposes of subsection (b)(2).

(3) Permitted insurance—The term "permitted insurance" means—

(A) insurance if substantially all of the coverage provided under such insurance relates to—

(i) liabilities incurred under workers' compensation laws,

(ii) tort liabilities,

(iii) liabilities relating to ownership or use of property, or

(iv) such other similar liabilities as the Secretary may specify by regulations,

(B) insurance for a specified disease or illness, and

(C) insurance paying a fixed amount per day (or other period) of hospitalization.

(4) Family coverage—The term "family coverage" means any coverage other than self-only coverage.

(5) Archer MSA—The term "Archer MSA" has the meaning given such term in section 220(d).

(d) Health savings account—For purposes of this section—

(1) In general—The term "health savings account" means a trust created or organized in the United States as a health savings account exclusively for the purpose of paying the qualified medical expenses of the account beneficiary, but only if the written governing instrument creating the trust meets the following requirements:

(A) Except in the case of a rollover contribution described in subsection (f)(5) or section 220(f)(5), no contribution will be accepted—

(i) unless it is in cash, or

(ii) to the extent such contribution, when added to previous contributions to the trust for the calendar year, exceeds the sum of—

(I) the dollar amount in effect under subsection (b)(2)(B), and

(II) the dollar amount in effect under subsection (b)(3)(B).

(B) The trustee is a bank (as defined in section 408(n)), an insurance company (as defined in section 816), or another person who demonstrates to the satisfaction of the Secretary that the manner in which such person will administer the trust will be consistent with the requirements of this section.

(C) No part of the trust assets will be invested in life insurance contracts.

(D) The assets of the trust will not be commingled with other property except in a common trust fund or common investment fund.

(E) The interest of an individual in the balance in his account is nonforfeitable.

(2) Qualified medical expenses—

(A) In general—The term "qualified medical expenses" means, with respect to an account beneficiary, amounts paid by such beneficiary for medical care (as defined in section 213(d) for such individual, the spouse of such individual, and any dependent (as defined in section 152) of such individual, but only to the extent such amounts are not compensated for by insurance or otherwise. Such term shall include an amount paid for medicine or a drug only if such medicine or drug is a prescribed drug (determined without regard to whether such drug is available without a prescription) or is insulin.

(B) Health insurance may not be purchased from account—Subparagraph (A) shall not apply to any payment for insurance.

(C) Exceptions—Subparagraph (B) shall not apply to any expense for coverage under—

(i) a health plan during any period of continuation coverage required under any Federal law,

(ii) a qualified long-term care insurance contract (as defined in section 7702B(b)),

(iii) a health plan during a period in which the individual is receiving unemployment compensation under any Federal or State law, or

(iv) in the case of an account beneficiary who has attained the age specified in section 1811 of the Social Security Act, any health insurance other than a medicare supplemental policy (as defined in section 1882 of the Social Security Act).

(3) Account beneficiary—The term "account beneficiary" means the individual on whose behalf the health savings account was established.

(4) Certain rules to apply—Rules similar to the following rules shall apply for purposes of this section:

(A) Section 219(d)(2) (relating to no deduction for rollovers).

(B) Section 219(f)(3) (relating to time when contributions deemed made).

(C) Except as provided in section 106(d), section 219(f)(5) (relating to employer payments).

(D) Section 408(g) (relating to community property laws).

(E) Section 408(h) (relating to custodial accounts).

(e) Tax treatment of accounts—

(1) In general—A health savings account is exempt from taxation under this subtitle unless such account has ceased to be a health savings account. Notwithstanding the preceding sentence, any such account is subject to the taxes imposed by section 511 (relating to imposition of tax on unrelated business income of charitable, etc. organizations).

(2) Account terminations—Rules similar to the rules of paragraphs (2) and (4) of section 408(e) shall apply to health savings accounts, and any amount treated as distributed under such rules shall be treated as not used to pay qualified medical expenses.

(f) Tax treatment of distributions—

(1) Amounts used for qualified medical expenses—Any amount paid or distributed out of a health savings account which is used exclusively to pay qualified medical expenses of any account beneficiary shall not be includible in gross income.

(2) Inclusion of amounts not used for qualified medical expenses—Any amount paid or distributed out of a health savings account which is not used exclusively to pay the qualified medical expenses of the account beneficiary shall be included in the gross income of such beneficiary.

(3) Excess contributions returned before due date of return—

(A) In general—If any excess contribution is contributed for a taxable year to any health savings account of an individual, paragraph (2) shall not apply to distributions from the health savings accounts of such individual (to the extent such distributions do not exceed the aggregate excess contributions to all such accounts of such individual for such year) if—

(i) such distribution is received by the individual on or before the last day prescribed by law (including extensions of time) for filing such individual's return for such taxable year, and

(ii) such distribution is accompanied by the amount of net income attributable to such excess contribution.

Any net income described in clause (ii) shall be included in the gross income of the individual for the taxable year in which it is received.

(B) Excess contribution—For purposes of subparagraph (A), the term "excess contribution" means any contribution (other than a rollover contribution described in paragraph (5) or section 220(f)(5)) which is neither excludable from gross income under section 106(d) nor deductible under this section.

(4) Additional tax on distributions not used for qualified medical expenses—

(A) In general—The tax imposed by this chapter on the account beneficiary for any taxable year in which there is a payment or distribution from a health savings account of such beneficiary which is includible in gross income under paragraph (2) shall be increased by 20 percent of the amount which is so includible.

(B) Exception for disability or death—Subparagraph (A) shall not apply if the payment or distribution is made after the account beneficiary becomes disabled within the meaning of section 72(m)(7) or dies.

(C) Exception for distributions after medicare eligibility—Subparagraph (A) shall not apply to any payment or distribution after the date on which the account beneficiary attains the age specified in section 1811 of the Social Security Act.

(5) Rollover contribution—An amount is described in this paragraph as a rollover contribution if it meets the requirements of subparagraphs (A) and (B).

(A) In general—Paragraph (2) shall not apply to any amount paid or distributed from a health savings account to the account beneficiary to the extent the amount received is paid into a health savings account for the benefit of such beneficiary not later than the 60th day after the day on which the beneficiary receives the payment or distribution.

(B) Limitation—This paragraph shall not apply to any amount described in subparagraph (A) received by an individual from a health savings account if, at any time during the 1-year period ending on the day of such receipt, such individual received any other amount described in subparagraph (A) from a health savings account which was not includible in the individual's gross income because of the application of this paragraph.

(6) Coordination with medical expense deduction—For purposes of determining the amount of the deduction under section 213, any payment or distribution out of a health savings account for qualified medical expenses shall not be treated as an expense paid for medical care.

(7) Transfer of account incident to divorce—The transfer of an individual's interest in a health savings account to an individual's spouse or former spouse under a divorce or separation instrument described in subparagraph (A) of section 71(b)(2) shall not be considered a taxable transfer made by such individual notwithstanding any other provision of this subtitle, and such interest shall, after such transfer, be treated as a health savings account with respect to which such spouse is the account beneficiary.

(8) Treatment after death of account beneficiary—

(A) Treatment if designated beneficiary is spouse—If the account beneficiary's surviving spouse acquires such beneficiary's interest in a health savings account by reason of being the designated beneficiary of such account at the death of the account beneficiary, such health savings account shall be treated as if the spouse were the account beneficiary.

(B) Other cases—

(i) In general—If, by reason of the death of the account beneficiary, any person acquires the account beneficiary's interest in a health savings account in a case to which subparagraph (A) does not apply—

(I) such account shall cease to be a health savings account as of the date of death, and

(II) an amount equal to the fair market value of the assets in such account on such date shall be includible if such person is not the estate of such beneficiary, in such person's gross income for the taxable year which includes such date, or if such person is the estate of such beneficiary, in such beneficiary's gross income for the last taxable year of such beneficiary.

(ii) Special rules—

(I) Reduction of inclusion for predeath expenses—The amount includible in gross income under clause (i) by any person (other than the estate) shall be reduced by the amount of qualified medical expenses which were incurred by the decedent before the date of the decedent's death and paid by such person within 1 year after such date.

(II) Deduction for estate taxes—An appropriate deduction shall be allowed under section 691(c) to any person (other than the decedent or the decedent's spouse) with respect to amounts included in gross income under clause (i) by such person.

(g) Cost-of-living adjustment—

(1) In general—Each dollar amount in subsections (b)(2) and (c)(2)(A) shall be increased by an amount equal to—

(A) such dollar amount, multiplied by

(B) the cost-of-living adjustment determined under section 1(f)(3) for the calendar year in which such taxable year begins determined by substituting for "calendar year 1992" in subparagraph (B) thereof—

(i) except as provided in clause (ii), "calendar year 1997", and

(ii) in the case of each dollar amount in subsection (c)(2)(A), "calendar year 2003".

In the case of adjustments made for any taxable year beginning after 2007, section 1(f)(4) shall be applied for purposes of this paragraph by substituting "March 31" for "August 31", and the Secretary shall publish the adjusted amounts under subsections (b)(2) and (c)(2)(A) for taxable years beginning in any calendar year no later than June 1 of the preceding calendar year.

(2) Rounding—If any increase under paragraph (1) is not a multiple of $50, such increase shall be rounded to the nearest multiple of $50.

* * *

§ 401. Qualified pension, profit-sharing, and stock bonus plans.

(a) Requirements for qualification—A trust created or organized in the United States and forming part of a stock bonus, pension, or profit-sharing plan of an employer for the exclusive benefit of his employees or their beneficiaries shall constitute a qualified trust under this section—

(1) if contributions are made to the trust by such employer, or employees, or both, or by another employer who is entitled to deduct his contributions under section 404(a)(3)(B) (relating to deduction for contributions to profit-sharing and stock bonus plans), or by a charitable remainder trust pursuant to a qualified gratuitous transfer (as defined in section 664(g)(1)), for the purpose of distributing to such employees or their beneficiaries the corpus and income of the fund accumulated by the trust in accordance with such plan;

(2) if under the trust instrument it is impossible, at any time prior to the satisfaction of all liabilities with respect to employees and their beneficiaries under the trust, for any part of the corpus or income to be (within the taxable year or thereafter) used for, or diverted to, purposes other than for the exclusive benefit of his employees or their beneficiaries (but this paragraph shall not be construed, in the case of a multiemployer plan, to prohibit the return of a contribution within 6 months after the plan administrator determines that the contribution was made by a mistake of fact or law (other than a mistake relating to whether the plan is described in section 401(a) or the trust which is part of such plan is exempt from taxation under section 501(a), or the return of any withdrawal liability payment determined to be an overpayment within 6 months of such determination));

(3) if the plan of which such trust is a part satisfies the requirements of section 410 (relating to minimum participation standards); and

(4) if the contributions or benefits provided under the plan do not discriminate in favor of highly compensated employees (within the meaning of section 414(q)). For purposes of this paragraph, there shall be excluded from consideration employees described in section 410(b)(3)(A) and (C).

(5) Special rules relating to nondiscrimination requirements—

(A) Salaried or clerical employees—A classification shall not be considered discriminatory within the meaning of paragraph (4) or section 410(b)(2)(A)(i) merely because it is limited to salaried or clerical employees.

(B) Contributions and benefits may bear uniform relationship to compensation—A plan shall not be considered discriminatory within the meaning of paragraph (4) merely because the contributions or benefits of, or on behalf of, the employees under the plan bear a uniform relationship to the compensation (within the meaning of section 414(s)) of such employees.

(C) Certain disparity permitted—A plan shall not be considered discriminatory within the meaning of paragraph (4) merely because the contributions or benefits of, or on behalf of, the employees under the plan favor highly compensated employees (as defined in section 414(q)) in the manner permitted under subsection (l).

(D) Integrated defined benefit plan—

(i) In general—A defined benefit plan shall not be considered discriminatory within the meaning of paragraph (4) merely because the plan provides that the employer-derived accrued retirement benefit for any participant under the plan may not exceed the excess (if any) of—

(I) the participant's final pay with the employer, over

(II) the employer-derived retirement benefit created under Federal law attributable to service by the participant with the employer.

For purposes of this clause, the employer-derived retirement benefit created under Federal law shall be treated as accruing ratably over 35 years.

(ii) Final pay—For purposes of this subparagraph, the participant's final pay is the compensation (as defined in section 414(q)(4)) paid to the participant by the employer for any year—

(I) which ends during the 5-year period ending with the year in which the participant separated from service for the employer, and

(II) for which the participant's total compensation from the employer was highest.

(E) 2 or more plans treated as single plan—For purposes of determining whether 2 or more plans of an employer satisfy the requirements of paragraph (4) when considered as a single plan—

(i) Contributions—If the amount of contributions on behalf of the employees allowed as a deduction under section 404 for the taxable year with respect to such plans, taken together, bears a uniform relationship to the compensation (within the meaning of section 414(s)) of such employees, the plans shall not be considered discriminatory merely because the rights of employees to, or derived from, the employer contributions under the separate plans do not become nonforfeitable at the same rate.

(ii) Benefits—If the employees' rights to benefits under the separate plans do not become nonforfeitable at the same rate, but the levels of benefits provided by the separate plans satisfy the requirements of regulations prescribed by the Secretary to take account of the differences in such rates, the plans shall not be considered discriminatory merely because of the difference in such rates.

(F) Social security retirement age—For purposes of testing for discrimination under paragraph (4)—

(i) the social security retirement age (as defined in section 415(b)(8)) shall be treated as a uniform retirement age, and

(ii) subsidized early retirement benefits and joint and survivor annuities shall not be treated as being unavailable to employees on the same terms merely because such benefits or annuities are based in whole or in part on an employee's social security retirement age (as so defined).

(G) Governmental plans—Paragraphs (3) and (4) shall not apply to a governmental plan (within the meaning of section 414(d)).

(6) A plan shall be considered as meeting the requirements of paragraph (3) during the whole of any taxable year of the plan if on one day in each quarter it satisfied such requirements.

(7) A trust shall not constitute a qualified trust under this section unless the plan of which such trust is a part satisfies the requirements of section 411 (relating to minimum vesting standards).

(8) A trust forming part of a defined benefit plan shall not constitute a qualified trust under this section unless the plan provides that forfeitures must not be applied to increase the benefits any employee would otherwise receive under the plan.

(9) Required distributions—

(A) In general—A trust shall not constitute a qualified trust under this subsection unless the plan provides that the entire interest of each employee—

(i) will be distributed to such employee not later than the required beginning date, or

(ii) will be distributed, beginning not later than the required beginning date, in accordance with regulations, over the life of such employee or over the lives of such employee and a designated beneficiary (or over a period not extending beyond the life expectancy of such employee or the life expectancy of such employee and a designated beneficiary).

(B) Required distribution where employee dies before entire interest is distributed—

(i) Where distributions have begun under subparagraph (A)(ii)—A trust shall not constitute a qualified trust under this section unless the plan provides that if—

(I) the distribution of the employee's interest has begun in accordance with subparagraph (A)(ii), and

(II) the employee dies before his entire interest has been distributed to him,

the remaining portion of such interest will be distributed at least as rapidly as under the method of distributions being used under subparagraph (A)(ii) as of the date of his death.

(ii) 5-year rule for other cases—A trust shall not constitute a qualified trust under this section unless the plan provides that, if an employee dies before the distribution of the employee's interest has begun in accordance with subparagraph (A)(ii), the entire interest of the employee will be distributed within 5 years after the death of such employee.

(iii) Exception to 5-year rule for certain amounts payable over life of beneficiary—If—

(I) any portion of the employee's interest is payable to (or for the benefit of) a designated beneficiary,

(II) such portion will be distributed (in accordance with regulations) over the life of such designated beneficiary (or over a period not extending beyond the life expectancy of such beneficiary), and

(III) such distributions begin not later than 1 year after the date of the employee's death or such later date as the Secretary may by regulations prescribe,

for purposes of clause (ii), the portion referred to in subclause (I) shall be treated as distributed on the date on which such distributions begin.

(iv) Special rule for surviving spouse of employee—If the designated beneficiary referred to in clause (iii)(I) is the surviving spouse of the employee—

(I) the date on which the distributions are required to begin under clause (iii)(III) shall not be earlier than the date on which the employee would have attained age 70½, and

(II) if the surviving spouse dies before the distributions to such spouse begin, this subparagraph shall be applied as if the surviving spouse were the employee.

(C) Required beginning date—For purposes of this paragraph—

(i) In general—The term "required beginning date" means April 1 of the calendar year following the later of—

(I) the calendar year in which the employee attains age 70½, or

(II) the calendar year in which the employee retires.

(ii) Exception—Subclause (II) of clause (i) shall not apply—

(I) except as provided in section 409(d), in the case of an employee who is a 5-percent owner (as defined in section 416) with respect to the plan year ending in the calendar year in which the employee attains age 70½, or

(II) for purposes of section 408(a)(6) or (b)(3).

(iii) Actuarial adjustment—In the case of an employee to whom clause (i)(II) applies who retires in a calendar year after the calendar year in which the employee attains age 70½, the employee's accrued benefit shall be actuarially increased to take into account the period after age 70½ in which the employee was not receiving any benefits under the plan.

(iv) Exception for governmental and church plans—Clauses (ii) and (iii) shall not apply in the case of a governmental plan or church plan. For purposes of this clause, the term "church plan" means a plan maintained by a church for church employees, and the term "church" means any church (as defined in section 3121(w)(3)(A)) or qualified church-controlled organization (as defined in section 3121(w)(3)(B)).

(D) Life expectancy—For purposes of this paragraph, the life expectancy of an employee and the employee's spouse (other than in the case of a life annuity) may be redetermined but not more frequently than annually.

(E) Designated beneficiary—For purposes of this paragraph, the term "designated beneficiary" means any individual designated as a beneficiary by the employee.

(F) Treatment of payments to children—Under regulations prescribed by the Secretary, for purposes of this paragraph, any amount paid to a child shall be treated as if it had been paid to the surviving spouse if such amount will become payable to the surviving spouse upon such child reaching majority (or other designated event permitted under regulations).

(G) Treatment of incidental death benefit distributions—For purposes of this title, any distribution required under the incidental death benefit requirements of this subsection shall be treated as a distribution required under this paragraph.

(H) Temporary waiver of minimum required distribution—

(i) In general—The requirements of this paragraph shall not apply for calendar year 2009 to—

(I) a defined contribution plan which is described in this subsection or in section 403(a) or 403(b),

(II) a defined contribution plan which is an eligible deferred compensation plan described in section 457(b) but only if such plan is maintained by an employer described in section 457(e)(1)(A), or

(III) an individual retirement plan.

(ii) Special rules regarding waiver period—For purposes of this paragraph—

(I) the required beginning date with respect to any individual shall be determined without regard to this subparagraph for purposes of applying this paragraph for calendar years after 2009, and

(II) if clause (ii) of subparagraph (B) applies, the 5-year period described in such clause shall be determined without regard to calendar year 2009.

(10) Other requirements—

(A) Plans benefiting owner-employees—In the case of any plan which provides contributions or benefits for employees some or all of whom are owner-employees (as defined in subsection (c)(3)), a trust forming part of such plan shall constitute a qualified trust under this section only if the requirements of subsection (d) are also met.

(B) Top-heavy plans—

(i) In general—In the case of any top-heavy plan, a trust forming part of such plan shall constitute a qualified trust under this section only if the requirements of section 416 are met.

(ii) Plans which may become top-heavy—Except to the extent provided in regulations, a trust forming part of a plan (whether or not a top-heavy plan) shall constitute a qualified trust under this section only if such plan contains provisions—

(I) which will take effect if such plan becomes a top-heavy plan, and

(II) which meet the requirements of section 416.

(iii) Exemption for governmental plans—This subparagraph shall not apply to any governmental plan.

(11) Requirement of joint and survivor annuity and preretirement survivor annuity—

(A) In general—In the case of any plan to which this paragraph applies, except as provided in section 417, a trust forming part of such plan shall not constitute a qualified trust under this section unless—

(i) in the case of a vested participant who does not die before the annuity starting date, the accrued benefit payable to such participant is provided in the form of a qualified joint and survivor annuity, and

(ii) in the case of a vested participant who dies before the annuity starting date and who has a surviving spouse, a qualified preretirement survivor annuity is provided to the surviving spouse of such participant.

(B) Plans to which paragraph applies—This paragraph shall apply to—

(i) any defined benefit plan,

(ii) any defined contribution plan which is subject to the funding standards of section 412, and

(iii) any participant under any other defined contribution plan unless—

(I) such plan provides that the participant's nonforfeitable accrued benefit (reduced by any security interest held by the plan by reason of a loan outstanding to such participant) is payable in full, on the death of the participant, to the participant's surviving spouse (or, if there is no surviving spouse or the surviving spouse consents in the manner required under section 417(a)(2), to a designated beneficiary),

(II) such participant does not elect a payment of benefits in the form of a life annuity, and

(III) with respect to such participant, such plan is not a direct or indirect transferee (in a transfer after December 31, 1984) of a plan which is described in clause (i) or (ii) or to which this clause applied with respect to the participant.

Clause (iii)(III) shall apply only with respect to the transferred assets (and income therefrom) if the plan separately accounts for such assets and any income therefrom.

(C) Exception for certain ESOP benefits—

(i) In general—In the case of—

(I) a tax credit employee stock ownership plan (as defined in section 409(a)), or

(II) an employee stock ownership plan (as defined in section 4975(e)(7)),

subparagraph (A) shall not apply to that portion of the employee's accrued benefit to which the requirements of section 409(h) apply.

(ii) Nonforfeitable benefit must be paid in full, etc—In the case of any participant, clause (i) shall apply only if the requirements of subclauses (I), (II), and (III) of subparagraph (B)(iii) are met with respect to such participant.

(D) Special rule where participant and spouse married less than 1 year—A plan shall not be treated as failing to meet the requirements of subparagraphs (B)(iii) or (C) merely because the plan provides that benefits will not be payable to the surviving spouse of the participant unless the participant and such spouse had been married throughout the 1-year period ending on the earlier of the participant's annuity starting date or the date of the participant's death.

(E) Exception for plans described in section 404(c)—This paragraph shall not apply to a plan which the Secretary has determined is a plan described in section 404(c) (or a continuation thereof) in which participation is substantially limited to individuals who, before January 1, 1976, ceased employment covered by the plan.

(F) Cross reference—For—

(i) provisions under which participants may elect to waive the requirements of this paragraph, and

(ii) other definitions and special rules for purposes of this paragraph,

see section 417.

(12) A trust shall not constitute a qualified trust under this section unless the plan of which such trust is a part provides that in the case of any merger or consolidation with, or transfer of assets or liabilities to, any other plan after September 2, 1974, each participant in the plan would (if the plan then terminated) receive a benefit immediately after the merger, consolidation, or transfer which is equal to or greater than the benefit he would have been entitled to receive immediately before the merger, consolidation, or transfer (if the plan had then terminated). The preceding sentence does not apply to any multiemployer plan with respect to any transaction to the extent that participants either before or after the transaction are covered under a multiemployer plan to which title IV of the Employee Retirement Income Security Act of 1974 applies.

(13) Assignment and alienation—

(A) In general—A trust shall not constitute a qualified trust under this section unless the plan of which such trust is a part provides that benefits provided under the plan may not be assigned or alienated. For purposes of the preceding sentence, there shall not be taken into account any voluntary and revocable assignment of not to exceed 10 percent of any benefit payment made by any participant who is receiving benefits under the plan unless the assignment or alienation is made for purposes of defraying plan administration costs. For purposes of this paragraph a loan made to a participant or beneficiary shall not be treated as an assignment or alienation if such loan is secured by the participant's accrued nonforfeitable benefit and is exempt from the tax imposed by section 4975 (relating to tax on prohibited transactions) by reason of section 4975(d)(1). This paragraph shall take effect on January 1, 1976 and shall not apply to assignments which were irrevocable on September 2, 1974.

(B) Special rules for domestic relations orders—Subparagraph (A) shall apply to the creation, assignment, or recognition of a right to any benefit payable with respect to a participant pursuant to a domestic relations order, except that subparagraph (A) shall not apply if the order is determined to be a qualified domestic relations order.

(C) Special rule for certain judgments and settlements—Subparagraph (A) shall not apply to any offset of a participant's benefits provided under a plan against an amount that the participant is ordered or required to pay to the plan if—

(i) the order or requirement to pay arises—

(I) under a judgment of conviction for a crime involving such plan,

(II) under a civil judgment (including a consent order or decree) entered by a court in an action brought in connection with a violation (or alleged violation) of part 4 of subtitle B of title I of the Employee Retirement Income Security Act of 1974, or

(III) pursuant to a settlement agreement between the Secretary of Labor and the participant, or a settlement agreement between the Pension Benefit Guaranty Corporation and the participant, in connection with a violation (or alleged violation) of part 4 of such subtitle by a fiduciary or any other person,

(ii) the judgment, order, decree, or settlement agreement expressly provides for the offset of all or part of the amount ordered or required to be paid to the plan against the participant's benefits provided under the plan, and

(iii) in a case in which the survivor annuity requirements of section 401(a)(11) apply with respect to distributions from the plan to the participant, if the participant has a spouse at the time at which the offset is to be made—

(I) either such spouse has consented in writing to such offset and such consent is witnessed by a notary public or representative of the plan (or it is established to the satisfaction of a plan representative that such consent may not be obtained by reason of circumstances described in section 417(a)(2)(B)), or an election to waive the right of the spouse to either a qualified joint and survivor annuity or a qualified preretirement survivor annuity is in effect in accordance with the requirements of section 417(a),

(II) such spouse is ordered or required in such judgment, order, decree, or settlement to pay an amount to the plan in connection with a violation of part 4 of such subtitle, or

(III) in such judgment, order, decree, or settlement, such spouse retains the right to receive the survivor annuity under a qualified joint and survivor annuity provided pursuant to section 401(a)(11)(A)(i) and under a qualified preretirement survivor annuity provided pursuant to section 401(a)(11)(A)(ii), determined in accordance with subparagraph (D).

A plan shall not be treated as failing to meet the requirements of this subsection, subsection (k), section 403(b), or section 409(d) solely by reason of an offset described in this subparagraph.

(D) Survivor annuity—

(i) In general—The survivor annuity described in subparagraph (C)(iii)(III) shall be determined as if—

(I) the participant terminated employment on the date of the offset,

(II) there was no offset,

(III) the plan permitted commencement of benefits only on or after normal retirement age,

(IV) the plan provided only the minimum-required qualified joint and survivor annuity, and

(V) the amount of the qualified preretirement survivor annuity under the plan is equal to the amount of the survivor annuity payable under the minimum-required qualified joint and survivor annuity.

(ii) Definition—For purposes of this subparagraph, the term "minimum-required qualified joint and survivor annuity" means the qualified joint and survivor annuity which is the actuarial equivalent of the participant's accrued benefit (within the meaning of section 411(a)(7)) and under which the survivor annuity is 50 percent of the amount of the annuity which is payable during the joint lives of the participant and the spouse.

(14) A trust shall not constitute a qualified trust under this section unless the plan of which such trust is a part provides that, unless the participant otherwise elects, the payment of benefits under the plan to the participant will begin not later than the 60th day after the latest of the close of the plan year in which—

(A) the date on which the participant attains the earlier of age 65 or the normal retirement age specified under the plan,

(B) occurs the 10th anniversary of the year in which the participant commenced participation in the plan, or

(C) the participant terminates his service with the employer.

In the case of a plan which provides for the payment of an early retirement benefit, a trust forming a part of such plan shall not constitute a qualified trust under this section unless a participant who satisfied the service requirements for such early retirement benefit, but separated from the service (with any nonforfeitable right to an accrued benefit) before satisfying the age requirement for such early retirement benefit, is entitled upon satisfaction of such age requirement to receive a benefit not less than the benefit to which he would be entitled at the normal retirement age, actuarially reduced under regulations prescribed by the Secretary.

(15) A trust shall not constitute a qualified trust under this section unless under the plan of which such trust is a part—

(A) in the case of a participant or beneficiary who is receiving benefits under such plan, or

(B) in the case of a participant who is separated from the service and who has nonforfeitable rights to benefits,

such benefits are not decreased by reason of any increase in the benefit levels payable under title II of the Social Security Act or any increase in the wage base under such title II, if such increase takes place after September 2, 1974, or (if later) the earlier of the date of first receipt of such benefits or the date of such separation, as the case may be.

(16) A trust shall not constitute a qualified trust under this section if the plan of which such trust is a part provides for benefits or contributions which exceed the limitations of section 415.

(17) Compensation limit—

(A) In general—A trust shall not constitute a qualified trust under this section unless, under the plan of which such trust is a part, the annual compensation of each employee taken into account under the plan for any year does not exceed $200,000.

(B) Cost-of-living adjustment—The Secretary shall adjust annually the $200,000 amount in subparagraph (A) for increases in the cost-of-living at the same time and in the same manner as adjustments under section 415(d) ; except that the base period shall be the calendar quarter beginning July 1, 2001, and any increase which is not a multiple of $5,000 shall be rounded to the next lowest multiple of $5,000.

(18) [Repealed]

(19) A trust shall not constitute a qualified trust under this section if under the plan of which such trust is a part any part of a participant's accrued benefit derived from employer contributions (whether or not otherwise nonforfeitable), is forfeitable solely because of withdrawal by such participant of any amount attributable to the benefit derived from contributions made by such participant. The preceding sentence shall not apply to the accrued benefit of any participant unless, at the time of such withdrawal, such participant has a nonforfeitable right to at least 50 percent of such accrued benefit (as determined under section 411). The first sentence of this paragraph shall not apply to the extent that an accrued benefit is permitted to be forfeited in accordance with section 411(a)(3)(D)(iii) (relating to proportional forfeitures of benefits accrued before September 2, 1974, in the event of withdrawal of certain mandatory contributions).

(20) A trust forming part of a pension plan shall not be treated as failing to constitute a qualified trust under this section merely because the pension plan of which such trust is a part makes 1 or more distributions within 1 taxable year to a distributee on account of a termination of the plan of which the trust is a part, or in the case of a profit-sharing or stock bonus plan, a complete discontinuance of contributions under such plan. This paragraph shall not apply to a defined benefit plan unless the employer maintaining such plan files a notice with the Pension Benefit Guaranty Corporation (at the time and in the manner prescribed by the Pension Benefit Guaranty Corporation) notifying the Corporation of such payment or distribution and the Corporation has approved such payment or distribution or, within 90 days after the date on which such notice was filed, has failed to disapprove such payment or distribution. For purposes of this paragraph, rules similar to the rules of section 402(a)(6)(B) (as in effect before its repeal by section 521 of the Unemployment Compensation Amendments of 1992) shall apply.

(21) [Repealed]

(22) If a defined contribution plan (other than a profit-sharing plan)—

(A) is established by an employer whose stock is not readily tradable on an established market, and

(B) after acquiring securities of the employer, more than 10 percent of the total assets of the plan are securities of the employer,

any trust forming part of such plan shall not constitute a qualified trust under this section unless the plan meets the requirements of subsection (e) of section 409. The requirements of subsection (e) of section 409 shall not apply to any employees of an employer who are participants in any defined contribution plan established and maintained by such employer if the stock of such employer is not readily tradable on an established market and the trade or business of such employer consists of publishing on a regular basis a newspaper for general circulation. For purposes of the preceding sentence, subsections (b), (c), (m), and (o) of section 414 shall not apply except for determining whether stock of the employer is not readily tradable on an established market.

(23) A stock bonus plan shall not be treated as meeting the requirements of this section unless such plan meets the requirements of subsections (h) and (o) of section 409, except that in applying section 409(h) for purposes of this paragraph, the term "employer securities" shall include any securities of the employer held by the plan.

(24) Any group trust which otherwise meets the requirements of this section shall not be treated as not meeting such requirements on account of the participation or inclusion in such trust of the moneys of any plan or governmental unit described in section 818(a)(6).

(25) Requirement that actuarial assumptions be specified—A defined benefit plan shall not be treated as providing definitely determinable benefits unless, whenever the amount of any benefit is to be determined on the basis of actuarial assumptions, such assumptions are specified in the plan in a way which precludes employer discretion.

(26) Additional participation requirements—

(A) In general—In the case of a trust which is a part of a defined benefit plan, such trust shall not constitute a qualified trust under this subsection unless on each day of the plan year such trust benefits at least the lesser of—

(i) 50 employees of the employer, or

(ii) the greater of—

(I) 40 percent of all employees of the employer, or

(II) 2 employees (or if there is only 1 employee, such employee).

(B) Treatment of excludable employees—

(i) In general—A plan may exclude from consideration under this paragraph employees described in paragraphs (3) and (4)(A) of section 410(b).

(ii) Separate application for certain excludable employees—If employees described in section 410(b)(4)(B) are covered under a plan which meets the requirements of subparagraph (A) separately with respect to such employees, such employees may be excluded from consideration in determining whether any plan of the employer meets such requirements if—

(I) the benefits for such employees are provided under the same plan as benefits for other employees,

(II) the benefits provided to such employees are not greater than comparable benefits provided to other employees under the plan, and

(III) no highly compensated employee (within the meaning of section 414(q)) is included in the group of such employees for more than 1 year.

(C) Special rule for collective bargaining units—Except to the extent provided in regulations, a plan covering only employees described in section 410(b)(3)(A) may exclude from consideration any employees who are not included in the unit or units in which the covered employees are included.

(D) Paragraph not to apply to multiemployer plans—Except to the extent provided in regulations, this paragraph shall not apply to employees in a multiemployer plan (within the meaning of section 414(f)) who are covered by collective bargaining agreements.

(E) Special rule for certain dispositions or acquisitions—Rules similar to the rules of section 410(b)(6)(C) shall apply for purposes of this paragraph.

(F) Separate lines of business—At the election of the employer and with the consent of the Secretary, this paragraph may be applied separately with respect to each separate line of business of the employer. For purposes of this paragraph, the term "separate line of business" has the meaning given such term by section 414(r) (without regard to paragraph (2)(A) or (7) thereof).

(G) Exception for governmental plans—This paragraph shall not apply to a governmental plan (within the meaning of section 414(d)).

(H) Regulations—The Secretary may by regulation provide that any separate benefit structure, any separate trust, or any other separate arrangement is to be treated as a separate plan for purposes of applying this paragraph.

(27) Determinations as to profit-sharing plans—

(A) Contributions need not be based on profits—The determination of whether the plan under which any contributions are made is a profit-sharing plan shall be made without regard to current or accumulated profits of the employer and without regard to whether the employer is a tax-exempt organization.

(B) Plan must designate type—In the case of a plan which is intended to be a money purchase pension plan or a profit-sharing plan, a trust forming part of such plan shall not constitute a qualified trust under this subsection unless the plan designates such intent at such time and in such manner as the Secretary may prescribe.

(28) Additional requirements relating to employee stock ownership plans—

(A) In general—In the case of a trust which is part of an employee stock ownership plan (within the meaning of section 4975(e)(7)) or a plan which meets the requirements of section 409(a), such trust shall not constitute a qualified trust under this section unless such plan meets the requirements of subparagraphs (B) and (C).

(B) Diversification of investments—

(i) In general—A plan meets the requirements of this subparagraph if each qualified participant in the plan may elect within 90 days after the close of each plan year in the qualified election period to direct the plan as to the investment of at least 25 percent of the participant's account in the plan (to the extent such portion exceeds the amount to which a prior election under this subparagraph applies). In the case of the election year in which the participant can make his last election, the preceding sentence shall be applied by substituting "50 percent" for "25 percent".

(ii) Method of meeting requirements—A plan shall be treated as meeting the requirements of clause (i) if—

(I) the portion of the participant's account covered by the election under clause (i) is distributed within 90 days after the period during which the election may be made, or

(II) the plan offers at least 3 investment options (not inconsistent with regulations prescribed by the Secretary) to each participant making an election under clause (i) and within 90 days after the period during which the election may be made, the plan invests the portion of the participant's account covered by the election in accordance with such election.

(iii) Qualified participant—For purposes of this subparagraph, the term "qualified participant" means any employee who has completed at least 10 years of participation under the plan and has attained age 55.

(iv) Qualified election period—For purposes of this subparagraph, the term "qualified election period" means the 6-plan-year period beginning with the later of—

(I) the 1st plan year in which the individual first became a qualified participant, or

(II) the 1st plan year beginning after December 31, 1986.

(v) Exception—This subparagraph shall not apply to an applicable defined contribution plan (as defined in paragraph (35)(E)).

For purposes of the preceding sentence, an employer may elect to treat an individual first becoming a qualified participant in the 1st plan year beginning in 1987 as having become a participant in the 1st plan year beginning in 1988.

(C) Use of independent appraiser—A plan meets the requirements of this subparagraph if all valuations of employer securities which are not readily tradable on an established securities market with respect to activities carried on by the plan are by an independent appraiser. For purposes of the preceding sentence, the term "independent appraiser" means any appraiser meeting requirements similar to the requirements of the regulations prescribed under section 170(a)(1).

(29) Benefit limitations—In the case of a defined benefit plan (other than a multiemployer plan) to which the requirements of section 412 apply, the trust of which the plan is a part shall not constitute a qualified trust under this subsection unless the plan meets the requirements of section 436.

(30) Limitations on elective deferrals—In the case of a trust which is part of a plan under which elective deferrals (within the meaning of section 402(g)(3)) may be made with respect to any individual during a calendar year, such trust shall not constitute a qualified trust under this subsection unless the plan provides that the amount of such deferrals under such plan and all other plans, contracts, or arrangements of an employer maintaining such plan may not exceed the amount of the limitation in effect under section 402(g)(1)(A) for taxable years beginning in such calendar year.

(31) Direct transfer of eligible rollover distributions—

(A) In general—A trust shall not constitute a qualified trust under this section unless the plan of which such trust is a part provides that if the distributee of any eligible rollover distribution—

(i) elects to have such distribution paid directly to an eligible retirement plan, and

(ii) specifies the eligible retirement plan to which such distribution is to be paid (in such form and at such time as the plan administrator may prescribe),

such distribution shall be made in the form of a direct trustee-to-trustee transfer to the eligible retirement plan so specified.

(B) Certain mandatory distributions—

(i) In general—In case of a trust which is part of an eligible plan, such trust shall not constitute a qualified trust under this section unless the plan of which such trust is a part provides that if—

(I) a distribution described in clause (ii) in excess of $1,000 is made, and

(II) the distributee does not make an election under subparagraph (A) and does not elect to receive the distribution directly,

the plan administrator shall make such transfer to an individual retirement plan of a designated trustee or issuer and shall notify the distributee in writing (either separately or as part of the notice under section 402(f)) that the distribution may be transferred to another individual retirement plan.

(ii) Eligible plan—For purposes of clause (i), the term "eligible plan" means a plan which provides that any nonforfeitable accrued benefit for which the present value (as determined under section 411(a)(11)) does not exceed $5,000 shall be immediately distributed to the participant.

(C) Limitation—Subparagraphs (A) and (B) shall apply only to the extent that the eligible rollover distribution would be includible in gross income if not transferred as provided in subparagraph (A) (determined without regard to sections 402(c), 403(a)(4), 403(b)(8), and 457(e)(16)). The preceding sentence shall not apply to such distribution if the plan to which such distribution is transferred—

(i) is a qualified trust which is part of a plan which is a defined contribution plan and agrees to separately account for amounts so transferred, including separately accounting for the portion of such distribution which is includible in gross income and the portion of such distribution which is not so includible, or

(ii) is an eligible retirement plan described in clause (i) or (ii) of section 402(c)(8)(B).

(D) Eligible rollover distribution—For purposes of this paragraph, the term "eligible rollover distribution" has the meaning given such term by section 402(f)(2)(A).

(E) Eligible retirement plan—For purposes of this paragraph, the term "eligible retirement plan" has the meaning given such term by section 402(c)(8)(B), except that a qualified trust shall be considered an eligible retirement plan only if it is a defined contribution plan, the terms of which permit the acceptance of rollover distributions.

(32) Treatment of failure to make certain payments if plan has liquidity shortfall—

(A) In general—A trust forming part of a pension plan to which section 430(j)(4) applies shall not be treated as failing to constitute a qualified trust under this section merely because such plan ceases to make any payment described in subparagraph (B) during any period that such plan has a liquidity shortfall (as defined in section 430(j)(4)).

(B) Payments described—A payment is described in this subparagraph if such payment is—

(i) any payment, in excess of the monthly amount paid under a single life annuity (plus any social security supplements described in the last sentence of section 411(a)(9)), to a participant or beneficiary whose annuity starting date (as defined in section 417(f)(2)) occurs during the period referred to in subparagraph (A),

(ii) any payment for the purchase of an irrevocable commitment from an insurer to pay benefits, and

(iii) any other payment specified by the Secretary by regulations.

(C) Period of shortfall—For purposes of this paragraph, a plan has a liquidity shortfall during the period that there is an underpayment of an installment under section 430(j)(3) by reason of section 430(j)(4)(A) thereof.

(33) Prohibition on benefit increases while sponsor is in bankruptcy—

(A) In general—A trust which is part of a plan to which this paragraph applies shall not constitute a qualified trust under this section if an amendment to such plan is adopted while the employer is a debtor in a case under title 11, United States Code, or similar Federal or State law, if such amendment increases liabilities of the plan by reason of—

(i) any increase in benefits,

(ii) any change in the accrual of benefits, or

(iii) any change in the rate at which benefits become nonforfeitable under the plan,

with respect to employees of the debtor, and such amendment is effective prior to the effective date of such employer's plan of reorganization.

(B) Exceptions—This paragraph shall not apply to any plan amendment if—

(i) the plan, were such amendment to take effect, would have a funding target attainment percentage (as defined in section 430(d)(2)) of 100 percent or more,

(ii) the Secretary determines that such amendment is reasonable and provides for only de minimis increases in the liabilities of the plan with respect to employees of the debtor,

(iii) such amendment only repeals an amendment described in section 412(d)(2), or

(iv) such amendment is required as a condition of qualification under this part.

(C) Plans to which this paragraph applies—This paragraph shall apply only to plans (other than multiemployer plans) covered under section 4021 of the Employee Retirement Income Security Act of 1974.

(D) Employer—For purposes of this paragraph, the term "employer" means the employer referred to in section 412(b)(1), without regard to section 412(b)(2).

(34) Benefits of missing participants on plan termination—In the case of a plan covered by title IV of the Employee Retirement Income Security Act of 1974, a trust forming part of such plan shall not be treated as failing to constitute a qualified trust under this section merely because the pension plan of which such trust is a part, upon its termination, transfers benefits of missing participants to the Pension Benefit Guaranty Corporation in accordance with section 4050 of such Act.

(35) Diversification requirements for certain defined contribution plans—

(A) In general—A trust which is part of an applicable defined contribution plan shall not be treated as a qualified trust unless the plan meets the diversification requirements of subparagraphs (B), (C), and (D).

(B) Employee contributions and elective deferrals invested in employer securities—In the case of the portion of an applicable individual's account attributable to employee contributions and elective deferrals which is invested in employer securities, a plan meets the requirements of this subparagraph if the applicable individual may elect to direct the plan to divest any such securities and to reinvest an equivalent amount in other investment options meeting the requirements of subparagraph (D).

(C) Employer contributions invested in employer securities—In the case of the portion of the account attributable to employer contributions other than elective deferrals which is invested in employer securities, a plan meets the requirements of this subparagraph if each applicable individual who—

(i) is a participant who has completed at least 3 years of service, or

(ii) is a beneficiary of a participant described in clause (i) or of a deceased participant, may elect to direct the plan to divest any such securities and to reinvest an equivalent amount in other investment options meeting the requirements of subparagraph (D).

(D) Investment options—

(i) In general—The requirements of this subparagraph are met if the plan offers not less than 3 investment options, other than employer securities, to which an applicable individual may direct the proceeds from the divestment of employer securities pursuant to this paragraph, each of which is diversified and has materially different risk and return characteristics.

(ii) Treatment of certain restrictions and conditions—

(I) Time for making investment choices—A plan shall not be treated as failing to meet the requirements of this subparagraph merely because the plan limits the time for divestment and reinvestment to periodic, reasonable opportunities occurring no less frequently than quarterly.

(II) Certain restrictions and conditions not allowed—Except as provided in regulations, a plan shall not meet the requirements of this subparagraph if the plan imposes restrictions or conditions with respect to the investment of employer securities which are not imposed on the investment of other assets of the plan. This subclause shall not apply to any restrictions or conditions imposed by reason of the application of securities laws.

(E) Applicable defined contribution plan—For purposes of this paragraph—

(i) In general—The term "applicable defined contribution plan" means any defined contribution plan which holds any publicly traded employer securities.

(ii) Exception for certain ESOPs—Such term does not include an employee stock ownership plan if—

(I) there are no contributions to such plan (or earnings thereunder) which are held within such plan and are subject to subsection (k) or (m), and

(II) such plan is a separate plan for purposes of section 414(l) with respect to any other defined benefit plan or defined contribution plan maintained by the same employer or employers.

(iii) Exception for one participant plans—Such term does not include a one-participant retirement plan.

(iv) One-participant retirement plan—For purposes of clause (iii), the term "one-participant retirement plan" means a retirement plan that on the first day of the plan year—

(I) covered only one individual (or the individual and the individual's spouse) and the individual (or the individual and the individual's spouse) owned 100 percent of the plan sponsor (whether or not incorporated), or

(II) covered only one or more partners (or partners and their spouses) in the plan sponsor.

(F) Certain plans treated as holding publicly traded employer securities—

(i) In general—Except as provided in regulations or in clause (ii), a plan holding employer securities which are not publicly traded employer securities shall be treated as holding publicly traded employer securities if any employer corporation, or any member of a controlled group of corporations which includes such employer corporation, has issued a class of stock which is a publicly traded employer security.

(ii) Exception for certain controlled groups with publicly traded securities—Clause (i) shall not apply to a plan if—

(I) no employer corporation, or parent corporation of an employer corporation, has issued any publicly traded employer security, and

(II) no employer corporation, or parent corporation of an employer corporation, has issued any special class of stock which grants particular rights to, or bears particular risks for, the holder or issuer with respect to any corporation described in clause (i) which has issued any publicly traded employer security.

(iii) Definitions—For purposes of this subparagraph, the term—

(I) "controlled group of corporations" has the meaning given such term by section 1563(a), except that "50 percent" shall be substituted for "80 percent" each place it appears,

(II) "employer corporation" means a corporation which is an employer maintaining the plan, and

(III) "parent corporation" has the meaning given such term by section 424(e).

(G) Other definitions—For purposes of this paragraph—

(i) Applicable individual—The term "applicable individual" means—

(I) any participant in the plan, and

(II) any beneficiary who has an account under the plan with respect to which the beneficiary is entitled to exercise the rights of a participant.

(ii) Elective deferral—The term "elective deferral" means an employer contribution described in section 402(g)(3)(A).

(iii) Employer security—The term "employer security" has the meaning given such term by section 407(d)(1) of the Employee Retirement Income Security Act of 1974.

(iv) Employee stock ownership plan—The term "employee stock ownership plan" has the meaning given such term by section 4975(e)(7).

(v) Publicly traded employer securities—The term "publicly traded employer securities" means employer securities which are readily tradable on an established securities market.

(vi) Year of service—The term "year of service" has the meaning given such term by section 411(a)(5).

(H) Transition rule for securities attributable to employer contributions—

(i) Rules phased in over 3 years—

(I) In general—In the case of the portion of an account to which subparagraph (C) applies and which consists of employer securities acquired in a plan year beginning before January 1, 2007, subparagraph (C) shall only apply to the applicable percentage of such securities. This subparagraph shall be applied separately with respect to each class of securities.

(II) Exception for certain participants aged 55 or over—Subclause (I) shall not apply to an applicable individual who is a participant who has attained age 55 and completed at least 3 years of service before the first plan year beginning after December 31, 2005.

(ii) Applicable percentage—For purposes of clause (i), the applicable percentage shall be determined as follows:

Plan year to which subparagraph (C) *applies:*	*The applicable percentage is:*
1st	33
2d	66
3d and following	100.

(36) Distributions during working retirement—A trust forming part of a pension plan shall not be treated as failing to constitute a qualified trust under this section solely because the plan provides that a distribution may be made from such trust to an employee who has attained age 62 and who is not separated from employment at the time of such distribution.

(37) Death benefits under USERRA-qualified active military service—A trust shall not constitute a qualified trust unless the plan provides that, in the case of a participant who dies while performing qualified military service (as defined in section 414(u)), the survivors of the participant are entitled to any additional benefits (other than benefit accruals relating to the period of qualified military service) provided under the plan had the participant resumed and then terminated employment on account of death.

Paragraphs (11), (12), (13), (14), (15), (19), and (20) shall apply only in the case of a plan to which section 411 (relating to minimum vesting standards) applies without regard to subsection (e)(2) of such section.

(b) Certain retroactive changes in plan—A stock bonus, pension, profit-sharing, or annuity plan shall be considered as satisfying the requirements of subsection (a) for the period beginning with the date on which it was put into effect, or for the period beginning with the earlier of the date on which there was adopted or put into effect any amendment which caused the plan to fail to satisfy such requirements, and ending with the time prescribed by law for filing the return of the employer for his taxable year in which such plan or amendment was adopted (including extensions thereof) or such later time as the Secretary may designate, if all provisions of the plan which are necessary to satisfy such requirements are in effect by the end of such period and have been made effective for all purposes for the whole of such period.

(c) Definitions and rules relating to self-employed individuals and owner-employees—For purposes of this section—

(1) Self-employed individual treated as employee—

(A) In general—The term "employee" includes, for any taxable year, an individual who is a self-employed individual for such taxable year.

(B) Self-employed individual—The term "self-employed individual" means, with respect to any taxable year, an individual who has earned income (as defined in paragraph (2)) for such taxable year. To the extent provided in regulations prescribed by the Secretary, such term also includes, for any taxable year—

(i) an individual who would be a self-employed individual within the meaning of the preceding sentence but for the fact that the trade or business carried on by such individual did not have net profits for the taxable year, and

(ii) an individual who has been a self-employed individual within the meaning of the preceding sentence for any prior taxable year.

(2) Earned income—

(A) In general—The term "earned income" means the net earnings from self-employment (as defined in section 1402(a)), but such net earnings shall be determined—

(i) only with respect to a trade or business in which personal services of the taxpayer are a material income-producing factor,

(ii) without regard to paragraphs (4) and (5) of section 1402(c),

(iii) in the case of any individual who is treated as an employee under sections 3121(d)(3)(A), (C), or (D), without regard to paragraph (2) of section 1402(c),

(iv) without regard to items which are not included in gross income for purposes of this chapter, and the deductions properly allocable to or chargeable against such items,

(v) with regard to the deductions allowed by section 404 to the taxpayer, and

(vi) with regard to the deduction allowed to the taxpayer by section 164(f).

For purposes of this subparagraph, section 1402, as in effect for a taxable year ending on December 31, 1962, shall be treated as having been in effect for all taxable years ending before such date. For purposes of this part only (other than sections 419 and 419A), this subparagraph shall be applied as if the term "trade or business" for purposes of section 1402 included service described in section 1402(c)(6).

(C)[B] Income from disposition of certain property—For purposes of this section, the term "earned income" includes gains (other than any gain which is treated under any provision of this chapter as gain from the sale or exchange of a capital asset) and net earnings derived from the sale or other disposition of, the transfer of any interest in, or the licensing of the use of property (other than good will) by an individual whose personal efforts created such property.

(3) Owner-employee—The term "owner-employee" means an employee who—

(A) owns the entire interest in an unincorporated trade or business, or

(B) in the case of a partnership, is a partner who owns more than 10 percent of either the capital interest or the profits interest in such partnership.

To the extent provided in regulations prescribed by the Secretary, such term also means an individual who has been an owner-employee within the meaning of the preceding sentence.

(4) Employer—An individual who owns the entire interest in an unincorporated trade or business shall be treated as his own employer. A partnership shall be treated as the employer of each partner who is an employee within the meaning of paragraph (1).

(5) Contributions on behalf of owner-employees—The term "contribution on behalf of an owner-employee" includes, except as the context otherwise requires, a contribution under a plan—

(A) by the employer for an owner-employee, and

(B) by an owner-employee as an employee.

(6) Special rule for certain fishermen—For purposes of this subsection, the term "self-employed individual" includes an individual described in section 3121(b)(20) (relating to certain fishermen).

(d) Contribution limit on owner-employees—A trust forming part of a pension or profit-sharing plan which provides contributions or benefits for employees some or all of whom are owner-employees shall constitute a qualified trust under this section only if, in addition to meeting the requirements of subsection (a), the plan provides that contributions on behalf of any owner-employee may be made only with respect to the earned income of such owner-employee which is derived from the trade or business with respect to which such plan is established.

(e) [Repealed]

(f) Certain custodial accounts and contracts—For purposes of this title, a custodial account, an annuity contract, or a contract (other than a life, health or accident, property, casualty, or liability insurance contract) issued by an insurance company qualified to do business in a State shall be treated as a qualified trust under this section if—

(1) the custodial account or contract would, except for the fact that it is not a trust, constitute a qualified trust under this section, and

(2) in the case of a custodial account the assets thereof are held by a bank (as defined in section 408(n)) or another person who demonstrates, to the satisfaction of the Secretary, that the manner in which he will hold the assets will be consistent with the requirements of this section.

For purposes of this title, in the case of a custodial account or contract treated as a qualified trust under this section by reason of this subsection, the person holding the assets of such account or holding such contract shall be treated as the trustee thereof.

(g) Annuity defined—For purposes of this section and sections 402, 403, and 404, the term "annuity" includes a face-amount certificate, as defined in section 2(a)(15) of the Investment Company Act of 1940 (15 U. S. C., sec. 80a-2); but does not include any contract or certificate issued after December 31, 1962, which is transferable, if any person other than the trustee of a trust described in section 401(a) which is exempt from tax under section 501(a) is the owner of such contract or certificate.

(h) Medical, etc., benefits for retired employees and their spouses and dependents—Under regulations prescribed by the Secretary, and subject to the provisions of section 420, a pension or annuity plan may provide for the payment of benefits for sickness, accident, hospitalization, and medical expenses of retired employees, their spouses and their dependents, but only if—

(1) such benefits are subordinate to the retirement benefits provided by the plan,

(2) a separate account is established and maintained for such benefits,

(3) the employer's contributions to such separate account are reasonable and ascertainable,

(4) it is impossible, at any time prior to the satisfaction of all liabilities under the plan to provide such benefits, for any part of the corpus or income of such separate account to be (within the taxable year or thereafter) used for, or diverted to, any purpose other than the providing of such benefits,

(5) notwithstanding the provisions of subsection (a)(2), upon the satisfaction of all liabilities under the plan to provide such benefits, any amount remaining in such separate account must, under the terms of the plan, be returned to the employer, and

(6) in the case of an employee who is a key employee, a separate account is established and maintained for such benefits payable to such employee (and his spouse and dependents) and such benefits (to the extent attributable to plan years beginning after March 31, 1984, for which the employee is a key employee) are only payable to such employee (and his spouse and dependents) from such separate account.

For purposes of paragraph (6), the term "key employee" means any employee, who at any time during the plan year or any preceding plan year during which contributions were made on behalf of such employee, is or was a key employee as defined in section 416(i). In no event shall the requirements of paragraph (1) be treated as met if the aggregate actual contributions for medical benefits, when added to actual contributions for life insurance protection under the plan, exceed 25 percent of the total actual contributions to the plan (other than contributions to fund past service credits) after the date on which the account is established. For purposes of this subsection, the term "dependent" shall include any individual who is a child (as defined in section 152(f)(1)) of a retired employee who as of the end of the calendar year has not attained age 27.

(i) Certain union-negotiated pension plans—In the case of a trust forming part of a pension plan which has been determined by the Secretary to constitute a qualified trust under subsection (a) and to be exempt from taxation under section 501(a) for a period beginning after contributions were first made to or for such trust, if it is shown to the satisfaction of the Secretary that—

(1) such trust was created pursuant to a collective bargaining agreement between employee representatives and one or more employers,

(2) any disbursements of contributions, made to or for such trust before the time as of which the Secretary determined that the trust constituted a qualified trust, substantially complied with the terms of the trust, and the plan of which the trust is a part, as subsequently qualified, and

(3) before the time as of which the Secretary determined that the trust constitutes a qualified trust, the contributions to or for such trust were not used in a manner which would jeopardize the interests of its beneficiaries,

then such trust shall be considered as having constituted a qualified trust under subsection (a) and as having been exempt from taxation under section 501(a) for the period beginning on the date on which contributions were first made to or for such trust and ending on the date such trust first constituted (without regard to this subsection) a qualified trust under subsection (a).

(j) [Repealed]

(k) Cash or deferred arrangements—

(1) General rule—A profit-sharing or stock bonus plan, a pre-ERISA money purchase plan, or a rural cooperative plan shall not be considered as not satisfying the requirements of subsection (a) merely because the plan includes a qualified cash or deferred arrangement.

(2) Qualified cash or deferred arrangement—A qualified cash or deferred arrangement is any arrangement which is part of a profit-sharing or stock bonus plan, a pre-ERISA money purchase plan, or a rural cooperative plan which meets the requirements of subsection (a)—

(A) under which a covered employee may elect to have the employer make payments as contributions to a trust under the plan on behalf of the employee, or to the employee directly in cash;

(B) under which amounts held by the trust which are attributable to employer contributions made pursuant to the employee's election—

(i) may not be distributable to participants or other beneficiaries earlier than—

(I) severance from employment, death, or disability,

(II) an event described in paragraph (10),

(III) in the case of a profit-sharing or stock bonus plan, the attainment of age 59½, or

(IV) in the case of contributions to a profit-sharing or stock bonus plan to which section 402(e)(3) applies, upon hardship of the employee, or

(V) in the case of a qualified reservist distribution (as defined in section 72(t)(2)(G)(iii)), the date on which a period referred to in subclause (III) of such section begins, and

(ii) will not be distributable merely by reason of the completion of a stated period of participation or the lapse of a fixed number of years;

(C) which provides that an employee's right to his accrued benefit derived from employer contributions made to the trust pursuant to his election is nonforfeitable, and

(D) which does not require, as a condition of participation in the arrangement, that an employee complete a period of service with the employer (or employers) maintaining the plan extending beyond the period permitted under section 410(a)(1) (determined without regard to subparagraph (B)(i) thereof).

(3) Application of participation and discrimination standards—

(A) A cash or deferred arrangement shall not be treated as a qualified cash or deferred arrangement unless—

(i) those employees eligible to benefit under the arrangement satisfy the provisions of section 410(b)(1), and

(ii) the actual deferral percentage for eligible highly compensated employees (as defined in paragraph (5)) for the plan year bears a relationship to the actual deferral percentage for all other eligible employees for the preceding plan year which meets either of the following tests:

(I) The actual deferral percentage for the group of eligible highly compensated employees is not more than the actual deferral percentage of all other eligible employees multiplied by 1.25.

(II) The excess of the actual deferral percentage for the group of eligible highly compensated employees over that of all other eligible employees is not more than 2 percentage points, and the actual deferral percentage for the group of eligible highly compensated employees is not more than the actual deferral percentage of all other eligible employees multiplied by 2.

If 2 or more plans which include cash or deferred arrangements are considered as 1 plan for purposes of section 401(a)(4) or 410(b), the cash or deferred arrangements included in such plans shall be treated as 1 arrangement for purposes of this subparagraph.

If any highly compensated employee is a participant under 2 or more cash or deferred arrangements of the employer, for purposes of determining the deferral percentage with respect to such employee, all such cash or deferred arrangements shall be treated as 1 cash or deferred arrangement. An arrangement may apply clause (ii) by using the plan year rather than the preceding plan year if the employer so elects, except that if such an election is made, it may not be changed except as provided by the Secretary.

(B) For purposes of subparagraph (A), the actual deferral percentage for a specified group of employees for a plan year shall be the average of the ratios (calculated separately for each employee in such group) of—

(i) the amount of employer contributions actually paid over to the trust on behalf of each such employee for such plan year, to

(ii) the employee's compensation for such plan year.

(C) A cash or deferred arrangement shall be treated as meeting the requirements of subsection (a)(4) with respect to contributions if the requirements of subparagraph (A)(ii) are met.

(D) For purposes of subparagraph (B), the employer contributions on behalf of any employee—

(i) shall include any employer contributions made pursuant to the employee's election under paragraph (2), and

(ii) under such rules as the Secretary may prescribe, may, at the election of employer, include—

(I) matching contributions (as defined in section 401(m)(4)(A)) which meet the requirements of paragraph (2)(B) and (C), and

(II) qualified nonelective contributions (within the meaning of section 401(m)(4)(C)).

(E) For purposes of this paragraph, in the case of the first plan year of any plan (other than a successor plan), the amount taken into account as the actual deferral percentage of nonhighly compensated employees for the preceding plan year shall be—

(i) 3 percent, or

(ii) if the employer makes an election under this subclause, the actual deferral percentage of nonhighly compensated employees determined for such first plan year.

(F) Special rule for early participation—If an employer elects to apply section 410(b)(4)(B) in determining whether a cash or deferred arrangement meets the requirements of subparagraph (A)(i), the employer may, in determining whether the arrangement meets the requirements of subparagraph (A)(ii), exclude from consideration all eligible employees (other than highly compensated employees) who have not met the minimum age and service requirements of section 410(a)(1)(A).

(G) Governmental plan—A governmental plan (within the meaning of section 414(d)) shall be treated as meeting the requirements of this paragraph.

(4) Other requirements—

(A) Benefits (other than matching contributions) must not be contingent on election to defer—A cash or deferred arrangement of any employer shall not be treated as a qualified cash or deferred arrangement if any other benefit is conditioned (directly or indirectly) on the employee electing to have the employer make or not make contributions under the arrangement in lieu of receiving cash. The preceding sentence shall not apply to any matching contribution (as defined in section 401(m)) made by reason of such an election.

(B) Eligibility of state and local governments and tax-exempt organizations—

(i) Tax-exempts eligible—Except as provided in clause (ii), any organization exempt from tax under this subtitle may include a qualified cash or deferred arrangement as part of a plan maintained by it.

(ii) Governments ineligible—A cash or deferred arrangement shall not be treated as a qualified cash or deferred arrangement if it is part of a plan maintained by a State or local government or political subdivision thereof, or any agency or instrumentality thereof. This clause shall not apply to a rural cooperative plan or to a plan of an employer described in clause (iii).

(iii) Treatment of Indian tribal governments—An employer which is an Indian tribal government (as defined in section 7701(a)(40)), a subdivision of an Indian tribal government (determined in accordance with section 7871(d)), an agency or instrumentality of an Indian tribal government or subdivision thereof, or a corporation chartered under Federal, State, or tribal law which is owned in whole or in part by any of the foregoing may include a qualified cash or deferred arrangement as part of a plan maintained by the employer.

(C) Coordination with other plans—Except as provided in section 401(m), any employer contribution made pursuant to an employee's election under a qualified cash or deferred arrangement shall not be taken into account for purposes of determining whether any other plan meets the requirements of section 401(a) or 410(b). This subparagraph shall not apply for purposes of determining whether a plan meets the average benefit requirement of section 410(b)(2)(A)(ii).

(5) Highly compensated employee—For purposes of this subsection, the term "highly compensated employee" has the meaning given such term by section 414(q).

(6) Pre-ERISA money purchase plan—For purposes of this subsection, the term "pre-ERISA money purchase plan" means a pension plan—

(A) which is a defined contribution plan (as defined in section 414(i)),

(B) which was in existence on June 27, 1974, and which, on such date, included a salary reduction arrangement, and

(C) under which neither the employee contributions nor the employer contributions may exceed the levels provided for by the contribution formula in effect under the plan on such date.

(7) Rural cooperative plan—For purposes of this subsection—

(A) In general—The term "rural cooperative plan" means any pension plan—

(i) which is a defined contribution plan (as defined in section 414(i)), and

(ii) which is established and maintained by a rural cooperative.

(B) Rural cooperative defined—For purposes of subparagraph (A), the term "rural cooperative" means—

(i) any organization which—

(I) is engaged primarily in providing electric service on a mutual or cooperative basis, or

(II) is engaged primarily in providing electric service to the public in its area of service and which is exempt from tax under this subtitle or which is a State or local government (or an agency or instrumentality thereof), other than a municipality (or an agency or instrumentality thereof),

(ii) any organization described in paragraph (4) or (6) of section 501(c) and at least 80 percent of the members of which are organizations described in clause (i),

(iii) a cooperative telephone company described in section 501(c)(12),

(iv) any organization which—

(I) is a mutual irrigation or ditch company described in section 501(c)(12) (without regard to the 85 percent requirement thereof), or

(II) is a district organized under the laws of a State as a municipal corporation for the purpose of irrigation, water conservation, or drainage, and

(v) an organization which is a national association of organizations described in clause (i), (ii), (iii), or (iv).

(C) Special rule for certain distributions—A rural cooperative plan which includes a qualified cash or deferred arrangement shall not be treated as violating the requirements of section 401(a) or of paragraph (2) merely by reason of a hardship distribution or a distribution to a participant after attainment of age 59½. For purposes of this section, the term "hardship distribution" means a distribution described in paragraph (2)(B)(i)(IV) (without regard to the limitation of its application to profit-sharing or stock bonus plans).

(8) Arrangement not disqualified if excess contributions distributed—

(A) In general—A cash or deferred arrangement shall not be treated as failing to meet the requirements of clause (ii) of paragraph (3)(A) for any plan year if, before the close of the following plan year—

(i) the amount of excess contributions for such plan year (and any income allocable to such contributions through the end of such year) is distributed, or

(ii) to the extent provided in regulations, the employee elects to treat the amount of the excess contributions as an amount distributed to the employee and then contributed by the employee to the plan.

Any distribution of excess contributions (and income) may be made without regard to any other provision of law.

(B) Excess contributions—For purposes of subparagraph (A), the term "excess contributions" means, with respect to any plan year, the excess of—

(i) the aggregate amount of employer contributions actually paid over to the trust on behalf of highly compensated employees for such plan year, over

(ii) the maximum amount of such contributions permitted under the limitations of clause (ii) of paragraph (3)(A) (determined by reducing contributions made on behalf of highly compensated employees in order of the actual deferral percentages beginning with the highest of such percentages).

(C) Method of distributing excess contributions—Any distribution of the excess contributions for any plan year shall be made to highly compensated employees on the basis of the amount of contributions by, or on behalf of, each of such employees.

(D) Additional tax under section 72(t) not to apply—No tax shall be imposed under section 72(t) on any amount required to be distributed under this paragraph.

(E) Treatment of matching contributions forfeited by reason of excess deferral or contribution or permissible withdrawal—For purposes of paragraph (2)(C), a matching contribution (within the meaning of subsection (m)) shall not be treated as forfeitable merely because such contribution is forfeitable if the contribution to which the matching contribution relates is treated as an excess contribution under subparagraph (B), an excess deferral under section 402(g)(2)(A), a permissible withdrawal under section 414(w), or an excess aggregate contribution under section 401(m)(6)(B).

(F) Cross reference—For excise tax on certain excess contributions, see section 4979.

(9) Compensation—For purposes of this subsection, the term "compensation" has the meaning given such term by section 414(s).

(10) Distributions upon termination of plan—

(A) In general—An event described in this subparagraph is the termination of the plan without establishment or maintenance of another defined contribution plan (other than an employee stock ownership plan as defined in section 4975(e)(7)).

(B) Distributions must be lump sum distributions—

(i) In general—A termination shall not be treated as described in subparagraph (A) with respect to any employee unless the employee receives a lump sum distribution by reason of the termination.

(ii) Lump-sum distribution—For purposes of this subparagraph, the term "lump-sum distribution" has the meaning given such term by section 402(e)(4)(D) (without regard to subclauses (I), (II), (III), and (IV) of clause (i) thereof). Such term includes a distribution of an annuity contract from—

(I) a trust which forms a part of a plan described in section 401(a) and which is exempt from tax under section 501(a), or

(II) an annuity plan described in section 403(a).

(11) Adoption of simple plan to meet nondiscrimination tests—

(A) In general—A cash or deferred arrangement maintained by an eligible employer shall be treated as meeting the requirements of paragraph (3)(A)(ii) if such arrangement meets—

(i) the contribution requirements of subparagraph (B),

(ii) the exclusive plan requirements of subparagraph (C), and

(iii) the vesting requirements of section 408(p)(3).

(B) Contribution requirements—

(i) In general—The requirements of this subparagraph are met if, under the arrangement—

(I) an employee may elect to have the employer make elective contributions for the year on behalf of the employee to a trust under the plan in an amount which is expressed as a percentage of compensation of the employee but which in no event exceeds the amount in effect under section 408(p)(2)(A)(ii),

(II) the employer is required to make a matching contribution to the trust for the year in an amount equal to so much of the amount the employee elects under subclause (I) as does not exceed 3 percent of compensation for the year, and

(III) no other contributions may be made other than contributions described in subclause (I) or (II).

(ii) Employer may elect 2-percent nonelective contribution—An employer shall be treated as meeting the requirements of clause (i)(II) for any year if, in lieu of the contributions described in such clause, the employer elects (pursuant to the terms of the arrangement) to make nonelective contributions of 2 percent of compensation for each employee who is eligible to participate in the arrangement and who has at least $5,000 of compensation from the employer for the year. If an employer makes an election under this subparagraph for any year, the employer shall notify employees of such election within a reasonable period of time before the 60th day before the beginning of such year.

(iii) Administrative requirements—

(I) In general—Rules similar to the rules of subparagraphs (B) and (C) of section 408(p)(5) shall apply for purposes of this subparagraph.

(II) Notice of election period—The requirements of this subparagraph shall not be treated as met with respect to any year unless the employer notifies each employee eligible to participate, within a reasonable period of time before the 60th day before the beginning of such year (and, for the first year the employee is so eligible, the 60th day before the first day such employee is so eligible), of the rules similar to the rules of section 408(p)(5)(C) which apply by reason of subclause (I).

(C) Exclusive plan requirement—The requirements of this subparagraph are met for any year to which this paragraph applies if no contributions were made, or benefits were accrued, for services during such year under any qualified plan of the employer on behalf of any employee eligible to participate in the cash or deferred arrangement, other than contributions described in subparagraph (B).

(D) Definitions and special rule—

(i) Definitions—For purposes of this paragraph, any term used in this paragraph which is also used in section 408(p) shall have the meaning given such term by such section.

(ii) Coordination with top-heavy rules—A plan meeting the requirements of this paragraph for any year shall not be treated as a top-heavy plan under section 416 for such year if such plan allows only contributions required under this paragraph.

(12) Alternative methods of meeting nondiscrimination requirements—

(A) In general—A cash or deferred arrangement shall be treated as meeting the requirements of paragraph (3)(A)(ii) if such arrangement—

(i) meets the contribution requirements of subparagraph (B) or (C), and

(ii) meets the notice requirements of subparagraph (D).

(B) Matching contributions—

(i) In general—The requirements of this subparagraph are met if, under the arrangement, the employer makes matching contributions on behalf of each employee who is not a highly compensated employee in an amount equal to—

(I) 100 percent of the elective contributions of the employee to the extent such elective contributions do not exceed 3 percent of the employee's compensation, and

(II) 50 percent of the elective contributions of the employee to the extent that such elective contributions exceed 3 percent but do not exceed 5 percent of the employee's compensation.

(ii) Rate for highly compensated employees—The requirements of this subparagraph are not met if, under the arrangement, the rate of matching contribution with respect to any elective contribution of a highly compensated employee at any rate of elective contribution is greater than that with respect to an employee who is not a highly compensated employee.

(iii) Alternative plan designs—If the rate of any matching contribution with respect to any rate of elective contribution is not equal to the percentage required under clause (i), an arrangement shall not be treated as failing to meet the requirements of clause (i) if—

(I) the rate of an employer's matching contribution does not increase as an employee's rate of elective contributions increase, and

(II) the aggregate amount of matching contributions at such rate of elective contribution is at least equal to the aggregate amount of matching contributions which would be made if matching contributions were made on the basis of the percentages described in clause (i).

(C) Nonelective contributions—The requirements of this subparagraph are met if, under the arrangement, the employer is required, without regard to whether the employee makes an elective contribution or employee contribution, to make a contribution to a defined contribution plan on behalf of each employee who is not a highly compensated employee and who is eligible to participate in the arrangement in an amount equal to at least 3 percent of the employee's compensation.

(D) Notice requirement—An arrangement meets the requirements of this paragraph if, under the arrangement, each employee eligible to participate is, within a reasonable period before any year, given written notice of the employee's rights and obligations under the arrangement which—

(i) is sufficiently accurate and comprehensive to appraise the employee of such rights and obligations, and

(ii) is written in a manner calculated to be understood by the average employee eligible to participate.

(E) Other requirements—

(i) Withdrawal and vesting restrictions—An arrangement shall not be treated as meeting the requirements of subparagraph (B) or (C) of this paragraph unless the requirements of subparagraphs (B) and (C) of paragraph (2) are met with respect to all employer contributions (including matching contributions) taken into account in determining whether the requirements of subparagraphs (B) and (C) of this paragraph are met.

(ii) Social security and similar contributions not taken into account—An arrangement shall not be treated as meeting the requirements of subparagraph (B) or (C) unless such requirements are met without regard to subsection (l), and, for purposes of subsection (l), employer contributions under subparagraph (B) or (C) shall not be taken into account.

(F) Other plans—An arrangement shall be treated as meeting the requirements under subparagraph (A)(i) if any other plan maintained by the employer meets such requirements with respect to employees eligible under the arrangement.

(13) Alternative method for automatic contribution arrangements to meet nondiscrimination requirements—

(A) In general—A qualified automatic contribution arrangement shall be treated as meeting the requirements of paragraph (3)(A)(ii).

(B) Qualified automatic contribution arrangement—For purposes of this paragraph, the term "qualified automatic contribution arrangement" means any cash or deferred arrangement which meets the requirements of subparagraphs (C) through (E).

(C) Automatic deferral—

(i) In general—The requirements of this subparagraph are met if, under the arrangement, each employee eligible to participate in the arrangement is treated as having elected to have the employer make elective contributions in an amount equal to a qualified percentage of compensation.

(ii) Election out—The election treated as having been made under clause (i) shall cease to apply with respect to any employee if such employee makes an affirmative election—

(I) to not have such contributions made, or

(II) to make elective contributions at a level specified in such affirmative election.

(iii) Qualified percentage—For purposes of this subparagraph, the term "qualified percentage" means, with respect to any employee, any percentage determined under the arrangement if such percentage is applied uniformly, does not exceed 10 percent, and is at least—

(I) 3 percent during the period ending on the last day of the first plan year which begins after the date on which the first elective contribution described in clause (i) is made with respect to such employee,

(II) 4 percent during the first plan year following the plan year described in subclause (I),

(III) 5 percent during the second plan year following the plan year described in subclause (I), and

(IV) 6 percent during any subsequent plan year.

(iv) Automatic deferral for current employees not required—Clause (i) may be applied without taking into account any employee who—

(I) was eligible to participate in the arrangement (or a predecessor arrangement) immediately before the date on which such arrangement becomes a qualified automatic contribution arrangement (determined after application of this clause), and

(II) had an election in effect on such date either to participate in the arrangement or to not participate in the arrangement.

(D) Matching or nonelective contributions—

(i) In general—The requirements of this subparagraph are met if, under the arrangement, the employer—

(I) makes matching contributions on behalf of each employee who is not a highly compensated employee in an amount equal to the sum of 100 percent of the elective contributions of the employee to the extent that such contributions do not exceed 1 percent of compensation plus 50 percent of so much of such contributions as exceed 1 percent but do not exceed 6 percent of compensation, or

(II) is required, without regard to whether the employee makes an elective contribution or employee contribution, to make a contribution to a defined contribution plan on behalf of each employee who is not a highly compensated employee and who is eligible to participate in the arrangement in an amount equal to at least 3 percent of the employee's compensation.

(ii) Application of rules for matching contributions—The rules of clauses (ii) and (iii) of paragraph (12)(B) shall apply for purposes of clause (i)(I).

(iii) Withdrawal and vesting restrictions—An arrangement shall not be treated as meeting the requirements of clause (i) unless, with respect to employer contributions (including matching contributions) taken into account in determining whether the requirements of clause (i) are met—

(I) any employee who has completed at least 2 years of service (within the meaning of section 411(a)) has a nonforfeitable right to 100 percent of the employee's accrued benefit derived from such employer contributions, and

(II) the requirements of subparagraph (B) of paragraph (2) are met with respect to all such employer contributions.

(iv) Application of certain other rules—The rules of subparagraphs (E)(ii) and (F) of paragraph (12) shall apply for purposes of subclauses (I) and (II) of clause (i).

(E) Notice requirements—

(i) In general—The requirements of this subparagraph are met if, within a reasonable period before each plan year, each employee eligible to participate in the arrangement for such year receives written notice of the employee's rights and obligations under the arrangement which—

(I) is sufficiently accurate and comprehensive to apprise the employee of such rights and obligations, and

(II) is written in a manner calculated to be understood by the average employee to whom the arrangement applies.

(ii) Timing and content requirements—A notice shall not be treated as meeting the requirements of clause (i) with respect to an employee unless—

(I) the notice explains the employee's right under the arrangement to elect not to have elective contributions made on the employee's behalf (or to elect to have such contributions made at a different percentage),

(II) in the case of an arrangement under which the employee may elect among 2 or more investment options, the notice explains how contributions made under the arrangement will be invested in the absence of any investment election by the employee, and

(III) the employee has a reasonable period of time after receipt of the notice described in subclauses (I) and (II) and before the first elective contribution is made to make either such election.

(l) Permitted disparity in plan contributions or benefits—

(1) In general—The requirements of this subsection are met with respect to a plan if—

(A) in the case of a defined contribution plan, the requirements of paragraph (2) are met, and

(B) in the case of a defined benefit plan, the requirements of paragraph (3) are met.

(2) Defined contribution plan—

(A) In general—A defined contribution plan meets the requirements of this paragraph if the excess contribution percentage does not exceed the base contribution percentage by more than the lesser of—

(i) the base contribution percentage, or

(ii) the greater of—

(I) 5.7 percentage points, or

(II) the percentage equal to the portion of the rate of tax under section 3111(a) (in effect as of the beginning of the year) which is attributable to old-age insurance.

(B) Contribution percentages—For purposes of this paragraph—

(i) Excess contribution percentage—The term "excess contribution percentage" means the percentage of compensation which is contributed by the employer under the plan with respect to that portion of each participant's compensation in excess of the integration level.

(ii) Base contribution percentage—The term "base contribution percentage" means the percentage of compensation contributed by the employer under the plan with respect to that portion of each participant's compensation not in excess of the integration level.

(3) Defined benefit plan—A defined benefit plan meets the requirements of this paragraph if—

(A) Excess plans—

(i) In general—In the case of a plan other than an offset plan—

(I) the excess benefit percentage does not exceed the base benefit percentage by more than the maximum excess allowance,

(II) any optional form of benefit, preretirement benefit, actuarial factor, or other benefit or feature provided with respect to compensation in excess of the integration level is provided with respect to compensation not in excess of such level, and

(III) benefits are based on average annual compensation.

(ii) Benefit percentages—For purposes of this subparagraph, the excess and base benefit percentages shall be computed in the same manner as the excess and base contribution percentages under paragraph (2)(B), except that such determination shall be made on the basis of benefits attributable to employer contributions rather than contributions.

(B) Offset plans—In the case of an offset plan, the plan provides that—

(i) a participant's accrued benefit attributable to employer contributions (within the meaning of section 411(c)(1)) may not be reduced (by reason of the offset) by more than the maximum offset allowance, and

(ii) benefits are based on average annual compensation.

(4) Definitions relating to paragraph (3)—For purposes of paragraph (3)—

(A) Maximum excess allowance—The maximum excess allowance is equal to—

(i) in the case of benefits attributable to any year of service with the employer taken into account under the plan, 3/4 of a percentage point, and

(ii) in the case of total benefits, 3/4 of a percentage point, multiplied by the participant's years of service (not in excess of 35) with the employer taken into account under the plan.

In no event shall the maximum excess allowance exceed the base benefit percentage.

(B) Maximum offset allowance—The maximum offset allowance is equal to—

(i) in the case of benefits attributable to any year of service with the employer taken into account under the plan, 3/4 percent of the participant's final average compensation, and

(ii) in the case of total benefits, 3/4 percent of the participant's final average compensation, multiplied by the participant's years of service (not in excess of 35) with the employer taken into account under the plan.

In no event shall the maximum offset allowance exceed 50 percent of the benefit which would have accrued without regard to the offset reduction.

(C) Reductions—

(i) In general—The Secretary shall prescribe regulations requiring the reduction of the 3/4 percentage factor under subparagraph (A) or (B)—

(I) in the case of a plan other than an offset plan which has an integration level in excess of covered compensation, or

(II) with respect to any participant in an offset plan who has final average compensation in excess of covered compensation.

(ii) Basis of reductions—Any reductions under clause (i) shall be based on the percentages of compensation replaced by the employer-derived portions of primary insurance amounts under the Social Security Act for participants with compensation in excess of covered compensation.

(D) Offset plan—The term "offset plan" means any plan with respect to which the benefit attributable to employer contributions for each participant is reduced by an amount specified in the plan.

(5) Other definitions and special rules—For purposes of this subsection—

(A) Integration level—

(i) In general—The term "integration level" means the amount of compensation specified under the plan (by dollar amount or formula) at or below which the rate at which contributions or benefits are provided (expressed as a percentage) is less than such rate above such amount.

(ii) Limitation—The integration level for any year may not exceed the contribution and benefit base in effect under section 230 of the Social Security Act for such year.

(iii) Level to apply to all participants—A plan's integration level shall apply with respect to all participants in the plan.

(iv) Multiple integration levels—Under rules prescribed by the Secretary, a defined benefit plan may specify multiple integration levels.

(B) Compensation—The term "compensation" has the meaning given such term by section 414(s).

(C) Average annual compensation—The term "average annual compensation" means the participant's highest average annual compensation for—

(i) any period of at least 3 consecutive years, or

(ii) if shorter, the participant's full period of service.

(D) Final average compensation—

(i) In general—The term "final average compensation" means the participant's average annual compensation for—

(I) the 3-consecutive year period ending with the current year, or

(II) if shorter, the participant's full period of service.

(ii) Limitation—A participant's final average compensation shall be determined by not taking into account in any year compensation in excess of the contribution and benefit base in effect under section 230 of the Social Security Act for such year.

(E) Covered compensation—

(i) In general—The term "covered compensation" means, with respect to an employee, the average of the contribution and benefit bases in effect under section 230 of the Social Security Act for each year in the 35-year period ending with the year in which the employee attains the social security retirement age.

(ii) Computation for any year—For purposes of clause (i), the determination for any year preceding the year in which the employee attains the social security retirement age shall be made by assuming that there is no increase in the bases described in clause (i) after the determination year and before the employee attains the social security retirement age.

(iii) Social security retirement age—For purposes of this subparagraph, the term "social security retirement age" has the meaning given such term by section 415(b)(8).

(F) Regulations—The Secretary shall prescribe such regulations as are necessary or appropriate to carry out the purposes of this subsection, including—

(i) in the case of a defined benefit plan which provides for unreduced benefits commencing before the social security retirement age (as defined in section 415(b)(8)), rules providing for the reduction of the maximum excess allowance and the maximum offset allowance, and

(ii) in the case of an employee covered by 2 or more plans of the employer which fail to meet the requirements of subsection (a)(4) (without regard to this subsection), rules preventing the multiple use of the disparity permitted under this subsection with respect to any employee.

For purposes of clause (i), unreduced benefits shall not include benefits for disability (within the meaning of section 223(d) of the Social Security Act).

(6) Special rule for plan maintained by railroads—In determining whether a plan which includes employees of a railroad employer who are entitled to benefits under the Railroad Retirement Act of 1974 meets the requirements of this subsection, rules similar to the rules set forth in this subsection shall apply. Such rules shall take into account the employer-derived portion of the employees' tier 2 railroad retirement benefits and any supplemental annuity under the Railroad Retirement Act of 1974.

(m) Nondiscrimination test for matching contributions and employee contributions—

(1) In general—A defined contribution plan shall be treated as meeting the requirements of subsection (a)(4) with respect to the amount of any matching contribution or employee contribution for any plan year only if the contribution percentage requirement of paragraph (2) of this subsection is met for such plan year.

(2) Requirements—

(A) Contribution percentage requirement—A plan meets the contribution percentage requirement of this paragraph for any plan year only if the contribution percentage for eligible highly compensated employees for such plan year does not exceed the greater of—

(i) 125 percent of such percentage for all other eligible employees for the preceding plan year, or

(ii) the lesser of 200 percent of such percentage for all other eligible employees for the preceding plan year, or such percentage for all other eligible employees for the preceding plan year plus 2 percentage points.

This subparagraph may be applied by using the plan year rather than the preceding plan year if the employer so elects, except that if such an election is made, it may not be changed except as provided the Secretary.

(B) Multiple plans treated as a single plan—If two or more plans of an employer to which matching contributions, employee contributions, or elective deferrals are made are treated as one plan for purposes of section 410(b), such plans shall be treated as one plan for purposes of this subsection. If a highly compensated employee participates in two or more plans of an employer to which contributions to which this subsection applies are made, all such contributions shall be aggregated for purposes of this subsection.

(3) Contribution percentage—For purposes of paragraph (2), the contribution percentage for a specified group of employees for a plan year shall be the average for the ratios (calculated separately for each employee in such group) of—

(A) the sum of the matching contributions and employee contributions paid under the plan on behalf of each such employee for such plan year, to

(B) the employee's compensation (within the meaning of section 414(s)) for such plan year.

Under regulations, an employer may elect to take into account (in computing the contribution percentage) elective deferrals and qualified nonelective contributions under the plan or any other plan of the employer. If matching contributions are taken into account for purposes of subsection (k)(3)(A)(ii) for any plan year, such contributions shall not be taken into account under subparagraph (A) for such year. Rules similar to the rules of subsection (k)(3)(E) shall apply for purposes of this subsection.

(4) Definitions—For purposes of this subsection—

(A) Matching contribution—The term "matching contribution" means—

(i) any employer contribution made to a defined contribution plan on behalf of an employee on account of an employee contribution made by such employee, and

(ii) any employer contribution made to a defined contribution plan on behalf of an employee on account of an employee's elective deferral.

(B) Elective deferral—The term "elective deferral" means any employer contribution described in section 402(g)(3).

(C) Qualified nonelective contributions—The term "qualified nonelective contribution" means any employer contribution (other than a matching contribution) with respect to which—

(i) the employee may not elect to have the contribution paid to the employee in cash instead of being contributed to the plan, and

(ii) the requirements of subparagraphs (B) and (C) of subsection (k)(2) are met.

(5) Employees taken into consideration—

(A) In general—Any employee who is eligible to make an employee contribution (or, if the employer takes elective contributions into account, elective contributions) or to receive a matching contribution under the plan being tested under paragraph (1) shall be considered an eligible employee for purposes of this subsection.

(B) Certain nonparticipants—If an employee contribution is required as a condition of participation in the plan, any employee who would be a participant in the plan if such employee made such a contribution shall be treated as an eligible employee on behalf of whom no employer contributions are made.

(C) Special rule for early participation—If an employer elects to apply section 410(b)(4)(B) in determining whether a plan meets the requirements of section 410(b), the employer may, in determining whether the plan meets the requirements of paragraph (2), exclude from consideration all eligible employees (other than highly compensated employees) who have not met the minimum age and service requirements of section 410(a)(1)(A).

(6) Plan not disqualified if excess aggregate contributions distributed before end of following plan year—

(A) In general—A plan shall not be treated as failing to meet the requirements of paragraph (1) for any plan year if, before the close of the following plan year, the amount of the excess aggregate contributions for such plan year (and any income allocable to such contributions through the end of such year) is distributed (or, if forfeitable, is forfeited). Such contributions (and such income) may be distributed without regard to any other provision of law.

(B) Excess aggregate contributions—For purposes of subparagraph (A), the term "excess aggregate contributions" means, with respect to any plan year, the excess of—

(i) the aggregate amount of the matching contributions and employee contributions (and any qualified nonelective contribution or elective contribution taken into account in computing the contribution percentage) actually made on behalf of highly compensated employees for such plan year, over

(ii) the maximum amount of such contributions permitted under the limitations of paragraph (2)(A) (determined by reducing contributions made on behalf of highly compensated employees in order of their contribution percentages beginning with the highest of such percentages).

(C) Method of distributing excess aggregate contributions—Any distribution of the excess aggregate contributions for any plan year shall be made to highly compensated employees on the basis of the amount of contributions on behalf of, or by, each such employee. Forfeitures of excess aggregate contributions may not be allocated to participants whose contributions are reduced under this paragraph.

(D) Coordination with subsection (k) and 402(g)—The determination of the amount of excess aggregate contributions with respect to a plan shall be made after—

(i) first determining the excess deferrals (within the meaning of section 402(g)), and

(ii) then determining the excess contributions under subsection (k).

(7) Treatment of distributions—

(A) Additional tax of section 72(t) not applicable—No tax shall be imposed under section 72(t) on any amount required to be distributed under paragraph (6).

(B) Exclusion of employee contributions—Any distribution attributable to employee contributions shall not be included in gross income except to the extent attributable to income on such contributions.

(8) Highly compensated employee—For purposes of this subsection, the term "highly compensated employee" has the meaning given to such term by section 414(q).

(9) Regulations—The Secretary shall prescribe such regulations as may be necessary to carry out the purposes of this subsection and subsection (k), including regulations permitting appropriate aggregation of plans and contributions.

(10) Alternative method of satisfying tests—A defined contribution plan shall be treated as meeting the requirements of paragraph (2) with respect to matching contributions if the plan—

(A) meets the contribution requirements of subparagraph (B) of subsection (k)(11),

(B) meets the exclusive plan requirements of subsection (k)(11)(C), and

(C) meets the vesting requirements of section 408(p)(3).

(11) Additional alternative method of satisfying tests—

(A) In general—A defined contribution plan shall be treated as meeting the requirements of paragraph (2) with respect to matching contributions if the plan—

(i) meets the contribution requirements of subparagraph (B) or (C) of subsection (k)(12),

(ii) meets the notice requirements of subsection (k)(12)(D), and

(iii) meets the requirements of subparagraph (B).

(B) Limitation on matching contributions—The requirements of this subparagraph are met if—

(i) matching contributions on behalf of any employee may not be made with respect to an employee's contributions or elective deferrals in excess of 6 percent of the employee's compensation,

(ii) the rate of an employer's matching contribution does not increase as the rate of an employee's contributions or elective deferrals increase, and

(iii) the matching contribution with respect to any highly compensated employee at any rate of an employee contribution or rate of elective deferral is not greater than that with respect to an employee who is not a highly compensated employee.

(12) Alternative method for automatic contribution arrangements—A defined contribution plan shall be treated as meeting the requirements of paragraph (2) with respect to matching contributions if the plan—

(A) is a qualified automatic contribution arrangement (as defined in subsection (k)(13)), and

(B) meets the requirements of paragraph (11)(B).

(13) Cross reference—For excise tax on certain excess contributions, see section 4979.

(n) Coordination with qualified domestic relations orders—The Secretary shall prescribe such rules or regulations as may be necessary to coordinate the requirements of subsection (a)(13)(B) and section 414(p) (and the regulations issued by the Secretary of Labor thereunder) with the other provisions of this chapter.

(o) Cross reference—For exemption from tax of a trust qualified under this section, see section 501(a).

§ 402. Taxability of beneficiary of employees' trust.

(a) Taxability of beneficiary of exempt trust—Except as otherwise provided in this section, any amount actually distributed to any distributee by any employees' trust described in section 401(a) which is exempt from tax under section 501(a) shall be taxable to the distributee, in the taxable year of the distributee in which distributed, under section 72 (relating to annuities).

(b) Taxability of beneficiary of nonexempt trust—

(1) Contributions—Contributions to an employees' trust made by an employer during a taxable year of the employer which ends with or within a taxable year of the trust for which the trust is not exempt from tax under section 501(a) shall be included in the gross income of the employee in accordance with section 83 (relating to property transferred in connection with performance of services), except that the value of the employee's interest in the trust shall be substituted for the fair market value of the property for purposes of applying such section.

(2) Distributions—The amount actually distributed or made available to any distributee by any trust described in paragraph (1) shall be taxable to the distributee, in the taxable year in which so distributed or made available, under section 72 (relating to annuities), except that distributions of income of such trust before the annuity starting date (as defined in section 72(c)(4)) shall be included in the gross income of the employee without regard to section 72(e)(5) (relating to amounts not received as annuities).

(3) Grantor trusts—A beneficiary of any trust described in paragraph (1) shall not be considered the owner of any portion of such trust under subpart E of part I of subchapter J (relating to grantors and others treated as substantial owners).

(4) Failure to meet requirements of section 410(b)—

(A) Highly compensated employees—If 1 of the reasons a trust is not exempt from tax under section 501(a) is the failure of the plan of which it is a part to meet the requirements of section 401(a)(26) or 410(b), then a highly compensated employee shall, in lieu of the amount determined under paragraph (1) or (2) include in gross income for the taxable year with or within which the taxable year of the trust ends an amount equal to the vested accrued benefit of such employee (other than the employee's investment in the contract) as of the close of such taxable year of the trust.

(B) Failure to meet coverage tests—If a trust is not exempt from tax under section 501(a) for any taxable year solely because such trust is part of a plan which fails to meet the requirements of section 401(a)(26) or 410(b), paragraphs (1) and (2) shall not apply by reason of such failure to any employee who was not a highly compensated employee during—

(i) such taxable year, or

(ii) any preceding period for which service was creditable to such employee under the plan.

(C) Highly compensated employee—For purposes of this paragraph, the term 'highly compensated employee' has the meaning given such term by section 414(q).

(c) Rules applicable to rollovers from exempt trusts—

(1) Exclusion from income—If—

(A) any portion of the balance to the credit of an employee in a qualified trust is paid to the employee in an eligible rollover distribution,

(B) the distributee transfers any portion of the property received in such distribution to an eligible retirement plan, and

(C) in the case of a distribution of property other than money, the amount so transferred consists of the property distributed,

then such distribution (to the extent so transferred) shall not be includible in gross income for the taxable year in which paid.

(2) Maximum amount which may be rolled over—In the case of any eligible rollover distribution, the maximum amount transferred to which paragraph (1) applies shall not exceed the portion of such distribution which is includible in gross income (determined without regard to paragraph (1)). The preceding sentence shall not apply to such distribution to the extent—

(A) such portion is transferred in a direct trustee-to-trustee transfer to a qualified trust or to an annuity contract described in section 403(b) and such trust or contract provides for separate accounting for amounts so transferred (and earnings thereon), including separately accounting for the portion of such distribution which is includible in gross income and the portion of such distribution which is not so includible, or

(B) such portion is transferred to an eligible retirement plan described in clause (i) or (ii) of paragraph (8)(B).

In the case of a transfer described in subparagraph (A) or (B), the amount transferred shall be treated as consisting first of the portion of such distribution that is includible in gross income (determined without regard to paragraph (1)).

(3) Transfer must be made within 60 days of receipt—

(A) In general—Except as provided in subparagraph (B), paragraph (1) shall not apply to any transfer of a distribution made after the 60th day following the day on which the distributee received the property distributed.

(B) Hardship exception—The Secretary may waive the 60-day requirement under subparagraph (A) where the failure to waive such requirement would be against equity or good conscience, including casualty, disaster, or other events beyond the reasonable control of the individual subject to such requirement.

(4) Eligible rollover distribution—For purposes of this subsection, the term "eligible rollover distribution" means any distribution to an employee of all or any portion of the balance to the credit of the employee in a qualified trust; except that such term shall not include—

(A) any distribution which is one of a series of substantially equal periodic payments (not less frequently than annually) made—

(i) for the life (or life expectancy) of the employee or the joint lives (or joint life expectancies) of the employee and the employee's designated beneficiary, or

(ii) for a specified period of 10 years or more,

(B) any distribution to the extent such distribution is required under section 401(a)(9), and

(C) any distribution which is made upon hardship of the employee.

If all or any portion of a distribution during 2009 is treated as an eligible rollover distribution but would not be so treated if the minimum distribution requirements under section 401(a)(9) had applied during 2009, such distribution shall not be treated as an eligible rollover distribution for purposes of section 401(a)(31) or 3405(c) or subsection (f) of this section.

(5) Transfer treated as rollover contribution under section 408—For purposes of this title, a transfer to an eligible retirement plan described in clause (i) or (ii) of paragraph (8)(B) resulting in any portion of a distribution being excluded from gross income under paragraph (1) shall be treated as a rollover contribution described in section 408(d)(3).

(6) Sales of distributed property—For purposes of this subsection—

(A) Transfer of proceeds from sale of distributed property treated as transfer of distributed property—The transfer of an amount equal to any portion of the proceeds from the sale of property received in the distribution shall be treated as the transfer of property received in the distribution.

(B) Proceeds attributable to increase in value—The excess of fair market value of property on sale over its fair market value on distribution shall be treated as property received in the distribution.

(C) Designation where amount of distribution exceeds rollover contribution—In any case where part or all of the distribution consists of property other than money—

(i) the portion of the money or other property which is to be treated as attributable to amounts not included in gross income, and

(ii) the portion of the money or other property which is to be treated as included in the rollover contribution,

shall be determined on a ratable basis unless the taxpayer designates otherwise. Any designation under this subparagraph for a taxable year shall be made not later than the time prescribed by law for filing the return for such taxable year (including extensions thereof). Any such designation, once made, shall be irrevocable.

(D) Nonrecognition of gain or loss—No gain or loss shall be recognized on any sale described in subparagraph (A) to the extent that an amount equal to the proceeds is transferred pursuant to paragraph (1).

(7) Special rule for frozen deposits—

(A) In general—The 60-day period described in paragraph (3) shall not—

(i) include any period during which the amount transferred to the employee is a frozen deposit, or

(ii) end earlier than 10 days after such amount ceases to be a frozen deposit.

(B) Frozen deposits—For purposes of this subparagraph, the term "frozen deposit" means any deposit which may not be withdrawn because of—

(i) the bankruptcy or insolvency of any financial institution, or

(ii) any requirement imposed by the State in which such institution is located by reason of the bankruptcy or insolvency (or threat thereof) of 1 or more financial institutions in such State.

A deposit shall not be treated as a frozen deposit unless on at least 1 day during the 60-day period described in paragraph (3) (without regard to this paragraph) such deposit is described in the preceding sentence.

(8) Definitions—For purposes of this subsection—

(A) Qualified trust—The term "qualified trust" means an employees' trust described in section 401(a) which is exempt from tax under section 501(a).

(B) Eligible retirement plan—The term "eligible retirement plan" means—

(i) an individual retirement account described in section 408(a),

(ii) an individual retirement annuity described in section 408(b) (other than an endowment contract),

(iii) a qualified trust,

(iv) an annuity plan described in section 403(a),

(v) an eligible deferred compensation plan described in section 457(b) which is maintained by an eligible employer described in section 457(e)(1)(A), and

(vi) an annuity contract described in section 403(b).

If any portion of an eligible rollover distribution is attributable to payments or distributions from a designated Roth account (as defined in section 402A), an eligible retirement plan with respect to such portion shall include only another designated Roth account and a Roth IRA.

(9) Rollover where spouse receives distribution after death of employee—If any distribution attributable to an employee is paid to the spouse of the employee after the employee's death, the preceding provisions of this subsection shall apply to such distribution in the same manner as if the spouse were the employee.

(10) Separate accounting—Unless a plan described in clause (v) of paragraph (8)(B) agrees to separately account for amounts rolled into such plan from eligible retirement plans not described in such clause, the plan described in such clause may not accept transfers or rollovers from such retirement plans.

(11) Distributions to inherited individual retirement plan of nonspouse beneficiary—

(A) In general—If, with respect to any portion of a distribution from an eligible retirement plan described in paragraph (8)(B)(iii) of a deceased employee, a direct trustee-to-trustee transfer is made to an individual retirement plan described in clause (i) or (ii) of paragraph (8)(B) established for the purposes of receiving the distribution on behalf of an individual who is a designated beneficiary (as defined by section 401(a)(9)(E)) of the employee and who is not the surviving spouse of the employee—

(i) the transfer shall be treated as an eligible rollover distribution,

(ii) the individual retirement plan shall be treated as an inherited individual retirement account or individual retirement annuity (within the meaning of section 408(d)(3)(C)) for purposes of this title, and

(iii) section 401(a)(9)(B) (other than clause (iv) thereof) shall apply to such plan.

(B) Certain trusts treated as beneficiaries—For purposes of this paragraph, to the extent provided in rules prescribed by the Secretary, a trust maintained for the benefit of one or more designated beneficiaries shall be treated in the same manner as a designated beneficiary.

(d) Taxability of beneficiary of certain foreign situs trusts—For purposes of subsections (a), (b), and (c), a stock bonus, pension, or profit-sharing trust which would qualify for exemption from tax under section 501(a) except for the fact that it is a trust created or organized outside the United States shall be treated as if it were a trust exempt from tax under section 501(a).

(e) Other rules applicable to exempt trusts—

(1) Alternate payees—

(A) Alternate payee treated as distributee—For purposes of subsection (a) and section 72, an alternate payee who is the spouse or former spouse of the participant shall be treated as the distributee of any distribution or payment made to the alternate payee under a qualified domestic relations order (as defined in section 414(p)).

(B) Rollovers—If any amount is paid or distributed to an alternate payee who is the spouse or former spouse of the participant by reason of any qualified domestic relations order (within the meaning of section 414(p)), subsection (c) shall apply to such distribution in the same manner as if such alternate payee were the employee.

(2) Distributions by united states to nonresident aliens—The amount includible under subsection (a) in the gross income of a nonresident alien with respect to a distribution made by the United States in respect of services performed by an employee of the United States shall not exceed an amount which bears the same ratio to the amount includible in gross income without regard to this paragraph as—

(A) the aggregate basic pay paid by the United States to such employee for such services, reduced by the amount of such basic pay which was not includible in gross income by reason of being from sources without the United States, bears to

(B) the aggregate basic pay paid by the United States to such employee for such services.

In the case of distributions under the civil service retirement laws, the term "basic pay" shall have the meaning provided in section 8331(3) of title 5, United States Code.

(3) Cash or deferred arrangements—For purposes of this title, contributions made by an employer on behalf of an employee to a trust which is a part of a qualified cash or deferred arrangement (as defined in section 401(k)(2)) or which is part of a salary reduction agreement under section 403(b) shall not be treated as distributed or made available to the employee nor as contributions made to the trust by the employee merely because the arrangement includes provisions under which the employee has an election whether the contribution will be made to the trust or received by the employee in cash.

(4) Net unrealized appreciation—

(A) Amounts attributable to employee contributions—For purposes of subsection (a) and section 72, in the case of a distribution other than a lump sum distribution, the amount actually distributed to any distributee from a trust described in subsection (a) shall not include any net unrealized appreciation in securities of the employer corporation attributable to amounts contributed by the employee (other than deductible employee contributions within the meaning of section 72(o)(5)). This subparagraph shall not apply to a distribution to which subsection (c) applies.

(B) Amounts attributable to employer contributions—For purposes of subsection (a) and section 72, in the case of any lump sum distribution which includes securities of the employer corporation, there shall be excluded from gross income the net unrealized appreciation attributable to that part of the distribution which consists of securities of the employer corporation. In accordance with rules prescribed by the Secretary, a taxpayer may elect, on the return of tax on which a lump sum distribution is required to be included, not to have this subparagraph apply to such distribution.

(C) Determination of amounts and adjustments—For purposes of subparagraphs (A) and (B), net unrealized appreciation and the resulting adjustments to basis shall be determined in accordance with regulations prescribed by the Secretary.

(D) Lump-sum distribution—For purposes of this paragraph—

(i) In general—The term "lump sum distribution" means the distribution or payment within one taxable year of the recipient of the balance to the credit of an employee which becomes payable to the recipient—

(I) on account of the employee's death,

(II) after the employee attains age 59½,

(III) on account of the employee's separation from service, or

(IV) after the employee has become disabled (within the meaning of section 72(m)(7)),

from a trust which forms a part of a plan described in section 401(a) and which is exempt from tax under section 501 or from a plan described in section 403(a). Subclause (III) of this clause shall be applied only with respect to an individual who is an employee without regard to section 401(c)(1), and subclause (IV) shall be applied only with respect to an employee within the meaning of section 401(c)(1). For purposes of this clause, a distribution to two or more trusts shall be treated as a distribution to one recipient. For purposes of this paragraph, the balance to the credit of the employee does not include the accumulated deductible employee contributions under the plan (within the meaning of section 72(o)(5)).

(ii) Aggregation of certain trusts and plans—For purposes of determining the balance to the credit of an employee under clause (i)—

(I) all trusts which are part of a plan shall be treated as a single trust, all pension plans maintained by the employer shall be treated as a single plan, all profit-sharing plans maintained by the employer shall be treated as a single plan, and all stock bonus plans maintained by the employer shall be treated as a single plan, and

(II) trusts which are not qualified trusts under section 401(a) and annuity contracts which do not satisfy the requirements of section 404(a)(2) shall not be taken into account.

(iii) Community property laws—The provisions of this paragraph shall be applied without regard to community property laws.

(iv) Amounts subject to penalty—This paragraph shall not apply to amounts described in subparagraph (A) of section 72(m)(5) to the extent that section 72(m)(5) applies to such amounts.

(v) Balance to credit of employee not to include amounts payable under qualified domestic relations order—For purposes of this paragraph, the balance to the credit of an employee shall not include any amount payable to an alternate payee under a qualified domestic relations order (within the meaning of section 414(p)).

(vi) Transfers to cost-of-living arrangement not treated as distribution—For purposes of this paragraph, the balance to the credit of an employee under a defined contribution plan shall not include any amount transferred from such defined contribution plan to a qualified cost-of-living arrangement (within the meaning of section 415(k)(2)) under a defined benefit plan.

(vii) Lump-sum distributions of alternate payees—If any distribution or payment of the balance to the credit of an employee would be treated as a lump-sum distribution, then, for purposes of this paragraph, the payment under a qualified domestic relations order (within the meaning of section 414(p)) of the balance to the credit of an alternate payee who is the spouse or former spouse of the employee shall be treated as a lump-sum distribution. For purposes of this clause, the balance to the credit of the alternate payee shall not include any amount payable to the employee.

(E) Definitions relating to securities—For purposes of this paragraph—

(i) Securities—The term "securities" means only shares of stock and bonds or debentures issued by a corporation with interest coupons or in registered form.

(ii) Securities of the employer—The term "securities of the employer corporation" includes securities of a parent or subsidiary corporation (as defined in subsections (e) and (f) of section 424) of the employer corporation.

(5) [Repealed]

(6) Direct trustee-to-trustee transfers—Any amount transferred in a direct trustee-to-trustee transfer in accordance with section 401(a)(31) shall not be includible in gross income for the taxable year of such transfer.

(f) Written explanation to recipients of distributions eligible for rollover treatment—

(1) In general—The plan administrator of any plan shall, within a reasonable period of time before making an eligible rollover distribution, provide a written explanation to the recipient—

(A) of the provisions under which the recipient may have the distribution directly transferred to an eligible retirement plan and that the automatic distribution by direct transfer applies to certain distributions in accordance with section 401(a)(31)(B),

(B) of the provision which requires the withholding of tax on the distribution if it is not directly transferred to an eligible retirement plan,

(C) of the provisions under which the distribution will not be subject to tax if transferred to an eligible retirement plan within 60 days after the date on which the recipient received the distribution,

(D) if applicable, of the provisions of subsections (d) and (e) of this section, and

(E) of the provisions under which distributions from the eligible retirement plan receiving the distribution may be subject to restrictions and tax consequences which are different from those applicable to distributions from the plan making such distribution.

(2) Definitions—For purposes of this subsection—

(A) Eligible rollover distribution—The term "eligible rollover distribution" has the same meaning as when used in subsection (c) of this section, paragraph (4) of section 403(a), subparagraph (A) of section 403(b)(8), or subparagraph (A) of section 457(e)(16). Such term shall include any distribution to a designated beneficiary which would be treated as an eligible rollover distribution by reason of subsection (c)(11), or section 403(a)(4)(B), 403(b)(8)(B), or 457(e)(16)(B), if the requirements of subsection (c)(11) were satisfied.

(B) Eligible retirement plan—The term "eligible retirement plan" has the meaning given such term by subsection (c)(8)(B).

(g) Limitation on exclusion for elective deferrals—

(1) In general—

(A) Limitation—Notwithstanding subsections (e)(3) and (h)(1)(B), the elective deferrals of any individual for any taxable year shall be included in such individual's gross income to the extent the amount of such deferrals for the taxable year exceeds the applicable dollar amount. The preceding sentence shall not apply the portion of such excess as does not exceed the designated Roth contributions of the individual for the taxable year.

(B) Applicable dollar amount—For purposes of subparagraph (A), the applicable dollar amount shall be the amount determined in accordance with the following table:

For taxable years beginning in calendar year:	*The applicable dollar amount:*

* * *

2006 or thereafter $15,000

(C) Catch-up contributions—In addition to subparagraph (A), in the case of an eligible participant (as defined in section 414(v)), gross income shall not include elective deferrals in excess of the applicable dollar amount under subparagraph (B) to the extent that the amount of such elective deferrals does not exceed the applicable dollar amount under section 414(v)(2)(B)(i) for the taxable year (without regard to the treatment of the elective deferrals by an applicable employer plan under section 414(v)).

(2) Distribution of excess deferrals—

(A) In general—If any amount (hereinafter in this paragraph referred to as "excess deferrals") is included in the gross income of an individual under paragraph (1) (or would be included but for the last sentence thereof) for any taxable year—

(i) not later than the 1st March 1 following the close of the taxable year, the individual may allocate the amount of such excess deferrals among the plans under which the deferrals were made and may notify each such plan of the portion allocated to it, and

(ii) not later than the 1st April 15 following the close of the taxable year, each such plan may distribute to the individual the amount allocated to it under clause (i) (and any income allocable to such amount through the end of such taxable year).

The distribution described in clause (ii) may be made notwithstanding any other provision of law.

(B) Treatment of distribution under section 401(k)—Except to the extent provided under rules prescribed by the Secretary, notwithstanding the distribution of any portion of an excess deferral from a plan under subparagraph (A)(ii), such portion shall, for purposes of applying section 401(k)(3)(A)(ii), be treated as an employer contribution.

(C) Taxation of distribution—In the case of a distribution to which subparagraph (A) applies—

(i) except as provided in clause (ii), such distribution shall not be included in gross income, and

(ii) any income on the excess deferral shall, for purposes of this chapter, be treated as earned and received in the taxable year in which such income is distributed.

No tax shall be imposed under section 72(t) on any distribution described in the preceding sentence.

(D) Partial distributions—If a plan distributes only a portion of any excess deferral and income allocable thereto, such portion shall be treated as having been distributed ratably from the excess deferral and the income.

(3) Elective deferrals—For purposes of this subsection, the term "elective deferrals" means, with respect to any taxable year, the sum of—

(A) any employer contribution under a qualified cash or deferred arrangement (as defined in section 401(k)) to the extent not includible in gross income for the taxable year under subsection (e)(3) (determined without regard to this subsection),

(B) any employer contribution to the extent not includible in gross income for the taxable year under subsection (h)(1)(B) (determined without regard to this subsection),

(C) any employer contribution to purchase an annuity contract under section 403(b) under a salary reduction agreement (within the meaning of section 3121(a)(5)(D)), and

(D) any elective employer contribution under section 408(p)(2)(A)(i).

An employer contribution shall not be treated as an elective deferral described in subparagraph (C) if under the salary reduction agreement such contribution is made pursuant to a one-time irrevocable election made by the employee at the time of initial eligibility to participate in the agreement or is made pursuant to a similar arrangement involving a one-time irrevocable election specified in regulations.

(4) Cost-of-living adjustment—In the case of taxable years beginning after December 31, 2006, the Secretary shall adjust the $15,000 amount under paragraph (1)(B) at the same time and in the same manner as under section 415(d), except that the base period shall be the calendar quarter beginning July 1, 2005, and any increase under this paragraph which is not a multiple of $500 shall be rounded to the next lowest multiple of $500.

(5) Disregard of community property laws—This subsection shall be applied without regard to community property laws.

(6) Coordination with section 72—For purposes of applying section 72, any amount includible in gross income for any taxable year under this subsection but which is not distributed from the plan during such taxable year shall not be treated as an investment in the contract.

(7) Special rule for certain organizations—

(A) In general—In the case of a qualified employee of a qualified organization, with respect to employer contributions described in paragraph (3)(C) made by such organization, the limitation of paragraph (1) for any taxable year shall be increased by whichever of the following is the least:

(i) $3,000,

(ii) $15,000 reduced by the sum of—

(I) the amounts not included in gross income for prior taxable years by reason of this paragraph, plus

(II) the aggregate amount of designated Roth contributions (as defined in section 402A(c)) permitted for prior taxable years by reason of this paragraph, or

(iii) the excess of $5,000 multiplied by the number of years of service of the employee with the qualified organization over the employer contributions described in paragraph (3) made by the organization on behalf of such employee for prior taxable years (determined in the manner prescribed by the Secretary).

(B) Qualified organization—For purposes of this paragraph, the term "qualified organization" means any educational organization, hospital, home health service agency, health and welfare service agency, church, or convention or association of churches. Such term includes any organization described in section 414(e)(3)(B)(ii). Terms used in this subparagraph shall have the same meaning as when used in section 415(c)(4) (as in effect before the enactment of the Economic Growth and Tax Relief Reconciliation Act of 2001).

(C) Qualified employee—For purposes of this paragraph, the term "qualified employee" means any employee who has completed 15 years of service with the qualified organization.

(D) Years of service—For purposes of this paragraph, the term "years of service" has the meaning given such term by section 403(b).

(8) Matching contributions on behalf of self-employed individuals not treated as elective employer contributions—Except as provided in section 401(k)(3)(D)(ii), any matching contribution described in section 401(m)(4)(A) which is made on behalf of a self-employed individual (as defined in section 401(c)) shall not be treated as an elective employer contribution under a qualified cash or deferred arrangement (as defined in section 401(k)) for purposes of this title.

(h) Special rules for simplified employee pensions—For purposes of this chapter—

(1) In general—Except as provided in paragraph (2), contributions made by an employer on behalf of an employee to an individual retirement plan pursuant to a simplified employee pension (as defined in section 408(k))—

(A) shall not be treated as distributed or made available to the employee or as contributions made by the employee, and

(B) if such contributions are made pursuant to an arrangement under section 408(k)(6) under which an employee may elect to have the employer make contributions to the simplified employer pension on behalf of the employee, shall not be treated as distributed or made available or as contributions made by the employee merely because the simplified employee pension includes provisions for such election.

(2) Limitations on employer contributions—Contributions made by an employer to a simplified employee pension with respect to an employee for any year shall be treated as distributed or made available to such employee and as contributions made by the employee to the extent such contributions exceed the lesser of—

(A) 25 percent of the compensation (within the meaning of section 414(s)) from such employer includible in the employee's gross income for the year (determined without regard to the employer contributions to the simplified employee pension), or

(B) the limitation in effect under section 415(c)(1)(A), reduced in the case of any highly compensated employee (within the meaning of section 414(q)) by the amount taken into account with respect to such employee under section 408(k)(3)(D).

(3) Distributions—Any amount paid or distributed out of an individual retirement plan pursuant to a simplified employee pension shall be included in gross income by the payee or distributee, as the case may be, in accordance with the provisions of section 408(d).

(i) Treatment of self-employed individuals—For purposes of this section, except as otherwise provided in subparagraph (A) of subsection (d)(4), the term "employee" includes a self-employed individual (as defined in section 401(c)(1)(B)) and the employer of such individual shall be the person treated as his employer under section 401(c)(4).

(j) Effect of disposition of stock by plan on net unrealized appreciation—

(1) In general—For purposes of subsection (e)(4), in the case of any transaction to which this subsection applies, the determination of net unrealized appreciation shall be made without regard to such transaction.

(2) Transaction to which subsection applies—This subsection shall apply to any transaction in which—

(A) the plan trustee exchanges the plan's securities of the employer corporation for other such securities, or

(B) the plan trustee disposes of securities of the employer corporation and uses the proceeds of such disposition to acquire securities of the employer corporation within 90 days (or such longer period as the Secretary may prescribe), except that this subparagraph shall not apply to any employee with respect to whom a distribution of money was made during the period after such disposition and before such acquisition.

(k) Treatment of simple retirement accounts—Rules similar to the rules of paragraphs (1) and (3) of subsection (h) shall apply to contributions and distributions with respect to a simple retirement account under section 408(p).

(l) Distributions from governmental plans for health and long-term care insurance—

(1) In general—In the case of an employee who is an eligible retired public safety officer who makes the election described in paragraph (6) with respect to any taxable year of such employee, gross income of such employee for such taxable year does not include any distribution from an eligible retirement plan maintained by the employer described in paragraph (4)(B) to the extent that the aggregate amount of such distributions does not exceed the amount paid by such employee for qualified health insurance premiums for such taxable year.

(2) Limitation—The amount which may be excluded from gross income for the taxable year by reason of paragraph (1) shall not exceed $3,000.

(3) Distributions must otherwise be includible—

(A) In general—An amount shall be treated as a distribution for purposes of paragraph (1) only to the extent that such amount would be includible in gross income without regard to paragraph (1).

(B) Application of section 72—Notwithstanding section 72, in determining the extent to which an amount is treated as a distribution for purposes of subparagraph (A), the aggregate amounts distributed from an eligible retirement plan in a taxable year (up to the amount excluded under paragraph (1)) shall be treated as includible in gross income (without regard to subparagraph (A)) to the extent that such amount does not exceed the aggregate amount which would have been so includible if all amounts to the credit of the eligible public safety officer in all eligible retirement plans maintained by the employer described in paragraph (4)(B) were distributed during such taxable year and all such plans were treated as 1 contract for purposes of determining under section 72 the aggregate amount which would have been so includible. Proper adjustments shall be made in applying section 72 to other distributions in such taxable year and subsequent taxable years.

(4) Definitions—For purposes of this subsection—

(A) Eligible retirement plan—For purposes of paragraph (1), the term "eligible retirement plan" means a governmental plan (within the meaning of section 414(d)) which is described in clause (iii), (iv), (v), or (vi) of subsection (c)(8)(B).

(B) Eligible retired public safety officer—The term "eligible retired public safety officer" means an individual who, by reason of disability or attainment of normal retirement age, is separated from service as a public safety officer with the employer who maintains the eligible retirement plan from which distributions subject to paragraph (1) are made.

(C) Public safety officer—The term "public safety officer" shall have the same meaning given such term by section 1204(9)(A) of the Omnibus Crime Control and Safe Streets Act of 1968 (42 U.S.C. 3796b(9)(A)).

(D) Qualified health insurance premiums—The term "qualified health insurance premiums" means premiums for coverage for the eligible retired public safety officer, his spouse, and dependents (as defined in section 152), by an accident or health plan or qualified long-term care insurance contract (as defined in section 7702B(b)).

(5) Special rules—For purposes of this subsection—

(A) Direct payment to insurer required—Paragraph (1) shall only apply to a distribution if payment of the premiums is made directly to the provider of the accident or health plan or qualified long-term care insurance contract by deduction from a distribution from the eligible retirement plan.

(B) Related plans treated as 1—All eligible retirement plans of an employer shall be treated as a single plan.

(6) Election described—

(A) In general—For purposes of paragraph (1), an election is described in this paragraph if the election is made by an employee after separation from service with respect to amounts not distributed from an eligible retirement plan to have amounts from such plan distributed in order to pay for qualified health insurance premiums.

(B) Special rule—A plan shall not be treated as violating the requirements of section 401, or as engaging in a prohibited transaction for purposes of section 503(b), merely because it provides for an election with respect to amounts that are otherwise distributable under the plan or merely because of a distribution made pursuant to an election described in subparagraph (A).

(7) Coordination with medical expense deduction—The amounts excluded from gross income under paragraph (1) shall not be taken into account under section 213.

(8) Coordination with deduction for health insurance costs of self-employed individuals—The amounts excluded from gross income under paragraph (1) shall not be taken into account under section 162(l).

§ 402A. Optional treatment of elective deferrals as Roth contributions.

(a) General rule—If an applicable retirement plan includes a qualified Roth contribution program—

(1) any designated Roth contribution made by an employee pursuant to the program shall be treated as an elective deferral for purposes of this chapter, except that such contribution shall not be excludable from gross income, and

(2) such plan (and any arrangement which is part of such plan) shall not be treated as failing to meet any requirement of this chapter solely by reason of including such program.

(b) Qualified Roth contribution program—For purposes of this section—

(1) In general—The term "qualified Roth contribution program" means a program under which an employee may elect to make designated Roth contributions in lieu of all or a portion of elective deferrals the employee is otherwise eligible to make under the applicable retirement plan.

(2) Separate accounting required—A program shall not be treated as a qualified Roth contribution program unless the applicable retirement plan—

(A) establishes separate accounts ("designated Roth account") for the designated Roth contributions of each employee and any earnings properly allocable to the contributions, and

(B) maintains separate recordkeeping with respect to each account.

(c) Definitions and rules relating to designated Roth contributions—For purposes of this section—

(1) Designated Roth contribution—The term "designated Roth contribution" means any elective deferral which—

(A) is excludable from gross income of an employee without regard to this section, and

(B) the employee designates (at such time and in such manner as the Secretary may prescribe) as not being so excludable.

(2) Designation limits—The amount of elective deferrals which an employee may designate under paragraph (1) shall not exceed the excess (if any) of—

(A) the maximum amount of elective deferrals excludable from gross income of the employee for the taxable year (without regard to this section), over

(B) the aggregate amount of elective deferrals of the employee for the taxable year which the employee does not designate under paragraph (1).

(3) Rollover contributions—

(A) In general—A rollover contribution of any payment or distribution from a designated Roth account which is otherwise allowable under this chapter may be made only if the contribution is to—

(i) another designated Roth account of the individual from whose account the payment or distribution was made, or

(ii) a Roth IRA of such individual.

(B) Coordination with limit—Any rollover contribution to a designated Roth account under subparagraph (A) shall not be taken into account for purposes of paragraph (1).

(4) Taxable rollovers to designated Roth accounts.

(A) In general. Notwithstanding sections 402(c), 403(b)(8), and 457(e)(16), in the case of any distribution to which this paragraph applies—

(i) there shall be included in gross income any amount which would be includible were it not part of a qualified rollover contribution,

(ii) section 72(t) shall not apply, and

(iii) unless the taxpayer elects not to have this clause apply, any amount required to be included in gross income for any taxable year beginning in 2010 by reason of this paragraph shall be so included ratably over the 2-taxable-year period beginning with the first taxable year beginning in 2011.

Any election under clause (iii) for any distributions during a taxable year may not be changed after the due date for such taxable year.

(B) Distributions to which paragraph applies. In the case of an applicable retirement plan which includes a qualified Roth contribution program, this paragraph shall apply to a distribution from such plan other than from a designated Roth account which is contributed in a qualified rollover contribution (within the meaning of section 408A(e)) to the designated Roth account maintained under such plan for the benefit of the individual to whom the distribution is made.

(C) Coordination with limit. Any distribution to which this paragraph applies shall not be taken into account for purposes of paragraph (1).

(D) Other rules. The rules of subparagraphs (D), (E), and (F) of section 408A(d)(3) (as in effect for taxable years beginning after 2009) shall apply for purposes of this paragraph.

(d) Distribution rules—For purposes of this title—

(1) Exclusion—Any qualified distribution from a designated Roth account shall not be includible in gross income.

(2) Qualified distribution—For purposes of this subsection—

(A) In general—The term "qualified distribution" has the meaning given such term by section 408A(d)(2)(A) (without regard to clause (iv) thereof).

(B) Distributions within nonexclusion period—A payment or distribution from a designated Roth account shall not be treated as a qualified distribution if such payment or distribution is made within the 5-taxable-year period beginning with the earlier of—

(i) the first taxable year for which the individual made a designated Roth contribution to any designated Roth account established for such individual under the same applicable retirement plan, or

(ii) if a rollover contribution was made to such designated Roth account from a designated Roth account previously established for such individual under another applicable retirement plan, the first taxable year for which the individual made a designated Roth contribution to such previously established account.

(C) Distributions of excess deferrals and contributions and earnings thereon—The term "qualified distribution" shall not include any distribution of any excess deferral under section 402(g)(2) or any excess contribution under section 401(k)(8), and any income on the excess deferral or contribution.

(3) Treatment of distributions of certain excess deferrals—Notwithstanding section 72, if any excess deferral under section 402(g)(2) attributable to a designated Roth contribution is not distributed on or before the 1st April 15 following the close of the taxable year in which such excess deferral is made, the amount of such excess deferral shall—

(A) not be treated as investment in the contract, and

(B) be included in gross income for the taxable year in which such excess is distributed.

(4) Aggregation rules—Section 72 shall be applied separately with respect to distributions and payments from a designated Roth account and other distributions and payments from the plan.

(e) Other definitions—For purposes of this section—

(1) Applicable retirement plan—The term "applicable retirement plan" means—

(A) an employees' trust described in section 401(a) which is exempt from tax under section 501(a),

(B) a plan under which amounts are contributed by an individual's employer for an annuity contract described in section 403(b), and

(C) an eligible deferred compensation plan (as defined in section 457(b) of an eligible employer described in section 457(e)(1)(A).

(2) Elective deferral—The term "elective deferral" means—

(A) any elective deferral described in subparagraph (A) or (C) of section 402(g)(3), and

(B) any elective deferral of compensation by an individual under an eligible deferred compensation plan (as defined in section 457(b)) of an eligible employer described in section 457(e)(1)(A).

§ 403. Taxation of employee annuities.

(a) Taxability of beneficiary under a qualified annuity plan—

(1) Distributee taxable under section 72—If an annuity contract is purchased by an employer for an employee under a plan which meets the requirements of section 404(a)(2) (whether or not the employer deducts the amounts paid for the contract under such section), the amount actually distributed to any distributee under the contract shall be taxable to the distributee (in the year in which so distributed) under section 72 (relating to annuities).

(2) Special rule for health and long-term care insurance—To the extent provided in section 402(l), paragraph (1) shall not apply to the amount distributed under the contract which is otherwise includible in gross income under this subsection.

(3) Self-employed individuals—For purposes of this subsection, the term "employee" includes an individual who is an employee within the meaning of section 401(c)(1), and the employer of such individual is the person treated as his employer under section 401(c)(4).

(4) Rollover amounts—

(A) General rule—If—

(i) any portion of the balance to the credit of an employee in an employee annuity described in paragraph (1) is paid to him in an eligible rollover distribution (within the meaning of section 402(c)(4)),

(ii) the employee transfers any portion of the property he receives in such distribution to an eligible retirement plan, and

(iii) in the case of a distribution of property other than money, the amount so transferred consists of the property distributed,

then such distribution (to the extent so transferred) shall not be includible in gross income for the taxable year in which paid.

(B) Certain rules made applicable— The rules of paragraphs (2) through (7) and (11) and (9) of section 402(c) and section 402(f) shall apply for purposes of subparagraph (A).

(5) Direct trustee-to-trustee transfer—Any amount transferred in a direct trustee-to-trustee transfer in accordance with section 401(a)(31) shall not be includible in gross income for the taxable year of such transfer.

(b) Taxability of beneficiary under annuity purchased by section 501(c)(3) organization or public school—

(1) General rule—If—

(A) an annuity contract is purchased—

(i) for an employee by an employer described in section 501(c)(3) which is exempt from tax under section 501(a),

(ii) for an employee (other than an employee described in clause (i)), who performs services for an educational organization described in section 170(b)(1)(A)(ii), by an employer which is a State, a political subdivision of a State, or an agency or instrumentality of any one or more of the foregoing, or

(iii) for the minister described in section 414(e)(5)(A) by the minister or by an employer,

(B) such annuity contract is not subject to subsection (a),

(C) the employee's rights under the contract are nonforfeitable, except for failure to pay future premiums,

(D) except in the case of a contract purchased by a church, such contract is purchased under a plan which meets the nondiscrimination requirements of paragraph 12, and

(E) in the case of a contract purchased under a salary reduction agreement, the contract meets the requirements of section 401(a)(30), then contributions and other additions by such employer for such annuity contract shall be excluded from the gross income of the employee for the taxable year to the extent that the aggregate of such contributions and additions (when expressed as an annual addition (within the meaning of section 415(c)(2))) does not exceed the applicable limit under section 415. The amount actually distributed to any distributee under such contract shall be taxable to the distributee (in the year in which so distributed) under section 72 (relating to annuities). For purposes of applying the rules of this subsection to contributions and other additions by an employer for a taxable year, amounts transferred to a contract described in this paragraph by reason of a rollover contribution described in paragraph (8) of this subsection or section 408(d)(3)(A)(ii) shall not be considered contributed by such employer.

(2) Special rule for health and long-term care insurance—To the extent provided in section 402(l), paragraph (1) shall not apply to the amount distributed under the contract which is otherwise includible in gross income under this subsection.

(3) Includible compensation—For purposes of this subsection, the term "includible compensation" means, in the case of any employee, the amount of compensation which is received from the employer described in paragraph (1)(A), and which is includible in gross income (computed without regard to section 911) for the most recent period (ending not later than the close of the taxable year) which under paragraph (4) may be counted as one year of service, and which precedes the taxable year by no more than five years. Such term does not include any amount contributed by the employer for any annuity contract to which this subsection applies. Such term includes—

(A) any elective deferral (as defined in section 402(g)(3)), and

(B) any amount which is contributed or deferred by the employer at the election of the employee and which is not includible in the gross income of the employee by reason of section 125, 132(f)(4), or 457.

(4) Years of service—In determining the number of years of service for purposes of this subsection, there shall be included—

(A) one year for each full year during which the individual was a full-time employee of the organization purchasing the annuity for him, and

(B) a fraction of a year (determined in accordance with regulations prescribed by the Secretary) for each full year during which such individual was a part-time employee of such organization and for each part of a year during which such individual was a full-time or part-time employee of such organization.

In no case shall the number of years of service be less than one.

(5) Application to more than one annuity contract—If for any taxable year of the employee this subsection applies to 2 or more annuity contracts purchased by the employer, such contracts shall be treated as one contract.

(6) [Repealed]

(7) Custodial accounts for regulated investment company stock—

(A) Amounts paid treated as contributions—For purposes of this title, amounts paid by an employer described in paragraph (1)(A) to a custodial account which satisfies the requirements of section 401(f)(2) shall be treated as amounts contributed by him for an annuity contract for his employee if—

(i) the amounts are to be invested in regulated investment company stock to be held in that custodial account, and

(ii) under the custodial account no such amounts may be paid or made available to any distributee (unless such amount is a distribution to which section 72(t)(2)(G) applies) before the employee dies, attains age 59½, has a severance from employment, becomes disabled (within the meaning of section 72(m)(7)), or in the case of contributions made pursuant to a salary reduction agreement (within the meaning of section 3121(a)(5)(D)), encounters financial hardship.

(B) Account treated as plan—For purposes of this title, a custodial account which satisfies the requirements of section 401(f)(2) shall be treated as an organization described in section 401(a) solely for purposes of subchapter F and subtitle F with respect to amounts received by it (and income from investment thereof).

(C) Regulated investment company—For purposes of this paragraph, the term "regulated investment company" means a domestic corporation which is a regulated investment company within the meaning of section 851(a).

(8) Rollover amounts—

(A) General rule—If—

(i) any portion of the balance to the credit of an employee in an annuity contract described in paragraph (1) is paid to him in an eligible rollover distribution (within the meaning of section 402(c)(4)),

(ii) the employee transfers any portion of the property he receives in such distribution to an eligible retirement plan described in section 402(c)(8)(B), and

(iii) in the case of a distribution of property other than money, the property so transferred consists of the property distributed,

then such distribution (to the extent so transferred) shall not be includible in gross income for the taxable year in which paid.

(B) Certain rules made applicable—The rules of paragraphs (2) through (7), (9), and (11) of section 402(c) and section 402(f) shall apply for purposes of subparagraph (A), except that section 402(f) shall be applied to the payor in lieu of the plan administrator.

(9) Retirement income accounts provided by churches, etc—

(A) Amounts paid treated as contributions—For purposes of this title—

(i) a retirement income account shall be treated as an annuity contract described in this subsection, and

(ii) amounts paid by an employer described in paragraph (1)(A) to a retirement income account shall be treated as amounts contributed by the employer for an annuity contract for the employee on whose behalf such account is maintained.

(B) Retirement income account—For purposes of this paragraph, the term "retirement income account" means a defined contribution program established or maintained by a church, or a convention or association of churches, including an organization described in section 414(e)(3)(A), to provide benefits under section 403(b) for an employee described in paragraph (1) or his beneficiaries.

(10) Distribution requirements—Under regulations prescribed by the Secretary, this subsection shall not apply to any annuity contract (or to any custodial account described in paragraph (7) or retirement income account described in paragraph (9)) unless requirements similar to the requirements of sections 401(a)(9) and 401(a)(31) are met (and requirements similar to the incidental death benefit requirements of section 401(a) are met) with respect to such annuity contract (or custodial account or retirement income account). Any amount transferred in a direct trustee-to-trustee transfer in accordance with section 401(a)(31) shall not be includible in gross income for the taxable year of the transfer.

(11) Requirement that distributions not begin before age 59½, severance from employment, death, or disability—This subsection shall not apply to any annuity contract unless under such contract distributions attributable to contributions made pursuant to a salary reduction agreement (within the meaning of section 402(g)(3)(C)) may be paid only—

(A) when the employee attains age 59½, has a severance from employment, dies, or becomes disabled (within the meaning of section 72(m)(7)), or

(B) in the case of hardship, or

(C) for distributions to which section 72(t)(2)(G) applies.

Such contract may not provide for the distribution of any income attributable to such contributions in the case of hardship.

(12) Nondiscrimination requirements—

(A) In general—For purposes of paragraph (1)(D), a plan meets the nondiscrimination requirements of this paragraph if—

(i) with respect to contributions not made pursuant to a salary reduction agreement, such plan meets the requirements of paragraphs (4), (5), (17), and (26) of section 401(a), section 401(m), and section 410(b) in the same manner as if such plan were described in section 401(a), and

(ii) all employees of the organization may elect to have the employer make contributions of more than $200 pursuant to a salary reduction agreement if any employee of the organization may elect to have the organization make contributions for such contracts pursuant to such agreement.

For purposes of clause (i), a contribution shall be treated as not made pursuant to a salary reduction agreement if under the agreement it is made pursuant to a 1-time irrevocable election made by the employee at the time of initial eligibility to participate in the agreement or is made pursuant to a similar arrangement involving a one-time irrevocable election specified in regulations. For purposes of clause (ii), there may be excluded any employee who is a participant in an eligible deferred compensation plan (within the meaning of section 457) or a qualified cash or deferred arrangement of the organization or another annuity contract described in this subsection. Any nonresident alien described in section 410(b)(3)(C) may also be excluded. Subject to the conditions applicable under section 410(b)(4), there may be excluded for purposes of this subparagraph employees who are students performing services described in section 3121(b)(10) and employees who normally work less than 20 hours per week.

(B) Church—For purposes of paragraph (1)(D), the term "church" has the meaning given to such term by section 3121(w)(3)(A). Such term shall include any qualified church-controlled organization (as defined in section 3121(w)(3)(B)).

(C) State and local governmental plans—For purposes of paragraph (1)(D), the requirements of subparagraph (A)(i) (other than those relating to section 401(a)(17)) shall not apply to a governmental plan (within the meaning of section 414(d)) maintained by a State or local government or political subdivision thereof (or agency or instrumentality thereof).

(13) Trustee-to-trustee transfers to purchase permissive service credit—No amount shall be includible in gross income by reason of a direct trustee-to-trustee transfer to a defined benefit governmental plan (as defined in section 414(d)) if such transfer is—

(A) for the purchase of permissive service credit (as defined in section 415(n)(3)(A)) under such plan, or

(B) a repayment to which section 415 does not apply by reason of subsection (k)(3) thereof.

(14) Death benefits under USERRA-qualified active military service—This subsection shall not apply to an annuity contract unless such contract meets the requirements of section 401(a)(37).

(c) Taxability of beneficiary under nonqualified annuities or under annuities purchased by exempt organizations—Premiums paid by an employer for an annuity contract which is not subject to subsection (a) shall be included in the gross income of the employee in accordance with section 83 (relating to property transferred in connection with performance of services), except that the value of such contract shall be substituted for the fair market value of the property for purposes of applying such section. The preceding sentence shall not apply to that portion of the premiums paid which is excluded from gross income under subsection (b). In the case of any portion of any contract which is attributable to premiums to which this subsection applies, the amount actually paid or made available under such contract to any beneficiary which is attributable to such premiums shall be taxable to the beneficiary (in the year in which so paid or made available) under section 72 (relating to annuities).

§ 404. Deduction for contributions of an employer to an employees' trust or annuity plan and compensation under a deferred-payment plan.

(a) General rule—If contributions are paid by an employer to or under a stock bonus, pension, profit-sharing, or annuity plan, or if compensation is paid or accrued on account of any employee under a plan deferring the receipt of such compensation, such contributions or compensation shall not be deductible under this chapter; but if they would otherwise be deductible, they shall be deductible under this section, subject, however, to the following limitations as to the amounts deductible in any year:

(1) Pension trusts—

(A) In general—In the taxable year when paid, if the contributions are paid into a pension trust (other than a trust to which paragraph (3) applies), and if such taxable year ends within or with a taxable year of the trust for which the trust is exempt under section 501(a), in the case of a defined benefit plan other than a multiemployer plan, in an amount determined under subsection (o), and in the case of any other plan in an amount determined as follows:

(i) the amount necessary to satisfy the minimum funding standard provided by section 412(a) for plan years ending within or with such taxable year (or for any prior plan year), if such amount is greater than the amount determined under clause (ii) or (iii) (whichever is applicable with respect to the plan),

(ii) the amount necessary to provide with respect to all of the employees under the trust the remaining unfunded cost of their past and current service credits distributed as a level amount, or a level percentage of compensation, over the remaining future service of each such employee, as determined under regulations prescribed by the Secretary, but if such remaining unfunded cost with respect to any 3 individuals is more than 50 percent of such remaining unfunded cost, the amount of such unfunded cost attributable to such individuals shall be distributed over a period of at least 5 taxable years,

(iii) an amount equal to the normal cost of the plan, as determined under regulations prescribed by the Secretary, plus, if past service or other supplementary pension or annuity credits are provided by the plan, an amount necessary to amortize the unfunded costs attributable to such credits in equal annual payments (until fully amortized) over 10 years, as determined under regulations prescribed by the Secretary.

In determining the amount deductible in such year under the foregoing limitations the funding method and the actuarial assumptions used shall be those used for such year under section 431, and the maximum amount deductible for such year shall be an amount equal to the full funding limitation for such year determined under section 431.

(B) Special rule in case of certain amendments—In the case of a multiemployer plan which the Secretary of Labor finds to be collectively bargained which makes an election under this subparagraph (in such manner and at such time as may be provided under regulations prescribed by the Secretary), if the full funding limitation determined under section 431(c)(6) for such year is zero, if as a result of any plan amendment applying to such plan year, the amount determined under section 431(c)(6)(A)(ii) exceeds the amount determined under section 431(c)(6)(A)(i), and if the funding method and the actuarial assumptions used are those used for such year under section 431, the maximum amount deductible in such year under the limitations of this paragraph shall be an amount equal to the lesser of—

(i) the full funding limitation for such year determined by applying section 431(c)(6) but increasing the amount referred to in subparagraph (A) thereof by the decrease in the present value of all unamortized liabilities resulting from such amendment, or

(ii) the normal cost under the plan reduced by the amount necessary to amortize in equal annual installments over 10 years (until fully amortized) the decrease described in clause (i).

In the case of any election under this subparagraph, the amount deductible under the limitations of this paragraph with respect to any of the plan years following the plan year for which such election was made shall be determined as provided under such regulations as may be prescribed by the Secretary to carry out the purposes of this subparagraph.

(C) Certain collectively-bargained plans—In the case of a plan which the Secretary of Labor finds to be collectively bargained, established or maintained by an employer doing business in not less than 40 States and engaged in the trade or business of furnishing or selling services described in section 168(i)(10)(C), with respect to which the rates have been established or approved by a State or political subdivision thereof, by any agency or instrumentality of the United States, or by a public service or public utility commission or other similar body of any State or political subdivision thereof, and in the case of any employer which is a member of a controlled group with such employer, subparagraph (B) shall be applied by substituting for the words "plan amendment" the words "plan amendment or increase in benefits payable under title II of the Social Security Act". For purposes of this subparagraph, the term "controlled group" has the meaning provided by section 1563(a), determined without regard to section 1563(a)(4) and (e)(3)(C).

(D) Amount determined on basis of unfunded current liability—In the case of a defined benefit plan which is a multiemployer plan, except as provided in regulations, the maximum amount deductible under the limitations of this paragraph shall not be less than the excess (if any) of—

(i) 140 percent of the current liability of the plan determined under section 431(c)(6)(D), over

(ii) the value of the plan's assets determined under section 431(c)(2).

(E) Carryover—Any amount paid in a taxable year in excess of the amount deductible in such year under the foregoing limitations shall be deductible in the succeeding taxable years in order of time to the extent of the difference between the amount paid and deductible in each such succeeding year and the maximum amount deductible for such year under the foregoing limitations.

(2) Employees' annuities—In the taxable year when paid, in an amount determined in accordance with paragraph (1), if the contributions are paid toward the purchase of retirement annuities, or retirement annuities and medical benefits as described in section 401(h), and such purchase is a part of a plan which meets the requirements of section 401(a)(3), (4), (5),(6), (7), (8), (9), (11), (12), (13), (14), (15), (16), (17), (19), (20), (22), (26), (27), (31), and (37) and, if applicable, the requirements of section 401(a)(10) and of section 401(d), and if refunds of premiums, if any, are applied within the current taxable year or next succeeding taxable year towards the purchase of such retirement annuities, or such retirement annuities and medical benefits.

(3) Stock bonus and profit-sharing trusts—

(A) Limits on deductible contributions—

(i) In general—In the taxable year when paid, if the contributions are paid into a stock bonus or profit-sharing trust, and if such taxable year ends within or with a taxable year of the trust with respect to which the trust is exempt under section 501(a), in an amount not in excess of the greater of—

(I) 25 percent of the compensation otherwise paid or accrued during the taxable year to the beneficiaries under the stock bonus or profit-sharing plan, or

(II) the amount such employer is required to contribute to such trust under section 401(k)(11) for such year.

(ii) Carryover of excess contributions—Any amount paid into the trust in any taxable year in excess of the limitation of clause (i) (or the corresponding provision of prior law) shall be deductible in the succeeding taxable years in order of time, but the amount so deductible under this clause in any 1 such succeeding taxable year together with the amount allowable under clause (i) shall not exceed the amount described in subclause (I) or (II) of clause (i), whichever is greater, with respect to such taxable year.

(iii) Certain retirement plans excluded—For purposes of this subparagraph, the term "stock bonus or profit-sharing trust" shall not include any trust designed to provide benefits upon retirement and covering a period of years, if under the plan the amounts to be contributed by the employer can be determined actuarially as provided in paragraph (1).

(iv) 2 or more trusts treated as 1 trust—If the contributions are made to 2 or more stock bonus or profit-sharing trusts, such trusts shall be considered a single trust for purposes of applying the limitations in this subparagraph.

(v) Defined contribution plans subject to the funding standards—Except as provided by the Secretary, a defined contribution plan which is subject to the funding standards of section 412 shall be treated in the same manner as a stock bonus or profit-sharing plan for purposes of this subparagraph.

(B) Profit-sharing plan of affiliated group—In the case of a profit-sharing plan, or a stock bonus plan in which contributions are determined with reference to profits, of a group of corporations which is an affiliated group within the meaning of section 1504, if any member of such affiliated group is prevented from making a contribution which it would otherwise have made under the plan, by reason of having no current or accumulated earnings or profits or because such earnings or profits are less than the contributions which it would otherwise have made, then so much of the contribution which such member was so prevented from making may be made, for the benefit of the employees of such member, by the other members of the group, to the extent of current or accumulated earnings or profits, except that such contribution by each such other member shall be limited, where the group does not file a consolidated return, to that proportion of its total current and accumulated earnings or profits remaining after adjustment for its contribution deductible without regard to this subparagraph which the total prevented contribution bears to the total current and accumulated earnings or profits of all the members of the group remaining after adjustment for all contributions deductible without regard to this subparagraph. Contributions made under the preceding sentence shall be deductible under subparagraph (A) of this paragraph by the employer making such contribution, and, for the purpose of determining amounts which may be carried forward and deducted under the second sentence of subparagraph (A) of this paragraph in succeeding taxable years, shall be deemed to have been made by the employer on behalf of whose employees such contributions were made.

(4) Trusts created or organized outside the united states—If a stock bonus, pension, or profit-sharing trust would qualify for exemption under section 501 (a) except for the fact that it is a trust created or organized outside the United States, contributions to such a trust by an employer which is a resident, or corporation, or other entity of the United States, shall be deductible under the preceding paragraphs.

(5) Other plans—If the plan is not one included in paragraph (1), (2), or (3), in the taxable year in which an amount attributable to the contribution is includible in the gross income of employees participating in the plan, but, in the case of a plan in which more than one employee participates only if separate accounts are maintained for each employee. For purposes of this section, any vacation pay which is treated as deferred compensation shall be deductible for the taxable year of the employer in which paid to the employee.

(6) Time when contributions deemed made—For purposes of paragraphs (1), (2), and (3), a taxpayer shall be deemed to have made a payment on the last day of the preceding taxable year if the payment is on account of such taxable year and is made not later than the time prescribed by law for filing the return for such taxable year (including extensions thereof).

(7) Limitation on deductions where combination of defined contribution plan and defined benefit plan—

(A) In general—If amounts are deductible under the foregoing paragraphs of this subsection (other than paragraph (5)) in connection with 1 or more defined contribution plans and 1 or more defined benefit plans or in connection with trusts or plans described in 2 or more of such paragraphs, the total amount deductible in a taxable year under such plans shall not exceed the greater of—

(i) 25 percent of the compensation otherwise paid or accrued during the taxable year to the beneficiaries under such plans, or

(ii) the amount of contributions made to or under the defined benefit plans to the extent such contributions do not exceed the amount of employer contributions necessary to satisfy the minimum funding standard provided by section 412 with respect to any such defined benefit plans for the plan year which ends with or within such taxable year (or for any prior plan year).

A defined contribution plan which is a pension plan shall not be treated as failing to provide definitely determinable benefits merely by limited employer contributions to amounts deductible under this section. In the case of a defined benefit plan which is a single employer plan, the amount necessary to satisfy the minimum funding standard provided by section 412 shall not be less than the excess (if any) of the plan's funding target (as defined in section 430(d)(1)) over the value of the plan's assets (as determined under section 430(g)(3)).

(B) Carryover of contributions in excess of the deductible limit—Any amount paid under the plans in any taxable year in excess of the limitation of subparagraph (A) shall be deductible in the succeeding taxable years in order of time, but the amount so deductible under this subparagraph in any 1 such succeeding taxable year together with the amount allowable under subparagraph (A) shall not exceed 25 percent of the compensation otherwise paid or accrued during such taxable year to the beneficiaries under the plans.

(C) Paragraph not to apply in certain cases—

(i) Beneficiary test—This paragraph shall not have the effect of reducing the amount otherwise deductible under paragraphs (1), (2), and (3), if no employee is a beneficiary under more than 1 trust or under a trust and an annuity plan.

(ii) Elective deferrals—If, in connection with 1 or more defined contribution plans and 1 or more defined benefit plans, no amounts (other than elective deferrals (as defined in section 402(g)(3))) are contributed to any of the defined contribution plans for the taxable year, then subparagraph (A) shall not apply with respect to any of such defined contribution plans and defined benefit plans.

(iii) Limitation—In the case of employer contributions to 1 or more defined contribution plans—

(I) if such contributions do not exceed 6 percent of the compensation otherwise paid or accrued during the taxable year to the beneficiaries under such plans, this paragraph shall not apply to such contributions or to employer contributions to the defined benefit plans to which this paragraph would otherwise apply by reason of contributions to the defined contribution plans, and

(II) if such contributions exceed 6 percent of such compensation, this paragraph shall be applied by only taking into account such contributions to the extent of such excess.

For purposes of this clause, amounts carried over from preceding taxable years under subparagraph (B) shall be treated as employer contributions to 1 or more defined contributions plans to the extent attributable to employer contributions to such plans in such preceding taxable years.

(iv) Guaranteed plans—In applying this paragraph, any single-employer plan covered under section 4021 of the Employee Retirement Income Security Act of 1974 shall not be taken into account.

(v) Multiemployer plans—In applying this paragraph, any multiemployer plan shall not be taken into account.

(D) Insurance contract plans—For purposes of this paragraph, a plan described in section 412(e)(3) shall be treated as a defined benefit plan.

(8) Self-employed individuals—In the case of a plan included in paragraph (1), (2), or (3) which provides contributions or benefits for employees some or all of whom are employees within the meaning of section 401(c)(1), for purposes of this section—

(A) the term "employee" includes an individual who is an employee within the meaning of section 401(c)(1), and the employer of such individual is the person treated as his employer under section 401(c)(4) ;

(B) the term "earned income" has the meaning assigned to it by section 401(c)(2) ;

(C) the contributions to such plan on behalf of an individual who is an employee within the meaning of section 401(c)(1) shall be considered to satisfy the conditions of section 162 or 212 to the extent that such contributions do not exceed the earned income of such individual (determined without regard to the deductions allowed by this section) derived from the trade or business with respect to which such plan is established, and to the extent that such contributions are not allocable (determined in accordance with regulations prescribed by the Secretary) to the purchase of life, accident, health, or other insurance; and

(D) any reference to compensation shall, in the case of an individual who is an employee within the meaning of section 401(c)(1), be considered to be a reference to the earned income of such individual derived from the trade or business with respect to which the plan is established.

(9) Certain contributions to employee stock ownership plans—

(A) Principal payments—Notwithstanding the provisions of paragraphs (3) and (7), if contributions are paid into a trust which forms a part of an employee stock ownership plan (as described in section 4975(e)(7)), and such contributions are, on or before the time prescribed in paragraph (6), applied by the plan to the repayment of the principal of a loan incurred for the purpose of acquiring qualifying employer securities (as described in section 4975(e)(8)), such contributions shall be deductible under this paragraph for the taxable year determined under paragraph (6). The amount deductible under this paragraph shall not, however, exceed 25 percent of the compensation otherwise paid or accrued during the taxable year to the employees under such employee stock ownership plan. Any amount paid into such trust in any taxable year in excess of the amount deductible under this paragraph shall be deductible in the succeeding taxable years in order of time to the extent of the difference between the amount paid and deductible in each such succeeding year and the maximum amount deductible for such year under the preceding sentence.

(B) Interest payment—Notwithstanding the provisions of paragraphs (3) and (7), if contributions are made to an employee stock ownership plan (described in subparagraph (A)) and such contributions are applied by the plan to the repayment of interest on a loan incurred for the purpose of acquiring qualifying employer securities (as described in subparagraph (A)), such contributions shall be deductible for the taxable year with respect to which such contributions are made as determined under paragraph (6).

(C) S corporations—This paragraph shall not apply to an S corporation.

(D) Qualified gratuitous transfers—A qualified gratuitous transfer (as defined in section 664(g)(1)) shall have no effect on the amount or amounts otherwise deductible under paragraph (3) or (7) or under this paragraph.

(10) Contributions by certain ministers to retirement income accounts—In the case of contributions made by a minister described in section 414(e)(5) to a retirement income account described in section 403(b)(9) and not by a person other than such minister, such contributions—

(A) shall be treated as made to a trust which is exempt from tax under section 501(a) and which is part of a plan which is described in section 401(a), and

(B) shall be deductible under this subsection to the extent such contributions do not exceed the limit on elective deferrals under section 402(g) or the limit on annual additions under section 415.

For purposes of this paragraph, all plans in which the minister is a participant shall be treated as one plan.

(11) Determinations relating to deferred compensation—For purposes of determining under this section—

(A) whether compensation of an employee is deferred compensation; and

(B) when deferred compensation is paid,

no amount shall be treated as received by the employee, or paid, until it is actually received by the employee.

(12) Definition of compensation—For purposes of paragraphs (3), (7), (8), and (9) and subsection (h)(1)(C), the term "compensation" shall include amounts treated as "participant's compensation" under subparagraph (C) or (D) of section 415(c)(3).

(b) Method of contributions, etc., having the effect of a plan; certain deferred benefits—

(1) Method of contributions, etc., having the effect of a plan—If—

(A) there is no plan, but

(B) there is a method or arrangement of employer contributions or compensation which has the effect of a stock bonus, pension, profit-sharing, or annuity plan, or other plan deferring the receipt of compensation (including a plan described in paragraph (2)),

subsection (a) shall apply as if there were such a plan.

(2) Plans providing certain deferred benefits—

(A) In general—For purposes of this section, any plan providing for deferred benefits (other than compensation) for employees, their spouses, or their dependents shall be treated as a plan deferring the receipt of compensation. In the case of such a plan, for purposes of this section, the determination of when an amount is includible in gross income shall be made without regard to any provisions of this chapter excluding such benefits from gross income.

(B) Exception—Subparagraph (A) shall not apply to any benefit provided through a welfare benefit fund (as defined in section 419(e)).

(c) Certain negotiated plans—If contributions are paid by an employer—

(1) under a plan under which such contributions are held in trust for the purpose of paying (either from principal or income or both) for the benefit of employees and their families and dependents at least medical or hospital care, or pensions on retirement or death of employees; and

(2) such plan was established prior to January 1, 1954, as a result of an agreement between employee representatives and the Government of the United States during a period of Government operation, under seizure powers, of a major part of the productive facilities of the industry in which such employer is engaged,

such contributions shall not be deductible under this section nor be made nondeductible by this section, but the deductibility thereof shall be governed solely by section 162 (relating to trade or business expenses). For purposes of this chapter and subtitle B, in the case of any individual who before July 1, 1974, was a participant in a plan described in the preceding sentence—

(A) such individual, if he is or was an employee within the meaning of section 401(c)(1), shall be treated (with respect to service covered by the plan) as being an employee other than an employee within the meaning of section 401(c)(1) and as being an employee of a participating employer under the plan,

(B) earnings derived from service covered by the plan shall be treated as not being earned income within the meaning of section 401(c)(2), and

(C) such individual shall be treated as an employee of a participating employer under the plan with respect to service before July 1, 1975, covered by the plan.

Section 277 (relating to deductions incurred by certain membership organizations in transactions with members) does not apply to any trust described in this subsection. The first and third sentences of this subsection shall have no application with respect to amounts contributed to a trust on or after any date on which such trust is qualified for exemption from tax under section 501(a).

(d) Deductibility of payments of deferred compensation, etc., to independent contractors—If a plan would be described in so much of subsection (a) as precedes paragraph (1) thereof (as modified by subsection (b)) but for the fact that there is no employer-employee relationship, the contributions or compensation—

(1) shall not be deductible by the payor thereof under this chapter, but

(2) shall (if they would be deductible under this chapter but for paragraph (1)) be deductible under this subsection for the taxable year in which an amount attributable to the contribution or compensation is includible in the gross income of the persons participating in the plan.

(e) Contributions allocable to life insurance protection for self-employed individuals— In the case of a self-employed individual described in section 401(c)(1), contributions which are allocable (determined under regulations prescribed by the Secretary) to the purchase of life, accident, health, or other insurance shall not be taken into account under paragraph (1), (2), or (3) of subsection (a).

(f) [Repealed]

(g) Certain employer liability payments considered as contributions—

(1) In general—For purposes of this section, any amount paid by an employer under section 4041(b), 4062, 4063, or 4064, or part 1 of subtitle E of title IV of the Employee Retirement Income Security Act of 1974 shall be treated as a contribution to which this section applies by such employer to or under a stock bonus, pension, profit-sharing, or annuity plan.

(2) Controlled group deductions—In the case of a payment described in paragraph (1) made by an entity which is liable because it is a member of a commonly controlled group of corporations, trades, or businesses, within the meaning of subsection (b) or (c) of section 414, the fact that the entity did not directly employ participants of the plan with respect to which the liability payment was made shall not affect the deductibility of a payment which otherwise satisfies the conditions of section 162 (relating to trade or business expenses) or section 212 (relating to expenses for the production of income).

(3) Timing of deduction of contributions—

(A) In general—Except as otherwise provided in this paragraph, any payment described in paragraph (1) shall (subject to the last sentence of subsection (a)(1)(A)) be deductible under this section when paid.

(B) Contributions under standard terminations—Subparagraph (A) shall not apply (and subsection (a)(1)(A) shall apply) to any payments described in paragraph (1) which are paid to terminate a plan under section 4041(b) of the Employee Retirement Income Security Act of 1974 to the extent such payments result in the assets of the plan being in excess of the total amount of benefits under such plan which are guaranteed by the Pension Benefit Guaranty Corporation under section 4022 of such Act.

(C) Contributions to certain trusts—Subparagraph (A) shall not apply to any payment described in paragraph (1) which is made under section 4062(c) of such Act and such payment shall be deductible at such time as may be prescribed in regulations which are based on principles similar to the principles of subsection (a)(1)(A).

(4) References to employee retirement income security act of 1974—For purposes of this subsection, any reference to a section of the Employee Retirement Income Security Act of 1974 shall be treated as a reference to such section as in effect on the date of the enactment of the Retirement Protection Act of 1994.

(h) Special rules for simplified employee pensions—

(1) In general—Employer contributions to a simplified employee pension shall be treated as if they are made to a plan subject to the requirements of this section. Employer contributions to a simplified employee pension are subject to the following limitations:

(A) Contributions made for a year are deductible—

(i) in the case of a simplified employee pension maintained on a calendar year basis, for the taxable year with or within which the calendar year ends, or

(ii) in the case of a simplified employee pension which is maintained on the basis of the taxable year of the employer, for such taxable year.

(B) Contributions shall be treated for purposes of this subsection as if they were made for a taxable year if such contributions are made on account of such taxable year and are made not later than the time prescribed by law for filing the return for such taxable year (including extensions thereof).

(C) The amount deductible in a taxable year for a simplified employee pension shall not exceed 25 percent of the compensation paid to the employees during the calendar year ending with or within the taxable year (or during the taxable year in the case of a taxable year described in subparagraph (A)(ii)). The excess of the amount contributed over the amount deductible for a taxable year shall be deductible in the succeeding taxable years in order of time, subject to the 25 percent limit of the preceding sentence.

(2) Effect on certain trusts—For any taxable year for which the employer has a deduction under paragraph (1), the otherwise applicable limitations in subsection (a)(3)(A) shall be reduced by the amount of the allowable deductions under paragraph (1) with respect to participants in the trust subject to subsection (a)(3)(A).

(3) Coordination with subsection (a)(7)—For purposes of subsection (a)(7), a simplified employee pension shall be treated as if it were a separate stock bonus or profit-sharing trust.

(i) [Repealed]

(j) Special rules relating to application with section 415—

(1) No deduction in excess of section 415 limitation—In computing the amount of any deduction allowable under paragraphs (1), (2), (3), (4), (7), or (9) of subsection (a) for any year—

(A) in the case of a defined benefit plan, there shall not be taken into account any benefits for any year in excess of any limitation on such benefits under section 415 for such year, or

(B) in the case of a defined contribution plan, the amount of any contributions otherwise taken into account shall be reduced by any annual additions in excess of the limitation under section 415 for such year.

(2) No advance funding of cost-of-living adjustments—For purposes of clause (i), (ii) or (iii) of subsection (a)(1)(A), and in computing the full funding limitation, there shall not be taken into account any adjustments under section 415(d)(1) for any year before the year for which such adjustment first takes effect.

(k) Deduction for dividends paid on certain employer securities—

(1) General rule—In the case of a C corporation, there shall be allowed as a deduction for a taxable year the amount of any applicable dividend paid in cash by such corporation with respect to applicable employer securities. Such deduction shall be in addition to the deductions allowed under subsection (a).

(2) Applicable dividend—For purposes of this subsection—

(A) In general—The term "applicable dividend" means any dividend which, in accordance with the plan provisions—

(i) is paid in cash to the participants in the plan or their beneficiaries,

(ii) is paid to the plan and is distributed in cash to participants in the plan or their beneficiaries not later than 90 days after the close of the plan year in which paid,

(iii) is, at the election of such participants or their beneficiaries—

(I) payable as provided in clause (i) or (ii), or

(II) paid to the plan and reinvested in qualifying employer securities, or

(iv) is used to make payments on a loan described in subsection (a)(9) the proceeds of which were used to acquire the employer securities (whether or not allocated to participants) with respect to which the dividend is paid.

(B) Limitation on certain dividends—A dividend described in subparagraph (A)(iv) which is paid with respect to any employer security which is allocated to a participant shall not be treated as an applicable dividend unless the plan provides that employer securities with a fair market value of not less than the amount of such dividend are allocated to such participant for the year which (but for subparagraph (A)) such dividend would have been allocated to such participant.

(3) Applicable employer securities—For purposes of this subsection, the term "applicable employer securities" means, with respect to any dividend, employer securities which are held on the record date for such dividend by an employee stock ownership plan which is maintained by—

(A) the corporation paying such dividend, or

(B) any other corporation which is a member of a controlled group of corporations (within the meaning of section 409(l)(4)) which includes such corporation.

(4) Time for deduction—

(A) In general—The deduction under paragraph (1) shall be allowable in the taxable year of the corporation in which the dividend is paid or distributed to a participant or his beneficiary.

(B) Reinvestment dividends—For purposes of subparagraph (A), an applicable dividend reinvested pursuant to clause (iii)(II) of paragraph (2)(A) shall be treated as paid in the taxable year of the corporation in which such dividend is reinvested in qualifying employer securities or in which the election under clause (iii) of paragraph (2)(A) is made, whichever is later.

(C) Repayment of loans—In the case of an applicable dividend described in clause (iv) of paragraph (2)(A), the deduction under paragraph (1) shall be allowable in the taxable year of the corporation in which such dividend is used to repay the loan described in such clause.

(5) Other rules—For purposes of this subsection—

(A) Disallowance of deduction—The Secretary may disallow the deduction under paragraph (1) for any dividend if the Secretary determines that such dividend constitutes, in substance, an avoidance or evasion of taxation.

(B) Plan qualification—A plan shall not be treated as violating the requirements of section 401, 409, or 4975(e)(7), or as engaging in a prohibited transaction for purposes of section 4975(d)(3), merely by reason of any payment or distribution described in paragraph (2)(A).

(6) Definitions—For purposes of this subsection—

(A) Employer securities—The term "employer securities" has the meaning given such term by section 409(l).

(B) Employee stock ownership plan—The term "employee stock ownership plan" has the meaning given such term by section 4975(e)(7). Such term includes a tax credit employee stock ownership plan (as defined in section 409).

(7) Full vesting—In accordance with section 411, an applicable dividend described in clause (iii)(II) of paragraph (2)(A) shall be subject to the requirements of section 411(a)(1).

(l) Limitation on amount of annual compensation taken into account—For purposes of applying the limitations of this section, the amount of annual compensation of each employee taken into account under the plan for any year shall not exceed $200,000. The Secretary shall adjust the $200,000 amount at the same time, and by the same amount, as the adjustment under section 401(a)(17)(B). For purposes of clause (i), (ii), or (iii) of subsection (a)(1)(A), and in computing the full funding limitation, any adjustment under the preceding sentence shall not be taken into account for any year before the year for which such adjustment first takes effect.

(m) Special rules for simple retirement accounts—

(1) In general—Employer contributions to a simple retirement account shall be treated as if they are made to a plan subject to the requirements of this section.

(2) Timing—

(A) Deduction—Contributions described in paragraph (1) shall be deductible in the taxable year of the employer with or within which the calendar year for which the contributions were made ends.

(B) Contributions after end of year—For purposes of this subsection, contributions shall be treated as made for a taxable year if they are made on account of the taxable year and are made not later than the time prescribed by law for filing the return for the taxable year (including extensions thereof).

(n) Elective deferrals not taken into account for purposes of deduction limits—Elective deferrals (as defined in section 402(g)(3)) shall not be subject to any limitation contained in paragraph (3), (7), or (9) of subsection (a) or paragraph (1)(C) of subsection (h), and such elective deferrals shall not be taken into account in applying any such limitation to any other contributions.

(o) Deduction limit for single-employer plans—For purposes of subsection (a)(1)(A)—

(1) In general—In the case of a defined benefit plan to which subsection (a)(1)(A) applies (other than a multiemployer plan), the amount determined under this subsection for any taxable year shall be equal to the greater of—

(A) the sum of the amounts determined under paragraph (2) with respect to each plan year ending with or within the taxable year, or

(B) the sum of the minimum required contributions under section 430 for such plan years.

(2) Determination of amount—

(A) In general—The amount determined under this paragraph for any plan year shall be equal to the excess (if any) of—

(i) the sum of—

(I) the funding target for the plan year,

(II) the target normal cost for the plan year, and

(III) the cushion amount for the plan year, over

(ii) the value (determined under section 430(g)(3)) of the assets of the plan which are held by the plan as of the valuation date for the plan year.

(B) Special rule for certain employers—If section 430(i) does not apply to a plan for a plan year, the amount determined under subparagraph (A)(i) for the plan year shall in no event be less than the sum of—

(i) the funding target for the plan year (determined as if section 430(i) applied to the plan), plus

(ii) the target normal cost for the plan year (as so determined).

(3) Cushion amount—For purposes of paragraph (2)(A)(i)(III)—

(A) In general—The cushion amount for any plan year is the sum of—

(i) 50 percent of the funding target for the plan year, and

(ii) the amount by which the funding target for the plan year would increase if the plan were to take into account—

(I) increases in compensation which are expected to occur in succeeding plan years, or

(II) if the plan does not base benefits for service to date on compensation, increases in benefits which are expected to occur in succeeding plan years (determined on the basis of the average annual increase in benefits over the 6 immediately preceding plan years).

(B) Limitations—

(i) In general—In making the computation under subparagraph (A)(ii), the plan's actuary shall assume that the limitations under subsection (l) and section 415(b) shall apply.

(ii) Expected increases—In the case of a plan year during which a plan is covered under section 4021 of the Employee Retirement Income Security Act of 1974, the plan's actuary may, notwithstanding subsection (l), take into account increases in the limitations which are expected to occur in succeeding plan years.

(4) Special rules for plans with 100 or fewer participants—

(A) In general—For purposes of determining the amount under paragraph (3) for any plan year, in the case of a plan which has 100 or fewer participants for the plan year, the liability of the plan attributable to benefit increases for highly compensated employees (as defined in section 414(q)) resulting from a plan amendment which is made or becomes effective, whichever is later, within the last 2 years shall not be taken into account in determining the target liability.

(B) Rule for determining number of participants—For purposes of determining the number of plan participants, all defined benefit plans maintained by the same employer (or any member of such employer's controlled group (within the meaning of section 412(d)(3))) shall be treated as one plan, but only participants of such member or employer shall be taken into account.

(5) Special rule for terminating plans—In the case of a plan which, subject to section 4041 of the Employee Retirement Income Security Act of 1974, terminates during the plan year, the amount determined under paragraph (2) shall in no event be less than the amount required to make the plan sufficient for benefit liabilities (within the meaning of section 4041(d) of such Act).

(6) Actuarial assumptions—Any computation under this subsection for any plan year shall use the same actuarial assumptions which are used for the plan year under section 430.

(7) Definitions—Any term used in this subsection which is also used in section 430 shall have the same meaning given such term by section 430.

§ 408. Individual retirement accounts.

(a) Individual retirement account—For purposes of this section, the term "individual retirement account" means a trust created or organized in the United States for the exclusive benefit of an individual or his beneficiaries, but only if the written governing instrument creating the trust meets the following requirements:

(1) Except in the case of a rollover contribution described in subsection (d)(3), in section 402(c), 403(a)(4), 403(b)(8), or 457(e)(16), no contribution will be accepted unless it is in cash, and contributions will not be accepted for the taxable year on behalf of any individual in excess of the amount in effect for such taxable year under section 219(b)(1)(A).

(2) The trustee is a bank (as defined in subsection (n)) or such other person who demonstrates to the satisfaction of the Secretary that the manner in which such other person will administer the trust will be consistent with the requirements of this section.

(3) No part of the trust funds will be invested in life insurance contracts.

(4) The interest of an individual in the balance of his account is nonforfeitable.

(5) The assets of the trust will not be commingled with other property except in a common trust fund or common investment fund.

(6) Under regulations prescribed by the Secretary, rules similar to the rules of section 401(a)(9) and the incidental death benefit requirements of section 401(a) shall apply to the distribution of the entire interest of an individual for whose benefit the trust is maintained.

(b) Individual retirement annuity—For purposes of this section, the term "individual retirement annuity" means an annuity contract, or an endowment contract (as determined under regulations prescribed by the Secretary), issued by an insurance company which meets the following requirements:

(1) The contract is not transferable by the owner.

(2) Under the contract—

(A) the premiums are not fixed,

(B) the annual premium on behalf of any individual will not exceed the dollar amount in effect under section 219(b)(1)(A), and

(C) any refund of premiums will be applied before the close of the calendar year following the year of the refund toward the payment of future premiums or the purchase of additional benefits.

(3) Under regulations prescribed by the Secretary, rules similar to the rules of section 401(a)(9) and the incidental death benefit requirements of section 401(a) shall apply to the distribution of the entire interest of the owner.

(4) The entire interest of the owner is nonforfeitable.

Such term does not include such an annuity contract for any taxable year of the owner in which it is disqualified on the application of subsection (e) or for any subsequent taxable year. For purposes of this subsection, no contract shall be treated as an endowment contract if it matures later than the taxable year in which the individual in whose name such contract is purchased attains age 70½; if it is not for the exclusive benefit of the individual in whose name it is purchased or his beneficiaries; or if the aggregate annual premiums under all such contracts purchased in the name of such individual for any taxable year exceed the dollar amount in effect under section 219(b)(1)(A).

(c) Accounts established by employers and certain associations of employees—A trust created or organized in the United States by an employer for the exclusive benefit of his employees or their beneficiaries, or by an association of employees (which may include employees within the meaning of section 401(c)(1)) for the exclusive benefit of its members or their beneficiaries, shall be treated as an individual retirement account (described in subsection (a)), but only if the written governing instrument creating the trust meets the following requirements:

(1) The trust satisfies the requirements of paragraphs (1) through (6) of subsection (a).

(2) There is a separate accounting for the interest of each employee or member (or spouse of an employee or member).

The assets of the trust may be held in a common fund for the account of all individuals who have an interest in the trust.

(d) Tax treatment of distributions—

(1) In general—Except as otherwise provided in this subsection, any amount paid or distributed out of an individual retirement plan shall be included in gross income by the payee or distributee, as the case may be, in the manner provided under section 72.

(2) Special rules for applying section 72—For purposes of applying section 72 to any amount described in paragraph (1)—

(A) all individual retirement plans shall be treated as 1 contract,

(B) all distributions during any taxable year shall be treated as 1 distribution, and

(C) the value of the contract, income on the contract, and investment in the contract shall be computed as of the close of the calendar year in which the taxable year begins.

For purposes of subparagraph (C), the value of the contract shall be increased by the amount of any distributions during the calendar year.

(3) Rollover contribution—An amount is described in this paragraph as a rollover contribution if it meets the requirements of subparagraphs (A) and (B).

(A) In general—Paragraph (1) does not apply to any amount paid or distributed out of an individual retirement account or individual retirement annuity to the individual for whose benefit the account or annuity is maintained if—

(i) the entire amount received (including money and any other property) is paid into an individual retirement account or individual retirement annuity (other than an endowment contract) for the benefit of such individual not later than the 60th day after the day on which he receives the payment or distribution; or

(ii) the entire amount received (including money and any other property) is paid into an eligible retirement plan for the benefit of such individual not later than the 60th day after the date on which the payment or distribution is received, except that the maximum amount which may be paid into such plan may not exceed the portion of the amount received which is includible in gross income (determined without regard to this paragraph).

For purposes of clause (ii), the term "eligible retirement plan" means an eligible retirement plan described in clause (iii), (iv), (v), or (vi) of section 402(c)(8)(B).

(B) Limitation—This paragraph does not apply to any amount described in subparagraph (A)(i) received by an individual from an individual retirement account or individual retirement annuity if at any time during the 1-year period ending on the day of such receipt such individual received any other amount described in that subparagraph from an individual retirement account or an individual retirement annuity which was not includible in his gross income because of the application of this paragraph.

(C) Denial of rollover treatment for inherited accounts, etc—

(i) In general—In the case of an inherited individual retirement account or individual retirement annuity—

(I) this paragraph shall not apply to any amount received by an individual from such an account or annuity (and no amount transferred from such account or annuity to another individual retirement account or annuity shall be excluded from gross income by reason of such transfer), and

(II) such inherited account or annuity shall not be treated as an individual retirement account or annuity for purposes of determining whether any other amount is a rollover contribution.

(ii) Inherited individual retirement account or annuity—An individual retirement account or individual retirement annuity shall be treated as inherited if—

(I) the individual for whose benefit the account or annuity is maintained acquired such account by reason of the death of another individual, and

(II) such individual was not the surviving spouse of such other individual.

(D) Partial rollovers permitted—

(i) In general—If any amount paid or distributed out of an individual retirement account or individual retirement annuity would meet the requirements of subparagraph (A) but for the fact that the entire amount was not paid into an eligible plan as required by clause (i) or (ii) of subparagraph (A), such amount shall be treated as meeting the requirements of subparagraph (A) to the extent it is paid into an eligible plan referred to in such clause not later than the 60th day referred to in such clause.

(ii) Eligible plan—For purposes of clause (i), the term "eligible plan" means any account, annuity, contract, or plan referred to in subparagraph (A).

(E) Denial of rollover treatment for required distributions—This paragraph shall not apply to any amount to the extent such amount is required to be distributed under subsection (a)(6) or (b)(3).

(F) Frozen deposits—For purposes of this paragraph, rules similar to the rules of section 402(c)(7) (relating to frozen deposits) shall apply.

(G) Simple retirement accounts—In the case of any payment or distribution out of a simple retirement account (as defined in subsection (p)) to which section 72(t)(6) applies, this paragraph shall not apply unless such payment or distribution is paid into another simple retirement account.

(H) Application of section 72—

(i) In general—If—

(I) a distribution is made from an individual retirement plan, and

(II) a rollover contribution is made to an eligible retirement plan described in section 402(c)(8)(B)(iii), (iv), (v), or (vi) with respect to all or part of such distribution,

then, notwithstanding paragraph (2), the rules of clause (ii) shall apply for purposes of applying section 72.

(ii) Applicable rules—In the case of a distribution described in clause (i)—

(I) section 72 shall be applied separately to such distribution,

(II) notwithstanding the pro rata allocation of income on, and investment in, the contract to distributions under section 72, the portion of such distribution rolled over to an eligible retirement plan described in clause (i) shall be treated as from income on the contract (to the extent of the aggregate income on the contract from all individual retirement plans of the distributee), and

(III) appropriate adjustments shall be made in applying section 72 to other distributions in such taxable year and subsequent taxable years.

(I) Waiver of 60-day requirement—The Secretary may waive the 60-day requirement under subparagraphs (A) and (D) where the failure to waive such requirement would be against equity or good conscience, including casualty, disaster, or other events beyond the reasonable control of the individual subject to such requirement.

(4) Contributions returned before due date of return—Paragraph (1) does not apply to the distribution of any contribution paid during a taxable year to an individual retirement account or for an individual retirement annuity if—

(A) such distribution is received on or before the day prescribed by law (including extensions of time) for filing such individual's return for such taxable year,

(B) no deduction is allowed under section 219 with respect to such contribution, and

(C) such distribution is accompanied by the amount of net income attributable to such contribution.

In the case of such a distribution, for purposes of section 61, any net income described in subparagraph (C) shall be deemed to have been earned and receivable in the taxable year in which such contribution is made.

(5) Distributions of excess contributions after due date for taxable year and certain excess rollover contributions—

(A) In general—In the case of any individual, if the aggregate contributions (other than rollover contributions) paid for any taxable year to an individual retirement account or for an individual retirement annuity do not exceed the dollar amount in effect under section 219(b)(1)(A), paragraph (1) shall not apply to the distribution of any such contribution to the extent that such contribution exceeds the amount allowable as a deduction under section 219 for the taxable year for which the contribution was paid—

(i) if such distribution is received after the date described in paragraph (4),

(ii) but only to the extent that no deduction has been allowed under section 219 with respect to such excess contribution.

If employer contributions on behalf of the individual are paid for the taxable year to a simplified employee pension, the dollar limitation of the preceding sentence shall be increased by the lesser of the amount of such contributions or the dollar limitation in effect under section 415(c)(1)(A) for such taxable year.

(B) Excess rollover contributions attributable to erroneous information—If—

(i) the taxpayer reasonably relies on information supplied pursuant to subtitle F for determining the amount of a rollover contribution, but

(ii) the information was erroneous,

subparagraph (A) shall be applied by increasing the dollar limit set forth therein by that portion of the excess contribution which was attributable to such information.

For purposes of this paragraph, the amount allowable as a deduction under section 219 shall be computed without regard to section 219(g).

(6) Transfer of account incident to divorce—The transfer of an individual's interest in an individual retirement account or an individual retirement annuity to his spouse or former spouse under a divorce or separation instrument described in subparagraph (A) of section 71(b)(2) is not to be considered a taxable transfer made by such individual notwithstanding any other provision of this subtitle, and such interest at the time of the transfer is to be treated as an individual retirement account of such spouse, and not of such individual. Thereafter such account or annuity for purposes of this subtitle is to be treated as maintained for the benefit of such spouse.

(7) Special rules for simplified employee pensions or simple retirement accounts—

(A) Transfer or rollover of contributions prohibited until deferral test met—Notwithstanding any other provision of this subsection or section 72(t), paragraph (1) and section 72(t)(1) shall apply to the transfer or distribution from a simplified employee pension of any contribution under a salary reduction arrangement described in subsection (k)(6) (or any income allocable thereto) before a determination as to whether the requirements of subsection (k)(6)(A)(iii) are met with respect to such contribution.

(B) Certain exclusions treated as deductions—For purposes of paragraphs (4) and (5) and section 4973, any amount excludable or excluded from gross income under section 402(h) or 402(k) shall be treated as an amount allowable or allowed as a deduction under section 219.

(8) Distributions for charitable purposes—

(A) In general—So much of the aggregate amount of qualified charitable distributions with respect to a taxpayer made during any taxable year which does not exceed $100,000 shall not be includible in gross income of such taxpayer for such taxable year.

(B) Qualified charitable distribution—For purposes of this paragraph, the term 'qualified charitable distribution' means any distribution from an individual retirement plan (other than a plan described in subsection (k) or (p))—

(i) which is made directly by the trustee to an organization described in section 170(b)(1)(A) (other than any organization described in section 509(a)(3) or any fund or account described in section 4966(d)(2)), and

(ii) which is made on or after the date that the individual for whose benefit the plan is maintained has attained age 70 1/2.

A distribution shall be treated as a qualified charitable distribution only to the extent that the distribution would be includible in gross income without regard to subparagraph (A).

(C) Contributions must be otherwise deductible—For purposes of this paragraph, a distribution to an organization described in subparagraph (B)(i) shall be treated as a qualified charitable distribution only if a deduction for the entire distribution would be allowable under section 170 (determined without regard to subsection (b) thereof and this paragraph).

(D) Application of section 72—Notwithstanding section 72, in determining the extent to which a distribution is a qualified charitable distribution, the entire amount of the distribution shall be treated as includible in gross income without regard to subparagraph (A) to the extent that such amount does not exceed the aggregate amount which would have been so includible if all amounts in all individual retirement plans of the individual were distributed during such taxable year and all such plans were treated as 1 contract for purposes of determining under section 72 the aggregate amount which would have been so includible. Proper adjustments shall be made in applying section 72 to other distributions in such taxable year and subsequent taxable years.

(E) Denial of deduction—Qualified charitable distributions which are not includible in gross income pursuant to subparagraph (A) shall not be taken into account in determining the deduction under section 170.

(F) Termination—This paragraph shall not apply to distributions made in taxable years beginning after December 31, 2011.

(9) Distribution for health savings account funding—

(A) In general—In the case of an individual who is an eligible individual (as defined in section 223(c)) and who elects the application of this paragraph for a taxable year, gross income of the individual for the taxable year does not include a qualified

HSA funding distribution to the extent such distribution is otherwise includible in gross income.

(B) Qualified HSA funding distribution—For purposes of this paragraph, the term "qualified HSA funding distribution" means a distribution from an individual retirement plan (other than a plan described in subsection (k) or (p)) of the employee to the extent that such distribution is contributed to the health savings account of the individual in a direct trustee-to-trustee transfer.

(C) Limitations—

(i) Maximum dollar limitation—The amount excluded from gross income by subparagraph (A) shall not exceed the excess of—

(I) the annual limitation under section 223(b) computed on the basis of the type of coverage under the high deductible health plan covering the individual at the time of the qualified HSA funding distribution, over

(II) in the case of a distribution described in clause (ii)(II), the amount of the earlier qualified HSA funding distribution.

(ii) One-time transfer—

(I) In general—Except as provided in subclause (II), an individual may make an election under subparagraph (A) only for one qualified HSA funding distribution during the lifetime of the individual. Such an election, once made, shall be irrevocable.

(II) Conversion from self-only to family coverage—If a qualified HSA funding distribution is made during a month in a taxable year during which an individual has self-only coverage under a high deductible health plan as of the first day of the month, the individual may elect to make an additional qualified HSA funding distribution during a subsequent month in such taxable year during which the individual has family coverage under a high deductible health plan as of the first day of the subsequent month.

(D) Failure to maintain high deductible health plan coverage—

(i) In general—If, at any time during the testing period, the individual is not an eligible individual, then the aggregate amount of all contributions to the health savings account of the individual made under subparagraph (A)—

(I) shall be includible in the gross income of the individual for the taxable year in which occurs the first month in the testing period for which such individual is not an eligible individual, and

(II) the tax imposed by this chapter for any taxable year on the individual shall be increased by 10 percent of the amount which is so includible.

(ii) Exception for disability or death—Subclauses (I) and (II) of clause (i) shall not apply if the individual ceased to be an eligible individual by reason of the death of the individual or the individual becoming disabled (within the meaning of section 72(m)(7)).

(iii) Testing period—The term "testing period" means the period beginning with the month in which the qualified HSA funding distribution is contributed to a health savings account and ending on the last day of the 12th month following such month.

(E) Application of section 72—Notwithstanding section 72, in determining the extent to which an amount is treated as otherwise includible in gross income for purposes of subparagraph (A), the aggregate amount distributed from an individual retirement plan shall be treated as includible in gross income to the extent that such amount does not exceed the aggregate amount which would have been so includible if all amounts from all individual retirement plans were distributed. Proper adjustments shall be made in applying section 72 to other distributions in such taxable year and subsequent taxable years.

(e) Tax treatment of accounts and annuities—

(1) Exemption from tax—Any individual retirement account is exempt from taxation under this subtitle unless such account has ceased to be an individual retirement account by reason of paragraph (2) or (3). Notwithstanding the preceding sentence, any such account is subject to the taxes imposed by section 511 (relating to imposition of tax on unrelated business income of charitable, etc. organizations).

(2) Loss of exemption of account where employee engages in prohibited transaction—

(A) In general—If, during any taxable year of the individual for whose benefit any individual retirement account is established, that individual or his beneficiary engages in any transaction prohibited by section 4975 with respect to such account, such account ceases to be an individual retirement account as of the first day of such taxable year. For purposes of this paragraph—

(i) the individual for whose benefit any account was established is treated as the creator of such account, and

(ii) the separate account for any individual within an individual retirement account maintained by an employer or association of employees is treated as a separate individual retirement account.

(B) Account treated as distributing all its assets—In any case in which any account ceases to be an individual retirement account by reason of subparagraph (A) as of the first day of any taxable year, paragraph (1) of subsection (d) applies as if there were a distribution on such first day in an amount equal to the fair market value (on such first day) of all assets in the account (on such first day).

(3) Effect of borrowing on annuity contract—If during any taxable year the owner of an individual retirement annuity borrows any money under or by use of such contract, the contract ceases to be an individual retirement annuity as of the first day of such taxable year. Such owner shall include in gross income for such year an amount equal to the fair market value of such contract as of such first day.

(4) Effect of pledging account as security—If, during any taxable year of the individual for whose benefit an individual retirement account is established, that individual uses the account or any portion thereof as security for a loan, the portion so used is treated as distributed to that individual.

(5) Purchase of endowment contract by individual retirement account—If the assets of an individual retirement account or any part of such assets are used to purchase an endowment contract for the benefit of the individual for whose benefit the account is established—

(A) to the extent that the amount of the assets involved in the purchase are not attributable to the purchase of life insurance, the purchase is treated as a rollover contribution described in subsection (d)(3), and

(B) to the extent that the amount of the assets involved in the purchase are attributable to the purchase of life, health, accident, or other insurance such amounts are treated as distributed to that individual (but the provisions of subsection (f) do not apply).

(6) Commingling individual retirement account amounts in certain common trust funds and common investment funds—Any common trust fund or common investment fund of individual retirement account assets which is exempt from taxation under this subtitle does not cease to be exempt on account of the participation or inclusion of assets of a trust exempt from taxation under section 501(a) which is described in section 401(a).

(f) [Repealed]

(g) Community property laws—This section shall be applied without regard to any community property laws.

(h) Custodial accounts—For purposes of this section, a custodial account shall be treated as a trust if the assets of such account are held by a bank (as defined in subsection (n)) or another person who demonstrates, to the satisfaction of the Secretary, that the manner in which he will administer the account will be consistent with the requirements of this section, and if the custodial account would, except for the fact that it is not a trust, constitute an individual retirement account described in subsection (a). For purposes of this title, in the case of a custodial account treated as a trust by reason of the preceding sentence, the custodian of such account shall be treated as the trustee thereof.

(i) Reports—The trustee of an individual retirement account and the issuer of an endowment contract described in subsection (b) or an individual retirement annuity shall make such reports regarding such account, contract, or annuity to the Secretary and to the individuals for whom the account, contract, or annuity is, or is to be, maintained with respect to contributions (and the years to which they relate), distributions aggregating $10 or more in any calendar year, and such other matters as the Secretary may require. The reports required by this subsection—

(1) shall be filed at such time and in such manner as the Secretary prescribes, and

(2) shall be furnished to individuals—

(A) not later than January 31 of the calendar year following the calendar year to which such reports relate, and

(B) in such manner as the Secretary prescribes.

In the case of a simple retirement account under subsection (p), only one report under this subsection shall be required to be submitted each calendar year to the Secretary (at the time provided under paragraph (2)) but, in addition to the report under this subsection, there shall be furnished, within 31 days after each calendar year, to the individual on whose behalf the account is maintained a statement with respect to the account balance as of the close of, and the account activity during, such calendar year.

(j) Increase in maximum limitations for simplified employee pensions—In the case of any simplified employee pension, subsections (a)(1) and (b)(2) of this section shall be applied by increasing the amounts contained therein by the amount of the limitation in effect under section 415(c)(1)(A).

(k) Simplified employee pension defined—

(1) In general—For purposes of this title, the term "simplified employee pension" means an individual retirement account or individual retirement annuity—

(A) with respect to which the requirements of paragraphs (2), (3), (4), and (5) of this subsection are met, and

(B) if such account or annuity is part of a top-heavy plan (as defined in section 416), with respect to which the requirements of section 416(c)(2) are met.

(2) Participation requirements—This paragraph is satisfied with respect to a simplified employee pension for a year only if for such year the employer contributes to the simplified employee pension of each employee who

(A) has attained age 21,

(B) has performed service for the employer during at least 3 of the immediately preceding 5 years, and

(C) received at least $450 in compensation (within the meaning of section 414(q)(4)) from the employer for the year.

For purposes of this paragraph, there shall be excluded from consideration employees described in subparagraph (A) or (C) of section 410(b)(3). For purposes of any arrangement described in subsection (k)(6), any employee who is eligible to have employer contributions made on the employee's behalf under such arrangement shall be treated as if such a contribution was made.

(3) Contributions may not discriminate in favor of the highly compensated, etc—

(A) In general—The requirements of this paragraph are met with respect to a simplified employee pension for a year if for such year the contributions made by the employer to simplified employee pensions for his employees do not discriminate in favor of any highly compensated employee (within the meaning of section 414(q)).

(B) Special rules—For purposes of subparagraph (A), there shall be excluded from consideration employees described in subparagraph (A) or (C) of section 410(b)(3).

(C) Contributions must bear uniform relationship to total compensation—For purposes of subparagraph (A), and except as provided in subparagraph (D), employer contributions, to simplified employee pensions (other than contributions under an arrangement described in paragraph (6)) shall be considered discriminatory unless contributions thereto bear a uniform relationship to the compensation (not in excess of the first $200,000) of each employee maintaining a simplified employee pension.

(D) Permitted disparity—For purposes of subparagraph (C), the rules of section 401(l)(2) shall apply to contributions to simplified employee pensions (other than contributions under an arrangement described in paragraph (6)).

(4) Withdrawals must be permitted—A simplified employee pension meets the requirements of this paragraph only if—

(A) employer contributions thereto are not conditioned on the retention in such pension of any portion of the amount contributed, and

(B) there is no prohibition imposed by the employer on withdrawals from the simplified employee pension.

(5) Contributions must be made under written allocation formula—The requirements of this paragraph are met with respect to a simplified employee pension only if employer contributions to such pension are determined under a definite written allocation formula which specifies—

(A) the requirements which an employee must satisfy to share in an allocation, and

(B) the manner in which the amount allocated is computed.

(6) Employee may elect salary reduction arrangement—

(A) Arrangements which qualify—

(i) In general—A simplified employee pension shall not fail to meet the requirements of this subsection for a year merely because, under the terms of the pension, an employee may elect to have the employer make payments—

(I) as elective employer contributions to the simplified employee pension on behalf of the employee, or

(II) to the employee directly in cash.

(ii) 50 percent of eligible employees must elect—Clause (i) shall not apply to a simplified employee pension unless an election described in clause (i)(I) is made or is in effect with respect to not less than 50 percent of the employees of the employer eligible to participate.

(iii) Requirements relating to deferral percentage—Clause (i) shall not apply to a simplified employee pension for any year unless the deferral percentage for such year of each highly compensated employee eligible to participate is not more than the product of—

(I) the average of the deferral percentages for such year of all employees (other than highly compensated employees) eligible to participate, multiplied by

(II) 1.25.

(iv) Limitations on elective deferrals—Clause (i) shall not apply to a simplified employee pension unless the requirements of section 401(a)(30) are met.

(B) Exception where more than 25 employees—This paragraph shall not apply with respect to any year in the case of a simplified employee pension maintained by an employer with more than 25 employees who were eligible to participate (or would have been required to be eligible to participate if a pension was maintained) at any time during the preceding year.

(C) Distributions of excess contributions—

(i) In general—Rules similar to the rules of section 401(k)(8) shall apply to any excess contribution under this paragraph. Any excess contribution under a simplified employee pension shall be treated as an excess contribution for purposes of section 4979.

(ii) Excess contribution—For purposes of clause (i), the term "excess contributions" means, with respect to a highly compensated employee, the excess of elective employer contributions under this paragraph over the maximum amount of such contributions allowable under subparagraph (A)(iii).

(D) Deferral percentage—For purposes of this paragraph, the deferral percentage for an employee for a year shall be the ratio of—

(i) the amount of elective employer contributions actually paid over to the simplified employee pension on behalf of the employee for the year, to

(ii) the employee's compensation (not in excess of the first $200,000) for the year.

(E) Exception for state and local and tax-exempt pensions—This paragraph shall not apply to a simplified employee pension maintained by—

(i) a State or local government or political subdivision thereof, or any agency or instrumentality thereof, or

(ii) an organization exempt from tax under this title.

(F) Exception where pension does not meet requirements necessary to insure distribution of excess contributions—This paragraph shall not apply with respect to any year for which the simplified employee pension does not meet such requirements as the Secretary may prescribe as are necessary to insure that excess contributions are distributed in accordance with subparagraph (C), including—

(i) reporting requirements, and

(ii) requirements which, notwithstanding paragraph (4), provide that contributions (and any income allocable thereto) may not be withdrawn from a simplified employee pension until a determination has been made that the requirements of subparagraph (A)(iii) have been met with respect to such contributions.

(G) Highly compensated employee—For purposes of this paragraph, the term "highly compensated employee" has the meaning given such term by section 414(q).

(H) Termination—This paragraph shall not apply to years beginning after December 31, 1996. The preceding sentence shall not apply to a simplified employee pension of an employer if the terms of simplified employee pensions of such employer, as in effect on December 31, 1996, provide that an employee may make the election described in subparagraph (A).

(7) Definitions—For purposes of this subsection and subsection (l)—

(A) Employee, employer, or owner-employee—The terms "employee", "employer", and "owner-employee" shall have the respective meanings given such terms by section 401(c).

(B) Compensation—Except as provided in paragraph (2)(C), the term "compensation" has the meaning given such term by section 414(s).

(C) Year—The term "year" means—

(i) the calendar year, or

(ii) if the employer elects, subject to such terms and conditions as the Secretary may prescribe, to maintain the simplified employee pension on the basis of the employer's taxable year.

(8) Cost-of-living adjustment—The Secretary shall adjust the $450 amount in paragraph (2)(C) at the same time and in the same manner as under section 415(d) and shall adjust the $200,000 amount in paragraphs (3)(C) and (6)(D)(ii) at the same time, and by the same amount, as any adjustment under section 401(a)(17)(B) ; except that any increase in the $450 amount which is not a multiple of $50 shall be rounded to the next lowest multiple of $50.

(9) Cross reference—For excise tax on certain excess contributions, see section 4979.

(l) Simplified employer reports—

(1) In general—An employer who makes a contribution on behalf of an employee to a simplified employee pension shall provide such simplified reports with respect to such contributions as the Secretary may require by regulations. The reports required by this subsection shall be filed at such time and in such manner, and information with respect to such contributions shall be furnished to the employee at such time and in such manner, as may be required by regulations.

(2) Simple retirement accounts—

(A) No employer reports—Except as provided in this paragraph, no report shall be required under this section by an employer maintaining a qualified salary reduction arrangement under subsection (p).

(B) Summary description—The trustee of any simple retirement account established pursuant to a qualified salary reduction arrangement under subsection (p) and the issuer of an annuity established under such an arrangement shall provide to the employer maintaining the arrangement, each year a description containing the following information:

(i) The name and address of the employer and the trustee or issuer.

(ii) The requirements for eligibility for participation.

(iii) The benefits provided with respect to the arrangement.

(iv) The time and method of making elections with respect to the arrangement.

(v) The procedures for, and effects of, withdrawals (including rollovers) from the arrangement.

(C) Employee notification—The employer shall notify each employee immediately before the period for which an election described in subsection (p)(5)(C) may be made of the employee's opportunity to make such election. Such notice shall include a copy of the description described in subparagraph (B).

(m) Investment in collectibles treated as distributions—

(1) In general—The acquisition by an individual retirement account or by an individually-directed account under a plan described in section 401(a) of any collectible shall be treated (for purposes of this section and section 402) as a distribution from such account in an amount equal to the cost to such account of such collectible.

(2) Collectible defined—For purposes of this subsection, the term "collectible" means—

(A) any work of art,

(B) any rug or antique,

(C) any metal or gem,

(D) any stamp or coin,

(E) any alcoholic beverage, or

(F) any other tangible personal property specified by the Secretary for purposes of this subsection.

(3) Exception for certain coins and bullion—For purposes of this subsection, the term "collectible" shall not include—

(A) any coin which is—

(i) a gold coin described in paragraph (7), (8), (9), or (10) of section 5112(a) of title 31, United States Code,

(ii) a silver coin described in section 5112(e) of title 31, United States Code,

(iii) a platinum coin described in section 5112(k) of title 31, United States Code, or

(iv) a coin issued under the laws of any State, or

(B) any gold, silver, platinum, or palladium bullion of a fineness equal to or exceeding the minimum fineness that a contract market (as described in section 7 of the Commodity Exchange Act, 7 U.S.C. 7) requires for metals which may be delivered in satisfaction of a regulated futures contract, if such bullion is in the physical possession of a trustee described under subsection (a) of this section.

(n) Bank—For purposes of subsection (a)(2), the term "bank" means—

(1) any bank (as defined in section 581),

(2) an insured credit union (within the meaning of paragraph (6) or (7) of section 101 of the Federal Credit Union Act), and

(3) a corporation which, under the laws of the State of its incorporation, is subject to supervision and examination by the Commissioner of Banking or other officer of such State in charge of the administration of the banking laws of such State.

(o) Definitions and rules relating to nondeductible contributions to individual retirement plans—

(1) In general—Subject to the provisions of this subsection, designated nondeductible contributions may be made on behalf of an individual to an individual retirement plan.

(2) Limits on amounts which may be contributed—

(A) In general—The amount of the designated nondeductible contributions made on behalf of any individual for any taxable year shall not exceed the nondeductible limit for such taxable year.

(B) Nondeductible limit—For purposes of this paragraph—

(i) In general—The term "nondeductible limit" means the excess of—

(I) the amount allowable as a deduction under section 219 (determined without regard to section 219(g)), over

(II) the amount allowable as a deduction under section 219 (determined with regard to section 219(g)).

(ii) Taxpayer may elect to treat deductible contributions as nondeductible—If a taxpayer elects not to deduct an amount which (without regard to this clause) is allowable as a deduction under section 219 for any taxable year, the nondeductible limit for such taxable year shall be increased by such amount.

(C) Designated nondeductible contributions—

(i) In general—For purposes of this paragraph, the term "designated nondeductible contribution" means any contribution to an individual retirement plan for the taxable year which is designated (in such manner as the Secretary may prescribe) as a contribution for which a deduction is not allowable under section 219.

(ii) Designation—Any designation under clause (i) shall be made on the return of tax imposed by chapter 1 for the taxable year.

(3) Time when contributions made—In determining for which taxable year a designated nondeductible contribution is made, the rule of section 219(f)(3) shall apply.

(4) Individual required to report amount of designated nondeductible contributions—

(A) In general—Any individual who—

(i) makes a designated nondeductible contribution to any individual retirement plan for any taxable year, or

(ii) receives any amount from any individual retirement plan for any taxable year,

shall include on his return of the tax imposed by chapter 1 for such taxable year and any succeeding taxable year (or on such other form as the Secretary may prescribe for any such taxable year) information described in subparagraph (B).

(B) Information required to be supplied—The following information is described in this subparagraph:

(i) The amount of designated nondeductible contributions for the taxable year.

(ii) The amount of distributions from individual retirement plans for the taxable year.

(iii) The excess (if any) of—

(I) the aggregate amount of designated nondeductible contributions for all preceding taxable years, over

(II) the aggregate amount of distributions from individual retirement plans which was excludable from gross income for such taxable years.

(iv) The aggregate balance of all individual retirement plans of the individual as of the close of the calendar year in which the taxable year begins.

(v) Such other information as the Secretary may prescribe.

(C) Penalty for reporting contributions not made—For penalty where individual reports designated nondeductible contributions not made, see section 6693(b).

(p) Simple retirement accounts—

(1) In general—For purposes of this title, the term "simple retirement account" means an individual retirement plan (as defined in section 7701(a)(37))—

(A) with respect to which the requirements of paragraphs (3), (4), and (5) are met; and

(B) with respect to which the only contributions allowed are contributions under a qualified salary reduction arrangement.

(2) Qualified salary reduction arrangement—

(A) In general—For purposes of this subsection, the term "qualified salary reduction arrangement" means a written arrangement of an eligible employer under which—

(i) an employee eligible to participate in the arrangement may elect to have the employer make payments—

(I) as elective employer contributions to a simple retirement account on behalf of the employee, or

(II) to the employee directly in cash,

(ii) the amount which an employee may elect under clause (i) for any year is required to be expressed as a percentage of compensation and may not exceed a total of the applicable dollar amount for any year,

(iii) the employer is required to make a matching contribution to the simple retirement account for any year in an amount equal to so much of the amount the employee elects under clause (i)(I) as does not exceed the applicable percentage of compensation for the year, and

(iv) no contributions may be made other than contributions described in clause (i) or (iii).

(B) Employer may elect 2-percent nonelective contribution—

(i) In general—An employer shall be treated as meeting the requirements of subparagraph (A)(iii) for any year if, in lieu of the contributions described in such clause, the employer elects to make nonelective contributions of 2 percent of compensation for each employee who is eligible to participate in the arrangement and who has at least $5,000 of compensation from the employer for the year. If an employer makes an election under this subparagraph for any year, the employer shall notify employees of such election within a reasonable period of time before the 60-day period for such year under paragraph (5)(C).

(ii) Compensation limitation—The compensation taken into account under clause (i) for any year shall not exceed the limitation in effect for such year under section 401(a)(17).

(C) Definitions—For purposes of this subsection—

(i) Eligible employer—

(I) In general—The term "eligible employer" means, with respect to any year, an employer which had no more than 100 employees who received at least $5,000 of compensation from the employer for the preceding year.

(II) 2-year grace period—An eligible employer who establishes and maintains a plan under this subsection for 1 or more years and who fails to be an eligible employer for any subsequent year shall be treated as an eligible employer for the 2 years following the last year the employer was an eligible employer. If such failure is due to any acquisition, disposition, or similar transaction involving an eligible employer, the preceding sentence shall not apply.

(ii) Applicable percentage—

(I) In general—The term "applicable percentage" means 3 percent.

(II) Election of lower percentage—An employer may elect to apply a lower percentage (not less than 1 percent) for any year for all employees eligible to participate in the plan for such year if the employer notifies the employees of such lower percentage within a reasonable period of time before the 60-day election period for such year under paragraph (5)(C). An employer may not elect a lower percentage under this subclause for any year if that election would result in the applicable percentage being lower than 3 percent in more than 2 of the years in the 5-year period ending with such year.

(III) Special rule for years arrangement not in effect—If any year in the 5-year period described in subclause (II) is a year prior to the first year for which any qualified salary reduction arrangement is in effect with respect to the employer (or any predecessor), the employer shall be treated as if the level of the employer matching contribution was at 3 percent of compensation for such prior year.

(D) Arrangement may be only plan of employer—

(i) In general—An arrangement shall not be treated as a qualified salary reduction arrangement for any year if the employer (or any predecessor employer) maintained a qualified plan with respect to which contributions were made, or benefits were accrued, for service in any year in the period beginning with the year such arrangement became effective and ending with the year for which the determination is being made. If only individuals other than employees described in subparagraph (A) of section 410(b)(3) are eligible to participate in such arrangement, then the preceding sentence shall be applied without regard to any qualified plan in which only employees so described are eligible to participate.

(ii) Qualified plan—For purposes of this subparagraph, the term "qualified plan" means a plan, contract, pension, or trust described in subparagraph (A) or (B) of section 219(g)(5).

(E) Applicable dollar amount; cost-of-living adjustment—

(i) In general—For purposes of subparagraph (A)(ii), the applicable dollar amount shall be the amount determined in accordance with the following table:

For years beginning in calendar year:	*The applicable dollar amount:*
* * *	
2005 or thereafter	$10,000

(ii) Cost-of-living adjustment—In the case of a year beginning after December 31, 2005, the Secretary shall adjust the $10,000 amount under clause (i) at the same time and in the same manner as under section 415(d), except that the base period taken into account shall be the calendar quarter beginning July 1, 2004, and any increase under this subparagraph which is not a multiple of $500 shall be rounded to the next lower multiple of $500.

(3) Vesting requirements—The requirements of this paragraph are met with respect to a simple retirement account if the employee's rights to any contribution to the simple retirement account are nonforfeitable. For purposes of this paragraph, rules similar to the rules of subsection (k)(4) shall apply.

(4) Participation requirements—

(A) In general—The requirements of this paragraph are met with respect to any simple retirement account for a year only if, under the qualified salary reduction arrangement, all employees of the employer who—

(i) received at least $5,000 in compensation from the employer during any 2 preceding years, and

(ii) are reasonably expected to receive at least $5,000 in compensation during the year,

are eligible to make the election under paragraph (2)(A)(i) or receive the nonelective contribution described in paragraph (2)(B).

(B) Excludable employees—An employer may elect to exclude from the requirement under subparagraph (A) employees described in section 410(b)(3).

(5) Administrative requirements—The requirements of this paragraph are met with respect to any simple retirement account if, under the qualified salary reduction arrangement—

(A) an employer must—

(i) make the elective employer contributions under paragraph (2)(A)(i) not later than the close of the 30-day period following the last day of the month with respect to which the contributions are to be made, and

(ii) make the matching contributions under paragraph (2)(A)(iii) or the nonelective contributions under paragraph (2)(B) not later than the date described in section 404(m)(2)(B),

(B) an employee may elect to terminate participation in such arrangement at any time during the year, except that if an employee so terminates, the arrangement may provide that the employee may not elect to resume participation until the beginning of the next year, and

(C) each employee eligible to participate may elect, during the 60-day period before the beginning of any year (and the 60-day period before the first day such employee is eligible to participate), to participate in the arrangement, or to modify the amounts subject to such arrangement, for such year.

(6) Definitions—For purposes of this subsection—

(A) Compensation—

(i) In general—The term "compensation" means amounts described in paragraphs (3) and (8) of section 6051(a). For purposes of the preceding sentence, amounts described in section 6051(a)(3) shall be determined without regard to section 3401(a)(3).

(ii) Self-employed—In the case of an employee described in subparagraph (B), the term "compensation" means net earnings from self-employment determined under section 1402(a) without regard to any contribution under this subsection. The preceding sentence shall be applied as if the term "trade or business" for purposes of section 1402 included service described in section 1402(c)(6).

(B) Employee—The term "employee" includes an employee as defined in section 401(c)(1).

(C) Year—The term "year" means the calendar year.

(7) Use of designated financial institution—A plan shall not be treated as failing to satisfy the requirements of this subsection or any other provision of this title merely because the employer makes all contributions to the individual retirement accounts or annuities of a designated trustee or issuer. The preceding sentence shall not apply unless each plan participant is notified in writing (either separately or as part of the notice under subsection (l)(2)(C)) that the participant's balance may be transferred without cost or penalty to another individual account or annuity in accordance with subsection (d)(3)(G).

(8) Coordination with maximum limitation under subsection (a)—In the case of any simple retirement account, subsections (a)(1) and (b)(2) shall be applied by substituting "the sum of the dollar amount in effect under paragraph (2)(A)(ii) of this subsection and the employer contribution required under subparagraph (A)(iii) or (B)(i) of paragraph (2) of this subsection, whichever is applicable" for "the dollar amount in effect under section 219(b)(1)(A) ".

(9) Matching contributions on behalf of self-employed individuals not treated as elective employer contributions—Any matching contribution described in paragraph (2)(A)(iii) which is made on behalf of a self-employed individual (as defined in section 401(c)) shall not be treated as an elective employer contribution to a simple retirement account for purposes of this title.

(10) Special rules for acquisitions, dispositions, and similar transactions—

(A) In general—An employer which fails to meet any applicable requirement by reason of an acquisition, disposition, or similar transaction shall not be treated as failing to meet such requirement during the transition period if—

(i) the employer satisfies requirements similar to the requirements of section 410(b)(6)(C)(i)(II) ; and

(ii) the qualified salary reduction arrangement maintained by the employer would satisfy the requirements of this subsection after the transaction if the employer which maintained the arrangement before the transaction had remained a separate employer.

(B) Applicable requirement—For purposes of this paragraph, the term "applicable requirement" means—

(i) the requirement under paragraph (2)(A)(i) that an employer be an eligible employer;

(ii) the requirement under paragraph (2)(D) that an arrangement be the only plan of an employer; and

(iii) the participation requirements under paragraph (4).

(C) Transition period—For purposes of this paragraph, the term "transition period" means the period beginning on the date of any transaction described in subparagraph (A) and ending on the last day of the second calendar year following the calendar year in which such transaction occurs.

(q) Deemed IRAs under qualified employer plans—

(1) General rule—If—

(A) a qualified employer plan elects to allow employees to make voluntary employee contributions to a separate account or annuity established under the plan, and

(B) under the terms of the qualified employer plan, such account or annuity meets the applicable requirements of this section or section 408A for an individual retirement account or annuity,

then such account or annuity shall be treated for purposes of this title in the same manner as an individual retirement plan and not as a qualified employer plan (and contributions to such account or annuity as contributions to an individual retirement plan and not to the qualified employer plan). For purposes of subparagraph (B), the requirements of subsection (a)(5) shall not apply.

(2) Special rules for qualified employer plans—For purposes of this title, a qualified employer plan shall not fail to meet any requirement of this title solely by reason of establishing and maintaining a program described in paragraph (1).

(3) Definitions—For purposes of this subsection—

(A) Qualified employer plan—The term "qualified employer plan" has the meaning given such term by section 72(p)(4)(A)(i); except that such term shall also include an eligible deferred compensation plan (as defined in section 457(b)) of an eligible employer described in section 457(e)(1)(A).

(B) Voluntary employee contribution—The term "voluntary employee contribution" means any contribution (other than a mandatory contribution within the meaning of section 411(c)(2)(C))—

(i) which is made by an individual as an employee under a qualified employer plan which allows employees to elect to make contributions described in paragraph (1), and

(ii) with respect to which the individual has designated the contribution as a contribution to which this subsection applies.

* * *

§ 408A. Roth IRAs.

(a) General rule—Except as provided in this section, a Roth IRA shall be treated for purposes of this title in the same manner as an individual retirement plan.

(b) Roth IRA—For purposes of this title, the term "Roth IRA" means an individual retirement plan (as defined in section 7701(a)(37)) which is designated (in such manner as the Secretary may prescribe) at the time of establishment of the plan as a Roth IRA. Such designation shall be made in such manner as the Secretary may prescribe.

(c) Treatment of contributions—

(1) No deduction allowed—No deduction shall be allowed under section 219 for a contribution to a Roth IRA.

(2) Contribution limit—The aggregate amount of contributions for any taxable year to all Roth IRAs maintained for the benefit of an individual shall not exceed the excess (if any) of—

(A) the maximum amount allowable as a deduction under section 219 with respect to such individual for such taxable year (computed without regard to subsection (d)(1) or (g) of such section), over

(B) the aggregate amount of contributions for such taxable year to all other individual retirement plans (other than Roth IRAs) maintained for the benefit of the individual.

(3) Limits based on modified adjusted gross income—

(A) Dollar limit—The amount determined under paragraph (2) for any taxable year shall not exceed an amount equal to the amount determined under paragraph (2)(A) for such taxable year, reduced (but not below zero) by the amount which bears the same ratio to such amount as—

(i) the excess of—

(I) the taxpayer's adjusted gross income for such taxable year, over

(II) the applicable dollar amount, bears to

(ii) $15,000 ($10,000 in the case of a joint return or a married individual filing a separate return).

The rules of subparagraphs (B) and (C) of section 219(g)(2) shall apply to any reduction under this subparagraph.

(B) Definitions—For purposes of this paragraph—

(i) adjusted gross income shall be determined in the same manner as under section 219(g)(3), except that any amount included in gross income under subsection (d)(3) shall not be taken into account, and

(ii) the applicable dollar amount is—

(I) in the case of a taxpayer filing a joint return, $150,000,

(II) in the case of any other taxpayer (other than a married individual filing a separate return), $95,000, and

(III) in the case of a married individual filing a separate return, zero.

(C) Marital status—Section 219(g)(4) shall apply for purposes of this paragraph.

(D) Inflation adjustment—In the case of any taxable year beginning in a calendar year after 2006, the dollar amounts in subclauses (I) and (II) of subparagraph (D)(ii) shall each be increased by an amount equal to—

(i) such dollar amount, multiplied by

(ii) the cost-of-living adjustment determined under section 1(f)(3) for the calendar year in which the taxable year begins, determined by substituting "calendar year 2005" for "calendar year 1992" in subparagraph (B) thereof.

Any increase determined under the preceding sentence shall be rounded to the nearest multiple of $1,000.

(4) Contributions permitted after age 70½—Contributions to a Roth IRA may be made even after the individual for whom the account is maintained has attained age 70½.

(5) Mandatory distribution rules not to apply before death—Notwithstanding subsections (a)(6) and (b)(3) of section 408 (relating to required distributions), the following provisions shall not apply to any Roth IRA:

(A) Section 401(a)(9)(A).

(B) The incidental death benefit requirements of section 401(a).

(6) Rollover contributions—

(A) In general—No rollover contribution may be made to a Roth IRA unless it is a qualified rollover contribution.

(B) Coordination with limit—A qualified rollover contribution shall not be taken into account for purposes of paragraph (2).

(7) Time when contributions made—For purposes of this section, the rule of section 219(f)(3) shall apply.

(d) Distribution rules—For purposes of this title—

(1) Exclusion—Any qualified distribution from a Roth IRA shall not be includible in gross income.

(2) Qualified distribution—For purposes of this subsection—

(A) In general—The term "qualified distribution" means any payment or distribution—

(i) made on or after the date on which the individual attains age 59½,

(ii) made to a beneficiary (or to the estate of the individual) on or after the death of the individual,

(iii) attributable to the individual's being disabled (within the meaning of section 72(m)(7)), or

(iv) which is a qualified special purpose distribution.

(B) Distributions within nonexclusion period—A payment or distribution from a Roth IRA shall not be treated as a qualified distribution under subparagraph (A) if such payment or distribution is made within the 5-taxable year period beginning with the 1st taxable year for which the individual made a contribution to a Roth IRA (or such individual's spouse made a contribution to a Roth IRA) established for such individual.

(C) Distributions of excess contributions and earnings—The term "qualified distribution" shall not include any distribution of any contribution described in section 408(d)(4) and any net income allocable to the contribution.

(3) Rollovers from an eligible retirement plan other than a Roth IRA—

(A) In general—Notwithstanding sections 402(c), 403(b)(8), 408(d)(3), and 457(e)(16), in the case of any distribution to which this paragraph applies—

(i) there shall be included in gross income any amount which would be includible were it not part of a qualified rollover contribution,

(ii) section 72(t) shall not apply, and

(iii) unless the taxpayer elects not to have this clause apply, any amount required to be included in gross income for any taxable year beginning in 2010 by reason of this paragraph shall be so included ratably over the 2-taxable-year period beginning with the first taxable year beginning in 2011.

Any election under clause (iii) for any distributions during a taxable year may not be changed after the due date for such taxable year.

(B) Distributions to which paragraph applies—This paragraph shall apply to a distribution from an eligible retirement plan (as defined by section 402(c)(8)(B)) maintained for the benefit of an individual which is contributed to a Roth IRA maintained for the benefit of such individual in a qualified rollover contribution. This paragraph shall not apply to a distribution which is a qualified rollover contribution from a Roth IRA or a qualified rollover contribution from a designated Roth account which is a rollover contribution described in section 402A(c)(3)(A).

(C) Conversions—The conversion of an individual retirement plan (other than a Roth IRA) to a Roth IRA shall be treated for purposes of this paragraph as a distribution to which this paragraph applies.

(D) Additional reporting requirements—Trustees of Roth IRAs, trustees of individual retirement plans, persons subject to section 6047(d)(1), or all of the foregoing persons, whichever is appropriate, shall include such additional information in reports required under section 408(i) or 6047 as the Secretary may require to ensure that amounts required to be included in gross income under subparagraph (A) are so included.

(E) Special rules for contributions to which 2-year averaging applies—In the case of a qualified rollover contribution to a Roth IRA of a distribution to which subparagraph (A)(iii) applied, the following rules shall apply:

(i) Acceleration of inclusion—

(I) In general—The amount otherwise required to be included in gross income for any taxable year beginning in 2010 or the first taxable year in the 2-year period under subparagraph (A)(iii) shall be increased by the aggregate distributions from Roth IRAs for such taxable year which are allocable under paragraph (4) to the portion of such qualified rollover contribution required to be included in gross income under subparagraph (A)(i).

(II) Limitation on aggregate amount included—The amount required to be included in gross income for any taxable year under subparagraph (A)(iii) shall not exceed the aggregate amount required to be included in gross income under subparagraph (A)(iii) for all taxable years in the 2-year period (without regard to subclause (I)) reduced by amounts included for all preceding taxable years.

(ii) Death of distributee—

(I) In general—If the individual required to include amounts in gross income under such subparagraph dies before all of such amounts are included, all remaining amounts shall be included in gross income for the taxable year which includes the date of death.

(II) Special rule for surviving spouse—If the spouse of the individual described in subclause (I) acquires the individual's entire interest in any Roth IRA to which such qualified rollover contribution is properly allocable, the spouse may elect to treat the remaining amounts described in subclause (I) as includible in the spouse's gross income in the taxable years of the spouse ending with or within the taxable years of such individual in which such amounts would otherwise have been includible. Any such election may not be made or changed after the due date for the spouse's taxable year which includes the date of death.

(F) Special rule for applying section 72—

(i) In general—If—

(I) any portion of a distribution from a Roth IRA is properly allocable to a qualified rollover contribution described in this paragraph; and

(II) such distribution is made within the 5-taxable year period beginning with the taxable year in which such contribution was made,

then section 72(t) shall be applied as if such portion were includible in gross income.

(ii) Limitation—Clause (i) shall apply only to the extent of the amount of the qualified rollover contribution includible in gross income under subparagraph (A)(i).

(4) Aggregation and ordering rules—

(A) Aggregation rules—Section 408(d)(2) shall be applied separately with respect to Roth IRAs and other individual retirement plans.

(B) Ordering rules—For purposes of applying this section and section 72 to any distribution from a Roth IRA, such distribution shall be treated as made—

(i) from contributions to the extent that the amount of such distribution, when added to all previous distributions from the Roth IRA, does not exceed the aggregate contributions to the Roth IRA; and

(ii) from such contributions in the following order:

(I) Contributions other than qualified rollover contributions to which paragraph (3) applies.

(II) Qualified rollover contributions to which paragraph (3) applies on a first-in, first-out basis.

Any distribution allocated to a qualified rollover contribution under clause (ii)(II) shall be allocated first to the portion of such contribution required to be included in gross income.

(5) Qualified special purpose distribution—For purposes of this section, the term "qualified special purpose distribution" means any distribution to which subparagraph (F) of section 72(t)(2) applies.

(6) Taxpayer may make adjustments before due date—

(A) In general—Except as provided by the Secretary, if, on or before the due date for any taxable year, a taxpayer transfers in a trustee-to-trustee transfer any contribution to an individual retirement plan made during such taxable year from such plan to any other individual retirement plan, then, for purposes of this chapter, such contribution shall be treated as having been made to the transferee plan (and not the transferor plan).

(B) Special rules—

(i) Transfer of earnings—Subparagraph (A) shall not apply to the transfer of any contribution unless such transfer is accompanied by any net income allocable to such contribution.

(ii) No deduction—Subparagraph (A) shall apply to the transfer of any contribution only to the extent no deduction was allowed with respect to the contribution to the transferor plan.

(7) Due date—For purposes of this subsection, the due date for any taxable year is the date prescribed by law (including extensions of time) for filing the taxpayer's return for such taxable year.

(e) Qualified rollover contribution—For purposes of this section—

(1) In general—The term “qualified rollover contribution” means a rollover contribution—

(A) to a Roth IRA from another such account,

(B) from an eligible retirement plan, but only if—

(i) in the case of an individual retirement plan, such rollover contribution meets the requirements of section 408(d)(3), and

(ii) in the case of any eligible retirement plan (as defined in section 402(c)(8)(B) other than clauses (i) and (ii) thereof), such rollover contribution meets the requirements of section 402(c), 403(b)(8), or 457(e)(16), as applicable.

For purposes of section 408(d)(3)(B), there shall be disregarded any qualified rollover contribution from an individual retirement plan (other than a Roth IRA) to a Roth IRA.

(2) Military death gratuity—

(A) In general—The term ‘qualified rollover contribution’ includes a contribution to a Roth IRA maintained for the benefit of an individual made before the end of the 1-year period beginning on the date on which such individual receives an amount under section 1477 of title 10, United States Code, or section 1967 of title 38 of such Code, with respect to a person, to the extent that such contribution does not exceed—

(i) the sum of the amounts received during such period by such individual under such sections with respect to such person, reduced by

(ii) the amounts so received which were contributed to a Coverdell education savings account under section 530(d)(9).

(B) Annual limit on number of rollovers not to apply—Section 408(d)(3)(B) shall not apply with respect to amounts treated as a rollover by the subparagraph (A).

(C) Application of section 72—For purposes of applying section 72 in the case of a distribution which is not a qualified distribution, the amount treated as a rollover by reason of subparagraph (A) shall be treated as investment in the contract.

(f) Individual retirement plan—For purposes of this section—

(1) a simplified employee pension or a simple retirement account may not be designated as a Roth IRA; and

(2) contributions to any such pension or account shall not be taken into account for purposes of subsection (c)(2)(B).

§ 409. Qualifications for tax credit employee stock ownership plans.

* * *

(e) Voting rights—

(1) In general—A plan meets the requirements of this subsection if it meets the requirements of paragraph (2) or (3), whichever is applicable.

(2) Requirements where employer has a registration-type class of securities—If the employer has a registration-type class of securities, the plan meets the requirements of this paragraph only if each participant or beneficiary in the plan is entitled to direct the plan as to the manner in which securities of the employer which are entitled to vote and are allocated to the account of such participant or beneficiary are to be voted.

(3) Requirement for other employers—If the employer does not have a registration-type class of securities, the plan meets the requirements of this paragraph only if each participant or beneficiary in the plan is entitled to direct the plan as to the manner in which voting rights under securities of the employer which are allocated to the account of such participant or beneficiary are to be exercised with respect to any corporate matter which involves the voting of such shares with respect to the approval or disapproval of any corporate merger or consolidation, recapitalization, reclassification, liquidation, dissolution, sale of substantially all assets of a trade or business, or such similar transaction as the Secretary may prescribe in regulations.

(4) Registration-type class of securities defined—For purposes of this subsection, the term "registration-type class of securities" means—

(A) a class of securities required to be registered under section 12 of the Securities Exchange Act of 1934, and

(B) a class of securities which would be required to be so registered except for the exemption from registration provided in subsection (g)(2)(H) of such section 12.

(5) 1 vote per participant—A plan meets the requirements of paragraph (3) with respect to an issue if—

(A) the plan permits each participant 1 vote with respect to such issue, and

(B) the trustee votes the shares held by the plan in the proportion determined after application of subparagraph (A).

* * *

(h) Right to demand employer securities; put option—

(1) In general—A plan meets the requirements of this subsection if a participant who is entitled to a distribution from the plan—

(A) has a right to demand that his benefits be distributed in the form of employer securities, and

(B) if the employer securities are not readily tradable on an established market, has a right to require that the employer repurchase employer securities under a fair valuation formula.

(2) Plan may distribute cash in certain cases—

(A) In general—A plan which otherwise meets the requirements of this subsection or of section 4975(e)(7) shall not be considered to have failed to meet the requirements of section 401(a) merely because under the plan the benefits may be distributed in cash or in the form of employer securities.

(B) Exception for certain plans restricted from distributing securities—

(i) In general—A plan to which this subparagraph applies shall not be treated as failing to meet the requirements of this subsection or section 401(a) merely because it does not permit a participant to exercise the right described in paragraph (1)(A) if such plan provides that the participant entitled to a distribution has a right to receive the distribution in cash, except that such plan may distribute employer securities subject to a requirement that such securities may be resold to the employer under terms which meet the requirements of paragraph (1)(B).

(ii) Applicable plans—This subparagraph shall apply to a plan which otherwise meets the requirements of this subsection or section 4975(e)(7) and which is established and maintained by—

(I) an employer whose charter or bylaws restrict the ownership of substantially all outstanding employer securities to employees or to a trust described in section 401(a), or

(II) an S corporation.

(3) Special rule for banks—In the case of a plan established and maintained by a bank (as defined in section 581) which is prohibited by law from redeeming or purchasing its own securities, the requirements of paragraph (1)(B) shall not apply if the plan provides that participants entitled to a distribution from the plan shall have a right to receive a distribution in cash.

(4) Put option period—An employer shall be deemed to satisfy the requirements of paragraph (1)(B) if it provides a put option for a period of at least 60 days following the date of distribution of stock of the employer and, if the put option is not exercised within such 60-day period, for an additional period of at least 60 days in the following plan year (as provided in regulations promulgated by the Secretary).

(5) Payment requirement for total distribution—If an employer is required to repurchase employer securities which are distributed to the employee as part of a total distribution, the requirements of paragraph (1)(B) shall be treated as met if—

(A) the amount to be paid for the employer securities is paid in substantially equal periodic payments (not less frequently than annually) over a period beginning not later than 30 days after the exercise of the put option described in paragraph (4) and not exceeding 5 years, and

(B) there is adequate security provided and reasonable interest paid on the unpaid amounts referred to in subparagraph (A).

For purposes of this paragraph, the term "total distribution" means the distribution within 1 taxable year to the recipient of the balance to the credit of the recipient's account.

(6) Payment requirement for installment distributions—If an employer is required to repurchase employer securities as part of an installment distribution, the requirements of paragraph (1)(B) shall be treated as met if the amount to be paid for the employer securities is paid not later than 30 days after the exercise of the put option described in paragraph (4).

(7) Exception where employee elected diversification—Paragraph (1)(A) shall not apply with respect to the portion of the participant's account which the employee elected to have reinvested under section 401(a)(28)(B) or subparagraph (B) or (C) of section 401(a)(35).

* * *

(l) Employer securities defined—For purposes of this section—

(1) In general—The term "employer securities" means common stock issued by the employer (or by a corporation which is a member of the same controlled group) which is readily tradable on an established securities market.

(2) Special rule where there is no readily tradable common stock—If there is no common stock which meets the requirements of paragraph (1), the term "employer securities" means common stock issued by the employer (or by a corporation which is a member of the same controlled group) having a combination of voting power and dividend rights equal to or in excess of—

(A) that class of common stock of the employer (or of any other such corporation) having the greatest voting power, and

(B) that class of common stock of the employer (or of any other such corporation) having the greatest dividend rights.

(3) Preferred stock may be issued in certain cases—Noncallable preferred stock shall be treated as employer securities if such stock is convertible at any time into stock which meets the requirements of paragraph (1) or (2) (whichever is applicable) and if such conversion is at a conversion price which (as of the date of the acquisition by the tax credit employee stock ownership plan) is reasonable. For purposes of the preceding sentence, under regulations prescribed by the Secretary, preferred stock shall be treated as noncallable if after the call there will be a reasonable opportunity for a conversion which meets the requirements of the preceding sentence.

(4) Application to controlled group of corporations—

(A) In general—For purposes of this subsection, the term "controlled group of corporations" has the meaning given to such term by section 1563(a) (determined without regard to subsections (a)(4) and (e)(3)(C) of section 1563).

(B) Where common parent owns at least 50 percent of first tier subsidiary—For purposes of subparagraph (A), if the common parent owns directly stock possessing at least 50 percent of the voting power of all classes of stock and at least 50 percent of each class of nonvoting stock in a first tier subsidiary, such subsidiary (and all other corporations below it in the chain which would meet the 80 percent test of section 1563(a) if the first tier subsidiary were the common parent) shall be treated as includible corporations.

(C) Where common parent owns 100 percent of first tier subsidiary—For purposes of subparagraph (A), if the common parent owns directly stock possessing all of the voting power of all classes of stock and all of the nonvoting stock, in a first tier subsidiary, and if the first tier subsidiary owns directly stock possessing at least 50 percent of the voting power of all classes of stock, and at least 50 percent of each class of nonvoting stock, in a second tier subsidiary of the common parent, such second tier subsidiary (and all other corporations below it in the chain which would meet the 80 percent test of section 1563(a) if the second tier subsidiary were the common parent) shall be treated as includible corporations.

(5) Nonvoting common stock may be acquired in certain cases—Nonvoting common stock of an employer described in the second sentence of section 401(a)(22) shall be treated as employer securities if an employer has a class of nonvoting common stock outstanding and the specific shares that the plan acquires have been issued and outstanding for at least 24 months.

* * *

(o) Distribution and payment requirements—A plan meets the requirements of this subsection if—

(1) Distribution requirement—

(A) In general—The plan provides that, if the participant and, if applicable pursuant to section 401(a)(11) and 417, with the consent of the participant's spouse elects the distribution of the participant's account balance in the plan will commence not later than 1 year after the close of the plan year—

(i) in which the participant separates from service by reason of the attainment of normal retirement age under the plan, disability, or death, or

(ii) which is the 5th plan year following the plan year in which the participant otherwise separates from service, except that this clause shall not apply if the participant is reemployed by the employer before distribution is required to begin under this clause.

(B) Exception for certain financed securities—For purposes of this subsection, the account balance of a participant shall not include any employer securities acquired with the proceeds of the loan described in section 404(a)(9) until the close of the plan year in which such loan is repaid in full.

(C) Limited distribution period—The plan provides that, unless the participant elects otherwise, the distribution of the participant's account balance will be in substantially equal periodic payments (not less frequently than annually) over a period not longer than the greater of—

(i) 5 years, or

(ii) in the case of a participant with an account balance in excess of $800,000, 5 years plus 1 additional year (but not more than 5 additional years) for each $160,000 or fraction thereof by which such balance exceeds $800,000.

(2) Cost-of-living adjustment—The Secretary shall adjust the dollar amounts under paragraph (1)(C) at the same time and in the same manner as under section 415(d).

* * *

§ 409A. Inclusion in gross income of deferred compensation under nonqualified deferred compensation plans

(a) Rules relating to constructive receipt—

(1) Plan failures—

(A) Gross income inclusion—

(i) In general—If at any time during a taxable year a nonqualified deferred compensation plan—

(I) fails to meet the requirements of paragraphs (2), (3), and (4), or

(II) is not operated in accordance with such requirements,

all compensation deferred under the plan for the taxable year and all preceding taxable years shall be includible in gross income for the taxable year to the extent not subject to a substantial risk of forfeiture and not previously included in gross income.

(ii) Application only to affected participants—Clause (i) shall only apply with respect to all compensation deferred under the plan for participants with respect to whom the failure relates.

(B) Interest and additional tax payable with respect to previously deferred compensation—

(i) In general—If compensation is required to be included in gross income under subparagraph (A) for a taxable year, the tax imposed by this chapter for the taxable year shall be increased by the sum of—

(I) the amount of interest determined under clause (ii), and

(II) an amount equal to 20 percent of the compensation which is required to be included in gross income.

(ii) Interest—For purposes of clause (i), the interest determined under this clause for any taxable year is the amount of interest at the underpayment rate plus 1 percentage point on the underpayments that would have occurred had the deferred compensation been includible in gross income for the taxable year in which first deferred or, if later, the first taxable year in which such deferred compensation is not subject to a substantial risk of forfeiture.

(2) Distributions—

(A) In general—The requirements of this paragraph are met if the plan provides that compensation deferred under the plan may not be distributed earlier than—

(i) separation from service as determined by the Secretary (except as provided in subparagraph (B)(i)),

(ii) the date the participant becomes disabled (within the meaning of subparagraph (C)),

(iii) death,

(iv) a specified time (or pursuant to a fixed schedule) specified under the plan at the date of the deferral of such compensation,

(v) to the extent provided by the Secretary, a change in the ownership or effective control of the corporation, or in the ownership of a substantial portion of the assets of the corporation, or

(vi) the occurrence of an unforeseeable emergency.

(B) Special rules—

(i) Specified employees—In the case of any specified employee, the requirement of subparagraph (A)(i) is met only if distributions may not be made before the date which is 6 months after the date of separation from service (or, if earlier, the date of death of the employee). For purposes of the preceding sentence, a specified employee is a key employee (as defined in section 416(i) without regard to paragraph (5) thereof) of a corporation any stock in which is publicly traded on an established securities market or otherwise.

(ii) Unforeseeable emergency—For purposes of subparagraph (A)(vi)—

(I) In general—The term 'unforeseeable emergency' means a severe financial hardship to the participant resulting from an illness or accident of the participant, the participant's spouse, or a dependent (as defined in section 152(a)) of the participant, loss of the participant's property due to casualty, or other similar extraordinary and unforeseeable circumstances arising as a result of events beyond the control of the participant.

(II) Limitation on distributions—The requirement of subparagraph (A)(vi) is met only if, as determined under regulations of the Secretary, the amounts distributed with respect to an emergency do not exceed the amounts necessary to satisfy such emergency plus amounts necessary to pay taxes reasonably anticipated as a result of the distribution, after taking into account the extent to which such hardship is or may be relieved through reimbursement or compensation by insurance or otherwise or by liquidation of the participant's assets (to the extent the liquidation of such assets would not itself cause severe financial hardship).

(C) Disabled—For purposes of subparagraph (A)(ii), a participant shall be considered disabled if the participant—

(i) is unable to engage in any substantial gainful activity by reason of any medically determinable physical or mental impairment which can be expected to result in death or can be expected to last for a continuous period of not less than 12 months, or

(ii) is, by reason of any medically determinable physical or mental impairment which can be expected to result in death or can be expected to last for a continuous period of not less than 12 months, receiving income replacement benefits for a period of not less than 3 months under an accident and health plan covering employees of the participant's employer.

(3) Acceleration of benefits—The requirements of this paragraph are met if the plan does not permit the acceleration of the time or schedule of any payment under the plan, except as provided in regulations by the Secretary.

(4) Elections—

(A) In general—The requirements of this paragraph are met if the requirements of subparagraphs (B) and (C) are met.

(B) Initial deferral decision—

(i) In general—The requirements of this subparagraph are met if the plan provides that compensation for services performed during a taxable year may be deferred at the participant's election only if the election to defer such compensation is made not later than the close of the preceding taxable year or at such other time as provided in regulations.

(ii) First year of eligibility—In the case of the first year in which a participant becomes eligible to participate in the plan, such election may be made with respect to services to be performed subsequent to the election within 30 days after the date the participant becomes eligible to participate in such plan.

(iii) Performance-based compensation—In the case of any performance-based compensation based on services performed over a period of at least 12 months, such election may be made no later than 6 months before the end of the period.

(C) Changes in time and form of distribution—The requirements of this subparagraph are met if, in the case of a plan which permits under a subsequent election a delay in a payment or a change in the form of payment—

(i) the plan requires that such election may not take effect until at least 12 months after the date on which the election is made,

(ii) in the case of an election related to a payment not described in clause (ii), (iii), or (vi) of paragraph (2)(A), the plan requires that the payment with respect to which such election is made be deferred for a period of not less than 5 years from the date such payment would otherwise have been made, and

(iii) the plan requires that any election related to a payment described in paragraph (2)(A)(iv) may not be made less than 12 months prior to the date of the first scheduled payment under such paragraph.

(b) Rules relating to funding—

(1) Offshore property in a trust—In the case of assets set aside (directly or indirectly) in a trust (or other arrangement determined by the Secretary) for purposes of paying deferred compensation under a nonqualified deferred compensation plan, for purposes of section 83 such assets shall be treated as property transferred in connection with the performance of services whether or not such assets are available to satisfy claims of general creditors—

(A) at the time set aside if such assets (or such trust or other arrangement) are located outside of the United States, or

(B) at the time transferred if such assets (or such trust or other arrangement) are subsequently transferred outside of the United States.

This paragraph shall not apply to assets located in a foreign jurisdiction if substantially all of the services to which the nonqualified deferred compensation relates are performed in such jurisdiction.

(2) Employer's financial health—In the case of compensation deferred under a nonqualified deferred compensation plan, there is a transfer of property within the meaning of section 83 with respect to such compensation as of the earlier of—

(A) the date on which the plan first provides that assets will become restricted to the provision of benefits under the plan in connection with a change in the employer's financial health, or

(B) the date on which assets are so restricted,

whether or not such assets are available to satisfy claims of general creditors.

(3) Treatment of employer's defined benefit plan during restricted period—

(A) In general—If—

(i) during any restricted period with respect to a single-employer defined benefit plan, assets are set aside or reserved (directly or indirectly) in a trust (or other arrangement as determined by the Secretary) or transferred to such a trust or other arrangement for purposes of paying deferred compensation of an applicable covered employee under a nonqualified deferred compensation plan of the plan sponsor or member of a controlled group which includes the plan sponsor, or

(ii) a nonqualified deferred compensation plan of the plan sponsor or member of a controlled group which includes the plan sponsor provides that assets will become restricted to the provision of benefits under the plan to an applicable covered employee in connection with such restricted period (or other similar financial measure determined by the Secretary) with respect to the defined benefit plan, or assets are so restricted,

such assets shall, for purposes of section 83, be treated as property transferred in connection with the performance of services whether or not such assets are available to satisfy claims of general creditors. Clause (i) shall not apply with respect to any assets which are so set aside before the restricted period with respect to the defined benefit plan.

(B) Restricted period—For purposes of this section, the term "restricted period" means, with respect to any plan described in subparagraph (A)—

(i) any period during which the plan is in at-risk status (as defined in section 430(i));

(ii) any period the plan sponsor is a debtor in a case under title 11, United States Code, or similar Federal or State law, and

(iii) the 12-month period beginning on the date which is 6 months before the termination date of the plan if, as of the termination date, the plan is not sufficient for benefit liabilities (within the meaning of section 4041 of the Employee Retirement Income Security Act of 1974).

(C) Special rule for payment of taxes on deferred compensation included in income—If an employer provides directly or indirectly for the payment of any Federal,

State, or local income taxes with respect to any compensation required to be included in gross income by reason of this paragraph—

(i) interest shall be imposed under subsection (a)(1)(B)(i)(I) on the amount of such payment in the same manner as if such payment was part of the deferred compensation to which it relates,

(ii) such payment shall be taken into account in determining the amount of the additional tax under subsection (a)(1)(B)(i)(II) in the same manner as if such payment was part of the deferred compensation to which it relates, and

(iii) no deduction shall be allowed under this title with respect to such payment.

(D) Other definitions—For purposes of this section—

(i) Applicable covered employee—The term "applicable covered employee" means any—

(I) covered employee of a plan sponsor,

(II) covered employee of a member of a controlled group which includes the plan sponsor, and

(III) former employee who was a covered employee at the time of termination of employment with the plan sponsor or a member of a controlled group which includes the plan sponsor.

(ii) Covered employee—The term "covered employee" means an individual described in section 162(m)(3) or an individual subject to the requirements of section 16(a) of the Securities Exchange Act of 1934.

(4) Income inclusion for offshore trusts and employer's financial health—For each taxable year that assets treated as transferred under this subsection remain set aside in a trust or other arrangement subject to paragraph (1), (2), or (3), any increase in value in, or earnings with respect to, such assets shall be treated as an additional transfer of property under this subsection (to the extent not previously included in income).

(5) Interest on tax liability payable with respect to transferred property—

(A) In general—If amounts are required to be included in gross income by reason of paragraph (1), (2), or (3) for a taxable year, the tax imposed by this chapter for such taxable year shall be increased by the sum of—

(i) the amount of interest determined under subparagraph (B), and

(ii) an amount equal to 20 percent of the amounts required to be included in gross income.

(B) Interest—For purposes of subparagraph (A), the interest determined under this subparagraph for any taxable year is the amount of interest at the underpayment rate plus 1 percentage point on the underpayments that would have occurred had the amounts so required to be included in gross income by paragraph (1), (2), or (3) been includible in gross income for the taxable year in which first deferred or, if later, the first taxable year in which such amounts are not subject to a substantial risk of forfeiture.

(c) No inference on earlier income inclusion or requirement of later inclusion—Nothing in this section shall be construed to prevent the inclusion of amounts in gross income under any other provision of this chapter or any other rule of law earlier than the time provided in this section. Any amount included in gross income under this section shall not be required to be included in gross income under any other provision of this chapter or any other rule of law later than the time provided in this section.

(d) Other definitions and special rules—For purposes of this section—

(1) Nonqualified deferred compensation plan—The term 'nonqualified deferred compensation plan' means any plan that provides for the deferral of compensation, other than—

(A) a qualified employer plan, and

(B) any bona fide vacation leave, sick leave, compensatory time, disability pay, or death benefit plan.

(2) Qualified employer plan—The term 'qualified employer plan' means—

(A) any plan, contract, pension, account, or trust described in subparagraph (A) or (B) of section 219(g)(5) (without regard to subparagraph (A)(iii)),

(B) any eligible deferred compensation plan (within the meaning of section 457(b)), and

(C) any plan described in section 415(m).

(3) Plan includes arrangements, etc—The term 'plan' includes any agreement or arrangement, including an agreement or arrangement that includes one person.

(4) Substantial risk of forfeiture—The rights of a person to compensation are subject to a substantial risk of forfeiture if such person's rights to such compensation are conditioned upon the future performance of substantial services by any individual.

(5) Treatment of earnings—References to deferred compensation shall be treated as including references to income (whether actual or notional) attributable to such compensation or such income.

(6) Aggregation rules—Except as provided by the Secretary, rules similar to the rules of subsections (b) and (c) of section 414 shall apply.

(e) Regulations—The Secretary shall prescribe such regulations as may be necessary or appropriate to carry out the purposes of this section, including regulations—

(1) providing for the determination of amounts of deferral in the case of a nonqualified deferred compensation plan which is a defined benefit plan,

(2) relating to changes in the ownership and control of a corporation or assets of a corporation for purposes of subsection (a)(2)(A)(v),

(3) exempting arrangements from the application of subsection (b) if such arrangements will not result in an improper deferral of United States tax and will not result in assets being effectively beyond the reach of creditors,

(4) defining financial health for purposes of subsection (b)(2), and

(5) disregarding a substantial risk of forfeiture in cases where necessary to carry out the purposes of this section.

§ 410. Minimum participation standards

(a) Participation—

(1) Minimum age and service conditions—

(A) General rule—A trust shall not constitute a qualified trust under section 401(a) if the plan of which it is a part requires, as a condition of participation in the plan, that an employee complete a period of service with the employer or employers maintaining the plan extending beyond the later of the following dates—

(i) the date on which the employee attains the age of 21; or

(ii) the date on which he completes 1 year of service.

(B) Special rules for certain plans—

(i) In the case of any plan which provides that after not more than 2 years of service each participant has a right to 100 percent of his accrued benefit under the plan which is nonforfeitable (within the meaning of section 411) at the time such benefit accrues, clause (ii) of subparagraph (A) shall be applied by substituting "2 years of service" for "1 year of service".

(ii) In the case of any plan maintained exclusively for employees of an educational institution (as defined in section 170(b)(1)(A)(ii)) by an employer which is exempt from tax under section 501(a) which provides that each participant having at least 1 year of service has a right to 100 percent of his accrued benefit under the plan which is nonforfeitable (within the meaning of section 411) at the time such benefit accrues, clause (i) of subparagraph (A) shall be applied by substituting "26" for "21". This clause shall not apply to any plan to which clause (i) applies.

(2) Maximum age conditions—A trust shall not constitute a qualified trust under section 401(a) if the plan of which it is a part excludes from participation (on the basis of age) employees who have attained a specified age.

(3) Definition of year of service—

(A) General rule—For purposes of this subsection, the term "year of service" means a 12-month period during which the employee has not less than 1,000 hours of service. For purposes of this paragraph, computation of any 12-month period shall be made with reference to the date on which the employee's employment commenced, except that, under regulations prescribed by the Secretary of Labor, such computation may be made by reference to the first day of a plan year in the case of an employee who does not complete 1,000 hours of service during the 12-month period beginning on the date his employment commenced.

(B) Seasonal industries—In the case of any seasonal industry where the customary period of employment is less than 1,000 hours during a calendar year, the term "year of service" shall be such period as may be determined under regulations prescribed by the Secretary of Labor.

(C) Hours of service—For purposes of this subsection, the term "hour of service" means a time of service determined under regulations prescribed by the Secretary of Labor.

(D) Maritime industries—For purposes of this subsection, in the case of any maritime industry, 125 days of service shall be treated as 1,000 hours of service. The Secretary of Labor may prescribe regulations to carry out this subparagraph.

(4) Time of participation—A plan shall be treated as not meeting the requirements of paragraph (1) unless it provides that any employee who has satisfied the minimum age and service requirements specified in such paragraph, and who is otherwise entitled to participate in the plan, commences participation in the plan no later than the earlier of—

(A) the first day of the first plan year beginning after the date on which such employee satisfied such requirements, or

(B) the date 6 months after the date on which he satisfied such requirements,

unless such employee was separated from the service before the date referred to in subparagraph (A) or (B), whichever is applicable.

(5) Breaks in service—

(A) General rule—Except as otherwise provided in subparagraphs (B), (C), and (D), all years of service with the employer or employers maintaining the plan shall be taken into account in computing the period of service for purposes of paragraph (1).

(B) Employees under 2-year 100 percent vesting—In the case of any employee who has any 1-year break in service (as defined in section 411(a)(6)(A)) under a plan to which the service requirements of clause (i) of paragraph (1)(B) apply, if such employee has not satisfied such requirements, service before such break shall not be required to be taken into account.

(C) 1-year break in service—In computing an employee's period of service for purposes of paragraph (1) in the case of any participant who has any 1-year break in service (as defined in section 411(a)(6)(A)), service before such break shall not be required to be taken into account under the plan until he has completed a year of service (as defined in paragraph (3)) after his return.

(D) Nonvested participants—

(i) In general—For purposes of paragraph (1), in the case of a nonvested participant, years of service with the employer or employers maintaining the plan before any period of consecutive 1-year breaks in service shall not be required to be taken into account in computing the period of service if the number of consecutive 1-year breaks in service within such period equals or exceeds the greater of—

(I) 5, or

(II) the aggregate number of years of service before such period.

(ii) Years of service not taken into account—If any years of service are not required to be taken into account by reason of a period of breaks in service to which clause (i) applies, such years of service shall not be taken into account in applying clause (i) to a subsequent period of breaks in service.

(iii) Nonvested participant defined—For purposes of clause (i), the term "nonvested participant" means a participant who does not have any nonforfeitable right under the plan to an accrued benefit derived from employer contributions.

(E) Special rule for maternity or paternity absences—

(i) General rule—In the case of each individual who is absent from work for any period—

(I) by reason of the pregnancy of the individual,

(II) by reason of the birth of a child of the individual,

(III) by reason of the placement of a child with the individual in connection with the adoption of such child by such individual, or

(IV) for purposes of caring for such child for a period beginning immediately following such birth or placement,

the plan shall treat as hours of service, solely for purposes of determining under this paragraph whether a 1-year break in service (as defined in section 411(a)(6)(A)) has occurred, the hours described in clause (ii).

(ii) Hours treated as hours of service—The hours described in this clause are—

(I) the hours of service which otherwise would normally have been credited to such individual but for such absence, or

(II) in any case in which the plan is unable to determine the hours described in subclause (I), 8 hours of service per day of such absence,

except that the total number of hours treated as hours of service under this clause by reason of any such pregnancy or placement shall not exceed 501 hours.

(iii) Year to which hours are credited—The hours described in clause (ii) shall be treated as hours of service as provided in this subparagraph—

(I) only in the year in which the absence from work begins, if a participant would be prevented from incurring a 1-year break in service in such year solely because the period of absence is treated as hours of service as provided in clause (i); or

(II) in any other case, in the immediately following year.

(iv) Year defined—For purposes of this subparagraph, the term "year" means the period used in computations pursuant to paragraph (3).

(v) Information required to be filed—A plan shall not fail to satisfy the requirements of this subparagraph solely because it provides that no credit will be given pursuant to this subparagraph unless the individual furnishes to the plan administrator such timely information as the plan may reasonably require to establish—

(I) that the absence from work is for reasons referred to in clause (i), and

(II) the number of days for which there was such an absence.

(b) Minimum coverage requirements—

(1) In general—A trust shall not constitute a qualified trust under section 401(a) unless such trust is designated by the employer as part of a plan which meets 1 of the following requirements:

(A) The plan benefits at least 70 percent of employees who are not highly compensated employees.

(B) The plan benefits—

(i) a percentage of employees who are not highly compensated employees which is at least 70 percent of

(ii) the percentage of highly compensated employees benefiting under the plan.

(C) The plan meets the requirements of paragraph (2).

(2) Average benefit percentage test—

(A) In general—A plan shall be treated as meeting the requirements of this paragraph if—

(i) the plan benefits such employees as qualify under a classification set up by the employer and found by the Secretary not to be discriminatory in favor of highly compensated employees, and

(ii) the average benefit percentage for employees who are not highly compensated employees is at least 70 percent of the average benefit percentage for highly compensated employees.

(B) Average benefit percentage—For purposes of this paragraph, the term "average benefit percentage" means, with respect to any group, the average of the benefit percentages calculated separately with respect to each employee in such group (whether or not a participant in any plan).

(C) Benefit percentage—For purposes of this paragraph—

(i) In general—The term "benefit percentage" means the employer-provided contribution or benefit of an employee under all qualified plans maintained by the employer, expressed as a percentage of such employee's compensation (within the meaning of section 414(s)).

(ii) Period for computing percentage—At the election of an employer, the benefit percentage for any plan year shall be computed on the basis of contributions or benefits for—

(I) such plan year, or

(II) any consecutive plan year period (not greater than 3 years) which ends with such plan year and which is specified in such election.

An election under this clause, once made, may be revoked or modified only with the consent of the Secretary.

(D) Employees taken into account—For purposes of determining who is an employee for purposes of determining the average benefit percentage under subparagraph (B)—

(i) except as provided in clause (ii), paragraph (4)(A) shall not apply, or

(ii) if the employer elects, paragraph (4)(A) shall be applied by using the lowest age and service requirements of all qualified plans maintained by the employer.

(E) Qualified plan—For purposes of this paragraph, the term "qualified plan" means any plan which (without regard to this subsection) meets the requirements of section 401(a).

(3) Exclusion of certain employees—For purposes of this subsection, there shall be excluded from consideration—

(A) employees who are included in a unit of employees covered by an agreement which the Secretary of Labor finds to be a collective bargaining agreement between employee representatives and one or more employers, if there is evidence that retirement benefits were the subject of good faith bargaining between such employee representatives and such employer or employers,

(B) in the case of a trust established or maintained pursuant to an agreement which the Secretary of Labor finds to be a collective bargaining agreement between air pilots represented in accordance with title II of the Railway Labor Act and one or more employers, all employees not covered by such agreement, and

(C) employees who are nonresident aliens and who receive no earned income (within the meaning of section 911(d)(2)) from the employer which constitutes income from sources within the United States (within the meaning of section 861(a)(3)).

Subparagraph (A) shall not apply with respect to coverage of employees under a plan pursuant to an agreement under such subparagraph. For purposes of subparagraph (B), management pilots who are not represented in accordance with title II of the Railway Labor Act shall be treated as covered by a collective bargaining agreement described in such subparagraph if the management pilots manage the flight operations of air pilots who are so represented and the management pilots are, pursuant to the terms of the agreement, included in the group of employees benefitting under the trust described in such subparagraph. Subparagraph (B) shall not apply in the case of a plan which provides contributions or benefits for employees whose principal duties are not customarily performed aboard an aircraft in flight (other than management pilots described in the preceding sentence).

(4) Exclusion of employees not meeting age and service requirements—

(A) In general—If a plan—

(i) prescribes minimum age and service requirements as a condition of participation, and

(ii) excludes all employees not meeting such requirements from participation,

then such employees shall be excluded from consideration for purposes of this subsection.

(B) Requirements may be met separately with respect to excluded group—If employees not meeting the minimum age or service requirements of subsection (a)(1) (without regard to subparagraph (B) thereof) are covered under a plan of the employer which meets the requirements of paragraph (1) separately with respect to such employees, such employees may be excluded from consideration in determining whether any plan of the employer meets the requirements of paragraph (1).

(C) Requirements not treated as being met before entry date—An employee shall not be treated as meeting the age and service requirements described in this paragraph until the first date on which, under the plan, any employee with the same age and service would be eligible to commence participation in the plan.

(5) Line of business exception—

(A) In general—If, under section 414(r), an employer is treated as operating separate lines of business for a year, the employer may apply the requirements of this subsection for such year separately with respect to employees in each separate line of business.

(B) Plan must be nondiscriminatory—Subparagraph (A) shall not apply with respect to any plan maintained by an employer unless such plan benefits such employees as qualify under a classification set up by the employer and found by the Secretary not to be discriminatory in favor of highly compensated employees.

(6) Definitions and special rules—For purposes of this subsection—

(A) Highly compensated employee—The term "highly compensated employee" has the meaning given such term by section 414(q).

(B) Aggregation rules—An employer may elect to designate—

(i) 2 or more trusts,

(ii) 1 or more trusts and 1 or more annuity plans, or

(iii) 2 or more annuity plans,

as part of 1 plan intended to qualify under section 401(a) to determine whether the requirements of this subsection are met with respect to such trusts or annuity plans. If an employer elects to treat any trusts or annuity plans as 1 plan under this subparagraph, such trusts or annuity plans shall be treated as 1 plan for purposes of section 401(a)(4).

(C) Special rules for certain dispositions or acquisitions—

(i) In general—If a person becomes, or ceases to be, a member of a group described in subsection (b), (c), (m), or (o) of section 414, then the requirements of this subsection shall be treated as having been met during the transition period with respect to any plan covering employees of such person or any other member of such group if—

(I) such requirements were met immediately before each such change, and

(II) the coverage under such plan is not significantly changed during the transition period (other than by reason of the change in members of a group) or such plan meets such other requirements as the Secretary may prescribe by regulation.

(ii) Transition period—For purposes of clause (i), the term "transition period" means the period—

(I) beginning on the date of the change in members of a group, and

(II) ending on the last day of the 1st plan year beginning after the date of such change.

(D) Special rule for certain employee stock ownership plans—A trust which is part of a tax credit employee stock ownership plan which is the only plan of an employer intended to qualify under section 401(a) shall not be treated as not a qualified trust under section 401(a) solely because it fails to meet the requirements of this subsection if—

(i) such plan benefits 50 percent or more of all the employees who are eligible under a nondiscriminatory classification under the plan, and

(ii) the sum of the amounts allocated to each participant's account for the year does not exceed 2 percent of the compensation of that participant for the year.

(E) Eligibility to contribute—In the case of contributions which are subject to section 401(k) or 401(m), employees who are eligible to contribute (or elect to have contributions made on their behalf) shall be treated as benefiting under the plan (other than for purposes of paragraph (2)(A)(ii)).

(F) Employers with only highly compensated employees—A plan maintained by an employer which has no employees other than highly compensated employees for any year shall be treated as meeting the requirements of this subsection for such year.

(G) Regulations—The Secretary shall prescribe such regulations as may be necessary or appropriate to carry out the purposes of this subsection.

(c) Application of participation standards to certain plans—

(1) The provisions of this section (other than paragraph (2) of this subsection) shall not apply to—

(A) a governmental plan (within the meaning of section 414(d)),

(B) a church plan (within the meaning of section 414(e)) with respect to which the election provided by subsection (d) of this section has not been made,

(C) a plan which has not at any time after September 2, 1974, provided for employer contributions, and

(D) a plan established and maintained by a society, order, or association described in section 501(c)(8) or (9) if no part of the contributions to or under such plan are made by employers of participants in such plan.

(2) A plan described in paragraph (1) shall be treated as meeting the requirements of this section for purposes of section 401(a), except that in the case of a plan described in subparagraph (B), (C), or (D) of paragraph (1), this paragraph shall apply only if such plan meets the requirements of section 401(a)(3) (as in effect on September 1, 1974).

(d) Election by church to have participation, vesting, funding, etc., provisions apply—

(1) In general—If the church or convention or association of churches which maintains any church plan makes an election under this subsection (in such form and manner as the Secretary may by regulations prescribe), then the provisions of this title relating to participation, vesting, funding, etc. (as in effect from time to time) shall apply to such church plan as if such provisions did not contain an exclusion for church plans.

(2) Election irrevocable—An election under this subsection with respect to any church plan shall be binding with respect to such plan, and, once made, shall be irrevocable.

§ 411. Minimum vesting standards.

(a) General rule—A trust shall not constitute a qualified trust under section 401(a) unless the plan of which such trust is a part provides that an employee's right to his normal retirement benefit is nonforfeitable upon the attainment of normal retirement age (as defined in paragraph (8)) and in addition satisfies the requirements of paragraphs (1), (2), and (11) of this subsection and the requirements of subsection (b)(3), and also satisfies, in the case of a defined benefit plan, the requirements of subsection (b)(1) and, in the case of a defined contribution plan, the requirements of subsection (b)(2).

(1) Employee contributions—A plan satisfies the requirements of this paragraph if an employee's rights in his accrued benefit derived from his own contributions are nonforfeitable.

(2) Employer contributions—

(A) Defined benefit plans—

(i) In general—In the case of a defined benefit plan, a plan satisfies the requirements of this paragraph if it satisfies the requirements of clause (ii) or (iii).

(ii) 5-year vesting—A plan satisfies the requirements of this clause if an employee who has completed at least 5 years of service has a nonforfeitable right to 100 percent of the employee's accrued benefit derived from employer contributions.

(iii) 3 to 7 year vesting—A plan satisfies the requirements of this clause if an employee has a nonforfeitable right to a percentage of the employee's accrued benefit derived from employer contributions determined under the following table:

Years of service:	*The nonforfeitable percentage is:*
3	20
4	40
5	60
6	80
7 or more	100.

(B) Defined contribution plans—

(i) In general—In the case of a defined contribution plan, a plan satisfies the requirements of this paragraph if it satisfies the requirements of clause (ii) or (iii).

(ii) 3-year vesting—A plan satisfies the requirements of this clause if an employee who has completed at least 3 years of service has a nonforfeitable right to 100 percent of the employee's accrued benefit derived from employer contributions.

(iii) 2 to 6 year vesting—A plan satisfies the requirements of this clause if an employee has a nonforfeitable right to a percentage of the employee's accrued benefit derived from employer contributions determined under the following table:

Years of service:	*The nonforfeitable percentage is:*
2	20
3	40
4	60
5	80
6 or more	100.

(3) Certain permitted forfeitures, suspensions, etc—For purposes of this subsection—

(A) Forfeiture on account of death—A right to an accrued benefit derived from employer contributions shall not be treated as forfeitable solely because the plan provides that it is not payable if the participant dies (except in the case of a survivor annuity which is payable as provided in section 401(a)(11)).

(B) Suspension of benefits upon reemployment of retiree—A right to an accrued benefit derived from employer contributions shall not be treated as forfeitable solely because the plan provides that the payment of benefits is suspended for such period as the employee is employed, subsequent to the commencement of payment of such benefits—

(i) in the case of a plan other than a multiemployer plan, by the employer who maintains the plan under which such benefits were being paid; and

(ii) in the case of a multiemployer plan, in the same industry, the same trade or craft, and the same geographic area covered by the plan as when such benefits commenced.

The Secretary of Labor shall prescribe such regulations as may be necessary to carry out the purposes of this subparagraph, including regulations with respect to the meaning of the term "employed".

(C) Effect of retroactive plan amendments—A right to an accrued benefit derived from employer contributions shall not be treated as forfeitable solely because plan amendments may be given retroactive application as provided in section 412(d)(2).

(D) Withdrawal of mandatory contributions—

(i) A right to an accrued benefit derived from employer contributions shall not be treated as forfeitable solely because the plan provides that, in the case of a participant who does not have a nonforfeitable right to at least 50 percent of his accrued benefit derived from employer contributions, such accrued benefit may be forfeited on account of the withdrawal by the participant of any amount attributable to the benefit derived from mandatory contributions (as defined in subsection (c)(2)(C)) made by such participant.

(ii) Clause (i) shall not apply to a plan unless the plan provides that any accrued benefit forfeited under a plan provision described in such clause shall be restored upon repayment by the participant of the full amount of the withdrawal described in such clause plus, in the case of a defined benefit plan, interest. Such interest shall be computed on such amount at the rate determined for purposes of subsection (c)(2)(C) on the date of such repayment (computed annually from the date of such withdrawal). The plan provision required under this clause may provide that such repayment must be made (I) in the case of a withdrawal on a account of separation from service, before the earlier of 5 years after the first date on which the participant is subsequently re-employed by the employer, or the close of the first period of 5 consecutive 1-year breaks in service commencing after the withdrawal; or (II) in the case of any other withdrawal, 5 years after the date of the withdrawal.

(iii) In the case of accrued benefits derived from employer contributions which accrued before September 2, 1974, a right to such accrued benefit derived from employer contributions shall not be treated as forfeitable solely because the plan provides that an amount of such accrued benefit may be forfeited on account of the withdrawal by the participant of an amount attributable to the benefit derived from mandatory contributions (as defined in subsection (c)(2)(C)) made by such participant before September 2, 1974 if such amount forfeited is proportional to such amount withdrawn. This clause shall not apply to any plan to which any mandatory contribution is made after September 2, 1974. The Secretary shall prescribe such regulations as may be necessary to carry out the purposes of this clause.

(iv) For purposes of this subparagraph, in the case of any class-year plan, a withdrawal of employee contributions shall be treated as a withdrawal of such contributions on a plan year by plan year basis in succeeding order of time.

(v) For nonforfeitability where the employee has a nonforfeitable right to at least 50 percent of his accrued benefit, see section 401(a)(19).

(E) Cessation of contributions under a multiemployer plan—A right to an accrued benefit derived from employer contributions under a multiemployer plan shall not be treated as forfeitable solely because the plan provides that benefits accrued as a result of service with the participant's employer before the employer had an obligation to contribute under the plan may not be payable if the employer ceases contributions to the multiemployer plan.

(F) Reduction and suspension of benefits by a multiemployer plan—A participant's right to an accrued benefit derived from employer contributions under a multiemployer plan shall not be treated as forfeitable solely because—

(i) the plan is amended to reduce benefits under section 418D or under section 4281 of the Employee Retirement Income Security Act of 1974, or

(ii) benefit payments under the plan may be suspended under section 418E or under section 4281 of the Employee Retirement Income Security Act of 1974.

(G) Treatment of matching contributions forfeited by reason of excess deferral or contribution or permissible withdrawal—A matching contribution (within the meaning of section 401(m)) shall not be treated as forfeitable merely because such contribution is forfeitable if the contribution to which the matching contribution relates is treated as an excess contribution under section 401(k)(8)(B), an excess deferral under section 402(g)(2)(A), a permissible withdrawal under section 414(w), or an excess aggregate contribution under section 401(m)(6)(B).

(4) Service included in determination of nonforfeitable percentage or erroneous automatic contribution—In computing the period of service under the plan for purposes of determining the nonforfeitable percentage under paragraph (2), all of an employee's years of service with the employer or employers maintaining the plan shall be taken into account, except that the following may be disregarded:

(A) years of service before age 18,

(B) years of service during a period for which the employee declined to contribute to a plan requiring employee contributions;

(C) years of service with an employer during any period for which the employer did not maintain the plan or a predecessor plan (as defined under regulations prescribed by the Secretary);

(D) service not required to be taken into account under paragraph (6);

(E) years of service before January 1, 1971, unless the employee has had at least 3 years of service after December 31, 1970;

(F) years of service before the first plan year to which this section applies, if such service would have been disregarded under the rules of the plan with regard to breaks in service as in effect on the applicable date; and

(G) in the case of a multiemployer plan, years of service—

(i) with an employer after—

(I) a complete withdrawal of that employer from the plan (within the meaning of section 4203 of the Employee Retirement Income Security Act of 1974), or

(II) to the extent permitted in regulations prescribed by the Secretary, a partial withdrawal described in section 4205(b)(2)(A)(i) of such Act in conjunction with the decertification of the collective bargaining representative, and

(ii) with any employer under the plan after the termination date of the plan under section 4048 of such Act.

(5) Year of service—

(A) General rule—For purposes of this subsection, except as provided in subparagraph (C), the term "year of service" means a calendar year, plan year, or other 12-consecutive month period designated by the plan (and not prohibited under regulations prescribed by the Secretary of Labor) during which the participant has completed 1,000 hours of service.

(B) Hours of service—For purposes of this subsection, the term "hours of service" has the meaning provided by section 410(a)(3)(C).

(C) Seasonal industries—In the case of any seasonal industry where the customary period of employment is less than 1,000 hours during a calendar year, the term "year of service" shall be such period as may be determined under regulations prescribed by the Secretary of Labor.

(D) Maritime industries—For purposes of this subsection, in the case of any maritime industry, 125 days of service shall be treated as 1,000 hours of service. The Secretary of Labor may prescribe regulations to carry out the purposes of this subparagraph.

(6) Breaks in service—

(A) Definition of 1-year break in service—For purposes of this paragraph, the term "1-year break in service" means a calendar year, plan year, or other 12-consecutive-month period designated by the plan (and not prohibited under regulations prescribed by the Secretary of Labor) during which the participant has not completed more than 500 hours of service.

(B) 1 year of service after 1-year break in service—For purposes of paragraph (4), in the case of any employee who has any 1-year break in service, years of service before such break shall not be required to be taken into account until he has completed a year of service after his return.

(C) 5 consecutive 1-year breaks in service under defined contribution plan—For purposes of paragraph (4), in the case of any participant in a defined contribution plan, or an insured defined benefit plan which satisfies the requirements of subsection (b)(1)(F), who has 5 consecutive 1-year breaks in service, years of service after such 5-year period shall not be required to be taken into account for purposes of determining the nonforfeitable percentage of his accrued benefit derived from employer contributions which accrued before such 5-year period.

(D) Nonvested participants—

(i) In general—For purposes of paragraph (4), in the case of a nonvested participant, years of service with the employer or employers maintaining the plan before any period of consecutive 1-year breaks in service shall not be required to be taken into account if the number of consecutive 1-year breaks in service within such period equals or exceeds the greater of—

(I) 5, or

(II) the aggregate number of years of service before such period.

(ii) Years of service not taken into account—If any years of service are not required to be taken into account by reason of a period of breaks in service to which clause (i) applies, such years of service shall not be taken into account in applying clause (i) to a subsequent period of breaks in service.

(iii) Nonvested participant defined—For purposes of clause (i), the term "nonvested participant" means a participant who does not have any nonforfeitable right under the plan to an accrued benefit derived from employer contributions.

(E) Special rule for maternity or paternity absences—

(i) General rule—In the case of each individual who is absent from work for any period—

(I) by reason of the pregnancy of the individual,

(II) by reason of the birth of a child of the individual,

(III) by reason of the placement of a child with the individual in connection with the adoption of such child by such individual, or

(IV) for purposes of caring for such child for a period beginning immediately following such birth or placement,

the plan shall treat as hours of service, solely for purposes of determining under this paragraph whether a 1-year break in service has occurred, the hours described in clause (ii).

(ii) Hours treated as hours of service—The hours described in this clause are—

(I) the hours of service which otherwise would normally have been credited to such individual but for such absence, or

(II) in any case in which the plan is unable to determine the hours described in subclause (I), 8 hours of service per day of absence,

except that the total number of hours treated as hours of service under this clause by reason of any such pregnancy or placement shall not exceed 501 hours.

(iii) Year to which hours are credited—The hours described in clause (ii) shall be treated as hours of service as provided in this subparagraph—

(I) only in the year in which the absence from work begins, if a participant would be prevented from incurring a 1-year break in service in such year solely because the period of absence is treated as hours of service as provided in clause (i); or

(II) in any other case, in the immediately following year.

(iv) Year defined—For purposes of this subparagraph, the term "year" means the period used in computations pursuant to paragraph (5).

(v) Information required to be filed—A plan shall not fail to satisfy the requirements of this subparagraph solely because it provides that no credit will be given pursuant to this subparagraph unless the individual furnishes to the plan administrator such timely information as the plan may reasonably require to establish—

(I) that the absence from work is for reasons referred to in clause (i), and

(II) the number of days for which there was such an absence.

(7) **Accrued benefit**—

(A) In general—For purposes of this section, the term "accrued benefit" means—

(i) in the case of a defined benefit plan, the employee's accrued benefit determined under the plan and, except as provided in subsection (c)(3), expressed in the form of an annual benefit commencing at normal retirement age, or

(ii) in the case of a plan which is not a defined benefit plan, the balance of the employee's account.

(B) Effect of certain distributions—Notwithstanding paragraph (4), for purposes of determining the employee's accrued benefit under the plan, the plan may disregard service performed by the employee with respect to which he has received—

(i) a distribution of the present value of his entire nonforfeitable benefit if such distribution was in an amount (not more than the dollar limit under section 411 (a)(11)(A)) permitted under regulations prescribed by the Secretary, or

(ii) a distribution of the present value of his nonforfeitable benefit attributable to such service which he elected to receive.

Clause (i) of this subparagraph shall apply only if such distribution was made on termination of the employee's participation in the plan. Clause (ii) of this subparagraph shall apply only if such distribution was made on termination of the employee's participation in the plan or under such other circumstances as may be provided under regulations prescribed by the Secretary.

(C) Repayment of subparagraph (b) distributions—For purposes of determining the employee's accrued benefit under a plan, the plan may not disregard service as provided in subparagraph (B) unless the plan provides an opportunity for the participant to repay the full amount of the distribution described in such subparagraph (B) with, in the case of a defined benefit plan, interest at the rate determined for purposes of subsection (c)(2)(C) and provides that upon such repayment the employee's accrued benefit shall be recomputed by taking into account service so disregarded. This subparagraph shall apply only in the case of a participant who—

(i) received such a distribution in any plan year to which this section applies, which distribution was less than the present value of his accrued benefit,

(ii) resumes employment covered under the plan, and

(iii) repays the full amount of such distribution with, in the case of a defined benefit plan, interest at the rate determined for purposes of subsection (c)(2)(C).

The plan provision required under this subparagraph may provide that such repayment must be made (I) in the case of a withdrawal on account of separation from service, before the earlier of 5 years after the first date on which the participant is subsequently re-employed by the employer, or the close of the first period of 5 consecutive 1-year breaks in service commencing after the withdrawal; or (II) in the case of any other withdrawal, 5 years after the date of the withdrawal.

(D) Accrued benefit attributable to employee contributions—The accrued benefit of an employee shall not be less than the amount determined under subsection (c)(2)(B) with respect to the employee's accumulated contributions.

(8) Normal retirement age—For purposes of this section, the term "normal retirement age" means the earlier of—

(A) the time a plan participant attains normal retirement age under the plan, or

(B) the later of—

(i) the time a plan participant attains age 65, or

(ii) the 5th anniversary of the time a plan participant commenced participation in the plan.

(9) Normal retirement benefit—For purposes of this section, the term "normal retirement benefit" means the greater of the early retirement benefit under the plan, or the benefit under the plan commencing at normal retirement age. The normal retirement benefit shall be determined without regard to—

(A) medical benefits, and

(B) disability benefits not in excess of the qualified disability benefit.

For purposes of this paragraph, a qualified disability benefit is a disability benefit provided by a plan which does not exceed the benefit which would be provided for the participant if he separated from the service at normal retirement age. For purposes of this paragraph, the early retirement benefit under a plan shall be determined without regard to any benefits commencing before benefits payable under title II of the Social Security Act become payable which—

(i) do not exceed such social security benefits, and

(ii) terminate when such social security benefits commence.

(10) Changes in vesting schedule—

(A) General rule—A plan amendment changing any vesting schedule under the plan shall be treated as not satisfying the requirements of paragraph (2) if the nonforfeitable percentage of the accrued benefit derived from employer contributions (determined as of the later of the date such amendment is adopted, or the date such amendment becomes effective) of any employee who is a participant in the plan is less than such nonforfeitable percentage computed under the plan without regard to such amendment.

(B) Election of former schedule—A plan amendment changing any vesting schedule under the plan shall be treated as not satisfying the requirements of paragraph (2) unless each participant having not less than 3 years of service is permitted to elect, within a reasonable period after the adoption of such amendment, to have his nonforfeitable percentage computed under the plan without regard to such amendment.

(11) Restrictions on certain mandatory distributions—

(A) In general—If the present value of any nonforfeitable accrued benefit exceeds $5,000 a plan meets the requirements of this paragraph only if such plan provides that such benefit may not be immediately distributed without the consent of the participant.

(B) Determination of present value—For purposes of subparagraph (A), the present value shall be calculated in accordance with section 417(e)(3).

(C) Dividend distributions of ESOPs arrangement—This paragraph shall not apply to any distribution of dividends to which section 404(k) applies.

(D) Special rule for rollover contributions—A plan shall not fail to meet the requirements of this paragraph if, under the terms of the plan, the present value of the nonforfeitable accrued benefit is determined without regard to that portion of such benefit which is attributable to rollover contributions (and earnings allocable thereto). For purposes of this subparagraph, the term "rollover contributions" means any rollover contribution under sections 402(c), 403(a)(4), 403(b)(8), 408(d)(3)(A)(ii), and 457(e)(16).

(12) [Repealed]

(13) Special rules for plans computing accrued benefits by reference to hypothetical account balance or equivalent amounts—

(A) In general—An applicable defined benefit plan shall not be treated as failing to meet—

(i) subject to subparagraph (B), the requirements of subsection (a)(2), or

(ii) the requirements of subsection (a)(11) or (c) or the requirements of section 417(e) with respect to accrued benefits derived from employer contributions,

solely because the present value of the accrued benefit (or any portion thereof) of any participant is, under the terms of the plan, equal to the amount expressed as the balance in the hypothetical account described in paragraph (3) or as an accumulated percentage of the participant's final average compensation.

(B) 3-year vesting—In the case of an applicable defined benefit plan, such plan shall be treated as meeting the requirements of subsection (a)(2) only if an employee who has completed at least 3 years of service has a nonforfeitable right to 100 percent of the employee's accrued benefit derived from employer contributions.

(C) Applicable defined benefit plan and related rules—For purposes of this subsection—

(i) In general—The term "applicable defined benefit plan" means a defined benefit plan under which the accrued benefit (or any portion thereof) is calculated as the balance of a hypothetical account maintained for the participant or as an accumulated percentage of the participant's final average compensation.

(ii) Regulations to include similar plans—The Secretary shall issue regulations which include in the definition of an applicable defined benefit plan any defined benefit plan (or any portion of such a plan) which has an effect similar to an applicable defined benefit plan.

(b) Accrued benefit requirements—

(1) Defined benefit plans—

(A) 3-percent method—A defined benefit plan satisfies the requirements of this paragraph if the accrued benefit to which each participant is entitled upon his separation from the service is not less than—

(i) 3 percent of the normal retirement benefit to which he would be entitled if he commenced participation at the earliest possible entry age under the plan and served continuously until the earlier of age 65 or the normal retirement age specified under the plan, multiplied by

(ii) the number of years (not in excess of 33⅓) of his participation in the plan.

In the case of a plan providing retirement benefits based on compensation during any period, the normal retirement benefit to which a participant would be entitled shall be determined as if he continued to earn annually the average rate of compensation which he earned during consecutive years of service, not in excess of 10, for which his compensation was the highest. For purposes of this subparagraph, social security benefits and all other relevant factors used to compute benefits shall be treated as remaining constant as of the current year for all years after such current year.

(B) 133⅓ percent rule—A defined benefit plan satisfies the requirements of this paragraph for a particular plan year if under the plan the accrued benefit payable at the normal retirement age is equal to the normal retirement benefit and the annual rate at which any individual who is or could be a participant can accrue the retirement benefits payable at normal retirement age under the plan for any later plan year is not more than 133⅓ percent of the annual rate at which he can accrue benefits for any plan year beginning on or after such particular plan year and before such later plan year. For purposes of this subparagraph—

(i) any amendment to the plan which is in effect for the current year shall be treated as in effect for all other plan years;

(ii) any change in an accrual rate which does not apply to any individual who is or could be a participant in the current year shall be disregarded;

(iii) the fact that benefits under the plan may be payable to certain employees before normal retirement age shall be disregarded; and

(iv) social security benefits and all other relevant factors used to compute benefits shall be treated as remaining constant as of the current year for all years after the current year.

(C) Fractional rule—A defined benefit plan satisfies the requirements of this paragraph if the accrued benefit to which any participant is entitled upon his separation from the service is not less than a fraction of the annual benefit commencing at normal retirement age to which he would be entitled under the plan as in effect on the date of his separation if he continued to earn annually until normal retirement age the same rate of compensation upon which his normal retirement benefit would be computed under the plan, determined as if he had attained normal retirement age on the date on which any such determination is made (but taking into account no more than the 10 years of service immediately preceding his separation from service). Such fraction shall be a fraction, not exceeding 1, the numerator of which is the total number of his years of participation in the plan (as of the date of his separation from the service) and the denominator of which is the total number of years he would have participated in the plan if he separated from the service at the normal retirement age. For purposes of this subparagraph, social security benefits and all other relevant factors used to compute benefits shall be treated as remaining constant as of the current year for all years after such current year.

(D) Accrual for service before effective date—Subparagraphs (A), (B), and (C) shall not apply with respect to years of participation before the first plan year to which this section applies, but a defined benefit plan satisfies the requirements of this subparagraph with respect to such years of participation only if the accrued benefit of any participant with respect to such years of participation is not less than the greater of—

(i) his accrued benefit determined under the plan, as in effect from time to time prior to September 2, 1974, or

(ii) an accrued benefit which is not less than one-half of the accrued benefit to which such participant would have been entitled if subparagraph (A), (B), or (C) applied with respect to such years of participation.

(E) First two years of service—Notwithstanding subparagraphs (A), (B), and (C) of this paragraph, a plan shall not be treated as not satisfying the requirements of this paragraph solely because the accrual of benefits under the plan does not become effective until the employee has two continuous years of service. For purposes of this subparagraph, the term "years of service" has the meaning provided by section 410(a)(3)(A).

(F) Certain insured defined benefit plans—Notwithstanding subparagraphs (A), (B), and (C), a defined benefit plan satisfies the requirements of this paragraph if such plan—

(i) is funded exclusively by the purchase of insurance contracts, and

(ii) satisfies the requirements of subparagraphs (B) and (C) of section 412(e)(3) (relating to certain insurance contract plans),

but only if an employee's accrued benefit as of any applicable date is not less than the cash surrender value his insurance contracts would have on such applicable date if the requirements of subparagraphs (D), (E), and (F) of section 412(e)(3) were satisfied.

(G) Accrued benefit may not decrease on account of increasing age or service—Notwithstanding the preceding subparagraphs, a defined benefit plan shall be treated as not satisfying the requirements of this paragraph if the participant's accrued benefit is reduced on account of any increase in his age or service. The preceding sentence shall not apply to benefits under the plan commencing before entitlement to benefits payable under title II of the Social Security Act which benefits under the plan—

(i) do not exceed such social security benefits, and

(ii) terminate when such social security benefits commence.

(H) Continued accrual beyond normal retirement age—

(i) In general—Notwithstanding the preceding subparagraphs, a defined benefit plan shall be treated as not satisfying the requirements of this paragraph if, under the plan, an employee's benefit accrual is ceased, or the rate of an employee's benefit accrual is reduced, because of the attainment of any age.

(ii) Certain limitations permitted—A plan shall not be treated as failing to meet the requirements of this subparagraph solely because the plan imposes (without regard to age) a limitation on the amount of benefits that the plan provides or a limitation on the number of years of service or years of participation which are taken into account for purposes of determining benefit accrual under the plan.

(iii) Adjustments under plan for delayed retirement taken into account—In the case of any employee who, as of the end of any plan year under a defined benefit plan, has attained normal retirement age under such plan—

(I) if distribution of benefits under such plan with respect to such employee has commenced as of the end of such plan year, then any requirement of this subparagraph for continued accrual of benefits under such plan with respect to such employee during such plan year shall be treated as satisfied to the extent of the actuarial equivalent of in-service distribution of benefits, and

(II) if distribution of benefits under such plan with respect to such employee has not commenced as of the end of such year in accordance with section 401(a)(14)(C), and the payment of benefits under such plan with respect to such employee is not suspended during such plan year pursuant to subsection (a)(3)(B), then any requirement of this subparagraph for continued accrual of benefits under such plan with respect to such employee during such plan year shall be treated as satisfied to the extent of any adjustment in the benefit payable under the plan during such plan year attributable to the delay in the distribution of benefits after the attainment of normal retirement age.

The preceding provisions of this clause shall apply in accordance with regulations of the Secretary. Such regulations may provide for the application of the preceding provisions of this clause, in the case of any such employee, with respect to any period of time within a plan year.

(iv) Disregard of subsidized portion of early retirement benefit—A plan shall not be treated as failing to meet the requirements of clause (i) solely because the subsidized portion of any early retirement benefit is disregarded in determining benefit accruals.

(v) Coordination with other requirements—The Secretary shall provide by regulation for the coordination of the requirements of this subparagraph with the requirements of subsection (a), sections 404, 410, and 415, and the provisions of this subchapter precluding discrimination in favor of highly compensated employees.

(2) Defined contribution plans—

(A) In general—A defined contribution plan satisfies the requirements of this paragraph if, under the plan, allocations to the employee's account are not ceased, and the rate at which amounts are allocated to the employee's account is not reduced, because of the attainment of any age.

(B) Application to target benefit plans—The Secretary shall provide by regulation for the application of the requirements of this paragraph to target benefit plans.

(C) Coordination with other requirements—The Secretary may provide by regulation for the coordination of the requirements of this paragraph with the requirements of subsection (a), sections 404, 410, and 415, and the provisions of this subchapter precluding discrimination in favor of highly compensated employees.

(3) Separate accounting required in certain cases—A plan satisfies the requirements of this paragraph if—

(A) in the case of a defined benefit plan, the plan requires separate accounting for the portion of each employee's accrued benefit derived from any voluntary employee contributions permitted under the plan; and

(B) in the case of any plan which is not a defined benefit plan, the plan requires separate accounting for each employee's accrued benefit.

(4) Year of participation—

(A) Definition—For purposes of determining an employee's accrued benefit, the term "year of participation" means a period of service (beginning at the earliest date on which the employee is a participant in the plan and which is included in a period of service required to be taken into account under section 410(a)(5) determined without regard to section 410(a)(5)(E)) as determined under regulations prescribed by the Secretary of Labor which provide for the calculation of such period on any reasonable and consistent basis.

(B) Less than full time service—For purposes of this paragraph, except as provided in subparagraph (C), in the case of any employee whose customary employment is less than full time, the calculation of such employee's service on any basis which provides less than a ratable portion of the accrued benefit to which he would be entitled under the plan if his customary employment were full time shall not be treated as made on a reasonable and consistent basis.

(C) Less than 1,000 hours of service during year—For purposes of this paragraph, in the case of any employee whose service is less than 1,000 hours during any calendar year, plan year or other 12-consecutive month period designated by the plan (and not prohibited under regulations prescribed by the Secretary of Labor) the calculation of his period of service shall not be treated as not made on a reasonable and consistent basis solely because such service is not taken into account.

(D) Seasonal industries—In the case of any seasonal industry where the customary period of employment is less than 1,000 hours during a calendar year, the term "year of participation" shall be such period as determined under regulations prescribed by the Secretary of Labor.

(E) Maritime industries—For purposes of this subsection, in the case of any maritime industry, 125 days of service shall be treated as a year of participation. The Secretary of Labor may prescribe regulations to carry out the purposes of this subparagraph.

(5) Special rules relating to age—

(A) Comparison to similarly situated younger individual—

(i) In general—A plan shall not be treated as failing to meet the requirements of paragraph (1)(H)(i) if a participant's accrued benefit, as determined as of any date under the terms of the plan, would be equal to or greater than that of any similarly situated, younger individual who is or could be a participant.

(ii) Similarly situated—For purposes of this subparagraph, a participant is similarly situated to any other individual if such participant is identical to such other individual in every respect (including period of service, compensation, position, date of hire, work history, and any other respect) except for age.

(iii) Disregard of subsidized early retirement benefits—In determining the accrued benefit as of any date for purposes of this subparagraph, the subsidized portion of any early retirement benefit or retirement-type subsidy shall be disregarded.

(iv) Accrued benefit—For purposes of this subparagraph, the accrued benefit may, under the terms of the plan, be expressed as an annuity payable at normal retirement age, the balance of a hypothetical account, or the current value of the accumulated percentage of the employee's final average compensation.

(B) Applicable defined benefit plans—

(i) Interest credits—

(I) In general—An applicable defined benefit plan shall be treated as failing to meet the requirements of paragraph (1)(H) unless the terms of the plan provide that any interest credit (or an equivalent amount) for any plan year shall be at a rate which is not greater than a market rate of return. A plan shall not be treated as failing to meet the requirements of this subclause merely because the plan provides for a reasonable minimum guaranteed rate of return or for a rate of return that is equal to the greater of a fixed or variable rate of return.

(II) Preservation of capital—An applicable defined benefit plan shall be treated as failing to meet the requirements of paragraph (1)(H) unless the plan provides that an interest credit (or equivalent amount) of less than zero shall in no event result in the account balance or similar amount being less than the aggregate amount of contributions credited to the account.

(III) Market rate of return—The Secretary may provide by regulation for rules governing the calculation of a market rate of return for purposes of subclause (I) and for permissible methods of crediting interest to the account (including fixed or variable interest rates) resulting in effective rates of return meeting the requirements of subclause (I).

(ii) Special rule for plan conversions—If, after June 29, 2005, an applicable plan amendment is adopted, the plan shall be treated as failing to meet **the** requirements of paragraph (1)(H) unless the requirements of clause (iii) are met with respect to each individual who was a participant in the plan immediately before the adoption of the amendment.

(iii) Rate of benefit accrual—Subject to clause (iv), **the** requirements of this clause are met with respect to any participant if the accrued benefit of the participant under the terms of the plan as in effect after the amendment is not less than the sum of—

(I) the participant's accrued benefit for years of service before the effective date of the amendment, determined under the terms of the plan as in effect before the amendment, plus

(II) the participant's accrued benefit for years of service after the effective date of the amendment, determined under the terms of the plan as in effect after the amendment.

(iv) Special rules for early retirement subsidies—For purposes of clause (iii)(I), the plan shall credit the accumulation account or similar amount with the amount of any early retirement benefit or retirement-type subsidy for the plan year in which the participant retires if, as of such time, the participant has met the age, years of service, and other requirements under the plan for entitlement to such benefit or subsidy.

(v) Applicable plan amendment—For purposes of this subparagraph—

(I) In general—The term "applicable plan amendment" means an amendment to a defined benefit plan which has the effect of converting the plan to an applicable defined benefit plan.

(II) Special rule for coordinated benefits—If the benefits of 2 or more defined benefit plans established or maintained by an employer are coordinated in such a manner as to have the effect of the adoption of an amendment described in subclause (I), the sponsor of the defined benefit plan or plans providing for such coordination shall be treated as having adopted such a plan amendment as of the date such coordination begins.

(III) Multiple amendments—The Secretary shall issue regulations to prevent the avoidance of the purposes of this subparagraph through the use of 2 or more plan amendments rather than a single amendment.

(IV) Applicable defined benefit plan—For purposes of this subparagraph, the term "applicable defined benefit plan" has the meaning given such term by section 411(a)(13).

(vi) Termination requirements—An applicable defined benefit plan shall not be treated as meeting the requirements of clause (i) unless the plan provides that, upon the termination of the plan—

(I) if the interest credit rate (or an equivalent amount) under the plan is a variable rate, the rate of interest used to determine accrued benefits under the plan shall be equal to the average of the rates of interest used under the plan during the 5-year period ending on the termination date, and

(II) the interest rate and mortality table used to determine the amount of any benefit under the plan payable in the form of an annuity payable at normal retirement age shall be the rate and table specified under the plan for such purpose as of the termination date, except that if such interest rate is a variable rate, the interest rate shall be determined under the rules of subclause (I).

(C) Certain offsets permitted—A plan shall not be treated as failing to meet the requirements of paragraph (1)(H)(i) solely because the plan provides offsets against benefits under the plan to the extent such offsets are otherwise allowable in applying the requirements of section 401(a).

(D) Permitted disparities in plan contributions or benefits—A plan shall not be treated as failing to meet the requirements of paragraph (1)(H) solely because the plan provides a disparity in contributions or benefits with respect to which the requirements of section 401(l) are met.

(E) Indexing permitted—

(i) In general—A plan shall not be treated as failing to meet the requirements of paragraph (1)(H) solely because the plan provides for indexing of accrued benefits under the plan.

(ii) Protection against loss—Except in the case of any benefit provided in the form of a variable annuity, clause (i) shall not apply with respect to any indexing which results in an accrued benefit less than the accrued benefit determined without regard to such indexing.

(iii) Indexing—For purposes of this subparagraph, the term "indexing" means, in connection with an accrued benefit, the periodic adjustment of the accrued benefit by means of the application of a recognized investment index or methodology.

(F) Early retirement benefit or retirement-type subsidy—For purposes of this paragraph, the terms "early retirement benefit" and "retirement-type subsidy" have the meaning given such terms in subsection (d)(6)(B)(i).

(G) Benefit accrued to date—For purposes of this paragraph, any reference to the accrued benefit shall be a reference to such benefit accrued to date.

(c) Allocation of accrued benefits between employer and employee contributions—

(1) Accrued benefit derived from employer contributions—For purposes of this section, an employee's accrued benefit derived from employer contributions as of any applicable date is the excess, if any, of the accrued benefit for such employee as of such applicable date over the accrued benefit derived from contributions made by such employee as of such date.

(2) Accrued benefit derived from employee contributions—

(A) Plans other than defined benefit plans—In the case of a plan other than a defined benefit plan, the accrued benefit derived from contributions made by an employee as of any applicable date is—

(i) except as provided in clause (ii), the balance of the employee's separate account consisting only of his contributions and the income, expenses, gains, and losses attributable thereto, or

(ii) if a separate account is not maintained with respect to an employee's contributions under such a plan, the amount which bears the same ratio to his total accrued benefit as the total amount of the employee's contributions (less withdrawals) bears to the sum of such contributions and the contributions made on his behalf by the employer (less withdrawals).

(B) Defined benefit plans—In the case of a defined benefit plan, the accrued benefit derived from contributions made by an employee as of any applicable date is the amount equal to the employee's accumulated contributions expressed as an annual benefit commencing at normal retirement age, using an interest rate which would be used under the plan under section 417(e)(3) (as of the determination date).

(C) Definition of accumulated contributions—For purposes of this subsection, the term "accumulated contributions" means the total of—

(i) all mandatory contributions made by the employee,

(ii) interest (if any) under the plan to the end of the last plan year to which subsection (a)(2) does not apply (by reason of the applicable effective date), and

(iii) interest on the sum of the amounts determined under clauses (i) and (ii) compounded annually—

(I) at the rate of 120 percent of the Federal mid-term rate (as in effect under section 1274 for the 1st month of a plan year) for the period beginning with the 1st plan year to which subsection (a)(2) applies (by reason of the applicable effective date) and ending with the date on which the determination is being made, and

(II) at the interest rate which would be used under the plan under section 417(e)(3) (as of the determination date) for the period beginning with the determination date and ending on the date on which the employee attains normal retirement age.

For purposes of this subparagraph, the term "mandatory contributions" means amounts contributed to the plan by the employee which are required as a condition of employment, as a condition of participation in such plan, or as a condition of obtaining benefits under the plan attributable to employer contributions.

(D) Adjustments—The Secretary is authorized to adjust by regulation the conversion factor described in subparagraph (B) from time to time as he may deem necessary.

(3) Actuarial adjustment—For purposes of this section, in the case of any defined benefit plan, if an employee's accrued benefit is to be determined as an amount other than an annual benefit commencing at normal retirement age, or if the accrued benefit derived from contributions made by an employee is to be determined with respect to a benefit other than an annual benefit in the form of a single life annuity (without ancillary benefits) commencing at normal retirement age, the employee's accrued benefit, or the accrued benefits derived from contributions made by an employee, as the case may be, shall be the actuarial equivalent of such benefit or amount determined under paragraph (1) or (2).

(d) Special rules—

(1) Coordination with section 401(a)(4)—A plan which satisfies the requirements of this section shall be treated as satisfying any vesting requirements resulting from the application of section 401(a)(4) unless—

(A) there has been a pattern of abuse under the plan (such as a dismissal of employees before their accrued benefits become nonforfeitable) tending to discriminate in favor of employees who are highly compensated employees (within the meaning of section 414(q)), or

(B) there have been, or there is reason to believe there will be, an accrual of benefits or forfeitures tending to discriminate in favor of employees who are highly compensated employees (within the meaning of section 414(q)).

(2) Prohibited discrimination—Subsection (a) shall not apply to benefits which may not be provided for designated employees in the event of early termination of the plan under provisions of the plan adopted pursuant to regulations prescribed by the Secretary to preclude the discrimination prohibited by section 401(a)(4).

(3) Termination or partial termination; discontinuance of contributions—Notwithstanding the provisions of subsection (a), a trust shall not constitute a qualified trust under section 401(a) unless the plan of which such trust is a part provides that—

(A) upon its termination or partial termination, or

(B) in the case of a plan to which section 412 does not apply, upon complete discontinuance of contributions under the plan,

the rights of all affected employees to benefits accrued to the date of such termination, partial termination, or discontinuance, to the extent funded as of such date, or the amounts credited to the employees' accounts, are nonforfeitable. This paragraph shall not apply to benefits or contributions which, under provisions of the plan adopted pursuant to regulations prescribed by the Secretary to preclude the discrimination prohibited by section 401(a)(4), may not be used for designated employees in the event of early termination of the plan. For purposes of this paragraph, in the case of the complete discontinuance of contributions under a profit-sharing or stock bonus plan, such plan shall be treated as having terminated on the day on which the plan administrator notifies the Secretary (in accordance with regulations) of the discontinuance.

(4) [Repealed]

(5) Treatment of voluntary employee contributions—In the case of a defined benefit plan which permits voluntary employee contributions, the portion of an employee's accrued benefit derived from such contributions shall be treated as an accrued benefit derived from employee contributions under a plan other than a defined benefit plan.

(6) Accrued benefit not to be decreased by amendment—

(A) In general—A plan shall be treated as not satisfying the requirements of this section if the accrued benefit of a participant is decreased by an amendment of the plan, other than an amendment described in section 412(d)(2), or section 4281 of the Employee Retirement Income Security Act of 1974.

(B) Treatment of certain plan amendments—For purposes of subparagraph (A), a plan amendment which has the effect of—

(i) eliminating or reducing an early retirement benefit or a retirement-type subsidy (as defined in regulations), or

(ii) eliminating an optional form of benefit,

with respect to benefits attributable to service before the amendment shall be treated as reducing accrued benefits. In the case of a retirement-type subsidy, the preceding sentence shall apply only with respect to a participant who satisfies (either before or after the amendment) the preamendment conditions for the subsidy. The Secretary shall by regulations provide that this subparagraph shall not apply to any plan amendment which reduces or eliminates benefits or subsidies which create significant burdens or complexities for the plan and plan participants, unless such amendment adversely affects the rights of any participant in a more than de minimis manner. The Secretary may by regulations provide that this subparagraph shall not apply to a plan amendment described in clause (ii) (other than a plan amendment having an effect described in clause (i)).

(C) Special rule for ESOPs—For purposes of this paragraph, any—

(i) tax credit employee stock ownership plan (as defined in section 409(a)), or

(ii) employee stock ownership plan (as defined in section 4975(e)(7)),

shall not be treated as failing to meet the requirements of this paragraph merely because it modifies distribution options in a nondiscriminatory manner.

(D) Plan transfers—

(i) In general—A defined contribution plan (in this subparagraph referred to as the "transferee plan") shall not be treated as failing to meet the requirements of this subsection merely because the transferee plan does not provide some or all of the forms of distribution previously available under another defined contribution plan (in this subparagraph referred to as the "transferor plan") to the extent that—

(I) the forms of distribution previously available under the transferor plan applied to the account of a participant or beneficiary under the transferor plan that was transferred from the transferor plan to the transferee plan pursuant to a direct transfer rather than pursuant to a distribution from the transferor plan,

(II) the terms of both the transferor plan and the transferee plan authorize the transfer described in subclause (I),

(III) the transfer described in subclause (I) was made pursuant to a voluntary election by the participant or beneficiary whose account was transferred to the transferee plan,

(IV) the election described in subclause (III) was made after the participant or beneficiary received a notice describing the consequences of making the election, and

(V) the transferee plan allows the participant or beneficiary described in subclause (III) to receive any distribution to which the participant or beneficiary is entitled under the transferee plan in the form of a single sum distribution.

(ii) Special rule for mergers, etc—Clause (i) shall apply to plan mergers and other transactions having the effect of a direct transfer, including consolidations of benefits attributable to different employers within a multiple employer plan.

(E) Elimination of form of distribution—Except to the extent provided in regulations, a defined contribution plan shall not be treated as failing to meet the requirements of this section merely because of the elimination of a form of distribution previously available thereunder. This subparagraph shall not apply to the elimination of a form of distribution with respect to any participant unless—

(i) a single sum payment is available to such participant at the same time or times as the form of distribution being eliminated, and

(ii) such single sum payment is based on the same or greater portion of the participant's account as the form of distribution being eliminated.

(e) Application of vesting standards to certain plans—

(1) The provisions of this section (other than paragraph (2)) shall not apply to—

(A) A governmental plan (within the meaning of section 414(d)),

(B) a church plan (within the meaning of section 414(e)) with respect to which the election provided by section 410(d) has not been made,

(C) a plan which has not, at any time after September 2, 1974, provided for employer contributions, and

(D) a plan established and maintained by a society, order, or association described in section 501(c)(8) or (9), if no part of the contributions to or under such plan are made by employers of participants in such plan.

(2) A plan described in paragraph (1) shall be treated as meeting the requirements of this section, for purposes of section 401(a), if such plan meets the vesting requirements resulting from the application of sections 401(a)(4) and 401(a)(7) as in effect on September 1, 1974.

§ 412. Minimum funding standards.

(a) Requirement to meet minimum funding standard—

(1) In general—A plan to which this section applies shall satisfy the minimum funding standard applicable to the plan for any plan year.

(2) Minimum funding standard—For purposes of paragraph (1), a plan shall be treated as satisfying the minimum funding standard for a plan year if—

(A) in the case of a defined benefit plan which is not a multiemployer plan, the employer makes contributions to or under the plan for the plan year which, in the aggregate, are not less than the minimum required contribution determined under section 430 for the plan for the plan year,

(B) in the case of a money purchase plan which is not a multiemployer plan, the employer makes contributions to or under the plan for the plan year which are required under the terms of the plan, and

(C) in the case of a multiemployer plan, the employers make contributions to or under the plan for any plan year which, in the aggregate, are sufficient to ensure that the plan does not have an accumulated funding deficiency under section 431 as of the end of the plan year.

(b) Liability for contributions—

(1) In general—Except as provided in paragraph (2), the amount of any contribution required by this section (including any required installments under paragraphs (3) and (4) of section 430(j)) shall be paid by the employer responsible for making contributions to or under the plan.

(2) Joint and several liability where employer member of controlled group— If the employer referred to in paragraph (1) is a member of a controlled group, each member of such group shall be jointly and severally liable for payment of such contributions.

(3) Multiemployer plans in critical status—Paragraph (1) shall not apply in the case of a multiemployer plan for any plan year in which the plan is in critical status pursuant to section 432. This paragraph shall only apply if the plan sponsor adopts a rehabilitation plan in accordance with section 432(e) and complies with such rehabilitation plan (and any modifications of the plan).

(c) Variance from minimum funding standards—

(1) Waiver in case of business hardship—

(A) In general—If—

(i) an employer is (or in the case of a multiemployer plan, 10 percent or more of the number of employers contributing to or under the plan are) unable to satisfy the minimum funding standard for a plan year without temporary substantial business hardship (substantial business hardship in the case of a multiemployer plan), and

(ii) application of the standard would be adverse to the interests of plan participants in the aggregate,

the Secretary may, subject to subparagraph (C), waive the requirements of subsection (a) for such year with respect to all or any portion of the minimum funding standard. The Secretary shall not waive the minimum funding standard with respect to a plan for more than 3 of any 15 (5 of any 15 in the case of a multiemployer plan) consecutive plan years

(B) Effects of waiver—If a waiver is granted under subparagraph (A) for any plan year—

(i) in the case of a defined benefit plan which is not a multiemployer plan, the minimum required contribution under section 430 for the plan year shall be reduced by the amount of the waived funding deficiency and such amount shall be amortized as required under section 430(e), and

(ii) in the case of a multiemployer plan, the funding standard account shall be credited under section 431(b)(3)(C) with the amount of the waived funding deficiency and such amount shall be amortized as required under section 431(b)(2)(C).

(C) Waiver of amortized portion not allowed—The Secretary may not waive under subparagraph (A) any portion of the minimum funding standard under subsection (a) for a plan year which is attributable to any waived funding deficiency for any preceding plan year.

(2) Determination of business hardship—For purposes of this subsection, the factors taken into account in determining temporary substantial business hardship (substantial business hardship in the case of a multiemployer plan) shall include (but shall not be limited to) whether or not—

(A) the employer is operating at an economic loss,

(B) there is substantial unemployment or underemployment in the trade or business and in the industry concerned,

(C) the sales and profits of the industry concerned are depressed or declining, and

(D) it is reasonable to expect that the plan will be continued only if the waiver is granted.

(3) Waived funding deficiency—For purposes of this section and part III of this subchapter, the term "waived funding deficiency" means the portion of the minimum funding standard under subsection (a) (determined without regard to the waiver) for a plan year waived by the Secretary and not satisfied by employer contributions.

(4) Security for waivers for single-employer plans, consultations—

(A) Security may be required—

(i) In general—Except as provided in subparagraph (C), the Secretary may require an employer maintaining a defined benefit plan which is a single-employer plan (within the meaning of section 4001(a)(15) of the Employee Retirement Income Security Act of 1974) to provide security to such plan as a condition for granting or modifying a waiver under paragraph (1).

(ii) Special rules—Any security provided under clause (i) may be perfected and enforced only by the Pension Benefit Guaranty Corporation, or at the direction of the Corporation, by a contributing sponsor (within the meaning of section 4001(a)(13) of the Employee Retirement Income Security Act of 1974), or a member of such sponsor's controlled group (within the meaning of section 4001(a)(14) of such Act).

(B) Consultation with the pension benefit guaranty corporation—Except as provided in subparagraph (C), the Secretary shall, before granting or modifying a waiver under this subsection with respect to a plan described in subparagraph (A)(i)—

(i) provide the Pension Benefit Guaranty Corporation with—

(I) notice of the completed application for any waiver or modification, and

(II) an opportunity to comment on such application within 30 days after receipt of such notice, and

(ii) consider—

(I) any comments of the Corporation under clause (i)(II), and

(II) any views of any employee organization (within the meaning of section 3(4) of the Employee Retirement Income Security Act of 1974) representing participants in the plan which are submitted in writing to the Secretary in connection with such application.

Information provided to the Corporation under this subparagraph shall be considered tax return information and subject to the safeguarding and reporting requirements of section 6103(p).

(C) Exception for certain waivers—

(i) In general—The preceding provisions of this paragraph shall not apply to any plan with respect to which the sum of—

(I) the aggregate unpaid minimum required contributions (within the meaning of section 4971(c)(4)) for the plan year and all preceding plan years, and

(II) the present value of all waiver amortization installments determined for the plan year and succeeding plan years under section 430(e)(2),

is less than $1,000,000.

(ii) Treatment of waivers for which applications are pending—The amount described in clause (i)(I) shall include any increase in such amount which would result if all applications for waivers of the minimum funding standard under this subsection which are pending with respect to such plan were denied.

(5) Special rules for single-employer plans—

(A) Application must be submitted before date 2 1/2 months after close of year—In the case of a defined benefit plan which is not a multiemployer plan, no waiver may be granted under this subsection with respect to any plan for any plan year unless an application therefor is submitted to the Secretary not later than the 15th day of the 3rd month beginning after the close of such plan year.

(B) Special rule if employer is member of controlled group—In the case of a defined benefit plan which is not a multiemployer plan, if an employer is a member of a controlled group, the temporary substantial business hardship requirements of paragraph (1) shall be treated as met only if such requirements are met—

(i) with respect to such employer, and

(ii) with respect to the controlled group of which such employer is a member (determined by treating all members of such group as a single employer).

The Secretary may provide that an analysis of a trade or business or industry of a member need not be conducted if the Secretary determines such analysis is not necessary because the taking into account of such member would not significantly affect the determination under this paragraph.

(6) Advance notice—

(A) In general—The Secretary shall, before granting a waiver under this subsection, require each applicant to provide evidence satisfactory to the Secretary that the applicant has provided notice of the filing of the application for such waiver to each affected party (as defined in section 4001(a)(21) of the Employee Retirement Income Security Act of 1974). Such notice shall include a description of the extent to which the plan is funded for benefits which are guaranteed under title IV of the Employee Retirement Income Security Act of 1974 and for benefit liabilities.

(B) Consideration of relevant information—The Secretary shall consider any relevant information provided by a person to whom notice was given under subparagraph (A).

(7) Restriction on plan amendments—

(A) In general—No amendment of a plan which increases the liabilities of the plan by reason of any increase in benefits, any change in the accrual of benefits, or any change in the rate at which benefits become nonforfeitable under the plan shall be adopted if a waiver under this subsection or an extension of time under section 431(d) is in effect with respect to the plan, or if a plan amendment described in subsection (d)(2) which reduces the accrued benefit of any participant has been made at any time in the preceding 12 months (24 months in the case of a multiemployer plan). If a plan is amended in violation of the preceding sentence, any such waiver, or extension of time, shall not apply to any plan year ending on or after the date on which such amendment is adopted.

(B) Exception—Subparagraph (A) shall not apply to any plan amendment which—

(i) the Secretary determines to be reasonable and which provides for only de minimis increases in the liabilities of the plan,

(ii) only repeals an amendment described in subsection (d)(2), or

(iii) is required as a condition of qualification under part I of subchapter D, of chapter 1.

(d) Miscellaneous rules—

(1) Change in method or year—If the funding method or a plan year for a plan is changed, the change shall take effect only if approved by the Secretary.

(2) Certain retroactive plan amendments—For purposes of this section, any amendment applying to a plan year which—

(A) is adopted after the close of such plan year but no later than 2 1/2 months after the close of the plan year (or, in the case of a multiemployer plan, no later than 2 years after the close of such plan year),

(B) does not reduce the accrued benefit of any participant determined as of the beginning of the first plan year to which the amendment applies, and

(C) does not reduce the accrued benefit of any participant determined as of the time of adoption except to the extent required by the circumstances,

shall, at the election of the plan administrator, be deemed to have been made on the first day of such plan year. No amendment described in this paragraph which reduces the accrued benefits of any participant shall take effect unless the plan administrator files a notice with the Secretary notifying him of such amendment and the Secretary has approved such amendment, or within 90 days after the date on which such notice was filed, failed to disapprove such amendment. No amendment described in this subsection shall be approved by the Secretary unless the Secretary determines that such amendment is necessary because of a temporary substantial business hardship (as determined under subsection (c)(2)) or a substantial business hardship (as so determined) in the case of a multiemployer plan and that a waiver under subsection (c) (or, in the case of a multiemployer plan, any extension of the amortization period under section 431(d)) is unavailable or inadequate.

(3) Controlled group—For purposes of this section, the term "controlled group" means any group treated as a single employer under subsection (b), (c), (m), or (o) of section 414.

(e) Plans to which section applies—

(1) In general—Except as provided in paragraphs (2) and (4), this section applies to a plan if, for any plan year beginning on or after the effective date of this section for such plan under the Employee Retirement Income Security Act of 1974—

(A) such plan included a trust which qualified (or was determined by the Secretary to have qualified) under section 401(a), or

(B) such plan satisfied (or was determined by the Secretary to have satisfied) the requirements of section 403(a).

(2) Exceptions—This section shall not apply to—

(A) any profit-sharing or stock bonus plan,

(B) any insurance contract plan described in paragraph (3),

(C) any governmental plan (within the meaning of section 414(d)),

(D) any church plan (within the meaning of section 414(e)) with respect to which the election provided by section 410(d) has not been made,

(E) any plan which has not, at any time after September 2, 1974, provided for employer contributions, or

(F) any plan established and maintained by a society, order, or association described in section 501(c)(8) or (9), if no part of the contributions to or under such plan are made by employers of participants in such plan.

No plan described in subparagraph (C), (D), or (F) shall be treated as a qualified plan for purposes of section 401(a) unless such plan meets the requirements of section 401(a)(7) as in effect on September 1, 1974.

(3) Certain insurance contract plans—A plan is described in this paragraph if—

(A) the plan is funded exclusively by the purchase of individual insurance contracts,

(B) such contracts provide for level annual premium payments to be paid extending not later than the retirement age for each individual participating in the plan, and commencing with the date the individual became a participant in the plan (or, in the case of an increase in benefits, commencing at the time such increase becomes effective),

(C) benefits provided by the plan are equal to the benefits provided under each contract at normal retirement age under the plan and are guaranteed by an insurance carrier (licensed under the laws of a State to do business with the plan) to the extent premiums have been paid,

(D) premiums payable for the plan year, and all prior plan years, under such contracts have been paid before lapse or there is reinstatement of the policy,

(E) no rights under such contracts have been subject to a security interest at any time during the plan year, and

(F) no policy loans are outstanding at any time during the plan year.

A plan funded exclusively by the purchase of group insurance contracts which is determined under regulations prescribed by the Secretary to have the same characteristics as contracts described in the preceding sentence shall be treated as a plan described in this paragraph.

(4) Certain terminated multiemployer plans—This section applies with respect to a terminated multiemployer plan to which section 4021 of the Employee Retirement Income Security Act of 1974 applies until the last day of the plan year in which the plan terminates (within the meaning of section 4041A(a)(2) of such Act).

§ 413. Collectively bargained plans, etc.

(a) Application of subsection (b)—Subsection (b) applies to—

(1) a plan maintained pursuant to an agreement which the Secretary of Labor finds to be a collective-bargaining agreement between employee representatives and one or more employers, and

(2) each trust which is a part of such plan.

(b) General rule—If this subsection applies to a plan, notwithstanding any other provision of this title—

(1) Participation—Section 410 shall be applied as if all employees of each of the employers who are parties to the collective-bargaining agreement and who are subject to the same benefit computation formula under the plan were employed by a single employer.

(2) Discrimination, etc—Sections 401(a)(4) and 411(d)(3) shall be applied as if all participants who are subject to the same benefit computation formula and who are employed by employers who are parties to the collective bargaining agreement were employed by a single employer.

(3) Exclusive benefit—For purposes of section 401(a), in determining whether the plan of an employer is for the exclusive benefit of his employees and their beneficiaries, all plan participants shall be considered to be his employees.

(4) Vesting—Section 411 (other than subsection (d)(3)) shall be applied as if all employers who have been parties to the collective-bargaining agreement constituted a single employer, except that the application of any rules with respect to breaks in service shall be made under regulations prescribed by the Secretary of Labor.

(5) Funding—The minimum funding standard provided by section 412 shall be determined as if all participants in the plan were employed by a single employer.

(6) Liability for funding tax—For a plan year the liability under section 4971 of each employer who is a party to the collective bargaining agreement shall be determined in a reasonable manner not inconsistent with regulations prescribed by the Secretary—

(A) first on the basis of their respective delinquencies in meeting required employer contributions under the plan, and

(B) then on the basis of their respective liabilities for contributions under the plan.

For purposes of this subsection and the last sentence of section 4971(a), an employer's withdrawal liability under part 1 of subtitle E of title IV of the Employee Retirement Income Security Act of 1974 shall not be treated as a liability for contributions under the plan.

(7) Deduction limitations—Each applicable limitation provided by section 404(a) shall be determined as if all participants in the plan were employed by a single employer. The amounts contributed to or under the plan by each employer who is a party to the agreement, for the portion of his taxable year which is included within such a plan year, shall be considered not to exceed such a limitation if the anticipated employer contributions for such plan year (determined in a manner consistent with the manner in which actual employer contributions for such plan year are determined) do not exceed such limitation. If such anticipated contributions exceed such a limitation, the portion of each such employer's contributions which is not deductible under section 404 shall be determined in accordance with regulations prescribed by the Secretary.

(8) Employees of labor unions—For purposes of this subsection, employees of employee representatives shall be treated as employees of an employer described in subsection (a)(1) if such representatives meet the requirements of sections 401(a)(4) and 410 with respect to such employees.

(9) Plans covering a professional employee—Notwithstanding subsection (a), in the case of a plan (and trust forming part thereof) which covers any professional employee, paragraph (1) shall be applied by substituting "section 410(a) " for "section 410 ", and paragraph (2) shall not apply.

(c) Plans maintained by more than one employer—In the case of a plan maintained by more than one employer—

(1) Participation—Section 410(a) shall be applied as if all employees of each of the employers who maintain the plan were employed by a single employer.

(2) Exclusive benefit—For purposes of section 401(a), in determining whether the plan of an employer is for the exclusive benefit of his employees and their beneficiaries all plan participants shall be considered to be his employees.

(3) Vesting—Section 411 shall be applied as if all employers who maintain the plan constituted a single employer, except that the application of any rules with respect to breaks in service shall be made under regulations prescribed by the Secretary of Labor.

(4) Funding—

(A) In general In the case of a plan established after December 31, 1988, each employer shall be treated as maintaining a separate plan for purposes of section 412 unless such plan uses a method for determining required contributions which provides that any employer contributes not less than the amount which would be required if such employer maintained a separate plan.

(B) Other plans—In the case of a plan not described in subparagraph (A), the requirements of section 412 shall be determined as if all participants in the plan were employed by a single employer unless the plan administrator elects not later than the close of the first plan year of the plan beginning after the date of enactment of the Technical and Miscellaneous Revenue Act of 1988 to have the provisions of subparagraph (A) apply. An election under the preceding sentence shall take effect for the plan year in which made and, once made, may be revoked only with the consent of the Secretary.

(5) Liability for funding tax—For a plan year the liability under section 4971 of each employer who maintains the plan shall be determined in a reasonable manner not inconsistent with regulations prescribed by the Secretary—

(A) first on the basis of their respective delinquencies in meeting required employer contributions under the plan, and

(B) then on the basis of their respective liabilities for contributions under the plan.

(6) Deduction limitations—

(A) In general—In the case of a plan established after December 31, 1988, each applicable limitation provided by section 404(a) shall be determined as if each employer were maintaining a separate plan.

(B) Other plans—

(i) In general—In the case of a plan not described in subparagraph (A), each applicable limitation provided by section 404(a) shall be determined as if all participants in the plan were employed by a single employer, except that if an election is made under paragraph (4)(B), subparagraph (A) shall apply to such plan.

(ii) Special rule—If this subparagraph applies, the amounts contributed to or under the plan by each employer who maintains the plan (for the portion of the taxable year included within a plan year) shall be considered not to exceed any such limitation if the anticipated employer contributions for such plan year (determined in a reasonable manner not inconsistent with regulations prescribed by the Secretary) do not exceed such limitation. If such anticipated contributions exceed such a limitation, the portion of each such employer's contributions which is not deductible under section 404 shall be determined in accordance with regulations prescribed by the Secretary.

(7) Allocations—

(A) In general—Except as provided in subparagraph (B), allocations of amounts under paragraphs (4), (5), and (6) among the employers maintaining the plan shall not be inconsistent with regulations prescribed for this purpose by the Secretary.

(B) Assets and liabilities of plan—For purposes of applying paragraphs (4)(A) and (6)(A), the assets and liabilities of each plan shall be treated as the assets and liabilities which would be allocated to a plan maintained by the employer if the employer withdrew from the multiple employer plan.

§ 414. Definitions and special rules.

(a) Service for predecessor employer—For purposes of this part—

(1) in any case in which the employer maintains a plan of a predecessor employer, service for such predecessor shall be treated as service for the employer, and

(2) in any case in which the employer maintains a plan which is not the plan maintained by a predecessor employer, service for such predecessor shall, to the extent provided in regulations prescribed by the Secretary, be treated as service for the employer.

(b) Employees of controlled group of corporations—For purposes of sections 401, 408(k), 408(p), 410, 411, 415, and 416, all employees of all corporations which are members of a controlled group of corporations (within the meaning of section 1563(a), determined without regard to section 1563(a)(4) and (e)(3)(C)) shall be treated as employed by a single employer. With respect to a plan adopted by more than one such corporation, the applicable limitations provided by section 404(a) shall be determined as if all such employers were a single employer, and allocated to each employer in accordance with regulations prescribed by the Secretary.

(c) Employees of partnerships, proprietorships, etc., which are under common control—For purposes of sections 401, 408(k), 408(p), 410, 411, 415, and 416, under regulations prescribed by the Secretary, all employees of trades or businesses (whether or not incorporated) which are under common control shall be treated as employed by a single employer. The regulations prescribed under this subsection shall be based on principles similar to the principles which apply in the case of subsection (b).

(d) Governmental plan—For purposes of this part, the term "governmental plan" means a plan established and maintained for its employees by the Government of the United States, by the government of any State or political subdivision thereof, or by any agency or instrumentality of any of the foregoing. The term "governmental plan" also includes any plan to which the Railroad Retirement Act of 1935 or 1937 applies and which is financed by contributions required under that Act and any plan of an international organization which is exempt from taxation by reason of the International Organizations Immunities Act (59 Stat. 669). The term "governmental plan" includes a plan which is established and maintained by an Indian tribal government (as defined in section 7701(a)(40)), a subdivision of an Indian tribal government (determined in accordance with section 7871(d)), or an agency or instrumentality of either, and all of the participants of which are employees of such entity substantially all of whose services as such an employee are in the performance of essential governmental functions but not in the performance of commercial activities (whether or not an essential government function).

(e) Church plan—

(1) In general—For purposes of this part, the term "church plan" means a plan established and maintained (to the extent required in paragraph (2)(B)) for its employees (or their beneficiaries) by a church or by a convention or association of churches which is exempt from tax under section 501.

(2) Certain plans excluded—The term "church plan" does not include a plan—

(A) which is established and maintained primarily for the benefit of employees (or their beneficiaries) of such church or convention or association of churches who are employed in connection with one or more unrelated trades or businesses (within the meaning of section 513); or

(B) if less than substantially all of the individuals included in the plan are individuals described in paragraph (1) or (3)(B) (or their beneficiaries).

* * *

(f) Multiemployer plan—

(1) Definition—For purposes of this part, the term "multiemployer plan" means a plan—

(A) to which more than one employer is required to contribute,

(B) which is maintained pursuant to one or more collective bargaining agreements between one or more employee organizations and more than one employer, and

(C) which satisfies such other requirements as the Secretary of Labor may prescribe by regulation.

(2) Cases of common control—For purposes of this subsection, all trades or businesses (whether or not incorporated) which are under common control within the meaning of subsection (c) are considered a single employer.

* * *

(h) Tax treatment of certain contributions—

(1) In general—Effective with respect to taxable years beginning after December 31, 1973, for purposes of this title, any amount contributed—

(A) to an employees' trust described in section 401(a), or

(B) under a plan described in section 403(a),

shall not be treated as having been made by the employer if it is designated as an employee contribution.

(2) Designation by units of government—For purposes of paragraph (1), in the case of any plan established by the government of any State or political subdivision thereof, or by any agency or instrumentality of any of the foregoing, or a governmental plan described in the last sentence of section 414(d) (relating to plans of Indian tribal governments), where the contributions of employing units are designated as employee contributions but where any employing unit picks up the contributions, the contributions so picked up shall be treated as employer contributions.

(i) Defined contribution plan—For purposes of this part, the term "defined contribution plan" means a plan which provides for an individual account for each participant and for benefits based solely on the amount contributed to the participant's account, and any income, expenses, gains and losses, and any forfeitures of accounts of other participants which may be allocated to such participant's account.

(j) Defined benefit plan—For purposes of this part, the term "defined benefit plan" means any plan which is not a defined contribution plan.

(k) Certain plans—A defined benefit plan which provides a benefit derived from employer contributions which is based partly on the balance of the separate account of a participant shall—

(1) for purposes of section 410 (relating to minimum participation standards), be treated as a defined contribution plan,

(2) for purposes of sections 72(d) (relating to treatment of employee contributions as separate contract), 411(a)(7)(A) (relating to minimum vesting standards), 415 (relating to limitations on benefits and contributions under qualified plans), and 401(m) (relating to nondiscrimination tests for matching requirements and employee contributions), be treated as consisting of a defined contribution plan to the extent benefits are based on the separate account of a participant and as a defined benefit plan with respect to the remaining portion of benefits under the plan, and

(3) for purposes of section 4975 (relating to tax on prohibited transactions), be treated as a defined benefit plan.

(l) Merger and consolidations of plans or transfers of plan assets—

(1) In general—A trust which forms a part of a plan shall not constitute a qualified trust under section 401 and a plan shall be treated as not described in section 403(a) unless in the case of any merger or consolidation of the plan with, or in the case of any transfer of assets or liabilities of such plan to, any other trust plan after September 2, 1974, each participant in the plan would (if the plan then terminated) receive a benefit immediately after the merger, consolidation, or transfer which is equal to or greater than the benefit he would have been entitled to receive immediately before the merger, consolidation, or transfer (if the plan had then terminated). The preceding sentence does not apply to any multiemployer plan with respect to any transaction to the extent that participants either before or after the transaction are covered under a multiemployer plan to which Title IV of the Employee Retirement Income Security Act of 1974 applies.

(2) Allocation of assets in plan spin-offs, etc—

(A) In general—In the case of a plan spin-off of a defined benefit plan, a trust which forms part of—

(i) the original plan, or

(ii) any plan spun off from such plan, shall not constitute a qualified trust under this section unless the applicable percentage of excess assets are allocated to each of such plans.

(B) Applicable percentage—For purposes of subparagraph (A), the term "applicable percentage" means, with respect to each of the plans described in clauses (i) and (ii) of subparagraph (A), the percentage determined by dividing—

(i) the excess (if any) of—

(I) the sum of the funding target and target normal cost determined under section 430, over

(II) the amount of the assets required to be allocated to the plan after the spin-off (without regard to this paragraph), by

(ii) the sum of the excess amounts determined separately under clause (i) for all such plans.

(C) Excess assets—For purposes of subparagraph (A), the term "excess assets" means an amount equal to the excess (if any) of—

(i) the fair market value of the assets of the original plan immediately before the spin-off, over

(ii) the amount of assets required to be allocated after the spin-off to all plans (determined without regard to this paragraph).

(D) Certain spun-off plans not taken into account—

(i) In general—A plan involved in a spin-off which is described in clause (ii), (iii), or (iv) shall not be taken into account for purposes of this paragraph, except that the amount determined under subparagraph (C)(ii) shall be increased by the amount of assets allocated to such plan.

(ii) Plans transferred out of controlled groups—A plan is described in this clause if, after such spin-off, such plan is maintained by an employer who is not a member of the same controlled group as the employer maintaining the original plan.

(iii) Plans transferred out of multiple employer plans—A plan as described in this clause if, after the spin-off, any employer maintaining such plan (and any member of the same controlled group as such employer) does not maintain any other plan remaining after the spin-off which is also maintained by another employer (or member of the same controlled group as such other employer) which maintained the plan in existence before the spin-off.

(iv) Terminated plans—A plan is described in this clause if, pursuant to the transaction involving the spin-off, the plan is terminated.

(v) Controlled group—For purposes of this subparagraph, the term "controlled group" means any group treated as a single employer under subsection (b), (c), (m), or (o).

(E) Paragraph not to apply to multiemployer plans—This paragraph does not apply to any multiemployer plan with respect to any spin-off to the extent that participants either before or after the spin-off are covered under a multiemployer plan to which title IV of the Employee Retirement Income Security Act of 1974 applies.

* * *

(m) Employees of an affiliated service group—

(1) In general—For purposes of the employee benefit requirements listed in paragraph (4), except to the extent otherwise provided in regulations, all employees of the members of an affiliated service group shall be treated as employed by a single employer.

(2) Affiliated service group—For purposes of this subsection, the term "affiliated service group" means a group consisting of a service organization (hereinafter in this paragraph referred to as the "first organization") and one or more of the following:

(A) any service organization which—

(i) is a shareholder or partner in the first organization, and

(ii) regularly performs services for the first organization or is regularly associated with the first organization in performing services for third persons, and

(B) any other organization if—

(i) a significant portion of the business of such organization is the performance of services (for the first organization, for organizations described in subparagraph (A), or for both) of a type historically performed in such service field by employees, and

(ii) 10 percent or more of the interests in such organization is held by persons who are highly compensated employees (within the meaning of section 414(q)) of the first organization or an organization described in subparagraph (A).

(3) Service organizations—For purposes of this subsection, the term "service organization" means an organization the principal business of which is the performance of services.

(4) Employee benefit requirements—For purposes of this subsection, the employee benefit requirements listed in this paragraph are—

(A) paragraphs (3), (4), (7), (16), (17), and (26) of section 401(a), and

(B) sections 408(k), 408(p), 410, 411, 415, and 416.

(5) Certain organizations performing management functions—For purposes of this subsection, the term "affiliated service group" also includes a group consisting of—

(A) an organization the principal business of which is performing, on a regular and continuing basis, management functions for 1 organization (or for 1 organization and other organizations related to such 1 organization), and

(B) the organization (and related organizations) for which such functions are so performed by the organization described in subparagraph (A).

For purposes of this paragraph, the term "related organizations" has the same meaning as the term "related persons" when used in section 144(a)(3).

(6) Other definitions—For purposes of this subsection—

(A) Organization defined—The term "organization" means a corporation, partnership, or other organization.

(B) Ownership—In determining ownership, the principles of section 318(a) shall apply.

(n) Employee leasing—

(1) In general—For purposes of the requirements listed in paragraph (3), with respect to any person (hereinafter in this subsection referred to as the "recipient") for whom a leased employee performs services—

(A) the leased employee shall be treated as an employee of the recipient, but

(B) contributions or benefits provided by the leasing organization which are attributable to services performed for the recipient shall be treated as provided by the recipient.

(2) Leased employee—For purposes of paragraph (1), the term "leased employee" means any person who is not an employee of the recipient and who provides services to the recipient if—

(A) such services are provided pursuant to an agreement between the recipient and any other person (in this subsection referred to as the "leasing organization"),

(B) such person has performed such services for the recipient (or for the recipient and related persons) on a substantially full-time basis for a period of at least 1 year, and

(C) such services are performed under primary direction or control by the recipient.

(3) Requirements—For purposes of this subsection, the requirements listed in this paragraph are—

(A) paragraphs (3), (4), (7), (16), (17), and (26) of section 401(a),

(B) sections 408(k), 408(p), 410, 411, 415, and 416, and

(C) sections 79, 106, 117(d), 120, 125, 127, 129, 132, 137, 274(j), 505, and 4980B.

(4) Time when first considered as employee—

(A) In general—In the case of any leased employee, paragraph (1) shall apply only for purposes of determining whether the requirements listed in paragraph (3) are met for periods after the close of the period referred to in paragraph (2)(B).

(B) Years of service—In the case of a person who is an employee of the recipient (whether by reason of this subsection or otherwise), for purposes of the requirements listed in paragraph (3), years of service for the recipient shall be determined by taking into account any period for which such employee would have been a leased employee but for the requirements of paragraph (2)(B).

(5) Safe harbor—

(A) In general—In the case of requirements described in subparagraphs (A) and (B) of paragraph (3), this subsection shall not apply to any leased employee with respect to services performed for a recipient if—

(i) such employee is covered by a plan which is maintained by the leasing organization and meets the requirements of subparagraph (B), and

(ii) leased employee (determined without regard to this paragraph) do not constitute more than 20 percent of the recipient's nonhighly compensated work force.

(B) Plan requirements—A plan meets the requirements of this subparagraph if—

(i) such plan is a money purchase pension plan with a nonintegrated employer contribution rate for each participant of at least 10 percent of compensation,

(ii) such plan provides for full and immediate vesting, and

(iii) each employee of the leasing organization (other than employees who perform substantially all of their services for the leasing organization) immediately participates in such plan.

Clause (iii) shall not apply to any individual whose compensation from the leasing organization in each plan year during the 4-year period ending with the plan year is less than $1,000.

* * *

(o) Regulations—The Secretary shall prescribe such regulations (which may provide rules in addition to the rules contained in subsections (m) and (n)) as may be necessary to prevent the avoidance of any employee benefit requirement listed in subsection (m)(4) or (n)(3) or any requirement under section 457 through the use of—

(1) separate organizations,

(2) employee leasing, or

(3) other arrangements.

The regulations prescribed under subsection (n) shall include provisions to minimize the recordkeeping requirements of subsection (n) in the case of an employer which has no top-heavy plans (within the meaning of section 416(g)) and which uses the services of persons (other than employees) for an insignificant percentage of the employer's total workload.

(p) Qualified domestic relations order defined—For purposes of this subsection and section 401(a)(13)—

(1) In general—

(A) Qualified domestic relations order—The term "qualified domestic relations order" means a domestic relations order—

(i) which creates or recognizes the existence of an alternate payee's right to, or assigns to an alternate payee the right to, receive all or a portion of the benefits payable with respect to a participant under a plan, and

(ii) with respect to which the requirements of paragraphs (2) and (3) are met.

(B) Domestic relations order—The term "domestic relations order" means any judgment, decree, or order (including approval of a property settlement agreement) which—

(i) relates to the provision of child support, alimony payments, or marital property rights to a spouse, former spouse, child, or other dependent of a participant, and

(ii) is made pursuant to a State domestic relations law (including a community property law).

(2) Order must clearly specify certain facts—A domestic relations order meets the requirements of this paragraph only if such order clearly specifies—

(A) the name and the last known mailing address (if any) of the participant and the name and mailing address of each alternate payee covered by the order,

(B) the amount or percentage of the participant's benefits to be paid by the plan to each such alternate payee, or the manner in which such amount or percentage is to be determined,

(C) the number of payments or period to which such order applies, and

(D) each plan to which such order applies.

(3) Order may not alter amount, form, etc., of benefits—A domestic relations order meets the requirements of this paragraph only if such order—

(A) does not require a plan to provide any type or form of benefit, or any option, not otherwise provided under the plan,

(B) does not require the plan to provide increased benefits (determined on the basis of actuarial value), and

(C) does not require the payment of benefits to an alternate payee which are required to be paid to another alternate payee under another order previously determined to be a qualified domestic relations order.

(4) Exception for certain payments made after earliest retirement age—

(A) In general—A domestic relations order shall not be treated as failing to meet the requirements of subparagraph (A) of paragraph (3) solely because such order requires that payment of benefits be made to an alternate payee—

(i) in the case of any payment before a participant has separated from service, on or after the date on which the participant attains (or would have attained) the earliest retirement age,

(ii) as if the participant had retired on the date on which such payment is to begin under such order (but taking into account only the present value of the benefits actually accrued and not taking into account the present value of any employer subsidy for early retirement), and

(iii) in any form in which such benefits may be paid under the plan to the participant (other than in the form of a joint and survivor annuity with respect to the alternate payee and his or her subsequent spouse).

For purposes of clause (ii), the interest rate assumption used in determining the present value shall be the interest rate specified in the plan or, if no rate is specified, 5 percent.

(B) Earliest retirement age—Purposes of this paragraph, the term "earliest retirement age" means the earlier of—

(i) the date on which the participant is entitled to a distribution under the plan, or

(ii) the later of—

(I) the date the participant attains age 50, or

(II) the earliest date on which the participant could begin receiving benefits under the plan if the participant separated from service.

(5) Treatment of former spouse as surviving spouse for purposes of determining survivor benefits—To the extent provided in any qualified domestic relations order—

(A) the former spouse of a participant shall be treated as a surviving spouse of such participant for purposes of sections 401(a)(11) and 417 (and any spouse of the participant shall not be treated as a spouse of the participant for such purposes), and

(B) if married for at least 1 year, the surviving former spouse shall be treated as meeting the requirements of section 417(d).

(6) Plan procedures with respect to orders—

(A) Notice and determination by administrator—In the case of any domestic relations order received by a plan—

(i) the plan administrator shall promptly notify the participant and each alternate payee of the receipt of such order and the plan's procedures for determining the qualified status of domestic relations orders, and

(ii) within a reasonable period after receipt of such order, the plan administrator shall determine whether such order is a qualified domestic relations order and notify the participant and each alternate payee of such determination.

(B) Plan to establish reasonable procedures—Each plan shall establish reasonable procedures to determine the qualified status of domestic relations orders and to administer distributions under such qualified orders.

(7) Procedures for period during which determination is being made—

(A) In general—During any period in which the issue of whether a domestic relations order is a qualified domestic relations order is being determined (by the plan administrator, by a court of competent jurisdiction, or otherwise), the plan administrator shall separately account for the amounts (hereinafter in this paragraph referred to as the "segregated amounts") which would have been payable to the alternate payee during such period if the order had been determined to be a qualified domestic relations order.

(B) Payment to alternate payee if order determined to be qualified domestic relations order—If within the 18-month period described in subparagraph (E) the order (or modification thereof) is determined to be a qualified domestic relations order, the plan administrator shall pay the segregated amounts (including any interest thereon) to the person or persons entitled thereto.

(C) Payment to plan participant in certain cases—If within the 18-month period described in subparagraph (E)—

(i) it is determined that the order is not a qualified domestic relations order, or

(ii) the issue as to whether such order is a qualified domestic relations order is not resolved,

then the plan administrator shall pay the segregated amounts (including any interest thereon) to the person or persons who would have been entitled to such amounts if there had been no order.

(D) Subsequent determination or order to be applied prospectively only—Any determination that an order is a qualified domestic relations order which is made after the close of the 18-month period described in subparagraph (E) shall be applied prospectively only.

(E) Determination of 18-month period—For purposes of this paragraph, the 18-month period described in this subparagraph is the 18-month period beginning with the date on which the first payment would be required to be made under the domestic relations order.

(8) Alternate payee defined—The term "alternate payee" means any spouse, former spouse, child or other dependent of a participant who is recognized by a domestic relations order as having a right to receive all, or a portion of, the benefits payable under a plan with respect to such participant.

(9) Subsection not to apply to plans to which section 401(a)(13) does not apply—This subsection shall not apply to any plan to which section 401(a)(13) does not apply. For purposes of this title, except as provided in regulations, any distribution from an annuity contract under section 403(b) pursuant to a qualified domestic relations order shall be treated in the same manner as a distribution from a plan to which section 401(a)(13) applies.

(10) Waiver of certain distribution requirements—With respect to the requirements of subsections (a) and (k) of section 401, section 403(b), section 409(d), and section 457(d), plan shall not be treated as failing to meet such requirements solely by reason of payments to an alternative payee pursuant to a qualified domestic relations order.

(11) Application of rules to certain other plans—For purposes of this title, a distribution or payment from a governmental plan (as defined in subsection (d)) or a church plan (as described in subsection (e)) or an eligible deferred compensation plan (within the meaning of section 457(b)) shall be treated as made pursuant to a qualified domestic relations order if it is made pursuant to a domestic relations order which meets the requirement of clause (i) of paragraph (1)(A).

(12) Tax treatment of payments from a section 457 plan—If a distribution or payment from an eligible deferred compensation plan described in section 457(b) is made pursuant to a qualified domestic relations order, rules similar to the rules of section 402(e)(1)(A) shall apply to such distribution or payment.

(13) Consultation with the Secretary—In prescribing regulations under this subsection and section 401(a)(13), the Secretary of Labor shall consult with the Secretary.

(q) Highly compensated employee—

(1) In general—The term "highly compensated employee" means any employee who—

(A) was a 5-percent owner at any time during the year or the preceding year, or

(B) for the preceding year—

(i) had compensation from the employer in excess of $80,000, and

(ii) if the employer elects the application of this clause for such preceding year, was in the top-paid group of employees for such preceding year.

The Secretary shall adjust the $80,000 amount under subparagraph (B) at the same time and in the same manner as under section 415(d), except that the base period shall be the calendar quarter ending September 30, 1996.

(2) 5-percent owner—An employee shall be treated as a 5-percent owner for any year if at any time during such year such employee was a 5-percent owner (as defined in section 416(i)(1)) of the employer.

(3) Top-paid group—An employee is in the top-paid group of employees for any year if such employee is in the group consisting of the top 20 percent of the employees when ranked on the basis of compensation paid during such year.

(4) Compensation—For purposes of this subsection, the term "compensation" has the meaning given such term by section 415(c)(3).

(5) Excluded employees—For purposes of subsection (r) and for purposes of determining the number of employees in the top-paid group, the following employees shall be excluded—

(A) employees who have not completed 6 months of service,

(B) employees who normally work less than 17½ hours per week,

(C) employees who normally work during not more than 6 months during any year,

(D) employees who have not attained age 21, and

(E) except to the extent provided in regulations, employees who are included in a unit of employees covered by an agreement which the Secretary of Labor finds to be a collective bargaining agreement between employee representatives and the employer.

Except as provided by the Secretary, the employer may elect to apply subparagraph (A), (B), (C), or (D) by substituting a shorter period of service, smaller number of hours or months, or lower age for the period of service, number of hours or months, or age (as the case may be) than that specified in such subparagraph.

(6) Former employees—A former employee shall be treated as a highly compensated employee if—

(A) such employee was a highly compensated employee when such employee separated from service, or

(B) such employee was a highly compensated employee at any time after attaining age 55.

(7) Coordination with other provisions—Subsections (b), (c), (m), (n), and (o) shall be applied before the application of this subsection.

(8) Special rule for nonresident aliens—For purposes of this subsection and subsection (r), employees who are nonresident aliens and who receive no earned income (within the meaning of section 911(d)(2)) from the employer which constitutes income from sources within the United States (within the meaning of section 861(a)(3)) shall not be treated as employees.

* * *

(r) Special rules for separate line of business—

(1) In general—For purposes of sections 129(d)(8) and 410(b), an employer shall be treated as operating separate lines of business during any year if the employer for bona fide business reasons operates separate lines of business.

(2) Line of business must have 50 employees, etc—A line of business shall not be treated as separate under paragraph (1) unless—

(A) such line of business has at least 50 employees who are not excluded under subsection (q)(5),

(B) the employer notifies the Secretary that such line of business is being treated as separate for purposes of paragraph (1), and

(C) such line of business meets guidelines prescribed by the Secretary or the employer receives a determination from the Secretary that such line of business may be treated as separate for purposes of paragraph (1).

(3) Safe harbor rule—

(A) In general—The requirements of subparagraph (C) of paragraph (2) shall not apply to any line of business if the highly compensated employee percentage with respect to such line of business is—

(i) not less than one-half, and

(ii) not more than twice,

the percentage which highly compensated employees are of all employees of the employer. An employer shall be treated as meeting the requirements of clause (i) if at least 10 percent of all highly compensated employees of the employer perform services solely for such line of business.

(B) Determination may be based on preceding year—The requirements of subparagraph (A) shall be treated as met with respect to any line of business if such requirements were met with respect to such line of business for the preceding year and if—

(i) no more than a de minimis number of employees were shifted to or from the line of business after the close of the preceding year, or

(ii) the employees shifted to or from the line of business after the close of the preceding year contained a substantially proportional number of highly compensated employees.

(4) Highly compensated employee percentage defined—For purposes of this subsection, the term "highly compensated employee percentage" means the percentage which highly compensated employees performing services for the line of business are of all employees performing services for the line of business.

(5) Allocation of benefits to line of business—For purposes of this subsection, benefits which are attributable to services provided to a line of business shall be treated as provided by such line of business.

(6) Headquarters personnel, etc—The Secretary shall prescribe rules providing for—

(A) the allocation of headquarters personnel among the lines of business of the employer, and

(B) the treatment of other employees providing services for more than 1 line of business of the employer or not in lines of business meeting the requirements of paragraph (2).

(7) Separate operating units—For purposes of this subsection, the term "separate line of business" includes an operating unit in a separate geographic area separately operated for a bona fide business reason.

(8) Affiliated service groups—This subsection shall not apply in the case of any affiliated service group (within the meaning of section 414(m)).

(s) Compensation—For purposes of any applicable provision—

(1) In general—Except as provided in this subsection, the term "compensation" has the meaning given such term by section 415(c)(3).

(2) Employer may elect not to treat certain deferrals as compensation—An employer may elect not to include as compensation any amount which is contributed by the employer pursuant to a salary reduction agreement and which is not includible in the gross income of an employee under section 125, 132(f)(4), 402(e)(3), 402(h) or 403(b).

(3) Alternative determination of compensation—The Secretary shall by regulation provide for alternative methods of determining compensation which may be used by an employer, except that such regulations shall provide that an employer may not use an alternative method if the use of such method discriminates in favor of highly compensated employees (within the meaning of subsection (q)).

(4) Applicable provision—For purposes of this subsection, the term "applicable provision" means any provision which specifically refers to this subsection.

(t) Application of controlled group rules to certain employee benefits—

(1) In general—All employees who are treated as employed by a single employer under subsection (b), (c), or (m) shall be treated as employed by a single employer for purposes of an applicable section. The provisions of subsection (o) shall apply with respect to the requirements of an applicable section.

(2) Applicable section—For purposes of this subsection, the term "applicable section" means section 79, 106, 117(d), 120, 125, 127, 129, 132, 137, 274(j), 505, or 4980B.

(u) Special rules relating to veterans' reemployment rights under USERRA and to differential wage payments to members on active duty—

(1) Treatment of certain contributions made pursuant to veterans' reemployment rights—If any contribution is made by an employer or an employee under an individual account plan with respect to an employee, or by an employee to a defined benefit plan that provides for employee contributions, and such contribution is required by reason of such employee's rights under chapter 43 of title 38, United States Code, resulting from qualified military service, then—

(A) such contribution shall not be subject to any otherwise applicable limitation contained in section 402(g), 402(h), 403(b), 404(a), 404(h), 408, 415, or 457, and shall not be taken into account in applying such limitations to other contributions or benefits under such plan or any other plan, with respect to the year in which the contribution is made,

(B) such contribution shall be subject to the limitations referred to in subparagraph (A) with respect to the year to which the contribution relates (in accordance with rules prescribed by the Secretary), and

(C) such plan shall not be treated as failing to meet the requirements of section 401(a)(4), 401(a)(26), 401(k)(3), 401(k)(11), 401(k)(12), 401(m), 403(b)(12), 408(k)(3), 408(k)(6), 408(p), 410(b), or 416 by reason of the making of (or the right to make) such contribution.

For purposes of the preceding sentence, any elective deferral or employee contribution made under paragraph (2) shall be treated as required by reason of the employee's rights under such chapter 43.

(2) Reemployment rights under USERRA with respect to elective deferrals—

(A) In general—For purposes of this subchapter and section 457, if an employee is entitled to the benefits of chapter 43 of title 38, United States Code, with respect to any plan which provides for elective deferrals, the employer sponsoring the plan shall be treated as meeting the requirements of such chapter 43 with respect to such elective deferrals only if such employer—

(i) permits such employee to make additional elective deferrals under such plan (in the amount determined under subparagraph (B) or such lesser amount as is elected by the employee) during the period which begins on the date of the reemployment of such employee with such employer and has the same length as the lesser of—

(I) the product of 3 and the period of qualified military service which resulted in such rights, and

(II) 5 years, and

(ii) makes a matching contribution with respect to any additional elective deferral made pursuant to clause (i) which would have been required had such deferral actually been made during the period of such qualified military service.

(B) Amount of makeup required—The amount determined under this subparagraph with respect to any plan is the maximum amount of the elective deferrals that the individual would have been permitted to make under the plan in accordance with the limitations referred to in paragraph (1)(A) during the period of qualified military service if the individual had continued to be employed by the employer during such period and received compensation as determined under paragraph (7). Proper adjustment shall be made to the amount determined under the preceding sentence for any elective deferrals actually made during the period of such qualified military service.

(C) Elective deferral—For purposes of this paragraph, the term "elective deferral" has the meaning given such term by section 402(g)(3); except that such term shall include any deferral of compensation under an eligible deferred compensation plan (as defined in section 457(b)).

(D) After-tax employee contributions—References in subparagraphs (A) and (B) to elective deferrals shall be treated as including references to employee contributions.

(3) Certain retroactive adjustments not required—For purposes of this subchapter and subchapter E, no provision of chapter 43 of title 38, United States Code, shall be construed as requiring—

(A) any crediting of earnings to an employee with respect to any contribution before such contribution is actually made, or

(B) any allocation of any forfeiture with respect to the period of qualified military service.

(4) Loan repayment suspensions permitted—If any plan suspends the obligation to repay any loan made to an employee from such plan for any part of any period during which such employee is performing service in the uniformed services (as defined in chapter 43 of title 38, United States Code), whether or not qualified military service, such suspension shall not be taken into account for purposes of section 72(p), 401(a), or 4975(d)(1).

(5) Qualified military service—For purposes of this subsection, the term "qualified military service" means any service in the uniformed services (as defined in chapter 43 of title 38, United States Code) by any individual if such individual is entitled to reemployment rights under such chapter with respect to such service.

(6) Individual account plan—For purposes of this subsection, the term "individual account plan" means any defined contribution plan (including any tax-sheltered annuity plan under section 403(b), any simplified employee pension under section 408(k), any qualified salary reduction arrangement under section 408(p), and any eligible deferred compensation plan (as defined in section 457(b)).

(7) Compensation—For purposes of sections 403(b)(3), 415(c)(3), and 457(e)(5), an employee who is in qualified military service shall be treated as receiving compensation from the employer during such period of qualified military service equal to—

(A) the compensation the employee would have received during such period if the employee were not in qualified military service, determined based on the rate of pay the employee would have received from the employer but for absence during the period of qualificd military service, or

(B) if the compensation the employee would have received during such period was not reasonably certain, the employee's average compensation from the employer during the 12-month period immediately preceding the qualified military service (or, if shorter, the period of employment immediately preceding the qualified military service).

(8) USERRA requirements for qualified retirement plans—For purposes of this subchapter and section 457, an employer sponsoring a retirement plan shall be treated as meeting the requirements of chapter 43 of title 38, United States Code, only if each of the following requirements is met:

(A) An individual reemployed under such chapter is treated with respect to such plan as not having incurred a break in service with the employer maintaining the plan by reason of such individual's period of qualified military service.

(B) Each period of qualified military service served by an individual is, upon reemployment under such chapter, deemed with respect to such plan to constitute service with the employer maintaining the plan for the purpose of determining the nonforfeitability of the individual's accrued benefits under such plan and for the purpose of determining the accrual of benefits under such plan.

(C) An individual reemployed under such chapter is entitled to accrued benefits that are contingent on the making of, or derived from, employee contributions or elective deferrals only to the extent the individual makes payment to the plan with respect to such contributions or deferrals. No such payment may exceed the amount the individual would have been permitted or required to contribute had the individual remained continuously employed by the employer throughout the period of qualified military service. Any payment to such plan shall be made during the period beginning with the date of reemployment and whose duration is 3 times the period of the qualified military service (but not greater than 5 years).

(9) Treatment in the case of death or disability resulting from active military service—

(A) In general—For benefit accrual purposes, an employer sponsoring a retirement plan may treat an individual who dies or becomes disabled (as defined under the terms of the plan) while performing qualified military service with respect to the employer maintaining the plan as if the individual has resumed employment in accordance with the individual's reemployment rights under chapter 43 of title 38, United States Code, on the day preceding death or disability (as the case may be) and terminated employment on the actual date of death or disability. In the case of any such treatment, and subject to subparagraphs (B) and (C), any full or partial compliance by such plan with respect to the benefit accrual requirements of paragraph (8) with respect to such individual shall be treated for purposes of paragraph (1) as if such compliance were required under such chapter 43.

(B) Nondiscrimination requirement—Subparagraph (A) shall apply only if all individuals performing qualified military service with respect to the employer maintaining the plan (as determined under subsections (b), (c), (m), and (o)) who die or became disabled as a result of performing qualified military service prior to reemployment by the employer are credited with service and benefits on reasonably equivalent terms.

(C) Determination of benefits—The amount of employee contributions and the amount of elective deferrals of an individual treated as reemployed under subparagraph (A) for purposes of applying paragraph (8)(C) shall be determined on the basis of the individual's average actual employee contributions or elective deferrals for the lesser of—

(i) the 12-month period of service with the employer immediately prior to qualified military service, or

(ii) if service with the employer is less than such 12-month period, the actual length of continuous service with the employer.

(10) Plans not subject to title 38—This subsection shall not apply to any retirement plan to which chapter 43 of title 38, United States Code, does not apply.

(11) References—For purposes of this section, any reference to chapter 43 of title 38, United States Code, shall be treated as a reference to such chapter as in effect on December 12, 1994 (without regard to any subsequent amendment).

(12) Treatment of differential wage payments—

(A) In general—Except as provided in this paragraph, for purposes of applying this title to a retirement plan to which this subsection applies—

(i) an individual receiving a differential wage payment shall be treated as an employee of the employer making the payment,

(ii) the differential wage payment shall be treated as compensation, and

(iii) the plan shall not be treated as failing to meet the requirements of any provision described in paragraph (1)(C) by reason of any contribution or benefit which is based on the differential wage payment.

(B) Special rule for distributions—

(i) In general—Notwithstanding subparagraph (A)(i), for purposes of section 401(k)(2)(B)(i)(I), 403(b)(7)(A)(ii), 403(b)(11)(A), or 457(d)(1)(A)(ii), an individual shall be treated as having been severed from employment during any period the individual is performing service in the uniformed services described in section 3401(h)(2)(A).

(ii) Limitation—If an individual elects to receive a distribution by reason of clause (i), the plan shall provide that the individual may not make an elective deferral or employee contribution during the 6-month period beginning on the date of the distribution.

(C) Nondiscrimination requirement—Subparagraph (A)(iii) shall apply only if all employees of an employer (as determined under subsections (b), (c), (m), and (o)) performing service in the uniformed services described in section 3401(h)(2)(A) are entitled to receive differential wage payments on reasonably equivalent terms and, if eligible to participate in a retirement plan maintained by the employer, to make contributions based on the payments on reasonably equivalent terms. For purposes of applying this subparagraph, the provisions of paragraphs (3), (4), and (5) of section 410(b) shall apply.

(D) Differential wage payment—For purposes of this paragraph, the term "differential wage payment" has the meaning given such term by section 3401(h)(2).

(v) Catch-up contributions for individuals age 50 or over—

(1) In general—An applicable employer plan shall not be treated as failing to meet any requirement of this title solely because the plan permits an eligible participant to make additional elective deferrals in any plan year.

(2) Limitation on amount of additional deferrals—

(A) In general—A plan shall not permit additional elective deferrals under paragraph (1) for any year in an amount greater than the lesser of—

(i) the applicable dollar amount, or

(ii) the excess (if any) of—

(I) the participant's compensation (as defined in section 415(c)(3)) for the year, over

(II) any other elective deferrals of the participant for such year which are made without regard to this subsection.

(B) Applicable dollar amount—For purposes of this paragraph—

(i) In the case of an applicable employer plan other than a plan described in section 401(k)(11) or 408(p), the applicable dollar amount shall be determined in accordance with the following table:

For taxable years beginning in:	*The applicable dollar amount is:*
* * *	
2006 or thereafter	$5,000

(ii) In the case of an applicable employer plan described in section 401(k)(11) or 408(p), the applicable dollar amount shall be determined in accordance with the following table:

For taxable years beginning in:	*The applicable dollar amount is:*
* * *	
2006 or thereafter	$2,500

(C) Cost-of-living adjustment—In the case of a year beginning after December 31, 2006, the Secretary shall adjust annually the $5,000 amount in subparagraph (B)(i) and the $2,500 amount in subparagraph (B)(ii) for increases in the cost-of-living at the same time and in the same manner as adjustments under section 415(d) ; except that the base period taken into account shall be the calendar quarter beginning July 1, 2005, and any increase under this subparagraph which is not a multiple of $500 shall be rounded to the next lower multiple of $500.

(D) Aggregation of plans—For purposes of this paragraph, plans described in clauses (i), (ii), and (iv) of paragraph (6)(A) that are maintained by the same employer (as determined under subsection (b), (c), (m) or (o)) shall be treated as a single plan, and plans described in clause (iii) of paragraph (6)(A) that are maintained by the same employer shall be treated as a single plan.

(3) Treatment of contributions—In the case of any contribution to a plan under paragraph (1)—

(A) such contribution shall not, with respect to the year in which the contribution is made—

(i) be subject to any otherwise applicable limitation contained in section 401(a)(30), 402(h), 403(b), 408, 415(c), and 457(b)(2) (determined without regard to section 457(b)(3)), or

(ii) be taken into account in applying such limitations to other contributions or benefits under such plan or any other such plan, and

(B) except as provided in paragraph (4), such plan shall not be treated as failing to meet the requirements of section 401(a)(4), 401(k)(3), 401(k)(11), 403(b)(12), 408(k), 410(b), or 416 by reason of the making of (or the right to make) such contribution.

(4) Application of nondiscrimination rules—

(A) In general—An applicable employer plan shall be treated as failing to meet the non-discrimination requirements under section 401(a)(4) with respect to benefits, rights, and features unless the plan allows all eligible participants to make the same election with respect to the additional elective deferrals under this subsection.

(B) Aggregation—For purposes of subparagraph (A), all plans maintained by employers who are treated as a single employer under subsection (b), (c), (m), or (o) of section 414 shall be treated as 1 plan, except that a plan described in clause (i) of section 410(b)(6)(C) shall not be treated as a plan of the employer until the expiration of the transition period with respect to such plan (as determined under clause (ii) of such section).

(5) Eligible participant—For purposes of this subsection, the term "eligible participant" means a participant in a plan—

(A) who would attain age 50 by the end of the taxable year,

(B) with respect to whom no other elective deferrals may (without regard to this subsection) be made to the plan for the plan (or other applicable) year by reason of the application of any limitation or other restriction described in paragraph (3) or comparable limitation or restriction contained in the terms of the plan.

(6) Other definitions and rules—For purposes of this subsection—

(A) Applicable employer plan—The term "applicable employer plan" means—

(i) an employees' trust described in section 401(a) which is exempt from tax under section 501(a),

(ii) a plan under which amounts are contributed by an individual's employer for an annuity contract described in section 403(b),

(iii) an eligible deferred compensation plan under section 457 of an eligible employer described in section 457(e)(1)(A), and

(iv) an arrangement meeting the requirements of section 408(k) or (p).

(B) Elective deferral—The term "elective deferral" has the meaning given such term by subsection (u)(2)(C).

(C) Exception for section 457 plans—This subsection shall not apply to a participant for any year for which a higher limitation applies to the participant under section 457(b)(3).

(w) Special rules for certain withdrawals from eligible automatic contribution arrangements—

(1) In general—If an eligible automatic contribution arrangement allows an employee to elect to make permissible withdrawals—

(A) the amount of any such withdrawal shall be includible in the gross income of the employee for the taxable year of the employee in which the distribution is made,

(B) no tax shall be imposed under section 72(t) with respect to the distribution, and

(C) the arrangement shall not be treated as violating any restriction on distributions under this title solely by reason of allowing the withdrawal.

In the case of any distribution to an employee by reason of an election under this paragraph, employer matching contributions shall be forfeited or subject to such other treatment as the Secretary may prescribe.

(2) Permissible withdrawal—For purposes of this subsection—

(A) In general—The term "permissible withdrawal" means any withdrawal from an eligible automatic contribution arrangement meeting the requirements of this paragraph which—

(i) is made pursuant to an election by an employee, and

(ii) consists of elective contributions described in paragraph (3)(B) (and earnings attributable thereto).

(B) Time for making election—Subparagraph (A) shall not apply to an election by an employee unless the election is made no later than the date which is 90 days after the date of the first elective contribution with respect to the employee under the arrangement.

(C) Amount of distribution—Subparagraph (A) shall not apply to any election by an employee unless the amount of any distribution by reason of the election is equal to the amount of elective contributions made with respect to the first payroll period to which the eligible automatic contribution arrangement applies to the employee and any succeeding payroll period beginning before the effective date of the election (and earnings attributable thereto).

(3) Eligible automatic contribution arrangement—For purposes of this subsection, the term "eligible automatic contribution arrangement" means an arrangement under an applicable employer plan—

(A) under which a participant may elect to have the employer make payments as contributions under the plan on behalf of the participant, or to the participant directly in cash,

(B) under which the participant is treated as having elected to have the employer make such contributions in an amount equal to a uniform percentage of compensation provided under the plan until the participant specifically elects not to have such contributions made (or specifically elects to have such contributions made at a different percentage), and

(C) which meets the requirements of paragraph (4).

(4) Notice requirements—

(A) In general—The administrator of a plan containing an arrangement described in paragraph (3) shall, within a reasonable period before each plan year, give to each employee to whom an arrangement described in paragraph (3) applies for such plan year notice of the employee's rights and obligations under the arrangement which—

(i) is sufficiently accurate and comprehensive to apprise the employee of such rights and obligations, and

(ii) is written in a manner calculated to be understood by the average employee to whom the arrangement applies.

(B) Time and form of notice—A notice shall not be treated as meeting the requirements of subparagraph (A) with respect to an employee unless—

(i) the notice includes an explanation of the employee's right under the arrangement to elect not to have elective contributions made on the employee's behalf (or to elect to have such contributions made at a different percentage),

(ii) the employee has a reasonable period of time after receipt of the notice described in clause (i) and before the first elective contribution is made to make such election, and

(iii) the notice explains how contributions made under the arrangement will be invested in the absence of any investment election by the employee.

(5) Applicable employer plan—For purposes of this subsection, the term "applicable employer plan" means—

(A) an employees' trust described in section 401(a) which is exempt from tax under section 501(a),

(B) a plan under which amounts are contributed by an individual's employer for an annuity contract described in section 403(b),

(C) an eligible deferred compensation plan described in section 457(b) which is maintained by an eligible employer described in section 457(e)(1)(A),

(D) a simplified employee pension the terms of which provide for a salary reduction arrangement described in section 408(k)(6), and

(E) a simple retirement account (as defined in section 408(p)).

(6) Special rule—A withdrawal described in paragraph (1) (subject to the limitation of paragraph (2)(C)) shall not be taken into account for purposes of section 401(k)(3).

(x) Special rules for eligible combined defined benefit plans and qualified cash or deferred arrangements—

(1) General rule—Except as provided in this subsection, the requirements of this title shall be applied to any defined benefit plan or applicable defined contribution plan which are part of an eligible combined plan in the same manner as if each such plan were not a part of the eligible combined plan. In the case of a termination of the defined benefit plan and the applicable defined contribution plan forming part of an eligible combined plan, the plan administrator shall terminate each such plan separately.

(2) Eligible combined plan—For purposes of this subsection—

(A) In general—The term "eligible combined plan" means a plan—

(i) which is maintained by an employer which, at the time the plan is established, is a small employer,

(ii) which consists of a defined benefit plan and an applicable defined contribution plan,

(iii) the assets of which are held in a single trust forming part of the plan and are clearly identified and allocated to the defined benefit plan and the applicable defined contribution plan to the extent necessary for the separate application of this title under paragraph (1), and

(iv) with respect to which the benefit, contribution, vesting, and nondiscrimination requirements of subparagraphs (B), (C), (D), (E), and (F) are met.

For purposes of this subparagraph, the term small employer has the meaning given such term by section 4980D(d)(2), except that such section shall be applied by substituting 500 for 50 each place it appears.

(B) Benefit requirements—

(i) In general—The benefit requirements of this subparagraph are met with respect to the defined benefit plan forming part of the eligible combined plan if the accrued benefit of each participant derived from employer contributions, when expressed as an annual retirement benefit, is not less than the applicable percentage of the participant's final average pay. For purposes of this clause, final average pay shall be determined using the period of consecutive years (not exceeding 5) during which the participant had the greatest aggregate compensation from the employer.

(ii) Applicable percentage—For purposes of clause (i), the applicable percentage is the lesser of—

(I) 1 percent multiplied by the number of years of service with the employer, or

(II) 20 percent.

(iii) Special rule for applicable defined benefit plans—If the defined benefit plan under clause (i) is an applicable defined benefit plan as defined in section 411(a)(13)(B) which meets the interest credit requirements of section 411(b)(5)(B)(i), the plan shall be treated as meeting the requirements of clause (i) with respect to any plan year if each participant receives a pay credit for the year which is not less than the percentage of compensation determined in accordance with the following table:

If the participant's age as of the beginning of the year is—	*The percentage is—*
30 or less	2
Over 30 but less than 40	4
40 or over but less than 50	6
50 or over	8.

(iv) Years of service—For purposes of this subparagraph, years of service shall be determined under the rules of paragraphs (4), (5), and (6) of section 411(a), except that the plan may not disregard any year of service because of a participant making, or failing to make, any elective deferral with respect to the qualified cash or deferred arrangement to which subparagraph (C) applies.

(C) Contribution requirements—

(i) In general—The contribution requirements of this subparagraph with respect to any applicable defined contribution plan forming part of an eligible combined plan are met if—

(I) the qualified cash or deferred arrangement included in such plan constitutes an automatic contribution arrangement, and

(II) the employer is required to make matching contributions on behalf of each employee eligible to participate in the arrangement in an amount equal to 50 percent of the elective contributions of the employee to the extent such elective contributions do not exceed 4 percent of compensation.

Rules similar to the rules of clauses (ii) and (iii) of section 401(k)(12)(B) shall apply for purposes of this clause.

(ii) Nonelective contributions—An applicable defined contribution plan shall not be treated as failing to meet the requirements of clause (i) because the employer makes nonelective contributions under the plan but such contributions shall not be taken into account in determining whether the requirements of clause (i)(II) are met.

(D) Vesting requirements—The vesting requirements of this subparagraph are met if—

(i) in the case of a defined benefit plan forming part of an eligible combined plan an employee who has completed at least 3 years of service has a nonforfeitable right to 100 percent of the employee's accrued benefit under the plan derived from employer contributions, and

(ii) in the case of an applicable defined contribution plan forming part of eligible combined plan—

(I) an employee has a nonforfeitable right to any matching contribution made under the qualified cash or deferred arrangement included in such plan by an employer with respect to any elective contribution, including matching contributions in excess of the contributions required under subparagraph (C)(i)(II), and

(II) an employee who has completed at least 3 years of service has a nonforfeitable right to 100 percent of the employee's accrued benefit derived under the arrangement from nonelective contributions of the employer.

For purposes of this subparagraph, the rules of section 411 shall apply to the extent not inconsistent with this subparagraph.

(E) Uniform provision of contributions and benefits—In the case of a defined benefit plan or applicable defined contribution plan forming part of an eligible combined plan, the requirements of this subparagraph are met if all contributions and benefits under each such plan, and all rights and features under each such plan, must be provided uniformly to all participants.

(F) Requirements must be met without taking into account social security and similar contributions and benefits or other plans—

(i) In general—The requirements of this subparagraph are met if the requirements of clauses (ii) and (iii) are met.

(ii) Social security and similar contributions—The requirements of this clause are met if—

(I) the requirements of subparagraphs (B) and (C) are met without regard to section 401(l), and

(II) the requirements of sections 401(a)(4) and 410(b) are met with respect to both the applicable defined contribution plan and defined benefit plan forming part of an eligible combined plan without regard to section 401(l).

(iii) Other plans and arrangements—The requirements of this clause are met if the applicable defined contribution plan and defined benefit plan forming part of an eligible combined plan meet the requirements of sections 401(a)(4) and 410(b) without being combined with any other plan.

(3) Nondiscrimination requirements for qualified cash or deferred arrangement—

(A) In general—A qualified cash or deferred arrangement which is included in an applicable defined contribution plan forming part of an eligible combined plan shall be treated as meeting the requirements of section 401(k)(3)(A)(ii) if the requirements of paragraph (2)(C) are met with respect to such arrangement.

(B) Matching contributions—In applying section 401(m)(11) to any matching contribution with respect to a contribution to which paragraph (2)(C) applies, the contribution requirement of paragraph (2)(C) and the notice requirements of paragraph (5)(B) shall be substituted for the requirements otherwise applicable under clauses (i) and (ii) of section 401(m)(11)(A).

(4) Satisfaction of top-heavy rules—A defined benefit plan and applicable defined contribution plan forming part of an eligible combined plan for any plan year shall be treated as meeting the requirements of section 416 for the plan year.

(5) Automatic contribution arrangement—For purposes of this subsection—

(A) In general—A qualified cash or deferred arrangement shall be treated as an automatic contribution arrangement if the arrangement—

(i) provides that each employee eligible to participate in the arrangement is treated as having elected to have the employer make elective contributions in an amount equal to 4 percent of the employee's compensation unless the employee specifically elects not to have such contributions made or to have such contributions made at a different rate, and

(ii) meets the notice requirements under subparagraph (B).

(B) Notice requirements—

(i) In general—The requirements of this subparagraph are met if the requirements of clauses (ii) and (iii) are met.

(ii) Reasonable period to make election—The requirements of this clause are met if each employee to whom subparagraph (A)(i) applies—

(I) receives a notice explaining the employee's right under the arrangement to elect not to have elective contributions made on the employee's behalf or to have the contributions made at a different rate, and

(II) has a reasonable period of time after receipt of such notice and before the first elective contribution is made to make such election.

(iii) Annual notice of rights and obligations—The requirements of this clause are met if each employee eligible to participate in the arrangement is, within a reasonable period before any year, given notice of the employee's rights and obligations under the arrangement.

The requirements of clauses (i) and (ii) of section 401(k)(12)(D) shall be met with respect to the notices described in clauses (ii) and (iii) of this subparagraph.

(6) Coordination with other requirements—

(A) Treatment of separate plans—Section 414(k) shall not apply to an eligible combined plan.

(B) Reporting—An eligible combined plan shall be treated as a single plan for purposes of sections 6058 and 6059.

(7) Applicable defined contribution plan—For purposes of this subsection—

(A) In general—The term "applicable defined contribution plan" means a defined contribution plan which includes a qualified cash or deferred arrangement.

(B) Qualified cash or deferred arrangement—The term "qualified cash or deferred arrangement" has the meaning given such term by section 401(k)(2).

§ 415. Limitations on benefits and contribution under qualified plans.

(a) General rule—

(1) Trusts—A trust which is a part of a pension, profit-sharing, or stock bonus plan shall not constitute a qualified trust under section 401(a) if—

(A) in the case of a defined benefit plan, the plan provides for the payment of benefits with respect to a participant which exceed the limitation of subsection (b), or

(B) in the case of a defined contribution plan, contributions and other additions under the plan with respect to any participant for any taxable year exceed the limitation of subsection (c).

(2) Section applies to certain annuities and accounts—In the case of—

(A) an employee annuity plan described in section 403(a),

(B) an annuity contract described in section 403(b), or

(C) a simplified employee pension described in section 408(k),

such a contract, plan, or pension shall not be considered to be described in section 403(a), 403(b), or 408(k), as the case may be, unless it satisfies the requirements of subparagraph (A) or subparagraph (B) of paragraph (1), whichever is appropriate, and has not been disqualified under subsection (g). In the case of an annuity contract described in section 403(b), the preceding sentence shall apply only to the portion of the annuity contract which exceeds the limitation of subsection (b) or the limitation of subsection (c), whichever is appropriate.

(b) Limitation for defined benefit plans—

(1) In general—Benefits with respect to a participant exceed the limitation of this subsection if, when expressed as an annual benefit (within the meaning of paragraph (2)), such annual benefit is greater than the lesser of—

(A) $160,000, or

(B) 100 percent of the participant's average compensation for his high 3 years.

(2) Annual benefit—

(A) In general—For purposes of paragraph (1), the term "annual benefit" means a benefit payable annually in the form of a straight life annuity (with no ancillary benefits) under a plan to which employees do not contribute and under which no rollover contributions (as defined in sections 402(c), 403(a)(4), 403(b)(8), 408(d)(3), and 457(e)(16)) are made.

(B) Adjustment for certain other forms of benefit—If the benefit under the plan is payable in any form other than the form described in subparagraph (A), or if the employees contribute to the plan or make rollover contributions (as defined in sections 402(c), 403(a)(4), 403(b)(8), 408(d)(3), and 457(e)(16)), the determinations as to whether the limitation described in paragraph (1) has been satisfied shall be made, in accordance with regulations prescribed by the Secretary, by adjusting such benefit so that it is equivalent to the benefit described in subparagraph (A). For purposes of this subparagraph, any ancillary benefit which is not directly related to retirement income benefits shall not be taken into account; and that portion of any joint and survivor annuity which constitutes a qualified joint and survivor annuity (as defined in section 417) shall not be taken into account.

(C) Adjustment to $160,000 limit where benefit begins before age 62—If the retirement income benefit under the plan begins before age 62, the determination as to whether the $160,000 limitation set forth in paragraph (1)(A) has been satisfied shall be made, in accordance with regulations prescribed by the Secretary, by reducing the limitation of paragraph (1)(A) so that such limitation (as so reduced) equals an annual benefit (beginning when such retirement income benefit begins) which is equivalent to a $160,000 annual benefit beginning at age 62.

(D) Adjustment to $160,000 limit where benefit begins after age 65—If the retirement income benefit under the plan begins after age 65, the determination as to whether the $160,000 limitation set forth in paragraph (1)(A) has been satisfied shall be made, in accordance with regulations prescribed by the Secretary, by increasing the limitation of paragraph (1)(A) so that such limitation (as so increased) equals an annual benefit (beginning when such retirement income benefit begins) which is equivalent to a $160,000 annual benefit beginning at age 65.

(E) Limitation on certain assumptions—

(i) For purposes of adjusting any limitation under subparagraph (C) and, except as provided in clause (ii), for purposes of adjusting any benefit under subparagraph (B), the interest rate assumption shall not be less than the greater of 5 percent or the rate specified in the plan.

(ii) For purposes of adjusting any benefit under subparagraph (B) for any form of benefit subject to section 417(e)(3), the interest rate assumption shall not be less than the greatest of—

(I) 5.5 percent,

(II) the rate that provides a benefit of not more than 105 percent of the benefit that would be provided if the applicable interest rate (as defined in section 417(e)(3)) were the interest rate assumption, or

(III) the rate specified under the plan.

(iii) For purposes of adjusting any limitation under subparagraph (D), the interest rate assumption shall not be greater than the lesser of 5 percent or the rate specified in the plan.

(iv) For purposes of this subsection, no adjustments under subsection (d)(1) shall be taken into account before the year for which such adjustment first takes effect.

(v) For purposes of adjusting any benefit or limitation under subparagraph (B), (C), or (D), the mortality table used shall be the applicable mortality table (within the meaning of section 417(e)(3)(B)).

(vi) In the case of a plan maintained by an eligible employer (as defined in section 408(p)(2)(C)(i)), clause (ii) shall be applied without regard to subclause (II) thereof.

(F) [Repealed]

(G) Special limitation for qualified police or firefighters—In the case of a qualified participant, subparagraph (C) of this paragraph shall not apply.

(H) Qualified participant defined—For purposes of subparagraph (G), the term "qualified participant" means a participant—

(i) in a defined benefit plan which is maintained by a State, Indian tribal government (as defined in section 7701(a)(40)), or any political subdivision thereof,

(ii) with respect to whom the period of service taken into account in determining the amount of the benefit under such defined benefit plan includes at least 15 years of service of the participant—

(I) as a full-time employee of any police department or fire department which is organized and operated by the State, Indian tribal government (as so defined), or any political subdivision maintaining such defined benefit plan to provide police protection, firefighting services, or emergency medical services for any area within the jurisdiction of such State, Indian tribal government (as so defined), or any political subdivision, or

(II) as a member of the Armed Forces of the United States.

(I) Exemption for survivor and disability benefits provided under governmental plans—Subparagraph (C) of this paragraph and paragraph (5) shall not apply to—

(i) income received from a governmental plan (as defined in section 414(d)) as a pension, annuity, or similar allowance as the result of the recipient becoming disabled by reason of personal injuries or sickness, or

(ii) amounts received from a governmental plan by the beneficiaries, survivors, or the estate of an employee as the result of the death of the employee.

(3) Average compensation for high 3 years—For purposes of paragraph (1), a participant's high 3 years shall be the period of consecutive calendar years (not more than 3) during which the participant had the greatest aggregate compensation from the employer. In the case of an employee within the meaning of section 401(c)(1), the preceding sentence shall be applied by substituting for "compensation from the employer" the following: "the participant's earned income (within the meaning of section 401(c)(2) but determined without regard to any exclusion under section 911)".

(4) Total annual benefits not in excess of $10,000—Notwithstanding the preceding provisions of this subsection, the benefits payable with respect to a participant under any defined benefit plan shall be deemed not to exceed the limitation of this subsection if—

(A) the retirement benefits payable with respect to such participant under such plan and under all other defined benefit plans of the employer do not exceed $10,000 for the plan year, or for any prior plan year, and

(B) the employer has not at any time maintained a defined contribution plan in which the participant participated.

(5) Reduction for participation or service of less than 10 years—

(A) Dollar limitation—In the case of an employee who has less than 10 years of participation in a defined benefit plan, the limitation referred to in paragraph (1)(A) shall be the limitation determined under such paragraph (without regard to this paragraph) multiplied by a fraction—

(i) the numerator of which is the number of years (or part thereof) of participation in the defined benefit plan of the employer, and

(ii) the denominator of which is 10.

(B) Compensation and benefits limitations—The provisions of subparagraph (A) shall apply to the limitations under paragraphs (1)(B) and (4), except that such subparagraph shall be applied with respect to years of service with an employer rather than years of participation in a plan.

(C) Limitation on reduction—In no event shall subparagraph (A) or (B) reduce the limitations referred to in paragraphs (1) and (4) to an amount less than 1/10 of such limitation (determined without regard to this paragraph).

(D) Application to changes in benefit structure—To the extent provided in regulations, subparagraph (A) shall be applied separately with respect to each change in the benefit structure of a plan.

(6) Computation of benefits and contributions—The computation of—

(A) benefits under a defined contribution plan, for purposes of section 401(a)(4),

(B) contributions made on behalf of a participant in a defined benefit plan, for purposes of section 401(a)(4), and

(C) contributions and benefits provided for a participant in a plan described in section 414(k), for purposes of this section

shall not be made on a basis inconsistent with regulations prescribed by the Secretary.

(7) Benefits under certain collectively bargained plans—For a year, the limitation referred to in paragraph (1)(B) shall not apply to benefits with respect to a participant under a defined benefit plan (other than a multiemployer plan)—

(A) which is maintained for such year pursuant to a collective bargaining agreement between employee representatives and one or more employers,

(B) which, at all times during such year, has at least 100 participants,

(C) under which benefits are determined solely by reference to length of service, the particular years during which service was rendered, age at retirement, and date of retirement,

(D) which provides that an employee who has at least 4 years of service has a nonforfeitable right to 100 percent of his accrued benefit derived from employer contributions, and

(E) which requires, as a condition of participation in the plan, that an employee complete a period of not more than 60 consecutive days of service with the employer or employers maintaining the plan.

This paragraph shall not apply to a participant whose compensation for any 3 years during the 10-year period immediately preceding the year in which he separates from service exceeded the average compensation for such 3 years of all participants in such plan. This paragraph shall not apply to a participant for any period for which he is a participant under another plan to which this section applies which is maintained by an employer maintaining this plan. For any year for which the paragraph applies to benefits with respect to a participant, paragraph (1)(A) and subsection (d)(1)(A) shall be applied with respect to such participant by substituting one-half the amount otherwise applicable for such year under paragraph (1)(A) for "$160,000".

(8) Social security retirement age defined—For purposes of this subsection, the term "social security retirement age" means the age used as the retirement age under section 216(l) of the Social Security Act, except that such section shall be applied—

(A) without regard to the age increase factor, and

(B) as if the early retirement age under section 216(l)(2) of such Act were 62.

(9) Special rule for commercial airline pilots—

(A) In general—Except as provided in subparagraph (B), in the case of any participant who is a commercial airline pilot, if, as of the time of the participant's retirement, regulations prescribed by the Federal Aviation Administration require an individual to separate from service as a commercial airline pilot after attaining any age occurring on or after age 60 and before age 62, paragraph (2)(C) shall be applied by substituting such age for age 62.

(B) Individuals who separate from service before age 60—If a participant described in subparagraph (A) separates from service before age 60, the rules of paragraph (2)(C) shall apply.

* * *

(11) Special limitation rule for governmental and multiemployer plans—In the case of a governmental plan (as defined in section 414(d)) or a multiemployer plan (as defined in section 414(f)), subparagraph (B) of paragraph (1) shall not apply. Subparagraph (B) of paragraph (1) shall not apply to a plan maintained by an organization described in section 3121(w)(3)(A) except with respect to highly compensated benefits. For purposes of this paragraph, the term "highly compensated benefits" means any benefits accrued for an employee in any year on or after the first year in which such employee is a highly compensated employee (as defined in section 414(q)) of the organization described in section 3121(w)(3)(A). For purposes of applying paragraph (1)(B) to highly compensated benefits, all benefits of the employee otherwise taken into account (without regard to this paragraph) shall be taken into account.

(c) Limitation for defined contribution plans—

(1) In general—Contributions and other additions with respect to a participant exceed the limitation of this subsection if, when expressed as an annual addition (within the meaning of paragraph (2)) to the participant's account, such annual addition is greater than the lesser of—

(A) $40,000, or

(B) 100 percent of the participant's compensation.

(2) Annual addition—For purposes of paragraph (1), the term "annual addition" means the sum for any year of—

(A) employer contributions,

(B) the employee contributions, and

(C) forfeitures.

For the purposes of this paragraph, employee contributions under subparagraph (B) are determined without regard to any rollover contributions (as defined in sections 402(c), 403(a)(4), 403(b)(8), 408(d)(3), and 457(e)(16)) without regard to employee contributions to a simplified employee pension which are excludable from gross income under section 408(k)(6). Subparagraph (B) of paragraph (1) shall not apply to any contribution for medical benefits (within the meaning of section 419A(f)(2)) after separation from service which is treated as an annual addition.

(3) Participant's compensation—For purposes of paragraph (1)—

(A) In general—The term "participant's compensation" means the compensation of the participant from the employer for the year.

(B) Special rule for self-employed individuals—In the case of an employee within the meaning of section 401(c)(1), subparagraph (A) shall be applied by substituting "the participant's earned income (within the meaning of section 401(c)(2) but determined without regard to any exclusion under section 911)" for "compensation of the participant from the employer".

(C) Special rules for permanent and total disability—In the case of a participant in any defined contribution plan—

(i) who is permanently and totally disabled (as defined in section 22(e)(3)),

(ii) who is not a highly compensated employee (within the meaning of section 414(q)), and

(iii) with respect to whom the employer elects, at such time and in such manner as the Secretary may prescribe, to have this subparagraph apply,

the term "participant's compensation" means the compensation the participant would have received for the year if the participant was paid at the rate of compensation paid immediately before becoming permanently and totally disabled. This subparagraph shall apply only if contributions made with respect to amounts treated as compensation under this subparagraph are nonforfeitable when made. If a defined contribution plan provides for the continuation of contributions on behalf of all participants described in clause (i) for a fixed or determinable period, this subparagraph shall be applied without regard to clauses (ii) and (iii).

(D) Certain deferrals included—The term "participant's compensation" shall include—

(i) any elective deferral (as defined in section 402(g)(3)), and

(ii) any amount which is contributed or deferred by the employer at the election of the employee and which is not includible in the gross income of the employee by reason of section 125, 132(f)(4), or 457.

(E) Annuity contracts—In the case of an annuity contract described in section 403(b), the term "participant's compensation" means the participant's includible compensation determined under section 403(b)(3).

* * *

(d) Cost-of-living adjustments—

(1) In general—The Secretary shall adjust annually—

(A) the $160,000 amount in subsection (b)(1)(A),

(B) in the case of a participant who separated from service, the amount taken into account under subsection (b)(1)(B), and

(C) the $40,000 amount in subsection (c)(1)(A),

for increases in the cost-of-living in accordance with regulations prescribed by the Secretary.

(2) Method—The regulations prescribed under paragraph (1) shall provide for—

(A) an adjustment with respect to any calendar year based on the increase in the applicable index for the calendar quarter ending September 30 of the preceding calendar year over such index for the base period, and

(B) adjustment procedures which are similar to the procedures used to adjust benefit amounts under section 215(i)(2)(A) of the Social Security Act.

(3) Base period—For purpose of paragraph (2)—

(A) $160,000 amount—The base period taken into account for purposes of paragraph (1)(A) is the calendar quarter beginning July 1, 2001.

(B) Separations after December 31, 1994—The base period taken into account for purposes of paragraph (1)(B) with respect to individuals separating from service with the employer after December 31, 1994, is the calendar quarter beginning July 1 of the calendar year preceding the calendar year in which such separation occurs.

(C) Separations before January 1, 1995—The base period taken into account for purposes of paragraph (1)(B) with respect to individuals separating from service with the employer before January 1, 1995, is the calendar quarter beginning October 1 of the calendar year preceding the calendar year in which such separation occurs.

(D) $40,000 amount—The base period taken into account for purposes of paragraph (1)(C) is the calendar quarter beginning July 1, 2001.

(4) Rounding—

(A) $160,000 amount—Any increase under subparagraph (A) of paragraph (1) which is not a multiple of $5,000 shall be rounded to the next lowest multiple of $5,000. This subparagraph shall also apply for purposes of any provision of this title that provides for adjustments in accordance with the method contained in this subsection, except to the extent provided in such provision.

(B) $40,000 amount—Any increase under subparagraph (C) of paragraph (1) which is not a multiple of $1,000 shall be rounded to the next lowest multiple of $1,000.

(e) [Repealed]

(f) Combining of plans—

(1) In general—For purposes of applying the limitations of subsections (b) and (c)—

(A) all defined benefit plans (whether or not terminated) of an employer are to be treated as one defined benefit plan, and

(B) all defined contribution plans (whether or not terminated) of an employer are to be treated as one defined contribution plan.

(2) Exception for multiemployer plans—Notwithstanding paragraph (1) and subsection (g), a multiemployer plan (as defined in section 414(f)) shall not be combined or aggregated—

(A) with any other plan which is not a multiemployer plan for purposes of applying subsection (b)(1)(B) to such other plan, or

(B) with any other multiemployer plan for purposes of applying the limitations established in this section.

(g) Aggregation of plans—Except as provided in subsection (f)(3), the Secretary, in applying the provisions of this section to benefits or contributions under more than one plan maintained by the same employer, and to any trusts, contracts, accounts, or bonds referred to in subsection (a)(2), with respect to which the participant has the control required under section 414(b) or (c), as modified by subsection (h), shall, under regulations prescribed by the Secretary, disqualify one or more trusts, plans, contracts, accounts, or bonds, or any combination thereof until such benefits or contributions do not exceed the limitations contained in this section. In addition to taking into account such other factors as may be necessary to carry out the purposes of subsection (f), the regulations prescribed under this paragraph shall provide that no plan which has been terminated shall be disqualified until all other trusts, plans, contracts, accounts, or bonds have been disqualified.

(h) 50 percent control—For purposes of applying subsections (b) and (c) of section 414 to this section, the phrase "more than 50 percent" shall be substituted for the phrase "at least 80 percent" each place it appears in section 1563(a)(1).

* * *

(k) Special rules—

(1) Defined benefit plan and defined contribution plan—For purposes of this title, the term "defined contribution plan" or "defined benefit plan" means a defined contribution plan (within the meaning of section 414(i)) or a defined plan (within the meaning of section 414(j)), whichever applies, which is—

(A) a plan described in section 401(a) which includes a trust which is exempt from tax under section 501(a),

(B) an annuity plan described in section 403(a),

(C) an annuity contract described in section 403(b), or

(D) a simplified employee pension.

* * *

(4) Special rules for sections 403(b) and 408—For purposes of this section, any annuity contract described in section 403(b) for the benefit of a participant shall be treated as a defined contribution plan maintained by each employer with respect to which the participant has the control required under subsection (b) or (c) of section 414 (as modified by subsection (h)). For purposes of this section, any contribution by an employer to a simplified employee pension plan for an individual for a taxable year shall be treated as an employer contribution to a defined contribution plan for such individual for such year.

(l) Treatment of certain medical benefits—

(1) In general—For purposes of this section, contributions allocated to any individual medical account which is part of a pension or annuity plan shall be treated as an annual addition to a defined contribution plan for purposes of subsection (c). Subparagraph (B) of subsection (c)(1) shall not apply to any amount treated as an annual addition under the preceding sentence.

(2) Individual medical benefit account—For purposes of paragraph (1), the term "individual medical benefit account" means any separate account—

(A) which is established for a participant under a pension or annuity plan, and

(B) from which benefits described in section 401(h) are payable solely to such participant, his spouse, or his dependents.

(m) Treatment of qualified governmental excess benefit arrangements—

(1) Governmental plan not affected—In determining whether a governmental plan (as defined in section 414(d)) meets the requirements of this section, benefits provided under a qualified governmental excess benefit arrangement shall not be taken into account. Income accruing to a governmental plan (or to a trust that is maintained solely for the purpose of providing benefits under a qualified governmental excess benefit arrangement) in respect of a qualified governmental excess benefit arrangement shall constitute income derived from the exercise of an essential governmental function upon which such governmental plan (or trust) shall be exempt from tax under section 115.

(2) Taxation of participant—For purposes of this chapter—

(A) the taxable year or years for which amounts in respect of a qualified governmental excess benefit arrangement are includible in gross income by a participant, and

(B) the treatment of such amounts when so includible by the participant,

shall be determined as if such qualified governmental excess benefit arrangement were treated as a plan for the deferral of compensation which is maintained by a corporation not exempt from tax under this chapter and which does not meet the requirements for qualification under section 401.

(3) Qualified governmental excess benefit arrangement—For purposes of this subsection, the term "qualified governmental excess benefit arrangement" means a portion of a governmental plan if—

(A) such portion is maintained solely for the purpose of providing to participants in the plan that part of the participant's annual benefit otherwise payable under the terms of the plan that exceeds the limitations on benefits imposed by this section,

(B) under such portion no election is provided at any time to the participant (directly or indirectly) to defer compensation, and

(C) benefits described in subparagraph (A) are not paid from a trust forming a part of such governmental plan unless such trust is maintained solely for the purpose of providing such benefits.

(n) Special rules relating to purchase of permissive service credit—

(1) In general—If a participant makes 1 or more contributions to a defined benefit governmental plan (within the meaning of section 414(d)) to purchase permissive service credit under such plan, then the requirements of this section shall be treated as met only if—

(A) the requirements of subsection (b) are met, determined by treating the accrued benefit derived from all such contributions as an annual benefit for purposes of subsection (b), or

(B) the requirements of subsection (c) are met, determined by treating all such contributions as annual additions for purposes of subsection (c).

(2) Application of limit—For purposes of—

(A) applying paragraph (1)(A), the plan shall not fail to meet the reduced limit under subsection (b)(2)(C) solely by reason of this subsection, and

(B) applying paragraph (1)(B), the plan shall not fail to meet the percentage limitation under subsection (c)(1)(B) solely by reason of this subsection.

(3) Permissive service credit—For purposes of this subsection—

(A) In general—The term "permissive service credit" means service credit—

(i) recognized by the governmental plan for purposes of calculating a participant's benefit under the plan,

(ii) which such participant has not received under such governmental plan, and

(iii) which such participant may receive only by making a voluntary additional contribution, in an amount determined under such governmental plan, which does not exceed the amount necessary to fund the benefit attributable to such service credit.

Such term may include service credit for periods for which there is no performance of service, and, notwithstanding clause (ii), may include service credited in order to provide an increased benefit for service credit which a participant is receiving under the plan.

(B) Limitation on nonqualified service credit—A plan shall fail to meet the requirements of this section if—

(i) more than 5 years of nonqualified service credit are taken into account for purposes of this subsection, or

(ii) any nonqualified service credit is taken into account under this subsection before the employee has at least 5 years of participation under the plan.

(C) Nonqualified service credit—For purposes of subparagraph (B), the term 'nonqualified service credit' means permissive service credit other than that allowed with respect to—

(i) service (including parental, medical, sabbatical, and similar leave) as an employee of the Government of the United States, any State or political subdivision thereof, or any agency or instrumentality of any of the foregoing (other than military service or service for credit which was obtained as a result of a repayment described in subsection (k)(3)),

(ii) service (including parental, medical, sabbatical, and similar leave) as an employee (other than as an employee described in clause (i)) of an educational organization described in section 170(b)(1)(A)(ii) which is a public, private, or sectarian school which provides elementary or secondary education (through grade 12), or a comparable level of education, as determined under the applicable law of the jurisdiction in which the service was performed,

(iii) service as an employee of an association of employees who are described in clause (i), or

(iv) military service (other than qualified military service under section 414(u)) recognized by such governmental plan.

In the case of service described in clauses (i), (ii), or (iii), such service will be nonqualified service if recognition of such service would cause a participant to receive a retirement benefit for the same service under more than one plan.

(D) Special rules for trustee-to-trustee transfers—In the case of a trustee-to-trustee transfer to which section 403(b)(13)(A) or 457(e)(17)(A) applies (without regard to whether the transfer is made between plans maintained by the same employer)—

(i) the limitations of subparagraph (B) shall not apply in determining whether the transfer is for the purchase of permissive service credit, and

(ii) the distribution rules applicable under this title to the defined benefit governmental plan to which any amounts are so transferred shall apply to such amounts and any benefits attributable to such amounts.

§ 416. Special rules for top heavy plans.

(a) General rule—A trust shall not constitute a qualified trust under section 401(a) for any plan year if the plan of which it is a part is a top-heavy plan for such plan year unless such plan meets—

(1) the vesting requirements of subsection (b), and

(2) the minimum benefit requirements of subsection (c).

(b) Vesting requirements—

(1) In general—A plan satisfies the requirements of this subsection if it satisfies the requirements of either of the following subparagraphs:

(A) 3-year vesting—A plan satisfies the requirements of this subparagraph if an employee who has completed at least 3 years of service with the employer or employers maintaining the plan has a nonforfeitable right to 100 percent of his accrued benefit derived from employer contributions.

(B) 6-year graded vesting—A plan satisfies the requirements of this subparagraph if an employee has a nonforfeitable right to a percentage of his accrued benefit derived from employer contributions determined under the following table:

Years of service:	*The nonforfeitable percentage is:*
2	20
3	40
4	60
5	80
6 or more	100

(2) Certain rules made applicable—Except to the extent inconsistent with the provisions of this subsection, the rules of section 411 shall apply for purposes of this subsection.

(c) Plan must provide minimum benefits—

(1) Defined benefit plans—

(A) In general—A defined benefit plan meets the requirements of this subsection if the accrued benefit derived from employer contributions of each participant who is a non-key employee, when expressed as an annual retirement benefit, is not less than the applicable percentage of the participant's average compensation for years in the testing period.

(B) Applicable percentage—For purposes of subparagraph (A), the term "applicable percentage" means the lesser of—

(i) 2 percent multiplied by the number of years of service with the employer, or

(ii) 20 percent.

(C) Years of service—For purposes of this paragraph—

(i) In general—Except as provided in clause (ii) or (iii), years of service shall be determined under the rules of paragraphs (4), (5), and (6) of section 411(a).

(ii) Exception for years during which plan was not top-heavy—A year of service with the employer shall not be taken into account under this paragraph if—

(I) the plan was not a top-heavy plan for any plan year ending during such year of service, or

(II) such year of service was completed in a plan year beginning before January 1, 1984.

(iii) Exception for plan under which no key employee (or former key employee) benefits for plan year—For purposes of determining an employee's years of service with the employer, any service with the employer shall be disregarded to the extent that such service occurs during a plan year when the plan benefits (within the meaning of section 410(b)) no key employee or former key employee.

(D) Average compensation for high 5 years—For purposes of this paragraph—

(i) In general—A participant's testing period shall be the period of consecutive years (not exceeding 5) during which the participant had the greatest aggregate compensation from the employer.

(ii) Year must be included in year of service—The years taken into account under clause (i) shall be properly adjusted for years not included in a year of service.

(iii) Certain years not taken into account—Except to the extent provided in the plan, a year shall not be taken into account under clause (i) if—

(I) such year ends in a plan year beginning before January 1, 1984, or

(II) such year begins after the close of the last year in which the plan was a top-heavy plan.

(E) Annual retirement benefit—For purposes of this paragraph, the term "annual retirement benefit" means a benefit payable annually in the form of a single life annuity (with no ancillary benefits) beginning at the normal retirement age under the plan.

(2) Defined contribution plans—

(A) In general—A defined contribution plan meets the requirements of the subsection if the employer contribution for the year for each participant who is a non-key employee is not less than 3 percent of such participant's compensation (within the meaning of section 415). Employer matching contributions (as defined in section 401(m)(4)(A)) shall be taken into account for purposes of this subparagraph (and any reduction under this sentence shall not be taken into account in determining whether section 401(k)(4)(A) applies).

(B) Special rule where maximum contribution less than 3 percent—

(i) In general—The percentage referred to in subparagraph (A) for any year shall not exceed the percentage at which contributions are made (or required to be made) under the plan for the year for the key employee for whom such percentage is the highest for the year.

(ii) Treatment of aggregation groups—

(I) For purposes of this subparagraph, all defined contribution plans required to be included in an aggregation group under subsection (g)(2)(A)(i) shall be treated as one plan.

(II) This subparagraph shall not apply to any plan required to be included in an aggregation group if such plan enables a defined benefit plan required to be included in such group to meet the requirements of section 401(a)(4) or 410.

(d) [Repealed]

(e) Plan must meet requirements without taking into account social security and similar contributions and benefits—A top-heavy plan shall not be treated as meeting the requirement of subsection (b) or (c) unless such plan meets such requirement without taking into account contributions or benefits under chapter 2 (relating to tax on self-employment income), chapter 21 (relating to Federal Insurance Contributions Act), title II of the Social Security Act, or any other Federal or State law.

(f) Coordination where employer has 2 or more plans—The Secretary shall prescribe such regulations as may be necessary or appropriate to carry out the purposes of this section where the employer has 2 or more plans including (but not limited to) regulations to prevent inappropriate omissions or required duplication of minimum benefits or contributions.

(g) Top-heavy plan defined—For purposes of this section—

(1) In general—

(A) Plans not required to be aggregated—Except as provided in subparagraph (B), the term "top-heavy plan" means, with respect to any plan year—

(i) any defined benefit plan if, as of the determination date, the present value of the cumulative accrued benefits under the plan for key employees exceeds 60 percent of the present value of the cumulative accrued benefits under the plan for all employees, and

(ii) any defined contribution plan if, as of the determination date, the aggregate of the accounts of key employees under the plan exceeds 60 percent of the aggregate of the accounts of all employees under such plan.

(B) Aggregated plans—Each plan of an employer required to be included in an aggregation group shall be treated as a top-heavy plan if such group is a top-heavy group.

(2) Aggregation—For purposes of this subsection—

(A) Aggregation group—

(i) Required aggregation—The term "aggregation group" means—

(I) each plan of the employer in which a key employee is a participant, and

(II) each other plan of the employer which enables any plan described in subclause (I) to meet the requirements of section 401(a)(4) or 410.

(ii) Permissive aggregation—The employer may treat any plan not required to be included in an aggregation group under clause (i) as being part of such group if such group would continue to meet the requirements of sections 401(a)(4) and 410 with such plan being taken into account.

(B) Top-heavy group—The term "top-heavy group" means any aggregation group if—

(i) the sum (as of the determination date) of—

(I) the present value of the cumulative accrued benefits for key employees under all defined benefit plans included in such group, and

(II) the aggregate of the accounts of key employees under all defined contribution plans included in such group,

(ii) exceeds 60 percent of a similar sum determined for all employees.

(3) Distributions during last year before determination date taken into account—

(A) In general—For purposes of determining—

(i) the present value of the cumulative accrued benefit for any employee, or

(ii) the amount of the account of any employee,

such present value or amount shall be increased by the aggregate distributions made with respect to such employee under the plan during the 1-year period ending on the determination date. The preceding sentence shall also apply to distributions under a terminated plan which if it had not been terminated would have been required to be included in an aggregation group.

(B) 5-year period in case of in-service distribution—In the case of any distribution made for a reason other than severance from employment, death, or disability, subparagraph (A) shall be applied by substituting "5-year period" for "1-year period".

(4) Other special rules—For purposes of this subsection—

(A) Rollover contributions to plan not taken into account—Except to the extent provided in regulations, any rollover contribution (or similar transfer) initiated by the employee and made after December 31, 1983, to a plan shall not be taken into account with respect to the transferee plan for purposes of determining whether such plan is a top-heavy plan (or whether any aggregation group which includes such plan is a top-heavy group).

(B) Benefits not taken into account if employee ceases to be key employee—If any individual is a non-key employee with respect to any plan for any plan year, but such individual was a key employee with respect to such plan for any prior plan year, any accrued benefit for such employee (and the account of such employee) shall not be taken into account.

(C) Determination date—The term "determination date" means, with respect to any plan year—

(i) the last day of the preceding plan year, or

(ii) in the case of the first plan year of any plan, the last day of such plan year.

(D) Years—To the extent provided in regulations, this section shall be applied on the basis of any year specified in such regulations in lieu of plan years.

(E) Benefits not taken into account if employee not employed for last year before determination date—If any individual has not performed services for the employer maintaining the plan at any time during the 1-year period ending on the determination date, any accrued benefit for such individual (and the account of such individual) shall not be taken into account.

(F) Accrued benefits treated as accruing ratably—The accrued benefit of any employee (other than a key employee) shall be determined—

(i) under the method which is used for accrual purposes for all plans of the employer, or

(ii) if there is no method described in clause (i), as if such benefit accrued not more rapidly than the slowest accrual rate permitted under section 411(b)(1)(C).

(G) Simple retirement accounts—The term "top-heavy plan" shall not include a simple retirement account under section 408(p).

(H) Cash or deferred arrangements using alternative methods of meeting nondiscrimination requirements—The term "top-heavy plan" shall not include a plan which consists solely of—

(i) a cash or deferred arrangement which meets the requirements of section 401(k)(12) or 401(k)(13), and

(ii) matching contributions with respect to which the requirements of section 401(m)(11) or 401(m)(12) are met.

If, but for this subparagraph, a plan would be treated as a top-heavy plan because it is a member of an aggregation group which is a top-heavy group, contributions under the plan may be taken into account in determining whether any other plan in the group meets the requirements of subsection (c)(2).

(h) [Repealed]

(i) Definitions—For purposes of this section—

(1) Key employee—

(A) In general—The term "key employee" means an employee who, at any time during the plan year, is—

(i) an officer of the employer having an annual compensation greater than $130,000,

(ii) a 5-percent owner of the employer, or

(iii) a 1-percent owner of the employer having an annual compensation from the employer of more than $150,000.

For purposes of clause (i), no more than 50 employees (or, if lesser, the greater of 3 or 10 percent of the employees) shall be treated as officers. In the case of plan years beginning after December 31, 2002, the $130,000 amount in clause (i) shall be adjusted at the same time and in the same manner as under section 415(d), except that the base period shall be the calendar quarter beginning July 1, 2001, and any increase under this sentence which is not a multiple of $5,000 shall be rounded to the next lower multiple of $5,000. Such term shall not include any officer or employee of an entity referred to in section 414(d) (relating to governmental plans). For purposes of determining the number of officers taken into account under clause (i), employees described in section 414(q)(5) shall be excluded.

(B) Percentage owners—

(i) 5-percent owner—For purposes of this paragraph, the term "5-percent owner" means—

(I) if the employer is a corporation, any person who owns (or is considered as owning within the meaning of section 318) more than 5 percent of the outstanding stock of the corporation or stock possessing more than 5 percent of the total combined voting power of all stock of the corporation, or

(II) if the employer is not a corporation, any person who owns more than 5 percent of the capital or profits interest in the employer.

(ii) 1-percent owner—For purposes of this paragraph, the term "1-percent owner" means any person who would be described in clause (i) if "1 percent" were substituted for "5 percent" each place it appears in clause (i).

(iii) Constructive ownership rules—For purposes of this subparagraph—

(I) subparagraph (C) of section 318(a)(2) shall be applied by substituting "5 percent" for "50 percent", and

(II) in the case of any employer which is not a corporation, ownership in such employer shall be determined in accordance with regulations prescribed by the Secretary which shall be based on principles similar to the principles of section 318 (as modified by subclause (I)).

(C) Aggregation rules do not apply for purposes of determining ownership in the employer—The rules of subsections (b), (c), and (m) of section 414 shall not apply for purposes of determining ownership in the employer.

(D) Compensation—For purposes of this paragraph, the term "compensation" has the meaning given such term by section 414(q)(4).

(2) Non-key employee—The term "non-key employee" means any employee who is not a key employee.

(3) Self-employed individuals—In the case of a self-employed individual described in section 401(c)(1)—

(A) such individual shall be treated as an employee, and

(B) such individual's earned income (within the meaning of section 401(c)(2)) shall be treated as compensation.

(4) Treatment of employees covered by collective bargaining agreements—The requirements of subsections (b), (c), and (d) shall not apply with respect to any employee included in a unit of employees covered by an agreement which the Secretary of Labor finds to be a collective bargaining agreement between employee representatives and 1 or more employers if there is evidence that retirement benefits were the subject of good faith bargaining between such employee representatives and such employer or employers.

(5) Treatment of beneficiaries—The terms "employee" and "key employee" include their beneficiaries.

(6) Treatment of simplified employee pensions—

(A) Treatment as defined contribution plans—A simplified employee pension shall be treated as a defined contribution plan.

(B) Election to have determinations based on employer contributions—In the case of a simplified employee pension, at the election of the employer, paragraphs (1)(A)(ii) and (2)(B) of subsection (g) shall bc applied by taking into account aggregate employer contributions in lieu of the aggregate of the accounts of employees.

§ 417. Definitions and special rules for purposes of minimum survivor annuity requirements.

(a) Election to waive qualified joint and survivor annuity or qualified preretirement survivor annuity—

(1) In general—A plan meets the requirements of section 401(a)(11) only if—

(A) under the plan, each participant—

(i) may elect at any time during the applicable election period to waive the qualified joint and survivor annuity form of benefit or the qualified preretirement survivor annuity form of benefit (or both),

(ii) if the participant elects a waiver under clause (i), may elect the qualified optional survivor annuity at any time during the applicable election period, and

(iii) may revoke any such election at any time during the applicable election period, and

(B) the plan meets the requirements of paragraphs (2), (3), and (4) of this subsection.

(2) Spouse must consent to election—Each plan shall provide that an election under paragraph (1)(A)(i) shall not take effect unless—

(A)(i) the spouse of the participant consents in writing to such election, (ii) such election designates a beneficiary (or a form of benefits) which may not be changed without spousal consent (or the consent of the spouse expressly permits designations by the participant without any requirement of further consent by the spouse), and (iii) the spouse's consent acknowledges the effect of such election and is witnessed by a plan representative or a notary public, or

(B) it is established to the satisfaction of a plan representative that the consent required under subparagraph (A) may not be obtained because there is no spouse, because the spouse cannot be located, or because of such other circumstances as the Secretary may by regulations prescribe.

Any consent by a spouse (or establishment that the consent of a spouse may not be obtained) under the preceding sentence shall be effective only with respect to such spouse.

(3) Plan to provide written explanations—

(A) Explanation of joint and survivor annuity—Each plan shall provide to each participant, within a reasonable period of time before the annuity starting date (and consistent with such regulations as the Secretary may prescribe), a written explanation of—

(i) the terms and conditions of the qualified joint and survivor annuity and of the qualified optional survivor annuity,

(ii) the participant's right to make, and the effect of, an election under paragraph (1) to waive the joint and survivor annuity form of benefit,

(iii) the rights of the participant's spouse under paragraph (2), and

(iv) the right to make, and the effect of, a revocation of an election under paragraph (1).

(B) Explanation of qualified preretirement survivor annuity—

(i) In general—Each plan shall provide to each participant, within the applicable period with respect to such participant (and consistent with such regulations as the Secretary may prescribe), a written explanation with respect to the qualified preretirement survivor annuity comparable to that required under subparagraph (A).

(ii) Applicable period—For purposes of clause (i), the term "applicable period" means, with respect to a participant, whichever of the following periods ends last:

(I) The period beginning with the first day of the plan year in which the participant attains age 32 and ending with the close of the plan year preceding the plan year in which the participant attains age 35.

(II) A reasonable period after the individual becomes a participant.

(III) A reasonable period ending after paragraph (5) ceases to apply to the participant.

(IV) A reasonable period ending after section 401(a)(11) applies to the participant.

In the case of a participant who separates from service before attaining age 35, the applicable period shall be a reasonable period after separation.

(4) Requirement of spousal consent for using plan assets as security for loans—Each plan shall provide that, if section 401(a)(11) applies to a participant when part or all of the participant's accrued benefit is to be used as security for a loan, no portion of the participant's accrued benefit may be used as security for such loan unless—

(A) the spouse of the participant (if any) consents in writing to such use during the 90-day period ending on the date on which the loan is to be so secured, and

(B) requirements comparable to the requirements of paragraph (2) are met with respect to such consent.

(5) Special rules where plan fully subsidizes costs—

(A) In general—The requirements of this subsection shall not apply with respect to the qualified joint and survivor annuity form of benefit or the qualified preretirement survivor annuity form of benefit, as the case may be, if such benefit may not be waived (or another beneficiary selected) and if the plan fully subsidizes the costs of such benefit.

(B) Definition—For purposes of subparagraph (A), a plan fully subsidizes the costs of a benefit if under the plan the failure to waive such benefit by a participant would not result in a decrease in any plan benefits with respect to such participant and would not result in increased contributions from such participant.

(6) Applicable election period defined—For purposes of this subsection, the term "applicable election period" means—

(A) in the case of an election to waive the qualified joint and survivor annuity form of benefit, the 180-day period ending on the annuity starting date, or

(B) in the case of an election to waive the qualified preretirement survivor annuity, the period which begins on the first day of the plan year in which the participant attains age 35 and ends on the date of the participant's death.

In the case of a participant who is separated from service, the applicable election period under subparagraph (B) with respect to benefits accrued before the date of such separation from service shall not begin later than such date.

(7) Special rules relating to time for written explanation—Notwithstanding any other provision of this subsection—

(A) Explanation may be provided after annuity starting date—

(i) In general—A plan may provide the written explanation described in paragraph (3)(A) after the annuity starting date. In any case to which this subparagraph applies, the applicable election period under paragraph (6) shall not end before the 30th day after the date on which such explanation is provided.

(ii) Regulatory authority—The Secretary may by regulations limit the application of clause (i), except that such regulations may not limit the period of time by which the annuity starting date precedes the provision of the written explanation other than by providing that the annuity starting date may not be earlier than termination of employment.

(B) Waiver of 30-day period—A plan may permit a participant to elect (with any applicable spousal consent) to waive any requirement that the written explanation be provided at least 30 days before the annuity starting date (or to waive the 30-day requirement under subparagraph (A)) if the distribution commences more than 7 days after such explanation is provided.

(b) Definition of qualified joint and survivor annuity—For purposes of this section and section 401(a)(11), the term "qualified joint and survivor annuity" means an annuity—

(1) for the life of the participant with a survivor annuity for the life of the spouse which is not less than 50 percent of (and is not greater than 100 percent of) the amount of the annuity which is payable during the joint lives of the participant and the spouse, and

(2) which is the actuarial equivalent of a single annuity for the life of the participant.

Such term also includes any annuity in a form having the effect of an annuity described in the preceding sentence.

(c) Definition of qualified preretirement survivor annuity—For purposes of this section and section 401(a)(11) —

(1) In general—Except as provided in paragraph (2), the term "qualified preretirement survivor annuity" means a survivor annuity for the life of the surviving spouse of the participant if—

(A) the payments to the surviving spouse under such annuity are not less than the amounts which would be payable as a survivor annuity under the qualified joint and survivor annuity under the plan (or the actuarial equivalent thereof) if—

(i) in the case of a participant who dies after the date on which the participant attained the earliest retirement age, such participant had retired with an immediate qualified joint and survivor annuity on the day before the participant's date of death, or

(ii) in the case of a participant who dies on or before the date on which the participant would have attained the earliest retirement age, such participant had—

(I) separated from service on the date of death,

(II) survived to the earliest retirement age,

(III) retired with an immediate qualified joint and survivor annuity at the earliest retirement age, and

(IV) died on the day after the day on which such participant would have attained the earliest retirement age, and

(B) under the plan, the earliest period for which the surviving spouse may receive a payment under such annuity is not later than the month in which the participant would have attained the earliest retirement age under the plan.

In the case of an individual who separated from service before the date of such individual's death, subparagraph (A)(ii)(I) shall not apply.

(2) Special rule for defined contribution plans—In the case of any defined contribution plan or participant described in clause (ii) or (iii) of section 401(a)(11)(B), the term "qualified preretirement survivor annuity" means an annuity for the life of the surviving spouse the actuarial equivalent of which is not less than 50 percent of the portion of the account balance of the participant (as of the date of death) to which the participant had a nonforfeitable right (within the meaning of section 411(a)).

(3) Security interests taken into account—For purposes of paragraphs (1) and (2), any security interest held by the plan by reason of a loan outstanding to the participant shall be taken into account in determining the amount of the qualified preretirement survivor annuity.

(d) Survivor annuities need not be provided if participant and spouse married less than 1 year—

(1) In general—Except as provided in paragraph (2), a plan shall not be treated as failing to meet the requirements of section 401(a)(11) merely because the plan provides that a qualified joint and survivor annuity (or a qualified preretirement survivor annuity) will not be provided unless the participant and spouse had been married throughout the 1-year period ending on the earlier of—

(A) the participant's annuity starting date, or

(B) the date of the participant's death.

(2) Treatment of certain marriages within 1 year of annuity starting date for purposes of qualified joint and survivor annuities—For purposes of paragraph (1), if—

(A) a participant marries within 1 year before the annuity starting date, and

(B) the participant and the participant's spouse in such marriage have been married for at least a 1-year period ending on or before the date of the participant's death,

such participant and such spouse shall be treated as having been married throughout the 1-year period ending on the participant's annuity starting date.

(e) Restrictions on cash-outs—

(1) Plan may require distribution if present value not in excess of dollar limit—A plan may provide that the present value of a qualified joint and survivor annuity or a qualified preretirement survivor annuity will be immediately distributed if such value does not exceed the amount that can be distributed without the participant's consent under section 411(a)(11). No distribution may be made under the preceding sentence after the annuity starting date unless the participant and the spouse of the participant (or where the participant has died, the surviving spouse) consents in writing to such distribution.

(2) Plan may distribute benefit in excess of dollar limit only with consent—If—

(A) the present value of the qualified joint and survivor annuity or the qualified preretirement survivor annuity exceeds the amount that can be distributed without the participant's consent under section 411(a)(11), and

(B) the participant and the spouse of the participant (or where the participant has died, the surviving spouse) consent in writing to the distribution,

the plan may immediately distribute the present value of such annuity.

(3) Determination of present value—

(A) In general—For purposes of paragraphs (1) and (2), the present value shall not be less than the present value calculated by using the applicable mortality table and the applicable interest rate.

(B) Applicable mortality table—For purposes of subparagraph (A), the term "applicable mortality table" means a mortality table, modified as appropriate by the Secretary, based on the mortality table specified for the plan year under subparagraph (A) of section 430(h)(3) (without regard to subparagraph (C) or (D) of such section).

(C) Applicable interest rate—For purposes of subparagraph (A), the term "applicable interest rate" means the adjusted first, second, and third segment rates applied under rules similar to the rules of section 430(h)(2)(C) for the month before the date of the distribution or such other time as the Secretary may by regulations prescribe.

(D) Applicable segment rates—For purposes of subparagraph (C), the adjusted first, second, and third segment rates are the first, second, and third segment rates which would be determined under section 430(h)(2)(C) if—

(i) section 430(h)(2)(D) were applied by substituting the average yields for the month described in subparagraph (C) for the average yields for the 24- month period described in such section,

(ii) section 430(h)(2)(G)(i)(II) were applied by substituting "section 417(e)(3)(A)(ii)(II)" for "section 412(b)(5)(B)(ii)(II)", and

(iii) the applicable percentage under section 430(h)(2)(G) were determined in accordance with the following table:

In the case of plan years beginning in:	*The applicable percentage is:*
2008	20 percent
2009	40 percent
2010	60 percent
2011	80 percent.

(f) Other definitions and special rules—For purposes of this section and section 401(a)(11) —

(1) Vested participant—The term "vested participant" means any participant who has a nonforfeitable right (within the meaning of section 411(a)) to any portion of such participant's accrued benefit.

(2) Annuity starting date—

(A) In general—The term "annuity starting date" means—

(i) the first day of the first period for which an amount is payable as an annuity, or

(ii) in the case of a benefit not payable in the form of an annuity, the first day on which all events have occurred which entitle the participant to such benefit.

(B) Special rule for disability benefits—For purposes of subparagraph (A), the first day of the first period for which a benefit is to be received by reason of disability shall be treated as the annuity starting date only if such benefit is not an auxiliary benefit.

(3) Earliest retirement age—The term "earliest retirement age" means the earliest date on which, under the plan, the participant could elect to receive retirement benefits.

(4) Plan may take into account increased costs—A plan may take into account in any equitable manner (as determined by the Secretary) any increased costs resulting from providing a qualified joint or survivor annuity or a qualified preretirement survivor annuity.

(5) Distributions by reason of security interests—If the use of any participant's accrued benefit (or any portion thereof) as security for a loan meets the requirements of subsection (a)(4), nothing in this section or section 411(a)(11) shall prevent any distribution required by reason of a failure to comply with the terms of such loan.

(6) Requirements for certain spousal consents—No consent of a spouse shall be effective for purposes of subsection (e)(1) or (e)(2) (as the case may be) unless requirements comparable to the requirements for spousal consent to an election under subsection (a)(1)(A) are met.

(7) Consultation with the Secretary of Labor—In prescribing regulations under this section and section 401(a)(11), the Secretary shall consult with the Secretary of Labor.

(g) Definition of qualified optional survivor annuity—

(1) In general—For purposes of this section, the term "qualified optional survivor annuity" means an annuity—

(A) for the life of the participant with a survivor annuity for the life of the spouse which is equal to the applicable percentage of the amount of the annuity which is payable during the joint lives of the participant and the spouse, and

(B) which is the actuarial equivalent of a single annuity for the life of the participant.

Such term also includes any annuity in a form having the effect of an annuity described in the preceding sentence.

(2) Applicable percentage—

(A) In general—For purposes of paragraph (1), if the survivor annuity percentage—

(i) is less than 75 percent, the applicable percentage is 75 percent, and

(ii) is greater than or equal to 75 percent, the applicable percentage is 50 percent.

(B) Survivor annuity percentage—For purposes of subparagraph (A), the term "survivor annuity percentage" means the percentage which the survivor annuity under the plan's qualified joint and survivor annuity bears to the annuity payable during the joint lives of the participant and the spouse.

§ 419. Treatment of funded welfare benefit plans.

(a) General rule—Contributions paid or accrued by an employer to a welfare benefit fund—

(1) shall not be deductible under this chapter, but

(2) if they would otherwise be deductible, shall (subject to the limitation of subsection (b)) be deductible under this section for the taxable year in which paid.

(b) Limitation—The amount of the deduction allowable under subsection (a)(2) for any taxable year shall not exceed the welfare benefit fund's qualified cost for the taxable year.

(c) Qualified cost—For purposes of this section—

(1) In general—Except as otherwise provided in this subsection, the term "qualified cost" means, with respect to any taxable year, the sum of—

(A) the qualified direct cost for such taxable year, and

(B) subject to the limitation of section 419A(b), any addition to a qualified asset account for the taxable year.

(2) Reduction for funds after-tax income—In the case of any welfare benefit fund, the qualified cost for any taxable year shall be reduced by such fund's after-tax income for such taxable year.

(3) Qualified direct cost—

(A) In general—The term "qualified direct cost" means, with respect to any taxable year, the aggregate amount (including administrative expenses) which would have been allowable as a deduction to the employer with respect to the benefits provided during the taxable year, if—

(i) such benefits were provided directly by the employer, and

(ii) the employer used the cash receipts and disbursements method of accounting.

(B) Time when benefits provided—For purposes of subparagraph (A), a benefit shall be treated as provided when such benefit would be includible in the gross income of the employee if provided directly by the employer (or would be so includible but for any provision of this chapter excluding such benefit from gross income).

* * *

(d) Carryover of excess contributions—If—

(1) the amount of the contributions paid (or deemed paid under this subsection) by the employer during any taxable year to a welfare benefit fund, exceeds

(2) the limitation of subsection (b),

such excess shall be treated as an amount paid by the employer to such fund during the succeeding taxable year.

(e) Welfare benefit fund—For purposes of this section—

(1) In general—The term "welfare benefit fund" means any fund—

(A) which is part of a plan of an employer, and

(B) through which the employer provides welfare benefits to employees or their beneficiaries.

(2) Welfare benefit—The term "welfare benefit" means any benefit other than a benefit with respect to which—

(A) section 83(h) applies,

(B) section 404 applies (determined without regard to section 404(b)(2)), or

(C) section 404A applies.

* * *

§ 419A. Qualified asset account; limitation on additions to account.

(a) General rule—For purposes of this subpart and section 512, the term "qualified asset account" means any account consisting of assets set aside to provide for the payment of—

(1) disability benefits,

(2) medical benefits,

(3) SUB or severance pay benefits, or

(4) life insurance benefits.

(b) Limitation on additions to account—No addition to any qualified asset account may be taken into account under section 419(c)(1)(B) to the extent such addition results in the amount in such account exceeding the account limit.

(c) Account limit—For purposes of this section—

(1) In general—Except as otherwise provided in this subsection, the account limit for any qualified asset account for any taxable year is the amount reasonably and actuarially necessary to fund—

(A) claims incurred but unpaid (as of the close of such taxable year) for benefits referred to in subsection (a), and

(B) administrative costs with respect to such claims.

(2) Additional reserve for post-retirement medical and life insurance benefits—The account limit for any taxable year may include a reserve funded over the working lives of the covered employees and actuarially determined on a level basis (using assumptions that are reasonable in the aggregate) as necessary for—

(A) post-retirement medical benefits to be provided to covered employees (determined on the basis of current medical costs), or

(B) post-retirement life insurance benefits to be provided to covered employees.

* * *

(f) Definitions and other special rules—For purposes of this section—

* * *

(5) Special rule for collective bargained and employee pay-all plans—No account limits shall apply in the case of any qualified asset account under a separate welfare benefit fund—

(A) under a collective bargaining agreement, or

(B) an employee pay-all plan under section 501(c)(9) if—

(i) such plan has at least 50 employees (determined without regard to subsection (h)(1)), and

(ii) no employee is entitled to a refund with respect to amounts in the fund, other than a refund based on the experience of the entire fund.

(6) Exception for 10-or-more employer plans—

(A) In general—This subpart shall not apply in the case of any welfare benefit fund which is part of a 10-or-more employer plan. The preceding sentence shall not apply to any plan which maintains experience-rating arrangements with respect to individual employers.

(B) 10 or more employer plan—For purposes of subparagraph (A), the term "10 or more employer plan" means a plan—

(i) to which more than 1 employer contributes, and

(ii) to which no employer normally contributes more than 10 percent of the total contributions contributed under the plan by all employers.

* * *

§ 420. Transfers of excess pension assets to retiree health accounts.

(a) General rule—If there is a qualified transfer of any excess pension assets of a defined benefit plan to a health benefits account which is part of such plan—

(1) a trust which is part of such plan shall not be treated as failing to meet the requirements of subsection (a) or (h) of section 401 solely by reason of such transfer (or any other action authorized under this section),

(2) no amount shall be includible in the gross income of the employer maintaining the plan solely by reason of such transfer,

(3) such transfer shall not be treated—

(A) as an employer reversion for purposes of section 4980, or

(B) as a prohibited transaction for purposes of section 4975, and

(4) the limitations of subsection (d) shall apply to such employer.

(b) Qualified transfer—For purposes of this section—

(1) In general—The term "qualified transfer" means a transfer—

(A) of excess pension assets of a defined benefit plan to a health benefits account which is part of such plan in a taxable year beginning after December 31, 1990,

(B) which does not contravene any other provision of law, and

(C) with respect to which the following requirements are met in connection with the plan—

(i) the use requirements of subsection (c)(1),

(ii) the vesting requirements of subsection (c)(2), and

(iii) the minimum cost requirements of subsection (c)(3).

(2) Only 1 transfer per year—

(A) In general—No more than 1 transfer with respect to any plan during a taxable year may be treated as a qualified transfer for purposes of this section.

(B) Exception—A transfer described in paragraph (4) shall not be taken into account for purposes of subparagraph (A).

(3) Limitation on amount transferred—The amount of excess pension assets which may be transferred in a qualified transfer shall not exceed the amount which is reasonably estimated to be the amount the employer maintaining the plan will pay (whether directly or through reimbursement) out of such account during the taxable year of the transfer for qualified current retiree health liabilities.

* * *

(5) Expiration—No transfer made after December 31, 2013, shall be treated as a qualified transfer.

(c) Requirements of plans transferring assets—

(1) Use of transferred assets—

(A) In general—Any assets transferred to a health benefits account in a qualified transfer (and any income allocable thereto) shall be used only to pay qualified current retiree health liabilities (other than liabilities of key employees not taken into account under subsection (e)(1)(D)) for the taxable year of the transfer (whether directly or through reimbursement). In the case of a qualified future transfer or collectively bargained transfer to which subsection (f) applies, any assets so transferred may also be used to pay liabilities described in subsection (f)(2)(C).

(B) Amounts not used to pay for health benefits—

(i) In general—Any assets transferred to a health benefits account in a qualified transfer (and any income allocable thereto) which are not used as provided in subparagraph (A) shall be transferred out of the account to the transferor plan.

(ii) Tax treatment of amounts—Any amount transferred out of an account under clause (i)—

(I) shall not be includible in the gross income of the employer for such taxable year, but

(II) shall be treated as an employer reversion for purposes of section 4980 (without regard to subsection (d) thereof).

(C) Ordering rule—For purposes of this section, any amount paid out of a health benefits account shall be treated as paid first out of the assets and income described in subparagraph (A).

(2) Requirements relating to pension benefits accruing before transfer—

(A) In general—The requirements of this paragraph are met if the plan provides that the accrued pension benefits of any participant or beneficiary under the plan become nonforfeitable in the same manner which would be required if the plan had terminated immediately before the qualified transfer (or in the case of a participant who separated during the 1-year period ending on the date of the transfer, immediately before such separation).

* * *

(3) Minimum cost requirements—

(A) In general—The requirements of this paragraph are met if each group health plan or arrangement under which applicable health benefits are provided provides that the applicable employer cost for each taxable year during the cost maintenance period shall not be less than the higher of the applicable employer costs for each of the 2 taxable years immediately preceding the taxable year of the qualified transfer or, in the case of a transfer which involves a plan maintained by an employer described in subsection (f)(2)(E)(i)(III), if the plan meets the requirements of subsection (f)(2)(D)(i)(II).

(B) Applicable employer cost—For purposes of this paragraph, the term "applicable employer cost" means, with respect to any taxable year, the amount determined by dividing—

(i) the qualified current retiree health liabilities of the employer for such taxable year determined—

(I) without regard to any reduction under subsection (e)(1)(B), and

(II) in the case of a taxable year in which there was no qualified transfer, in the same manner as if there had been such a transfer at the end of the taxable year, by

(ii) the number of individuals to whom coverage for applicable health benefits was provided during such taxable year.

* * *

(D) Cost maintenance period—For purposes of this paragraph, the term "cost maintenance period" means the period of 5 taxable years beginning with the taxable year in which the qualified transfer occurs. If a taxable year is in two or more overlapping cost maintenance periods, this paragraph shall be applied by taking into account the highest applicable employer cost required to be provided under subparagraph (A) for such taxable year.

(E) Regulations—

(i) In general—The Secretary shall prescribe such regulations as may be necessary to prevent an employer who significantly reduces retiree health coverage during the cost maintenance period from being treated as satisfying the minimum cost requirement of this subsection.

(ii) Insignificant cost reductions permitted—

(I) In general—An eligible employer shall not be treated as failing to meet the requirements of this paragraph for any taxable year if, in lieu of any reduction of retiree health coverage permitted under the regulations prescribed under clause (i), the employer reduces applicable employer cost by an amount not in excess of the reduction in costs which would have occurred if the employer had made the maximum permissible reduction in retiree health coverage under such regulations. In applying such regulations to any subsequent taxable year, any reduction in applicable employer cost under this clause shall be treated as if it were an equivalent reduction in retiree health coverage.

(II) Eligible employer—For purposes of subclause (I), an employer shall be treated as an eligible employer for any taxable year if, for the preceding taxable year, the qualified current retiree health liabilities of the employer were at least 5 percent of the gross receipts of the employer. For purposes of this subclause, the rules of paragraphs (2), (3)(B), and (3)(C) of section 448(c) shall apply in determining the amount of an employer's gross receipts.

(d) Limitations on employer—For purposes of this title—

(1) Deduction limitations—No deduction shall be allowed—

(A) for the transfer of any amount to a health benefits account in a qualified transfer (or any retransfer to the plan under subsection (c)(1)(B)),

(B) for qualified current retiree health liabilities paid out of the assets (and income) described in subsection (c)(1), or

(C) for any amounts to which subparagraph (B) does not apply and which are paid for qualified current retiree health liabilities for the taxable year to the extent such amounts are not greater than the excess (if any) of—

(i) the amount determined under subparagraph (A) (and income allocable thereto), over

(ii) the amount determined under subparagraph (B).

(2) No contributions allowed—An employer may not contribute after December 31, 1990, any amount to a health benefits account or welfare benefit fund (as defined in section 419(e)(1)) with respect to qualified current retiree health liabilities for which transferred assets are required to be used under subsection (c)(1).

(e) Definition and special rules—For purposes of this section—

(1) Qualified current retiree health liabilities—For purposes of this section—

(A) In general—The term "qualified current retiree health liabilities" means, with respect to any taxable year, the aggregate amounts (including administrative expenses) which would have been allowable as a deduction to the employer for such taxable year with respect to applicable health benefits provided during such taxable year if—

(i) such benefits were provided directly by the employer, and

(ii) the employer used the cash receipts and disbursements method of accounting.

For purposes of the preceding sentence, the rule of section 419(c)(3)(B) shall apply.

(B) Reductions for amounts previously set aside—The amount determined under subparagraph (A) shall be reduced by the amount which bears the same ratio to such amount as—

(i) the value (as of the close of the plan year preceding the year of the qualified transfer) of the assets in all health benefits accounts or welfare benefit funds (as defined in section 419(e)(1)) set aside to pay for the qualified current retiree health liability, bears to

(ii) the present value of the qualified current retiree health liabilities for all plan years (determined without regard to this subparagraph).

(C) Applicable health benefits—The term "applicable health benefits" means health benefits or coverage which are provided to—

(i) retired employees who, immediately before the qualified transfer, are entitled to receive such benefits upon retirement and who are entitled to pension benefits under the plan, and

(ii) their spouses and dependents.

(D) Key employees excluded—If an employee is a key employee (within the meaning of section 416(i)(1)) with respect to any plan year ending in a taxable year, such employee shall not be taken into account in computing qualified current retiree health liabilities for such taxable year or in calculating applicable employer cost under subsection (c)(3)(B).

(2) Excess pension assets— The term "excess pension assets" means the excess (if any) of—

(A) the lesser of—

(i) the fair market value of the plan's assets (reduced by the prefunding balance and funding standard carryover balance determined under section 430(f)), or

(ii) the value of plan assets as determined under section 430(g)(3) after reduction under section 430(f), over

(B) 125 percent of the sum of the funding target and the target normal cost determined under section 430 for such plan year.

The determination under this paragraph shall be made as of the most recent valuation date of the plan preceding the qualified transfer.

(3) Health benefits account—The term "health benefits account" means an account established and maintained under section 401(h).

(4) Coordination with section 430—In the case of a qualified transfer, any assets so transferred shall not, for purposes of this section and section 430, be treated as assets in the plan.

(5) Application to multiemployer plans—In the case of a multiemployer plan, this section shall be applied to any such plan—

(A) by treating any reference in this section to an employer as a reference to all employers maintaining the plan (or, if appropriate, the plan sponsor), and

(B) in accordance with such modifications of this section (and the provisions of this title relating to this section) as the Secretary determines appropriate to reflect the fact the plan is not maintained by a single employer.

(f) Qualified transfers to cover future retiree health costs and collectively bargained retiree health benefits—

(1) In general—An employer maintaining a defined benefit plan (other than a multiemployer plan) may, in lieu of a qualified transfer, elect for any taxable year to have the plan make—

(A) a qualified future transfer, or

(B) a collectively bargained transfer.

Except as provided in this subsection, a qualified future transfer and a collectively bargained transfer shall be treated for purposes of this title and the Employee Retirement Income Security Act of 1974 as if it were a qualified transfer.

(2) Qualified future and collectively bargained transfers—For purposes of this subsection—

(A) In general—The terms "qualified future transfer" and "collectively bargained transfer" mean a transfer which meets all of the requirements for a qualified transfer, except that—

(i) the determination of excess pension assets shall be made under subparagraph (B),

(ii) the limitation on the amount transferred shall be determined under subparagraph (C),

(iii) the minimum cost requirements of subsection (c)(3) shall be modified as provided under subparagraph (D), and

(iv) in the case of a collectively bargained transfer, the requirements of subparagraph (E) shall be met with respect to the transfer.

(B) Excess pension assets—

(i) In general—In determining excess pension assets for purposes of this subsection, subsection (e)(2) shall be applied by substituting "120 percent" for "125 percent".

(ii) Requirement to maintain funded status—If, as of any valuation date of any plan year in the transfer period, the amount determined under subsection (e)(2)(B) (after application of clause (i)) exceeds the amount determined under subsection (e)(2)(A), either—

(I) the employer maintaining the plan shall make contributions to the plan in an amount not less than the amount required to reduce such excess to zero as of such date, or

(II) there is transferred from the health benefits account to the plan an amount not less than the amount required to reduce such excess to zero as of such date.

(C) Limitation on amount transferred—Notwithstanding subsection (b)(3), the amount of the excess pension assets which may be transferred—

(i) in the case of a qualified future transfer shall be equal to the sum of—

(I) if the transfer period includes the taxable year of the transfer, the amount determined under subsection (b)(3) for such taxable year, plus

(II) in the case of all other taxable years in the transfer period, the sum of the qualified current retiree health liabilities which the plan reasonably estimates, in accordance with guidance issued by the Secretary, will be incurred for each of such years, and

(ii) in the case of a collectively bargained transfer, shall not exceed the amount which is reasonably estimated, in accordance with the provisions of the collective bargaining agreement and generally accepted accounting principles, to be the amount the employer maintaining the plan will pay (whether directly or through reimbursement) out of such account during the collectively bargained cost maintenance period for collectively bargained retiree health liabilities.

(D) Minimum cost requirements—

(i) In general—The requirements of subsection (c)(3) shall be treated as met if—

(I) in the case of a qualified future transfer, each group health plan or arrangement under which applicable health benefits are provided provides applicable health benefits during the period beginning with the first year of the transfer period and ending with the last day of the 4th year following the transfer period such that the annual average amount of the applicable employer cost during such period is not less than the applicable employer cost determined under subsection (c)(3)(A) with respect to the transfer, and

(II) in the case of a collectively bargained transfer, each collectively bargained group health plan under which collectively bargained health benefits are provided provides that the collectively bargained employer cost for each taxable year during the collectively bargained cost maintenance period shall not be less than the amount specified by the collective bargaining agreement.

(ii) Election to maintain benefits for future transfers—An employer may elect, in lieu of the requirements of clause (i)(I), to meet the requirements of subsection (c)(3) by meeting the requirements of such subsection (as in effect before the amendments made by section 535 of the Tax Relief Extension Act of 1999) for each of the years described in the period under clause (i)(I).

(iii) Collectively bargained employer cost—For purposes of this subparagraph, the term "collectively bargained employer cost" means the average cost per covered individual of providing collectively bargained retiree health benefits as determined in accordance with the applicable collective bargaining agreement. Such agreement may provide for an appropriate reduction in the collectively bargained employer cost to take into account any portion of the collectively bargained retiree health benefits that is provided or financed by a government program or other source.

(E) Special rules for collectively bargained transfers—

(i) In general—A collectively bargained transfer shall only include a transfer which—

(I) is made in accordance with a collective bargaining agreement,

(II) before the transfer, the employer designates, in a written notice delivered to each employee organization that is a party to the collective bargaining agreement, as a collectively bargained transfer in accordance with this section, and

(III) involves a plan maintained by an employer which, in its taxable year ending in 2005, provided health benefits or coverage to retirees and their spouses and dependents under all of the benefit plans maintained by the employer, but only if the aggregate cost (including administrative expenses) of such benefits or coverage which would have been allowable as a deduction to the employer (if such benefits or coverage had been provided directly by the employer and the employer used the cash receipts and disbursements method of accounting) is at least 5 percent of the gross receipts of the employer (determined in accordance with the last sentence of subsection (c)(3)(E)(ii)(II)) for such taxable year, or a plan maintained by a successor to such employer.

(ii) Use of assets—Any assets transferred to a health benefits account in a collectively bargained transfer (and any income allocable thereto) shall be used only to pay collectively bargained retiree health liabilities (other than liabilities of key employees not taken into account under paragraph (6)(B)(iii)) for the taxable year of the transfer or for any subsequent taxable year during the collectively bargained cost maintenance period (whether directly or through reimbursement).

(3) Coordination with other transfers—In applying subsection (b)(3) to any subsequent transfer during a taxable year in a transfer period or collectively bargained cost maintenance period, qualified current retiree health liabilities shall be reduced by any such liabilities taken into account with respect to the qualified future transfer or collectively bargained transfer to which such period relates.

(4) Special deduction rules for collectively bargained transfers—In the case of a collectively bargained transfer—

(A) the limitation under subsection (d)(1)(C) shall not apply, and

(B) notwithstanding subsection (d)(2), an employer may contribute an amount to a health benefits account or welfare benefit fund (as defined in section 419(e)(1)) with respect to collectively bargained retiree health liabilities for which transferred assets are required to be used under subsection (c)(1)(B), and the deductibility of any such contribution shall be governed by the limits applicable to the deductibility of contributions to a welfare benefit fund under a collective bargaining agreement (as determined under section 419A(f)(5)(A)) without regard to whether such contributions are made to a health benefits account or welfare benefit fund and without regard to the provisions of section 404 or the other provisions of this section.

The Secretary shall provide rules to ensure that the application of this paragraph does not result in a deduction being allowed more than once for the same contribution or for 2 or more contributions or expenditures relating to the same collectively bargained retiree health liabilities.

(5) Transfer period—For purposes of this subsection, the term "transfer period" means, with respect to any transfer, a period of consecutive taxable years (not less than 2) specified in the election under paragraph (1) which begins and ends during the 10-taxable-year period beginning with the taxable year of the transfer.

(6) Terms relating to collectively bargained transfers—For purposes of this subsection—

(A) Collectively bargained cost maintenance period—The term "collectively bargained cost maintenance period" means, with respect to each covered retiree and his covered spouse and dependents, the shorter of—

(i) the remaining lifetime of such covered retiree and his covered spouse and dependents, or

(ii) the period of coverage provided by the collectively bargained health plan (determined as of the date of the collectively bargained transfer) with respect to such covered retiree and his covered spouse and dependents.

(B) Collectively bargained retiree health liabilities—

(i) In general—The term "collectively bargained retiree health liabilities" means the present value, as of the beginning of a taxable year and determined in accordance with the applicable collective bargaining agreement, of all collectively bargained health benefits (including administrative expenses) for such taxable year and all subsequent taxable years during the collectively bargained cost maintenance period.

(ii) Reduction for amounts previously set aside—The amount determined under clause (i) shall be reduced by the value (as of the close of the plan year preceding the year of the collectively bargained transfer) of the assets in all health benefits accounts or welfare benefit funds (as defined in section 419(e)(1)) set aside to pay for the collectively bargained retiree health liabilities.

(iii) Key employees excluded—If an employee is a key employee (within the meaning of section 416(I)(1)) with respect to any plan year ending in a taxable year, such employee shall not be taken into account in computing collectively bargained retiree health liabilities for such taxable year or in calculating collectively bargained employer cost under subsection (c)(3)(C).

(C) Collectively bargained health benefits—The term "collectively bargained health benefits" means health benefits or coverage which are provided to—

(i) retired employees who, immediately before the collectively bargained transfer, are entitled to receive such benefits upon retirement and who are entitled to pension benefits under the plan, and their spouses and dependents, and

(ii) if specified by the provisions of the collective bargaining agreement governing the collectively bargained transfer, active employees who, following their retirement, are entitled to receive such benefits and who are entitled to pension benefits under the plan, and their spouses and dependents.

(D) Collectively bargained health plan—The term "collectively bargained health plan" means a group health plan or arrangement for retired employees and their spouses and dependents that is maintained pursuant to 1 or more collective bargaining agreements.

§ 421. General rules.

(a) Effect of qualifying transfer—If a share of stock is transferred to an individual in a transfer in respect of which the requirements of section 422(a) or 423(a) are met—

(1) no income shall result at the time of the transfer of such share to the individual upon his exercise of the option with respect to such share;

(2) no deduction under section 162 (relating to trade or business expenses) shall be allowable at any time to the employer corporation, a parent or subsidiary corporation of such corporation, or a corporation issuing or assuming a stock option in a transaction to which section 424(a) applies, with respect to the share so transferred; and

(3) no amount other than the price paid under the option shall be considered as received by any of such corporations for the share so transferred.

(b) Effect of disqualifying disposition—If the transfer of a share of stock to an individual pursuant to his exercise of an option would otherwise meet the requirements of section 422(a) or 423(a) except that there is a failure to meet any of the holding period requirements of section 422(a)(1) or 423(a)(1), then any increase in the income of such individual or deduction from the income of his employer corporation for the taxable year in which such exercise occurred attributable to such disposition, shall be treated as an increase in income or a deduction from income in the taxable year of such individual or of such employer corporation in which such disposition occurred. No amount shall be required to be deducted and withheld under chapter 24 with respect to any increase in income attributable to a disposition described in the preceding sentence.

* * *

§ 423. Employee stock purchase plans.

(a) General rule—Section 421(a) shall apply with respect to the transfer of a share of stock to an individual pursuant to his exercise of an option granted after December 31, 1963, under an employee stock purchase plan (as defined in subsection (b)) if—

(1) no disposition of such share is made by him within 2 years after the date of the granting of the option nor within 1 year after the transfer of such share to him; and

(2) at all times during the period beginning with the date of the granting of the option and ending on the day 3 months before the date of such exercise, he is an employee of the corporation granting such option, a parent or subsidiary corporation of such corporation, or a corporation or a parent or subsidiary corporation of such corporation issuing or assuming a stock option in a transaction to which section 424(a) applies.

(b) Employee stock purchase plan—For purposes of this part, the term "employee stock purchase plan" means a plan which meets the following requirements:

(1) the plan provides that options are to be granted only to employees of the employer corporation or of its parent or subsidiary corporation to purchase stock in any such corporation;

(2) such plan is approved by the stockholders of the granting corporation within 12 months before or after the date such plan is adopted;

(3) under the terms of the plan, no employee can be granted an option if such employee, immediately after the option is granted, owns stock possessing 5 percent or more of the total combined voting power or value of all classes of stock of the employer corporation or of its parent or subsidiary corporation. For purposes of this paragraph, the rules of section 424(d) shall apply in determining the stock ownership of an individual, and stock which the employee may purchase under outstanding options shall be treated as stock owned by the employee;

(4) under the terms of the plan, options are to be granted to all employees of any corporation whose employees are granted any of such options by reason of their employment by such corporation, except that there may be excluded—

(A) employees who have been employed less than 2 years,

(B) employees whose customary employment is 20 hours or less per week,

(C) employees whose customary employment is for not more than 5 months in any calendar year, and

(D) highly compensated employees (within the meaning of section 414(q));

(5) under the terms of the plan, all employees granted such options shall have the same rights and privileges, except that the amount of stock which may be purchased by any employee under such option may bear a uniform relationship to the total compensation, or the basic or regular rate of compensation, of employees, and the plan may provide that no employee may purchase more than a maximum amount of stock fixed under the plan;

(6) under the terms of the plan, the option price is not less than the lesser of—

(A) an amount equal to 85 percent of the fair market value of the stock at the time such option is granted, or

(B) an amount which under the terms of the option may not be less than 85 percent of the fair market value of the stock at the time such option is exercised;

(7) under the terms of the plan, such option cannot be exercised after the expiration of—

(A) 5 years from the date such option is granted if, under the terms of such plan, the option price is to be not less than 85 percent of the fair market value of such stock at the time of the exercise of the option, or

(B) 27 months from the date such option is granted, if the option price is not determinable in the manner described in subparagraph (A);

(8) under the terms of the plan, no employee may be granted an option which permits his rights to purchase stock under all such plans of his employer corporation and its parent and subsidiary corporations to accrue at a rate which exceeds $25,000 of fair market value of such stock (determined at the time such option is granted) for each calendar year in which such option is outstanding at any time. For purposes of this paragraph—

(A) the right to purchase stock under an option accrues when the option (or any portion thereof) first becomes exercisable during the calendar year;

(B) the right to purchase stock under an option accrues at the rate provided in the option, but in no case may such rate exceed $25,000 of fair market value of such stock (determined at the time such option is granted) for any one calendar year; and

(C) a right to purchase stock which has accrued under one option granted pursuant to the plan may not be carried over to any other option; and

(9) under the terms of the plan, such option is not transferable by such individual otherwise than by will or the laws of descent and distribution, and is exercisable, during his lifetime, only by him.

For purposes of paragraphs (3) to (9), inclusive, where additional terms are contained in an offering made under a plan, such additional terms shall, with respect to options exercised under such offering, be treated as a part of the terms of such plan.

(c) Special rule where option price is between 85 percent and 100 percent of value of stock—If the option price of a share of stock acquired by an individual pursuant to a transfer to which subsection (a) applies was less than 100 percent of the fair market value of such share at the time such option was granted, then, in the event of any disposition of such share by him which meets the holding period requirements of subsection (a), or in the event of his death (whenever occurring) while owning such share, there shall be included as compensation (and not as gain upon the sale or exchange of a capital asset) in his gross income, for the taxable year in which falls the date of such disposition or for the taxable year closing with his death, whichever applies, an amount equal to the lesser of—

(1) the excess of the fair market value of the share at the time of such disposition or death over the amount paid for the share under the option, or

(2) the excess of the fair market value of the share at the time the option was granted over the option price.

If the option price is not fixed or determinable at the time the option is granted, then for purposes of this subsection, the option price shall be determined as if the option were exercised at such time. In the case of the disposition of such share by the individual, the basis of the share in his hands at the time of such disposition shall be increased by an amount equal to the amount so includible in his gross income. No amount shall be required to be deducted and withheld under chapter 24 with respect to any amount treated as compensation under this subsection.

§ 430. Minimum funding standards for single-employer defined benefit pension plans.

(a) Minimum required contribution—For purposes of this section and section 412(a)(2)(A), except as provided in subsection (f), the term "minimum required contribution" means, with respect to any plan year of a defined benefit plan which is not a multiemployer plan—

(1) in any case in which the value of plan assets of the plan (as reduced under subsection (f)(4)(B)) is less than the funding target of the plan for the plan year, the sum of—

(A) the target normal cost of the plan for the plan year,

(B) the shortfall amortization charge (if any) for the plan for the plan year determined under subsection (c), and

(C) the waiver amortization charge (if any) for the plan for the plan year as determined under subsection (e);

(2) in any case in which the value of plan assets of the plan (as reduced under subsection (f)(4)(B)) equals or exceeds the funding target of the plan for the plan year, the target normal cost of the plan for the plan year reduced (but not below zero) by such excess.

(b) Target normal cost—For purposes of this section:

(1) In general—Except as provided in subsection (i)(2) with respect to plans in at-risk status, the term "target normal cost" means, for any plan year, the excess of—

(A) the sum of—

(i) the present value of all benefits which are expected to accrue or to be earned under the plan during the plan year, plus

(ii) the amount of plan-related expenses expected to be paid from plan assets during the plan year, over

(B) the amount of mandatory employee contributions expected to be made during the plan year.

(2) Special rule for increase in compensation—For purposes of this subsection, if any benefit attributable to services performed in a preceding plan year is increased by reason of any increase in compensation during the current plan year, the increase in such benefit shall be treated as having accrued during the current plan year.

(c) Shortfall amortization charge—

(1) In general—For purposes of this section, the shortfall amortization charge for a plan for any plan year is the aggregate total (not less than zero) of any shortfall amortization base which has not been fully amortized under this subsection.

(2) Shortfall amortization installment—For purposes of paragraph (1)—

(A) Determination—The shortfall amortization installments are the amounts necessary to amortize the shortfall amortization base of the plan for any plan year in level annual installments over the 7-plan-year period beginning with such plan year.

(B) Shortfall installment—The shortfall amortization installment for any plan year in the 7-plan-year period under subparagraph (A) with respect to any shortfall amortization base is the annual installment determined under subparagraph (A) for that year for that base.

(C) Segment rates—In determining any shortfall amortization installment under this paragraph, the plan sponsor shall use the segment rates determined under subparagraph (C) of subsection (h)(2), applied under rules similar to the rules of subparagraph (B) of subsection (h)(2).

(D) Special election for eligible plan years.

(i) In general. If a plan sponsor elects to apply this subparagraph with respect to the shortfall amortization base of a plan for any eligible plan year (in this subparagraph and paragraph (7) referred to as an "election year"), then, notwithstanding subparagraphs (A) and (B)—

(I) the shortfall amortization installments with respect to such base shall be determined under clause (ii) or (iii), whichever is specified in the election, and

(II) the shortfall amortization installment for any plan year in the 9-plan-year period described in clause (ii) or the 15-plan-year period described in clause (iii), respectively, with respect to such shortfall amortization base is the annual installment determined under the applicable clause for that year for that base.

(ii) 2 plus 7 amortization schedule. The shortfall amortization installments determined under this clause are—

(I) in the case of the first 2 plan years in the 9-plan-year period beginning with the election year, interest on the shortfall amortization base of the plan for the election year (determined using the effective interest rate for the plan for the election year), and

(II) in the case of the last 7 plan years in such 9-plan-year period, the amounts necessary to amortize the remaining balance of the shortfall amortization base of the plan for the election year in level annual installments over such last 7 plan years (using the segment rates under subparagraph (C) for the election year).

(iii) 15-year amortization. The shortfall amortization installments determined under this subparagraph are the amounts necessary to amortize the shortfall amortization base of the plan for the election year in level annual installments over the 15-plan-year period beginning with the election year (using the segment rates under subparagraph (C) for the election year).

(iv) Election.

(I) In general. The plan sponsor of a plan may elect to have this subparagraph apply to not more than 2 eligible plan years with respect to the plan, except that in the case of a plan described in section 106 of the Pension Protection Act of 2006, the plan sponsor may only elect to have this subparagraph apply to a plan year beginning in 2011.

(II) Amortization schedule. Such election shall specify whether the amortization schedule under clause (ii) or (iii) shall apply to an election year, except that if a plan sponsor elects to have this subparagraph apply to 2 eligible plan years, the plan sponsor must elect the same schedule for both years.

(III) Other rules. Such election shall be made at such time, and in such form and manner, as shall be prescribed by the Secretary, and may be revoked only with the consent of the Secretary. The Secretary shall, before granting a revocation request, provide the Pension Benefit Guaranty Corporation an opportunity to comment on the conditions applicable to the treatment of any portion of the election year shortfall amortization base that remains unamortized as of the revocation date.

(v) Eligible plan year. For purposes of this subparagraph, the term "eligible plan year" means any plan year beginning in 2008, 2009, 2010, or 2011, except that a plan year shall only be treated as an eligible plan year if the due date under subsection (j)(1) for the payment of the minimum required contribution for such plan year occurs on or after the date of the enactment of this subparagraph.

(vi) Reporting. A plan sponsor of a plan who makes an election under clause (i) shall—

(I) give notice of the election to participants and beneficiaries of the plan, and

(II) inform the Pension Benefit Guaranty Corporation of such election in such form and manner as the Director of the Pension Benefit Guaranty Corporation may prescribe.

(vii) Increases in required installments in certain cases. For increases in required contributions in cases of excess compensation or extraordinary dividends or stock redemptions, see paragraph (7).

(3) Shortfall amortization base—For purposes of this section, the shortfall amortization base of a plan for a plan year is—

(A) the funding shortfall of such plan for such plan year, minus

(B) the present value (determined using the segment rates determined under subparagraph (C) of subsection (h)(2), applied under rules similar to the rules of subparagraph (B) of subsection (h)(2)) of the aggregate total of the shortfall amortization installments and waiver amortization installments which have been determined for such plan year and any succeeding plan year with respect to the shortfall amortization bases and waiver amortization bases of the plan for any plan year preceding such plan year.

(4) Funding shortfall—For purposes of this section, the funding shortfall of a plan for any plan year is the excess (if any) of—

(A) the funding target of the plan for the plan year, over

(B) the value of plan assets of the plan (as reduced under subsection (f)(4)(B)) for the plan year which are held by the plan on the valuation date.

(5) Exemption from new shortfall amortization base—

(A) In general—In any case in which the value of plan assets of the plan (as reduced under subsection (f)(4)(A)) is equal to or greater than the funding target of the plan for the plan year, the shortfall amortization base of the plan for such plan year shall be zero.

(B) Transition rule—

(i) In general—Except as provided in clause (iii), in the case of plan years beginning after 2007 and before 2011, only the applicable percentage of the funding target shall be taken into account under paragraph (3)(A) in determining the funding shortfall for the plan year for purposes of paragraph (3)(A) and subparagraph (A).

(ii) Applicable percentage—For purposes of subparagraph (A), the applicable percentage shall be determined in accordance with the following table:

In the case of a plan year beginning in calendar year:	*The applicable percentage is*
2008	92
2009	94
2010	96

(iii) Transition relief not available for new or deficit reduction plans—Clause (i) shall not apply to a plan—

(I) which was not in effect for a plan year beginning in 2007, or

(II) which was in effect for a plan year beginning in 2007 and which was subject to section 412(l) (as in effect for plan years beginning in 2007) for such year, determined after the application of paragraphs (6) and (9) thereof.

(6) Early deemed amortization upon attainment of funding target—In any case in which the funding shortfall of a plan for a plan year is zero, for purposes of determining the shortfall amortization charge for such plan year and succeeding plan years, the shortfall amortization bases for all preceding plan years (and all shortfall amortization installments determined with respect to such bases) shall be reduced to zero.

(7) Increases in alternate required installments in cases of excess compensation or extraordinary dividends or stock redemptions.

(A) In general. If there is an installment acceleration amount with respect to a plan for any plan year in the restriction period with respect to an election year under paragraph (2)(D), then the shortfall amortization installment otherwise determined and payable under such paragraph for such plan year shall, subject to the limitation under subparagraph (B), be increased by such amount.

(B) Total installments limited to shortfall base. Subject to rules prescribed by the Secretary, if a shortfall amortization installment with respect to any shortfall amortization base for an election year is required to be increased for any plan year under subparagraph (A)—

(i) such increase shall not result in the amount of such installment exceeding the present value of such installment and all succeeding installments with respect to such base (determined without regard to such increase but after application of clause (ii)), and

(ii) subsequent shortfall amortization installments with respect to such base shall, in reverse order of the otherwise required installments, be reduced to the extent necessary to limit the present value of such subsequent shortfall amortization installments (after application of this paragraph) to the present value of the remaining unamortized shortfall amortization base.

(C) Installment acceleration amount. For purposes of this paragraph—

(i) In general. The term "installment acceleration amount" means, with respect to any plan year in a restriction period with respect to an election year, the sum of—

(I) the aggregate amount of excess employee compensation determined under subparagraph (D) with respect to all employees for the plan year, plus

(II) the aggregate amount of extraordinary dividends and redemptions determined under subparagraph (E) for the plan year.

(ii) Annual limitation. The installment acceleration amount for any plan year shall not exceed the excess (if any) of—

(I) the sum of the shortfall amortization installments for the plan year and all preceding plan years in the amortization period elected under paragraph (2)(D) with respect to the shortfall amortization base with respect to an election year, determined without regard to paragraph (2)(D) and this paragraph, over

(II) the sum of the shortfall amortization installments for such plan year and all such preceding plan years, determined after application of paragraph (2)(D) (and in the case of any preceding plan year, after application of this paragraph).

(iii) Carryover of excess installment acceleration amounts.

(I) In general. If the installment acceleration amount for any plan year (determined without regard to clause (ii)) exceeds the limitation under clause (ii), then, subject to subclause (II), such excess shall be treated as an installment acceleration amount with respect to the succeeding plan year.

(II) Cap to apply. If any amount treated as an installment acceleration amount under subclause (I) or this subclause with respect any succeeding plan year, when added to other installment acceleration amounts (determined without regard to clause (ii)) with respect to the plan year, exceeds the limitation under clause (ii), the portion of such amount representing such excess shall be treated as an installment acceleration amount with respect to the next succeeding plan year.

(III) Limitation on years to which amounts carried for. No amount shall be carried under subclause (I) or (II) to a plan year which begins after the first plan year following the last plan year in the restriction period (or after the second plan year following such last plan year in the case of an election year with respect to which 15-year amortization was elected under paragraph (2)(D)).

(IV) Ordering rules. For purposes of applying subclause (II), installment acceleration amounts for the plan year (determined without regard to any carryover under this clause) shall be applied first against the limitation under clause (ii) and then carryovers to such plan year shall be applied against such limitation on a first-in, first-out basis.

(D) Excess employee compensation. For purposes of this paragraph—

(i) In general. The term "excess employee compensation" means, with respect to any employee for any plan year, the excess (if any) of—

(I) the aggregate amount includible in income under this chapter for remuneration during the calendar year in which such plan year begins for services performed by the employee for the plan sponsor (whether or not performed during such calendar year), over

(II) $ 1,000,000.

(ii) Amounts set aside for nonqualified deferred compensation. If during any calendar year assets are set aside or reserved (directly or indirectly) in a trust (or other arrangement as determined by the Secretary), or transferred to such a trust or other arrangement, by a plan sponsor for purposes of paying deferred compensation of an employee under a nonqualified deferred compensation plan (as defined in section 409A) of the plan sponsor, then, for purposes of clause (i), the amount of such assets shall be treated as remuneration of the employee includible in income for the calendar year unless such amount is otherwise includible in income for such year. An amount to which the preceding sentence applies shall not be taken into account under this paragraph for any subsequent calendar year.

(iii) Only remuneration for certain post-2009 services counted. Remuneration shall be taken into account under clause (i) only to the extent attributable to services performed by the employee for the plan sponsor after February 28, 2010.

(iv) Exception for certain equity payments.

(I) In general. There shall not be taken into account under clause (i)(I) any amount includible in income with respect to the granting after February 28, 2010, of service recipient stock (within the meaning of section 409A) that, upon such grant, is subject to a substantial risk of forfeiture (as defined under section 83(c)(1)) for at least 5 years from the date of such grant.

(II) Secretarial authority. The Secretary may by regulation provide for the application of this clause in the case of a person other than a corporation.

(v) Other exceptions. The following amounts includible in income shall not be taken into account under clause (i)(I):

(I) Commissions. Any remuneration payable on a commission basis solely on account of income directly generated by the individual performance of the individual to whom such remuneration is payable.

(II) Certain payments under existing contracts. Any remuneration consisting of nonqualified deferred compensation, restricted stock, stock options, or stock appreciation rights payable or granted under a written binding contract that was in effect on March 1, 2010, and which was not modified in any material respect before such remuneration is paid.

(vi) Self-employed individual treated as employee. The term "employee" includes, with respect to a calendar year, a self-employed individual who is treated as an employee under section 401(c) for the taxable year ending during such calendar year, and the term "compensation" shall include earned income of such individual with respect to such self-employment.

(vii) Indexing of amount. In the case of any calendar year beginning after 2010, the dollar amount under clause (i)(II) shall be increased by an amount equal to--

(I) such dollar amount, multiplied by

(II) the cost-of-living adjustment determined under section 1(f)(3) for the calendar year, determined by substituting "calendar year 2009" for "calendar year 1992" in subparagraph (B) thereof. If the amount of any increase under clause (i) is not a multiple of $ 1,000, such increase shall be rounded to the next lowest multiple of $ 1,000.

(E) Extraordinary dividends and redemptions.

(i) In general. The amount determined under this subparagraph for any plan year is the excess (if any) of the sum of the dividends declared during the plan year by the plan sponsor plus the aggregate amount paid for the redemption of stock of the plan sponsor redeemed during the plan year over the greater of—

(I) the adjusted net income (within the meaning of section 4043 of the Employee Retirement Income Security Act of 1974) of the plan sponsor for the preceding plan year, determined without regard to any reduction by reason of interest, taxes, depreciation, or amortization, or

(II) in the case of a plan sponsor that determined and declared dividends in the same manner for at least 5 consecutive years immediately preceding such plan year, the aggregate amount of dividends determined and declared for such plan year using such manner.

(ii) Only certain post-2009 dividends and redemptions counted. For purposes of clause (i), there shall only be taken into account dividends declared, and redemptions occurring, after February 28, 2010.

(iii) Exception for intra-group dividends. Dividends paid by one member of a controlled group (as defined in section 412(d)(3)) to another member of such group shall not be taken into account under clause (i).

(iv) Exception for certain redemptions. Redemptions that are made pursuant to a plan maintained with respect to employees, or that are made on account of the death, disability, or termination of employment of an employee or shareholder, shall not be taken into account under clause (i).

(v) Exception for certain preferred stock.

(I) In general. Dividends and redemptions with respect to applicable preferred stock shall not be taken into account under clause (i) to the extent that dividends accrue with respect to such stock at a specified rate in all events and without regard to the plan sponsor's income, and interest accrues on any unpaid dividends with respect to such stock.

(II) Applicable preferred stock. For purposes of subclause (I), the term "applicable preferred stock" means preferred stock which was issued before March 1, 2010 (or which was issued after such date and is held by an employee benefit plan subject to the provisions of title I of Employee Retirement Income Security Act of 1974).

(F) Other definitions and rules. For purposes of this paragraph—

(i) Plan sponsor. The term "plan sponsor" includes any member of the plan sponsor's controlled group (as defined in section 412(d)(3)).

(ii) Restriction period. The term "restriction period" means, with respect to any election year—

(I) except as provided in subclause (II), the 3-year period beginning with the election year (or, if later, the first plan year beginning after December 31, 2009), and

(II) if the plan sponsor elects 15-year amortization for the shortfall amortization base for the election year, the 5-year period beginning with the election year (or, if later, the first plan year beginning after December 31, 2009).

(iii) Elections for multiple plans. If a plan sponsor makes elections under paragraph (2)(D) with respect to 2 or more plans, the Secretary shall provide rules for the application of this paragraph to such plans, including rules for the ratable allocation of any installment acceleration amount among such plans on the basis of each plan's relative reduction in the plan's shortfall amortization installment for the first plan year in the amortization period described in subparagraph (A) (determined without regard to this paragraph).

(iv) Mergers and acquisitions. The Secretary shall prescribe rules for the application of paragraph (2)(D) and this paragraph in any case where there is a merger or acquisition involving a plan sponsor making the election under paragraph (2)(D).

(d) Rules relating to funding target—For purposes of this section—

(1) Funding target—Except as provided in subsection (i)(1) with respect to plans in at-risk status, the funding target of a plan for a plan year is the present value of all benefits accrued or earned under the plan as of the beginning of the plan year.

(2) Funding target attainment percentage—The "funding target attainment percentage" of a plan for a plan year is the ratio (expressed as a percentage) which—

(A) the value of plan assets for the plan year (as reduced under subsection (f)(4)(B)), bears to

(B) the funding target of the plan for the plan year (determined without regard to subsection (i)(1)).

(e) Waiver amortization charge—

(1) Determination of waiver amortization charge—The waiver amortization charge (if any) for a plan for any plan year is the aggregate total of the waiver amortization installments for such plan year with respect to the waiver amortization bases for each of the 5 preceding plan years.

(2) Waiver amortization installment—For purposes of paragraph (1)—

(A) Determination—The waiver amortization installments are the amounts necessary to amortize the waiver amortization base of the plan for any plan year in level annual installments over a period of 5 plan years beginning with the succeeding plan year.

(B) Waiver installment—The waiver amortization installment for any plan year in the 5-year period under subparagraph (A) with respect to any waiver amortization base is the annual installment determined under subparagraph (A) for that year for that base.

(3) Interest rate—In determining any waiver amortization installment under this subsection, the plan sponsor shall use the segment rates determined under subparagraph (C) of subsection (h)(2), applied under rules similar to the rules of subparagraph (B) of subsection (h)(2).

(4) Waiver amortization base—The waiver amortization base of a plan for a plan year is the amount of the waived funding deficiency (if any) for such plan year under section 412(c).

(5) Early deemed amortization upon attainment of funding target—In any case in which the funding shortfall of a plan for a plan year is zero, for purposes of determining the waiver amortization charge for such plan year and succeeding plan years, the waiver amortization bases for all preceding plan years (and all waiver amortization installments determined with respect to such bases) shall be reduced to zero.

(f) Reduction of minimum required contribution by prefunding balance and funding standard carryover balance—

(1) Election to maintain balances—

(A) Prefunding balance—The plan sponsor of a defined benefit plan which is not a multiemployer plan may elect to maintain a prefunding balance.

(B) Funding standard carryover balance—

(i) In general—In the case of a defined benefit plan (other than a multiemployer plan) described in clause (ii), the plan sponsor may elect to maintain a funding standard carryover balance, until such balance is reduced to zero.

(ii) Plans maintaining funding standard account in 2007—A plan is described in this clause if the plan—

(I) was in effect for a plan year beginning in 2007, and

(II) had a positive balance in the funding standard account under section 412(b) as in effect for such plan year and determined as of the end of such plan year.

(2) Application of balances—A prefunding balance and a funding standard carryover balance maintained pursuant to this paragraph—

(A) shall be available for crediting against the minimum required contribution, pursuant to an election under paragraph (3),

(B) shall be applied as a reduction in the amount treated as the value of plan assets for purposes of this section, to the extent provided in paragraph (4), and

(C) may be reduced at any time, pursuant to an election under paragraph (5).

(3) Election to apply balances against minimum required contribution—

(A) In general—Except as provided in subparagraphs (B) and (C), in the case of any plan year in which the plan sponsor elects to credit against the minimum required contribution for the current plan year all or a portion of the prefunding balance or the funding standard carryover balance for the current plan year (not in excess of such minimum required contribution), the minimum required contribution for the plan year shall be reduced as of the first day of the plan year by the amount so credited by the plan sponsor. For purposes of the preceding sentence, the minimum required contribution shall be determined after taking into account any waiver under section 412(c).

(B) Coordination with funding standard carryover balance—To the extent that any plan has a funding standard carryover balance greater than zero, no amount of the prefunding balance of such plan may be credited under this paragraph in reducing the minimum required contribution.

(C) Limitation for underfunded plans—The preceding provisions of this paragraph shall not apply for any plan year if the ratio (expressed as a percentage) which—

(i) the value of plan assets for the preceding plan year (as reduced under paragraph (4)(C)), bears to

(ii) the funding target of the plan for the preceding plan year (determined without regard to subsection (i)(1)),

is less than 80 percent. In the case of plan years beginning in 2008, the ratio under this subparagraph may be determined using such methods of estimation as the Secretary may prescribe.

(D) Special rule for certain years of plans maintained by charities.

(i) In general. For purposes of applying subparagraph (C) for plan years beginning after August 31, 2009, and before September 1, 2011, the ratio determined under such subparagraph for the preceding plan year of a plan shall be the greater of—

(I) such ratio, as determined without regard to this subsection, or

(II) the ratio for such plan for the plan year beginning after August 31,

2007 and before September 1, 2008, as determined under rules prescribed by the Secretary.

(ii) Special rule. In the case of a plan for which the valuation date is not the first day of the plan year—

(I) clause (i) shall apply to plan years beginning after December 31, 2007, and before January 1, 2010, and

(II) clause (i)(II) shall apply based on the last plan year beginning before September 1, 2007, as determined under rules prescribed by the Secretary.

(iii) Limitation to charities. This subparagraph shall not apply to any plan unless such plan is maintained exclusively by one or more organizations described in section 501(c)(3).

(4) Effect of balances on amounts treated as value of plan assets—In the case of any plan maintaining a prefunding balance or a funding standard carryover balance pursuant to this subsection, the amount treated as the value of plan assets shall be deemed to be such amount, reduced as provided in the following subparagraphs:

(A) Applicability of shortfall amortization base—For purposes of subsection (c)(5), the value of plan assets is deemed to be such amount, reduced by the amount of the prefunding balance, but only if an election under paragraph (3) applying any portion of the prefunding balance in reducing the minimum required contribution is in effect for the plan year.

(B) Determination of excess assets, funding shortfall, and funding target attainment percentage—

(i) In general—For purposes of subsections (a), (c)(4)(B), and (d)(2)(A), the value of plan assets is deemed to be such amount, reduced by the amount of the prefunding balance and the funding standard carryover balance.

(ii) Special rule for certain binding agreements with PBGC—For purposes of subsection (c)(4)(B), the value of plan assets shall not be deemed to be reduced for a plan year by the amount of the specified balance if, with respect to such balance, there is in effect for a plan year a binding written agreement with the Pension Benefit Guaranty Corporation which provides that such balance is not available to reduce the minimum required contribution for the plan year. For purposes of the preceding sentence, the term "specified balance" means the prefunding balance or the funding standard carryover balance, as the case may be.

(C) Availability of balances in plan year for crediting against minimum required contribution—For purposes of paragraph (3)(C)(i) of this subsection, the value of plan assets is deemed to be such amount, reduced by the amount of the prefunding balance.

(5) Election to reduce balance prior to determinations of value of plan assets and crediting against minimum required contribution—

(A) In general—The plan sponsor may elect to reduce by any amount the balance of the prefunding balance and the funding standard carryover balance for any plan year (but not below zero). Such reduction shall be effective prior to any determination of the value of plan assets for such plan year under this section and application of the balance in reducing the minimum required contribution for such plan for such plan year pursuant to an election under paragraph (2).

(B) Coordination between prefunding balance and funding standard carryover balance—To the extent that any plan has a funding standard carryover balance greater than zero, no election may be made under subparagraph (A) with respect to the prefunding balance.

(6) Prefunding balance—

(A) In general—A prefunding balance maintained by a plan shall consist of a beginning balance of zero, increased and decreased to the extent provided in subparagraphs (B) and (C), and adjusted further as provided in paragraph (8).

(B) Increases—

(i) In general—As of the first day of each plan year beginning after 2008, the prefunding balance of a plan shall be increased by the amount elected by the plan sponsor for the plan year. Such amount shall not exceed the excess (if any) of—

(I) the aggregate total of employer contributions to the plan for the preceding plan year, over—

(II) the minimum required contribution for such preceding plan year.

(ii) Adjustments for interest—Any excess contributions under clause (i) shall be properly adjusted for interest accruing for the periods between the first day of the current plan year and the dates on which the excess contributions were made, determined by using the effective interest rate for the preceding plan year and by treating contributions as being first used to satisfy the minimum required contribution.

(iii) Certain contributions necessary to avoid benefit limitations disregarded—The excess described in clause (i) with respect to any preceding plan year shall be reduced (but not below zero) by the amount of contributions an employer would be required to make under subsection (b), (c), or (e) of section 436 to avoid a benefit limitation which would otherwise be imposed under such paragraph for the preceding plan year. Any contribution which may be taken into account in satisfying the requirements of more than 1 of such paragraphs shall be taken into account only once for purposes of this clause.

(C) Decreases—The prefunding balance of a plan shall be decreased (but not below zero) by—

(i) as of the first day of each plan year after 2008, the amount of such balance credited under paragraph (2) (if any) in reducing the minimum required contribution of the plan for the preceding plan year, and

(ii) as of the time specified in paragraph (5)(A), any reduction in such balance elected under paragraph (5).

(7) Funding standard carryover balance—

(A) In general—A funding standard carryover balance maintained by a plan shall consist of a beginning balance determined under subparagraph (B), decreased to the extent provided in subparagraph (C), and adjusted further as provided in paragraph (8).

(B) Beginning balance—The beginning balance of the funding standard carryover balance shall be the positive balance described in paragraph (1)(B)(ii)(II).

(C) Decreases—The funding standard carryover balance of a plan shall be decreased (but not below zero) by—

(i) as of the first day of each plan year after 2008, the amount of such balance credited under paragraph (2) (if any) in reducing the minimum required contribution of the plan for the preceding plan year, and

(ii) as of the time specified in paragraph (5)(A), any reduction in such balance elected under paragraph (5).

(8) Adjustments for investment experience—In determining the prefunding balance or the funding standard carryover balance of a plan as of the first day of the plan year, the plan sponsor shall, in accordance with regulations prescribed by the Secretary, adjust such balance to reflect the rate of return on plan assets for the preceding plan year. Notwithstanding subsection (g)(3), such rate of return shall be determined on the basis of fair market value and shall properly take into account, in accordance with such regulations, all contributions, distributions, and other plan payments made during such period.

(9) Elections—Elections under this subsection shall be made at such times, and in such form and manner, as shall be prescribed in regulations of the Secretary.

(g) Valuation of plan assets and liabilities—

(1) Timing of determinations—Except as otherwise provided under this subsection, all determinations under this section for a plan year shall be made as of the valuation date of the plan for such plan year.

(2) Valuation date—For purposes of this section—

(A) In general—Except as provided in subparagraph (B), the valuation date of a plan for any plan year shall be the first day of the plan year.

(B) Exception for small plans—If, on each day during the preceding plan year, a plan had 100 or fewer participants, the plan may designate any day during the plan year as its valuation date for such plan year and succeeding plan years. For purposes of this subparagraph, all defined benefit plans (other than multiemployer plans) maintained by the same employer (or any member of such employer's controlled group) shall be treated as 1 plan, but only participants with respect to such employer or member shall be taken into account.

(C) Application of certain rules in determination of plan size—For purposes of this paragraph—

(i) Plans not in existence in preceding year—In the case of the first plan year of any plan, subparagraph (B) shall apply to such plan by taking into account the number of participants that the plan is reasonably expected to have on days during such first plan year.

(ii) Predecessors—Any reference in subparagraph (B) to an employer shall include a reference to any predecessor of such employer.

(3) Determination of value of plan assets—For purposes of this section—

(A) In general—Except as provided in subparagraph (B), the value of plan assets shall be the fair market value of the assets.

(B) Averaging allowed—A plan may determine the value of plan assets on the basis of the averaging of fair market values, but only if such method—

(i) is permitted under regulations prescribed by the Secretary,

(ii) does not provide for averaging of such values over more than the period beginning on the last day of the 25th month preceding the month in which the valuation date occurs and ending on the valuation date (or a similar period in the case of a valuation date which is not the 1st day of a month), and

(iii) does not result in a determination of the value of plan assets which, at any time, is lower than 90 percent or greater than 110 percent of the fair market value of such assets at such time.

Any such averaging shall be adjusted for contributions, distributions, and expected earnings (as determined by the plan's actuary on the basis of an assumed earnings rate specified by the actuary but not in excess of the third segment rate applicable under subsection (h)(2)(C)(iii)), as specified by the Secretary.

(4) Accounting for contribution receipts—For purposes of determining the value of assets under paragraph (3)—

(A) Prior year contributions—If—

(i) an employer makes any contribution to the plan after the valuation date for the plan year in which the contribution is made, and

(ii) the contribution is for a preceding plan year,

the contribution shall be taken into account as an asset of the plan as of the valuation date, except that in the case of any plan year beginning after 2008, only the present value (determined as of the valuation date) of such contribution may be taken into account. For purposes of the preceding sentence, present value shall be determined using the effective interest rate for the preceding plan year to which the contribution is properly allocable.

(B) Special rule for current year contributions made before valuation date—If any contributions for any plan year are made to or under the plan during the plan year but before the valuation date for the plan year, the assets of the plan as of the valuation date shall not include—

(i) such contributions, and

(ii) interest on such contributions for the period between the date of the contributions and the valuation date, determined by using the effective interest rate for the plan year.

(h) Actuarial assumptions and methods—

(1) In general—Subject to this subsection, the determination of any present value or other computation under this section shall be made on the basis of actuarial assumptions and methods—

(A) each of which is reasonable (taking into account the experience of the plan and reasonable expectations), and

(B) which, in combination, offer the actuary's best estimate of anticipated experience under the plan.

(2) Interest rates—

(A) Effective interest rate—For purposes of this section, the term "effective interest rate" means, with respect to any plan for any plan year, the single rate of interest which, if used to determine the present value of the plan's accrued or earned benefits referred to in subsection (d)(1), would result in an amount equal to the funding target of the plan for such plan year.

(B) Interest rates for determining funding target—For purposes of determining the funding target and target normal cost of a plan for any plan year, the interest rate used in determining the present value of the benefits of the plan shall be—

(i) in the case of benefits reasonably determined to be payable during the 5-year period beginning on the first day of the plan year, the first segment rate with respect to the applicable month,

(ii) in the case of benefits reasonably determined to be payable during the 15-year period beginning at the end of the period described in clause (i), the second segment rate with respect to the applicable month, and

(iii) in the case of benefits reasonably determined to be payable after the period described in clause (ii), the third segment rate with respect to the applicable month.

(C) Segment rates—For purposes of this paragraph—

(i) First segment rate—The term "first segment rate" means, with respect to any month, the single rate of interest which shall be determined by the Secretary for such month on the basis of the corporate bond yield curve for such month, taking into account only that portion of such yield curve which is based on bonds maturing during the 5-year period commencing with such month.

(ii) Second segment rate—The term "second segment rate" means, with respect to any month, the single rate of interest which shall be determined by the Secretary for such month on the basis of the corporate bond yield curve for such month, taking into account only that portion of such yield curve which is based on bonds maturing during the 15-year period beginning at the end of the period described in clause (i).

(iii) Third segment rate—The term "third segment rate" means, with respect to any month, the single rate of interest which shall be determined by the Secretary for such month on the basis of the corporate bond yield curve for such month, taking into account only that portion of such yield curve which is based on bonds maturing during periods beginning after the period described in clause (ii).

(D) Corporate bond yield curve—For purposes of this paragraph—

(i) In general—The term "corporate bond yield curve" means, with respect to any month, a yield curve which is prescribed by the Secretary for such month and which reflects the average, for the 24-month period ending with the month preceding such month, of monthly yields on investment grade corporate bonds with varying maturities and that are in the top 3 quality levels available.

(ii) Election to use yield curve—Solely for purposes of determining the minimum required contribution under this section, the plan sponsor may, in lieu of the segment rates determined under subparagraph (C), elect to use interest rates under the corporate bond yield curve. For purposes of the preceding sentence such curve shall be determined without regard to the 24-month averaging described in clause (i). Such election, once made, may be revoked only with the consent of the Secretary.

(E) Applicable month—For purposes of this paragraph, the term "applicable month" means, with respect to any plan for any plan year, the month which includes the valuation date of such plan for such plan year or, at the election of the plan sponsor, any of the 4 months which precede such month. Any election made under this subparagraph shall apply to the plan year for which the election is made and all succeeding plan years, unless the election is revoked with the consent of the Secretary.

(F) Publication requirements—The Secretary shall publish for each month the corporate bond yield curve (and the corporate bond yield curve reflecting the modification described in section 417(e)(3)(D)(i) for such month) and each of the rates determined under subparagraph (C) for such month. The Secretary shall also publish a description of the methodology used to determine such yield curve and such rates which is sufficiently detailed to enable plans to make reasonable projections regarding the yield curve and such rates for future months based on the plan's projection of future interest rates.

* * *

(3) Mortality tables—

(A) In general—Except as provided in subparagraph (C) or (D), the Secretary shall by regulation prescribe mortality tables to be used in determining any present value or making any computation under this section. Such tables shall be based on the actual experience of pension plans and projected trends in such experience. In prescribing such tables, the Secretary shall take into account results of available independent studies of mortality of individuals covered by pension plans.

(B) Periodic revision—The Secretary shall (at least every 10 years) make revisions in any table in effect under subparagraph (A) to reflect the actual experience of pension plans and projected trends in such experience.

(C) Substitute mortality table—

(i) In general—Upon request by the plan sponsor and approval by the Secretary, a mortality table which meets the requirements of clause (iii) shall be used in determining any present value or making any computation under this section during the period of consecutive plan years (not to exceed 10) specified in the request.

(ii) Early termination of period—Notwithstanding clause (i), a mortality table described in clause (i) shall cease to be in effect as of the earliest of—

(I) the date on which there is a significant change in the participants in the plan by reason of a plan spinoff or merger or otherwise, or

(II) the date on which the plan actuary determines that such table does not meet the requirements of clause (iii).

(iii) Requirements—A mortality table meets the requirements of this clause if—

(I) there is a sufficient number of plan participants, and the pension plans have been maintained for a sufficient period of time, to have credible information necessary for purposes of subclause (II), and

(II) such table reflects the actual experience of the pension plans maintained by the sponsor and projected trends in general mortality experience.

(iv) All plans in controlled group must use separate table—Except as provided by the Secretary, a plan sponsor may not use a mortality table under this subparagraph for any plan maintained by the plan sponsor unless—

(I) a separate mortality table is established and used under this subparagraph for each other plan maintained by the plan sponsor and if the plan sponsor is a member of a controlled group, each member of the controlled group, and

(II) the requirements of clause (iii) are met separately with respect to the table so established for each such plan, determined by only taking into account the participants of such plan, the time such plan has been in existence, and the actual experience of such plan.

(v) Deadline for submission and disposition of application—

(I) Submission—The plan sponsor shall submit a mortality table to the Secretary for approval under this subparagraph at least 7 months before the 1st day of the period described in clause (i).

(II) Disposition—Any mortality table submitted to the Secretary for approval under this subparagraph shall be treated as in effect as of the 1st day of the period described in clause (i) unless the Secretary, during the 180-day period beginning on the date of such submission, disapproves of such table and provides the reasons that such table fails to meet the requirements of clause (iii). The 180-day period shall be extended upon mutual agreement of the Secretary and the plan sponsor.

(D) Separate mortality tables for the disabled—Notwithstanding subparagraph (A)—

(i) In general—The Secretary shall establish mortality tables which may be used (in lieu of the tables under subparagraph (A)) under this subsection for individuals who are entitled to benefits under the plan on account of disability. The Secretary shall establish separate tables for individuals whose disabilities occur in plan years beginning before January 1, 1995, and for individuals whose disabilities occur in plan years beginning on or after such date.

(ii) Special rule for disabilities occurring after 1994—In the case of disabilities occurring in plan years beginning after December 31, 1994, the tables under clause (i) shall apply only with respect to individuals described in such subclause who are disabled within the meaning of title II of the Social Security Act and the regulations thereunder.

(iii) Periodic revision—The Secretary shall (at least every 10 years) make revisions in any table in effect under clause (i) to reflect the actual experience of pension plans and projected trends in such experience.

(4) Probability of benefit payments in the form of lump sums or other optional forms—For purposes of determining any present value or making any computation under this section, there shall be taken into account—

(A) the probability that future benefit payments under the plan will be made in the form of optional forms of benefits provided under the plan (including lump sum distributions, determined on the basis of the plan's experience and other related assumptions), and

(B) any difference in the present value of such future benefit payments resulting from the use of actuarial assumptions, in determining benefit payments in any such optional form of benefits, which are different from those specified in this subsection.

(5) Approval of large changes in actuarial assumptions—

(A) In general—No actuarial assumption used to determine the funding target for a plan to which this paragraph applies may be changed without the approval of the Secretary.

(B) Plans to which paragraph applies—This paragraph shall apply to a plan only if—

(i) the plan is a defined benefit plan (other than a multiemployer plan) to which title IV of the Employee Retirement Income Security Act of 1974 applies,

(ii) the aggregate unfunded vested benefits as of the close of the preceding plan year (as determined under section 4006(a)(3)(E)(iii) of the Employee Retirement Income Security Act of 1974) of such plan and all other plans maintained by the contributing sponsors (as defined in section 4001(a)(13) of such Act) and members of such sponsors' controlled groups (as defined in section 4001(a)(14) of such Act) which are covered by title IV (disregarding plans with no unfunded vested benefits) exceed $50,000,000, and

(iii) the change in assumptions (determined after taking into account any changes in interest rate and mortality table) results in a decrease in the funding shortfall of the plan for the current plan year that exceeds $50,000,000, or that exceeds $5,000,000 and that is 5 percent or more of the funding target of the plan before such change.

(i) Special rules for at-risk plans—

(1) Funding target for plans in at-risk status—

(A) In general—In the case of a plan which is in at-risk status for a plan year, the funding target of the plan for the plan year shall be equal to the sum of—

(i) the present value of all benefits accrued or earned under the plan as of the beginning of the plan year, as determined by using the additional actuarial assumptions described in subparagraph (B), and

(ii) in the case of a plan which also has been in at-risk status for at least 2 of the 4 preceding plan years, a loading factor determined under subparagraph (C).

(B) Additional actuarial assumptions—The actuarial assumptions described in this subparagraph are as follows:

(i) All employees who are not otherwise assumed to retire as of the valuation date but who will be eligible to elect benefits during the plan year and the 10 succeeding plan years shall be assumed to retire at the earliest retirement date under the plan but not before the end of the plan year for which the at-risk funding target and at-risk target normal cost are being determined.

(ii) All employees shall be assumed to elect the retirement benefit available under the plan at the assumed retirement age (determined after application of clause (i)) which would result in the highest present value of benefits.

(C) Loading factor—The loading factor applied with respect to a plan under this paragraph for any plan year is the sum of—

(i) $700, times the number of participants in the plan, plus

(ii) 4 percent of the funding target (determined without regard to this paragraph) of the plan for the plan year.

(2) Target normal cost of at-risk plans—In the case of a plan which is in at-risk status for a plan year, the target normal cost of the plan for such plan year shall be equal to the sum of—

(A) the excess of—

(i) the sum of—

(I) the present value of all benefits which are expected to accrue or to be earned under the plan during the plan year, determined using the additional actuarial assumptions described in paragraph (1)(B), plus

(II) the amount of plan-related expenses expected to be paid from plan assets during the plan year, over

(ii) the amount of mandatory employee contributions expected to be made during the plan year, plus

(B) in the case of a plan which also has been in at-risk status for at least 2 of the 4 preceding plan years, a loading factor equal to 4 percent of the amount determined under subsection (b)(1)(A)(i) with respect to the plan for the plan year.

(3) Minimum amount—In no event shall—

(A) the at-risk funding target be less than the funding target, as determined without regard to this subsection, or

(B) the at-risk target normal cost be less than the target normal cost, as determined without regard to this subsection.

(4) Determination of at-risk status—For purposes of this subsection—

(A) In general—A plan is in at-risk status for a plan year if—

(i) the funding target attainment percentage for the preceding plan year (determined under this section without regard to this subsection) is less than 80 percent, and

(ii) the funding target attainment percentage for the preceding plan year (determined under this section by using the additional actuarial assumptions described in paragraph (1)(B) in computing the funding target) is less than 70 percent.

(B) Transition rule—In the case of plan years beginning in 2008, 2009, and 2010, subparagraph (A)(i) shall be applied by substituting the following percentages for "80 percent":

(i) 65 percent in the case of 2008.

(ii) 70 percent in the case of 2009.

(iii) 75 percent in the case of 2010.

In the case of plan years beginning in 2008, the funding target attainment percentage for the preceding plan year under subparagraph (A) may be determined using such methods of estimation as the Secretary may provide.

* * *

(5) Transition between applicable funding targets and between applicable target normal costs—

(A) In general—In any case in which a plan which is in at-risk status for a plan year has been in such status for a consecutive period of fewer than 5 plan years, the applicable amount of the funding target and of the target normal cost shall be, in lieu of the amount determined without regard to this paragraph, the sum of—

(i) the amount determined under this section without regard to this subsection, plus

(ii) the transition percentage for such plan year of the excess of the amount determined under this subsection (without regard to this paragraph) over the amount determined under this section without regard to this subsection.

(B) Transition percentage—For purposes of subparagraph (A), the transition percentage shall be determined in accordance with the following table:

If the consecutive number of years (including the plan year) the plan is in at-risk status is—	*The transition percentage is—*
1	20
2	40
3	60
4	80.

(C) Years before effective date—For purposes of this paragraph, plan years beginning before 2008 shall not be taken into account.

(6) Small plan exception—If, on each day during the preceding plan year, a plan had 500 or fewer participants, the plan shall not be treated as in at-risk status for the plan year. For purposes of this paragraph, all defined benefit plans (other than multiemployer plans) maintained by the same employer (or any member of such employer's controlled group) shall be treated as 1 plan, but only participants with respect to such employer or member shall be taken into account and the rules of subsection (g)(2)(C) shall apply.

(j) Payment of minimum required contributions—

(1) In general—For purposes of this section, the due date for any payment of any minimum required contribution for any plan year shall be 8 1/2 months after the close of the plan year.

(2) Interest—Any payment required under paragraph (1) for a plan year that is made on a date other than the valuation date for such plan year shall be adjusted for interest accruing for the period between the valuation date and the payment date, at the effective rate of interest for the plan for such plan year.

(3) Accelerated quarterly contribution schedule for underfunded plans—

(A) Failure to timely make required installment—In any case in which the plan has a funding shortfall for the preceding plan year, the employer maintaining the plan shall make the required installments under this paragraph and if the employer fails to pay the full amount of a required installment for the plan year, then the amount of interest charged under paragraph (2) on the underpayment for the period of underpayment shall be determined by using a rate of interest equal to the rate otherwise used under paragraph (2) plus 5 percentage points. In the case of plan years beginning in 2008, the funding shortfall for the preceding plan year may be determined using such methods of estimation as the Secretary may provide.

(B) Amount of underpayment, period of underpayment—For purposes of subparagraph (A)—

(i) Amount—The amount of the underpayment shall be the excess of—

(I) the required installment, over

(II) the amount (if any) of the installment contributed to or under the plan on or before the due date for the installment.

(ii) Period of underpayment—The period for which any interest is charged under this paragraph with respect to any portion of the underpayment shall run from the due date for the installment to the date on which such portion is contributed to or under the plan.

(iii) Order of crediting contributions—For purposes of clause (i)(II), contributions shall be credited against unpaid required installments in the order in which such installments are required to be paid.

(C) Number of required installments; due dates—For purposes of this paragraph—

(i) Payable in 4 installments—There shall be 4 required installments for each plan year.

(ii) Time for payment of installments—The due dates for required installments are set forth in the following table:

In the case of the following required installment:	*The due date is:*
1st	April 15
2nd	July 15
3rd	October 15
4th	January 15 of the following year.

(D) Amount of required installment—For purposes of this paragraph—

(i) In general—The amount of any required installment shall be 25 percent of the required annual payment.

(ii) Required annual payment—For purposes of clause (i), the term "required annual payment" means the lesser of—

(I) 90 percent of the minimum required contribution (determined without regard to this subsection) to the plan for the plan year under this section, or

(II) 100 percent of the minimum required contribution (determined without regard to this subsection or to any waiver under section 412(c)) to the plan for the preceding plan year.

Subclause (II) shall not apply if the preceding plan year referred to in such clause was not a year of 12 months.

(E) Fiscal years, short years, and years with alternate valuation date—

(i) Fiscal years—In applying this paragraph to a plan year beginning on any date other than January 1, there shall be substituted for the months specified in this paragraph, the months which correspond thereto.

(ii) Short plan year—This subparagraph shall be applied to plan years of less than 12 months in accordance with regulations prescribed by the Secretary.

(iii) Plan with alternate valuation date—The Secretary shall prescribe regulations for the application of this paragraph in the case of a plan which has a valuation date other than the first day of the plan year.

(F) Quarterly contributions not to include certain increased contributions. Subparagraph (D) shall be applied without regard to any increase under subsection (c)(7).

(4) Liquidity requirement in connection with quarterly contributions—

(A) In general—A plan to which this paragraph applies shall be treated as failing to pay the full amount of any required installment under paragraph (3) to the extent that the value of the liquid assets paid in such installment is less than the liquidity shortfall (whether or not such liquidity shortfall exceeds the amount of such installment required to be paid but for this paragraph).

(B) Plans to which paragraph applies—This paragraph shall apply to a plan (other than a plan described in subsection (g)(2)(B)) which—

(i) is required to pay installments under paragraph (3) for a plan year, and

(ii) has a liquidity shortfall for any quarter during such plan year.

(C) Period of underpayment—For purposes of paragraph (3)(A), any portion of an installment that is treated as not paid under subparagraph (A) shall continue to be treated as unpaid until the close of the quarter in which the due date for such installment occurs.

(D) Limitation on increase—If the amount of any required installment is increased by reason of subparagraph (A), in no event shall such increase exceed the amount which, when added to prior installments for the plan year, is necessary to increase the funding target attainment percentage of the plan for the plan year (taking into account the expected increase in funding target due to benefits accruing or earned during the plan year) to 100 percent.

(E) Definitions—For purposes of this paragraph—

(i) Liquidity shortfall—The term "liquidity shortfall" means, with respect to any required installment, an amount equal to the excess (as of the last day of the quarter for which such installment is made) of—

(I) the base amount with respect to such quarter, over

(II) the value (as of such last day) of the plan's liquid assets.

(ii) Base amount—

(I) In general—The term "base amount" means, with respect to any quarter, an amount equal to 3 times the sum of the adjusted disbursements from the plan for the 12 months ending on the last day of such quarter.

(II) Special rule—If the amount determined under subclause (I) exceeds an amount equal to 2 times the sum of the adjusted disbursements from the plan for the 36 months ending on the last day of the quarter and an enrolled actuary certifies to the satisfaction of the Secretary that such excess is the result of nonrecurring circumstances, the base amount with respect to such quarter shall be determined without regard to amounts related to those nonrecurring circumstances.

(iii) Disbursements from the plan—The term "disbursements from the plan" means all disbursements from the trust, including purchases of annuities, payments of single sums and other benefits, and administrative expenses.

(iv) Adjusted disbursements—The term "adjusted disbursements" means disbursements from the plan reduced by the product of—

(I) the plan's funding target attainment percentage for the plan year, and

(II) the sum of the purchases of annuities, payments of single sums, and such other disbursements as the Secretary shall provide in regulations.

(v) Liquid assets—The term "liquid assets" means cash, marketable securities, and such other assets as specified by the Secretary in regulations.

(vi) Quarter—The term "quarter" means, with respect to any required installment, the 3-month period preceding the month in which the due date for such installment occurs.

(F) Regulations—The Secretary may prescribe such regulations as are necessary to carry out this paragraph.

(k) Imposition of lien where failure to make required contributions—

(1) In general—In the case of a plan to which this subsection applies (as provided under paragraph (2)), if—

(A) any person fails to make a contribution payment required by section 412 and this section before the due date for such payment, and

(B) the unpaid balance of such payment (including interest), when added to the aggregate unpaid balance of all preceding such payments for which payment was not made before the due date (including interest), exceeds $1,000,000, then there shall be a lien in favor of the plan in the amount determined under paragraph (3) upon all property and rights to property, whether real or personal, belonging to such person and any other person who is a member of the same controlled group of which such person is a member.

(2) Plans to which subsection applies—This subsection shall apply to a defined benefit plan (other than a multiemployer plan) covered under section 4021 of the Employee Retirement Income Security Act of 1974 for any plan year for which the funding target attainment percentage (as defined in subsection (d)(2)) of such plan is less than 100 percent.

(3) Amount of lien—For purposes of paragraph (1), the amount of the lien shall be equal to the aggregate unpaid balance of contribution payments required under this section and section 412 for which payment has not been made before the due date.

(4) Notice of failure; lien—

(A) Notice of failure—A person committing a failure described in paragraph (1) shall notify the Pension Benefit Guaranty Corporation of such failure within 10 days of the due date for the required contribution payment.

(B) Period of lien—The lien imposed by paragraph (1) shall arise on the due date for the required contribution payment and shall continue until the last day of the first plan year in which the plan ceases to be described in paragraph (1)(B). Such lien shall continue to run without regard to whether such plan continues to be described in paragraph (2) during the period referred to in the preceding sentence.

(C) Certain rules to apply—Any amount with respect to which a lien is imposed under paragraph (1) shall be treated as taxes due and owing the United States and rules similar to the rules of subsections (c), (d), and (e) of section 4068 of the Employee Retirement Income Security Act of 1974 shall apply with respect to a lien imposed by subsection (a) and the amount with respect to such lien.

(5) Enforcement—Any lien created under paragraph (1) may be perfected and enforced only by the Pension Benefit Guaranty Corporation, or at the direction of the Pension Benefit Guaranty Corporation, by the contributing sponsor (or any member of the controlled group of the contributing sponsor).

(6) Definitions—For purposes of this subsection—

(A) Contribution payment—The term "contribution payment" means, in connection with a plan, a contribution payment required to be made to the plan, including any required installment under paragraphs (3) and (4) of subsection (j).

(B) Due date; required installment—The terms "due date" and "required installment" have the meanings given such terms by subsection (j).

(C) Controlled group—The term "controlled group" means any group treated as a single employer under subsections (b), (c), (m), and (o) of section 414.

(l) Qualified transfers to health benefit accounts—In the case of a qualified transfer (as defined in section 420), any assets so transferred shall not, for purposes of this section, be treated as assets in the plan.

§ 431. Minimum funding standards for multiemployer plans.

(a) In general—For purposes of section 412, the accumulated funding deficiency of a multiemployer plan for any plan year is—

(1) except as provided in paragraph (2), the amount, determined as of the end of the plan year, equal to the excess (if any) of the total charges to the funding standard account of the plan for all plan years (beginning with the first plan year for which this part applies to the plan) over the total credits to such account for such years, and

(2) if the multiemployer plan is in reorganization for any plan year, the accumulated funding deficiency of the plan determined under section 4243 of the Employee Retirement Income Security Act of 1974.

(b) Funding standard account—

(1) Account required—Each multiemployer plan to which this part applies shall establish and maintain a funding standard account. Such account shall be credited and charged solely as provided in this section.

(2) Charges to account—For a plan year, the funding standard account shall be charged with the sum of—

(A) the normal cost of the plan for the plan year,

(B) the amounts necessary to amortize in equal annual installments (until fully amortized)—

(i) in the case of a plan which comes into existence on or after January 1, 2008, the unfunded past service liability under the plan on the first day of the first plan year to which this section applies, over a period of 15 plan years,

(ii) separately, with respect to each plan year, the net increase (if any) in unfunded past service liability under the plan arising from plan amendments adopted in such year, over a period of 15 plan years,

(iii) separately, with respect to each plan year, the net experience loss (if any) under the plan, over a period of 15 plan years, and

(iv) separately, with respect to each plan year, the net loss (if any) resulting from changes in actuarial assumptions used under the plan, over a period of 15 plan years,

(C) the amount necessary to amortize each waived funding deficiency (within the meaning of section 412(c)(3)) for each prior plan year in equal annual installments (until fully amortized) over a period of 15 plan years,

(D) the amount necessary to amortize in equal annual installments (until fully amortized) over a period of 5 plan years any amount credited to the funding standard account under section 412(b)(3)(D) (as in effect on the day before the date of the enactment of the Pension Protection Act of 2006), and

(E) the amount necessary to amortize in equal annual installments (until fully amortized) over a period of 20 years the contributions which would be required to be made under the plan but for the provisions of section 412(c)(7)(A)(i)(I) (as in effect on the day before the date of the enactment of the Pension Protection Act of 2006).

(3) Credits to account—For a plan year, the funding standard account shall be credited with the sum of—

(A) the amount considered contributed by the employer to or under the plan for the plan year,

(B) the amount necessary to amortize in equal annual installments (until fully amortized)—

(i) separately, with respect to each plan year, the net decrease (if any) in unfunded past service liability under the plan arising from plan amendments adopted in such year, over a period of 15 plan years,

(ii) separately, with respect to each plan year, the net experience gain (if any) under the plan, over a period of 15 plan years, and

(iii) separately, with respect to each plan year, the net gain (if any) resulting from changes in actuarial assumptions used under the plan, over a period of 15 plan years,

(C) the amount of the waived funding deficiency (within the meaning of section 412(c)(3)) for the plan year, and

(D) in the case of a plan year for which the accumulated funding deficiency is determined under the funding standard account if such plan year follows a plan year for which such deficiency was determined under the alternative minimum funding standard under section 412(g) (as in effect on the day before the date of the enactment of the Pension Protection Act of 2006), the excess (if any) of any debit balance in the funding standard account (determined without regard to this subparagraph) over any debit balance in the alternative minimum funding standard account.

(4) Special rule for amounts first amortized in plan years before 2008—In the case of any amount amortized under section 412(b) (as in effect on the day before the date of the enactment of the Pension Protection Act of 2006) over any period beginning with a plan year beginning before 2008 in lieu of the amortization described in paragraphs (2)(B) and (3)(B), such amount shall continue to be amortized under such section as so in effect.

(5) Combining and offsetting amounts to be amortized—Under regulations prescribed by the Secretary, amounts required to be amortized under paragraph (2) or paragraph (3), as the case may be—

(A) may be combined into one amount under such paragraph to be amortized over a period determined on the basis of the remaining amortization period for all items entering into such combined amount, and

(B) may be offset against amounts required to be amortized under the other such paragraph, with the resulting amount to be amortized over a period determined on the basis of the remaining amortization periods for all items entering into whichever of the two amounts being offset is the greater.

(6) Interest—The funding standard account (and items therein) shall be charged or credited (as determined under regulations prescribed by the Secretary of the Treasury) with interest at the appropriate rate consistent with the rate or rates of interest used under the plan to determine costs.

(7) Special rules relating to charges and credits to funding standard account—For purposes of this part—

(A) Withdrawal liability—Any amount received by a multiemployer plan in payment of all or part of an employer's withdrawal liability under part 1 of subtitle E of title IV of the Employee Retirement Income Security Act of 1974 shall be considered an amount contributed by the employer to or under the plan. The Secretary may prescribe by regulation additional charges and credits to a multiemployer plan's funding standard account to the extent necessary to prevent withdrawal liability payments from being unduly reflected as advance funding for plan liabilities.

(B) Adjustments when a multiemployer plan leaves reorganization—If a multiemployer plan is not in reorganization in the plan year but was in reorganization in the immediately preceding plan year, any balance in the funding standard account at the close of such immediately preceding plan year—

(i) shall be eliminated by an offsetting credit or charge (as the case may be), but

(ii) shall be taken into account in subsequent plan years by being amortized in equal annual installments (until fully amortized) over 30 plan years.

The preceding sentence shall not apply to the extent of any accumulated funding deficiency under section 4243(a) of such Act as of the end of the last plan year that the plan was in reorganization.

(C) Plan payments to supplemental program or withdrawal liability payment fund—Any amount paid by a plan during a plan year to the Pension Benefit Guaranty Corporation pursuant to section 4222 of such Act or to a fund exempt under section 501(c)(22) pursuant to section 4223 of such Act shall reduce the amount of contributions considered received by the plan for the plan year.

(D) Interim withdrawal liability payments—Any amount paid by an employer pending a final determination of the employer's withdrawal liability under part 1 of subtitle E of title IV of such Act and subsequently refunded to the employer by the plan shall be charged to the funding standard account in accordance with regulations prescribed by the Secretary.

(E) Election for deferral of charge for portion of net experience loss—If an election is in effect under section 412(b)(7)(F) (as in effect on the day before the date of the enactment of the Pension Protection Act of 2006) for any plan year, the funding standard account shall be charged in the plan year to which the portion of the net experience loss deferred by such election was deferred with the amount so deferred (and paragraph (2)(B)(iii) shall not apply to the amount so charged).

(F) Financial assistance—Any amount of any financial assistance from the Pension Benefit Guaranty Corporation to any plan, and any repayment of such amount, shall be taken into account under this section and section 412 in such manner as is determined by the Secretary.

(G) Short-term benefits—To the extent that any plan amendment increases the unfunded past service liability under the plan by reason of an increase in benefits which are not payable as a life annuity but are payable under the terms of the plan for a period that does not exceed 14 years from the effective date of the amendment, paragraph (2)(B)(ii) shall be applied separately with respect to such increase in unfunded past service liability by substituting the number of years of the period during which such benefits are payable for "15".

(8) Special relief rules. Notwithstanding any other provision of this subsection—

(A) Amortization of net investment losses.

(i) In general. A multiemployer plan with respect to which the solvency test under subparagraph (C) is met may treat the portion of any experience loss or gain attributable to net investment losses incurred in either or both of the first two plan years ending after August 31, 2008, as an item separate from other experience losses, to be amortized in equal annual installments (until fully amortized) over the period –

(I) beginning with the plan year in which such portion is first recognized in the actuarial value of assets, and

(II) ending with the last plan year in the 30-plan year period beginning with the plan year in which such net investment loss was incurred.

(ii) Coordination with extensions. If this subparagraph applies for any plan year—

(I) no extension of the amortization period under clause (i) shall be allowed under subsection (d), and

(II) if an extension was granted under subsection (d) for any plan year before the election to have this subparagraph apply to the plan year, such extension shall not result in such amortization period exceeding 30 years.

(iii) Net investment losses. For purposes of this subparagraph—

(I) In general. Net investment losses shall be determined in the manner prescribed by the Secretary on the basis of the difference between actual and expected returns (including any difference attributable to any criminally fraudulent investment arrangement).

(II) **Criminally fraudulent investment arrangements.** The determination as to whether an arrangement is a criminally fraudulent investment arrangement shall be made under rules substantially similar to the rules prescribed by the Secretary for purposes of section 165.

(B) Expanded smoothing period.

(i) In general. A multiemployer plan with respect to which the solvency test under subparagraph (C) is met may change its asset valuation method in a manner which—

(I) spreads the difference between expected and actual returns for either or both of the first 2 plan years ending after August 31, 2008, over a period of not more than 10 years,

(II) provides that for either or both of the first 2 plan years beginning after August 31, 2008, the value of plan assets at any time shall not be less than 80 percent or greater than 130 percent of the fair market value of such assets at such time, or

(III) makes both changes described in subclauses (I) and (II) to such method.

(ii) Asset valuation methods. If this subparagraph applies for any plan year—

(I) the Secretary shall not treat the asset valuation method of the plan as unreasonable solely because of the changes in such method described in clause (i), and

(II) such changes shall be deemed approved by the Secretary under section 302(d)(1) of the Employee Retirement Income Security Act of 1974 and section 412(d)(1).

(iii) Amortization of reduction in unfunded accrued liability. If this subparagraph and subparagraph (A) both apply for any plan year, the plan shall treat any reduction in unfunded accrued liability resulting from the application of this subparagraph as a separate experience amortization base, to be amortized in equal annual installments (until fully amortized) over a period of 30 plan years rather than the period such liability would otherwise be amortized over.

(C) Solvency test. The solvency test under this paragraph is met only if the plan actuary certifies that the plan is projected to have sufficient assets to timely pay expected benefits and anticipated expenditures over the amortization period, taking into account the changes in the funding standard account under this paragraph.

(D) Restriction on benefit increases. If subparagraph (A) or (B) apply to a multiemployer plan for any plan year, then, in addition to any other applicable restrictions on benefit increases, a plan amendment increasing benefits may not go into effect during either of the 2 plan years immediately following such plan year unless—

(i) the plan actuary certifies that—

(I) any such increase is paid for out of additional contributions not allocated to the plan immediately before the application of this paragraph to the plan, and

(II) the plan's funded percentage and projected credit balances for such 2 plan years are reasonably expected to be at least as high as such percentage and balances would have been if the benefit increase had not been adopted, or

(ii) the amendment is required as a condition of qualification under part I of subchapter D or to comply with other applicable law.

(E) Reporting. A plan sponsor of a plan to which this paragraph applies shall—

(i) give notice of such application to participants and beneficiaries of the plan, and

(ii) inform the Pension Benefit Guaranty Corporation of such application in such form and manner as the Director of the Pension Benefit Guaranty Corporation may prescribe.

(c) Additional rules—

(1) Determinations to be made under funding method—For purposes of this part, normal costs, accrued liability, past service liabilities, and experience gains and losses shall be determined under the funding method used to determine costs under the plan.

(2) Valuation of assets—

(A) In general—For purposes of this part, the value of the plan's assets shall be determined on the basis of any reasonable actuarial method of valuation which takes into account fair market value and which is permitted under regulations prescribed by the Secretary.

(B) Election with respect to bonds—The value of a bond or other evidence of indebtedness which is not in default as to principal or interest may, at the election of the plan administrator, be determined on an amortized basis running from initial cost at purchase to par value at maturity or earliest call date. Any election under this subparagraph shall be made at such time and in such manner as the Secretary shall by regulations provide, shall apply to all such evidences of indebtedness, and may be revoked only with the consent of the Secretary.

(3) Actuarial assumptions must be reasonable—For purposes of this section, all costs, liabilities, rates of interest, and other factors under the plan shall be determined on the basis of actuarial assumptions and methods—

(A) each of which is reasonable (taking into account the experience of the plan and reasonable expectations), and

(B) which, in combination, offer the actuary's best estimate of anticipated experience under the plan.

(4) Treatment of certain changes as experience gain or loss—For purposes of this section, if—

(A) a change in benefits under the Social Security Act or in other retirement benefits created under Federal or State law, or

(B) a change in the definition of the term "wages" under section 3121, or a change in the amount of such wages taken into account under regulations prescribed for purposes of section 401(a)(5),

results in an increase or decrease in accrued liability under a plan, such increase or decrease shall be treated as an experience loss or gain.

(5) Full funding—If, as of the close of a plan year, a plan would (without regard to this paragraph) have an accumulated funding deficiency in excess of the full funding limitation—

(A) the funding standard account shall be credited with the amount of such excess, and

(B) all amounts described in subparagraphs (B), (C), and (D) of subsection (b)(2) and subparagraph (B) of subsection (b)(3) which are required to be amortized shall be considered fully amortized for purposes of such subparagraphs.

(6) Full-funding limitation—

(A) In general—For purposes of paragraph (5), the term "full-funding limitation" means the excess (if any) of—

(i) the accrued liability (including normal cost) under the plan (determined under the entry age normal funding method if such accrued liability cannot be directly calculated under the funding method used for the plan), over

(ii) the lesser of—

(I) the fair market value of the plan's assets, or

(II) the value of such assets determined under paragraph (2).

(B) Minimum amount—

(i) In general—In no event shall the full-funding limitation determined under subparagraph (A) be less than the excess (if any) of—

(I) 90 percent of the current liability of the plan (including the expected increase in current liability due to benefits accruing during the plan year), over

(II) the value of the plan's assets determined under paragraph (2).

(ii) Assets—For purposes of clause (i), assets shall not be reduced by any credit balance in the funding standard account.

(C) Full funding limitation—For purposes of this paragraph, unless otherwise provided by the plan, the accrued liability under a multiemployer plan shall not include benefits which are not nonforfeitable under the plan after the termination of the plan (taking into consideration section 411(d)(3)).

(D) Current liability—For purposes of this paragraph—

(i) In general—The term "current liability" means all liabilities to employees and their beneficiaries under the plan.

(ii) Treatment of unpredictable contingent event benefits—For purposes of clause (i), any benefit contingent on an event other than—

(I) age, service, compensation, death, or disability, or

(II) an event which is reasonably and reliably predictable (as determined by the Secretary),

shall not be taken into account until the event on which the benefit is contingent occurs.

(iii) Interest rate used—The rate of interest used to determine current liability under this paragraph shall be the rate of interest determined under subparagraph (E).

(iv) Mortality tables—

(I) Commissioners' standard table—In the case of plan years beginning before the first plan year to which the first tables prescribed under subclause (II) apply, the mortality table used in determining current liability under this paragraph shall be the table prescribed by the Secretary which is based on the prevailing commissioners' standard table (described in section 807(d)(5)(A)) used to determine reserves for group annuity contracts issued on January 1, 1993.

(II) Secretarial authority—The Secretary may by regulation prescribe for plan years beginning after December 31, 1999, mortality tables to be used in determining current liability under this subsection. Such tables shall be based upon the actual experience of pension plans and projected trends in such experience. In prescribing such tables, the Secretary shall take into account results of available independent studies of mortality of individuals covered by pension plans.

(v) Separate mortality tables for the disabled—Notwithstanding clause (iv)—

(I) In general—The Secretary shall establish mortality tables which may be used (in lieu of the tables under clause (iv)) to determine current liability under this subsection for individuals who are entitled to benefits under the plan on account of disability. The Secretary shall establish separate tables for individuals whose disabilities occur in plan years beginning before January 1, 1995, and for individuals whose disabilities occur in plan years beginning on or after such date.

(II) Special rule for disabilities occurring after 1994—In the case of disabilities occurring in plan years beginning after December 31, 1994, the tables under subclause (I) shall apply only with respect to individuals described in such subclause who are disabled within the meaning of title II of the Social Security Act and the regulations thereunder.

(vi) Periodic review—The Secretary shall periodically (at least every 5 years) review any tables in effect under this subparagraph and shall, to the extent such Secretary determines necessary, by regulation update the tables to reflect the actual experience of pension plans and projected trends in such experience.

(E) Required change of interest rate—For purposes of determining a plan's current liability for purposes of this paragraph—

(i) In general—If any rate of interest used under the plan under subsection (b)(6) to determine cost is not within the permissible range, the plan shall establish a new rate of interest within the permissible range.

(ii) Permissible range—For purposes of this subparagraph—

(I) In general—Except as provided in subclause (II), the term "permissible range" means a rate of interest which is not more than 5 percent above, and not more than 10 percent below, the weighted average of the rates of interest on 30-year Treasury securities during the 4-year period ending on the last day before the beginning of the plan year.

(II) Secretarial authority—If the Secretary finds that the lowest rate of interest permissible under subclause (I) is unreasonably high, the Secretary may prescribe a lower rate of interest, except that such rate may not be less than 80 percent of the average rate determined under such subclause.

(iii) Assumptions—Notwithstanding paragraph (3)(A), the interest rate used under the plan shall be—

(I) determined without taking into account the experience of the plan and reasonable expectations, but

(II) consistent with the assumptions which reflect the purchase rates which would be used by insurance companies to satisfy the liabilities under the plan.

(7) Annual valuation—

(A) In general—For purposes of this section, a determination of experience gains and losses and a valuation of the plan's liability shall be made not less frequently than once every year, except that such determination shall be made more frequently to the extent required in particular cases under regulations prescribed by the Secretary.

(B) Valuation date—

(i) Current year—Except as provided in clause (ii), the valuation referred to in subparagraph (A) shall be made as of a date within the plan year to which the valuation refers or within one month prior to the beginning of such year.

(ii) Use of prior year valuation—The valuation referred to in subparagraph (A) may be made as of a date within the plan year prior to the year to which the valuation refers if, as of such date, the value of the assets of the plan are not less than 100 percent of the plan's current liability (as defined in paragraph (6)(D) without regard to clause (iv) thereof).

(iii) Adjustments—Information under clause (ii) shall, in accordance with regulations, be actuarially adjusted to reflect significant differences in participants.

(iv) Limitation—A change in funding method to use a prior year valuation, as provided in clause (ii), may not be made unless as of the valuation date within the prior plan year, the value of the assets of the plan are not less than 125 percent of the plan's current liability (as defined in paragraph (6)(D) without regard to clause (iv) thereof).

(8) Time when certain contributions deemed made—For purposes of this section, any contributions for a plan year made by an employer after the last day of such plan year, but not later than two and one-half months after such day, shall be deemed to have been made on such last day. For purposes of this subparagraph, such two and one-half month period may be extended for not more than six months under regulations prescribed by the Secretary.

(d) Extension of amortization periods for multiemployer plans—

(1) Automatic extension upon application by certain plans—

(A) In general—If the plan sponsor of a multiemployer plan—

(i) submits to the Secretary an application for an extension of the period of years required to amortize any unfunded liability described in any clause of subsection (b)(2)(B) or described in subsection (b)(4), and

(ii) includes with the application a certification by the plan's actuary described in subparagraph (B),

the Secretary shall extend the amortization period for the period of time (not in excess of 5 years) specified in the application. Such extension shall be in addition to any extension under paragraph (2).

(B) Criteria—A certification with respect to a multiemployer plan is described in this subparagraph if the plan's actuary certifies that, based on reasonable assumptions—

(i) absent the extension under subparagraph (A), the plan would have an accumulated funding deficiency in the current plan year or any of the 9 succeeding plan years,

(ii) the plan sponsor has adopted a plan to improve the plan's funding status,

(iii) the plan is projected to have sufficient assets to timely pay expected benefits and anticipated expenditures over the amortization period as extended, and

(iv) the notice required under paragraph (3)(A) has been provided.

(C) Termination—The preceding provisions of this paragraph shall not apply with respect to any application submitted after December 31, 2014.

(2) Alternative extension—

(A) In general—If the plan sponsor of a multiemployer plan submits to the Secretary an application for an extension of the period of years required to amortize any unfunded liability described in any clause of subsection (b)(2)(B) or described in subsection (b)(4), the Secretary may extend the amortization period for a period of time (not in excess of 10 years reduced by the number of years of any extension under paragraph (1) with respect to such unfunded liability) if the Secretary makes the determination described in subparagraph (B). Such extension shall be in addition to any extension under paragraph (1).

(B) Determination—The Secretary may grant an extension under subparagraph (A) if the Secretary determines that—

(i) such extension would carry out the purposes of this Act and would provide adequate protection for participants under the plan and their beneficiaries, and

(ii) the failure to permit such extension would—

(I) result in a substantial risk to the voluntary continuation of the plan, or a substantial curtailment of pension benefit levels or employee compensation, and

(II) be adverse to the interests of plan participants in the aggregate.

(C) Action by secretary—The Secretary shall act upon any application for an extension under this paragraph within 180 days of the submission of such application. If the Secretary rejects the application for an extension under this paragraph, the Secretary shall provide notice to the plan detailing the specific reasons for the rejection, including references to the criteria set forth above.

(3) Advance notice—

(A) In general—The Secretary shall, before granting an extension under this subsection, require each applicant to provide evidence satisfactory to such Secretary that the applicant has provided notice of the filing of the application for such extension to each affected party (as defined in section 4001(a)(21) of the Employee Retirement Income Security Act of 1974) with respect to the affected plan. Such notice shall include a description of the extent to which the plan is funded for benefits which are guaranteed under title IV of such Act and for benefit liabilities.

(B) Consideration of relevant information—The Secretary shall consider any relevant information provided by a person to whom notice was given under paragraph (1)

§ 432. Additional funding rules for multiemployer plans in endangered status or critical status.

(a) General rule—For purposes of this part, in the case of a multiemployer plan in effect on July 16, 2006—

(1) if the plan is in endangered status—

(A) the plan sponsor shall adopt and implement a funding improvement plan in accordance with the requirements of subsection (c), and

(B) the requirements of subsection (d) shall apply during the funding plan adoption period and the funding improvement period, and

(2) if the plan is in critical status—

(A) the plan sponsor shall adopt and implement a rehabilitation plan in accordance with the requirements of subsection (e), and

(B) the requirements of subsection (f) shall apply during the rehabilitation plan adoption period and the rehabilitation period.

(b) Determination of endangered and critical status—For purposes of this section—

(1) Endangered status—A multiemployer plan is in endangered status for a plan year if, as determined by the plan actuary under paragraph (3), the plan is not in critical status for the plan year and, as of the beginning of the plan year, either—

(A) the plan's funded percentage for such plan year is less than 80 percent, or

(B) the plan has an accumulated funding deficiency for such plan year, or is projected to have such an accumulated funding deficiency for any of the 6 succeeding plan years, taking into account any extension of amortization periods under section 431(d).

For purposes of this section, a plan shall be treated as in seriously endangered status for a plan year if the plan is described in both subparagraphs (A) and (B).

(2) Critical status—A multiemployer plan is in critical status for a plan year if, as determined by the plan actuary under paragraph (3), the plan is described in 1 or more of the following subparagraphs as of the beginning of the plan year:

(A) A plan is described in this subparagraph if—

(i) the funded percentage of the plan is less than 65 percent, and

(ii) the sum of—

(I) the fair market value of plan assets, plus

(II) the present value of the reasonably anticipated employer contributions for the current plan year and each of the 6 succeeding plan years, assuming that the terms of all collective bargaining agreements pursuant to which the plan is maintained for the current plan year continue in effect for succeeding plan years,

is less than the present value of all nonforfeitable benefits projected to be payable under the plan during the current plan year and each of the 6 succeeding plan years (plus administrative expenses for such plan years).

(B) A plan is described in this subparagraph if—

(i) the plan has an accumulated funding deficiency for the current plan year, not taking into account any extension of amortization periods under section 431(d), or

(ii) the plan is projected to have an accumulated funding deficiency for any of the 3 succeeding plan years (4 succeeding plan years if the funded percentage of the plan is 65 percent or less), not taking into account any extension of amortization periods under section 431(d).

(C) A plan is described in this subparagraph if—

(i)(I) the plan's normal cost for the current plan year, plus interest (determined at the rate used for determining costs under the plan) for the current plan year on the amount of unfunded benefit liabilities under the plan as of the last date of the preceding plan year, exceeds

(II) the present value of the reasonably anticipated employer and employee contributions for the current plan year,

(ii) the present value, as of the beginning of the current plan year, of nonforfeitable benefits of inactive participants is greater than the present value of nonforfeitable benefits of active participants, and

(iii) the plan has an accumulated funding deficiency for the current plan year, or is projected to have such a deficiency for any of the 4 succeeding plan years, not taking into account any extension of amortization periods under section 431(d).

(D) A plan is described in this subparagraph if the sum of—

(i) the fair market value of plan assets, plus

(ii) the present value of the reasonably anticipated employer contributions for the current plan year and each of the 4 succeeding plan years, assuming that the terms of all collective bargaining agreements pursuant to which the plan is maintained for the current plan year continue in effect for succeeding plan years, is less than the present value of all benefits projected to be payable under the plan during the current plan year and each of the 4 succeeding plan years (plus administrative expenses for such plan years).

* * *

§ 436. Funding-based limits on benefits and benefit accruals under single-employer plans.

(a) General rule—For purposes of section 401(a)(29), a defined benefit plan which is a single-employer plan shall be treated as meeting the requirements of this section if the plan meets the requirements of subsections (b), (c), (d), and (e).

(b) Funding-based limitation on shutdown benefits and other unpredictable contingent event benefits under single-employer plans—

(1) In general—If a participant of a defined benefit plan which is a single-employer plan is entitled to an unpredictable contingent event benefit payable with respect to any event occurring during any plan year, the plan shall provide that such benefit may not be provided if the adjusted funding target attainment percentage for such plan year—

(A) is less than 60 percent, or

(B) would be less than 60 percent taking into account such occurrence.

(2) Exemption—Paragraph (1) shall cease to apply with respect to any plan year, effective as of the first day of the plan year, upon payment by the plan sponsor of a contribution (in addition to any minimum required contribution under section 430) equal to—

(A) in the case of paragraph (1)(A), the amount of the increase in the funding target of the plan (under section 430) for the plan year attributable to the occurrence referred to in paragraph (1), and

(B) in the case of paragraph (1)(B), the amount sufficient to result in an adjusted funding target attainment percentage of 60 percent.

(3) Unpredictable contingent event—For purposes of this subsection, the term "unpredictable contingent event benefit" means any benefit payable solely by reason of—

(A) a plant shutdown (or similar event, as determined by the Secretary), or

(B) an event other than the attainment of any age, performance of any service, receipt or derivation of any compensation, or occurrence of death or disability.

(c) Limitations on plan amendments increasing liability for benefits—

(1) In general—No amendment to a defined benefit plan which is a single-employer plan which has the effect of increasing liabilities of the plan by reason of increases in benefits, establishment of new benefits, changing the rate of benefit accrual, or changing the rate at which benefits become nonforfeitable may take effect during any plan year if the adjusted funding target attainment percentage for such plan year is—

(A) less than 80 percent, or

(B) would be less than 80 percent taking into account such amendment.

(2) Exemption—Paragraph (1) shall cease to apply with respect to any plan year, effective as of the first day of the plan year (or if later, the effective date of the amendment), upon payment by the plan sponsor of a contribution (in addition to any minimum required contribution under section 430) equal to—

(A) in the case of paragraph (1)(A), the amount of the increase in the funding target of the plan (under section 430) for the plan year attributable to the amendment, and

(B) in the case of paragraph (1)(B), the amount sufficient to result in an adjusted funding target attainment percentage of 80 percent.

(3) Exception for certain benefit increases—Paragraph (1) shall not apply to any amendment which provides for an increase in benefits under a formula which is not based on a participant's compensation, but only if the rate of such increase is not in excess of the contemporaneous rate of increase in average wages of participants covered by the amendment.

(d) Limitations on accelerated benefit distributions—

(1) Funding percentage less than 60 percent—A defined benefit plan which is a single-employer plan shall provide that, in any case in which the plan's adjusted funding target attainment percentage for a plan year is less than 60 percent, the plan may not pay any prohibited payment after the valuation date for the plan year.

(2) Bankruptcy—A defined benefit plan which is a single-employer plan shall provide that, during any period in which the plan sponsor is a debtor in a case under title 11, United States Code, or similar Federal or State law, the plan may not pay any prohibited payment. The preceding sentence shall not apply on or after the date on which the enrolled actuary of the plan certifies that the adjusted funding target attainment percentage of such plan is not less than 100 percent.

(3) Limited payment if percentage at least 60 percent but less than 80 percent—

(A) In general—A defined benefit plan which is a single-employer plan shall provide that, in any case in which the plan's adjusted funding target attainment percentage for a plan year is 60 percent or greater but less than 80 percent, the plan may not pay any prohibited payment after the valuation date for the plan year to the extent the amount of the payment exceeds the lesser of—

(i) 50 percent of the amount of the payment which could be made without regard to this section, or

(ii) the present value (determined under guidance prescribed by the Pension Benefit Guaranty Corporation, using the interest and mortality assumptions under section 417(e)) of the maximum guarantee with respect to the participant under section 4022 of the Employee Retirement Income Security Act of 1974.

(B) One-time application—

(i) In general—The plan shall also provide that only 1 prohibited payment meeting the requirements of subparagraph (A) may be made with respect to any participant during any period of consecutive plan years to which the limitations under either paragraph (1) or (2) or this paragraph applies.

(ii) Treatment of beneficiaries—For purposes of this subparagraph, a participant and any beneficiary on his behalf (including an alternate payee, as defined in section 414(p)(8)) shall be treated as 1 participant. If the accrued benefit of a participant is allocated to such an alternate payee and 1 or more other persons, the amount under subparagraph (A) shall be allocated among such persons in the same manner as the accrued benefit is allocated unless the qualified domestic relations order (as defined in section 414(p)(1)(A)) provides otherwise.

(4) Exception—This subsection shall not apply to any plan for any plan year if the terms of such plan (as in effect for the period beginning on September 1, 2005, and ending with such plan year) provide for no benefit accruals with respect to any participant during such period.

(5) Prohibited payment—For purpose of this subsection, the term "prohibited payment" means—

(A) any payment, in excess of the monthly amount paid under a single life annuity (plus any social security supplements described in the last sentence of section 411(a)(9)), to a participant or beneficiary whose annuity starting date (as defined in section 417(f)(2)) occurs during any period a limitation under paragraph (1) or (2) is in effect,

(B) any payment for the purchase of an irrevocable commitment from an insurer to pay benefits, and

(C) any other payment specified by the Secretary by regulations.

Such term shall not include the payment of a benefit which under section 411(a)(11) may be immediately distributed without the consent of the participant.

(e) Limitation on benefit accruals for plans with severe funding shortfalls—

(1) In general—A defined benefit plan which is a single-employer plan shall provide that, in any case in which the plan's adjusted funding target attainment percentage for a plan year is less than 60 percent, benefit accruals under the plan shall cease as of the valuation date for the plan year.

(2) Exemption—Paragraph (1) shall cease to apply with respect to any plan year, effective as of the first day of the plan year, upon payment by the plan sponsor of a contribution (in addition to any minimum required contribution under section 430) equal to the amount sufficient to result in an adjusted funding target attainment percentage of 60 percent.

(f) Rules relating to contributions required to avoid benefit limitations—

(1) Security may be provided—

(A) In general—For purposes of this section, the adjusted funding target attainment percentage shall be determined by treating as an asset of the plan any security provided by a plan sponsor in a form meeting the requirements of subparagraph (B).

(B) Form of security—The security required under subparagraph (A) shall consist of—

(i) a bond issued by a corporate surety company that is an acceptable surety for purposes of section 412 of the Employee Retirement Income Security Act of 1974,

(ii) cash, or United States obligations which mature in 3 years or less, held in escrow by a bank or similar financial institution, or

(iii) such other form of security as is satisfactory to the Secretary and the parties involved.

(C) Enforcement—Any security provided under subparagraph (A) may be perfected and enforced at any time after the earlier of—

(i) the date on which the plan terminates,

(ii) if there is a failure to make a payment of the minimum required contribution for any plan year beginning after the security is provided, the due date for the payment under section 430(j), or

(iii) if the adjusted funding target attainment percentage is less than 60 percent for a consecutive period of 7 years, the valuation date for the last year in the period.

(D) Release of security—The security shall be released (and any amounts thereunder shall be refunded together with any interest accrued thereon) at such time as the Secretary may prescribe in regulations, including regulations for partial releases of the security by reason of increases in the adjusted funding target attainment percentage.

(2) Prefunding balance or funding standard carryover balance may not be used—No prefunding balance or funding standard carryover balance under section 430(f) may be used under subsection (b), (c), or (e) to satisfy any payment an employer may make under any such subsection to avoid or terminate the application of any limitation under such subsection.

(3) Deemed reduction of funding balances—

(A) In general—Subject to subparagraph (C), in any case in which a benefit limitation under subsection (b), (c), (d), or (e) would (but for this subparagraph and determined without regard to subsection (b)(2), (c)(2), or (e)(2)) apply to such plan for the plan year, the plan sponsor of such plan shall be treated for purposes of this title as having made an election under section 430(f) to reduce the prefunding balance or funding standard carryover balance by such amount as is necessary for such benefit limitation to not apply to the plan for such plan year.

(B) Exception for insufficient funding balances—Subparagraph (A) shall not apply with respect to a benefit limitation for any plan year if the application of subparagraph (A) would not result in the benefit limitation not applying for such plan year.

(C) Restrictions of certain rules to collectively bargained plans—With respect to any benefit limitation under subsection (b), (c), or (e), subparagraph (A) shall only apply in the case of a plan maintained pursuant to 1 or more collective bargaining agreements between employee representatives and 1 or more employers.

(g) New plans—Subsections (b), (c), and (e) shall not apply to a plan for the first 5 plan years of the plan. For purposes of this subsection, the reference in this subsection to a plan shall include a reference to any predecessor plan.

(h) Presumed underfunding for purposes of benefit limitations—

(1) Presumption of continued underfunding—In any case in which a benefit limitation under subsection (b), (c), (d), or (e) has been applied to a plan with respect to the plan year preceding the current plan year, the adjusted funding target attainment percentage of the plan for the current plan year shall be presumed to be equal to the adjusted funding target attainment percentage of the plan for the preceding plan year until the enrolled actuary of the plan certifies the actual adjusted funding target attainment percentage of the plan for the current plan year.

(2) Presumption of underfunding after 10th month—In any case in which no certification of the adjusted funding target attainment percentage for the current plan year is made with respect to the plan before the first day of the 10th month of such year, for purposes of subsections (b), (c), (d), and (e), such first day shall be deemed, for purposes of such subsection, to be the valuation date of the plan for the current plan year and the plan's adjusted funding target attainment percentage shall be conclusively presumed to be less than 60 percent as of such first day.

(3) Presumption of underfunding after 4th month for nearly underfunded plans— In any case in which—

(A) a benefit limitation under subsection (b), (c), (d), or (e) did not apply to a plan with respect to the plan year preceding the current plan year, but the adjusted funding target attainment percentage of the plan for such preceding plan year was not more than 10 percentage points greater than the percentage which would have caused such subsection to apply to the plan with respect to such preceding plan year, and

(B) as of the first day of the 4th month of the current plan year, the enrolled actuary of the plan has not certified the actual adjusted funding target attainment percentage of the plan for the current plan year,

until the enrolled actuary so certifies, such first day shall be deemed, for purposes of such subsection, to be the valuation date of the plan for the current plan year and the adjusted funding target attainment percentage of the plan as of such first day shall, for purposes of such subsection, be presumed to be equal to 10 percentage points less than the adjusted funding target attainment percentage of the plan for such preceding plan year.

(i) Treatment of plan as of close of prohibited or cessation period—For purposes of applying this title—

(1) Operation of plan after period—Unless the plan provides otherwise, payments and accruals will resume effective as of the day following the close of the period for which any limitation of payment or accrual of benefits under subsection (d) or (e) applies.

(2) Treatment of affected benefits—Nothing in this subsection shall be construed as affecting the plan's treatment of benefits which would have been paid or accrued but for this section.

(j) Terms relating to funding target attainment percentage—For purposes of this section—

(1) In general—The term "funding target attainment percentage" has the same meaning given such term by section 430(d)(2).

(2) Adjusted funding target attainment percentage—The term "adjusted funding target attainment percentage" means the funding target attainment percentage which is determined under paragraph (1) by increasing each of the amounts under subparagraphs (A) and (B) of section 430(d)(2) by the aggregate amount of purchases of annuities for employees other than highly compensated employees (as defined in section 414(q)) which were made by the plan during the preceding 2 plan years.

(3) Application to plans which are fully funded without regard to reductions for funding balances—

(A) In general—In the case of a plan for any plan year, if the funding target attainment percentage is 100 percent or more (determined without regard to the reduction in the value of assets under section 430(f)(4)), the funding target attainment percentage for purposes of paragraphs (1) and (2) shall be determined without regard to such reduction.

(B) Transition rule—Subparagraph (A) shall be applied to plan years beginning after 2007 and before 2011 by substituting for "100 percent" the applicable percentage determined in accordance with the following table:

In the case of a plan year beginning in calendar year:	*The applicable percentage is*
2008	92
2009	94
2010	96

(C) Limitation—Subparagraph (B) shall not apply with respect to any plan year beginning after 2008 unless the funding target attainment percentage (determined without regard to the reduction in the value of assets under section 430(f)(4)) of the plan for each preceding plan year beginning after 2007 was not less than the applicable percentage with respect to such preceding plan year determined under subparagraph (B).

(4) Special rule for certain years. Solely for purposes of any applicable provision—

(A) In general. For plan years beginning on or after October 1, 2008, and before October 1, 2010, the adjusted funding target attainment percentage of a plan shall be the greater of—

(i) such percentage, as determined without regard to this paragraph, or

(ii) the adjusted funding target attainment percentage for such plan for the plan year beginning after October 1, 2007, and before October 1, 2008, as determined under rules prescribed by the Secretary.

(B) Special rule. In the case of a plan for which the valuation date is not the first day of the plan year—

(i) subparagraph (A) shall apply to plan years beginning after December 31, 2007, and before January 1, 2010, and

(ii) subparagraph (A)(ii) shall apply based on the last plan year beginning before November 1, 2007, as determined under rules prescribed by the Secretary.

(C) Applicable provision. For purposes of this paragraph, the term "applicable provision" means—

(i) subsection (d), but only for purposes of applying such paragraph to a payment which, as determined under rules prescribed by the Secretary, is a payment under a social security leveling option which accelerates payments under the plan before, and reduces payments after, a participant starts receiving social security benefits in order to provide substantially similar aggregate payments both before and after such benefits are received, and

(ii) subsection (e).

* * *

§ 457. Deferred compensation plans of state and local governments and tax-exempt organizations.

(a) Year of inclusion in gross income—

(1) In general—Any amount of compensation deferred under an eligible deferred compensation plan, and any income attributable to the amounts so deferred, shall be includible in gross income only for the taxable year in which such compensation or other income—

(A) is paid to the participant or other beneficiary, in the case of a plan of an eligible employer described in subsection (e)(1)(A), and

(B) is paid or otherwise made available to the participant or other beneficiary, in the case of a plan of an eligible employer described in subsection (e)(1)(B).

(2) Special rule for rollover amounts—To the extent provided in section 72(t)(9), section 72(t) shall apply to any amount includible in gross income under this subsection.

(3) Special rule for health and long-term care insurance—In the case of a plan of an eligible employer described in subsection (e)(1)(A), to the extent provided in section 402(l), paragraph (1) shall not apply to amounts otherwise includible in gross income under this subsection.

(b) Eligible deferred compensation plan defined—For purposes of this section, the term "eligible deferred compensation plan" means a plan established and maintained by an eligible employer—

(1) in which only individuals who perform service for the employer may be participants,

(2) which provides that (except as provided in paragraph (3)) the maximum amount which may be deferred under the plan for the taxable year (other than rollover amounts) shall not exceed the lesser of—

(A) the applicable dollar amount, or

(B) 100 percent of the participant's includible compensation,

(3) which may provide that, for 1 or more of the participant's last 3 taxable years ending before he attains normal retirement age under the plan, the ceiling set forth in paragraph (2) shall be the lesser of—

(A) twice the dollar amount in effect under subsection (b)(2)(A), or

(B) the sum of—

(i) the plan ceiling established for purposes of paragraph (2) for the taxable year (determined without regard to this paragraph), plus

(ii) so much of the plan ceiling established for purposes of paragraph (2) for taxable years before the taxable year as has not previously been used under paragraph (2) or this paragraph,

(4) which provides that compensation will be deferred for any calendar month only if an agreement providing for such deferral has been entered into before the beginning of such month,

(5) which meets the distribution requirements of subsection (d), and

(6) except as provided in subsection (g), which provides that—

(A) all amounts of compensation deferred under the plan,

(B) all property and rights purchased with such amounts, and

(C) all income attributable to such amounts, property, or rights,

shall remain (until made available to the participant or other beneficiary) solely the property and rights of the employer (without being restricted to the provision of benefits under the plan), subject only to the claims of the employer's general creditors.

A plan which is established and maintained by an employer which is described in subsection (e)(1)(A) and which is administered in a manner which is inconsistent with the requirements of any of the preceding paragraphs shall be treated as not meeting the requirements of such paragraph as of the 1st plan year beginning more than 180 days after the date of notification by the Secretary of the inconsistency unless the employer corrects the inconsistency before the 1st day of such plan year.

(c) Limitation—The maximum amount of the compensation of any one individual which may be deferred under subsection (a) during any taxable year shall not exceed the amount in effect under subsection (b)(2)(A) (as modified by any adjustment provided under subsection (b)(3)).

(d) Distribution requirements—

(1) In general—For purposes of subsection (b)(5), a plan meets the distribution requirements of this subsection if—

(A) under the plan amounts will not be made available to participants or beneficiaries earlier than—

(i) the calendar year in which the participant attains age 70½,

(ii) when the participant has a severance from employment with the employer, or

(iii) when the participant is faced with an unforeseeable emergency (determined in the manner prescribed by the Secretary in regulations),

(B) the plan meets the minimum distribution requirements of paragraph (2), and

(C) in the case of a plan maintained by an employer described in subsection (e)(1)(A), the plan meets requirements similar to the requirements of section 401(a)(31).

Any amount transferred in a direct trustee-to-trustee transfer in accordance with section 401(a)(31) shall not be includible in gross income for the taxable year of transfer.

(2) Minimum distribution requirements—A plan meets the minimum distribution requirements of this paragraph if such plan meets the requirements of section 401(a)(9).

(3) Special rule for government plan—An eligible deferred compensation plan of an employer described in subsection (e)(1)(A) shall not be treated as failing to meet the requirements of this subsection solely by reason of making a distribution described in subsection (e)(9)(A).

(e) Other definitions and special rules—For purposes of this section—

(1) Eligible employer—The term "eligible employer" means—

(A) a State, political subdivision of a State, and any agency or instrumentality of a State or political subdivision of a State, and

(B) any other organization (other than a governmental unit) exempt from tax under this subtitle.

(2) Performance of service—The performance of service includes performance of service as an independent contractor and the person (or governmental unit) for whom such services are performed shall be treated as the employer.

(3) Participant—The term "participant" means an individual who is eligible to defer compensation under the plan.

(4) Beneficiary—The term "beneficiary" means a beneficiary of the participant, his estate, or any other person whose interest in the plan is derived from the participant.

(5) Includible compensation—The term "includible compensation" has the meaning given to the term "participant's compensation" by section 415(c)(3).

(6) Compensation taken into account at present value—Compensation shall be taken into account at its present value.

(7) Community property laws—The amount of includible compensation shall be determined without regard to any community property laws.

(8) Income attributable—Gains from the disposition of property shall be treated as income attributable to such property.

(9) Benefits of tax exempt organization plans not treated as made available by reason of certain elections, etc—In the case of an eligible deferred compensation plan of an employer described in subsection (e)(1)(B)—

(A) Total amount payable is dollar limit or less—The total amount payable to a participant under the plan shall not be treated as made available merely because the participant may elect to receive such amount (or the plan may distribute such amount without the participant's consent) if—

(i) the portion of such amount which is not attributable to rollover contributions (as defined in section 411(a)(11)(D)) does not exceed the dollar limit under section 411(a)(11)(A), and

(ii) such amount may be distributed only if—

(I) no amount has been deferred under the plan with respect to such participant during the 2-year period ending on the date of the distribution, and

(II) there has been no prior distribution under the plan to such participant to which this subparagraph applied.

A plan shall not be treated as failing to meet the distribution requirements of subsection (d) by reason of a distribution to which this subparagraph applies.

(B) Election to defer commencement of distributions—The total amount payable to a participant under the plan shall not be treated as made available merely because the participant may elect to defer commencement of distributions under the plan if—

(i) such election is made after amounts may be available under the plan in accordance with subsection (d)(1)(A) and before commencement of such distributions, and

(ii) the participant may make only 1 such election.

(10) Transfers between plans—A participant shall not be required to include in gross income any portion of the entire amount payable to such participant solely by reason of the transfer of such portion from 1 eligible deferred compensation plan to another eligible deferred compensation plan.

(11) Certain plans excluded—

(A) In general—The following plans shall be treated as not providing for the deferral of compensation:

(i) Any bona fide vacation leave, sick leave, compensatory time, severance pay, disability pay, or death benefit plan.

(ii) Any plan paying solely length of service awards to bona fide volunteers (or their beneficiaries) on account of qualified services performed by such volunteers.

* * *

(12) Exception for nonelective deferred compensation of nonemployees—

(A) In general—This section shall not apply to nonelective deferred compensation attributable to services not performed as an employee.

(B) Nonelective deferred compensation—For purposes of subparagraph (A), deferred compensation shall be treated as nonelective only if all individuals (other than those who have not satisfied any applicable initial service requirement) with the same relationship to the payor are covered under the same plan with no individual variations or options under the plan.

* * *

(14) Treatment of qualified governmental excess benefit arrangements—Subsections (b)(2) and (c)(1) shall not apply to any qualified governmental excess benefit arrangement (as defined in section 415(m)(3)), and benefits provided under such an arrangement shall not be taken into account in determining whether any other plan is an eligible deferred compensation plan.

(15) Applicable dollar amount—

(A) In general—The applicable dollar amount shall be the amount determined in accordance with the following table:

For taxable years beginning in calendar year:	*The applicable dollar amount:*
* * *	
2006 or thereafter	$15,000

(B) Cost-of-living adjustments—In the case of taxable years beginning after December 31, 2006, the Secretary shall adjust the $15,000 amount under subparagraph (A) at the same time and in the same manner as under section 415(d), except that the base period shall be the calendar quarter beginning July 1, 2005, and any increase under this paragraph which is not a multiple of $500 shall be rounded to the next lowest multiple of $500.

(16) Rollover amounts—

(A) General rule—In the case of an eligible deferred compensation plan established and maintained by an employer described in subsection (e)(1)(A), if—

(i) any portion of the balance to the credit of an employee in such plan is paid to such employee in an eligible rollover distribution (within the meaning of section 402(c)(4)),

(ii) the employee transfers any portion of the property such employee receives in such distribution to an eligible retirement plan described in section 402(c)(8)(B), and

(iii) in the case of a distribution of property other than money, the amount so transferred consists of the property distributed,

then such distribution (to the extent so transferred) shall not be includible in gross income for the taxable year in which paid.

(B) Certain rules made applicable—The rules of paragraphs (2) through (7), (9), and (11) of section 402(c) and section 402(f) shall apply for purposes of subparagraph (A).

(C) Reporting—Rollovers under this paragraph shall be reported to the Secretary in the same manner as rollovers from qualified retirement plans (as defined in section 4974(c)).

(17) Trustee-to-trustee transfers to purchase permissive service credit—No amount shall be includible in gross income by reason of a direct trustee-to-trustee transfer to a defined benefit governmental plan (as defined in section 414(d)) if such transfer is—

(A) for the purchase of permissive service credit (as defined in section 415(n)(3)(A)) under such plan, or

(B) a repayment to which section 415 does not apply by reason of subsection (k)(3) thereof.

(18) Coordination with catch-up contributions for individuals age 50 or older—In the case of an individual who is an eligible participant (as defined by section 414(v)) and who is a participant in an eligible deferred compensation plan of an employer described in paragraph (1)(A), subsections (b)(3) and (c) shall be applied by substituting for the amount otherwise determined under the applicable subsection the greater of—

(A) the sum of—

(i) the plan ceiling established for purposes of subsection (b)(2) (without regard to subsection (b)(3)), plus

(ii) the applicable dollar amount for the taxable year determined under section 414(v)(2)(B)(i), or

(B) the amount determined under the applicable subsection (without regard to this paragraph).

(f) Tax treatment of participants where plan or arrangement of employer is not eligible—

(1) In general—In the case of a plan of an eligible employer providing for a deferral of compensation, if such plan is not an eligible deferred compensation plan, then—

(A) the compensation shall be included in the gross income of the participant or beneficiary for the 1st taxable year in which there is no substantial risk of forfeiture of the rights to such compensation, and

(B) the tax treatment of any amount made available under the plan to a participant or beneficiary shall be determined under section 72 (relating to annuities, etc.).

(2) Exceptions—Paragraph (1) shall not apply to—

(A) a plan described in section 401(a) which includes a trust exempt from tax under section 501(a),

(B) an annuity plan or contract described in section 403,

(C) that portion of any plan which consists of a transfer of property described in section 83,

(D) that portion of any plan which consists of a trust to which section 402(b) applies,

(E) a qualified governmental excess benefit arrangement described in section 415(m), and

(F) that portion of any applicable employment retention plan described in paragraph (4) with respect to any participant.

(3) Definitions—For purposes of this subsection—

(A) Plan includes arrangements, etc—The term "plan" includes any agreement or arrangement.

(B) Substantial risk of forfeiture—The rights of a person to compensation are subject to a substantial risk of forfeiture if such person's rights to such compensation are conditioned upon the future performance of substantial services by any individual.

(4) Employment retention plans—For purposes of paragraph (2)(F)—

(A) In general—The portion of an applicable employment retention plan described in this paragraph with respect to any participant is that portion of the plan which provides benefits payable to the participant not in excess of twice the applicable dollar limit determined under subsection (e)(15).

(B) Other rules—

(i) Limitation—Paragraph (2)(F) shall only apply to the portion of the plan described in subparagraph (A) for years preceding the year in which such portion is paid or otherwise made available to the participant.

(ii) Treatment—A plan shall not be treated for purposes of this title as providing for the deferral of compensation for any year with respect to the portion of the plan described in subparagraph (A).

(C) Applicable employment retention plan—The term "applicable employment retention plan" means an employment retention plan maintained by—

(i) a local educational agency (as defined in section 9101 of the Elementary and Secondary Education Act of 1965 (20 U.S.C. 7801), or

(ii) an education association which principally represents employees of 1 or more agencies described in clause (i) and which is described in section 501(c) (5) or (6) and exempt from taxation under section 501(a).

(D) Employment retention plan—The term "employment retention plan" means a plan to pay, upon termination of employment, compensation to an employee of a local educational agency or education association described in subparagraph (C) for purposes of—

(i) retaining the services of the employee, or

(ii) rewarding such employee for the employee's service with 1 or more such agencies or associations.

(g) Governmental plans must maintain set-asides for exclusive benefit of participants—

(1) In general—A plan maintained by an eligible employer described in subsection (e)(1)(A) shall not be treated as an eligible deferred compensation plan unless all assets and income of the plan described in subsection (b)(6) are held in trust for the exclusive benefit of participants and their beneficiaries.

(2) Taxability of trusts and participants—For purposes of this title—

(A) a trust described in paragraph (1) shall be treated as an organization exempt from taxation under section 501(a), and

(B) notwithstanding any other provision of this title, amounts in the trust shall be includible in the gross income of participants and beneficiaries only to the extent, and at the time, provided in this section.

(3) Custodial accounts and contracts—For purposes of this subsection, custodial accounts and contracts described in section 401(f) shall be treated as trusts under rules similar to the rules under section 401(f).

(4) Death benefits under USERRA-qualified active military service—A plan described in paragraph (1) shall not be treated as an eligible deferred compensation plan unless such plan meets the requirements of section 401(a)(37).

§ 501. Exemption from tax on corporations, certain trusts, etc.

(a) Exemption from taxation—An organization described in subsection (c) or (d) or section 401(a) shall be exempt from taxation under this subtitle unless such exemption is denied under section 502 or 503.

(b) Tax on unrelated business income and certain other activities—An organization exempt from taxation under subsection (a) shall be subject to tax to the extent provided in parts II, III, and VI of this subchapter, but (notwithstanding parts II, III, and VI of this subchapter) shall be considered an organization exempt from income taxes for the purpose of any law which refers to organizations exempt from income taxes.

(c) List of exempt organizations—The following organizations are referred to in subsection (a):

* * *

(9) Voluntary employees' beneficiary associations providing for the payment of life, sick, accident, or other benefits to the members of such association or their dependents or designated beneficiaries, if no part of the net earnings of such association inures (other than through such payments) to the benefit of any private shareholder or individual. For purposes of providing for the payment of sick and accident benefits to members of such an association and their dependents, the term "dependent" shall include any individual who is a child (as defined in section 152(f)(1)) of a member who as of the end of the calendar year has not attained age 27.

* * *

§ 3121. Definitions.

(a) Wages—For purposes of this chapter, the term "wages" means all remuneration for employment, including the cash value of all remuneration (including benefits) paid in any medium other than cash; except that such term shall not include—

* * *

(5) any payment made to, or on behalf of, an employee or his beneficiary—

(A) from or to a trust described in section 401(a) which is exempt from tax under section 501(a) at the time of such payment unless such payment is made to an employee of the trust as remuneration for services rendered as such employee and not as a beneficiary of the trust,

(B) under or to an annuity plan which, at the time of such payment, is a plan described in section 403(a),

(C) under a simplified employee pension (as defined in section 408(k)(1)), other than any contributions described in section 408(k)(6),

(D) under or to an annuity contract described in section 403(b), other than a payment for the purchase of such contract which is made by reason of a salary reduction agreement (whether evidenced by a written instrument or otherwise),

(E) under or to an exempt governmental deferred compensation plan (as defined in subsection (v)(3)),

(F) to supplement pension benefits under a plan or trust described in any of the foregoing provisions of this paragraph to take into account some portion or all of the increase in the cost of living (as determined by the Secretary of Labor) since retirement but only if such supplemental payments are under a plan which is treated as a welfare plan under section 3(2)(B)(ii) of the Employee Retirement Income Security Act of 1974,

(G) under a cafeteria plan (within the meaning of section 125) if such payment would not be treated as wages without regard to such plan and it is reasonable to believe that (if section 125 applied for purposes of this section) section 125 would not treat any wages as constructively received,

(H) under an arrangement to which section 408(p) applies, other than any elective contributions under paragraph (2)(A)(i) thereof, or

(I) under a plan described in section 457(e)(11)(A)(ii) and maintained by an eligible employer (as defined in section 457(e)(1));

* * *

(v) Treatment of certain deferred compensation and salary reduction arrangements—

(1) Certain employer contributions treated as wages—Nothing in any paragraph of subsection (a) (other than paragraph (1)) shall exclude from the term "wages"—

(A) any employer contribution under a qualified cash or deferred arrangement (as defined in section 401(k)) to the extent not included in gross income by reason of section 402(e)(3) or consisting of designated Roth contributions (as defined in section 402A(c)), or

(B) any amount treated as an employer contribution under section 414(h)(2) where the pickup referred to in such section is pursuant to a salary reduction agreement (whether evidenced by a written instrument or otherwise).

(2) Treatment of certain nonqualified deferred compensation plans—

(A) In general—Any amount deferred under a nonqualified deferred compensation plan shall be taken into account for purposes of this chapter as of the later of—

(i) when the services are performed, or

(ii) when there is no substantial risk of forfeiture of the rights to such amount.

The preceding sentence shall not apply to any excess parachute payment (as defined in section 280G(b)).

(B) Taxed only once—Any amount taken into account as wages by reason of subparagraph (A) (and the income attributable thereto) shall not thereafter be treated as wages for purposes of this chapter.

(C) Nonqualified deferred compensation plan—For purposes of this paragraph, the term "nonqualified deferred compensation plan" means any plan or other arrangement for deferral of compensation other than a plan described in subsection (a)(5).

(3) Exempt governmental deferred compensation plan—For purposes of subsection (a)(5), the term "exempt governmental deferred compensation plan" means any plan providing for deferral of compensation established and maintained for its employees by the United States, by a State or political subdivision thereof, or by an agency or instrumentality of any of the foregoing. Such term shall not include—

(A) any plan to which section 83, 402(b), 403(c), 457(a), or 457(f)(1) applies,

(B) any annuity contract described in section 403(b), and

(C) the Thrift Savings Fund (within the meaning of subchapter III of chapter 84 of title 5, United States Code).

* * *

§ 3405. Special rules for pensions, annuities, and certain other deferred income.

(a) Periodic payments—

(1) Withholding as if payment were wages—The payor of any periodic payment (as defined in subsection (e)(2)) shall withhold from such payment the amount which would be required to be withheld from such payment if such payment were a payment of wages by an employer to an employee for the appropriate payroll period.

(2) Election of no withholding—An individual may elect to have paragraph (1) not apply with respect to periodic payments made to such individual. Such an election shall remain in effect until revoked by such individual.

(3) When election takes effect—Any election under this subsection (and any revocation of such an election) shall take effect as provided by subsection (f)(3) of section 3402 for withholding exemption certificates.

(4) Amount withheld where no withholding exemption certificate in effect—In the case of any payment with respect to which a withholding exemption certificate is not in effect, the amount withheld under paragraph (1) shall be determined by treating the payee as a married individual claiming 3 withholding exemptions.

(b) Nonperiodic distribution—

(1) Withholding—The payor of any nonperiodic distribution (as defined in subsection (e)(3)) shall withhold from such distribution an amount equal to 10 percent of such distribution.

(2) Election of no withholding—

(A) In general—An individual may elect not to have paragraph (1) apply with respect to any nonperiodic distribution.

(B) Scope of election—An election under subparagraph (A)—

(i) except as provided in clause (ii), shall be on a distribution-by-distribution basis, or

(ii) to the extent provided in regulations, may apply to subsequent nonperiodic distributions made by the payor to the payee under the same arrangement.

(c) Eligible rollover distributions—

(1) In general—In the case of any designated distribution which is an eligible rollover distribution—

(A) subsections (a) and (b) shall not apply, and

(B) the payor of such distribution shall withhold from such distribution an amount equal to 20 percent of such distribution.

(2) Exception—Paragraph (1)(B) shall not apply to any distribution if the distributee elects under section 401(a)(31)(A) to have such distribution paid directly to an eligible retirement plan.

(3) Eligible rollover distribution—For purposes of this subsection, the term "eligible rollover distribution" has the meaning given such term by section 402(f)(2)(A).

* * *

(e) Definitions and special rules—For purposes of this section—

(1) Designated distribution—

(A) In general—Except as provided in subparagraph (B), the term "designated distribution" means any distribution or payment from or under—

(i) an employer deferred compensation plan,

(ii) an individual retirement plan (as defined in section 7701(a)(37)), or

(iii) a commercial annuity.

(B) Exceptions—The term "designated distribution" shall not include—

(i) any amount which is wages without regard to this section,

(ii) the portion of a distribution or payment which it is reasonable to believe is not includible in gross income,

(iii) any amount which is subject to withholding under subchapter A of chapter 3 (relating to withholding of tax on nonresident aliens and foreign corporations) by the person paying such amount or which would be so subject but for a tax treaty, or

(iv) any distribution described in section 404(k)(2).

For purposes of clause (ii), any distribution or payment from or under an individual retirement plan (other than a Roth IRA) shall be treated as includible in gross income.

* * *

(8) Maximum amount withheld—The maximum amount to be withheld under this section on any designated distribution shall not exceed the sum of the amount of money and the fair market value of other property (other than securities of the employer corporation) received in the distribution. No amount shall be required to be withheld under this section in the case of any designated distribution which consists only of securities of the employer corporation and cash (not in excess of $200) in lieu of financial shares. For purposes of this paragraph, the term "securities of the employer corporation" has the meaning given such term by section 402(e)(4)(E).

* * *

§ 4971. Taxes on failure to meet minimum funding standards.

(a) Initial tax—If at any time during any taxable year an employer maintains a plan to which section 412 applies, there is hereby imposed for the taxable year a tax equal to—

(1) in the case of a single-employer plan, 10 percent of the aggregate unpaid minimum required contributions for all plan years remaining unpaid as of the end of any plan year ending with or within the taxable year, and

(2) in the case of a multiemployer plan, 5 percent of the accumulated funding deficiency determined under section 431 as of the end of any plan year ending with or within the taxable year.

(b) Additional tax—If—

(1) a tax is imposed under subsection (a)(1) on any unpaid minimum required contribution and such amount remains unpaid as of the close of the taxable period, or

(2) a tax is imposed under subsection (a)(2) on any accumulated funding deficiency and the accumulated funding deficiency is not corrected within the taxable period,

there is hereby imposed a tax equal to 100 percent of the unpaid minimum required contribution or accumulated funding deficiency, whichever is applicable, to the extent not so paid or corrected.

(c) Definitions—For purposes of this section—

(1) Accumulated funding deficiency—The term "accumulated funding deficiency" has the meaning given to such term by section 431.

(2) Correct—The term "correct" means, with respect to an accumulated funding deficiency, the contribution, to or under the plan, of the amount necessary to reduce such accumulated funding deficiency as of the end of a plan year in which such deficiency arose to zero.

(3) Taxable period—The term "taxable period" means, with respect to an accumulated funding deficiency or unpaid minimum required contribution, whichever is applicable, the period beginning with the end of the plan year in which there is an accumulated funding deficiency or unpaid minimum required contribution, whichever is applicable and ending on the earlier of—

(A) the date of mailing of a notice of deficiency with respect to the tax imposed by subsection (a), or

(B) the date on which the tax imposed by subsection (a) is assessed.

(4) Unpaid minimum required contribution—

(A) In general—The term "unpaid minimum required contribution" means, with respect to any plan year, any minimum required contribution under section 430 for the plan year which is not paid on or before the due date (as determined under section 430(j)(1)) for the plan year.

(B) Ordering rule—Any payment to or under a plan for any plan year shall be allocated first to unpaid minimum required contributions for all preceding plan years on a first-in, first-out basis and then to the minimum required contribution under section 430 for the plan year.

* * *

(e) Liability for tax—

(1) In general—Except as provided in paragraph (2), the tax imposed by subsection (a), (b), or (f) shall be paid by the employer responsible for contributing to or under the plan the amount described in section 412(a)(2).

(2) Joint and several liability where employer member of controlled group—

(A) In general—If an employer referred to in paragraph (1) is a member of a controlled group, each member of such group shall be jointly and severally liable for the tax imposed by subsection (a), (b), (f), or (g).

(B) Controlled group—For purposes of subparagraph (A), the term "controlled group" means any group treated as a single employer under subsection (b), (c), (m), or (o) of section 414.

(f) Failure to pay liquidity shortfall—

(1) In general—In the case of a plan to which section 430(j)(4) applies, there is hereby imposed a tax of 10 percent of the excess (if any) of—

(A) the amount of the liquidity shortfall for any quarter, over

(B) the amount of such shortfall which is paid by the required installment under section 430(j) for such quarter (but only if such installment is paid on or before the due date for such installment).

(2) Additional tax—If the plan has a liquidity shortfall as of the close of any quarter and as of the close of each of the following 4 quarters, there is hereby imposed a tax equal to 100 percent of the amount on which tax was imposed by paragraph (1) for such first quarter.

(3) Definitions and special rule—

(A) Liquidity shortfall; quarter—For purposes of this subsection, the terms "liquidity shortfall" and "quarter" have the respective meanings given such terms by section 412(m)(5).

(B) Special rule—If the tax imposed by paragraph (2) is paid with respect to any liquidity shortfall for any quarter, no further tax shall be imposed by this subsection on such shortfall for such quarter.

(4) Waiver by Secretary—If the taxpayer establishes to the satisfaction of the Secretary that—

(A) the liquidity shortfall described in paragraph (1) was due to reasonable cause and not willful neglect, and

(B) reasonable steps have been taken to remedy such liquidity shortfall,

the Secretary may waive all or part of the tax imposed by this subsection.

* * *

§ 4972. Tax on nondeductible contributions to qualified employer plans.

(a) Tax imposed—In the case of any qualified employer plan, there is hereby imposed a tax equal to 10 percent of the nondeductible contributions under the plan (determined as of the close of the taxable year of the employer).

(b) Employer liable for tax—The tax imposed by this section shall be paid by the employer making the contributions.

(c) Nondeductible contributions—For purposes of this section—

(1) In general—The term "nondeductible contributions" means, with respect to any qualified employer plan, the sum of—

(A) the excess (if any) of—

(i) the amount contributed for the taxable year by the employer to or under such plan, over

(ii) the amount allowable as a deduction under section 404 for such contributions (determined without regard to subsection (e) thereof), and

(B) the amount determined under this subsection for the preceding taxable year reduced by the sum of—

(i) the portion of the amount so determined returned to the employer during the taxable year, and

(ii) the portion of the amount so determined deductible under section 404 for the taxable year (determined without regard to subsection (e) thereof).

* * *

(4) Special rule for self-employed individuals—For purposes of paragraph (1), if—

(A) the amount which is required to be contributed to a plan under section 412 on behalf of an individual who is an employee (within the meaning of section 401(c)(1)), exceeds

(B) the earned income (within the meaning of section 404(a)(8)) of such individual derived from the trade or business with respect to which such plan is established,

such excess shall be treated as an amount allowable as a deduction under section 404.

* * *

(6) Exceptions—In determining the amount of nondeductible contributions for any taxable year, there shall not be taken into account—

(A) so much of the contributions to 1 or more defined contribution plans which are not deductible when contributed solely because of section 404(a)(7) as does not exceed the amount of contributions described in section 401(m)(4)(A), or

(B) so much of the contributions to a simple retirement account (within the meaning of section 408(p)) or a simple plan (within the meaning of section 401(k)(11)) which are not deductible when contributed solely because such contributions are not made in connection with a trade or business of the employer.

For purposes of subparagraph (A), the deductible limits under section 404(a)(7) shall first be applied to amounts contributed to a defined benefit plan and then to amounts described in subparagraph (A). Subparagraph (B) shall not apply to contributions made on behalf of the employer or a member of the employer's family (as defined in section 447(e)(1)).

(7) Defined benefit plan exception—In determining the amount of nondeductible contributions for any taxable year, an employer may elect for such year not to take into account any contributions to a defined benefit plan except, in the case of a multiemployer plan, to the extent that such contributions exceed the full-funding limitation (as defined in section 431(c)(6)). For purposes of this paragraph, the deductible limits under section 404(a)(7) shall first be applied to amounts contributed to defined contribution plans and then to amounts described in this paragraph. If an employer makes an election under this paragraph for a taxable year, paragraph (6) shall not apply to such employer for such taxable year.

(d) Definitions—For purposes of this section—

(1) Qualified employer plan—

(A) In general—The term "qualified employer plan" means—

(i) any plan meeting the requirements of section 401(a) which includes a trust exempt from tax under section 501(a),

(ii) an annuity plan described in section 403(a),

(iii) any simplified employee pension (within the meaning of section 408(k)), and

(iv) any simple retirement account (within the meaning of section 408(p)).

(B) Exemption for governmental and tax exempt plans—The term "qualified employer plan" does not include a plan described in subparagraph (A) or (B) of section 4980(c)(1).

(2) Employer—In the case of a plan which provides contributions or benefits for employees some or all of whom are self-employed individuals within the meaning of section 401(c)(1), the term "employer" means the person treated as the employer under section 401(c)(4).

§ 4973. Tax on excess contributions to certain tax-favored accounts and annuities.

(a) Tax imposed—In the case of—

(1) an individual retirement account (within the meaning of section 408(a)),

(2) an Archer MSA (within the meaning of section 220(d)),

(3) an individual retirement annuity (within the meaning of section 408(b)), a custodial account treated as an annuity contract under section 403(b)(7)(A) (relating to custodial accounts for regulated investment company stock), or

(4) a Cloverdell education savings account (as defined in section 530),

(5) a health savings account (within the meaning of section 223(d)),

there is imposed for each taxable year a tax in an amount equal to 6 percent of the amount of the excess contributions to such individual's accounts or annuities (determined as of the close of the taxable year). The amount of such tax for any taxable year shall not exceed 6 percent of the value of the account or annuity (determined as of the close of the taxable year). In the case of an endowment contract described in section 408(b), the tax imposed by this section does not apply to any amount allocable to life, health, accident, or other insurance under such contract. The tax imposed by this subsection shall be paid by such individual.

(b) Excess contributions—For purposes of this section, in the case of individual retirement accounts, or individual retirement annuities the term "excess contributions" means the sum of—

(1) the excess (if any) of—

(A) the amount contributed for the taxable year to the accounts or for the annuities or bonds (other than a contribution to a Roth IRA or a rollover contribution described in section 402(c), 403(a)(4), 403(b)(8), 408(d)(3), or 457(e)(16)), over

(B) the amount allowable as a deduction under section 219 for such contributions, and

(2) the amount determined under this subsection for the preceding taxable year, reduced by the sum of—

(A) the distributions out of the account for the taxable year which were included in the gross income of the payee under section 408(d)(1),

(B) the distributions out of the account for the taxable year to which section 408(d)(5) applies, and

(C) the excess (if any) of the maximum amount allowable as a deduction under section 219 for the taxable year over the amount contributed (determined without regard to section 219(f)(6)) to the accounts or for the annuities (including the amount contributed to a Roth IRA) or bonds for the taxable year.

For purposes of this subsection, any contribution which is distributed from the individual retirement account or the individual retirement annuity in a distribution to which section 408(d)(4) applies shall be treated as an amount not contributed. For purposes of paragraphs (1)(B) and (2)(C), the amount allowable as a deduction under section 219 shall be computed without regard to section 219(g).

* * *

(f) Excess contributions to Roth IRAs—For purposes of this section, in the case of contributions to a Roth IRA (within the meaning of section 408A(b)), the term "excess contributions" means the sum of—

(1) the excess (if any) of—

(A) the amount contributed for the taxable year to Roth IRAs (other than a qualified rollover contribution described in section 408A(e)), over

(B) the amount allowable as a contribution under sections 408A (c)(2) and (c)(3), and

(2) the amount determined under this subsection for the preceding taxable year, reduced by the sum of—

(A) the distributions out of the accounts for the taxable year, and

(B) the excess (if any) of the maximum amount allowable as a contribution under sections 408A (c)(2) and (c)(3) for the taxable year over the amount contributed by the individual to all individual retirement plans for the taxable year.

For purposes of this subsection, any contribution which is distributed from a Roth IRA in a distribution described in section 408(d)(4) shall be treated as an amount not contributed.

§ 4974. Excise tax on certain accumulations in qualified retirement plans.

(a) General rule—If the amount distributed during the taxable year of the payee under any qualified retirement plan or any eligible deferred compensation plan (as defined in section 457(b)) is less than the minimum required distribution for such taxable year, there is hereby imposed a tax equal to 50 percent of the amount by which such minimum required distribution exceeds the actual amount distributed during the taxable year. The tax imposed by this section shall be paid by the payee.

(b) Minimum required distribution—For purposes of this section, the term "minimum required distribution" means the minimum amount required to be distributed during a taxable year under section 401(a)(9), 403(b)(10), 408(a)(6), 408(b)(3), or 457(d)(2), as the case may be, as determined under regulations prescribed by the Secretary.

(c) Qualified retirement plan—For purposes of this section, the term "qualified retirement plan" means—

(1) a plan described in section 401(a) which includes a trust exempt from tax under section 501(a),

(2) an annuity plan described in section 403(a),

(3) an annuity contract described in section 403(b),

(4) an individual retirement account described in section 408(a), or

(5) an individual retirement annuity described in section 408(b).

Such term includes any plan, contract, account, or annuity which, at any time, has been determined by the Secretary to be such a plan, contract, account, or annuity.

(d) Waiver of tax in certain cases—If the taxpayer establishes to the satisfaction of the Secretary that—

(1) the shortfall described in subsection (a) in the amount distributed during any taxable year was due to reasonable error, and

(2) reasonable steps are being taken to remedy the shortfall, the Secretary may waive the tax imposed by subsection (a) for the taxable year.

§ 4975. Tax on prohibited transactions.

(a) Initial taxes on disqualified person—There is hereby imposed a tax on each prohibited transaction. The rate of tax shall be equal to 15 percent of the amount involved with respect to the prohibited transaction for each year (or part thereof) in the taxable period. The tax imposed by this subsection shall be paid by any disqualified person who participates in the prohibited transaction (other than a fiduciary acting only as such).

(b) Additional taxes on disqualified person—In any case in which an initial tax is imposed by subsection (a) on a prohibited transaction and the transaction is not corrected within the taxable period, there is hereby imposed a tax equal to 100 percent of the amount involved. The tax imposed by this subsection shall be paid by any disqualified person who participated in the prohibited transaction (other than a fiduciary acting only as such).

(c) Prohibited transaction—

(1) General rule—For purposes of this section, the term "prohibited transaction" means any direct or indirect—

(A) sale or exchange, or leasing, of any property between a plan and a disqualified person;

(B) lending of money or other extension of credit between a plan and a disqualified person;

(C) furnishing of goods, services, or facilities between a plan and a disqualified person;

(D) transfer to, or use by or for the benefit of, a disqualified person of the income or assets of a plan;

(E) act by a disqualified person who is a fiduciary whereby he deals with the income or assets of a plan in his own interest or for his own account; or

(F) receipt of any consideration for his own personal account by any disqualified person who is a fiduciary from any party dealing with the plan in connection with a transaction involving the income or assets of the plan.

(2) Special exemption—The Secretary shall establish an exemption procedure for purposes of this subsection. Pursuant to such procedure, he may grant a conditional or unconditional exemption of any disqualified person or transaction or class of disqualified persons or transactions, from all or part of the restrictions imposed by paragraph (1) of this subsection. Action under this subparagraph may be taken only after consultation and coordination with the Secretary of Labor. The Secretary may not grant an exemption under this paragraph unless he finds that such exemption is—

(A) administratively feasible,

(B) in the interests of the plan and of its participants and beneficiaries, and

(C) protective of the rights of participants and beneficiaries of the plan.

Before granting an exemption under this paragraph, the Secretary shall require adequate notice to be given to interested persons and shall publish notice in the Federal Register of the pendency of such exemption and shall afford interested persons an opportunity to present views. No exemption may be granted under this paragraph with respect to a transaction described in subparagraph (E) or (F) of paragraph (1) unless the Secretary affords an opportunity for a hearing and makes a determination on the record with respect to the findings required under subparagraphs (A), (B), and (C) of this paragraph, except that in lieu of such hearing the Secretary may accept any record made by the Secretary of Labor with respect to an application for exemption under section 408(a) of title I of the Employee Retirement Income Security Act of 1974.

* * *

(d) Exemptions—Except as provided in subsection (f)(6), the prohibitions provided in subsection (c) shall not apply to—

(1) any loan made by the plan to a disqualified person who is a participant or beneficiary of the plan if such loan—

(A) is available to all such participants or beneficiaries on a reasonably equivalent basis,

(B) is not made available to highly compensated employees (within the meaning of section 414(q) of the Internal Revenue Code of 1986) in an amount greater than the amount made available to other employees,

(C) is made in accordance with specific provisions regarding such loans set forth in the plan,

(D) bears a reasonable rate of interest, and

(E) is adequately secured;

(2) any contract, or reasonable arrangement, made with a disqualified person for office space, or legal, accounting, or other services necessary for the establishment or operation of the plan, if no more than reasonable compensation is paid therefor; 4975(d)(3) any loan to a leveraged employee stock ownership plan (as defined in subsection (e)(7)), if—

(A) such loan is primarily for the benefit of participants and beneficiaries of the plan, and

(B) such loan is at a reasonable rate of interest, and any collateral which is given to a disqualified person by the plan consists only of qualifying employer securities (as defined in subsection (e)(8));

* * *

(17) Any transaction in connection with the provision of investment advice described in subsection (e)(3)(B) to a participant or beneficiary in a plan that permits such participant or beneficiary to direct the investment of plan assets in an individual account, if—

(A) the transaction is—

(i) the provision of the investment advice to the participant or beneficiary of the plan with respect to a security or other property available as an investment under the plan,

(ii) the acquisition, holding, or sale of a security or other property available as an investment under the plan pursuant to the investment advice, or

(iii) the direct or indirect receipt of fees or other compensation by the fiduciary adviser or an affiliate thereof (or any employee, agent, or registered representative of the fiduciary adviser or affiliate) in connection with the provision of the advice or in connection with an acquisition, holding, or sale of a security or other property available as an investment under the plan pursuant to the investment advice; and

(B) the requirements of subsection (f)(8) are met.

* * *

(e) **Definitions**—

(1) Plan—For purposes of this section, the term "plan" means—

(A) a trust described in section 401(a) which forms a part of a plan, or a plan described in section 403(a), which trust or plan is exempt from tax under section 501(a),

(B) an individual retirement account described in section 408(a),

(C) an individual retirement annuity described in section 408(b),

(D) an Archer MSA described in section 220(d),

(E) a health savings account described in section 223(d),

(F) a Cloverdell education savings account described in section 530, or

(G) a trust, plan, account, or annuity which, at any time, has been determined by the Secretary to be described in any preceding subparagraph of this paragraph.

(2) Disqualified person—For purposes of this section, the term "disqualified person" means a person who is—

(A) a fiduciary;

(B) a person providing services to the plan;

(C) an employer any of whose employees are covered by the plan;

(D) an employee organization any of whose members are covered by the plan;

(E) an owner, direct or indirect, of 50 percent or more of—

(i) the combined voting power of all classes of stock entitled to vote or the total value of shares of all classes of stock of a corporation,

(ii) the capital interest or the profits interest of a partnership, or

(iii) the beneficial interest of a trust or unincorporated enterprise, which is an employer or an employee organization described in subparagraph (C) or (D);

(F) a member of the family (as defined in paragraph (6)) of any individual described in subparagraph (A), (B), (C), or (E);

(G) a corporation, partnership, or trust or estate of which (or in which) 50 percent or more of—

(i) the combined voting power of all classes of stock entitled to vote or the total value of shares of all classes of stock of such corporation,

(ii) the capital interest or profits interest of such partnership, or

(iii) the beneficial interest of such trust or estate, is owned directly or indirectly, or held by persons described in subparagraph (A), (B), (C), (D), or (E);

(H) an officer, director (or an individual having powers or responsibilities similar to those of officers or directors), a 10 percent or more shareholder, or a highly compensated employee (earning 10 percent or more of the yearly wages of an employer) of a person described in subparagraph (C), (D), (E), or (G); or

(I) a 10 percent or more (in capital or profits) partner or joint venturer of a person described in subparagraph (C), (D), (E), or (G).

The Secretary, after consultation and coordination with the Secretary of Labor or his delegate, may by regulation prescribe a percentage lower than 50 percent for subparagraphs (E) and (G) and lower than 10 percent for subparagraphs (H) and (I).

(3) Fiduciary—For purposes of this section, the term "fiduciary" means any person who—

(A) exercises any discretionary authority or discretionary control respecting management of such plan or exercises any authority or control respecting management or disposition of its assets,

(B) renders investment advice for a fee or other compensation, direct or indirect, with respect to any moneys or other property of such plan, or has any authority or responsibility to do so, or

(C) has any discretionary authority or discretionary responsibility in the administration of such plan. Such term includes any person designated under section 405(c)(1)(B) of the Employee Retirement Income Security Act of 1974.

(4) Stockholdings—For purposes of paragraphs (2)(E)(i), and (G)(i) there shall be taken into account indirect stockholdings which would be taken into account under section 267(c), except that, for purposes of this paragraph, section 267(c)(4) shall be treated as providing that the members of the family of an individual are the members within the meaning of paragraph (6).

(5) Partnerships; trusts—For purposes of paragraphs (2)(E)(ii) and (iii), (G)(ii) and (iii), and (I) the ownership of profits or beneficial interests shall be determined in accordance with the rules for constructive ownership of stock provided in section 267(c) (other than paragraph (3) thereof), except that section 267(c)(4) shall be treated as providing that the members of the family of an individual are the members within the meaning of paragraph (6).

(6) Member of family—For purposes of paragraph (2)(F), the family of any individual shall include his spouse, ancestor, lineal descendant, and any spouse of a lineal descendant.

(7) Employee stock ownership plan—The term "employee stock ownership plan" means a defined contribution plan—

(A) which is a stock bonus plan which is qualified, or a stock bonus and a money purchase plan both of which are qualified under section 401(a) and which are designed to invest primarily in qualifying employer securities; and

(B) which is otherwise defined in regulations prescribed by the Secretary.

A plan shall not be treated as an employee stock ownership plan unless it meets the requirements of section 409(h), section 409(o), and, if applicable, section 409(n), section 409(p), and section 664(g) and, if the employer has a registration-type class of securities (as defined in section 409(e)(4)), it meets the requirements of section 409(e).

(8) Qualifying employer security—The term "qualifying employer security" means an employer security within the meaning of section 409(l).

If any moneys or other property of a plan are invested in shares of an investment company registered under the Investment Company Act of 1940, the investment shall not cause that investment company or that investment company's investment adviser or principal underwriter to be treated as a fiduciary or a disqualified person for purposes of this section, except when an investment company or its investment adviser or principal underwriter acts in connection with a plan covering employees of the investment company, its investment adviser, or its principal underwriter.

* * *

(f) Other definitions and special rules—For purposes of this section—

(1) Joint and several liability—If more than one person is liable under subsection (a) or (b) with respect to any one prohibited transaction, all such persons shall be jointly and severally liable under such subsection with respect to such transaction.

(2) Taxable period—The term "taxable period" means, with respect to any prohibited transaction, the period beginning with the date on which the prohibited transaction occurs and ending on the earliest of—

(A) the date of mailing a notice of deficiency with respect to the tax imposed by subsection (a) under section 6212,

(B) the date on which the tax imposed by subsection (a) is assessed, or

(C) the date on which correction of the prohibited transaction is completed.

(3) Sale or exchange; encumbered property—A transfer of real or personal property by a disqualified person to a plan shall be treated as a sale or exchange if the property is subject to a mortgage or similar lien which the plan assumes or if it is subject to a mortgage or similar lien which a disqualified person placed on the property within the 10-year period ending on the date of the transfer.

(4) Amount involved—The term "amount involved" means, with respect to a prohibited transaction, the greater of the amount of money and the fair market value of the other property given or the amount of money and the fair market value of the other property received; except that, in the case of services described in paragraphs (2) and (10) of subsection (d) the amount involved shall be only the excess compensation. For purposes of the preceding sentence, the fair market value—

(A) in the case of the tax imposed by subsection (a), shall be determined as of the date on which the prohibited transaction occurs; and

(B) in the case of the tax imposed by subsection (b), shall be the highest fair market value during the taxable period.

(5) Correction—The terms "correction" and "correct" mean, with respect to a prohibited transaction, undoing the transaction to the extent possible, but in any case placing the plan in a financial position not worse than that in which it would be if the disqualified person were acting under the highest fiduciary standards.

(6) Exemptions not to apply to certain transactions—

(A) In general—In the case of a trust described in section 401(a) which is part of a plan providing contributions or benefits for employees some or all of whom are owner-employees (as defined in section 401(c)(3)), the exemptions provided by subsection (d) (other than paragraphs (9) and (12)) shall not apply to a transaction in which the plan directly or indirectly—

(i) lends any part of the corpus or income of the plan to,

(ii) pays any compensation for personal services rendered to the plan to, or

(iii) acquires for the plan any property from, or sells any property to,

any such owner-employee, a member of the family (as defined in section 267(c)(4)) of any such owner-employee, or any corporation in which any such owner-employee owns, directly or indirectly, 50 percent or more of the total combined voting power of all classes of stock entitled to vote or 50 percent or more of the total value of shares of all classes of stock of the corporation.

(B) Special rules for shareholder-employees, etc—

(i) In general—For purposes of subparagraph (A), the following shall be treated as owner-employees:

(I) A shareholder-employee.

(II) A participant or beneficiary of an individual retirement plan (as defined in section 7701(a)(37)).

(III) An employer or association of employees which establishes such an individual retirement plan under section 408(c).

(ii) Exception for certain transactions involving shareholder-employees— Subparagraph (A)(iii) shall not apply to a transaction which consists of a sale of employer securities to an employee stock ownership plan (as defined in subsection (e)(7)) by a shareholder-employee, a member of the family (as defined in section 267(c)(4)) of such shareholder-employee, or a corporation in which such a shareholder-employee owns stock representing a 50 percent or greater interest described in subparagraph (A).

(iii) Loan exception—For purposes of subparagraph (A)(i), the term "owner-employee" shall only include a person described in subclause (II) or (III) of clause (i).

(C) Shareholder-employee—For purposes of subparagraph (B), the term "shareholder-employee" means an employee or officer of an S corporation who owns (or is considered as owning within the meaning of section 318(a)(1)) more than 5 percent of the outstanding stock of the corporation on any day during the taxable year of such corporation.

(7) S corporation repayment of loans for qualifying employer securities—A plan shall not be treated as violating the requirements of section 401 or 409 or subsection (e)(7), or as engaging in a prohibited transaction for purposes of subsection (d)(3), merely by reason of any distribution (as described in section 1368(a)) with respect to S corporation stock that constitutes qualifying employer securities, which in accordance with the plan provisions is used to make payments on a loan described in subsection (d)(3) the proceeds of which were used to acquire such qualifying employer securities (whether or not allocated to participants). The preceding sentence shall not apply in the case of a distribution which is paid with respect to any employer security which is allocated to a participant unless the plan provides that employer securities with a fair market value of not less than the amount of such distribution are allocated to such participant for the year which (but for the preceding sentence) such distribution would have been allocated to such participant.

(8) Provision of investment advice to participant and beneficiaries—

(A) In general—The prohibitions provided in subsection (c) shall not apply to transactions described in subsection (d)(17) if the investment advice provided by a fiduciary adviser is provided under an eligible investment advice arrangement.

(B) Eligible investment advice arrangement—For purposes of this paragraph, the term "eligible investment advice arrangement" means an arrangement—

(i) which either—

(I) provides that any fees (including any commission or other compensation) received by the fiduciary adviser for investment advice or with respect to the sale, holding, or acquisition of any security or other property for purposes of investment of plan assets do not vary depending on the basis of any investment option selected, or

(II) uses a computer model under an investment advice program meeting the requirements of subparagraph (C) in connection with the provision of investment advice by a fiduciary adviser to a participant or beneficiary, and

(ii) with respect to which the requirements of subparagraphs (D), (E), (F), (G), (H), and (I) are met.

(C) Investment advice program using computer model—

(i) In general—An investment advice program meets the requirements of this subparagraph if the requirements of clauses (ii), (iii), and (iv) are met.

(ii) Computer model—The requirements of this clause are met if the investment advice provided under the investment advice program is provided pursuant to a computer model that—

(I) applies generally accepted investment theories that take into account the historic returns of different asset classes over defined periods of time,

(II) utilizes relevant information about the participant, which may include age, life expectancy, retirement age, risk tolerance, other assets or sources of income, and preferences as to certain types of investments,

(III) utilizes prescribed objective criteria to provide asset allocation portfolios comprised of investment options available under the plan,

(IV) operates in a manner that is not biased in favor of investments offered by the fiduciary adviser or a person with a material affiliation or contractual relationship with the fiduciary adviser, and

(V) takes into account all investment options under the plan in specifying how a participant's account balance should be invested and is not inappropriately weighted with respect to any investment option.

(iii) Certification—

(I) In general—The requirements of this clause are met with respect to any investment advice program if an eligible investment expert certifies, prior to the utilization of the computer model and in accordance with rules prescribed by the Secretary of Labor, that the computer model meets the requirements of clause (ii).

(II) Renewal of certifications—If, as determined under regulations prescribed by the Secretary of Labor, there are material modifications to a computer model, the requirements of this clause are met only if a certification described in subclause (I) is obtained with respect to the computer model as so modified.

(III) Eligible investment expert—The term "eligible investment expert" means any person which meets such requirements as the Secretary of Labor may provide and which does not bear any material affiliation or contractual relationship with any investment adviser or a related person thereof (or any employee, agent, or registered representative of the investment adviser or related person).

(iv) Exclusivity of recommendation—The requirements of this clause are met with respect to any investment advice program if—

(I) the only investment advice provided under the program is the advice generated by the computer model described in clause (ii), and

(II) any transaction described in subsection (d)(17)(A)(ii) occurs solely at the direction of the participant or beneficiary.

Nothing in the preceding sentence shall preclude the participant or beneficiary from requesting investment advice other than that described in clause (i), but only if such request has not been solicited by any person connected with carrying out the arrangement.

(D) Express authorization by separate fiduciary—The requirements of this subparagraph are met with respect to an arrangement if the arrangement is expressly authorized by a plan fiduciary other than the person offering the investment advice program, any person providing investment options under the plan, or any affiliate of either.

(E) Audits—

(i) In general—The requirements of this subparagraph are met if an independent auditor, who has appropriate technical training or experience and proficiency and so represents in writing—

(I) conducts an annual audit of the arrangement for compliance with the requirements of this paragraph, and

(II) following completion of the annual audit, issues a written report to the fiduciary who authorized use of the arrangement which presents its specific findings regarding compliance of the arrangement with the requirements of this paragraph.

(ii) Special rule for individual retirement and similar plans—In the case of a plan described in subparagraphs (B) through (F) (and so much of subparagraph (G) as relates to such subparagraphs) of subsection (e)(1), in lieu of the requirements of clause (i), audits of the arrangement shall be conducted at such times and in such manner as the Secretary of Labor may prescribe.

(iii) Independent auditor—For purposes of this subparagraph, an auditor is considered independent if it is not related to the person offering the arrangement to the plan and is not related to any person providing investment options under the plan.

(F) Disclosure—The requirements of this subparagraph are met if—

(i) the fiduciary adviser provides to a participant or a beneficiary before the initial provision of the investment advice with regard to any security or other property offered as an investment option, a written notification (which may consist of notification by means of electronic communication)—

(I) of the role of any party that has a material affiliation or contractual relationship with the fiduciary adviser in the development of the investment advice program and in the selection of investment options available under the plan,

(II) of the past performance and historical rates of return of the investment options available under the plan,

(III) of all fees or other compensation relating to the advice that the fiduciary adviser or any affiliate thereof is to receive (including compensation provided by any third party) in connection with the provision of the advice or in connection with the sale, acquisition, or holding of the security or other property,

(IV) of any material affiliation or contractual relationship of the fiduciary adviser or affiliates thereof in the security or other property,

(V) the manner, and under what circumstances, any participant or beneficiary information provided under the arrangement will be used or disclosed,

(VI) of the types of services provided by the fiduciary adviser in connection with the provision of investment advice by the fiduciary adviser,

(VII) that the adviser is acting as a fiduciary of the plan in connection with the provision of the advice, and

(VIII) that a recipient of the advice may separately arrange for the provision of advice by another adviser, that could have no material affiliation with and receive no fees or other compensation in connection with the security or other property, and

(ii) at all times during the provision of advisory services to the participant or beneficiary, the fiduciary adviser—

(I) maintains the information described in clause (i) in accurate form and in the manner described in subparagraph (H),

(II) provides, without charge, accurate information to the recipient of the advice no less frequently than annually,

(III) provides, without charge, accurate information to the recipient of the advice upon request of the recipient, and

(IV) provides, without charge, accurate information to the recipient of the advice concerning any material change to the information required to be provided to the recipient of the advice at a time reasonably contemporaneous to the change in information.

(G) Other conditions—The requirements of this subparagraph are met if—

(i) the fiduciary adviser provides appropriate disclosure, in connection with the sale, acquisition, or holding of the security or other property, in accordance with all applicable securities laws,

(ii) the sale, acquisition, or holding occurs solely at the direction of the recipient of the advice,

(iii) the compensation received by the fiduciary adviser and affiliates thereof in connection with the sale, acquisition, or holding of the security or other property is reasonable, and

(iv) the terms of the sale, acquisition, or holding of the security or other property are at least as favorable to the plan as an arm's length transaction would be.

(H) Standards for presentation of information—

(i) In general—The requirements of this subparagraph are met if the notification required to be provided to participants and beneficiaries under subparagraph (F)(i) is written in a clear and conspicuous manner and in a manner calculated to be understood by the average plan participant and is sufficiently accurate and comprehensive to reasonably apprise such participants and beneficiaries of the information required to be provided in the notification.

(ii) Model form for disclosure of fees and other compensation—The Secretary of Labor shall issue a model form for the disclosure of fees and other compensation required in subparagraph (F)(i)(III) which meets the requirements of clause (i).

(I) Maintenance for 6 years of evidence of compliance—The requirements of this subparagraph are met if a fiduciary adviser who has provided advice referred to in subparagraph (A) maintains, for a period of not less than 6 years after the provision of the advice, any records necessary for determining whether the requirements of the preceding provisions of this paragraph and of subsection (d)(17) have been met. A transaction prohibited under subsection (c) shall not be considered to have occurred solely because the records are lost or destroyed prior to the end of the 6-year period due to circumstances beyond the control of the fiduciary adviser.

(J) Definitions—For purposes of this paragraph and subsection (d)(17)—

(i) Fiduciary adviser—The term "fiduciary adviser" means, with respect to a plan, a person who is a fiduciary of the plan by reason of the provision of investment advice referred to in subsection (e)(3)(B) by the person to a participant or beneficiary of the plan and who is—

(I) registered as an investment adviser under the Investment Advisers Act of 1940 (15 U.S.C. 80b-1 et seq.) or under the laws of the State in which the fiduciary maintains its principal office and place of business,

(II) a bank or similar financial institution referred to in subsection (d)(4) or a savings association (as defined in section 3(b)(1) of the Federal Deposit Insurance Act (12 U.S.C. 1813(b)(1)), but only if the advice is provided through a trust department of the bank or similar financial institution or savings association which is subject to periodic examination and review by Federal or State banking authorities,

(III) an insurance company qualified to do business under the laws of a State,

(IV) a person registered as a broker or dealer under the Securities Exchange Act of 1934 (15 U.S.C. 78a et seq.),

(V) an affiliate of a person described in any of subclauses (I) through (IV), or

(VI) an employee, agent, or registered representative of a person described in subclauses (I) through (V) who satisfies the requirements of applicable insurance, banking, and securities laws relating to the provision of the advice.

For purposes of this title, a person who develops the computer model described in subparagraph (C)(ii) or markets the investment advice program or computer model shall be treated as a person who is a fiduciary of the plan by reason of the provision of investment advice referred to in subsection (e)(3)(B) to a participant or beneficiary and shall be treated as a fiduciary adviser for purposes of this paragraph and subsection (d)(17), except that the Secretary of Labor may prescribe rules under which only 1 fiduciary adviser may elect to be treated as a fiduciary with respect to the plan.

(ii) Affiliate—The term "affiliate" of another entity means an affiliated person of the entity (as defined in section 2(a)(3) of the Investment Company Act of 1940 (15 U.S.C. 80a-2(a)(3))).

(iii) Registered representative—The term "registered representative" of another entity means a person described in section 3(a)(18) of the Securities Exchange Act of 1934 (15 U.S.C. 78c(a)(18)) (substituting the entity for the broker or dealer referred to in such section) or a person described in section 202(a)(17) of the Investment Advisers Act of 1940 (15 U.S.C. 80b-2(a)(17)) (substituting the entity for the investment adviser referred to in such section).

* * *

(g) Application of section—This section shall not apply—

(1) in the case of a plan to which a guaranteed benefit policy (as defined in section 401(b)(2)(B) of the Employee Retirement Income Security Act of 1974) is issued, to any assets of the insurance company, insurance service, or insurance organization merely because of its issuance of such policy;

(2) to a governmental plan (within the meaning of section 414(d)); or

(3) to a church plan (within the meaning of section 414(e)) with respect to which the election provided by section 410(d) has not been made. In the case of a plan which invests in any security issued by an investment company registered under the Investment Company Act of 1940, the assets of such plan shall be deemed to include such security but shall not, by reason of such investment, be deemed to include any assets of such company.

(h) Notification of Secretary of Labor—Before sending a notice of deficiency with respect to the tax imposed by subsection (a) or (b), the Secretary shall notify the Secretary of Labor and provide him a reasonable opportunity to obtain a correction of the prohibited transaction or to comment on the imposition of such tax.

* * *

§ 4979. Tax on certain excess contributions.

(a) General rule—In the case of any plan, there is hereby imposed a tax for the taxable year equal to 10 percent of the sum of—

(1) any excess contributions under such plan for the plan year ending in such taxable year, and

(2) any excess aggregate contributions under the plan for the plan year ending in such taxable year.

(b) Liability for tax—The tax imposed by subsection (a) shall be paid by the employer.

(c) Excess contributions—For purposes of this section, the term "excess contributions" has the meaning given such term by sections 401(k)(8)(B), 408(k)(6)(C), and 501(c)(18).

(d) Excess aggregate contribution—For purposes of this section, the term "excess aggregate contribution" has the meaning given to such term by section 401(m)(6)(B). For purposes of determining excess aggregate contributions under an annuity contract described in section 403(b), such contract shall be treated as a plan described in subsection (e)(1).

(e) Plan—For purposes of this section, the term "plan" means—

(1) a plan described in section 401(a) which includes a trust exempt from tax under section 501(a),

(2) any annuity plan described in section 403(a),

(3) any annuity contract described in section 403(b),

(4) a simplified employee pension of an employer which satisfies the requirements of section 408(k), and 4979(e)(5) a plan described in section 501(c)(18).

Such term includes any plan which, at any time, has been determined by the Secretary to be such a plan.

(f) No tax where excess distributed within specified period after close of year—

(1) In general—No tax shall be imposed under this section on any excess contribution or excess aggregate contribution, as the case may be, to the extent such contribution (together with any income allocable thereto through the end of the plan year for which the contribution was made) is distributed (or, if forfeitable, is forfeited) before the close of the first 2½ months (6 months in the case of an excess contribution or excess aggregate contribution to an eligible automatic contribution arrangement (as defined in section 414(w)(3))) of the following plan year.

(2) Year of inclusion—Any amount distributed as provided in paragraph (1) shall be treated as earned and received by the recipient in the recipient's taxable year in which such distributions were made.

§ 4980. Tax on reversion of qualified plan assets to employer.

(a) Imposition of tax—There is hereby imposed a tax of 20 percent of the amount of any employer reversion from a qualified plan.

(b) Liability for tax—The tax imposed by subsection (a) shall be paid by the employer maintaining the plan.

(c) Definitions and special rules—For purposes of this section—

(1) Qualified plan—The term "qualified plan" means any plan meeting the requirements of section 401(a) or 403(a), other than—

(A) a plan maintained by an employer if such employer has, at all times, been exempt from tax under subtitle A, or

(B) a governmental plan (within the meaning of section 414(d)).

Such term shall include any plan which, at any time, has been determined by the Secretary to be a qualified plan.

(2) Employer reversion—

(A) In general—The term "employer reversion" means the amount of cash and the fair market value of other property received (directly or indirectly) by an employer from the qualified plan.

(B) Exceptions—The term "employer reversion" shall not include—

(i) except as provided in regulations, any amount distributed to or on behalf of any employee (or his beneficiaries) if such amount could have been so distributed before termination of such plan without violating any provision of section 401, or

(ii) any distribution to the employer which is allowable under section 401(a)(2) —

(I) in the case of a multiemployer plan, by reason of mistakes of law or fact or the return of any withdrawal liability payment,

(II) in the case of a plan other than a multiemployer plan, by reason of mistake of fact, or

(III) in the case of a plan, by reason of the failure of the plan to initially qualify or the failure of contributions to be deductible; or

(iii) any transfer described in section 420(f)(2)(B)(ii)(II).

* * *

(d) Increase in tax for failure to establish replacement plan or increase benefits—

(1) In general—Subsection (a) shall be applied by substituting "50 percent" for "20 percent" with respect to any employer reversion from a qualified plan unless—

(A) the employer establishes or maintains a qualified replacement plan, or

(B) the plan provides benefit increases meeting the requirements of paragraph (3).

(2) Qualified replacement plan—For purposes of this subsection, the term "qualified replacement plan" means a qualified plan established or maintained by the employer in connection with a qualified plan termination (hereinafter referred to as the "replacement plan") with respect to which the following requirements are met:

(A) Participation requirement—At least 95 percent of the active participants in the terminated plan who remain as employees of the employer after the termination are active participants in the replacement plan.

(B) Asset transfer requirement—

(i) 25 percent cushion—A direct transfer from the terminated plan to the replacement plan is made before any employer reversion, and the transfer is in an amount equal to the excess (if any) of—

(I) 25 percent of the maximum amount which the employer could receive as an employer reversion without regard to this subsection, over

(II) the amount determined under clause (ii).

(ii) Reduction for increase in benefits—The amount determined under this clause is an amount equal to the present value of the aggregate increases in the accrued benefits under the terminated plan of any participants or beneficiaries pursuant to a plan amendment which—

(I) is adopted during the 60-day period ending on the date of termination of the qualified plan, and

(II) takes effect immediately on the termination date.

(iii) Treatment of amount transferred—In the case of the transfer of any amount under clause (i)—

(I) such amount shall not be includible in the gross income of the employer,

(II) no deduction shall be allowable with respect to such transfer, and

(III) such transfer shall not be treated as an employer reversion for purposes of this section.

(C) Allocation requirements—

(i) In general—In the case of any defined contribution plan, the portion of the amount transferred to the replacement plan under subparagraph (B)(i) is—

(I) allocated under the plan to the accounts of participants in the plan year in which the transfer occurs, or

(II) credited to a suspense account and allocated from such account to accounts of participants no less rapidly than ratably over the 7-plan-year period beginning with the year of the transfer.

* * *

(3) Pro rata benefit increases—

(A) In general—The requirements of this paragraph are met if a plan amendment to the terminated plan is adopted in connection with the termination of the plan which provides pro rata increases in the accrued benefits of all qualified participants which—

(i) have an aggregate present value not less than 20 percent of the maximum amount which the employer could receive as an employer reversion without regard to this subsection, and

(ii) take effect immediately on the termination date.

* * *

(6) Subsection not to apply to employer in bankruptcy—This subsection shall not apply to an employer who, as of the termination date of the qualified plan, is in bankruptcy liquidation under chapter 7 of title 11 of the United States Code or in similar proceedings under State law.

§ 4980F. Failure of applicable plans reducing benefit accruals to satisfy notice requirements.

(a) Imposition of tax—There is hereby imposed a tax on the failure of any applicable pension plan to meet the requirements of subsection (e) with respect to any applicable individual.

(b) Amount of tax—

(1) In general—The amount of the tax imposed by subsection (a) on any failure with respect to any applicable individual shall be $100 for each day in the noncompliance period with respect to such failure.

(2) Noncompliance period—For purposes of this section, the term "noncompliance period" means, with respect to any failure, the period beginning on the date the failure first occurs and ending on the date the notice to which the failure relates is provided or the failure is otherwise corrected.

(c) Limitations on amount of tax—

(1) Tax not to apply where failure not discovered and reasonable diligence exercised—No tax shall be imposed by subsection (a) on any failure during any period for which it is established to the satisfaction of the Secretary that any person subject to liability for the tax under subsection (d) did not know that the failure existed and exercised reasonable diligence to meet the requirements of subsection (e).

(2) Tax not to apply to failures corrected within 30 days—No tax shall be imposed by subsection (a) on any failure if—

(A) any person subject to liability for the tax under subsection (d) exercised reasonable diligence to meet the requirements of subsection (e), and

(B) such person provides the notice described in subsection (e) during the 30-day period beginning on the first date such person knew, or exercising reasonable diligence would have known, that such failure existed.

(3) Overall limitation for unintentional failures—

(A) In general—If the person subject to liability for tax under subsection (d) exercised reasonable diligence to meet the requirements of subsection (e), the tax imposed by subsection (a) for failures during the taxable year of the employer (or, in the case of a multiemployer plan, the taxable year of the trust forming part of the plan) shall not exceed $500,000. For purposes of the preceding sentence, all multiemployer plans of which the same trust forms a part shall be treated as 1 plan.

(B) Taxable years in the case of certain controlled groups—For purposes of this paragraph, if all persons who are treated as a single employer for purposes of this section do not have the same taxable year, the taxable years taken into account shall be determined under principles similar to the principles of section 1561.

(4) Waiver by secretary—In the case of a failure which is due to reasonable cause and not to willful neglect, the Secretary may waive part or all of the tax imposed by subsection (a) to the extent that the payment of such tax would be excessive or otherwise inequitable relative to the failure involved.

(d) Liability for tax—The following shall be liable for the tax imposed by subsection (a):

(1) In the case of a plan other than a multiemployer plan, the employer.

(2) In the case of a multiemployer plan, the plan.

(e) Notice requirements for plans significantly reducing benefit accruals—

(1) In general—If an applicable pension plan is amended to provide for a significant reduction in the rate of future benefit accrual, the plan administrator shall provide the notice described in paragraph (2) to each applicable individual (and to each employee organization representing applicable individuals) and to each employer who has an obligation to contribute to the plan.

(2) Notice—The notice required by paragraph (1) shall be written in a manner calculated to be understood by the average plan participant and shall provide sufficient information (as determined in accordance with regulations prescribed by the Secretary) to allow applicable individuals to understand the effect of the plan amendment. The Secretary may provide a simplified form of notice for, or exempt from any notice requirement, a plan—

(A) which has fewer than 100 participants who have accrued a benefit under the plan, or

(B) which offers participants the option to choose between the new benefit formula and the old benefit formula.

(3) Timing of notice—Except as provided in regulations, the notice required by paragraph (1) shall be provided within a reasonable time before the effective date of the plan amendment.

(4) Designees—Any notice under paragraph (1) may be provided to a person designated, in writing, by the person to which it would otherwise be provided.

(5) Notice before adoption of amendment—A plan shall not be treated as failing to meet the requirements of paragraph (1) merely because notice is provided before the adoption of the plan amendment if no material modification of the amendment occurs before the amendment is adopted.

(f) Definitions and special rules—For purposes of this section—

(1) Applicable individual—The term "applicable individual" means, with respect to any plan amendment—

(A) each participant in the plan, and

(B) any beneficiary who is an alternate payee (within the meaning of section 414(p)(8)) under an applicable qualified domestic relations order (within the meaning of section 414(p)(1)(A)),

whose rate of future benefit accrual under the plan may reasonably be expected to be significantly reduced by such plan amendment.

(2) Applicable pension plan—The term "applicable pension plan" means—

(A) any defined benefit plan described in section 401(a) which includes a trust exempt from tax under section 501(a), or

(B) an individual account plan which is subject to the funding standards of section 412.

Such term shall not include a governmental plan (within the meaning of section 414(d)) or a church plan (within the meaning of section 414(e)) with respect to which the election provided by section 410(d) has not been made.

(3) Early retirement—A plan amendment which eliminates or reduces any early retirement benefit or retirement-type subsidy (within the meaning of section 411(d)(6)(B)(i)) shall be treated as having the effect of reducing the rate of future benefit accrual.

(g) New technologies—The Secretary may by regulations allow any notice under subsection (e) to be provided by using new technologies.

§ 7476. Declaratory judgments relating to qualification of certain retirement plans.

(a) Creation of remedy—In a case of actual controversy involving—

(1) a determination by the Secretary with respect to the initial qualification or continuing qualification of a retirement plan under subchapter D of chapter 1, or

(2) a failure by the Secretary to make a determination with respect to

(A) such initial qualification, or

(B) such continuing qualification if the controversy arises from a plan amendment or plan termination,

upon the filing of an appropriate pleading, the Tax Court may make a declaration with respect to such initial qualification or continuing qualification. Any such declaration shall have the force and effect of a decision of the Tax Court and shall be reviewable as such. For purposes of this section, a determination with respect to a continuing qualification includes any revocation of or other change in a qualification.

(b) Limitations—

(1) Petitioner—A pleading may be filed under this section only by a petitioner who is the employer, the plan administrator, an employee who has qualified under regulations prescribed by the Secretary as an interested party for purposes of pursuing administrative remedies within the Internal Revenue Service, or the Pension Benefit Guaranty Corporation.

(2) Notice—For purposes of this section, the filing of a pleading by any petitioner may be held by the Tax Court to be premature, unless the petitioner establishes to the satisfaction of the court that he has complied with the requirements prescribed by regulations of the Secretary with respect to notice to other interested parties of the filing of the request for a determination referred to in subsection (a).

(3) Exhaustion of administrative remedies—The Tax Court shall not issue a declaratory judgment or decree under this section in any proceeding unless it determines that the petitioner has exhausted administrative remedies available to him within the Internal Revenue Service. A petitioner shall not be deemed to have exhausted his administrative remedies with respect to a failure by the Secretary to make a determination with respect to initial qualification or continuing qualification of a retirement plan before the expiration of 270 days after the request for such determination was made.

(4) Plan put into effect—No proceeding may be maintained under this section unless the plan (and, in the case of a controversy involving the continuing qualification of the plan because of an amendment to the plan, the amendment) with respect to which a decision of the Tax Court is sought has been put into effect before the filing of the pleading. A plan or amendment shall not be treated as not being in effect merely because under the plan the funds contributed to the plan may be refunded if the plan (or the plan as so amended) is found to be not qualified.

(5) Time for bringing action—If the Secretary sends by certified or registered mail notice of his determination with respect to the qualification of the plan to the persons referred to in paragraph (1) (or, in the case of employees referred to in paragraph (1), to any individual designated under regulations prescribed by the Secretary as a representative of such employee), no proceeding may be initiated under this section by any person unless the pleading is filed before the ninety-first day after the day after such notice is mailed to such person (or to his designated representative, in the case of an employee).

(c) Retirement plan—For purposes of this section, the term "retirement plan" means—

(1) a pension, profit-sharing, or stock bonus plan described in section 401(a) or a trust which is part of such a plan, or

(2) an annuity plan described in section 403(a).

* * *

EMPLOYEE RETIREMENT INCOME SECURITY ACT OF 1974

29 U.S.C. § 1001 et seq.

Title I—Protection of Employee Benefit Rights

Subtitle A—General Provisions

§ 2. Findings and declaration of policy (§ 1001)

(a) The Congress finds that the growth in size, scope, and numbers of employee benefit plans in recent years has been rapid and substantial; that the operational scope and economic impact of such plans is increasingly interstate; that the continued well-being and security of millions of employees and their dependents are directly affected by these plans; that they are affected with a national public interest; that they have become an important factor affecting the stability of employment and the successful development of industrial relations; that they have become an important factor in commerce because of the interstate character of their activities, and of the activities of their participants, and the employers, employee organizations, and other entities by which they are established or maintained; that a large volume of the activities of such plans are carried on by means of the mails and instrumentalities of interstate commerce; that owing to the lack of employee information and adequate safeguards concerning their operation, it is desirable in the interests of employees and their beneficiaries, and to provide for the general welfare and the free flow of commerce, that disclosure be made and safeguards be provided with respect to the establishment, operation, and administration of such plans; that they substantially affect the revenues of the United States because they are afforded preferential Federal tax treatment; that despite the enormous growth in such plans many employees with long years of employment are losing anticipated retirement benefits owing to the lack of vesting provisions in such plans; that owing to the inadequacy of current minimum standards, the soundness and stability of plans with respect to adequate funds to pay promised benefits may be endangered; that owing to the termination of plans before requisite funds have been accumulated, employees and their beneficiaries have been deprived of anticipated benefits; and that it is therefore desirable in the interests of employees and their beneficiaries, for the protection of the revenue of the United States, and to provide for the free flow of commerce, that minimum standards be provided assuring the equitable character of such plans and their financial soundness.

(b) It is hereby declared to be the policy of this Act to protect interstate commerce and the interests of participants in employee benefit plans and their beneficiaries, by requiring the disclosure and reporting to participants and beneficiaries of financial and other information with respect thereto, by establishing standards of conduct, responsibility, and obligation for fiduciaries of employee benefit plans, and by providing for appropriate remedies, sanctions, and ready access to the Federal courts.

(c) It is hereby further declared to be the policy of this Act to protect interstate commerce, the Federal taxing power, and the interests of participants in private pension plans and their beneficiaries by improving the equitable character and the soundness of such plans by requiring them to vest the accrued benefits of employees with significant periods of service, to meet minimum standards of funding, and by requiring plan termination insurance.

§ 3. Definitions (§ 1002)

For purposes of this title:

(1) The terms "employee welfare benefit plan" and "welfare plan" mean any plan, fund, or program which was heretofore or is hereafter established or maintained by an employer or by an employee organization, or by both, to the extent that such plan, fund, or program was established or is maintained for the purpose of providing for its participants or their beneficiaries, through the purchase of insurance or otherwise, (A) medical, surgical, or hospital care or benefits, or benefits in the event of sickness, accident, disability, death or unemployment, or vacation benefits, apprenticeship or other training programs, or day care centers, scholarship funds, or prepaid legal services, or (B) any benefit described in section 302(c) of the Labor Management Relations Act, 1947 (other than pensions on retirement or death, and insurance to provide such pensions).

(2)(A) Except as provided in subparagraph (B), the terms "employee pension benefit plan" and "pension plan" mean any plan, fund, or program which was heretofore or is hereafter established or maintained by an employer or by an employee organization, or by both, to the extent that by its express terms or as a result of surrounding circumstances such plan, fund, or program—

(i) provides retirement income to employees, or

(ii) results in a deferral of income by employees for periods extending to the termination of covered employment or beyond,

regardless of the method of calculating the contributions made to the plan, the method of calculating the benefits under the plan or the method of distributing benefits from the plan. A distribution from a plan, fund, or program shall not be treated as made in a form other than retirement income or as a distribution prior to termination of covered employment solely because such distribution is made to an employee who has attained age 62 and who is not separated from employment at the time of such distribution.

(B) The Secretary may by regulation prescribe rules consistent with the standards and purposes of this Act providing one or more exempt categories under which—

(i) severance pay arrangements, and

(ii) supplemental retirement income payments, under which the pension benefits of retirees or their beneficiaries are supplemented to take into account some portion or all of the increases in the cost of living (as determined by the Secretary of Labor) since retirement,

shall, for purposes of this title, be treated as welfare plans rather than pension plans. In the case of any arrangement or payment a principal effect of which is the evasion of the standards or purposes of this Act applicable to pension plans, such arrangement or payment shall be treated as a pension plan. An applicable voluntary early retirement incentive plan (as defined in section 457(e)(11)(D)(ii) of the Internal Revenue Code of 1986) making payments or supplements described in section 457(e)(11)(D)(i) of such Code, and an applicable employment retention plan (as defined in section 457(f)(4)(C) of such Code) making payments of benefits described in section 457(f)(4)(A) of such Code, shall, for purposes of this title, be treated as a welfare plan (and not a pension plan) with respect to such payments and supplements.

(3) The term "employee benefit plan" or "plan" means an employee welfare benefit plan or an employee pension benefit plan or a plan which is both an employee welfare benefit plan and an employee pension benefit plan.

(4) The term "employee organization" means any labor union or any organization of any kind, or any agency or employee representation committee, association, group, or plan, in which employees participate and which exists for the purpose, in whole or in part, of dealing with employers concerning an employee benefit plan, or other matters incidental to employment relationships; or any employees' beneficiary association organized for the purpose in whole or in part, of establishing such a plan.

(5) The term "employer" means any person acting directly as an employer, or indirectly in the interest of an employer, in relation to an employee benefit plan; and includes a group or association of employers acting for an employer in such capacity.

(6) The term "employee" means any individual employed by an employer.

(7) The term "participant" means any employee or former employee of an employer, or any member or former member of an employee organization, who is or may become eligible to receive a benefit of any type from an employee benefit plan which covers employees of such employer or members of such organization, or whose beneficiaries may be eligible to receive any such benefit.

(8) The term "beneficiary" means a person designated by a participant, or by the terms of an employee benefit plan, who is or may become entitled to a benefit thereunder.

(9) The term "person" means an individual, partnership, joint venture, corporation, mutual company, joint-stock company, trust, estate, unincorporated organization, association, or employee organization.

(10) The term "State" includes any State of the United States, the District of Columbia, Puerto Rico, the Virgin Islands, American Samoa, Guam, Wake Island, and the Canal Zone. The term "United States" when used in the geographic sense means the States and the Outer Continental Shelf lands defined in the Outer Continental Shelf Lands Act (43 U.S.C. 1331-1343).

(11) The term "commerce" means trade, traffic, commerce, transportation, or communication between any State and any place outside thereof.

(12) The term "industry or activity affecting commerce" means any activity, business, or industry in commerce or in which a labor dispute would hinder or obstruct commerce or the free flow of commerce, and includes any activity or industry "affecting commerce" within the meaning of the Labor Management Relations Act, 1947, or the Railway Labor Act.

(13) The term "Secretary" means the Secretary of Labor.

(14) The term "party in interest" means, as to an employee benefit plan—

(A) any fiduciary (including, but not limited to, any administrator, officer, trustee, or custodian), counsel, or employee of such employee benefit plan;

(B) a person providing services to such plan;

(C) an employer any of whose employees are covered by such plan;

(D) an employee organization any of whose members are covered by such plan;

(E) an owner, direct or indirect, of 50 percent or more of—

(i) the combined voting power of all classes of stock entitled to vote or the total value of shares of all classes of stock of a corporation.

(ii) the capital interest or the profits interest of a partnership, or

(iii) the beneficial interest of a trust or unincorporated enterprise,

which is an employer or an employee organization described in subparagraph (C) or (D);

(F) a relative (as defined in paragraph (15)) of any individual described in subparagraph (A), (B), (C), or (E);

(G) a corporation, partnership, or trust or estate of which (or in which) 50 percent or more of—

(i) the combined voting power of all classes of stock entitled to vote or the total value of shares of all classes of stock of such corporation,

(ii) the capital interest or profits interest of such partnership, or

(iii) the beneficial interest of such trust or estate,

is owned directly or indirectly, or held by persons described in subparagraph (A), (B), (C), (D), or (E);

(H) an employee, officer, director (or an individual having powers or responsibilities similar to those of officers or directors), or a 10 percent or more shareholder directly or indirectly, of a person described in subparagraph (B), (C), (D), (E), or (G), or of the employee benefit plan; or

(I) a 10 percent or more (directly or indirectly in capital or profits) partner or joint venturer of a person described in subparagraph (B), (C), (D), (E), or (G).

The Secretary, after consultation and coordination with the Secretary of the Treasury, may by regulation prescribe a percentage lower than 50 percent for subparagraph (E) and (G) and lower than 10 percent for subparagraph (H) or (I). The Secretary may prescribe regulations for determining the ownership (direct or indirect) of profits and beneficial interests, and the manner in which indirect stockholdings are taken into account. Any person who is a party in interest with respect to a plan to which a trust described in section 501(c)(22) of Internal Revenue Code of 1986 is permitted to make payments under section 4223 shall be treated as a party in interest with respect to such trust.

(15) The term "relative" means a spouse, ancestor, lineal descendant, or spouse of a lineal descendant.

(16)(A) The term "administrator" means—

(i) the person specifically so designated by the terms of the instrument under which the plan is operated;

(ii) if an administrator is not so designated, the plan sponsor; or

(iii) in the case of a plan for which an administrator is not designated and a plan sponsor cannot be identified, such other person as the Secretary may by regulation prescribe.

(B) The term "plan sponsor" means (i) the employer in the case of an employee benefit plan established or maintained by a single employer, (ii) the employee organization in the case of a plan established or maintained by an employee organization, or (iii) in the case of a plan established or maintained by two or more employers or jointly by one or more employers and one or more employee organizations, the association, committee, joint board of trustees, or other similar group of representatives of the parties who establish or maintain the plan.

(17) The term "separate account" means an account established or maintained by an insurance company under which income, gains, and losses, whether or not realized, from assets allocated to such account, are, in accordance with the applicable contract, credited to or charged against such account without regard to other income, gains, or losses of the insurance company.

(18) The term "adequate consideration" when used in part 4 of subtitle B means (A) in the case of a security for which there is a generally recognized market, either (i) the price of the security prevailing on a national securities exchange which is registered under section 6 of the Securities Exchange Act of 1934, or (ii) if the security is not traded on such a national securities exchange, a price not less favorable to the plan than the offering price for the security as established by the current bid and asked prices quoted by persons independent of the issuer and of any party in interest; and (B) in the case of an asset other than a security for which there is a generally recognized market, the fair market value of the asset as determined in good faith by the trustee or named fiduciary pursuant to the terms of the plan and in accordance with regulations promulgated by the Secretary.

(19) The term "nonforfeitable" when used with respect to a pension benefit or right means a claim obtained by a participant or his beneficiary to that part of an immediate or deferred benefit under a pension plan which arises from the participant's service, which is unconditional, and which is legally enforceable against the plan. For purposes of this paragraph, a right to an accrued benefit derived from employer contributions shall not be treated as forfeitable merely because the plan contains a provision described in section 203(a)(3).

(20) The term "security" has the same meaning as such term has under section 2(1) of the Securities Act of 1933 (15 U.S.C. 77b(1)).

(21)(A) Except as otherwise provided in subparagraph (B), a person is a fiduciary with respect to a plan to the extent (i) he exercises any discretionary authority or discretionary control respecting management of such plan or exercises any authority or control respecting management or disposition of its assets, (ii) he renders investment advice for a fee or other compensation, direct or indirect, with respect to any moneys or other property of such plan, or has any authority or responsibility to do so, or (iii) he has any discretionary authority or discretionary responsibility in the administration of such plan. Such term includes any person designated under section 405(c)(1)(B).

(B) If any money or other property of an employee benefit plan is invested in securities issued by an investment company registered under the Investment Company Act of 1940, such investment shall not by itself cause such investment company or such investment company's investment adviser or principal underwriter to be deemed to be a fiduciary or a party in interest as those terms are defined in this title, except insofar as such investment company or its investment adviser or principal underwriter acts in connection with an employee benefit plan covering employees of the investment company, the investment adviser, or its principal underwriter. Nothing contained in this subparagraph shall limit the duties imposed on such investment company, investment adviser, or principal underwriter by any other law.

(22) The term "normal retirement benefit" means the greater of the early retirement benefit under the plan, or the benefit under the plan commencing at normal retirement age. The normal retirement benefit shall be determined without regard to—

(A) medical benefits, and

(B) disability benefits not in excess of the qualified disability benefit.

For purposes of this paragraph, a qualified disability benefit is a disability benefit provided by a plan which does not exceed the benefit which would be provided for the participant if he separated from the service at normal retirement age. For purposes of this paragraph, the early retirement benefit under a plan shall be determined without regard to any benefit under the plan which the Secretary of the Treasury finds to be a benefit described in section 204(b)(1)(G).

(23) The term "accrued benefit" means—

(A) in the case of a defined benefit plan, the individual's accrued benefit determined under the plan and, except as provided in section 204(c)(3), expressed in the form of an annual benefit commencing at normal retirement age, or

(B) in the case of a plan which is an individual account plan, the balance of the individual's account.

The accrued benefit of an employee shall not be less than the amount determined under section 204(c)(2)(B) with respect to the employee's accumulated contribution.

(24) The term "normal retirement age" means the earlier of—

(A) the time a plan participant attains normal retirement age under the plan, or

(B) the later of—

(i) the time a plan participant attains age 65, or

(ii) the 5th anniversary of the time a plan participant commenced participation in the plan.

(25) The term "vested liabilities" means the present value of the immediate or deferred benefits available at normal retirement age for participants and their beneficiaries which are nonforfeitable.

(26) The term "current value" means fair market value where available and otherwise the fair value as determined in good faith by a trustee or a named fiduciary (as defined in section 402(a)(2)) pursuant to the terms of the plan and in accordance with regulations of the Secretary, assuming an orderly liquidation at the time of such determination.

(27) The term "present value", with respect to a liability, means the value adjusted to reflect anticipated events. Such adjustments shall conform to such regulations as the Secretary of the Treasury may prescribe.

(28) The term "normal service cost" or "normal cost" means the annual cost of future pension benefits and administrative expenses assigned, under an actuarial cost method, to years subsequent to a particular valuation date of a pension plan. The Secretary of the Treasury may prescribe regulations to carry out this paragraph.

(29) The term "accrued liability" means the excess of the present value, as of a particular valuation date of a pension plan, of the projected future benefit costs and administrative expenses for all plan participants and beneficiaries over the present value of future contributions for the normal cost of all applicable plan participants and beneficiaries. The Secretary of the Treasury may prescribe regulations to carry out this paragraph.

(30) The term "unfunded accrued liability" means the excess of the accrued liability, under an actuarial cost method which so provides, over the present value of the assets of a pension plan. The Secretary of the Treasury may prescribe regulations to carry out this paragraph.

(31) The term "advance funding actuarial cost method" or "actuarial cost method" means a recognized actuarial technique utilized for establishing the amount and incidence of the annual actuarial cost of pension plan benefits and expenses. Acceptable actuarial cost methods shall include the accrued benefit cost method (unit credit method), the entry age normal cost method, the individual level premium cost method, the aggregate cost method, the attained age normal cost method, and the frozen initial liability cost method. The terminal funding cost method and the current funding (pay-as-you-go) cost method are not acceptable actuarial cost methods. The Secretary of the Treasury shall issue regulations to further define acceptable actuarial cost methods.

(32) The term "governmental plan" means a plan established or maintained for its employees by the Government of the United States, by the government of any State or political subdivision thereof, or by any agency or instrumentality of any of the foregoing. The term "governmental plan" also includes any plan to which the Railroad Retirement Act of 1935, or 1937 applies, and which is financed by contributions required under that Act and any plan of an international organization which is exempt from taxation under the provisions of the International Organizations Immunities Act (59 Stat. 669). The term "governmental plan" includes a plan which is established and maintained by an Indian tribal government (as defined in section 7701(a)(40) of the Internal Revenue Code of 1986), a subdivision of an Indian tribal government (determined in accordance with section 7871(d) of such Code), or an agency or instrumentality of either, and all of the participants of which are employees of such entity substantially all of whose services as such an employee are in the performance of essential governmental functions but not in the performance of commercial activities (whether or not an essential government function).

(33)(A) The term "church plan" means a plan established and maintained (to the extent required in clause (ii) of subparagraph (B)) for its employees (or their beneficiaries) by a church or by a convention or association of churches which is exempt from tax under section 501 of the Internal Revenue Code of 1986.

* * *

(34) The term "individual account plan" or "defined contribution plan" means a pension plan which provides for an individual account for each participant and for benefits based solely upon the amount contributed to the participant's account, and any income, expenses, gains and losses, and any forfeitures of accounts of other participants which may be allocated to such participant's account.

(35) The term "defined benefit plan" means a pension plan other than an individual account plan; except that a pension plan which is not an individual account plan and which provides a benefit derived from employer contributions which is based partly on the balance of the separate account of a participant—

(A) for the purposes of section 202, shall be treated as an individual account plan, and

(B) for the purposes of paragraph (23) of this section and section 204, shall be treated as an individual account plan to the extent benefits are based upon the separate account of a participant and as a defined benefit plan with respect to the remaining portion of benefits under the plan.

(36) The term "excess benefit plan" means a plan maintained by an employer solely for the purpose of providing benefits for certain employees in excess of the limitations on contributions and benefits imposed by section 415 of the Internal Revenue Code of 1986 on plans to which that section applies without regard to whether the plan is funded. To the extent that a separable part of a plan (as determined by the Secretary of Labor) maintained by an employer is maintained for such purpose, that part shall be treated as a separate plan which is an excess benefit plan.

(37)(A) The term "multiemployer plan" means a plan—

(i) to which more than one employer is required to contribute,

(ii) which is maintained pursuant to one or more collective bargaining agreements between one or more employee organizations and more than one employer, and

(iii) which satisfies such other requirements as the Secretary may prescribe by regulation.

(B) For purposes of this paragraph, all trades or businesses (whether or not incorporated) which are under common control within the meaning of section 4001(b)(1) are considered a single employer.

* * *

(38) The term "investment manager" means any fiduciary (other than a trustee or named fiduciary, as defined in section 402(a)(2))—

(A) who has the power to manage, acquire, or dispose of any asset of a plan;

(B) who (i) is registered as an investment adviser under the Investment Advisers Act of 1940; (ii) is not registered as an investment adviser under such Act by reason of paragraph (1) of section203A(a) of such Act, is registered as an investment adviser under the laws of the State (referred to in such paragraph (1)) in which it maintains its principal office and place of business, and, at the time the fiduciary last filed the registration form most recently filed by the fiduciary with such State in order to maintain the fiduciary's registration under the laws of such State, also filed a copy of such form with the Secretary; (iii) is a bank, as defined in that Act; or (iv) is an insurance company qualified to perform services described in subparagraph (A) under the laws of more than one State; and

(C) has acknowledged in writing that he is a fiduciary with respect to the plan.

(39) The terms "plan year" and "fiscal year of the plan" mean, with respect to a plan, the calendar, policy, or fiscal year on which the records of the plan are kept.

(40)(A) The term "multiple employer welfare arrangement" means an employee welfare benefit plan, or any other arrangement (other than an employee welfare benefit plan), which is established or maintained for the purpose of offering or providing any benefit described in paragraph (1) to the employees of two or more employers (including one or more self-employed individuals), or to their beneficiaries, except that such term does not include any such plan or other arrangement which is established or maintained—

(i) under or pursuant to one or more agreements which the Secretary finds to be collective bargaining agreements,

(ii) by a rural electric cooperative, or

(iii) by a rural telephone cooperative association.

* * *

(41) The term "single employer plan" means a plan which is not a multiemployer plan.

(42) the term "plan assets" means plan assets as defined by such regulations as the Secretary may prescribe, except that under such regulations the assets of any entity shall not be treated as plan assets if, immediately after the most recent acquisition of any equity interest in the entity, less than 25 percent of the total value of each class of equity interest in the entity is held by benefit plan investors. For purposes of determinations pursuant to this paragraph, the value of any equity interest held by a person (other than such a benefit plan investor) who has discretionary authority or control with respect to the assets of the entity or any person who provides investment advice for a fee (direct or indirect) with respect to such assets, or any affiliate of such a person, shall be disregarded for purposes of calculating the 25 percent threshold. An entity shall be considered to hold plan assets only to the extent of the percentage of the equity interest held by benefit plan investors. For purposes of this paragraph, the term "benefit plan investor" means an employee benefit plan subject to part 4, any plan to which section 4975 of the Internal Revenue Code of 1986 applies, and any entity whose underlying assets include plan assets by reason of a plan's investment in such entity.

§ 4. Coverage (§ 1003)

(a) Except as provided in subsection (b) or (c) of this section and in sections 201, 301, and 401, this title shall apply to any employee benefit plan if it is established or maintained—

(1) by any employer engaged in commerce or in any industry or activity affecting commerce; or

(2) by any employee organization or organizations representing employees engaged in commerce or in any industry or activity affecting commerce; or

(3) by both.

(b) The provisions of this title shall not apply to any employee benefit plan if—

(1) such plan is a governmental plan (as defined in section 3(32));

(2) such plan is a church plan (as defined in section 3(33)) with respect to which no election has been made under section 410(d) of the Internal Revenue Code of 1986;

(3) such plan is maintained solely for the purpose of complying with applicable workmen's compensation laws or unemployment compensation or disability insurance laws;

(4) such plan is maintained outside of the United States primarily for the benefit of persons substantially all of whom are nonresident aliens; or

(5) such plan is an excess benefit plan (as defined in section 3(36)) and is unfunded.

* * *

(c) If a pension plan allows an employee to elect to make voluntary employee contributions to accounts and annuities as provided in section 408(q) of the Internal Revenue Code of 1986, such accounts and annuities (and contributions thereto) shall not be treated as part of such plan (or as a separate pension plan) for purposes of any provision of this title other than section 403(c), 404, or 405 (relating to exclusive benefit, and fiduciary and co-fiduciary responsibilities) and part 5 (relating to administration and enforcement). Such provisions shall apply to such accounts and annuities in a manner similar to their application to a simplified employee pension under section 408(k) of the Internal Revenue Code of 1986.

Subtitle B—Regulatory Provisions

Part 1—Reporting and Disclosure

§ 101. Duty of disclosure and reporting (§ 1021)

(a) The administrator of each employee benefit plan shall cause to be furnished in accordance with section 104(b) to each participant covered under the plan and to each beneficiary who is receiving benefits under the plan—

(1) a summary plan description described in section 102(a)(1); and

(2) the information described in subsection (f) and sections 104(b)(3) and 105(a) and (c).

(b) The administrator shall, in accordance with section 104(a), file with the Secretary—

(1) the annual report containing the information required by section 103; and

(2) terminal and supplementary reports as required by subsection (c) of this section.

(c)(1) Each administrator of an employee pension benefit plan which is winding up its affairs (without regard to the number of participants remaining in the plan) shall, in accordance with regulations prescribed by the Secretary, file such terminal reports as the Secretary may consider necessary. A copy of such report shall also be filed with the Pension Benefit Guaranty Corporation.

(2) The Secretary may require terminal reports to be filed with regard to any employee welfare benefit plan which is winding up its affairs in accordance with regulations promulgated by the Secretary.

(3) The Secretary may require that a plan described in paragraph (1) or (2) file a supplementary or terminal report with the annual report in the year such plan is terminated and that a copy of such supplementary or terminal report in the case of a plan described in paragraph (1) be also filed with the Pension Benefit Guaranty Corporation.

* * *

(f) Defined benefit plan funding notices—

(1) In general—The administrator of a defined benefit plan to which title IV applies shall for each plan year provide a plan funding notice to the Pension Benefit Guaranty Corporation, to each plan participant and beneficiary, to each labor organization representing such participants or beneficiaries, and, in the case of a multiemployer plan, to each employer that has an obligation to contribute to the plan.

* * *

(i) Notice of blackout periods to participant or beneficiary under individual account plan—

(1) Duties of plan administrator—In advance of the commencement of any blackout period with respect to an individual account plan, the plan administrator shall notify the plan participants and beneficiaries who are affected by such action in accordance with this subsection.

(2) Notice requirements—

(A) In general—The notices described in paragraph (1) shall be written in a manner calculated to be understood by the average plan participant and shall include—

(i) the reasons for the blackout period,

(ii) an identification of the investments and other rights affected,

(iii) the expected beginning date and length of the blackout period,

(iv) in the case of investments affected, a statement that the participant or beneficiary should evaluate the appropriateness of their current investment decisions in light of their inability to direct or diversify assets credited to their accounts during the blackout period, and

(v) such other matters as the Secretary may require by regulation.

(B) Notice to participants and beneficiaries—Except as otherwise provided in this subsection, notices described in paragraph (1) shall be furnished to all participants and beneficiaries under the plan to whom the blackout period applies at least 30 days in advance of the blackout period.

(C) Exception to 30-day notice requirement—In any case in which—

(i) a deferral of the blackout period would violate the requirements of subparagraph (A) or (B) of section 404(a)(1), and a fiduciary of the plan reasonably so determines in writing, or

(ii) the inability to provide the 30-day advance notice is due to events that were unforeseeable or circumstances beyond the reasonable control of the plan administrator, and a fiduciary of the plan reasonably so determines in writing,

subparagraph (B) shall not apply, and the notice shall be furnished to all participants and beneficiaries under the plan to whom the blackout period applies as soon as reasonably possible under the circumstances unless such a notice in advance of the termination of the blackout period is impracticable.

(D) Written notice—The notice required to be provided under this subsection shall be in writing, except that such notice may be in electronic or other form to the extent that such form is reasonably accessible to the recipient.

(E) Notice to issuers of employer securities subject to blackout period—In the case of any blackout period in connection with an individual account plan, the plan administrator shall provide timely notice of such blackout period to the issuer of any employer securities subject to such blackout period.

(3) Exception for blackout periods with limited applicability—In any case in which the blackout period applies only to 1 or more participants or beneficiaries in connection with a merger, acquisition, divestiture, or similar transaction involving the plan or plan sponsor and occurs solely in connection with becoming or ceasing to be a participant or beneficiary under the plan by reason of such merger, acquisition, divestiture, or transaction, the requirement of this subsection that the notice be provided to all participants and beneficiaries shall be treated as met if the notice required under paragraph (1) is provided to such participants or beneficiaries to whom the blackout period applies as soon as reasonably practicable.

(4) Changes in length of blackout period—If, following the furnishing of the notice pursuant to this subsection, there is a change in the beginning date or length of the blackout period (specified in such notice pursuant to paragraph (2)(A)(iii)), the administrator shall provide affected participants and beneficiaries notice of the change as soon as reasonably practicable. In relation to the extended blackout period, such notice shall meet the requirements of paragraph (2)(D) and shall specify any material change in the matters referred to in clauses (i) through (v) of paragraph (2)(A).

(5) Regulatory exceptions—The Secretary may provide by regulation for additional exceptions to the requirements of this subsection which the Secretary determines are in the interests of participants and beneficiaries.

(6) Guidance and model notices—The Secretary shall issue guidance and model notices which meet the requirements of this subsection.

(7) Blackout period—For purposes of this subsection—

(A) In general—The term 'blackout period' means, in connection with an individual account plan, any period for which any ability of participants or beneficiaries under the plan, which is otherwise available under the terms of such plan, to direct or diversify assets credited to their accounts, to obtain loans from the plan, or to obtain distributions from the plan is temporarily suspended, limited, or restricted, if such suspension, limitation, or restriction is for any period of more than 3 consecutive business days.

(B) Exclusions—The term 'blackout period' does not include a suspension, limitation, or restriction—

(i) which occurs by reason of the application of the securities laws (as defined in section 3(a)(47) of the Securities Exchange Act of 1934),

(ii) which is a change to the plan which provides for a regularly scheduled suspension, limitation, or restriction which is disclosed to participants or beneficiaries through any summary of material modifications, any materials describing specific investment alternatives under the plan, or any changes thereto, or

(iii) which applies only to 1 or more individuals, each of whom is the participant, an alternate payee (as defined in section 206(d)(3)(K)), or any other beneficiary pursuant to a qualified domestic relations order (as defined in section 206(d)(3)(B)(i)).

(8) Individual account plan—

(A) In general—For purposes of this subsection, the term 'individual account plan' shall have the meaning provided such term in section 3(34), except that such term shall not include a one-participant retirement plan.

(B) One-participant retirement plan—For purposes of subparagraph (A), the term 'one-participant retirement plan' means a retirement plan that on the first day of the plan year —

(i) covered only one individual (or the individual and the individual's spouse) and the individual (or the individual and the individual's spouse) owned 100 percent of the plan sponsor (whether or not incorporated), or

(ii) covered only one or more partners (or partners and their spouses) in the plan sponsor.

(j) Notice of funding-based limitation on certain forms of distribution—The plan administrator of a single-employer plan shall provide a written notice to plan participants and beneficiaries within 30 days—

(1) after the plan has become subject to a restriction described in paragraph (1) or (3) of section 206(g)),

(2) in the case of a plan to which section 206(g)(4) applies, after the valuation date for the plan year described in section 206(g)(4)(A) for which the plan's adjusted funding target attainment percentage for the plan year is less than 60 percent (or, if earlier, the date such percentage is deemed to be less than 60 percent under section 206(g)(7)), and

(3) at such other time as may be determined by the Secretary of the Treasury.

The notice required to be provided under this subsection shall be in writing, except that such notice may be in electronic or other form to the extent that such form is reasonably accessible to the recipient. The Secretary of the Treasury, in consultation with the Secretary, shall have the authority to prescribe rules applicable to the notices required under this subsection.

* * *

(m) Notice of right to divest—Not later than 30 days before the first date on which an applicable individual of an applicable individual account plan is eligible to exercise the right under section 204(j) to direct the proceeds from the divestment of employer securities with respect to any type of contribution, the administrator shall provide to such individual a notice—

(1) setting forth such right under such section, and

(2) describing the importance of diversifying the investment of retirement account assets.

The notice required by this subsection shall be written in a manner calculated to be understood by the average plan participant and may be delivered in written, electronic, or other appropriate form to the extent that such form is reasonably accessible to the recipient.

* * *

§ 102. Summary plan description (§ 1022)

(a) A summary plan description of any employee benefit plan shall be furnished to participants and beneficiaries as provided in section 104(b). The summary plan description shall include the information described in subsection (b), shall be written in a manner calculated to be understood by the average plan participant, and shall be sufficiently accurate and comprehensive to reasonably apprise such participants and beneficiaries of their rights and obligations under the plan. A summary of any material modification in the terms of the plan and any change in the information required under subsection (b) shall be written in a manner calculated to be understood by the average plan participant and shall be furnished in accordance with section 104(b)(1).

(b) The summary plan description shall contain the following information: The name and type of administration of the plan; in the case of a group health plan (as defined in section

706(a)(1)), whether a health insurance issuer (as defined in section 706(b)(2)) is responsible for the financing or administration (including payment of claims) of the plan and (if so) the name and address of such issuer; the name and address of the person designated as agent for the service of legal process, if such person is not the administrator; the name and address of the administrator; names, titles, and addresses of any trustee or trustees (if they are persons different from the administrator); a description of the relevant provisions of any applicable collective bargaining agreement; the plan's requirements respecting eligibility for participation and benefits; a description of the provisions providing for nonforfeitable pension benefits; circumstances which may result in disqualification, ineligibility, or denial or loss of benefits; the source of financing of the plan and the identity of any organization through which benefits are provided; the date of the end of the plan year and whether the records of the plan are kept on a calendar, policy, or fiscal year basis; the procedures to be followed in presenting claims for benefits under the plan including the office at the Department of Labor through which participants and beneficiaries may seek assistance or information regarding their rights under this Act and the Health Insurance Portability and Accountability Act of 1996 with respect to health benefits that are offered through a group health plan (as defined in section 706(a)(1)), the remedies available under the plan for the redress of claims which are denied in whole or in part (including procedures required under section 503 of this Act), and if the employer so elects for purposes of complying with section 701(f)(3)(B)(i), the model notice applicable to the State in which the participants and beneficiaries reside.

§ 103. Annual reports (§ 1023)

(a)(1)(A) An annual report shall be published with respect to every employee benefit plan to which this part applies. Such report shall be filed with the Secretary in accordance with section 104(a), and shall be made available and furnished to participants in accordance with section 104(b).

(B) The annual report shall include the information described in subsections (b) and (c) and where applicable subsections (d), (e) and (f) and shall also include—

(i) a financial statement and opinion, as required by paragraph (3) of this subsection, and

(ii) an actuarial statement and opinion, as required by paragraph (4) of this subsection.

* * *

(3)(A) Except as provided in subparagraph (C), the administrator of an employee benefit plan shall engage, on behalf of all plan participants, an independent qualified public accountant, who shall conduct such an examination of any financial statements of the plan, and of other books and records of the plan, as the accountant may deem necessary to enable the accountant to form an opinion as to whether the financial statements and schedules required to be included in the annual reports by subsection (b) of this section are presented fairly in conformity with generally accepted accounting principles applied on a basis consistent with that of the preceding year. Such examination shall be conducted in accordance with generally accepted auditing standards, and shall involve such tests of the books and records of the plan as are considered necessary by the independent qualified public accountant. The independent qualified public accountant shall also offer his opinion as to whether the separate schedules specified in subsection (b)(3) of this section and the summary material required under section 104(b)(3) present fairly, and in all material respects the information contained therein when considered in conjunction with the financial statements taken as a whole. The opinion by the independent qualified public accountant shall be made a part of the annual report. In a case where a plan is not required to file an annual report, the requirements of this paragraph shall not apply. In a case where by reason of section 104(a)(2) a plan is required only to file a simplified annual report, the Secretary may waive the requirements of this paragraph.

* * *

(4)(A) The administrator of an employee pension benefit plan subject to the reporting requirement of subsection (d) of this section shall engage, on behalf of all plan participants, an enrolled actuary who shall be responsible for the preparation of the materials comprising the actuarial statement required under subsection (d) of this section. In a case where a plan is not required to file an annual report, the requirement of this paragraph shall not apply, and, in a case where by reason of section 104(a)(2), a plan is required only to file a simplified report, the Secretary may waive the requirement of this paragraph.

(B) The enrolled actuary shall utilize such assumptions and techniques as are necessary to enable him to form an opinion as to whether the contents of the matters reported under subsection (d) of this section—

(i) are in the aggregate reasonably related to the experience of the plan and to reasonable expectations; and

(ii) represent his best estimate of anticipated experience under the plan.

* * *

§ 104. Filing and furnishing of information (§ 1024)

(a)(1) The administrator of any employee benefit plan subject to this part shall file with the Secretary the annual report for a plan year within 210 days after the close of such year (or within such time as may be required by regulations promulgated by the Secretary in order to reduce duplicative filing). The Secretary shall make copies of such annual reports available for inspection in the public document room of the Department of Labor.

(2)(A) With respect to annual reports required to be filed with the Secretary under this part, he may by regulation prescribe simplified annual reports for any pension plan which covers less than 100 participants.

* * *

(b) Publication of the summary plan descriptions and annual reports shall be made to participants and beneficiaries of the particular plan as follows:

(1) The administrator shall furnish to each participant, and each beneficiary receiving benefits under the plan, a copy of the summary plan description, and all modifications and changes referred to in section 102(a)—

(A) within 90 days after he becomes a participant, or (in the case of a beneficiary) within 90 days after he first receives benefits, or

(B) if later, within 120 days after the plan becomes subject to this part.

The administrator shall furnish to each participant, and each beneficiary receiving benefits under the plan, every fifth year after the plan becomes subject to this part an updated summary plan description described in section 102 which integrates all plan amendments made within such five-year period, except that in a case where no amendments have been made to a plan during such five-year period this sentence shall not apply. Notwithstanding the foregoing, the administrator shall furnish to each participant, and to each beneficiary receiving benefits under the plan, the summary plan description described in section 102 every tenth year after the plan becomes subject to this part. If there is a modification or change described in section 102(a) (other than a material reduction in covered services or benefits provided in the case of a group health plan (as defined in section 706(a)(1))), a summary description of such modification or change shall be furnished not later than 210 days after the end of the plan year in which the change is adopted to each participant, and to each beneficiary who is receiving benefits under the plan. If there is a modification or change described in section 102(a) that is a material reduction in covered services or benefits provided under a group health plan (as defined in section 706(a)(1)), a summary description of such modification or change shall be furnished to participants and beneficiaries not later than 60 days after the date of the adoption of the modification or change. In the alternative, the plan sponsors may provide such description at regular intervals of not more than 90 days.

* * *

(2) The administrator shall make copies of the latest updated summary plan description and the latest annual report and the bargaining agreement, trust agreement, contract, or other instruments under which the plan was established or is operated available for examination by any plan participant or beneficiary in the principal office of the administrator and in such other places as may be necessary to make available all pertinent information to all participants (including such places as the Secretary may prescribe by regulations).

(3) Within 210 days after the close of the fiscal year of the plan, the administrator (other than an administrator of a defined benefit plan to which the requirements of section 101(f) applies) shall furnish to each participant, and to each beneficiary receiving benefits under the plan, a copy of the statements and schedules, for such fiscal year, described in subparagraphs (A) and (B) of section 103(b)(3) and such other material (including the percentage determined under section 103(d)(11)) as is necessary to fairly summarize the latest annual report.

(4) The administrator shall, upon written request of any participant or beneficiary, furnish a copy of the latest updated summary plan description, and the latest annual report, any terminal report, the bargaining agreement, trust agreement, contract, or other instruments under which the plan is established or operated. The administrator may make a reasonable charge to cover the cost of furnishing such complete copies. The Secretary may by regulation prescribe the maximum amount which will constitute a reasonable charge under the preceding sentence.

(5) Identification and basic plan information and actuarial information included in the annual report for any plan year shall be filed with the Secretary in an electronic format which accommodates display on the Internet, in accordance with regulations which shall be prescribed by the Secretary. The Secretary shall provide for display of such information included in the annual report, within 90 days after the date of the filing of the annual report, on an Internet website maintained by the Secretary and other appropriate media. Such information shall also be displayed on any Intranet website maintained by the plan sponsor (or by the plan administrator on behalf of the plan sponsor) for the purpose of communicating with employees and not the public, in accordance with regulations which shall be prescribed by the Secretary.

* * *

§ 105. Reporting of participant's benefit rights (§ 1025)

(a) Requirements to provide pension benefit statements—

(1) Requirements—

(A) Individual account plan—The administrator of an individual account plan (other than a one-participant retirement plan described in section 101(i)(8)(B)) shall furnish a pension benefit statement—

(i) at least once each calendar quarter to a participant or beneficiary who has the right to direct the investment of assets in his or her account under the plan,

(ii) at least once each calendar year to a participant or beneficiary who has his or her own account under the plan but does not have the right to direct the investment of assets in that account, and

(iii) upon written request to a plan beneficiary not described in clause (i) or (ii).

(B) Defined benefit plan—The administrator of a defined benefit plan (other than a one-participant retirement plan described in section 101(i)(8)(B)) shall furnish a pension benefit statement—

(i) at least once every 3 years to each participant with a nonforfeitable accrued benefit and who is employed by the employer maintaining the plan at the time the statement is to be furnished, and

(ii) to a participant or beneficiary of the plan upon written request.

Information furnished under clause (i) to a participant may be based on reasonable estimates determined under regulations prescribed by the Secretary, in consultation with the Pension Benefit Guaranty Corporation.

(2) Statements—

(A) In general—A pension benefit statement under paragraph (1)—

(i) shall indicate, on the basis of the latest available information—

(I) the total benefits accrued, and

(II) the nonforfeitable pension benefits, if any, which have accrued, or the earliest date on which benefits will become nonforfeitable,

(ii) shall include an explanation of any permitted disparity under section 401(l) of the Internal Revenue Code of 1986 or any floor-offset arrangement that may be applied in determining any accrued benefits described in clause (i),

(iii) shall be written in a manner calculated to be understood by the average plan participant, and

(iv) may be delivered in written, electronic, or other appropriate form to the extent such form is reasonably accessible to the participant or beneficiary.

(B) Additional information—In the case of an individual account plan, any pension benefit statement under clause (i) or (ii) of paragraph (1)(A) shall include—

(i) the value of each investment to which assets in the individual account have been allocated, determined as of the most recent valuation date under the plan, including the value of any assets held in the form of employer securities, without regard to whether such securities were contributed by the plan sponsor or acquired at the direction of the plan or of the participant or beneficiary, and

(ii) in the case of a pension benefit statement under paragraph (1)(A)(i)—

(I) an explanation of any limitations or restrictions on any right of the participant or beneficiary under the plan to direct an investment,

(II) an explanation, written in a manner calculated to be understood by the average plan participant, of the importance, for the long-term retirement security of participants and beneficiaries, of a well-balanced and diversified investment portfolio, including a statement of the risk that holding more than 20 percent of a portfolio in the security of one entity (such as employer securities) may not be adequately diversified, and

(III) a notice directing the participant or beneficiary to the Internet website of the Department of Labor for sources of information on individual investing and diversification.

(C) Alternative notice—The requirements of subparagraph (A)(i)(II) are met if, at least annually and in accordance with requirements of the Secretary, the plan—

(i) updates the information described in such paragraph which is provided in the pension benefit statement, or

(ii) provides in a separate statement such information as is necessary to enable a participant or beneficiary to determine their nonforfeitable vested benefits.

(3) Defined benefit plans—

(A) Alternative notice—In the case of a defined benefit plan, the requirements of paragraph (1)(B)(i) shall be treated as met with respect to a participant if at least once each year the administrator provides to the participant notice of the availability of the pension benefit statement and the ways in which the participant may obtain such statement. Such notice may be delivered in written, electronic, or other appropriate form to the extent such form is reasonably accessible to the participant.

(B) Years in which no benefits accrue—The Secretary may provide that years in which no employee or former employee benefits (within the meaning of section 410(b) of the Internal Revenue Code of 1986) under the plan need not be taken into account in determining the 3-year period under paragraph (1)(B)(i).

* * *

Part 2—Participation and Vesting

§ 201. Coverage (§ 1051)

This part shall apply to any employee benefit plan described in section 4(a) (and not exempted under section 4(b)) other than—

(1) an employee welfare benefit plan;

(2) a plan which is unfunded and is maintained by an employer primarily for the purpose of providing deferred compensation for a select group of management or highly compensated employees;

(3)(A) a plan established and maintained by a society, order, or association described in section 501(c)(8) or (9) of the Internal Revenue Code of 1986, if no part of the contributions to or under such plan are made by employers of participants in such plan, or

(B) a trust described in section 501(c)(18) of such Code of 1986;

(4) a plan which is established and maintained by a labor organization described in section 501(c)(5) of the Internal Revenue Code of 1986 and which does not at any time after September 2, 1974, provide for employer contributions;

(5) any agreement providing payments to a retired partner or a deceased partner's successor in interest, as described in section 736 of the Internal Revenue Code of 1986;

(6) an individual retirement account or annuity described in section 408 of the Internal Revenue Code of 1954, or a retirement bond described in section 409 of the Internal Revenue Code of 1954 (as effective for obligations issued before January 1, 1984);

(7) an excess benefit plan; or

(8) any plan, fund or program under which an employer, all of whose stock is directly or indirectly owned by employees, former employees or their beneficiaries, proposes through an unfunded arrangement to compensate retired employees for benefits which were forfeited by such employees under a pension plan maintained by a former employer prior to the date such pension plan became subject to this Act.

§ 202. Minimum participation standards (§ 1052)

(a)(1)(A) No pension plan may require, as a condition of participation in the plan, that an employee complete a period of service with the employer or employers maintaining the plan extending beyond the later of the following dates—

(i) the date on which the employee attains the age of 21; or

(ii) the date on which he completes 1 year of service.

(B)(i) In the case of any plan which provides that after not more than 2 years of service each participant has a right to 100 percent of his accrued benefit under the plan which is nonforfeitable at the time such benefit accrues, clause (ii) of subparagraph (A) shall be applied by substituting "2 years of service" for "1 year of service".

(ii) In the case of any plan maintained exclusively for employees of an educational organization (as defined in section 170(b)(1)(A)(ii) of the Internal Revenue Code of 1986) by an employer which is exempt from tax under section 501(a) of such Code, which provides that each participant having at least 1 year of service has a right to 100 percent of his accrued benefit under the plan which is nonforfeitable at the time such benefit accrues, clause (i) of subparagraph (A) shall be applied by substituting "26" for "21". This clause shall not apply to any plan to which clause (i) applies.

(2) No pension plan may exclude from participation (on the basis of age) employees who have attained a specified age.

(3)(A) For purposes of this section, the term "year of service" means a 12- month period during which the employee has not less than 1,000 hours of service. For purposes of this paragraph, computation of any 12-month period shall be made with reference to the date on which the employee's employment commenced, except that, in accordance with regulations prescribed by the Secretary, such computation may be made by reference to the first day of a plan year in the case of an employee who does not complete 1,000 hours of service during the 12-month period beginning on the date his employment commenced.

(B) In the case of any seasonal industry where the customary period of employment is less than 1,000 hours during a calendar year, the term "year of service" shall be such period as may be determined under regulations prescribed by the Secretary.

(C) For purposes of this section, the term "hour of service" means a time of service determined under regulations prescribed by the Secretary.

(D) For purposes of this section, in the case of any maritime industry, 125 days of service shall be treated as 1,000 hours of service. The Secretary may prescribe regulations to carry out the purposes of this subparagraph.

(4) A plan shall be treated as not meeting the requirements of paragraph (1) unless it provides that any employee who has satisfied the minimum age and service requirements specified in such paragraph, and who is otherwise entitled to participate in the plan, commences participation in the plan no later than the earlier of—

(A) the first day of the first plan year beginning after the date on which such employee satisfied such requirements, or

(B) the date 6 months after the date on which he satisfied such requirements,

unless such employee was separated from the service before the date referred to in subparagraph (A) or (B), whichever is applicable.

(b)(1) Except as otherwise provided in paragraphs (2), (3), and (4) all years of service with the employer or employers maintaining the plan shall be taken into account in computing the period of service for purposes of subsection (a)(1).

(2) In the case of any employee who has any 1-year break in service (as defined in section 203(b)(3)(A)) under a plan to which the service requirements of clause (i) of subsection (a)(1)(B) apply, if such employee has not satisfied such requirements, service before such break shall not be required to be taken into account.

(3) In computing an employee's period of service for purposes of subsection (a)(1) in the case of any participant who has any 1-year break in service (as defined in section 203(b)(3)(A)), service before such break shall not be required to be taken into account under the plan until he has completed a year of service (as defined in subsection (a)(3)) after his return.

(4)(A) For purposes of paragraph (1), in the case of a nonvested participant, years of service with the employer or employers maintaining the plan before any period of consecutive 1-year breaks in service shall not be required to be taken into account in computing the period of service if the number of consecutive 1-year breaks in service within such period equals or exceeds the greater of—

(i) 5, or

(ii) the aggregate number of years of service before such period.

(B) If any years of service are not required to be taken into account by reason of a period of breaks in service to which subparagraph (A) applies, such years of service shall not be taken into account in applying subparagraph (A) to a subsequent period of breaks in service.

(C) For purposes of subparagraph (A), the term "nonvested participant" means a participant who does not have any nonforfeitable right under the plan to an accrued benefit derived from employer contributions.

* * *

§ 203. Minimum vesting standards (§ 1053)

(a) Each pension plan shall provide that an employee's right to his normal retirement benefit is nonforfeitable upon the attainment of normal retirement age and in addition shall satisfy the requirements of paragraphs (1) and (2) of this subsection.

(1) A plan satisfies the requirements of this paragraph if an employee's rights in his accrued benefit derived from his own contributions are nonforfeitable.

(2)(A)(i) In the case of a defined benefit plan, a plan satisfies the requirements of this paragraph if it satisfies the requirements of clause (ii) or (iii).

(ii) A plan satisfies the requirements of this clause if an employee who has completed at least 5 years of service has a nonforfeitable right to 100 percent of the employee's accrued benefit derived from employer contributions.

(iii) A plan satisfies the requirements of this clause if an employee has a nonforfeitable right to a percentage of the employee's accrued benefit derived from employer contributions determined under the following table:

Years of service:	*The nonforfeitable percentage is:*
3	20
4	40
5	60
6	80
7 or more	100.

(B)(i) In the case of an individual account plan, a plan satisfies the requirements of this paragraph if it satisfies the requirements of clause (ii) or (iii).

(ii) A plan satisfies the requirements of this clause if an employee who has completed at least 3 years of service has a nonforfeitable right to 100 percent of the employee's accrued benefit derived from employer contributions.

(iii) A plan satisfies the requirements of this clause if an employee has a nonforfeitable right to a percentage of the employee's accrued benefit derived from employer contributions determined under the following table:

Years of service:	*The nonforfeitable percentage is:*
2	20
3	40
4	60
5	80
6 or more	100.

(3)(A) A right to an accrued benefit derived from employer contributions shall not be treated as forfeitable solely because the plan provides that it is not payable if the participant dies (except in the case of a survivor annuity which is payable as provided in section 205).

(B) A right to an accrued benefit derived from employer contributions shall not be treated as forfeitable solely because the plan provides that the payment of benefits is suspended for such period as the employee is employed, subsequent to the commencement of payment of such benefits—

(i) in the case of a plan other than a multiemployer plan, by an employer who maintains the plan under which such benefits were being paid; and

(ii) in the case of a multiemployer plan, in the same industry, in the same trade or craft, and the same geographic area covered by the plan, as when such benefits commenced.

The Secretary shall prescribe such regulations as may be necessary to carry out the purposes of this subparagraph, including regulations with respect to the meaning of the term "employed".

(C) A right to an accrued benefit derived from employer contributions shall not be treated as forfeitable solely because plan amendments may be given retroactive application as provided in section 302(d)(2).

* * *

(b)(1) In computing the period of service under the plan for purposes of determining the nonforfeitable percentage under subsection (a)(2), all of an employee's years of service with the employer or employers maintaining the plan shall be taken into account, except that the following may be disregarded:

(A) years of service before age 18,

(B) years of service during a period for which the employee declined to contribute to a plan requiring employee contributions,

(C) years of service with an employer during any period for which the employer did not maintain the plan or a predecessor plan, defined by the Secretary of the Treasury;

(D) service not required to be taken into account under paragraph (3);

(E) years of service before January 1, 1971, unless the employee has had at least 3 years of service after December 31, 1970;

(F) years of service before this part first applies to the plan if such service would have been disregarded under the rules of the plan with regard to breaks in service, as in effect on the applicable date; and

(G) in the case of a multiemployer plan, years of service—

(i) with an employer after—

(I) a complete withdrawal of such employer from the plan (within the meaning of section 4203), or

(II) to the extent permitted by regulations prescribed by the Secretary of the Treasury, a partial withdrawal described in section 4205(b)(2)(A)(i) in connection with the decertification of the collective bargaining representative; and

(ii) with any employer under the plan after the termination date of the plan under section 4048.

(2)(A) For purposes of this section, except as provided in subparagraph (C), the term "year of service" means a calendar year, plan year, or other 12- consecutive month period designated by the plan (and not prohibited under regulations prescribed by the Secretary) during which the participant has completed 1,000 hours of service.

(B) For purposes of this section, the term "hour of service" has the meaning provided by section 202(a)(3)(C).

(C) In the case of any seasonal industry where the customary period of employment is less than 1,000 hours during a calendar year, the term "year of service" shall be such period as determined under regulations of the Secretary.

(D) For purposes of this section, in the case of any maritime industry, 125 days of service shall be treated as 1,000 hours of service. The Secretary may prescribe regulations to carry out the purposes of this subparagraph.

(3)(A) For purposes of this paragraph, the term "1-year break in service" means a calendar year, plan year, or other 12-consecutive-month period designated by the plan (and not prohibited under regulations prescribed by the Secretary) during which the participant has not completed more than 500 hours of service.

(B) For purposes of paragraph (1), in the case of any employee who has any 1- year break in service, years of service before such break shall not be required to be taken into account until he has completed a year of service after his return.

(C) For purposes of paragraph (1), in the case of any participant in an individual account plan or an insured defined benefit plan which satisfies the requirements of subsection 204(b)(1)(F) who has 5 consecutive 1-year breaks in service, years of service after such 5-year period shall not be required to be taken into account for purposes of determining the nonforfeitable percentage of his accrued benefit derived from employer contributions which accrued before such 5-year period.

(D)(i) For purposes of paragraph (1), in the case of a nonvested participant, years of service with the employer or employers maintaining the plan before any period of consecutive 1-year breaks in service shall not be required to be taken into account if the number of consecutive 1-year breaks in service within such period equals or exceeds the greater of—

(I) 5, or

(II) the aggregate number of years of service before such period.

(ii) If any years of service are not required to be taken into account by reason of a period of breaks in service to which clause (i) applies, such years of service shall not be taken into account in applying clause (i) to a subsequent period of breaks in service.

(iii) For purposes of clause (i), the term "nonvested participant" means a participant who does not have any nonforfeitable right under the plan to an accrued benefit derived from employer contributions.

* * *

(c)(1)(A) A plan amendment changing any vesting schedule under the plan shall be treated as not satisfying the requirements of subsection (a)(2) if the nonforfeitable percentage of the accrued benefit derived from employer contributions (determined as of the later of the date such amendment is adopted, or the date such amendment becomes effective) of any employee who is a participant in the plan is less than such nonforfeitable percentage computed under the plan without regard to such amendment.

(B) A plan amendment changing any vesting schedule under the plan shall be treated as not satisfying the requirements of subsection (a)(2) unless each participant having not less than 3 years of service is permitted to elect, within a reasonable period after adoption of such amendment, to have his nonforfeitable percentage computed under the plan without regard to such amendment.

(2) Subsection (a) shall not apply to benefits which may not be provided for designated employees in the event of early termination of the plan under provisions of the plan adopted pursuant to regulations prescribed by the Secretary of the Treasury to preclude the discrimination prohibited by section 401(a)(4) of the Internal Revenue Code of 1986.

(d) A pension plan may allow for nonforfeitable benefits after a lesser period and in greater amounts than are required by this part.

(e)(1) If the present value of any nonforfeitable benefit with respect to a participant in a plan exceeds $5,000, the plan shall provide that such benefit may not be immediately distributed without the consent of the participant.

(2) For purposes of paragraph (1), the present value shall be calculated in accordance with section 205(g)(3).

(3) This subsection shall not apply to any distribution of dividends to which section 404(k) of the Internal Revenue Code of 1986 applies.

(4) A plan shall not fail to meet the requirements of this subsection if, under the terms of the plan, the present value of the nonforfeitable accrued benefit is determined without regard to that portion of such benefit which is attributable to rollover contributions (and earnings allocable thereto). For purposes of this subparagraph, the term "rollover contributions" means any rollover contribution under sections 402(c), 403(a)(4), 403(b)(8), 408(d)(3)(A)(ii), and 457(e)(16) of the Internal Revenue Code of 1986.

(f) Special rules for plans computing accrued benefits by reference to hypothetical account balance or equivalent amounts—

(1) In general—An applicable defined benefit plan shall not be treated as failing to meet—

(A) subject to paragraph (2), the requirements of subsection (a)(2), or

(B) the requirements of section 204(c) or section 205(g), or the requirements of subsection (e), with respect to accrued benefits derived from employer contributions,

solely because the present value of the accrued benefit (or any portion thereof) of any participant is, under the terms of the plan, equal to the amount expressed as the balance in the hypothetical account described in paragraph (3) or as an accumulated percentage of the participant's final average compensation.

(2) 3-year vesting—In the case of an applicable defined benefit plan, such plan shall be treated as meeting the requirements of subsection (a)(2) only if an employee who has completed at least 3 years of service has a nonforfeitable right to 100 percent of the employee's accrued benefit derived from employer contributions.

(3) Applicable defined benefit plan and related rules—For purposes of this subsection—

(A) In general—The term "applicable defined benefit plan" means a defined benefit plan under which the accrued benefit (or any portion thereof) is calculated as the balance of a hypothetical account maintained for the participant or as an accumulated percentage of the participant's final average compensation.

(B) Regulations to include similar plans—The Secretary of the Treasury shall issue regulations which include in the definition of an applicable defined benefit plan any defined benefit plan (or any portion of such a plan) which has an effect similar to an applicable defined benefit plan.

§ 204. Benefit accrual requirements (§ 1054)

(a) Each pension plan shall satisfy the requirements of subsection (b)(3), and—

(1) in the case of a defined benefit plan, shall satisfy the requirements of subsection (b)(1); and

(2) in the case of a defined contribution plan, shall satisfy the requirements of subsection (b)(2).

(b)(1)(A) A defined benefit plan satisfies the requirements of this paragraph if the accrued benefit to which each participant is entitled upon his separation from the service is not less than—

(i) 3 percent of the normal retirement benefit to which he would be entitled at the normal retirement age if he commenced participation at the earliest possible entry age under the plan and served continuously until the earlier of age 65 or the normal retirement age specified under the plan, multiplied by

(ii) the number of years (not in excess of 33 1/3) of his participation in the plan.

In the case of a plan providing retirement benefits based on compensation during any period, the normal retirement benefit to which a participant would be entitled shall be determined as if he continued to earn annually the average rate of compensation which he earned during consecutive years of service, not in excess of 10, for which his compensation was the highest. For purposes of this subparagraph, social security benefits and all other relevant factors used to compute benefits shall be treated as remaining constant as of the current year for all years after such current year.

(B) A defined benefit plan satisfies the requirements of this paragraph of a particular plan year if under the plan the accrued benefit payable at the normal retirement age is equal to the normal retirement benefit and the annual rate at which any individual who is or could be a participant can accrue the retirement benefits payable at normal retirement age under the plan for any later plan year is not more than 133 1/3 percent of the annual rate at which he can accrue benefits for any plan year beginning on or after such particular plan year and before such later plan year. For purposes of this subparagraph—

(i) any amendment to the plan which is in effect for the current year shall be treated as in effect for all other plan years;

(ii) any change in an accrual rate which does not apply to any individual who is or could be a participant in the current year shall be disregarded;

(iii) the fact that benefits under the plan may be payable to certain employees before normal retirement age shall be disregarded; and

(iv) social security benefits and all other relevant factors used to compute benefits shall be treated as remaining constant as of the current year for all years after the current year.

(C) A defined benefit plan satisfies the requirements of this paragraph if the accrued benefit to which any participant is entitled upon his separation from the service is not less than a fraction of the annual benefit commencing at normal retirement age to which he would be entitled under the plan as in effect on the date of his separation if he continued to earn annually until normal retirement age the same rate of compensation upon which his normal retirement benefit would be computed under the plan, determined as if he had attained normal retirement age on the date any such determination is made (but taking into account no more than the 10 years of service immediately preceding his separation from service). Such fraction shall be a fraction, not exceeding 1, the numerator of which is the total number of his years of participation in the plan (as of the date of his separation from the service) and the denominator of which is the total number of years he would have participated in the plan if he separated from the service at the normal retirement age. For purposes of this subparagraph, social security benefits and all other relevant factors used to compute benefits shall be treated as remaining constant as of the current year for all years after such current year.

* * *

(G) Notwithstanding the preceding subparagraphs, a defined benefit plan shall be treated as not satisfying the requirements of this paragraph if the participant's accrued benefit is reduced on account of any increase in his age or service. The preceding sentence shall not apply to benefits under the plan commencing before benefits payable under title II of the Social Security Act which benefits under the plan—

(i) do not exceed social security benefits, and

(ii) terminate when such social security benefits commence.

(H)(i) Notwithstanding the preceding subparagraphs, a defined benefit plan shall be treated as not satisfying the requirements of this paragraph if, under the plan, an employee's benefit accrual is ceased, or the rate of an employee's benefit accrual is reduced, because of the attainment of any age.

(ii) A plan shall not be treated as failing to meet the requirements of this subparagraph solely because the plan imposes (without regard to age) a limitation on the amount of benefits that the plan provides or a limitation on the number of years of service or years of participation which are taken into account for purposes of determining benefit accrual under the plan.

(iii) In the case of any employee who, as of the end of any plan year under a defined benefit plan, has attained normal retirement age under such plan—

(I) if distribution of benefits under such plan with respect to such employee has commenced as of the end of such plan year, then any requirement of this subparagraph for continued accrual of benefits under such plan with respect to such employee during such plan year shall be treated as satisfied to the extent of the actuarial equivalent of in-service distribution of benefits, and

(II) if distribution of benefits under such plan with respect to such employee has not commenced as of the end of such year in accordance with section 206(a)(3), and the payment of benefits under such plan with respect to such employee is not suspended during such plan year pursuant to section 203(a)(3)(B), then any requirement of this subparagraph for continued accrual of benefits under such plan with respect to such employee during such plan year shall be treated as satisfied to the extent of any adjustment in the benefit payable under the plan during such plan year attributable to the delay in the distribution of benefits after the attainment of normal retirement age.

The preceding provisions of this clause shall apply in accordance with regulations of the Secretary of the Treasury. Such regulations may provide for the application of the preceding provisions of this clause, in the case of any such employee, with respect to any period of time within a plan year.

(iv) Clause (i) shall not apply with respect to any employee who is a highly compensated employee (within the meaning of section 414(q) of the Internal Revenue Code of 1986) to the extent provided in regulations prescribed by the Secretary of the Treasury for purposes of precluding discrimination in favor of highly compensated employees within the meaning of subchapter D of chapter 1 of the Internal Revenue Code of 1986.

(v) A plan shall not be treated as failing to meet the requirements of clause (i) solely because the subsidized portion of any early retirement benefit is disregarded in determining benefit accruals.

(vi) Any regulations prescribed by the Secretary of the Treasury pursuant to clause (v) of section 411(b)(1)(H) of the Internal Revenue Code of 1986 shall apply with respect to the requirements of this subparagraph in the same manner and to the same extent as such regulations apply with respect to the requirements of such section 411(b)(1)(H).

(2)(A) A defined contribution plan satisfies the requirements of this paragraph if, under the plan, allocations to the employee's account are not ceased, and the rate at which amounts are allocated to the employee's account is not reduced, because of the attainment of any age.

(B) A plan shall not be treated as failing to meet the requirements of subparagraph (A) solely because the subsidized portion of any early retirement benefit is disregarded in determining benefit accruals.

(C) Any regulations prescribed by the Secretary of the Treasury pursuant to subparagraphs (B) and (C) of section 411(b)(2) of the Internal Revenue Code of 1986 shall apply with respect to the requirements of this paragraph in the same manner and to the same extent as such regulations apply with respect to the requirements of such section 411(b)(2).

* * *

(5) Special rules relating to age—

(A) Comparison to similarly situated younger individual—

(i) In general—A plan shall not be treated as failing to meet the requirements of paragraph (1)(H)(i) if a participant's accrued benefit, as determined as of any date under the terms of the plan, would be equal to or greater than that of any similarly situated, younger individual who is or could be a participant.

(ii) Similarly situated—For purposes of this subparagraph, a participant is similarly situated to any other individual if such participant is identical to such other individual in every respect (including period of service, compensation, position, date of hire, work history, and any other respect) except for age.

(iii) Disregard of subsidized early retirement benefits—In determining the accrued benefit as of any date for purposes of this subparagraph, the subsidized portion of any early retirement benefit or retirement-type subsidy shall be disregarded.

(iv) Accrued benefit—For purposes of this subparagraph, the accrued benefit may, under the terms of the plan, be expressed as an annuity payable at normal retirement age, the balance of a hypothetical account, or the current value of the accumulated percentage of the employee's final average compensation.

(B) Applicable defined benefit plans—

(i) Interest credits—

(I) In general—An applicable defined benefit plan shall be treated as failing to meet the requirements of paragraph (1)(H) unless the terms of the plan provide that any interest credit (or an equivalent amount) for any plan year shall be at a rate which is not greater than a market rate of return. A plan shall not be treated as failing to meet the requirements of this subclause merely because the plan provides for a reasonable minimum guaranteed rate of return or for a rate of return that is equal to the greater of a fixed or variable rate of return.

(II) Preservation of capital—An applicable defined benefit plan shall be treated as failing to meet the requirements of paragraph (1)(H) unless the plan provides that an interest credit (or equivalent amount) of less than zero shall in no event result in the account balance or similar amount being less than the aggregate amount of contributions credited to the account.

(III) Market rate of return—The Secretary of the Treasury may provide by regulation for rules governing the calculation of a market rate of return for purposes of subclause (I) and for permissible methods of crediting interest to the account (including fixed or variable interest rates) resulting in effective rates of return meeting the requirements of subclause (I).

(ii) Special rule for plan conversions—If, after June 29, 2005, an applicable plan amendment is adopted, the plan shall be treated as failing to meet the requirements of paragraph (1)(H) unless the requirements of clause (iii) are met with respect to each individual who was a participant in the plan immediately before the adoption of the amendment.

(iii) Rate of benefit accrual—Subject to clause (iv), the requirements of this clause are met with respect to any participant if the accrued benefit of the participant under the terms of the plan as in effect after the amendment is not less than the sum of—

(I) the participant's accrued benefit for years of service before the effective date of the amendment, determined under the terms of the plan as in effect before the amendment, plus

(II) the participant's accrued benefit for years of service after the effective date of the amendment, determined under the terms of the plan as in effect after the amendment.

(iv) Special rules for early retirement subsidies—For purposes of clause (iii)(I), the plan shall credit the accumulation account or similar amount with the amount of any early retirement benefit or retirement-type subsidy for the plan year in which the participant retires if, as of such time, the participant has met the age, years of service, and other requirements under the plan for entitlement to such benefit or subsidy.

(v) Applicable plan amendment—For purposes of this subparagraph—

(I) In general—The term "applicable plan amendment" means an amendment to a defined benefit plan which has the effect of converting the plan to an applicable defined benefit plan.

(II) Special rule for coordinated benefits—If the benefits of 2 or more defined benefit plans established or maintained by an employer are coordinated in such a manner as to have the effect of the adoption of an amendment described in subclause (I), the sponsor of the defined benefit plan or plans providing for such coordination shall be treated as having adopted such a plan amendment as of the date such coordination begins.

(III) Multiple amendments—The Secretary of the Treasury shall issue regulations to prevent the avoidance of the purposes of this subparagraph through the use of 2 or more plan amendments rather than a single amendment.

(IV) Applicable defined benefit plan—For purposes of this subparagraph, the term "applicable defined benefit plan" has the meaning given such term by section 203(f)(3).

(vi) Termination requirements—An applicable defined benefit plan shall not be treated as meeting the requirements of clause (i) unless the plan provides that, upon the termination of the plan—

(I) if the interest credit rate (or an equivalent amount) under the plan is a variable rate, the rate of interest used to determine accrued benefits under the plan shall be equal to the average of the rates of interest used under the plan during the 5-year period ending on the termination date, and

(II) the interest rate and mortality table used to determine the amount of any benefit under the plan payable in the form of an annuity payable at normal retirement age shall be the rate and table specified under the plan for such purpose as of the termination date, except that if such interest rate is a variable rate, the interest rate shall be determined under the rules of subclause (I).

(C) Certain offsets permitted—A plan shall not be treated as failing to meet the requirements of paragraph (1)(H)(i) solely because the plan provides offsets against benefits under the plan to the extent such offsets are otherwise allowable in applying the requirements of section 401(a) of the Internal Revenue Code of 1986.

(D) Permitted disparities in plan contributions or benefits—A plan shall not be treated as failing to meet the requirements of paragraph (1)(H) solely because the plan provides a disparity in contributions or benefits with respect to which the requirements of section 401(l) of the Internal Revenue Code of 1986 are met.

(E) Indexing permitted—

(i) In general—A plan shall not be treated as failing to meet the requirements of paragraph (1)(H) solely because the plan provides for indexing of accrued benefits under the plan.

(ii) Protection against loss—Except in the case of any benefit provided in the form of a variable annuity, clause (i) shall not apply with respect to any indexing which results in an accrued benefit less than the accrued benefit determined without regard to such indexing.

(iii) Indexing—For purposes of this subparagraph, the term "indexing" means, in connection with an accrued benefit, the periodic adjustment of the accrued benefit by means of the application of a recognized investment index or methodology.

(F) Early retirement benefit or retirement-type subsidy—For purposes of this paragraph, the terms "early retirement benefit" and "retirement-type subsidy" have the meaning given such terms in subsection (g)(2)(A).

(G) Benefit accrued to date—For purposes of this paragraph, any reference to the accrued benefit shall be a reference to such benefit accrued to date.

(c)(1) For purposes of this section and section 203 an employee's accrued benefit derived from employer contributions as of any applicable date is the excess (if any) of the accrued benefit for such employee as of such applicable date over the accrued benefit derived from contributions made by such employee as of such date.

* * *

(d) Notwithstanding section 203(b)(1), for purposes of determining the employee's accrued benefit under the plan, the plan may disregard service performed by the employee with respect to which he has received—

(1) a distribution of the present value of his entire nonforfeitable benefit if such distribution was in an amount (not more than the dollar limit under section 203(e)(1)) permitted under regulations prescribed by the Secretary of the Treasury, or

(2) a distribution of the present value of his nonforfeitable benefit attributable to such service which he elected to receive.

Paragraph (1) shall apply only if such distribution was made on termination of the employee's participation in the plan. Paragraph (2) shall apply only if such distribution was made on termination of the employee's participation in the plan or under such other circumstances as may be provided under regulations prescribed by the Secretary of the Treasury.

(e) For purposes of determining the employee's accrued benefit, the plan shall not disregard service as provided in subsection (d) unless the plan provides an opportunity for the participant to repay the full amount of a distribution described in subsection (d) with, in the case of a defined benefit plan, interest at the rate determined for purposes of subsection (c)(2)(C) and provides that upon such repayment the employee's accrued benefit shall be recomputed by taking into account service so disregarded. This subsection shall apply only in the case of a participant who—

(1) received such a distribution in any plan year to which this section applies, which distribution was less than the present value of his accrued benefit,

(2) resumes employment covered under the plan, and

(3) repays the full amount of such distribution with, in the case of a defined benefit plan, interest at the rate determined for purposes of subsection (c)(2)(C).

The plan provision required under this subsection may provide that such repayment must be made (A) in the case of a withdrawal on account of separation from service, before the earlier of 5 years after the first date on which the participant is subsequently re-employed by the employer, or the close of the first period of 5 consecutive 1-year breaks in service commencing after the withdrawal; or (B) in the case of any other withdrawal, 5 years after the date of the withdrawal.

* * *

(g)(1) The accrued benefit of a participant under a plan may not be decreased by an amendment of the plan, other than an amendment described in section 302(d)(2) or 4281.

(2) For purposes of paragraph (1), a plan amendment which has the effect of—

(A) eliminating or reducing an early retirement benefit or a retirement-type subsidy (as defined in regulations), or

(B) eliminating an optional form of benefit,

with respect to benefits attributable to service before the amendment shall be treated as reducing accrued benefits. In the case of a retirement-type subsidy, the preceding sentence shall apply only with respect to a participant who satisfies (either before or after the amendment) the preamendment conditions for the subsidy. The Secretary of the Treasury shall by regulations provide that this paragraph shall not apply to any plan amendment which reduces or eliminates benefits or subsidies which create significant burdens or complexities for the plan and plan participants, unless such amendment adversely affects the rights of any participant in a more than de minimis manner. The Secretary of the Treasury may by regulations provide that this subparagraph shall not apply to a plan amendment described in subparagraph (B) (other than a plan amendment having an effect described in subparagraph (A)).

* * *

(4)(A) A defined contribution plan (in this subparagraph referred to as the "transferee plan") shall not be treated as failing to meet the requirements of this subsection merely because the transferee plan does not provide some or all of the forms of distribution previously available under another defined contribution plan (in this subparagraph referred to as the "transferor plan") to the extent that

(i) the forms of distribution previously available under the transferor plan applied to the account of a participant or beneficiary under the transferor plan that was transferred from the transferor plan to the transferee plan pursuant to a direct transfer rather than pursuant to a distribution from the transferor plan;

(ii) the terms of both the transferor plan and the transferee plan authorize the transfer described in clause (i);

(iii) the transfer described in clause (i) was made pursuant to a voluntary election by the participant or beneficiary whose account was transferred to the transferee plan;

(iv) the election described in clause (iii) was made after the participant or beneficiary received a notice describing the consequences of making the election; and

(v) the transferee plan allows the participant or beneficiary described in clause (iii) to receive any distribution to which the participant or beneficiary is entitled under the transferee plan in the form of a single sum distribution.

(B) Subparagraph (A) shall apply to plan mergers and other transactions having the effect of a direct transfer, including consolidations of benefits attributable to different employers within a multiple employer plan.

(5) Except to the extent provided in regulations promulgated by the Secretary of the treasury, a defined contribution plan shall not be treated as failing to meet the requirements of this subsection merely because of the elimination of a form of distribution previously available thereunder. this paragraph shall not apply to the elimination of a form of distribution with respect to any participant unless

(A) a single sum payment is available to such participant at the same time or times as the form of distribution being eliminated; and

(B) such single sum payment is based on the same or greater portion of the participant's account as the form of distribution being eliminated.

(h)(1) An applicable pension plan may not be amended so as to provide for a significant reduction in the rate of future benefit accrual unless the plan administrator provides the notice described in paragraph (2) to each applicable individual (and to each employee organization representing applicable individuals) and to each employer who has an obligation to contribute to the plan.

(2) The notice required by paragraph (1) shall be written in a manner calculated to be understood by the average plan participant and shall provide sufficient information (as determined in accordance with regulations prescribed by the Secretary of the treasury) to allow applicable individuals to understand the effect of the plan amendment. the Secretary of the treasury may provide a simplified form of notice for, or exempt from any notice requirement, a plan

(A) which has fewer than 100 participants who have accrued a benefit under the plan, or

(B) which offers participants the option to choose between the new benefit formula and the old benefit formula.

(3) Except as provided in regulations prescribed by the Secretary of the Treasury, the notice required by paragraph (1) shall be provided within a reasonable time before the effective date of the plan amendment.

* * *

(6)(A) In the case of any egregious failure to meet any requirement of this subsection with respect to any plan amendment, the provisions of the applicable pension plan shall be applied as if such plan amendment entitled all applicable individuals to the greater of

(i) the benefits to which they would have been entitled without regard to such amendment, or

(ii) the benefits under the plan with regard to such amendment.

(B) For purposes of subparagraph (a), there is an egregious failure to meet the requirements of this subsection if such failure is within the control of the plan sponsor and is

(i) an intentional failure (including any failure to promptly provide the required notice or information after the plan administrator discovers an unintentional failure to meet the requirements of this subsection),

(ii) a failure to provide most of the individuals with most of the information they are entitled to receive under this subsection, or

(iii) a failure which is determined to be egregious under regulations prescribed by the Secretary of the Treasury.

(7) The Secretary of the Treasury may by regulations allow any notice under this subsection to be provided by using new technologies.

(8) For purposes of this subsection

(A) The term "applicable individual" means, with respect to any plan amendment—

(i) each participant in the plan; and

(ii) any beneficiary who is an alternate payee (within the meaning of section 206(d)(3)(K)) under an applicable qualified domestic relations order (within the meaning of section 206(d)(3)(B)(i)),

whose rate of future benefit accrual under the plan may reasonably be expected to be significantly reduced by such plan amendment.

(B) The term "applicable pension plan" means—

(i) any defined benefit plan; or

(ii) an individual account plan which is subject to the funding standards of section 412 of the Internal Revenue Code of 1986.

(9) For purposes of this subsection, a plan amendment which eliminates or reduces any early retirement benefit or retirement-type subsidy (within the meaning of subsection (g)(2)(A)) shall be treated as having the effect of reducing the rate of future benefit accrual.

(i)(1) In the case of a plan described in paragraph (3) which is maintained by an employer that is a debtor in a case under Title 11 or similar Federal or State law, no amendment of the plan which increases the liabilities of the plan by reason of—

(A) any increase in benefits,

(B) any change in the accrual of benefits, or

(C) any change in the rate at which benefits become nonforfeitable under the plan,

with respect to employees of the debtor, shall be effective prior to the effective date of such employer's plan of reorganization.

(2) Paragraph (1) shall not apply to any plan amendment that—

(A) the Secretary of the Treasury determines to be reasonable and that provides for only de minimis increases in the liabilities of the plan with respect to employees of the debtor,

(B) only repeals an amendment described in section 302(d)(2),

(C) is required as a condition of qualification under part I of subchapter D of chapter 1 of the Internal Revenue Code of 1986, or

(D) was adopted prior to, or pursuant to a collective bargaining agreement entered into prior to, the date on which the employer became a debtor in a case under Title 11 or similar Federal or State law.

(3) This subsection shall apply only to plans (other than multiemployer plans) covered under section 4021 of this Act for which the funding target attainment percentage (as defined in section 303(d)(2)) is less than 100 percent after taking into account the effect of the amendment.

(4) For purposes of this subsection, the term "employer" has the meaning set forth in section 302(b)(1), without regard to section 302(b)(2).

(j) Diversification requirements for certain individual account plans—

(1) In general—An applicable individual account plan shall meet the diversification requirements of paragraphs (2), (3), and (4).[**]

* * *

§ 205. Requirement of joint and survivor annuity and preretirement survivor annuity (§ 1055)

(a) Each pension plan to which this section applies shall provide that—

(1) in the case of a vested participant who does not die before the annuity starting date, the accrued benefit payable to such participant shall be provided in the form of a qualified joint and survivor annuity, and

(2) in the case of a vested participant who dies before the annuity starting date and who has a surviving spouse, a qualified preretirement survivor annuity shall be provided to the surviving spouse of such participant.

(b)(1) This section shall apply to—

(A) any defined benefit plan,

(B) any individual account plan which is subject to the funding standards of section 302, and

(C) any participant under any other individual account plan unless—

(i) such plan provides that the participant's nonforfeitable accrued benefit (reduced by any security interest held by the plan by reason of a loan outstanding to such participant) is payable in full, on the death of the participant, to the participant's surviving spouse (or, if there is no surviving spouse or the surviving spouse consents in the manner required under subsection (c)(2), to a designated beneficiary),

[**] Paragraphs (2)-(7) of § 204(j) are omitted, but IRC § 401(a)(35) mirrors the requirements of these paragraphs.

(ii) such participant does not elect the payment of benefits in the form of a life annuity, and

(iii) with respect to such participant, such plan is not a direct or indirect transferee (in a transfer after December 31, 1984) of a plan which is described in subparagraph (A) or (B) or to which this clause applied with respect to the participant.

Clause (iii) of subparagraph (C) shall apply only with respect to the transferred assets (and income therefrom) if the plan separately accounts for such assets and any income therefrom.

* * *

(3) A plan shall not be treated as failing to meet the requirements of paragraph (1)(C) or (2) merely because the plan provides that benefits will not be payable to the surviving spouse of the participant unless the participant and such spouse had been married throughout the 1-year period ending on the earlier of the participant's annuity starting date or the date of the participant's death.

* * *

(c)(1) A plan meets the requirements of this section only if—

(A) under the plan, each participant—

(i) may elect at any time during the applicable election period to waive the qualified joint and survivor annuity form of benefit or the qualified preretirement survivor annuity form of benefit (or both),

(ii) if the participant elects a waiver under clause (i), may elect the qualified optional survivor annuity at any time during the applicable election period, and

(iii) may revoke any such election at any time during the applicable election period, and

(B) the plan meets the requirements of paragraphs (2), (3), and (4).

(2) Each plan shall provide that an election under paragraph (1)(A)(i) shall not take effect unless—

(A)(i) the spouse of the participant consents in writing to such election, (ii) such election designates a beneficiary (or a form of benefits) which may not be changed without spousal consent (or the consent of the spouse expressly permits designations by the participant without any requirement of further consent by the spouse), and (iii) the spouse's consent acknowledges the effect of such election and is witnessed by a plan representative or a notary public, or

(B) it is established to the satisfaction of a plan representative that the consent required under subparagraph (A) may not be obtained because there is no spouse, because the spouse cannot be located, or because of such other circumstances as the Secretary of the Treasury may by regulations prescribe.

Any consent by a spouse (or establishment that the consent of a spouse may not be obtained) under the preceding sentence shall be effective only with respect to such spouse.

(3)(A) Each plan shall provide to each participant, within a reasonable period of time before the annuity starting date (and consistent with such regulations as the Secretary of the Treasury may prescribe) a written explanation of—

(i) the terms and conditions of the qualified joint and survivor annuity and of the qualified optional survivor annuity,

(ii) the participant's right to make, and the effect of, an election under paragraph (1) to waive the joint and survivor annuity form of benefit,

(iii) the rights of the participant's spouse under paragraph (2), and

(iv) the right to make, and the effect of, a revocation of an election under paragraph (1).

(B)(i) Each plan shall provide to each participant, within the applicable period with respect to such participant (and consistent with such regulations as the Secretary may prescribe), a written explanation with respect to the qualified preretirement survivor annuity comparable to that required under subparagraph (A).

* * *

(4) Each plan shall provide that, if this section applies to a participant when part or all of the participant's accrued benefit is to be used as security for a loan, no portion of the participant's accrued benefit may be used as security for such loan unless—

(A) the spouse of the participant (if any) consents in writing to such use during the 90-day period ending on the date on which the loan is to be so secured, and

(B) requirements comparable to the requirements of paragraph (2) are met with respect to such consent.

(5)(A) The requirements of this subsection shall not apply with respect to the qualified joint and survivor annuity form of benefit or the qualified preretirement survivor annuity form of benefit, as the case may be, if such benefit may not be waived (or another beneficiary selected) and if the plan fully subsidizes the costs of such benefit.

(B) For purposes of subparagraph (A), a plan fully subsidizes the costs of a benefit if under the plan the failure to waive such benefit by a participant would not result in a decrease in any plan benefits with respect to such participant and would not result in increased contributions from such participant.

(6) If a plan fiduciary acts in accordance with part 4 of this subtitle in—

(A) relying on a consent or revocation referred to in paragraph (1)(A), or

(B) making a determination under paragraph (2),

then such consent, revocation, or determination shall be treated as valid for purposes of discharging the plan from liability to the extent of payments made pursuant to such Act.

(7) For purposes of this subsection, the term "applicable election period" means—

(A) in the case of an election to waive the qualified joint and survivor annuity form of benefit, the 180-day period ending on the annuity starting date, or

(B) in the case of an election to waive the qualified preretirement survivor annuity, the period which begins on the first day of the plan year in which the participant attains age 35 and ends on the date of the participant's death.

In the case of a participant who is separated from service, the applicable election period under subparagraph (B) with respect to benefits accrued before the date of such separation from service shall not begin later than such date.

* * *

(d)(1) For purposes of this section, the term "qualified joint and survivor annuity" means an annuity—

(A) for the life of the participant with a survivor annuity for the life of the spouse which is not less than 50 percent of (and is not greater than 100 percent of) the amount of the annuity which is payable during the joint lives of the participant and the spouse, and

(B) which is the actuarial equivalent of a single annuity for the life of the participant.

Such term also includes any annuity in a form having the effect of an annuity described in the preceding sentence.

(2)(A) For purposes of this section, the term 'qualified optional survivor annuity' means an annuity—

(i) for the life of the participant with a survivor annuity for the life of the spouse which is equal to the applicable percentage of the amount of the annuity which is payable during the joint lives of the participant and the spouse, and

(ii) which is the actuarial equivalent of a single annuity for the life of the participant.

Such term also includes any annuity in a form having the effect of an annuity described in the preceding sentence.

(B)(i) For purposes of subparagraph (A), if the survivor annuity percentage—

(I) is less than 75 percent, the applicable percentage is 75 percent, and

(II) is greater than or equal to 75 percent, the applicable percentage is 50 percent.

(ii) For purposes of clause (i), the term 'survivor annuity percentage' means the percentage which the survivor annuity under the plan's qualified joint and survivor annuity bears to the annuity payable during the joint lives of the participant and the spouse.

(e) For purposes of this section—

(1) Except as provided in paragraph (2), the term "qualified preretirement survivor annuity" means a survivor annuity for the life of the surviving spouse of the participant if—

(A) the payments to the surviving spouse under such annuity are not less than the amounts which would be payable as a survivor annuity under the qualified joint and survivor annuity under the plan (or the actuarial equivalent thereof) if—

(i) in the case of a participant who dies after the date on which the participant attained the earliest retirement age, such participant had retired with an immediate qualified joint and survivor annuity on the day before the participant's date of death, or

(ii) in the case of a participant who dies on or before the date on which the participant would have attained the earliest retirement age, such participant had—

(I) separated from service on the date of death,

(II) survived to the earliest retirement age,

(III) retired with an immediate qualified joint and survivor annuity at the earliest retirement age, and

(IV) died on the day after the day on which such participant would have attained the earliest retirement age, and

(B) under the plan, the earliest period for which the surviving spouse may receive a payment under such annuity is not later than the month in which the participant would have attained the earliest retirement age under the plan.

In the case of an individual who separated from service before the date of such individual's death, subparagraph (A)(ii)(I) shall not apply.

(2) In the case of any individual account plan or participant described in subparagraph (B) or (C) of subsection (b)(1), the term "qualified preretirement survivor annuity" means an annuity for the life of the surviving spouse the actuarial equivalent of which is not less than 50 percent of the portion of the account balance of the participant (as of the date of death) to which the participant had a nonforfeitable right (within the meaning of section 203).

(3) For purposes of paragraphs (1) and (2), any security interest held by the plan by reason of a loan outstanding to the participant shall be taken into account in determining the amount of the qualified preretirement survivor annuity.

(f)(1) Except as provided in paragraph (2), a plan may provide that a qualified joint and survivor annuity (or a qualified preretirement survivor annuity) will not be provided unless the participant and spouse had been married throughout the 1-year period ending on the earlier of—

(A) the participant's annuity starting date, or

(B) the date of the participant's death.

(2) For purposes of paragraph (1), if—

(A) a participant marries within 1 year before the annuity starting date, and

(B) the participant and the participant's spouse in such marriage have been married for at least a 1-year period ending on or before the date of the participant's death,

such participant and such spouse shall be treated as having been married throughout the 1-year period ending on the participant's annuity starting date.

(g)(1) A plan may provide that the present value of a qualified joint and survivor annuity or a qualified preretirement survivor annuity will be immediately distributed if such value does not exceed the amount that can be distributed without the participant's consent under section 203(e). No distribution may be made under the preceding sentence after the annuity starting date unless the participant and the spouse of the participant (or where the participant has died, the surviving spouse) consent in writing to such distribution.

(2) If—

(A) the present value of the qualified joint and survivor annuity or the qualified preretirement survivor annuity exceeds the amount that can be distributed without the participant's consent under section 203(e), and

(B) the participant and the spouse of the participant (or where the participant has died, the surviving spouse) consent in writing to the distribution, the plan may immediately distribute the present value of such annuity.

(3)(A) For purposes of paragraphs (1) and (2), the present value shall not be less than the present value calculated by using the applicable mortality table and the applicable interest rate.

(B) For purposes of subparagraph (A)—

(i) The term "applicable mortality table" means a mortality table, modified as appropriate by the Secretary of the Treasury, based on the mortality table specified for the plan year under subparagraph (A) of section 303(h)(3) (without regard to subparagraph (C) or (D) of such section).

(ii) The term "applicable interest rate" means the adjusted first, second, and third segment rates applied under rules similar to the rules of section 303(h)(2)(C) for the month before the date of the distribution or such other time as the Secretary of the Treasury may by regulations prescribe.

(iii) For purposes of clause (ii), the adjusted first, second, and third segment rates are the first, second, and third segment rates which would be determined under section 303(h)(2)(C) if—

(I) section 303(h)(2)(D) were applied by substituting the average yields for the month described in clause (ii) for the average yields for the 24-month period described in such section,

(II) section 303(h)(2)(G)(i)(II) were applied by substituting "section 205(g)(3)(A)(ii)(II)" for "section 302(b)(5)(B)(ii)(II)", and

(III) the applicable percentage under section 303(h)(2)(G) were determined in accordance with the following table:

In the case of plan years beginning in:	*The applicable percentage is:*
2008	20 percent
2009	40 percent
2010	60 percent
2011	80 percent.

(h) For purposes of this section—

(1) The term "vested participant" means any participant who has a nonforfeitable right (within the meaning of section 3(19)) to any portion of such participant's accrued benefit.

(2)(A) The term "annuity starting date" means—

(i) the first day of the first period for which an amount is payable as an annuity, or

(ii) in the case of a benefit not payable in the form of an annuity, the first day on which all events have occurred which entitle the participant to such benefit.

(B) For purposes of subparagraph (A), the first day of the first period for which a benefit is to be received by reason of disability shall be treated as the annuity starting date only if such benefit is not an auxiliary benefit.

(3) The term "earliest retirement age" means the earliest date on which, under the plan, the participant could elect to receive retirement benefits.

(i) A plan may take into account in any equitable manner (as determined by the Secretary of the Treasury) any increased costs resulting from providing a qualified joint or survivor annuity or a qualified preretirement survivor annuity.

(j) If the use of any participant's accrued benefit (or any portion thereof) as security for a loan meets the requirements of subsection (c)(4), nothing in this section shall prevent any distribution required by reason of a failure to comply with the terms of such loan.

(k) No consent of a spouse shall be effective for purposes of subsection (g)(1) or (g)(2) (as the case may be) unless requirements comparable to the requirements for spousal consent to an election under subsection (c)(1)(A) are met.

* * *

§ 206. Form and payment of benefits (§ 1056)

(a) Each pension plan shall provide that unless the participant otherwise elects, the payment of benefits under the plan to the participant shall begin not later than the 60th day after the latest of the close of the plan year in which—

(1) occurs the date on which the participant attains the earlier of age 65 or the normal retirement age specified under the plan,

(2) occurs the 10th anniversary of the year in which the participant commenced participation in the plan, or

(3) the participant terminates his service with the employer.

In the case of a plan which provides for the payment of an early retirement benefit, such plan shall provide that a participant who satisfied the service requirements for such early retirement benefit, but separated from the service (with any nonforfeitable right to an accrued benefit) before satisfying the age requirement for such early retirement benefit, is entitled upon satisfaction of such age requirement to receive a benefit not less than the benefit to which he would be entitled at the normal retirement age, actuarially reduced under regulations prescribed by the Secretary of the Treasury.

(b) If—

(1) a participant or beneficiary is receiving benefits under a pension plan, or

(2) a participant is separated from the service and has nonforfeitable rights to benefits,

a plan may not decrease benefits of such a participant by reason of any increase in the benefit levels payable under title II of the Social Security Act or the Railroad Retirement Act of 1937, or any increase in the wage base under such title II, if such increase takes place after September 2, 1974, or (if later) the earlier of the date of first entitlement of such benefits or the date of such separation.

(c) No pension plan may provide that any part of a participant's accrued benefit derived from employer contributions (whether or not otherwise nonforfeitable) is forfeitable solely because of withdrawal by such participant of any amount attributable to the benefit derived from contributions made by such participant. The preceding sentence shall not apply (1) to the accrued benefit of any participant unless, at the time of such withdrawal, such participant has a nonforfeitable right to at least 50 percent of such accrued benefit, or (2) to the extent that an accrued benefit is permitted to be forfeited in accordance with section 203(a)(3)(D)(iii).

(d)(1) Each pension plan shall provide that benefits provided under the plan may not be assigned or alienated.

(2) For the purposes of paragraph (1) of this subsection, there shall not be taken into account any voluntary and revocable assignment of not to exceed 10 percent of any benefit payment, or of any irrevocable assignment or alienation of benefits executed before September 2, 1974. The preceding sentence shall not apply to any assignment or alienation made for the purposes of defraying plan administration costs. For purposes of this paragraph a loan made to a participant or beneficiary shall not be treated as an assignment or alienation if such loan is secured by the participant's accrued nonforfeitable benefit and is exempt from the tax imposed by section 4975 of the Internal Revenue Code of 1986 (relating to tax on prohibited transactions) by reason of section 4975(d)(1) of such Code.

(3)(A) Paragraph (1) shall apply to the creation, assignment, or recognition of a right to any benefit payable with respect to a participant pursuant to a domestic relations order, except that paragraph (1) shall not apply if the order is determined to be a qualified domestic relations order. Each pension plan shall provide for the payment of benefits in accordance with the applicable requirements of any qualified domestic relations order.

(B) For purposes of this paragraph—

(i) the term "qualified domestic relations order" means a domestic relations order—

(I) which creates or recognizes the existence of an alternate payee's right to, or assigns to an alternate payee the right to, receive all or a portion of the benefits payable with respect to a participant under a plan, and

(II) with respect to which the requirements of subparagraphs (C) and (D) are met, and

(ii) the term "domestic relations order" means any judgment, decree, or order (including approval of a property settlement agreement) which—

(I) relates to the provision of child support, alimony payments, or marital property rights to a spouse, former spouse, child, or other dependent of a participant, and

(II) is made pursuant to a State domestic relations law (including a community property law).

(C) A domestic relations order meets the requirements of this subparagraph only if such order clearly specifies—

(i) the name and the last known mailing address (if any) of the participant and the name and mailing address of each alternate payee covered by the order,

(ii) the amount or percentage of the participant's benefits to be paid by the plan to each such alternate payee, or the manner in which such amount or percentage is to be determined,

(iii) the number of payments or period to which such order applies, and

(iv) each plan to which such order applies.

(D) A domestic relations order meets the requirements of this subparagraph only if such order—

(i) does not require a plan to provide any type or form of benefit, or any option, not otherwise provided under the plan,

(ii) does not require the plan to provide increased benefits (determined on the basis of actuarial value), and

(iii) does not require the payment of benefits to an alternate payee which are required to be paid to another alternate payee under another order previously determined to be a qualified domestic relations order.

(E)(i) A domestic relations order shall not be treated as failing to meet the requirements of clause (i) of subparagraph (D) solely because such order requires that payment of benefits be made to an alternate payee—

(I) in the case of any payment before a participant has separated from service, on or after the date on which the participant attains (or would have attained) the earliest retirement age,

(II) as if the participant had retired on the date on which such payment is to begin under such order (but taking into account only the present value of benefits actually accrued and not taking into account the present value of any employer subsidy for early retirement), and

(III) in any form in which such benefits may be paid under the plan to the participant (other than in the form of a joint and survivor annuity with respect to the alternate payee and his or her subsequent spouse).

For purposes of subclause (II), the interest rate assumption used in determining the present value shall be the interest rate specified in the plan or, if no rate is specified, 5 percent.

(ii) For purposes of this subparagraph, the term "earliest retirement age" means the earlier of—

(I) the date on which the participant is entitled to a distribution under the plan, or

(II) the later of the date of the participant attains age 50 or the earliest date on which the participant could begin receiving benefits under the plan if the participant separated from service.

(F) To the extent provided in any qualified domestic relations order—

(i) the former spouse of a participant shall be treated as a surviving spouse of such participant for purposes of section 205 (and any spouse of the participant shall not be treated as a spouse of the participant for such purposes), and

(ii) if married for at least 1 year, the surviving former spouse shall be treated as meeting the requirements of section 205(f).

(G)(i) In the case of any domestic relations order received by a plan—

(I) the plan administrator shall promptly notify the participant and each alternate payee of the receipt of such order and the plan's procedures for determining the qualified status of domestic relations orders, and

(II) within a reasonable period after receipt of such order, the plan administrator shall determine whether such order is a qualified domestic relations order and notify the participant and each alternate payee of such determination.

(ii) Each plan shall establish reasonable procedures to determine the qualified status of domestic relations orders and to administer distributions under such qualified orders. Such procedures—

(I) shall be in writing,

(II) shall provide for the notification of each person specified in a domestic relations order as entitled to payment of benefits under the plan (at the address included in the domestic relations order) of such procedures promptly upon receipt by the plan of the domestic relations order, and

(III) shall permit an alternate payee to designate a representative for receipt of copies of notices that are sent to the alternate payee with respect to a domestic relations order.

(H)(i) During any period in which the issue of whether a domestic relations order is a qualified domestic relations order is being determined (by the plan administrator, by a court of competent jurisdiction, or otherwise), the plan administrator shall separately account for the amounts (hereinafter in this subparagraph referred to as the "segregated amounts") which would have been payable to the alternate payee during such period if the order had been determined to be a qualified domestic relations order.

(ii) If within the 18-month period described in clause (v) the order (or modification thereof) is determined to be a qualified domestic relations order, the plan administrator shall pay the segregated amounts (including any interest thereon) to the person or persons entitled thereto.

(iii) If within the 18-month period described in clause (v)—

(I) it is determined that the order is not a qualified domestic relations order, or

(II) the issue as to whether such order is a qualified domestic relations order is not resolved,

then the plan administrator shall pay the segregated amounts (including any interest thereon) to the person or persons who would have been entitled to such amounts if there had been no order.

(iv) Any determination that an order is a qualified domestic relations order which is made after the close of the 18-month period described in clause (v) shall be applied prospectively only.

(v) For purposes of this subparagraph, the 18-month period described in this clause is the 18-month period beginning with the date on which the first payment would be required to be made under the domestic relations order.

(I) If a plan fiduciary acts in accordance with part 4 of this subtitle in—

(i) treating a domestic relations order as being (or not being) a qualified domestic relations order, or

(ii) taking action under subparagraph (H),

then the plan's obligation to the participant and each alternate payee shall be discharged to the extent of any payment made pursuant to such Act.

(J) A person who is an alternate payee under a qualified domestic relations order shall be considered for purposes of any provision of this Act a beneficiary under the plan. Nothing in the preceding sentence shall permit a requirement under section 4001 of the payment of more than 1 premium with respect to a participant for any period.

(K) The term "alternate payee" means any spouse, former spouse, child, or other dependent of a participant who is recognized by a domestic relations order as having a right to receive all, or a portion of, the benefits payable under a plan with respect to such participant.

(L) This paragraph shall not apply to any plan to which paragraph (1) does not apply.

* * *

(4) Paragraph (1) shall not apply to any offset of a participant's benefits provided under an employee pension benefit plan against an amount that the participant is ordered or required to pay to the plan if—

(A) the order or requirement to pay arises—

(i) under a judgment of conviction for a crime involving such plan,

(ii) under a civil judgment (including a consent order or decree) entered by a court in an action brought in connection with a violation (or alleged violation) of part 4 of this subtitle, or

(iii) pursuant to a settlement agreement between the Secretary and the participant, or a settlement agreement between the Pension Benefit Guaranty Corporation and the participant, in connection with a violation (or alleged violation) of part 4 of this subtitle by a fiduciary or any other person,

(B) the judgment, order, decree, or settlement agreement expressly provides for the offset of all or part of the amount ordered or required to be paid to the plan against the participant's benefits provided under the plan, and

(C) in a case in which the survivor annuity requirements of section 205 apply with respect to distributions from the plan to the participant, if the participant has a spouse at the time at which the offset is to be made—

(i) either—

(I) such spouse has consented in writing to such offset and such consent is witnessed by a notary public or representative of the plan (or it is established to the satisfaction of a plan representative that such consent may not be obtained by reason of circumstances described in section 205(c)(2)(B)), or

(II) an election to waive the right of the spouse to a qualified joint and survivor annuity or a qualified preretirement survivor annuity is in effect in accordance with the requirements of section 205(c),

(ii) such spouse is ordered or required in such judgment, order, decree, or settlement to pay an amount to the plan in connection with a violation of part 4 of this subtitle, or

(iii) in such judgment, order, decree, or settlement, such spouse retains the right to receive the survivor annuity under a qualified joint and survivor annuity provided pursuant to section 205(a)(1) and under a qualified preretirement survivor annuity provided pursuant to section 205(a)(2), determined in accordance with paragraph (5).

A plan shall not be treated as failing to meet the requirements of section 205 solely by reason of an offset under this paragraph.

* * *

(g) Funding-based limits on benefits and benefit accruals under single-employer plans—

(1) Funding-based limitation on shutdown benefits and other unpredictable contingent event benefits under single-employer plans—

(A) In general—If a participant of a defined benefit plan which is a single-employer plan is entitled to an unpredictable contingent event benefit payable with respect to any event occurring during any plan year, the plan shall provide that such benefit may not be provided if the adjusted funding target attainment percentage for such plan year—

(i) is less than 60 percent, or

(ii) would be less than 60 percent taking into account such occurrence.

(B) Exemption—Subparagraph (A) shall cease to apply with respect to any plan year, effective as of the first day of the plan year, upon payment by the plan sponsor of a contribution (in addition to any minimum required contribution under section 303) equal to—

(i) in the case of subparagraph (A)(i), the amount of the increase in the funding target of the plan (under section 303) for the plan year attributable to the occurrence referred to in subparagraph (A), and

(ii) in the case of subparagraph (A)(ii), the amount sufficient to result in an adjusted funding target attainment percentage of 60 percent.

(C) Unpredictable contingent event benefit—For purposes of this paragraph, the term "unpredictable contingent event benefit" means any benefit payable solely by reason of—

(i) a plant shutdown (or similar event, as determined by the Secretary of the Treasury), or

(ii) an event other than the attainment of any age, performance of any service, receipt or derivation of any compensation, or occurrence of death or disability.

(2) Limitations on plan amendments increasing liability for benefits—

(A) In general—No amendment to a defined benefit plan which is a single-employer plan which has the effect of increasing liabilities of the plan by reason of increases in benefits, establishment of new benefits, changing the rate of benefit accrual, or changing the rate at which benefits become nonforfeitable may take effect during any plan year if the adjusted funding target attainment percentage for such plan year is—

(i) less than 80 percent, or

(ii) would be less than 80 percent taking into account such amendment.

(B) Exemption—Subparagraph (A) shall cease to apply with respect to any plan year, effective as of the first day of the plan year (or if later, the effective date of the amendment), upon payment by the plan sponsor of a contribution (in addition to any minimum required contribution under section 303) equal to—

(i) in the case of subparagraph (A)(i), the amount of the increase in the funding target of the plan (under section 303) for the plan year attributable to the amendment, and

(ii) in the case of subparagraph (A)(ii), the amount sufficient to result in an adjusted funding target attainment percentage of 80 percent.

(C) Exception for certain benefit increases—Subparagraph (A) shall not apply to any amendment which provides for an increase in benefits under a formula which is not based on a participant's compensation, but only if the rate of such increase is not in excess of the contemporaneous rate of increase in average wages of participants covered by the amendment.

(3) Limitations on accelerated benefit distributions—

(A) Funding percentage less than 60 percent—A defined benefit plan which is a single-employer plan shall provide that, in any case in which the plan's adjusted funding target attainment percentage for a plan year is less than 60 percent, the plan may not pay any prohibited payment after the valuation date for the plan year.

(B) Bankruptcy—A defined benefit plan which is a single-employer plan shall provide that, during any period in which the plan sponsor is a debtor in a case under title 11, United States Code, or similar Federal or State law, the plan may not pay any prohibited payment. The preceding sentence shall not apply on or after the date on which the enrolled actuary of the plan certifies that the adjusted funding target attainment percentage of such plan is not less than 100 percent.

(C) Limited payment if percentage at least 60 percent but less than 80 percent—

(i) In general—A defined benefit plan which is a single-employer plan shall provide that, in any case in which the plan's adjusted funding target attainment percentage for a plan year is 60 percent or greater but less than 80 percent, the plan may not pay any prohibited payment after the valuation date for the plan year to the extent the amount of the payment exceeds the lesser of—

(I) 50 percent of the amount of the payment which could be made without regard to this subsection, or

(II) the present value (determined under guidance prescribed by the Pension Benefit Guaranty Corporation, using the interest and mortality assumptions under section 205(g)) of the maximum guarantee with respect to the participant under section 4022.

(ii) One-time application—

(I) In general—The plan shall also provide that only 1 prohibited payment meeting the requirements of clause (i) may be made with respect to any participant during any period of consecutive plan years to which the limitations under either subparagraph (A) or (B) or this subparagraph applies.

(II) Treatment of beneficiaries—For purposes of this clause, a participant and any beneficiary on his behalf (including an alternate payee, as defined in section 206(d)(3)(K)) shall be treated as 1 participant. If the accrued benefit of a participant is allocated to such an alternate payee and 1 or more other persons, the amount under clause (i) shall be allocated among such persons in the same manner as the accrued benefit is allocated unless the qualified domestic relations order (as defined in section 206(d)(3)(B)(i)) provides otherwise.

(D) Exception—This paragraph shall not apply to any plan for any plan year if the terms of such plan (as in effect for the period beginning on September 1, 2005, and ending with such plan year) provide for no benefit accruals with respect to any participant during such period.

(E) Prohibited payment—For purpose of this paragraph, the term "prohibited payment" means—

(i) any payment, in excess of the monthly amount paid under a single life annuity (plus any social security supplements described in the last sentence of section 204(b)(1)(G)), to a participant or beneficiary whose annuity starting date (as defined in section 205(h)(2)) occurs during any period a limitation under subparagraph (A) or (B) is in effect,

(ii) any payment for the purchase of an irrevocable commitment from an insurer to pay benefits, and

(iii) any other payment specified by the Secretary of the Treasury by regulations.

Such term shall not include the payment of a benefit which under section 203(e) of this title may be immediately distributed without the consent of the participant.

(4) Limitation on benefit accruals for plans with severe funding shortfalls—

(A) In general—A defined benefit plan which is a single-employer plan shall provide that, in any case in which the plan's adjusted funding target attainment percentage for a plan year is less than 60 percent, benefit accruals under the plan shall cease as of the valuation date for the plan year.

(B) Exemption—Subparagraph (A) shall cease to apply with respect to any plan year, effective as of the first day of the plan year, upon payment by the plan sponsor of a contribution (in addition to any minimum required contribution under section 303) equal to the amount sufficient to result in an adjusted funding target attainment percentage of 60 percent.

(5) Rules relating to contributions required to avoid benefit limitations—

(A) Security may be provided—

(i) In general—For purposes of this subsection, the adjusted funding target attainment percentage shall be determined by treating as an asset of the plan any security provided by a plan sponsor in a form meeting the requirements of clause (ii).

(ii) Form of security—The security required under clause (i) shall consist of—

(I) a bond issued by a corporate surety company that is an acceptable surety for purposes of section 412 of this Act,

(II) cash, or United States obligations which mature in 3 years or less, held in escrow by a bank or similar financial institution, or

(III) such other form of security as is satisfactory to the Secretary of the Treasury and the parties involved.

(iii) Enforcement—Any security provided under clause (i) may be perfected and enforced at any time after the earlier of—

(I) the date on which the plan terminates,

(II) if there is a failure to make a payment of the minimum required contribution for any plan year beginning after the security is provided, the due date for the payment under section 303(j), or

(III) if the adjusted funding target attainment percentage is less than 60 percent for a consecutive period of 7 years, the valuation date for the last year in the period.

(iv) Release of security—The security shall be released (and any amounts thereunder shall be refunded together with any interest accrued thereon) at such time as the Secretary of the Treasury may prescribe in regulations, including regulations for partial releases of the security by reason of increases in the adjusted funding target attainment percentage.

(B) Prefunding balance or funding standard carryover balance may not be used—No prefunding balance or funding standard carryover balance under section 303(f) may be used under paragraph (1), (2), or (4) to satisfy any payment an employer may make under any such paragraph to avoid or terminate the application of any limitation under such paragraph.

(C) Deemed reduction of funding balances—

(i) In general—Subject to clause (iii), in any case in which a benefit limitation under paragraph (1), (2), (3), or (4) would (but for this subparagraph and determined without regard to paragraph (1)(B), (2)(B), or (4)(B)) apply to such plan for the plan year, the plan sponsor of such plan shall be treated for purposes of this Act as having made an election under section 303(f) to reduce the prefunding balance or funding standard carryover balance by such amount as is necessary for such benefit limitation to not apply to the plan for such plan year.

(ii) Exception for insufficient funding balances—Clause (i) shall not apply with respect to a benefit limitation for any plan year if the application of clause (i) would not result in the benefit limitation not applying for such plan year.

(iii) Restrictions of certain rules to collectively bargained plans—With respect to any benefit limitation under paragraph (1), (2), or (4), clause (i) shall only apply in the case of a plan maintained pursuant to 1 or more collective bargaining agreements between employee representatives and 1 or more employers.

(6) New plans—Paragraphs (1), (2), and (4) shall not apply to a plan for the first 5 plan years of the plan. For purposes of this paragraph, the reference in this paragraph to a plan shall include a reference to any predecessor plan.

(7) Presumed underfunding for purposes of benefit limitations—

(A) Presumption of continued underfunding—In any case in which a benefit limitation under paragraph (1), (2), (3), or (4) has been applied to a plan with respect to the plan year preceding the current plan year, the adjusted funding target attainment percentage of the plan for the current plan year shall be presumed to be equal to the adjusted funding target attainment percentage of the plan for the preceding plan year until the enrolled actuary of the plan certifies the actual adjusted funding target attainment percentage of the plan for the current plan year.

(B) Presumption of underfunding after 10th month—In any case in which no certification of the adjusted funding target attainment percentage for the current plan year is made with respect to the plan before the first day of the 10th month of such year, for purposes of paragraphs (1), (2), (3), and (4), such first day shall be deemed, for purposes of such paragraph, to be the valuation date of the plan for the current plan year and the plan's adjusted funding target attainment percentage shall be conclusively presumed to be less than 60 percent as of such first day.

(C) Presumption of underfunding after 4th month for nearly underfunded plans—In any case in which—

(i) a benefit limitation under paragraph (1), (2), (3), or (4) did not apply to a plan with respect to the plan year preceding the current plan year, but the adjusted funding target attainment percentage of the plan for such preceding plan year was not more than 10 percentage points greater than the percentage which would have caused such paragraph to apply to the plan with respect to such preceding plan year, and

(ii) as of the first day of the 4th month of the current plan year, the enrolled actuary of the plan has not certified the actual adjusted funding target attainment percentage of the plan for the current plan year,

until the enrolled actuary so certifies, such first day shall be deemed, for purposes of such paragraph, to be the valuation date of the plan for the current plan year and the adjusted funding target attainment percentage of the plan as of such first day shall, for purposes of such paragraph, be presumed to be equal to 10 percentage points less than the adjusted funding target attainment percentage of the plan for such preceding plan year.

(8) Treatment of plan as of close of prohibited or cessation period—For purposes of applying this part—

(A) Operation of plan after period—Unless the plan provides otherwise, payments and accruals will resume effective as of the day following the close of the period for which any limitation of payment or accrual of benefits under paragraph (3) or (4) applies.

(B) Treatment of affected benefits—Nothing in this paragraph shall be construed as affecting the plan's treatment of benefits which would have been paid or accrued but for this subsection.

(9) Terms relating to funding target attainment percentage—For purposes of this subsection—

(A) In general—The term "funding target attainment percentage" has the same meaning given such term by section 303(d)(2).

(B) Adjusted funding target attainment percentage—The term "adjusted funding target attainment percentage" means the funding target attainment percentage which is determined under subparagraph (A) by increasing each of the amounts under subparagraphs (A) and (B) of section 303(d)(2) by the aggregate amount of purchases of annuities for employees other than highly compensated employees (as defined in section 414(q) of the Internal Revenue Code of 1986) which were made by the plan during the preceding 2 plan years.

(C) Application to plans which are fully funded without regard to reductions for funding balances—

(i) In general—In the case of a plan for any plan year, if the funding target attainment percentage is 100 percent or more (determined without regard to the reduction in the value of assets under section 303(f)(4)), the funding target attainment percentage for purposes of subparagraphs (A) and (B) shall be determined without regard to such reduction.

(ii) Transition rule—Clause (i) shall be applied to plan years beginning after 2007 and before 2011 by substituting for "100 percent" the applicable percentage determined in accordance with the following table:

In the case of a plan year beginning in calendar year:	*The applicable percentage is*
2008	92
2009	94
2010	96.

(iii) Limitation—Clause (ii) shall not apply with respect to any plan year beginning after 2008 unless the funding target attainment percentage (determined without regard to without regard to the reduction in the value of assets under section 303(f)(4)) of the plan for each preceding plan year beginning after 2007 was not less than the applicable percentage with respect to such preceding plan year determined under clause (ii).

(D) Special rule for certain years. Solely for purposes of any applicable provision—

(i) In general. For plan years beginning on or after October 1, 2008, and before October 1, 2010, the adjusted funding target attainment percentage of a plan shall be the greater of—

(I) such percentage, as determined without regard to this subparagraph, or

(II) the adjusted funding target attainment percentage for such plan for the plan year beginning after October 1, 2007, and before October 1, 2008, as determined under rules prescribed by the Secretary of the Treasury.

(ii) Special rule. In the case of a plan for which the valuation date is not the first day of the plan year—

(I) clause (i) shall apply to plan years beginning after December 31, 2007, and before January 1, 2010, and

(II) clause (i)(II) shall apply based on the last plan year beginning before November 1, 2007, as determined under rules prescribed by the Secretary of the Treasury.

(iii) Applicable provision. For purposes of this subparagraph, the term "applicable provision" means—

(I) paragraph (3), but only for purposes of applying such paragraph to a payment which, as determined under rules prescribed by the Secretary of the Treasury, is a payment under a social security leveling option which accelerates payments under the plan before, and reduces payments after, a participant starts receiving social security benefits in order to provide substantially similar aggregate payments both before and after such benefits are received, and

(II) paragraph (4).

* * *

§ 208. Mergers and consolidations of plans or transfers of plan assets (§ 1058)

A pension plan may not merge or consolidate with, or transfer its assets or liabilities to, any other plan after September 2, 1974, unless each participant in the plan would (if the plan then terminated) receive a benefit immediately after the merger, consolidation, or transfer which is equal to or greater than the benefit he would have been entitled to receive immediately before the merger, consolidation, or transfer (if the plan had then terminated). The preceding sentence shall not apply to any transaction to the extent that participants either before or after the transaction are covered under a multiemployer plan to which title IV of this Act applies.

Part 3—Funding

§ 301. Coverage (§ 1081)

(a) This part shall apply to any employee pension benefit plan described in section 4(a), (and not exempted under section 4(b)), other than—

(1) an employee welfare benefit plan;

(2) an insurance contract plan described in subsection (b);

(3) a plan which is unfunded and is maintained by an employer primarily for the purpose of providing deferred compensation for a select group of management or highly compensated employees;

(4)(A) a plan which is established and maintained by a society, order, or association described in section 501(c)(8) or (9) of the Internal Revenue Code of 1986, if no part of the contributions to or under such plan are made by employers of participants in such plan; or

(B) a trust described in section 501(c)(18) of such Code;

(5) a plan which has not at any time after September 2, 1974, provided for employer contributions;

(6) an agreement providing payments to a retired partner or deceased partner or a deceased partner's successor in interest as described in section 736 of the Internal Revenue Code of 1986;

(7) an individual retirement account or annuity as described in section 408(a) of the Internal Revenue Code of 1954, or a retirement bond described in section 409 of the Internal Revenue Code of 1954 (as effective for obligations issued before January 1, 1984);

(8) an individual account plan (other than a money purchase plan) and a defined benefit plan to the extent it is treated as an individual account plan (other than a money purchase plan) under section 3(35)(B) of this title;

(9) an excess benefit plan; or

(10) any plan, fund or program under which an employer, all of whose stock is directly or indirectly owned by employees, former employees or their beneficiaries, proposes through an unfunded arrangement to compensate retired employees for benefits which were forfeited by such employees under a pension plan maintained by a former employer prior to the date such pension plan became subject to this Act.

* * *

§ 302. Minimum funding standards (§ 1082)

(a) Requirement to meet minimum funding standard—

(1) In general—A plan to which this part applies shall satisfy the minimum funding standard applicable to the plan for any plan year.

(2) Minimum funding standard—For purposes of paragraph (1), a plan shall be treated as satisfying the minimum funding standard for a plan year if—

(A) in the case of a defined benefit plan which is a single-employer plan, the employer makes contributions to or under the plan for the plan year which, in the aggregate, are not less than the minimum required contribution determined under section 303 for the plan for the plan year,

(B) in the case of a money purchase plan which is a single-employer plan, the employer makes contributions to or under the plan for the plan year which are required under the terms of the plan, and

(C) in the case of a multiemployer plan, the employers make contributions to or under the plan for any plan year which, in the aggregate, are sufficient to ensure that the plan does not have an accumulated funding deficiency under section 304 as of the end of the plan year.

(b) Liability for contributions—

(1) In general—Except as provided in paragraph (2), the amount of any contribution required by this section (including any required installments under paragraphs (3) and (4) of section 303(j)) shall be paid by the employer responsible for making contributions to or under the plan.

(2) Joint and several liability where employer member of controlled group— If the employer referred to in paragraph (1) is a member of a controlled group, each member of such group shall be jointly and severally liable for payment of such contributions.

(3) Multiemployer plans in critical status—Paragraph (1) shall not apply in the case of a multiemployer plan for any plan year in which the plan is in critical status pursuant to section 305. This paragraph shall only apply if the plan sponsor adopts a rehabilitation plan in accordance with section 305(e) and complies with the terms of such rehabilitation plan (and any updates or modifications of the plan).

(c) Variance from minimum funding standards—

(1) Waiver in case of business hardship—

(A) In general—If—

(i) an employer is (or in the case of a multiemployer plan, 10 percent or more of the number of employers contributing to or under the plan are) unable to satisfy the minimum funding standard for a plan year without temporary substantial business hardship (substantial business hardship in the case of a multiemployer plan), and

(ii) application of the standard would be adverse to the interests of plan participants in the aggregate,

the Secretary of the Treasury may, subject to subparagraph (C), waive the requirements of subsection (a) for such year with respect to all or any portion of the minimum funding standard. The Secretary of the Treasury shall not waive the minimum funding standard with respect to a plan for more than 3 of any 15 (5 of any 15 in the case of a multiemployer plan) consecutive plan years.

(B) Effects of waiver—If a waiver is granted under subparagraph (A) for any plan year—

(i) in the case of a single-employer plan, the minimum required contribution under section 303 for the plan year shall be reduced by the amount of the waived funding deficiency and such amount shall be amortized as required under section 303(e), and

(ii) in the case of a multiemployer plan, the funding standard account shall be credited under section 304(b)(3)(C) with the amount of the waived funding deficiency and such amount shall be amortized as required under section 304(b)(2)(C).

(C) Waiver of amortized portion not allowed—The Secretary of the Treasury may not waive under subparagraph (A) any portion of the minimum funding standard under subsection (a) for a plan year which is attributable to any waived funding deficiency for any preceding plan year.

(2) Determination of business hardship—For purposes of this subsection, the factors taken into account in determining temporary substantial business hardship (substantial business hardship in the case of a multiemployer plan) shall include (but shall not be limited to) whether or not—

(A) the employer is operating at an economic loss,

(B) there is substantial unemployment or underemployment in the trade or business and in the industry concerned,

(C) the sales and profits of the industry concerned are depressed or declining, and

(D) it is reasonable to expect that the plan will be continued only if the waiver is granted.

(3) Waived funding deficiency—For purposes of this part, the term "waived funding deficiency" means the portion of the minimum funding standard under subsection (a) (determined without regard to the waiver) for a plan year waived by the Secretary of the Treasury and not satisfied by employer contributions.

(4) Security for waivers for single-employer plans, consultations—

(A) Security may be required—

(i) In general—Except as provided in subparagraph (C), the Secretary of the Treasury may require an employer maintaining a defined benefit plan which is a single-employer plan (within the meaning of section 4001(a)(15)) to provide security to such plan as a condition for granting or modifying a waiver under paragraph (1).

(ii) Special rules—Any security provided under clause (i) may be perfected and enforced only by the Pension Benefit Guaranty Corporation, or at the direction of the Corporation, by a contributing sponsor (within the meaning of section 4001(a)(13)), or a member of such sponsor's controlled group (within the meaning of section 4001(a)(14)).

(B) Consultation with the pension benefit guaranty corporation—Except as provided in subparagraph (C), the Secretary of the Treasury shall, before granting or modifying a waiver under this subsection with respect to a plan described in subparagraph (A)(i)—

(i) provide the Pension Benefit Guaranty Corporation with—

(I) notice of the completed application for any waiver or modification, and

(II) an opportunity to comment on such application within 30 days after receipt of such notice, and

(ii) consider—

(I) any comments of the Corporation under clause (i)(II), and

(II) any views of any employee organization (within the meaning of section 3(4)) representing participants in the plan which are submitted in writing to the Secretary of the Treasury in connection with such application.

Information provided to the Corporation under this subparagraph shall be considered tax return information and subject to the safeguarding and reporting requirements of section 6103(p) of the Internal Revenue Code of 1986.

(C) Exception for certain waivers—

(i) In general—The preceding provisions of this paragraph shall not apply to any plan with respect to which the sum of—

(I) the aggregate unpaid minimum required contributions for the plan year and all preceding plan years, and

(II) the present value of all waiver amortization installments determined for the plan year and succeeding plan years under section 303(e)(2),

is less than $1,000,000.

(ii) Treatment of waivers for which applications are pending—The amount described in clause (i)(I) shall include any increase in such amount which would result if all applications for waivers of the minimum funding standard under this subsection which are pending with respect to such plan were denied.

(iii) Unpaid minimum required contribution—For purposes of this subparagraph—

(I) In general—The term "unpaid minimum required contribution" means, with respect to any plan year, any minimum required contribution under section 303 for the plan year which is not paid on or before the due date (as determined under section 303(j)(1)) for the plan year.

(II) Ordering rule—For purposes of subclause (I), any payment to or under a plan for any plan year shall be allocated first to unpaid minimum required contributions for all preceding plan years on a first-in, first-out basis and then to the minimum required contribution under section 303 for the plan year.

(5) Special rules for single-employer plans—

(A) Application must be submitted before date 2 1/2 months after close of year—In the case of a single-employer plan, no waiver may be granted under this subsection with respect to any plan for any plan year unless an application therefor is submitted to the Secretary of the Treasury not later than the 15th day of the 3rd month beginning after the close of such plan year.

(B) Special rule if employer is member of controlled group—In the case of a single-employer plan, if an employer is a member of a controlled group, the temporary substantial business hardship requirements of paragraph (1) shall be treated as met only if such requirements are met—

(i) with respect to such employer, and

(ii) with respect to the controlled group of which such employer is a member (determined by treating all members of such group as a single employer).

The Secretary of the Treasury may provide that an analysis of a trade or business or industry of a member need not be conducted if such Secretary determines such analysis is not necessary because the taking into account of such member would not significantly affect the determination under this paragraph.

(6) Advance notice—

(A) In general—The Secretary of the Treasury shall, before granting a waiver under this subsection, require each applicant to provide evidence satisfactory to such Secretary that the applicant has provided notice of the filing of the application for such waiver to each affected party (as defined in section 4001(a)(21)). Such notice shall include a description of the extent to which the plan is funded for benefits which are guaranteed under title IV and for benefit liabilities.

(B) Consideration of relevant information—The Secretary of the Treasury shall consider any relevant information provided by a person to whom notice was given under subparagraph (A).

(7) Restriction on plan amendments—

(A) In general—No amendment of a plan which increases the liabilities of the plan by reason of any increase in benefits, any change in the accrual of benefits, or any change in the rate at which benefits become nonforfeitable under the plan shall be adopted if a waiver under this subsection or an extension of time under section 304(d) is in effect with respect to the plan, or if a plan amendment described in subsection (d)(2) which reduces the accrued benefit of any participant has been made at any time in the preceding 12 months (24 months in the case of a multiemployer plan). If a plan is amended in violation of the preceding sentence, any such waiver, or extension of time, shall not apply to any plan year ending on or after the date on which such amendment is adopted.

(B) Exception—Subparagraph (A) shall not apply to any plan amendment which—

(i) the Secretary of the Treasury determines to be reasonable and which provides for only de minimis increases in the liabilities of the plan,

(ii) only repeals an amendment described in subsection (d)(2), or

(iii) is required as a condition of qualification under part I of subchapter D of chapter 1 of the Internal Revenue Code of 1986.

(8) Cross reference—For corresponding duties of the Secretary of the Treasury with regard to implementation of the Internal Revenue Code of 1986, see section 412(c) of such Code.

(d) Miscellaneous rules—

(1) Change in method or year—If the funding method or a plan year for a plan is changed, the change shall take effect only if approved by the Secretary of the Treasury.

(2) Certain retroactive plan amendments—For purposes of this section, any amendment applying to a plan year which—

(A) is adopted after the close of such plan year but no later than 2 1/2 months after the close of the plan year (or, in the case of a multiemployer plan, no later than 2 years after the close of such plan year),

(B) does not reduce the accrued benefit of any participant determined as of the beginning of the first plan year to which the amendment applies, and

(C) does not reduce the accrued benefit of any participant determined as of the time of adoption except to the extent required by the circumstances, shall, at the election of the plan administrator, be deemed to have been made on the first day of such plan year. No amendment described in this paragraph which reduces the accrued benefits of any participant shall take effect unless the plan administrator files a notice with the Secretary of the Treasury notifying him of such amendment and such Secretary has approved such amendment, or within 90 days after the date on which such notice was filed, failed to disapprove such amendment. No amendment described in this subsection shall be approved by the Secretary of the Treasury unless such Secretary determines that such amendment is necessary because of a temporary substantial business hardship (as determined under subsection (c)(2)) or a substantial business hardship (as so determined) in the case of a multiemployer plan and that a waiver under subsection (c) (or, in the case of a multiemployer plan, any extension of the amortization period under section 304(d)) is unavailable or inadequate.

(3) Controlled group—For purposes of this section, the term "controlled group" means any group treated as a single employer under subsection (b), (c), (m), or (o) of section 414 of the Internal Revenue Code of 1986.

§ 303. Minimum funding standards for single-employer defined benefit pension plans (§ 1083)

(a) Minimum required contribution—For purposes of this section and section 302(a)(2)(A), except as provided in subsection (f), the term "minimum required contribution" means, with respect to any plan year of a single-employer plan—

(1) in any case in which the value of plan assets of the plan (as reduced under subsection (f)(4)(B)) is less than the funding target of the plan for the plan year, the sum of—

(A) the target normal cost of the plan for the plan year,

(B) the shortfall amortization charge (if any) for the plan for the plan year determined under subsection (c), and

(C) the waiver amortization charge (if any) for the plan for the plan year as determined under subsection (e); or

(2) in any case in which the value of plan assets of the plan (as reduced under subsection (f)(4)(B)) equals or exceeds the funding target of the plan for the plan year, the target normal cost of the plan for the plan year reduced (but not below zero) by such excess.

(b) Target normal cost—For purposes of this section:

(1) In general— Except as provided in subsection (i)(2) with respect to plans in at-risk status, the term “target normal cost” means, for any plan year, the excess of—

(A) the sum of—

(i) the present value of all benefits which are expected to accrue or to be earned under the plan during the plan year, plus

(ii) the amount of plan-related expenses expected to be paid from plan assets during the plan year, over

(B) the amount of mandatory employee contributions expected to be made during the plan year.

(2) Special rule for increase in compensation—For purposes of this subsection, if any benefit attributable to services performed in a preceding plan year is increased by reason of any increase in compensation during the current plan year, the increase in such benefit shall be treated as having accrued during the current plan year.

(c) Shortfall amortization charge—

(1) In general—For purposes of this section, the shortfall amortization charge for a plan for any plan year is the aggregate total (not less than zero) of the shortfall amortization installments for such plan year with respect to any shortfall amortization base which has not been fully amortized under this subsection.

(2) Shortfall amortization installment—For purposes of paragraph (1)—

(A) Determination—The shortfall amortization installments are the amounts necessary to amortize the shortfall amortization base of the plan for any plan year in level annual installments over the 7-plan-year period beginning with such plan year.

(B) Shortfall installment—The shortfall amortization installment for any plan year in the 7-plan-year period under subparagraph (A) with respect to any shortfall amortization base is the annual installment determined under subparagraph (A) for that year for that base.

(C) Segment rates—In determining any shortfall amortization installment under this paragraph, the plan sponsor shall use the segment rates determined under subparagraph (C) of subsection (h)(2), applied under rules similar to the rules of subparagraph (B) of subsection (h)(2).

(D) Special election for eligible plan years.

(i) In general. If a plan sponsor elects to apply this subparagraph with respect to the shortfall amortization base of a plan for any eligible plan year (in this subparagraph and paragraph (7) referred to as an 'election year'), then, notwithstanding subparagraphs (A) and (B)—

(I) the shortfall amortization installments with respect to such base shall be determined under clause (ii) or (iii), whichever is specified in the election, and

(II) the shortfall amortization installment for any plan year in the 9-plan-year period described in clause (ii) or the 15-plan-year period described in clause (iii), respectively, with respect to such shortfall amortization base is the annual installment determined under the applicable clause for that year for that base.

(ii) 2 plus 7 amortization schedule. The shortfall amortization installments determined under this clause are—

(I) in the case of the first 2 plan years in the 9-plan-year period beginning with the election year, interest on the shortfall amortization base of the plan for the election year (determined using the effective interest rate for the plan for the election year), and

(II) in the case of the last 7 plan years in such 9-plan-year period, the amounts necessary to amortize the remaining balance of the shortfall amortization base of the plan for the election year in level annual installments over such last 7 plan years (using the segment rates under subparagraph (C) for the election year).

(iii) 15-year amortization. The shortfall amortization installments determined under this subparagraph are the amounts necessary to amortize the shortfall amortization base of the plan for the election year in level annual installments over the 15-plan-year period beginning with the election year (using the segment rates under subparagraph (C) for the election year).

(iv) Election.

(I) In general. The plan sponsor of a plan may elect to have this subparagraph apply to not more than 2 eligible plan years with respect to the plan, except that in the case of a plan described in section 106 of the Pension Protection Act of 2006, the plan sponsor may only elect to have this subparagraph apply to a plan year beginning in 2011.

(II) Amortization schedule. Such election shall specify whether the amortization schedule under clause (ii) or (iii) shall apply to an election year, except that if a plan sponsor elects to have this subparagraph apply to 2 eligible plan years, the plan sponsor must elect the same schedule for both years.

(III) Other rules. Such election shall be made at such time, and in such form and manner, as shall be prescribed by the Secretary of the Treasury, and may be revoked only with the consent of the Secretary of the Treasury. The Secretary of the Treasury shall, before granting a revocation request, provide the Pension Benefit Guaranty Corporation an opportunity to comment on the conditions applicable to the treatment of any portion of the election year shortfall amortization base that remains unamortized as of the revocation date.

(v) Eligible plan year. For purposes of this subparagraph, the term "eligible plan year" means any plan year beginning in 2008, 2009, 2010, or 2011, except that a plan year shall only be treated as an eligible plan year if the due date under subsection (j)(1) for the payment of the minimum required contribution for such plan year occurs on or after the date of the enactment of this subparagraph.

(vi) Reporting. A plan sponsor of a plan who makes an election under clause (i) shall—

(I) give notice of the election to participants and beneficiaries of the plan, and

(II) inform the Pension Benefit Guaranty Corporation of such election in such form and manner as the Director of the Pension Benefit Guaranty Corporation may prescribe.

(vii) Increases in required installments in certain cases. For increases in required contributions in cases of excess compensation or extraordinary dividends or stock redemptions, see paragraph (7).

(3) Shortfall amortization base—For purposes of this section, the shortfall amortization base of a plan for a plan year is—

(A) the funding shortfall of such plan for such plan year, minus

(B) the present value (determined using the segment rates determined under subparagraph (C) of subsection (h)(2), applied under rules similar to the rules of subparagraph (B) of subsection (h)(2)) of the aggregate total of the shortfall amortization installments and waiver amortization installments which have been determined for such plan year and any succeeding plan year with respect to the shortfall amortization bases and waiver amortization bases of the plan for any plan year preceding such plan year.

(4) Funding shortfall—For purposes of this section, the funding shortfall of a plan for any plan year is the excess (if any) of—

(A) the funding target of the plan for the plan year, over

(B) the value of plan assets of the plan (as reduced under subsection (f)(4)(B)) for the plan year which are held by the plan on the valuation date.

(5) Exemption from new shortfall amortization base—

(A) In general—In any case in which the value of plan assets of the plan (as reduced under subsection (f)(4)(A)) is equal to or greater than the funding target of the plan for the plan year, the shortfall amortization base of the plan for such plan year shall be zero.

(B) Transition rule—

(i) In general—Except as provided in clause (iii), in the case of plan years beginning after 2007 and before 2011, only the applicable percentage of the funding target shall be taken into account under paragraph (3)(A) in determining the funding shortfall for purposes of paragraph (3)(A) and subparagraph (A).

(ii) Applicable percentage—For purposes of subparagraph (A), the applicable percentage shall be determined in accordance with the following table:

In the case of a plan year beginning in calendar year:	*The applicable percentage is*
2008	92
2009	94
2010	96.

(iii) Transition relief not available for new or deficit reduction plans— Clause (i) shall not apply to a plan—

(I) which was not in effect for a plan year beginning in 2007, or

(II) which was in effect for a plan year beginning in 2007 and which was subject to section 302(d) (as in effect for plan years beginning in 2007) for such year, determined after the application of paragraphs (6) and (9) thereof.

(6) Early deemed amortization upon attainment of funding target—In any case in which the funding shortfall of a plan for a plan year is zero, for purposes of determining the shortfall amortization charge for such plan year and succeeding plan years, the shortfall amortization bases for all preceding plan years (and all shortfall amortization installments determined with respect to such bases) shall be reduced to zero.

(7) Increases in alternate required installments in cases of excess compensation or extraordinary dividends or stock redemptions.

(A) In general. If there is an installment acceleration amount with respect to a plan for any plan year in the restriction period with respect to an election year under paragraph (2)(D), then the shortfall amortization installment otherwise determined and payable under such paragraph for such plan year shall, subject to the limitation under subparagraph (B), be increased by such amount.

(B) Total installments limited to shortfall base. Subject to rules prescribed by the Secretary of the Treasury, if a shortfall amortization installment with respect to any shortfall amortization base for an election year is required to be increased for any plan year under subparagraph (A)—

(i) such increase shall not result in the amount of such installment exceeding the present value of such installment and all succeeding installments with respect to such base (determined without regard to such increase but after application of clause (ii)), and

(ii) subsequent shortfall amortization installments with respect to such base shall, in reverse order of the otherwise required installments, be reduced to the extent necessary to limit the present value of such subsequent shortfall amortization installments (after application of this paragraph) to the present value of the remaining unamortized shortfall amortization base.

(C) Installment acceleration amount. For purposes of this paragraph—

(i) In general. The term "installment acceleration amount" means, with respect to any plan year in a restriction period with respect to an election year, the sum of—

(I) the aggregate amount of excess employee compensation determined under subparagraph (D) with respect to all employees for the plan year, plus

(II) the aggregate amount of extraordinary dividends and redemptions determined under subparagraph (E) for the plan year.

(ii) Annual limitation. The installment acceleration amount for any plan year shall not exceed the excess (if any) of—

(I) the sum of the shortfall amortization installments for the plan year and all preceding plan years in the amortization period elected under paragraph (2)(D) with respect to the shortfall amortization base with respect to an election year, determined without regard to paragraph (2)(D) and this paragraph, over

(II) the sum of the shortfall amortization installments for such plan year and all such preceding plan years, determined after application of paragraph (2)(D) (and in the case of any preceding plan year, after application of this paragraph).

(iii) Carryover of excess installment acceleration amounts.

(I) In general. If the installment acceleration amount for any plan year (determined without regard to clause (ii)) exceeds the limitation under clause (ii), then, subject to subclause (II), such excess shall be treated as an installment acceleration amount with respect to the succeeding plan year.

(II) Cap to apply. If any amount treated as an installment acceleration amount under subclause (I) or this subclause with respect any succeeding plan year, when added to other installment acceleration amounts (determined without regard to clause (ii)) with respect to the plan year, exceeds the limitation under clause (ii), the portion of such amount representing such excess shall be treated as an installment acceleration amount with respect to the next succeeding plan year.

(III) Limitation on years to which amounts carried for. No amount shall be carried under subclause (I) or (II) to a plan year which begins after the first plan year following the last plan year in the restriction period (or after the second plan year following such last plan year in the case of an election year with respect to which 15-year amortization was elected under paragraph (2)(D)).

(IV) Ordering rules. For purposes of applying subclause (II), installment acceleration amounts for the plan year (determined without regard to any carryover under this clause) shall be applied first against the limitation under clause (ii) and then carryovers to such plan year shall be applied against such limitation on a first-in, first-out basis.

(D) Excess employee compensation. For purposes of this paragraph—

(i) In general. The term "excess employee compensation" means, with respect to any employee for any plan year, the excess (if any) of—

(I) the aggregate amount includible in income under chapter 1 of the Internal Revenue Code of 1986 for remuneration during the calendar year in which such plan year begins for services performed by the employee for the plan sponsor (whether or not performed during such calendar year), over

(II) $ 1,000,000.

(ii) Amounts set aside for nonqualified deferred compensation. If during any calendar year assets are set aside or reserved (directly or indirectly) in a trust (or other arrangement as determined by the Secretary of the Treasury), or transferred to such a trust or other arrangement, by a plan sponsor for purposes of paying deferred compensation of an employee under a nonqualified deferred compensation plan (as defined in section 409A of such Code) of the plan sponsor, then, for purposes of clause (i), the amount of such assets shall be treated as remuneration of the employee includible in income for the calendar year unless such amount is otherwise includible in income for such year. An amount to which the preceding sentence applies shall not be taken into account under this paragraph for any subsequent calendar year.

(iii) Only remuneration for certain post-2009 services counted. Remuneration shall be taken into account under clause (i) only to the extent attributable to services performed by the employee for the plan sponsor after February 28, 2010.

(iv) Exception for certain equity payments.

(I) In general. There shall not be taken into account under clause (i)(I) any amount includible in income with respect to the granting after February 28, 2010, of service recipient stock (within the meaning of section 409A of the Internal Revenue Code of 1986) that, upon such grant, is subject to a substantial risk of forfeiture (as defined under section 83(c)(1) of such Code) for at least 5 years from the date of such grant.

(II) Secretarial authority. The Secretary of the Treasury may by regulation provide for the application of this clause in the case of a person other than a corporation.

(v) Other exceptions. The following amounts includible in income shall not be taken into account under clause (i)(I):

(I) Commissions. Any remuneration payable on a commission basis solely on account of income directly generated by the individual performance of the individual to whom such remuneration is payable.

(II) Certain payments under existing contracts. Any remuneration consisting of nonqualified deferred compensation, restricted stock, stock options, or stock appreciation rights payable or granted under a written binding contract that was in effect on March 1, 2010, and which was not modified in any material respect before such remuneration is paid.

(vi) Self-employed individual treated as employee. The term "employee" includes, with respect to a calendar year, a self-employed individual who is treated as an employee under section 401(c) of such Code for the taxable year ending during such calendar year, and the term 'compensation' shall include earned income of such individual with respect to such self-employment.

(vii) Indexing of amount. In the case of any calendar year beginning after 2010, the dollar amount under clause (i)(II) shall be increased by an amount equal to—

(I) such dollar amount, multiplied by

(II) the cost-of-living adjustment determined under section 1(f)(3) of such Code for the calendar year, determined by substituting "calendar year 2009" for "calendar year 1992" in subparagraph (B) thereof.

If the amount of any increase under clause (i) is not a multiple of $ 1,000, such increase shall be rounded to the next lowest multiple of $ 1,000.

(E) Extraordinary dividends and redemptions.

(i) In general. The amount determined under this subparagraph for any plan year is the excess (if any) of the sum of the dividends declared during the plan year by the plan sponsor plus the aggregate amount paid for the redemption of stock of the plan sponsor redeemed during the plan year over the greater of—

(I) the adjusted net income (within the meaning of section 4043) of the plan sponsor for the preceding plan year, determined without regard to any reduction by reason of interest, taxes, depreciation, or amortization, or

(II) in the case of a plan sponsor that determined and declared dividends in the same manner for at least 5 consecutive years immediately preceding such plan year, the aggregate amount of dividends determined and declared for such plan year using such manner.

(ii) Only certain post-2009 dividends and redemptions counted. For purposes of clause (i), there shall only be taken into account dividends declared, and redemptions occurring, after February 28, 2010.

(iii) Exception for intra-group dividends. Dividends paid by one member of a controlled group (as defined in section 302(d)(3)) to another member of such group shall not be taken into account under clause (i).

(iv) Exception for certain redemptions. Redemptions that are made pursuant to a plan maintained with respect to employees, or that are made on account of the death, disability, or termination of employment of an employee or shareholder, shall not be taken into account under clause (i).

(v) Exception for certain preferred stock.

(I) In general. Dividends and redemptions with respect to applicable preferred stock shall not be taken into account under clause (i) to the extent that dividends accrue with respect to such stock at a specified rate in all events and without regard to the plan sponsor's income, and interest accrues on any unpaid dividends with respect to such stock.

(II) Applicable preferred stock. For purposes of subclause (I), the term "applicable preferred stock" means preferred stock which was issued before March 1, 2010 (or which was issued after such date and is held by an employee benefit plan subject to the provisions of this title).

(F) Other definitions and rules. For purposes of this paragraph—

(i) Plan sponsor. The term " plan sponsor" includes any member of the plan sponsor's controlled group (as defined in section 302(d)(3)).

(ii) Restriction period. The term "restriction period" means, with respect to any election year—

(I) except as provided in subclause (II), the 3-year period beginning with the election year (or, if later, the first plan year beginning after December 31, 2009), and

(II) if the plan sponsor elects 15-year amortization for the shortfall amortization base for the election year, the 5-year period beginning with the election year (or, if later, the first plan year beginning after December 31, 2009).

(iii) Elections for multiple plans. If a plan sponsor makes elections under paragraph (2)(D) with respect to 2 or more plans, the Secretary of the Treasury shall provide rules for the application of this paragraph to such plans, including rules for the ratable allocation of any installment acceleration amount among such plans on the basis of each plan's relative reduction in the plan's shortfall amortization installment for the first plan year in the amortization period described in subparagraph (A) (determined without regard to this paragraph).

(iv) Mergers and acquisitions. The Secretary of the Treasury shall prescribe rules for the application of paragraph (2)(D) and this paragraph in any case where there is a merger or acquisition involving a plan sponsor making the election under paragraph (2)(D).

(d) Rules relating to funding target—For purposes of this section—

(1) Funding target—Except as provided in subsection (i)(1) with respect to plans in at-risk status, the funding target of a plan for a plan year is the present value of all benefits accrued or earned under the plan as of the beginning of the plan year.

(2) Funding target attainment percentage—The "funding target attainment percentage" of a plan for a plan year is the ratio (expressed as a percentage) which—

(A) the value of plan assets for the plan year (as reduced under subsection (f)(4)(B)), bears to

(B) the funding target of the plan for the plan year (determined without regard to subsection (i)(1)).

(e) Waiver amortization charge—

(1) Determination of waiver amortization charge—The waiver amortization charge (if any) for a plan for any plan year is the aggregate total of the waiver amortization installments for such plan year with respect to the waiver amortization bases for each of the 5 preceding plan years.

(2) Waiver amortization installment—For purposes of paragraph (1)—

(A) Determination—The waiver amortization installments are the amounts necessary to amortize the waiver amortization base of the plan for any plan year in level annual installments over a period of 5 plan years beginning with the succeeding plan year.

(B) Waiver installment—The waiver amortization installment for any plan year in the 5-year period under subparagraph (A) with respect to any waiver amortization base is the annual installment determined under subparagraph (A) for that year for that base.

(3) Interest rate—In determining any waiver amortization installment under this subsection, the plan sponsor shall use the segment rates determined under subparagraph (C) of subsection (h)(2), applied under rules similar to the rules of subparagraph (B) of subsection (h)(2).

(4) Waiver amortization base—The waiver amortization base of a plan for a plan year is the amount of the waived funding deficiency (if any) for such plan year under section 302(c).

(5) Early deemed amortization upon attainment of funding target—In any case in which the funding shortfall of a plan for a plan year is zero, for purposes of determining the waiver amortization charge for such plan year and succeeding plan years, the waiver amortization bases for all preceding plan years (and all waiver amortization installments determined with respect to such bases) shall be reduced to zero.

(f) Reduction of minimum required contribution by prefunding balance and funding standard carryover balance—

(1) Election to maintain balances—

(A) Prefunding balance—The plan sponsor of a single-employer plan may elect to maintain a prefunding balance.

(B) Funding standard carryover balance—

(i) In general—In the case of a single-employer plan described in clause (ii), the plan sponsor may elect to maintain a funding standard carryover balance, until such balance is reduced to zero.

(ii) Plans maintaining funding standard account in 2007—A plan is described in this clause if the plan—

(I) was in effect for a plan year beginning in 2007, and

(II) had a positive balance in the funding standard account under section 302(b) as in effect for such plan year and determined as of the end of such plan year.

(2) Application of balances—A prefunding balance and a funding standard carryover balance maintained pursuant to this paragraph—

(A) shall be available for crediting against the minimum required contribution, pursuant to an election under paragraph (3),

(B) shall be applied as a reduction in the amount treated as the value of plan assets for purposes of this section, to the extent provided in paragraph (4), and

(C) may be reduced at any time, pursuant to an election under paragraph (5).

(3) Election to apply balances against minimum required contribution—

(A) In general—Except as provided in subparagraphs (B) and (C), in the case of any plan year in which the plan sponsor elects to credit against the minimum required contribution for the current plan year all or a portion of the prefunding balance or the funding standard carryover balance for the current plan year (not in excess of such minimum required contribution), the minimum required contribution for the plan year shall be reduced as of the first day of the plan year by the amount so credited by the plan sponsor. For purposes of the preceding sentence, the minimum required contribution shall be determined after taking into account any waiver under section 302(c).

(B) Coordination with funding standard carryover balance—To the extent that any plan has a funding standard carryover balance greater than zero, no amount of the prefunding balance of such plan may be credited under this paragraph in reducing the minimum required contribution.

(C) Limitation for underfunded plans—The preceding provisions of this paragraph shall not apply for any plan year if the ratio (expressed as a percentage) which—

(i) the value of plan assets for the preceding plan year (as reduced under paragraph (4)(C)), bears to

(ii) the funding target of the plan for the preceding plan year (determined without regard to subsection (i)(1)),

is less than 80 percent. In the case of plan years beginning in 2008, the ratio under this subparagraph may be determined using such methods of estimation as the Secretary of the Treasury may prescribe.

(D) Special rule for certain years of plans maintained by charities.

(i) In general. For purposes of applying subparagraph (C) for plan years beginning after August 31, 2009, and before September 1, 2011, the ratio determined under such subparagraph for the preceding plan year shall be the greater of—

(I) such ratio, as determined without regard to this subparagraph, or

(II) the ratio for such plan for the plan year beginning after August 31, 2007, and before September 1, 2008, as determined under rules prescribed by the Secretary of the Treasury.

(ii) Special rule. In the case of a plan for which the valuation date is not the first day of the plan year—

(I) clause (i) shall apply to plan years beginning after December 31, 2008, and before January 1, 2011, and

(II) clause (i)(II) shall apply based on the last plan year beginning before September 1, 2007, as determined under rules prescribed by the Secretary of the Treasury.

(iii) Limitation to charities. This subparagraph shall not apply to any plan unless such plan is maintained exclusively by one or more organizations described in section 501(c)(3) of the Internal Revenue Code of 1986.

(4) Effect of balances on amounts treated as value of plan assets—In the case of any plan maintaining a prefunding balance or a funding standard carryover balance pursuant to this subsection, the amount treated as the value of plan assets shall be deemed to be such amount, reduced as provided in the following subparagraphs:

(A) Applicability of shortfall amortization base—For purposes of subsection (c)(5), the value of plan assets is deemed to be such amount, reduced by the amount of the prefunding balance, but only if an election under paragraph (3) applying any portion of the prefunding balance in reducing the minimum required contribution is in effect for the plan year.

(B) Determination of excess assets, funding shortfall, and funding target attainment percentage—

(i) In general—For purposes of subsections (a), (c)(4)(B), and (d)(2)(A), the value of plan assets is deemed to be such amount, reduced by the amount of the prefunding balance and the funding standard carryover balance.

(ii) Special rule for certain binding agreements with PBGC—For purposes of subsection (c)(4)(B), the value of plan assets shall not be deemed to be reduced for a plan year by the amount of the specified balance if, with respect to such balance, there is in effect for a plan year a binding written agreement with the Pension Benefit Guaranty Corporation which provides that such balance is not available to reduce the minimum required contribution for the plan year. For purposes of the preceding sentence, the term "specified balance" means the prefunding balance or the funding standard carryover balance, as the case may be.

(C) Availability of balances in plan year for crediting against minimum required contribution—For purposes of paragraph (3)(C)(i) of this subsection, the value of plan assets is deemed to be such amount, reduced by the amount of the prefunding balance.

(5) Election to reduce balance prior to determinations of value of plan assets and crediting against minimum required contribution—

(A) In general—The plan sponsor may elect to reduce by any amount the balance of the prefunding balance and the funding standard carryover balance for any plan year (but not below zero). Such reduction shall be effective prior to any determination of the value of plan assets for such plan year under this section and application of the balance in reducing the minimum required contribution for such plan for such plan year pursuant to an election under paragraph (2).

(B) Coordination between prefunding balance and funding standard carryover balance—To the extent that any plan has a funding standard carryover balance greater than zero, no election may be made under subparagraph (A) with respect to the prefunding balance.

(6) Prefunding balance—

(A) In general—A prefunding balance maintained by a plan shall consist of a beginning balance of zero, increased and decreased to the extent provided in subparagraphs (B) and (C), and adjusted further as provided in paragraph (8).

(B) Increases—

(i) In general—As of the first day of each plan year beginning after 2008, the prefunding balance of a plan shall be increased by the amount elected by the plan sponsor for the plan year. Such amount shall not exceed the excess (if any) of—

(I) the aggregate total of employer contributions to the plan for the preceding plan year, over—

(II) the minimum required contribution for such preceding plan year.

(ii) Adjustments for interest—Any excess contributions under clause (i) shall be properly adjusted for interest accruing for the periods between the first day of the current plan year and the dates on which the excess contributions were made, determined by using the effective interest rate for the preceding plan year and by treating contributions as being first used to satisfy the minimum required contribution.

(iii) Certain contributions necessary to avoid benefit limitations disregarded—The excess described in clause (i) with respect to any preceding plan year shall be reduced (but not below zero) by the amount of contributions an employer would be required to make under paragraph (1), (2), or (4) of section 206(g) to avoid a benefit limitation which would otherwise be imposed under such paragraph for the preceding plan year. Any contribution which may be taken into account in satisfying the requirements of more than 1 of such paragraphs shall be taken into account only once for purposes of this clause.

(C) Decrease—The prefunding balance of a plan shall be decreased (but not below zero) by—

(i) as of the first day of each plan year after 2008, the amount of such balance credited under paragraph (2) (if any) in reducing the minimum required contribution of the plan for the preceding plan year, and

(ii) as of the time specified in paragraph (5)(A), any reduction in such balance elected under paragraph (5).

(7) Funding standard carryover balance—

(A) In general—A funding standard carryover balance maintained by a plan shall consist of a beginning balance determined under subparagraph (B), decreased to the extent provided in subparagraph (C), and adjusted further as provided in paragraph (8).

(B) Beginning balance—The beginning balance of the funding standard carryover balance shall be the positive balance described in paragraph (1)(B)(ii)(II).

(C) Decreases—The funding standard carryover balance of a plan shall be decreased (but not below zero) by—

(i) as of the first day of each plan year after 2008, the amount of such balance credited under paragraph (2) (if any) in reducing the minimum required contribution of the plan for the preceding plan year, and

(ii) as of the time specified in paragraph (5)(A), any reduction in such balance elected under paragraph (5).

(8) Adjustments for investment experience—In determining the prefunding balance or the funding standard carryover balance of a plan as of the first day of the plan year, the plan sponsor shall, in accordance with regulations prescribed by the Secretary of the Treasury, adjust such balance to reflect the rate of return on plan assets for the preceding plan year. Notwithstanding subsection (g)(3), such rate of return shall be determined on the basis of fair market value and shall properly take into account, in accordance with such regulations, all contributions, distributions, and other plan payments made during such period.

(9) Elections—Elections under this subsection shall be made at such times, and in such form and manner, as shall be prescribed in regulations of the Secretary of the Treasury.

(g) Valuation of plan assets and liabilities—

(1) Timing of determinations—Except as otherwise provided under this subsection, all determinations under this section for a plan year shall be made as of the valuation date of the plan for such plan year.

(2) Valuation date—For purposes of this section—

(A) In general—Except as provided in subparagraph (B), the valuation date of a plan for any plan year shall be the first day of the plan year.

(B) Exception for small plans—If, on each day during the preceding plan year, a plan had 100 or fewer participants, the plan may designate any day during the plan year as its valuation date for such plan year and succeeding plan years. For purposes of this subparagraph, all defined benefit plans which are single-employer plans and are maintained by the same employer (or any member of such employer's controlled group) shall be treated as 1 plan, but only participants with respect to such employer or member shall be taken into account.

(C) Application of certain rules in determination of plan size—For purposes of this paragraph—

(i) Plans not in existence in preceding year—In the case of the first plan year of any plan, subparagraph (B) shall apply to such plan by taking into account the number of participants that the plan is reasonably expected to have on days during such first plan year.

(ii) Predecessors—Any reference in subparagraph (B) to an employer shall include a reference to any predecessor of such employer.

(3) Determination of value of plan assets—For purposes of this section—

(A) In general—Except as provided in subparagraph (B), the value of plan assets shall be the fair market value of the assets.

(B) Averaging allowed—A plan may determine the value of plan assets on the basis of the averaging of fair market values, but only if such method—

(i) is permitted under regulations prescribed by the Secretary of the Treasury,

(ii) does not provide for averaging of such values over more than the period beginning on the last day of the 25th month preceding the month in which the valuation date occurs and ending on the valuation date (or a similar period in the case of a valuation date which is not the 1st day of a month), and

(iii) does not result in a determination of the value of plan assets which, at any time, is lower than 90 percent or greater than 110 percent of the fair market value of such assets at such time.

Any such averaging shall be adjusted for contributions, distributions, and expected earnings (as determined by the plan's actuary on the basis of an assumed earnings rate specified by the actuary but not in excess of the third segment rate applicable under subsection (h)(2)(C)(iii)), as specified by the Secretary of the Treasury.

(4) Accounting for contribution receipts—For purposes of determining the value of assets under paragraph (3)—

(A) Prior year contributions—If—

(i) an employer makes any contribution to the plan after the valuation date for the plan year in which the contribution is made, and

(ii) the contribution is for a preceding plan year,

the contribution shall be taken into account as an asset of the plan as of the valuation date, except that in the case of any plan year beginning after 2008, only the present value (determined as of the valuation date) of such contribution may be taken into account. For purposes of the preceding sentence, present value shall be determined using the effective interest rate for the preceding plan year to which the contribution is properly allocable.

(B) Special rule for current year contributions made before valuation date—If any contributions for any plan year are made to or under the plan during the plan year but before the valuation date for the plan year, the assets of the plan as of the valuation date shall not include—

(i) such contributions, and

(ii) interest on such contributions for the period between the date of the contributions and the valuation date, determined by using the effective interest rate for the plan year.

(h) Actuarial assumptions and methods—

(1) In general—Subject to this subsection, the determination of any present value or other computation under this section shall be made on the basis of actuarial assumptions and methods—

(A) each of which is reasonable (taking into account the experience of the plan and reasonable expectations), and

(B) which, in combination, offer the actuary's best estimate of anticipated experience under the plan.

(2) Interest rates—

(A) Effective interest rate—For purposes of this section, the term "effective interest rate" means, with respect to any plan for any plan year, the single rate of interest which, if used to determine the present value of the plan's accrued or earned benefits referred to in subsection (d)(1), would result in an amount equal to the funding target of the plan for such plan year.

(B) Interest rates for determining funding target—For purposes of determining the funding target and normal cost of a plan for any plan year, the interest rate used in determining the present value of the benefits of the plan shall be—

(i) in the case of benefits reasonably determined to be payable during the 5-year period beginning on the first day of the plan year, the first segment rate with respect to the applicable month,

(ii) in the case of benefits reasonably determined to be payable during the 15-year period beginning at the end of the period described in clause (i), the second segment rate with respect to the applicable month, and

(iii) in the case of benefits reasonably determined to be payable after the period described in clause (ii), the third segment rate with respect to the applicable month.

(C) Segment rates—For purposes of this paragraph—

(i) First segment rate—The term "first segment rate" means, with respect to any month, the single rate of interest which shall be determined by the Secretary of the Treasury for such month on the basis of the corporate bond yield curve for such month, taking into account only that portion of such yield curve which is based on bonds maturing during the 5-year period commencing with such month.

(ii) Second segment rate—The term "second segment rate" means, with respect to any month, the single rate of interest which shall be determined by the Secretary of the Treasury for such month on the basis of the corporate bond yield curve for such month, taking into account only that portion of such yield curve which is based on bonds maturing during the 15- year period beginning at the end of the period described in clause (i).

(iii) Third segment rate—The term "third segment rate" means, with respect to any month, the single rate of interest which shall be determined by the Secretary of the Treasury for such month on the basis of the corporate bond yield curve for such month, taking into account only that portion of such yield curve which is based on bonds maturing during periods beginning after the period described in clause (ii).

(D) Corporate bond yield curve—For purposes of this paragraph—

(i) In general—The term "corporate bond yield curve" means, with respect to any month, a yield curve which is prescribed by the Secretary of the Treasury for such month and which reflects the average, for the 24-month period ending with the month preceding such month, of monthly yields on investment grade corporate bonds with varying maturities and that are in the top 3 quality levels available.

(ii) Election to use yield curve—Solely for purposes of determining the minimum required contribution under this section, the plan sponsor may, in lieu of the segment rates determined under subparagraph (C), elect to use interest rates under the corporate bond yield curve. For purposes of the preceding sentence such curve shall be determined without regard to the 24- month averaging described in clause (i). Such election, once made, may be revoked only with the consent of the Secretary of the Treasury.

(E) Applicable month—For purposes of this paragraph, the term "applicable month" means, with respect to any plan for any plan year, the month which includes the valuation date of such plan for such plan year or, at the election of the plan sponsor, any of the 4 months which precede such month. Any election made under this subparagraph shall apply to the plan year for which the election is made and all succeeding plan years, unless the election is revoked with the consent of the Secretary of the Treasury.

(F) Publication requirements—The Secretary of the Treasury shall publish for each month the corporate bond yield curve (and the corporate bond yield curve reflecting the modification described in section 205(g)(3)(B)(iii)(I) for such month) and each of the rates determined under subparagraph (C) for such month. The Secretary of the Treasury shall also publish a description of the methodology used to determine such yield curve and such rates which is sufficiently detailed to enable plans to make reasonable projections regarding the yield curve and such rates for future months based on the plan's projection of future interest rates.

* * *

(3) Mortality tables—

(A) In general—Except as provided in subparagraph (C) or (D), the Secretary of the Treasury shall by regulation prescribe mortality tables to be used in determining any present value or making any computation under this section. Such tables shall be based on the actual experience of pension plans and projected trends in such experience. In prescribing such tables, the Secretary of the Treasury shall take into account results of available independent studies of mortality of individuals covered by pension plans.

(B) Periodic revision—The Secretary of the Treasury shall (at least every 10 years) make revisions in any table in effect under subparagraph (A) to reflect the actual experience of pension plans and projected trends in such experience.

(C) Substitute mortality table—

(i) In general—Upon request by the plan sponsor and approval by the Secretary of the Treasury, a mortality table which meets the requirements of clause (iii) shall be used in determining any present value or making any computation under this section during the period of consecutive plan years (not to exceed 10) specified in the request.

(ii) Early termination of period—Notwithstanding clause (i), a mortality table described in clause (i) shall cease to be in effect as of the earliest of—

(I) the date on which there is a significant change in the participants in the plan by reason of a plan spinoff or merger or otherwise, or

(II) the date on which the plan actuary determines that such table does not meet the requirements of clause (iii).

(iii) Requirements—A mortality table meets the requirements of this clause if—

(I) there is a sufficient number of plan participants, and the pension plans have been maintained for a sufficient period of time, to have credible information necessary for purposes of subclause (II), and

(II) such table reflects the actual experience of the pension plans maintained by the sponsor and projected trends in general mortality experience.

(iv) All plans in controlled group must use separate table—Except as provided by the Secretary of the Treasury, a plan sponsor may not use a mortality table under this subparagraph for any plan maintained by the plan sponsor unless—

(I) a separate mortality table is established and used under this subparagraph for each other plan maintained by the plan sponsor and if the plan sponsor is a member of a controlled group, each member of the controlled group, and

(II) the requirements of clause (iii) are met separately with respect to the table so established for each such plan, determined by only taking into account the participants of such plan, the time such plan has been in existence, and the actual experience of such plan.

(v) Deadline for submission and disposition of application—

(I) Submission—The plan sponsor shall submit a mortality table to the Secretary of the Treasury for approval under this subparagraph at least 7 months before the 1st day of the period described in clause (i).

(II) Disposition—Any mortality table submitted to the Secretary of the Treasury for approval under this subparagraph shall be treated as in effect as of the 1st day of the period described in clause (i) unless the Secretary of the Treasury, during the 180-day period beginning on the date of such submission, disapproves of such table and provides the reasons that such table fails to meet the requirements of clause (iii). The 180-day period shall be extended upon mutual agreement of the Secretary of the Treasury and the plan sponsor.

(D) Separate mortality tables for the disabled—Notwithstanding subparagraph (A)—

(i) In general—The Secretary of the Treasury shall establish mortality tables which may be used (in lieu of the tables under subparagraph (A)) under this subsection for individuals who are entitled to benefits under the plan on account of disability. The Secretary of the Treasury shall establish separate tables for individuals whose disabilities occur in plan years beginning before January 1, 1995, and for individuals whose disabilities occur in plan years beginning on or after such date.

(ii) Special rule for disabilities occurring after 1994—In the case of disabilities occurring in plan years beginning after December 31, 1994, the tables under clause (i) shall apply only with respect to individuals described in such subclause who are disabled within the meaning of title II of the Social Security Act and the regulations thereunder.

(iii) Periodic revision—The Secretary of the Treasury shall (at least every 10 years) make revisions in any table in effect under clause (i) to reflect the actual experience of pension plans and projected trends in such experience.

(4) Probability of benefit payments in the form of lump sums or other optional forms—For purposes of determining any present value or making any computation under this section, there shall be taken into account—

(A) the probability that future benefit payments under the plan will be made in the form of optional forms of benefits provided under the plan (including lump sum distributions, determined on the basis of the plan's experience and other related assumptions), and

(B) any difference in the present value of such future benefit payments resulting from the use of actuarial assumptions, in determining benefit payments in any such optional form of benefits, which are different from those specified in this subsection.

(5) Approval of large changes in actuarial assumptions—

(A) In general—No actuarial assumption used to determine the funding target for a plan to which this paragraph applies may be changed without the approval of the Secretary of the Treasury.

(B) Plans to which paragraph applies—This paragraph shall apply to a plan only if—

(i) the plan is a single-employer plan to which title IV applies,

(ii) the aggregate unfunded vested benefits as of the close of the preceding plan year (as determined under section 4006(a)(3)(E)(iii)) of such plan and all other plans maintained by the contributing sponsors (as defined in section 4001(a)(13)) and members of such sponsors' controlled groups (as defined in section 4001(a)(14)) which are covered by title IV (disregarding plans with no unfunded vested benefits) exceed $50,000,000, and

(iii) the change in assumptions (determined after taking into account any changes in interest rate and mortality table) results in a decrease in the funding shortfall of the plan for the current plan year that exceeds $50,000,000, or that exceeds $5,000,000 and that is 5 percent or more of the funding target of the plan before such change.

(i) Special rules for at-risk plans—

(1) Funding target for plans in at-risk status—

(A) In general—In the case of a plan which is in at-risk status for a plan year, the funding target of the plan for the plan year shall be equal to the sum of—

(i) the present value of all benefits accrued or earned under the plan as of the beginning of the plan year, as determined by using the additional actuarial assumptions described in subparagraph (B), and

(ii) in the case of a plan which also has been in at-risk status for at least 2 of the 4 preceding plan years, a loading factor determined under subparagraph (C).

(B) Additional actuarial assumptions—The actuarial assumptions described in this subparagraph are as follows:

(i) All employees who are not otherwise assumed to retire as of the valuation date but who will be eligible to elect benefits during the plan year and the 10 succeeding plan years shall be assumed to retire at the earliest retirement date under the plan but not before the end of the plan year for which the at-risk funding target and at-risk target normal cost are being determined.

(ii) All employees shall be assumed to elect the retirement benefit available under the plan at the assumed retirement age (determined after application of clause (i)) which would result in the highest present value of benefits.

(C) Loading factor—The loading factor applied with respect to a plan under this paragraph for any plan year is the sum of—

(i) $700, times the number of participants in the plan, plus

(ii) 4 percent of the funding target (determined without regard to this paragraph) of the plan for the plan year.

(2) Target normal cost of at-risk plans—In the case of a plan which is in at-risk status for a plan year, the target normal cost of the plan for such plan year shall be equal to the sum of—

(A) the excess of—

(i) the sum of—

(I) the present value of all benefits which are expected to accrue or to be earned under the plan during the plan year, determined using the additional actuarial assumptions described in paragraph (1)(B), plus

(II) the amount of plan-related expenses expected to be paid from plan assets during the plan year, over

(ii) the amount of mandatory employee contributions expected to be made during the plan year, plus

(B) in the case of a plan which also has been in at-risk status for at least 2 of the 4 preceding plan years, a loading factor equal to 4 percent of the amount determined under subsection (b)(1)(A)(i) with respect to the plan for the plan year.

(3) Minimum amount—In no event shall—

(A) the at-risk funding target be less than the funding target, as determined without regard to this subsection, or

(B) the at-risk target normal cost be less than the target normal cost, as determined without regard to this subsection.

(4) Determination of at-risk status—For purposes of this subsection—

(A) In general—A plan is in at-risk status for a plan year if—

(i) the funding target attainment percentage for the preceding plan year (determined under this section without regard to this subsection) is less than 80 percent, and

(ii) the funding target attainment percentage for the preceding plan year (determined under this section by using the additional actuarial assumptions described in paragraph (1)(B) in computing the funding target) is less than 70 percent.

(B) Transition rule—In the case of plan years beginning in 2008, 2009, and 2010, subparagraph (A)(i) shall be applied by substituting the following percentages for "80 percent":

(i) 65 percent in the case of 2008.

(ii) 70 percent in the case of 2009.

(iii) 75 percent in the case of 2010.

In the case of plan years beginning in 2008, the funding target attainment percentage for the preceding plan year under subparagraph (A) may be determined using such methods of estimation as the Secretary of the Treasury may provide.

(C) Special rule for employees offered early retirement in 2006—

(i) In general—For purposes of subparagraph (A)(ii), the additional actuarial assumptions described in paragraph (1)(B) shall not be taken into account with respect to any employee if—

(I) such employee is employed by a specified automobile manufacturer,

(II) such employee is offered a substantial amount of additional cash compensation, substantially enhanced retirement benefits under the plan, or materially reduced employment duties on the condition that by a specified date (not later than December 31, 2010) the employee retires (as defined under the terms of the plan),

(III) such offer is made during 2006 and pursuant to a bona fide retirement incentive program and requires, by the terms of the offer, that such offer can be accepted not later than a specified date (not later than December 31, 2006), and

(IV) such employee does not elect to accept such offer before the specified date on which the offer expires.

(ii) Specified automobile manufacturer—For purposes of clause (i), the term "specified automobile manufacturer" means—

(I) any manufacturer of automobiles, and

(II) any manufacturer of automobile parts which supplies such parts directly to a manufacturer of automobiles and which, after a transaction or series of transactions ending in 1999, ceased to be a member of a controlled group which included such manufacturer of automobiles.

(5) Transition between applicable funding targets and between applicable target normal costs—

(A) In general—In any case in which a plan which is in at-risk status for a plan year has been in such status for a consecutive period of fewer than 5 plan years, the applicable amount of the funding target and of the target normal cost shall be, in lieu of the amount determined without regard to this paragraph, the sum of—

(i) the amount determined under this section without regard to this subsection, plus

(ii) the transition percentage for such plan year of the excess of the amount determined under this subsection (without regard to this paragraph) over the amount determined under this section without regard to this subsection.

(B) Transition percentage—For purposes of subparagraph (A), the transition percentage shall be determined in accordance with the following table:

If the consecutive number of years (including the plan year) the plan is in at-risk status is—	*The transition percentage is—*
1	20
2	40
3	60
4	80.

(C) Years before effective date—For purposes of this paragraph, plan years beginning before 2008 shall not be taken into account.

(6) Small plan exception—If, on each day during the preceding plan year, a plan had 500 or fewer participants, the plan shall not be treated as in at-risk status for the plan year. For purposes of this paragraph, all defined benefit plans (other than multiemployer plans) maintained by the same employer (or any member of such employer's controlled group) shall be treated as 1 plan, but only participants with respect to such employer or member shall be taken into account and the rules of subsection (g)(2)(C) shall apply.

(j) Payment of minimum required contributions—

(1) In general—For purposes of this section, the due date for any payment of any minimum required contribution for any plan year shall be 8 1/2 months after the close of the plan year.

(2) Interest—Any payment required under paragraph (1) for a plan year that is made on a date other than the valuation date for such plan year shall be adjusted for interest accruing for the period between the valuation date and the payment date, at the effective rate of interest for the plan for such plan year.

(3) Accelerated quarterly contribution schedule for underfunded plans—

(A) Failure to timely make required installment—In any case in which the plan has a funding shortfall for the preceding plan year, the employer maintaining the plan shall make the required installments under this paragraph and if the employer fails to pay the full amount of a required installment for the plan year, then the amount of interest charged under paragraph (2) on the underpayment for the period of underpayment shall be determined by using a rate of interest equal to the rate otherwise used under paragraph (2) plus 5 percentage points. In the case of plan years beginning in 2008, the funding shortfall for the preceding plan year may be determined using such methods of estimation as the Secretary of the Treasury may provide.

(B) Amount of underpayment, period of underpayment—For purposes of subparagraph (A)—

(i) Amount—The amount of the underpayment shall be the excess of—

(I) the required installment, over

(II) the amount (if any) of the installment contributed to or under the plan on or before the due date for the installment.

(ii) Period of underpayment—The period for which any interest is charged under this paragraph with respect to any portion of the underpayment shall run from the due date for the installment to the date on which such portion is contributed to or under the plan.

(iii) Order of crediting contributions—For purposes of clause (i)(II), contributions shall be credited against unpaid required installments in the order in which such installments are required to be paid.

(C) Number of required installments; due dates—For purposes of this paragraph—

(i) Payable in 4 installments—There shall be 4 required installments for each plan year.

(ii) Time for payment of installments—The due dates for required installments are set forth in the following table:

In the case of the following required installment:	*The due date is:*
1st	April 15
2nd	July 15
3rd	October 15
4th	January 15 of the following year.

(D) Amount of required installment—For purposes of this paragraph—

(i) In general—The amount of any required installment shall be 25 percent of the required annual payment.

(ii) Required annual payment—For purposes of clause (i), the term "required annual payment" means the lesser of—

(I) 90 percent of the minimum required contribution (determined without regard to this subsection) to the plan for the plan year under this section, or

(II) 100 percent of the minimum required contribution (determined without regard to this subsection or to any waiver under section 302(c)) to the plan for the preceding plan year.

Subclause (II) shall not apply if the preceding plan year referred to in such clause was not a year of 12 months.

(E) Fiscal years, short years, and years with alternate valuation date—

(i) Fiscal years—In applying this paragraph to a plan year beginning on any date other than January 1, there shall be substituted for the months specified in this paragraph, the months which correspond thereto.

(ii) Short plan year—This subparagraph shall be applied to plan years of less than 12 months in accordance with regulations prescribed by the Secretary of the Treasury.

(ii) **Plan with alternate valuation date**—The Secretary of the Treasury shall prescribe regulations for the application of this paragraph in the case of a plan which has a valuation date other than the first day of the plan year.

(F) Quarterly contributions not to include certain increased contributions. Subparagraph (D) shall be applied without regard to any increase under subsection (c)(7).

(4) Liquidity requirement in connection with quarterly contributions—

(A) In general—A plan to which this paragraph applies shall be treated as failing to pay the full amount of any required installment under paragraph (3) to the extent that the value of the liquid assets paid in such installment is less than the liquidity shortfall (whether or not such liquidity shortfall exceeds the amount of such installment required to be paid but for this paragraph).

(B) Plans to which paragraph applies—This paragraph shall apply to a plan (other than a plan described in subsection (g)(2)(B)) which—

(i) is required to pay installments under paragraph (3) for a plan year, and

(ii) has a liquidity shortfall for any quarter during such plan year.

(C) Period of underpayment—For purposes of paragraph (3)(A), any portion of an installment that is treated as not paid under subparagraph (A) shall continue to be treated as unpaid until the close of the quarter in which the due date for such installment occurs.

(D) Limitation on increase—If the amount of any required installment is increased by reason of subparagraph (A), in no event shall such increase exceed the amount which, when added to prior installments for the plan year, is necessary to increase the funding target attainment percentage of the plan for the plan year (taking into account the expected increase in funding target due to benefits accruing or earned during the plan year) to 100 percent.

(E) Definitions—For purposes of this paragraph—

(i) Liquidity shortfall—The term "liquidity shortfall" means, with respect to any required installment, an amount equal to the excess (as of the last day of the quarter for which such installment is made) of—

(I) the base amount with respect to such quarter, over

(II) the value (as of such last day) of the plan's liquid assets.

(ii) Base amount—

(I) In general—The term "base amount" means, with respect to any quarter, an amount equal to 3 times the sum of the adjusted disbursements from the plan for the 12 months ending on the last day of such quarter.

(II) Special rule—If the amount determined under subclause (I) exceeds an amount equal to 2 times the sum of the adjusted disbursements from the plan for the 36 months ending on the last day of the quarter and an enrolled actuary certifies to the satisfaction of the Secretary of the Treasury that such excess is the result of nonrecurring circumstances, the base amount with respect to such quarter shall be determined without regard to amounts related to those nonrecurring circumstances.

(iii) Disbursements from the plan—The term "disbursements from the plan" means all disbursements from the trust, including purchases of annuities, payments of single sums and other benefits, and administrative expenses.

(iv) Adjusted disbursements—The term "adjusted disbursements" means disbursements from the plan reduced by the product of—

(I) the plan's funding target attainment percentage for the plan year, and

(II) the sum of the purchases of annuities, payments of single sums, and such other disbursements as the Secretary of the Treasury shall provide in regulations.

(v) Liquid assets—The term "liquid assets" means cash, marketable securities, and such other assets as specified by the Secretary of the Treasury in regulations.

(vi) Quarter—The term "quarter" means, with respect to any required installment, the 3-month period preceding the month in which the due date for such installment occurs.

(F) Regulations—The Secretary of the Treasury may prescribe such regulations as are necessary to carry out this paragraph.

(k) Imposition of lien where failure to make required contributions—

(1) In general—In the case of a plan to which this subsection applies (as provided under paragraph (2)), if—

(A) any person fails to make a contribution payment required by section 302 and this section before the due date for such payment, and

(B) the unpaid balance of such payment (including interest), when added to the aggregate unpaid balance of all preceding such payments for which payment was not made before the due date (including interest), exceeds $1,000,000,

then there shall be a lien in favor of the plan in the amount determined under paragraph (3) upon all property and rights to property, whether real or personal, belonging to such person and any other person who is a member of the same controlled group of which such person is a member.

(2) Plans to which subsection applies—This subsection shall apply to a single-employer plan covered under section 4021 for any plan year for which the funding target attainment percentage (as defined in subsection (d)(2)) of such plan is less than 100 percent.

(3) Amount of lien—For purposes of paragraph (1), the amount of the lien shall be equal to the aggregate unpaid balance of contribution payments required under this section and section 302 for which payment has not been made before the due date.

(4) Notice of failure; lien—

(A) Notice of failure—A person committing a failure described in paragraph (1) shall notify the Pension Benefit Guaranty Corporation of such failure within 10 days of the due date for the required contribution payment.

(B) Period of lien—The lien imposed by paragraph (1) shall arise on the due date for the required contribution payment and shall continue until the last day of the first plan year in which the plan ceases to be described in paragraph (1)(B). Such lien shall continue to run without regard to whether such plan continues to be described in paragraph (2) during the period referred to in the preceding sentence.

(C) Certain rules to apply—Any amount with respect to which a lien is imposed under paragraph (1) shall be treated as taxes due and owing the United States and rules similar to the rules of subsections (c), (d), and (e) of section 4068 shall apply with respect to a lien imposed by subsection (a) and the amount with respect to such lien.

(5) Enforcement—Any lien created under paragraph (1) may be perfected and enforced only by the Pension Benefit Guaranty Corporation, or at the direction of the Pension Benefit Guaranty Corporation, by the contributing sponsor (or any member of the controlled group of the contributing sponsor).

(6) Definitions—For purposes of this subsection—

(A) Contribution payment—The term "contribution payment" means, in connection with a plan, a contribution payment required to be made to the plan, including any required installment under paragraphs (3) and (4) of subsection (j).

(B) Due date; required installment—The terms "due date" and "required installment" have the meanings given such terms by subsection (j).

(C) Controlled group—The term "controlled group" means any group treated as a single employer under subsections (b), (c), (m), and (o) of section 414 of the Internal Revenue Code of 1986.

(l) Qualified transfers to health benefit accounts—In the case of a qualified transfer (as defined in section 420 of the Internal Revenue Code of 1986), any assets so transferred shall not, for purposes of this section, be treated as assets in the plan.

§ 304. Minimum funding standards for multiemployer plans (§ 1084)

(a) In general—For purposes of section 302, the accumulated funding deficiency of a multiemployer plan for any plan year is—

(1) except as provided in paragraph (2), the amount, determined as of the end of the plan year, equal to the excess (if any) of the total charges to the funding standard account of the plan for all plan years (beginning with the first plan year for which this part applies to the plan) over the total credits to such account for such years, and

(2) if the multiemployer plan is in reorganization for any plan year, the accumulated funding deficiency of the plan determined under section 4243.

* * *

§ 305. Additional funding rules for multiemployer plans in endangered status or critical status (§ 1085)

(a) General rule—For purposes of this part, in the case of a multiemployer plan in effect on July 16, 2006—

(1) if the plan is in endangered status—

(A) the plan sponsor shall adopt and implement a funding improvement plan in accordance with the requirements of subsection (c), and

(B) the requirements of subsection (d) shall apply during the funding plan adoption period and the funding improvement period, and

(2) if the plan is in critical status—

(A) the plan sponsor shall adopt and implement a rehabilitation plan in accordance with the requirements of subsection (e), and

(B) the requirements of subsection (f) shall apply during the rehabilitation plan adoption period and the rehabilitation period.

* * *

Part 4—Fiduciary Responsibility

§ 401. Coverage (§ 1101)

(a) This part shall apply to any employee benefit plan described in section 4(a) (and not exempted under section 4(b)), other than—

(1) a plan which is unfunded and is maintained by an employer primarily for the purpose of providing deferred compensation for a select group of management or highly compensated employees; or

(2) any agreement described in section 736 of the Internal Revenue Code of 1986, which provides payments to a retired partner or deceased partner or a deceased partner's successor in interest.

(b) For purposes of this part:

(1) In the case of a plan which invests in any security issued by an investment company registered under the Investment Company Act of 1940, the assets of such plan shall be deemed to include such security but shall not, solely by reason of such investment, be deemed to include any assets of such investment company.

(2) In the case of a plan to which a guaranteed benefit policy is issued by an insurer, the assets of such plan shall be deemed to include such policy, but shall not, solely by reason of the issuance of such policy, be deemed to include any assets of such insurer. For purposes of this paragraph:

(A) The term "insurer" means an insurance company, insurance service, or insurance organization, qualified to do business in a State.

(B) The term "guaranteed benefit policy" means an insurance policy or contract to the extent that such policy or contract provides for benefits the amount of which is guaranteed by the insurer. Such term includes any surplus in a separate account, but excludes any other portion of a separate account

(c)(1)(A) Not later than June 30, 1997, the Secretary shall issue proposed regulations to provide guidance for the purpose of determining, in cases where an insurer issues 1 or more policies to or for the benefit of an employee benefit plan (and such policies are supported by assets of such insurer's general account), which assets held by the insurer (other than plan assets held in its separate accounts) constitute assets of the plan for purposes of this part and section 4975 of the Internal Revenue Code of 1986 and to provide guidance with respect to the application of this subchapter to the general account assets of insurers.

(B) The proposed regulations under subparagraph (A) shall be subject to public notice and comment until September 30, 1997.

(C) The Secretary shall issue final regulations providing the guidance described in subparagraph (A) not later than December 31, 1997.

(D) Such regulations shall only apply with respect to policies which are issued by an insurer on or before December 31, 1998, to or for the benefit of an employee benefit plan which is supported by assets of such insurer's general account. With respect to policies issued on or before December 31, 1998, such regulations shall take effect at the end of the 18-month period following the date on which such regulations become final.

(2) The Secretary shall ensure that the regulations issued under paragraph (1)—

(A) are administratively feasible, and

(B) protect the interests and rights of the plan and of its participants and beneficiaries (including meeting the requirements of paragraph (3)).

(3) The regulations prescribed by the Secretary pursuant to paragraph (1) shall require, in connection with any policy issued by an insurer to or for the benefit of an employee benefit plan to the extent that the policy is not a guaranteed benefit policy (as defined in subsection (b)(2)(B))—

(A) that a plan fiduciary totally independent of the insurer authorize the purchase of such policy (unless such purchase is a transaction exempt under section 408(b)(5)),

(B) that the insurer describe (in such form and manner as shall be prescribed in such regulations), in annual reports and in policies issued to the policyholder after the date on which such regulations are issued in final form pursuant to paragraph (1)(C)—

(i) a description of the method by which any income and expenses of the insurer's general account are allocated to the policy during the term of the policy and upon the termination of the policy, and

(ii) for each report, the actual return to the plan under the policy and such other financial information as the Secretary may deem appropriate for the period covered by each such annual report,

(C) that the insurer disclose to the plan fiduciary the extent to which alternative arrangements supported by assets of separate accounts of the insurer (which generally hold plan assets) are available, whether there is a right under the policy to transfer funds to a separate account and the terms governing any such right, and the extent to which support by assets of the insurer's general account and support by assets of separate accounts of the insurer might pose differing risks to the plan, and

(D) that the insurer manage those assets of the insurer which are assets of such insurer's general account (irrespective of whether any such assets are plan assets) with the care, skill, prudence, and diligence under the circumstances then prevailing that a prudent man acting in a like capacity and familiar with such matters would use in the conduct of an enterprise of a like character and with like aims, taking into account all obligations supported by such enterprise.

(4) Compliance by the insurer with all requirements of the regulations issued by the Secretary pursuant to paragraph (1) shall be deemed compliance by such insurer with sections 404, 406, and 407 with respect to those assets of the insurer's general account which support a policy described in paragraph (3).

(5)(A) Subject to subparagraph (B), any regulations issued under paragraph (1) shall not take effect before the date on which such regulations become final.

(B) No person shall be subject to liability under this part or section 4975 of the Internal Revenue Code of 1986 for conduct which occurred before the date which is 18 months following the date described in subparagraph (A) on the basis of a claim that the assets of an insurer (other than plan assets held in a separate account) constitute assets of the plan, except—

(i) as otherwise provided by the Secretary in regulations intended to prevent avoidance of the regulations issued under paragraph (1), or

(ii) as provided in an action brought by the Secretary pursuant to paragraph (2) or (5) of section 502(a) for a breach of fiduciary responsibilities which would also constitute a violation of Federal or State criminal law.

The Secretary shall bring a cause of action described in clause (ii) if a participant, beneficiary, or fiduciary demonstrates to the satisfaction of the Secretary that a breach described in clause (ii) has occurred.

(6) Nothing in this subsection shall preclude the application of any Federal criminal law.

(7) For purposes of this subsection, the term "policy" includes a contract.

§ 402. Establishment of plan (§ 1102)

(a)(1) Every employee benefit plan shall be established and maintained pursuant to a written instrument. Such instrument shall provide for one or more named fiduciaries who jointly or severally shall have authority to control and manage the operation and administration of the plan.

(2) For purposes of this title, the term "named fiduciary" means a fiduciary who is named in the plan instrument, or who, pursuant to a procedure specified in the plan, is identified as a fiduciary (A) by a person who is an employer or employee organization with respect to the plan or (B) by such an employer and such an employee organization acting jointly.

(b) Every employee benefit plan shall—

(1) provide a procedure for establishing and carrying out a funding policy and method consistent with the objectives of the plan and the requirements of this title,

(2) describe any procedure under the plan for the allocation of responsibilities for the operation and administration of the plan (including any procedure described in section 405(c)(1)),

(3) provide a procedure for amending such plan, and for identifying the persons who have authority to amend the plan, and

(4) specify the basis on which payments are made to and from the plan.

(c) Any employee benefit plan may provide—

(1) that any person or group of persons may serve in more than one fiduciary capacity with respect to the plan (including service both as trustee and administrator);

(2) that a named fiduciary, or a fiduciary designated by a named fiduciary pursuant to a plan procedure described in section 405(c)(1), may employ one or more persons to render advice with regard to any responsibility such fiduciary has under the plan; or

(3) that a person who is a named fiduciary with respect to control or management of the assets of the plan may appoint an investment manager or managers to manage (including the power to acquire and dispose of) any assets of a plan.

§ 403. Establishment of trust (§ 1103)

(a) Except as provided in subsection (b), all assets of an employee benefit plan shall be held in trust by one or more trustees. Such trustee or trustees shall be either named in the trust instrument or in the plan instrument described in section 402(a) or appointed by a person who is a named fiduciary, and upon acceptance of being named or appointed, the trustee or trustees shall have exclusive authority and discretion to manage and control the assets of the plan, except to the extent that—

(1) the plan expressly provides that the trustee or trustees are subject to the direction of a named fiduciary who is not a trustee, in which case the trustees shall be subject to proper directions of such fiduciary which are made in accordance with the terms of the plan and which are not contrary to this Act, or

(2) authority to manage, acquire, or dispose of assets of the plan is delegated to one or more investment managers pursuant to section 402(c)(3).

(b) The requirements of subsection (a) of this section shall not apply—

(1) to any assets of a plan which consist of insurance contracts or policies issued by an insurance company qualified to do business in a State;

(2) to any assets of such an insurance company or any assets of a plan which are held by such an insurance company;

(3) to a plan—

(A) some or all of the participants of which are employees described in section 401(c)(1) of the Internal Revenue Code of 1986; or

(B) which consists of one or more individual retirement accounts described in section 408 of the Internal Revenue Code of 1986;

to the extent that such plan's assets are held in one or more custodial accounts which qualify under section 401(f) or 408(h) of such Code, whichever is applicable.

(4) to a plan which the Secretary exempts from the requirement of subsection (a) and which is not subject to any of the following provisions of this Act—

(A) part 2 of this subtitle,

(B) part 3 of this subtitle, or

(C) title IV of this Act;

(5) to a contract established and maintained under section 403(b) of the Internal Revenue Code of 1986 to the extent that the assets of the contract are held in one or more custodial accounts pursuant to section 403(b)(7) of such Code; or

(6) Any plan, fund or program under which an employer, all of whose stock is directly or indirectly owned by employees, former employees or their beneficiaries, proposes through an unfunded arrangement to compensate retired employees for benefits which were forfeited by such employees under a pension plan maintained by a former employer prior to the date such pension plan became subject to this Act.

(c)(1) Except as provided in paragraph (2), (3), or (4) or subsection (d), or under sections 4042 and 4044 (relating to termination of insured plans), or under section 420 of the Internal Revenue Code of 1986 (as in effect on the date of enactment of Pension Protection Act of 2006), the assets of a plan shall never inure to the benefit of any employer and shall be held for the exclusive purposes of providing benefits to participants in the plan and their beneficiaries and defraying reasonable expenses of administering the plan.

(2)(A) In the case of a contribution, or a payment of withdrawal liability under part 1 of subtitle E of title IV—

(i) if such contribution or payment is made by an employer to a plan (other than a multiemployer plan) by a mistake of fact, paragraph (1) shall not prohibit the return of such contribution to the employer within one year after the payment of the contribution, and

(ii) if such contribution or payment is made by an employer to a multiemployer plan by a mistake of fact or law (other than a mistake relating to whether the plan is described in section 401(a) of the Internal Revenue Code of 1986 or the trust which is part of such plan is exempt from taxation under section 501(a) of such Code), paragraph (1) shall not prohibit the return of such contribution or payment to the employer within 6 months after the plan administrator determines that the contribution was made by such a mistake.

(B) If a contribution is conditioned on initial qualification of the plan under section 401 or 403(a) of the Internal Revenue Code of 1986, and if the plan receives an adverse determination with respect to its initial qualification, then paragraph (1) shall not prohibit the return of such contribution to the employer within one year after such determination, but only if the application for the determination is made by the time prescribed by law for filing the employer's return for the taxable year in which such plan was adopted, or such later date as the Secretary of the Treasury may prescribe.

(C) If a contribution is conditioned upon the deductibility of the contribution under section 404 of the Internal Revenue Code of 1986, then, to the extent the deduction is disallowed, paragraph (1) shall not prohibit the return to the employer of such contribution (to the extent disallowed) within one year after the disallowance of the deduction.

(3) In the case of a withdrawal liability payment which has been determined to be an overpayment, paragraph (1) shall not prohibit the return of such payment to the employer within 6 months after the date of such determination.

(d)(1) Upon termination of a pension plan to which section 4021 does not apply at the time of termination and to which this part applies (other than a plan to which no employer contributions have been made) the assets of the plan shall be allocated in accordance with the provisions of section 4044, except as otherwise provided in regulations of the Secretary.

(2) The assets of a welfare plan which terminates shall be distributed in accordance with the terms of the plan, except as otherwise provided in regulations of the Secretary.

§ 404. Fiduciary duties (§ 1104)

(a)(1) Subject to sections 403(c) and (d), 4042, and 4044, a fiduciary shall discharge his duties with respect to a plan solely in the interest of the participants and beneficiaries and—

(A) for the exclusive purpose of:

(i) providing benefits to participants and their beneficiaries; and

(ii) defraying reasonable expenses of administering the plan;

(B) with the care, skill, prudence, and diligence under the circumstances then prevailing that a prudent man acting in a like capacity and familiar with such matters would use in the conduct of an enterprise of a like character and with like aims;

(C) by diversifying the investments of the plan so as to minimize the risk of large losses, unless under the circumstances it is clearly prudent not to do so; and

(D) in accordance with the documents and instruments governing the plan insofar as such documents and instruments are consistent with the provisions of this title and Title IV.

(2) In the case of an eligible individual account plan (as defined in section 407(d)(3)), the diversification requirement of paragraph (1)(C) and the prudence requirement (only to the extent that it requires diversification) of paragraph (1)(B) is not violated by acquisition or holding of qualifying employer real property or qualifying employer securities (as defined in section 407(d)(4) and (5)).

(b) Except as authorized by the Secretary by regulations, no fiduciary may maintain the indicia of ownership of any assets of a plan outside the jurisdiction of the district courts of the United States.

(c)(1)(A) In the case of a pension plan which provides for individual accounts and permits a participant or beneficiary to exercise control over the assets in his account, if a participant or beneficiary exercises control over the assets in his account (as determined under regulations of the Secretary)—

(i) such participant or beneficiary shall not be deemed to be a fiduciary by reason of such exercise, and

(ii) no person who is otherwise a fiduciary shall be liable under this part for any loss, or by reason of any breach, which results from such participant's or beneficiary's exercise of control, except that this clause shall not apply in connection with such participant or beneficiary for any blackout period during which the ability of such participant or beneficiary to direct the investment of the assets in his or her account is suspended by a plan sponsor or fiduciary.

(B) If a person referred to in subparagraph (A)(ii) meets the requirements of this title in connection with authorizing and implementing the blackout period, any person who is otherwise a fiduciary shall not be liable under this title for any loss occurring during such period.

(C) For purposes of this paragraph, the term 'blackout period' has the meaning given such term by section 101(i)(7).

(2) In the case of a simple retirement account established pursuant to a qualified salary reduction arrangement under section 408(p) of the Internal Revenue Code of 1986, a participant or beneficiary shall, for purposes of paragraph (1), be treated as exercising control over the assets in the account upon the earliest of—

(A) an affirmative election among investment options with respect to the initial investment of any contribution,

(B) a rollover to any other simple retirement account or individual retirement plan, or

(C) one year after the simple retirement account is established.

No reports, other than those required under section 101(g), shall be required with respect to a simple retirement account established pursuant to such a qualified salary reduction arrangement.

(3) In the case of a pension plan which makes a transfer to an individual retirement account or annuity of a designated trustee or issuer under section 401(a)(31)(B) of the Internal Revenue Code of 1986, the participant or beneficiary shall, for purposes of paragraph (1), be treated as exercising control over the assets in the account or annuity upon—

(A) the earlier of—

(i) a rollover of all or a portion of the amount to another individual retirement account or annuity; or

(ii) one year after the transfer is made; or

(B) a transfer that is made in a manner consistent with guidance provided by the Secretary.

(4)(A) In any case in which a qualified change in investment options occurs in connection with an individual account plan, a participant or beneficiary shall not be treated for purposes of paragraph (1) as not exercising control over the assets in his account in connection with such change if the requirements of subparagraph (C) are met in connection with such change.

(B) For purposes of subparagraph (A), the term "qualified change in investment options" means, in connection with an individual account plan, a change in the investment options offered to the participant or beneficiary under the terms of the plan, under which—

(i) the account of the participant or beneficiary is reallocated among one or more remaining or new investment options which are offered in lieu of one or more investment options offered immediately prior to the effective date of the change, and

(ii) the stated characteristics of the remaining or new investment options provided under clause (i), including characteristics relating to risk and rate of return, are, as of immediately after the change, reasonably similar to those of the existing investment options as of immediately before the change.

(C) The requirements of this subparagraph are met in connection with a qualified change in investment options if—

(i) at least 30 days and no more than 60 days prior to the effective date of the change, the plan administrator furnishes written notice of the change to the participants and beneficiaries, including information comparing the existing and new investment options and an explanation that, in the absence of affirmative investment instructions from the participant or beneficiary to the contrary, the account of the participant or beneficiary will be invested in the manner described in subparagraph (B),

(ii) the participant or beneficiary has not provided to the plan administrator, in advance of the effective date of the change, affirmative investment instructions contrary to the change, and

(iii) the investments under the plan of the participant or beneficiary as in effect immediately prior to the effective date of the change were the product of the exercise by such participant or beneficiary of control over the assets of the account within the meaning of paragraph (1).

(5) Default investment arrangements—

(A) In general—For purposes of paragraph (1), a participant or beneficiary in an individual account plan meeting the notice requirements of subparagraph (B) shall be treated as exercising control over the assets in the account with respect to the amount of contributions and earnings which, in the absence of an investment election by the participant or beneficiary, are invested by the plan in accordance with regulations prescribed by the Secretary. The regulations under this subparagraph shall provide guidance on the appropriateness of designating default investments that include a mix of asset classes consistent with capital preservation or long-term capital appreciation, or a blend of both.

(B) Notice requirements—

(i) In general—The requirements of this subparagraph are met if each participant or beneficiary—

(I) receives, within a reasonable period of time before each plan year, a notice explaining the employee's right under the plan to designate how contributions and earnings will be invested and explaining how, in the absence of any investment election by the participant or beneficiary, such contributions and earnings will be invested, and

(II) has a reasonable period of time after receipt of such notice and before the beginning of the plan year to make such designation.

(ii) Form of notice—The requirements of clauses (i) and (ii) of section 401(k)(12)(D) of the Internal Revenue Code of 1986 shall apply with respect to the notices described in this subparagraph.

* * *

§ 405. Liability for breach of co-fiduciary (§ 1105)

(a) In addition to any liability which he may have under any other provisions of this part, a fiduciary with respect to a plan shall be liable for a breach of fiduciary responsibility of another fiduciary with respect to the same plan in the following circumstances:

(1) if he participates knowingly in, or knowingly undertakes to conceal, an act or omission of such other fiduciary, knowing such act or omission is a breach;

(2) if, by his failure to comply with section 404(a)(1) in the administration of his specific responsibilities which give rise to his status as a fiduciary, he has enabled such other fiduciary to commit a breach; or

(3) if he has knowledge of a breach by such other fiduciary, unless he makes reasonable efforts under the circumstances to remedy the breach.

(b)(1) Except as otherwise provided in subsection (d) and in section 403(a)(1) and (2), if the assets of a plan are held by two or more trustees—

(A) each shall use reasonable care to prevent a co-trustee from committing a breach; and

(B) they shall jointly manage and control the assets of the plan, except that nothing in this subparagraph (B) shall preclude any agreement, authorized by the trust instrument, allocating specific responsibilities, obligations, or duties among trustees, in which event a trustee to whom certain responsibilities, obligations, or duties have not been allocated shall not be liable by reason of this subparagraph (B) either individually or as a trustee for any loss resulting to the plan arising from the acts or omissions on the part of another trustee to whom such responsibilities, obligations, or duties have been allocated.

(2) Nothing in this subsection shall limit any liability that a fiduciary may have under subsection (a) or any other provision of this part.

(3)(A) In the case of a plan the assets of which are held in more than one trust, a trustee shall not be liable under paragraph (1) except with respect to an act or omission of a trustee of a trust of which he is a trustee.

(B) No trustee shall be liable under this subsection for following instructions referred to in section 403(a)(1).

(c)(1) The instrument under which a plan is maintained may expressly provide for procedures (A) for allocating fiduciary responsibilities (other than trustee responsibilities) among named fiduciaries, and (B) for named fiduciaries to designate persons other than named fiduciaries to carry out fiduciary responsibilities (other than trustee responsibilities) under the plan.

(2) If a plan expressly provides for a procedure described in paragraph (1), and pursuant to such procedure any fiduciary responsibility of a named fiduciary is allocated to any person, or a person is designated to carry out any such responsibility, then such named fiduciary shall not be liable for an act or omission of such person in carrying out such responsibility except to the extent that—

(A) the named fiduciary violated section 404(a)(1)—

(i) with respect to such allocation or designation,

(ii) with respect to the establishment or implementation of the procedure under paragraph (1), or

(iii) in continuing the allocation or designation; or

(B) the named fiduciary would otherwise be liable in accordance with subsection (a).

(3) For purposes of this subsection, the term "trustee responsibility" means any responsibility provided in the plan's trust instrument (if any) to manage or control the assets of the plan, other than a power under the trust instrument of a named fiduciary to appoint an investment manager in accordance with section 402(c)(3).

(d)(1) If an investment manager or managers have been appointed under section 402(c)(3), then, notwithstanding subsections (a)(2) and (3) and subsection (b), no trustee shall be liable for the acts or omissions of such investment manager or managers, or be under an obligation to invest or otherwise manage any asset of the plan which is subject to the management of such investment manager.

(2) Nothing in this subsection shall relieve any trustee of any liability under this part for any act of such trustee.

§ 406. Prohibited transactions (§ 1106)

(a) Except as provided in section 408:

(1) A fiduciary with respect to a plan shall not cause the plan to engage in a transaction, if he knows or should know that such transaction constitutes a direct or indirect—

(A) sale or exchange, or leasing, of any property between the plan and a party in interest;

(B) lending of money or other extension of credit between the plan and a party in interest;

(C) furnishing of goods, services, or facilities between the plan and a party in interest;

(D) transfer to, or use by or for the benefit of, a party in interest, of any assets of the plan; or

(E) acquisition, on behalf of the plan, of any employer security or employer real property in violation of section 407(a).

(2) No fiduciary who has authority or discretion to control or manage the assets of a plan shall permit the plan to hold any employer security or employer real property if he knows or should know that holding such security or real property violates section 407(a).

(b) A fiduciary with respect to a plan shall not—

(1) deal with the assets of the plan in his own interest or for his own account,

(2) in his individual or in any other capacity act in any transaction involving the plan on behalf of a party (or represent a party) whose interests are adverse to the interests of the plan or the interests of its participants or beneficiaries, or

(3) receive any consideration for his own personal account from any party dealing with such plan in connection with a transaction involving the assets of the plan.

(c) A transfer of real or personal property by a party in interest to a plan shall be treated as a sale or exchange if the property is subject to a mortgage or similar lien which the plan assumes or if it is subject to a mortgage or similar lien which a party-in-interest placed on the property within the 10-year period ending on the date of the transfer.

§ 407. Limitation with respect to acquisition and holding of employer securities and employer real property by certain plans (§ 1107)

(a) Except as otherwise provided in this section and section 414:

(1) A plan may not acquire or hold—

(A) any employer security which is not a qualifying employer security, or

(B) any employer real property which is not qualifying employer real property.

(2) A plan may not acquire any qualifying employer security or qualifying employer real property, if immediately after such acquisition the aggregate fair market value of employer securities and employer real property held by the plan exceeds 10 percent of the fair market value of the assets of the plan.

* * *

(b)(1) Subsection (a) of this section shall not apply to any acquisition or holding of qualifying employer securities or qualifying employer real property by an eligible individual account plan.

(2)(A) If this paragraph applies to an eligible individual account plan, the portion of such plan which consists of applicable elective deferrals (and earnings allocable thereto) shall be treated as a separate plan—

(i) which is not an eligible individual account plan, and

(ii) to which the requirements of this section apply.

(B)(i) This paragraph shall apply to any eligible individual account plan if any portion of the plan's applicable elective deferrals (or earnings allocable thereto) are required to be invested in qualifying employer securities or qualifying employer real property or both—

(I) pursuant to the terms of the plan, or

(II) at the direction of a person other than the participant on whose behalf such elective deferrals are made to the plan (or a beneficiary).

(ii) This paragraph shall not apply to an individual account plan for a plan year if, on the last day of the preceding plan year, the fair market value of the assets of all individual account plans maintained by the employer equals not more than 10 percent of the fair market value of the assets of all pension plans (other than multiemployer plans) maintained by the employer.

(iii) This paragraph shall not apply to an individual account plan that is an employee stock ownership plan as defined in section 4975(e)(7) of the Internal Revenue Code of 1986.

(iv) This paragraph shall not apply to an individual account plan if, pursuant to the terms of the plan, the portion of any employee's applicable elective deferrals which is required to be invested in qualifying employer securities and qualifying employer real property for any year may not exceed 1 percent of the employee's compensation which is taken into account under the plan in determining the maximum amount of the employee's applicable elective deferrals for such year.

(C) For purposes of this paragraph, the term "applicable elective deferral" means any elective deferral (as defined in section 402(g)(3)(A) of the Internal Revenue Code of 1986) which is made pursuant to a qualified cash or deferred arrangement as defined in section 401(k) of the Internal Revenue Code of 1986.

* * *

(d) For purposes of this section—

(1) The term "employer security" means a security issued by an employer of employees covered by the plan, or by an affiliate of such employer. A contract to which section 408(b)(5) applies shall not be treated as a security for purposes of this section.

(2) The term "employer real property" means real property (and related personal property) which is leased to an employer of employees covered by the plan, or to an affiliate of such employer. For purposes of determining the time at which a plan acquires employer real property for purposes of this section, such property shall be deemed to be acquired by the plan on the date on which the plan acquires the property or on the date on which the lease to the employer (or affiliate) is entered into, whichever is later.

(3)(A) The term "eligible individual account plan" means an individual account plan which is (i) a profit-sharing, stock bonus, thrift, or savings plan; (ii) an employee stock ownership plan; or (iii) a money purchase plan which was in existence on September 2, 1974, and which on such date invested primarily in qualifying employer securities. Such term excludes an individual retirement account or annuity described in section 408 of the Internal Revenue Code of 1986.

(B) Notwithstanding subparagraph (A), a plan shall be treated as an eligible individual account plan with respect to the acquisition or holding of qualifying employer real property or qualifying employer securities only if such plan explicitly provides for acquisition and holding of qualifying employer securities or qualifying employer real property (as the case may be). In the case of a plan in existence on September 2, 1974, this subparagraph shall not take effect until January 1, 1976.

(C) The term "eligible individual account plan" does not include any individual account plan the benefits of which are taken into account in determining the benefits payable to a participant under any defined benefit plan.

(4) The term "qualifying employer real property" means parcels of employer real property—

(A) if a substantial number of the parcels are dispersed geographically;

(B) if each parcel of real property and the improvements thereon are suitable (or adaptable without excessive cost) for more than one use;

(C) even if all of such real property is leased to one lessee (which may be an employer, or an affiliate of an employer); and

(D) if the acquisition and retention of such property comply with the provisions of this part (other than section 404(a)(1)(B) to the extent it requires diversification, and sections 404(a)(1)(C), 406, and subsection (a) of this section).

(5) The term "qualifying employer security" means an employer security which is—

(A) stock,

(B) a marketable obligation (as defined in subsection (e)), or

(C) an interest in a publicly traded partnership (as defined in section 7704(b) of the Internal Revenue Code of 1986), but only if such partnership is an existing partnership as defined in section 10211(c)(2)(A) of the Revenue Act of 1987 (Public Law 100-203).

After December 17, 1987, in the case of a plan other than an eligible individual account plan, an employer security described in subparagraph (A) or (C) shall be considered a qualifying employer security only if such employer security satisfies the requirements of subsection (f)(1).

(6) The term "employee stock ownership plan" means an individual account plan—

(A) which is a stock bonus plan which is qualified, or a stock bonus plan and money purchase plan both of which are qualified, under section 401 of the Internal Revenue Code of 1986, and which is designed to invest primarily in qualifying employer securities, and

(B) which meets such other requirements as the Secretary of the Treasury may prescribe by regulation.

(7) A corporation is an affiliate of an employer if it is a member of any controlled group of corporations (as defined in section 1563(a) of the Internal Revenue Code of 1986, except that "applicable percentage" shall be substituted for "80 percent" wherever the latter percentage appears in such section) of which the employer who maintains the plan is a member. For purposes of the preceding sentence, the term "applicable percentage" means 50 percent, or such lower percentage as the Secretary may prescribe by regulation.

* * *

(e) For purposes of subsection (d)(5) of this section, the term "marketable obligation" means a bond, debenture, note, or certificate, or other evidence of indebtedness (hereinafter in this subsection referred to as "obligation") if—

(1) such obligation is acquired—

(A) on the market, either (i) at the price of the obligation prevailing on a national securities exchange which is registered with the Securities and Exchange Commission, or (ii) if the obligation is not traded on such a national securities exchange, at a price not less favorable to the plan than the offering price for the obligation as established by current bid and asked prices quoted by persons independent of the issuer;

(B) from an underwriter, at a price (i) not in excess of the public offering price for the obligation as set forth in a prospectus or offering circular filed with the Securities and Exchange Commission, and (ii) at which a substantial portion of the same issue is acquired by persons independent of the issuer; or

(C) directly from the issuer, at a price not less favorable to the plan than the price paid currently for a substantial portion of the same issue by persons independent of the issuer;

(2) immediately following acquisition of such obligation—

(A) not more than 25 percent of the aggregate amount of obligations issued in such issue and outstanding at the time of acquisition is held by the plan, and

(B) at least 50 percent of the aggregate amount referred to in subparagraph (A) is held by persons independent of the issuer; and

(3) immediately following acquisition of the obligation, not more than 25 percent of the assets of the plan is invested in obligations of the employer or an affiliate of the employer.

(f)(1) Stock satisfies the requirements of this paragraph if, immediately following the acquisition of such stock—

(A) no more than 25 percent of the aggregate amount of stock of the same class issued and outstanding at the time of acquisition is held by the plan, and

(B) at least 50 percent of the aggregate amount referred to in subparagraph (A) is held by persons independent of the issuer.

* * *

§ 408. Exemptions from prohibited transactions (§ 1108)

(a) The Secretary shall establish an exemption procedure for purposes of this subsection. Pursuant to such procedure, he may grant a conditional or unconditional exemption of any fiduciary or transaction, or class of fiduciaries or transactions, from all or part of the restrictions imposed by sections 406 and 407(a). Action under this subsection may be taken only after consultation and coordination with the Secretary of the Treasury. An exemption granted under this section shall not relieve a fiduciary from any other applicable provision of this Act. The Secretary may not grant an exemption under this subsection unless he finds that such exemption is—

(1) administratively feasible,

(2) in the interests of the plan and of its participants and beneficiaries, and

(3) protective of the rights of participants and beneficiaries of such plan.

Before granting an exemption under this subsection from section 406(a) or 407(a), the Secretary shall publish notice in the Federal Register of the pendency of the exemption, shall require that adequate notice be given to interested persons, and shall afford interested persons opportunity to present views. The Secretary may not grant an exemption under this subsection from section 406(b) unless he affords an opportunity for a hearing and makes a determination on the record with respect to the findings required by paragraphs (1), (2), and (3) of this subsection.

(b) The prohibitions provided in section 406 shall not apply to any of the following transactions:

(1) Any loans made by the plan to parties in interest who are participants or beneficiaries of the plan if such loans (A) are available to all such participants and beneficiaries on a reasonably equivalent basis, (B) are not made available to highly compensated employees (within the meaning of section 414(q) of the Internal Revenue Code of 1986) in an amount greater than the amount made available to other employees, (C) are made in accordance with specific provisions regarding such loans set forth in the plan, (D) bear a reasonable rate of interest, and (E) are adequately secured. A loan made by a plan shall not fail to meet the requirements of the preceding sentence by reason of a loan repayment suspension described under section 414(u)(4) of the Internal Revenue Code of 1986.

(2) Contracting or making reasonable arrangements with a party in interest for office space, or legal, accounting, or other services necessary for the establishment or operation of the plan, if no more than reasonable compensation is paid therefor.

(3) A loan to an employee stock ownership plan (as defined in section 407(d)(6)), if—

(A) such loan is primarily for the benefit of participants and beneficiaries of the plan, and

(B) such loan is at an interest rate which is not in excess of a reasonable rate.

If the plan gives collateral to a party in interest for such loan, such collateral may consist only of qualifying employer securities (as defined in section 407(d)(5)).

(4) The investment of all or part of a plan's assets in deposits which bear a reasonable interest rate in a bank or similar financial institution supervised by the United States or a State, if such bank or other institution is a fiduciary of such plan and if—

(A) the plan covers only employees of such bank or other institution and employees of affiliates of such bank or other institution, or

(B) such investment is expressly authorized by a provision of the plan or by a fiduciary (other than such bank or institution or affiliate thereof) who is expressly empowered by the plan to so instruct the trustee with respect to such investment.

(5) Any contract for life insurance, health insurance, or annuities with one or more insurers which are qualified to do business in a State, if the plan pays no more than adequate consideration, and if each such insurer or insurers is—

(A) the employer maintaining the plan, or

(B) a party in interest which is wholly owned (directly or indirectly) by the employer maintaining the plan, or by any person which is a party in interest with respect to the plan, but only if the total premiums and annuity considerations written by such insurers for life insurance, health insurance, or annuities for all plans (and their employers) with respect to which such insurers are parties in interest (not including premiums or annuity considerations written by the employer maintaining the plan) do not exceed 5 percent of the total premiums and annuity considerations written for all lines of insurance in that year by such insurers (not including premiums or annuity considerations written by the employer maintaining the plan).

(6) The providing of any ancillary service by a bank or similar financial institution supervised by the United States or a State, if such bank or other institution is a fiduciary of such plan, and if—

(A) such bank or similar financial institution has adopted adequate internal safeguards which assure that the providing of such ancillary service is consistent with sound banking and financial practice, as determined by Federal or State supervisory authority, and

(B) the extent to which such ancillary service is provided is subject to specific guidelines issued by such bank or similar financial institution (as determined by the Secretary after consultation with Federal and State supervisory authority), and adherence to such guidelines would reasonably preclude such bank or similar financial institution from providing such ancillary service (i) in an excessive or unreasonable manner, and (ii) in a manner that would be inconsistent with the best interests of participants and beneficiaries of employee benefit plans.

Such ancillary services shall not be provided at more than reasonable compensation.

(7) The exercise of a privilege to convert securities, to the extent provided in regulations of the Secretary, but only if the plan receives no less than adequate consideration pursuant to such conversion.

(8) Any transaction between a plan and (i) a common or collective trust fund or pooled investment fund maintained by a party in interest which is a bank or trust company supervised by a State or Federal agency or (ii) a pooled investment fund of an insurance company qualified to do business in a State, if—

(A) the transaction is a sale or purchase of an interest in the fund,

(B) the bank, trust company, or insurance company receives not more than reasonable compensation, and

(C) such transaction is expressly permitted by the instrument under which the plan is maintained, or by a fiduciary (other than the bank, trust company, or insurance company, or an affiliate thereof) who has authority to manage and control the assets of the plan.

(9) The making by a fiduciary of a distribution of the assets of the plan in accordance with the terms of the plan if such assets are distributed in the same manner as provided under section 4044 of this Act (relating to allocation of assets).

* * *

(14) Any transaction in connection with the provision of investment advice described in section 3(21)(A)(ii) to a participant or beneficiary of an individual account plan that permits such participant or beneficiary to direct the investment of assets in their individual account, if—

(A) the transaction is—

(i) the provision of the investment advice to the participant or beneficiary of the plan with respect to a security or other property available as an investment under the plan,

(ii) the acquisition, holding, or sale of a security or other property available as an investment under the plan pursuant to the investment advice, or

(iii) the direct or indirect receipt of fees or other compensation by the fiduciary adviser or an affiliate thereof (or any employee, agent, or registered representative of the fiduciary adviser or affiliate) in connection with the provision of the advice or in connection with an acquisition, holding, or sale of a security or other property available as an investment under the plan pursuant to the investment advice; and

(B) the requirements of subsection (g)* are met.

* * *

(c) Nothing in section 406 shall be construed to prohibit any fiduciary from—

(1) receiving any benefit to which he may be entitled as a participant or beneficiary in the plan, so long as the benefit is computed and paid on a basis which is consistent with the terms of the plan as applied to all other participants and beneficiaries;

(2) receiving any reasonable compensation for services rendered, or for the reimbursement of expenses properly and actually incurred, in the performance of his duties with the plan; except that no person so serving who already receives full-time pay from an employer or an association of employers, whose employees are participants in the plan, or from an employee organization whose members are participants in such plan shall receive compensation from such plan, except for reimbursement of expenses properly and actually incurred; or

(3) serving as a fiduciary in addition to being an officer, employee, agent, or other representative of a party in interest.

---

* Subsection (g) of § 408 is omitted, but its provisions are mirrored by IRC § 4975(f)(8).

(d)(1) Section 407(b) and subsections (b), (c), and (e) of this section shall not apply to a transaction in which a plan directly or indirectly—

(A) lends any part of the corpus or income of the plan to,

(B) pays any compensation for personal services rendered to the plan to, or

(C) acquires for the plan any property from, or sells any property to,

any person who is with respect to the plan an owner-employee (as defined in section 401(c)(3) of the Internal Revenue Code of 1986), a member of the family (as defined in section 267(c)(4) of such Code) of any such owner-employee, or any corporation in which any such owner-employee owns, directly or indirectly, 50 percent or more of the total combined voting power of all classes of stock entitled to vote or 50 percent or more of the total value of shares of all classes of stock of the corporation.

(2)(A) For purposes of paragraph (1), the following shall be treated as owner- employees:

(i) A shareholder-employee.

(ii) A participant or beneficiary of an individual retirement plan (as defined in section 7701(a)(37) of the Internal Revenue Code of 1986).

(iii) An employer or association of employees which establishes such an individual retirement plan under section 408(c) of such Code.

(B) Paragraph (1)(C) shall not apply to a transaction which consists of a sale of employer securities to an employee stock ownership plan (as defined in section 407(d)(6)) by a shareholder-employee, a member of the family (as defined in section 267(c)(4) of such Code) of any such owner- employee, or a corporation in which such a shareholder-employee owns stock representing a 50 percent or greater interest described in paragraph (1).

(C) For purposes of paragraph (1)(A), the term "owner-employee" shall only include a person described in clause (ii) or (iii) of subparagraph (A).

(3) For purposes of paragraph (2), the term "shareholder-employee" means an employee or officer of an S corporation (as defined in section 1361(a)(1) of such Code) who owns (or is considered as owning within the meaning of section 318(a)(1) of such Code) more than 5 percent of the outstanding stock of the corporation on any day during the taxable year of such corporation.

(e) Sections 406 and 407 shall not apply to the acquisition or sale by a plan of qualifying employer securities (as defined in section 407(d)(5)) or acquisition, sale or lease by a plan of qualifying employer real property (as defined in section 407(d)(4))—

(1) if such acquisition, sale, or lease is for adequate consideration (or in the case of a marketable obligation, at a price not less favorable to the plan than the price determined under section 407(e)(1)),

(2) if no commission is charged with respect thereto, and

(3) if—

(A) the plan is an eligible individual account plan (as defined in section 407(d)(3)), or

(B) in the case of an acquisition or lease of qualifying employer real property by a plan which is not an eligible individual account plan, or of an acquisition of qualifying employer securities by such a plan, the lease or acquisition is not prohibited by section 407(a).

* * *

§ 409. Liability for breach of fiduciary duty (§ 1109)

(a) Any person who is a fiduciary with respect to a plan who breaches any of the responsibilities, obligations, or duties imposed upon fiduciaries by this title shall be personally liable to make good to such plan any losses to the plan resulting from each such breach, and to restore to such plan any profits of such fiduciary which have been made through use of assets of the plan by the fiduciary, and shall be subject to such other equitable or remedial relief as the court may deem appropriate, including removal of such fiduciary. A fiduciary may also be removed for a violation of section 411 of this Act.

(b) No fiduciary shall be liable with respect to a breach of fiduciary duty under this title if such breach was committed before he became a fiduciary or after he ceased to be a fiduciary.

§ 410. Exculpatory provisions; insurance (§ 1110)

(a) Except as provided in sections 405(b)(1) and 405(d), any provision in an agreement or instrument which purports to relieve a fiduciary from responsibility or liability for any responsibility, obligation, or duty under this part shall be void as against public policy.

(b) Nothing in this subpart shall preclude—

(1) a plan from purchasing insurance for its fiduciaries or for itself to cover liability or losses occurring by reason of the act or omission of a fiduciary, if such insurance permits recourse by the insurer against the fiduciary in the case of a breach of a fiduciary obligation by such fiduciary;

(2) a fiduciary from purchasing insurance to cover liability under this part from and for his own account; or

(3) an employer or an employee organization from purchasing insurance to cover potential liability of one or more persons who serve in a fiduciary capacity with regard to an employee benefit plan.

§ 411. Prohibition against certain persons holding certain positions (§ 1111)

(a) No person who has been convicted of, or has been imprisoned as a result of his conviction of, robbery, bribery, extortion, embezzlement, fraud, grand larceny, burglary, arson, a felony violation of Federal or State law involving substances defined in section 102(6) of the Drug Abuse Prevention and Control Act of 1970, murder, rape, kidnaping, perjury, assault with intent to kill, any crime described in section 9(a)(1) of the Investment Company Act of 1940 (15 U.S.C. 80a-9(a)(1)), a violation of any provision of this Act, a violation of section 302 of the Labor-Management Relations Act, 1947 (29 U.S.C. 186), a violation of chapter 63 of title 18, United States Code, a violation of section 874, 1027, 1503, 1505, 1506, 1510, 1951, or 1954 of title 18, United States Code, a violation of the Labor-Management Reporting and Disclosure Act of 1959 (29 U.S.C. 401), any felony involving abuse or misuse of such person's position or employment in a labor organization or employee benefit plan to seek or obtain an illegal gain at the expense of the members of the labor organization or the beneficiaries of the employee benefit plan, or conspiracy to commit any such crimes or attempt to commit any such crimes, or a crime in which any of the foregoing crimes is an element, shall serve or be permitted to serve—

(1) as an administrator, fiduciary, officer, trustee, custodian, counsel, agent, employee, or representative in any capacity of any employee benefit plan,

(2) as a consultant or adviser to an employee benefit plan, including but not limited to any entity whose activities are in whole or substantial part devoted to providing goods or services to any employee benefit plan, or

(3) in any capacity that involves decisionmaking authority or custody or control of the moneys, funds, assets, or property of any employee benefit plan,

during or for the period of thirteen years after such conviction or after the end of such imprisonment, whichever is later, unless the sentencing court on the motion of the person convicted sets a lesser period of at least three years after such conviction or after the end of such imprisonment, whichever is later, or unless prior to the end of such period, in the case of a person so convicted or imprisoned (A) his citizenship rights, having been revoked as a result of such conviction, have been fully restored, or (B) if the offense is a Federal offense, the sentencing judge or, if the offense is a State or local offense, the United States district court for the district in which the offense was committed, pursuant to sentencing guidelines and policy statements under section 994(a) of title 28, United States Code, determines that such person's service in any capacity referred to in paragraphs (1) through (3) would not be contrary to the purposes of this title. Prior to making any such determination the court shall hold a hearing and shall give notice to such proceeding by certified mail to the Secretary of Labor and to State, county, and Federal prosecuting officials in the jurisdiction or jurisdictions in which such person was convicted. The court's determination in any such proceeding shall be final. No person shall knowingly hire, retain, employ, or otherwise place any other person to serve in any capacity in violation of this subsection. Notwithstanding the preceding provisions of this subsection, no corporation or partnership will be precluded from acting as an administrator, fiduciary, officer, trustee, custodian, counsel, agent, or employee of any employee benefit plan or as a consultant to any employee benefit plan without a notice, hearing, and determination by such court that such service would be inconsistent with the intention of this section.

(b) Any person who intentionally violates this section shall be fined not more than $10,000 or imprisoned for not more than five years, or both.

(c) For the purpose of this section—

(1) A person shall be deemed to have been "convicted" and under the disability of "conviction" from the date of the judgment of the trial court, regardless of whether that judgment remains under appeal.

(2) The term "consultant" means any person who, for compensation, advises, or

represents an employee benefit plan or who provides other assistance to such plan, concerning the establishment or operation of such plan.

(3) A period of parole or supervised release shall not be considered as part of a period of imprisonment.

(d) Whenever any person—

(1) by operation of this section, has been barred from office or other position in an employee benefit plan as a result of a conviction, and

(2) has filed an appeal of that conviction,

any salary which would be otherwise due such person by virtue of such office or position, shall be placed in escrow by the individual or organization responsible for payment of such salary. Payment of such salary into escrow shall continue for the duration of the appeal or for the period of time during which such salary would be otherwise due, whichever period is shorter. Upon the final reversal of such person's conviction on appeal, the amounts in escrow shall be paid to such person. Upon the final sustaining of that person's conviction on appeal, the amounts in escrow shall be returned to the individual or organization responsible for payments of those amounts. Upon final reversal of such person's conviction, such person shall no longer be barred by this statute from assuming any position from which such person was previously barred.

§ 413. Limitation of actions (§ 1113)

No action may be commenced under this title with respect to a fiduciary's breach of any responsibility, duty, or obligation under this part, or with respect to a violation of this part, after the earlier of—

(1) six years after (A) the date of the last action which constituted a part of the breach or violation, or (B) in the case of an omission, the latest date on which the fiduciary could have cured the breach or violation, or

(2) three years after the earliest date on which the plaintiff had actual knowledge of the breach or violation;

except that in the case of fraud or concealment, such action may be commenced not later than six years after the date of discovery of such breach or violation.

* * *

Part 5—Administration and Enforcement

§ 501. Criminal penalties (§ 1131)

(a) Any person who willfully violates any provision of part 1 of this subtitle, or any regulation or order issued under any such provision, shall upon conviction be fined not more than $ 100,000 or imprisoned not more than 10 years, or both; except that in the case of such violation by a person not an individual, the fine imposed upon such person shall be a fine not exceeding $ 500,000.

(b) Any person that violates section 519 shall upon conviction be imprisoned not more than 10 years or fined under title 18, United States Code, or both. Any person who willfully violates any provision of part 1 of this subtitle, or any regulation or order issued under any such provision, shall upon conviction be fined not more than $100,000 or imprisoned not more than 10 years, or both; except that in the case of such violation by a person not an individual, the fine imposed upon such person shall be a fine not exceeding $500,000.

§ 502. Civil enforcement (§ 1132)

(a) A civil action may be brought—

(1) by a participant or beneficiary—

(A) for the relief provided for in subsection (c) of this section, or

(B) to recover benefits due to him under the terms of his plan, to enforce his rights under the terms of the plan, or to clarify his rights to future benefits under the terms of the plan;

(2) by the Secretary, or by a participant, beneficiary or fiduciary for appropriate relief under section 409;

(3) by a participant, beneficiary, or fiduciary (A) to enjoin any act or practice which violates any provision of this title or the terms of the plan, or (B) to obtain other appropriate equitable relief (i) to redress such violations or (ii) to enforce any provisions of this title or the terms of the plan;

(4) by the Secretary, or by a participant, or beneficiary for appropriate relief in the case of a violation of 105(c);

(5) except as otherwise provided in subsection (b), by the Secretary (A) to enjoin any act or practice which violates any provision of this title, or (B) to obtain other appropriate equitable relief (i) to redress such violation or (ii) to enforce any provision of this title;

(6) by the Secretary to collect any civil penalty under paragraph (2), (4), (5), (6). (7), (8), or (9) of subsection (c) or under subsection (i) or (l);

(7) by a State to enforce compliance with a qualified medical child support order (as defined in section 609(a)(2)(A));

(8) by the Secretary, or by an employer or other person referred to in section 101(f)(1), (A) to enjoin any act or practice which violates subsection (f) of section 101, or (B) to obtain appropriate equitable relief (i) to redress such violation or (ii) to enforce such subsection; or

(9) in the event that the purchase of an insurance contract or insurance annuity in connection with termination of an individual's status as a participant covered under a pension plan with respect to all or any portion of the participant's pension benefit under such plan constitutes a violation of part 4 of this title or the terms of the plan, by the Secretary, by any individual who was a participant or beneficiary at the time of the alleged violation, or by a fiduciary, to obtain appropriate relief, including the posting of security if necessary, to assure receipt by the participant or beneficiary of the amounts provided or to be provided by such insurance contract or annuity, plus reasonable prejudgment interest on such amounts.

(10) in the case of a multiemployer plan that has been certified by the actuary to be in endangered or critical status under section 305, if the plan sponsor—

(A) has not adopted a funding improvement or rehabilitation plan under that section by the deadline established in such section, or

(B) fails to update or comply with the terms of the funding improvement or rehabilitation plan in accordance with the requirements of such section,

by an employer that has an obligation to contribute with respect to the multiemployer plan or an employee organization that represents active participants in the multiemployer plan, for an order compelling the plan sponsor to adopt a funding improvement or rehabilitation plan or to update or comply with the terms of the funding improvement or rehabilitation plan in accordance with the requirements of such section and the funding improvement or rehabilitation plan.

* * *

(c)(1) Any administrator (A) who fails to meet the requirements of paragraph (1) or (4) of section 606, section 101(e)(1), section 101(f), or section 105(a) with respect to a participant or beneficiary, or (B) who fails or refuses to comply with a request for any information which such administrator is required by this title to furnish to a participant or beneficiary (unless such failure or refusal results from matters reasonably beyond the control of the administrator) by mailing the material requested to the last known address of the requesting participant or beneficiary within 30 days after such request may in the court's discretion be personally liable to such participant or beneficiary in the amount of up to $100 a day from the date of such failure or refusal, and the court may in its discretion order such other relief as it deems proper. For purposes of this paragraph, each violation described in subparagraph (A) with respect to any single participant, and each violation described in subparagraph (B) with respect to any single participant or beneficiary, shall be treated as a separate violation.

(2) The Secretary may assess a civil penalty against any plan administrator of up to $1,000 a day from the date of such plan administrator's failure or refusal to file the annual report required to be filed with the Secretary under section 101(b)(4). For purposes of this paragraph, an annual report that has been rejected under section 104(a)(4) for failure to provide material information shall not be treated as having been filed with the Secretary.

(3) Any employer maintaining a plan who fails to meet the notice requirement of section 101(d) with respect to any participant or beneficiary or who fails to meet the requirements of section 101(e)(2) with respect to any person or who fails to meet the requirements of section 302(d)(12)(E) with respect to any person may in the court's discretion be liable to such participant or beneficiary or to such person in the amount of up to $100 a day from the date of such failure, and the court may in its discretion order such other relief as it deems proper.

(4) The Secretary may assess a civil penalty of not more than $1,000 a day for each violation by any person of subsection (j), (k), or (l) of section 101, section 302(b)(7)(F)(vi), or section 514(e)(3).

(5) The Secretary may assess a civil penalty against any person of up to $1,000 a day from the date of the person's failure or refusal to file the information required to be filed by such person with the Secretary under regulations prescribed pursuant to section 101(g).

(6) If, within 30 days of a request by the Secretary to a plan administrator for documents under section 104(a)(6), the plan administrator fails to furnish the material requested to the Secretary, the Secretary may assess a civil penalty against the plan administrator of up to $100 a day from the date of such failure (but in no event in excess of $1,000 per request). No penalty shall be imposed under this paragraph for any failure resulting from matters reasonably beyond the control of the plan administrator.

(7) The Secretary may assess a civil penalty against a plan administrator of up to $100 a day from the date of the plan administrator's failure or refusal to provide notice to participants and beneficiaries in accordance with subsection (i) or (m) of section 101. For purposes of this paragraph, each violation with respect to any single participant or beneficiary shall be treated as a separate violation.

(8) The Secretary may assess against any plan sponsor of a multiemployer plan a civil penalty of not more than $1,100 per day—

(A) for each violation by such sponsor of the requirement under section 305 to adopt by the deadline established in that section a funding improvement plan or rehabilitation plan with respect to a multiemployer which is in endangered or critical status, or

(B) in the case of a plan in endangered status which is not in seriously endangered status, for failure by the plan to meet the applicable benchmarks under section 305 by the end of the funding improvement period with respect to the plan.

(9)(A) The Secretary may assess a civil penalty against any employer of up to $100 a day from the date of the employer's failure to meet the notice requirement of section 701(f)(3)(B)(i)(I). For purposes of this subparagraph, each violation with respect to any single employee shall be treated as a separate violation.

(B) The Secretary may assess a civil penalty against any plan administrator of up to $100 a day from the date of the plan administrator's failure to timely provide to any State the information required to be disclosed under section 701(f)(3)(B)(ii). For purposes of this subparagraph, each violation with respect to any single participant or beneficiary shall be treated as a separate violation.

(10)* Secretarial enforcement authority relating to use of genetic information—

(A) General rule—The Secretary may impose a penalty against any plan sponsor of a group health plan, or any health insurance issuer offering health insurance coverage in connection with the plan, for any failure by such sponsor or issuer to meet the requirements of subsection (a)(1)(F), (b)(3), (c), or (d) of section 702 or section 701 or 702(b)(1) with respect to genetic information, in connection with the plan.

* * *

(10)* The Secretary and the Secretary of Health and Human Services shall maintain such ongoing consultation as may be necessary and appropriate to coordinate enforcement under this subsection with enforcement under section 1144(c)(8) of the Social Security Act.

(d)(1) An employee benefit plan may sue or be sued under this title as an entity. Service of summons, subpoena, or other legal process of a court upon a trustee or an administrator of an employee benefit plan in his capacity as such shall constitute service upon the employee benefit plan. In a case where a plan has not designated in the summary plan description of the plan an individual as agent for the service of legal process, service upon the Secretary shall constitute such service. The Secretary, not later than 15 days after receipt of service under the preceding sentence, shall notify the administrator or any trustee of the plan of receipt of such service.

(2) Any money judgment under this title against an employee benefit plan shall be enforceable only against the plan as an entity and shall not be enforceable against any other person unless liability against such person is established in his individual capacity under this title.

(e)(1) Except for actions under subsection (a)(1)(B) of this section, the district courts of the United States shall have exclusive jurisdiction of civil actions under this title brought by the Secretary or by a participant, beneficiary, fiduciary, or any person referred to in section 101(f)(1). State courts of competent jurisdiction and district courts of the United States shall have concurrent jurisdiction of actions under paragraphs (1)(B) and (7) of subsection (a) of this section.

(2) Where an action under this title is brought in a district court of the United States, it may be brought in the district where the plan is administered, where the breach took place, or where a defendant resides or may be found, and process may be served in any other district where a defendant resides or may be found.

---

* So in original. Two paragraphs (10) have been enacted.

(f) The district courts of the United States shall have jurisdiction, without respect to the amount in controversy or the citizenship of the parties, to grant the relief provided for in subsection (a) of this section in any action.

(g)(1) In any action under this title (other than an action described in paragraph (2)) by a participant, beneficiary, or fiduciary, the court in its discretion may allow a reasonable attorney's fee and costs of action to either party.

(2) In any action under this title by a fiduciary for or on behalf of a plan to enforce section 515 in which a judgment in favor of the plan is awarded, the court shall award the plan—

(A) the unpaid contributions,

(B) interest on the unpaid contributions,

(C) an amount equal to the greater of—

(i) interest on the unpaid contributions, or

(ii) liquidated damages provided for under the plan in an amount not in excess of 20 percent (or such higher percentage as may be permitted under Federal or State law) of the amount determined by the court under subparagraph (A),

(D) reasonable attorney's fees and costs of the action, to be paid by the defendant, and

(E) such other legal or equitable relief as the court deems appropriate.

For purposes of this paragraph, interest on unpaid contributions shall be determined by using the rate provided under the plan, or, if none, the rate prescribed under section 6621 of the Internal Revenue Code of 1986.

(h) A copy of the complaint in any action under this title by a participant, beneficiary, or fiduciary (other than an action brought by one or more participants or beneficiaries under subsection (a)(1)(B) which is solely for the purpose of recovering benefits due such participants under the terms of the plan) shall be served upon the Secretary and the Secretary of the Treasury by certified mail. Either Secretary shall have the right in his discretion to intervene in any action, except that the Secretary of the Treasury may not intervene in any action under part 4 of this subtitle. If the Secretary brings an action under subsection (a) on behalf of a participant or beneficiary, he shall notify the Secretary of the Treasury.

(i) In the case of a transaction prohibited by section 406 by a party in interest with respect to a plan to which this part applies, the Secretary may assess a civil penalty against such party in interest. The amount of such penalty may not exceed 5 percent of the amount involved in each such transaction (as defined in section 4975(f)(4) of the Internal Revenue Code of 1986) for each year or part thereof during which the prohibited transaction continues, except that, if the transaction is not corrected (in such manner as the Secretary shall prescribe in regulations which shall be consistent with section 4975(f)(5) of such Code) within 90 days after notice from the Secretary (or such longer period as the Secretary may permit), such penalty may be in an amount not more than 100 percent of the amount involved. This subsection shall not apply to a transaction with respect to a plan described in section 4975(e)(1) of such Code.

(j) In all civil actions under this title, attorneys appointed by the Secretary may represent the Secretary (except as provided in section 518(a) of title 28), but all such litigation shall be subject to the direction and control of the Attorney General.

(k) Suits by an administrator, fiduciary, participant, or beneficiary of an employee benefit plan to review a final order of the Secretary, to restrain the Secretary from taking any action contrary to the provisions of this Act, or to compel him to take action required under this Act, may be brought in the district court of the United States for the district where the plan has its principal office, or in the United States District Court for the District of Columbia.

(l)(1) In the case of—

(A) any breach of fiduciary responsibility under (or other violation of) part 4 by a fiduciary, or

(B) any knowing participation in such a breach or violation by any other person,

the Secretary shall assess a civil penalty against such fiduciary or other person in an amount equal to 20 percent of the applicable recovery amount.

(2) For purposes of paragraph (1), the term "applicable recovery amount" means any amount which is recovered from a fiduciary or other person with respect to a breach or violation described in paragraph (1)—

(A) pursuant to any settlement agreement with the Secretary, or

(B) ordered by a court to be paid by such fiduciary or other person to a plan or its participants and beneficiaries in a judicial proceeding instituted by the Secretary under subsection (a)(2) or (a)(5).

(3) The Secretary may, in the Secretary's sole discretion, waive or reduce the penalty under paragraph (1) if the Secretary determines in writing that—

(A) the fiduciary or other person acted reasonably and in good faith, or

(B) it is reasonable to expect that the fiduciary or other person will not be able to restore all losses to the plan (or to provide the relief ordered pursuant to subsection (a)(9)) without severe financial hardship unless such waiver or reduction is granted.

(4) The penalty imposed on a fiduciary or other person under this subsection with respect to any transaction shall be reduced by the amount of any penalty or tax imposed on such fiduciary or other person with respect to such transaction under subsection (i) of this section and section 4975 of the Internal Revenue Code of 1986.

(m) In the case of a distribution to a pension plan participant or beneficiary in violation of section 206(e) by a plan fiduciary, the Secretary shall assess a penalty against such fiduciary in an amount equal to the value of the distribution. Such penalty shall not exceed $10,000 for each such distribution.

§ 503. Claims procedure (§ 1133)

In accordance with regulations of the Secretary, every employee benefit plan shall—

(1) provide adequate notice in writing to any participant or beneficiary whose claim for benefits under the plan has been denied, setting forth the specific reasons for such denial, written in a manner calculated to be understood by the participant, and

(2) afford a reasonable opportunity to any participant whose claim for benefits has been denied for a full and fair review by the appropriate named fiduciary of the decision denying the claim.

§ 504. Investigative authority (§ 1134)

(a) The Secretary shall have the power, in order to determine whether any person has violated or is about to violate any provision of this title or any regulation or order thereunder—

(1) to make an investigation, and in connection therewith to require the submission of reports, books, and records, and the filing of data in support of any information required to be filed with the Secretary under this title, and

(2) to enter such places, inspect such books and records and question such persons as he may deem necessary to enable him to determine the facts relative to such investigation, if he has reasonable cause to believe there may exist a violation of this title or any rule or regulation issued thereunder or if the entry is pursuant to an agreement with the plan.

The Secretary may make available to any person actually affected by any matter which is the subject of an investigation under this section, and to any department or agency of the United States, information concerning any matter which may be the subject of such investigation; except that any information obtained by the Secretary pursuant to section 6103(g) of the Internal Revenue Code of 1986 shall be made available only in accordance with regulations prescribed by the Secretary of the Treasury.

(b) The Secretary may not under the authority of this section require any plan to submit to the Secretary any books or records of the plan more than once in any 12 month period, unless the Secretary has reasonable cause to believe there may exist a violation of this subchapter or any regulation or order thereunder.

* * *

§ 510. Interference with protected rights (§ 1140)

It shall be unlawful for any person to discharge, fine, suspend, expel, discipline, or discriminate against a participant or beneficiary for exercising any right to which he is entitled under the provisions of an employee benefit plan, this title, section 3001, or the Welfare and Pension Plans Disclosure Act, or for the purpose of interfering with the attainment of any right to which such participant may become entitled under the plan, this title, or the Welfare and Pension Plans Disclosure Act. It shall be unlawful for any person to discharge, fine, suspend, expel, or discriminate against any person because he has given information or has testified or is about to testify in any inquiry or proceeding relating to this Act or the Welfare and Pension Plans Disclosure Act. In the case of a multiemployer plan, it shall be unlawful for the plan sponsor or any other person to discriminate against any contributing employer for exercising rights under this Act or for giving information or testifying in any inquiry or proceeding relating to this Act before Congress. The provisions of section 502 shall be applicable in the enforcement of this section.

§ 511. Coercive interference (§ 1141)

It shall be unlawful for any person through the use of fraud, force, violence, or threat of the use of force or violence, to restrain, coerce, intimidate, or attempt to restrain, coerce, or intimidate any participant or beneficiary for the purpose of interfering with or preventing the exercise of any right to which he is or may become entitled under the plan, this title, section 3001, or the Welfare and Pension Plans Disclosure Act. Any person who willfully violates this section shall be fined $100,000 or imprisoned for not more than 10 years, or both.

* * *

§ 514. Other laws (§ 1144)

(a) Except as provided in subsection (b) of this section, the provisions of this title and title IV shall supersede any and all State laws insofar as they may now or hereafter relate to any employee benefit plan described in section 4(a) and not exempt under section 4(b). This section shall take effect on January 1, 1975.

(b)(1) This section shall not apply with respect to any cause of action which arose, or any act or omission which occurred, before January 1, 1975.

(2)(A) Except as provided in subparagraph (B), nothing in this title shall be construed to exempt or relieve any person from any law of any State which regulates insurance, banking, or securities.

(B) Neither an employee benefit plan described in section 4(a), which is not exempt under section 4(b) (other than a plan established primarily for the purpose of providing death benefits), nor any trust established under such a plan, shall be deemed to be an insurance company or other insurer, bank, trust company, or investment company or to be engaged in the business of insurance or banking for purposes of any law of any State purporting to regulate insurance companies, insurance contracts, banks, trust companies, or investment companies.

(3) Nothing in this section shall be construed to prohibit use by the Secretary of services or facilities of a State agency as permitted under section 506 of this Act.

(4) Subsection (a) shall not apply to any generally applicable criminal law of a State.

(5)(A) Except as provided in subparagraph (B), subsection (a) shall not apply to the Hawaii Prepaid Health Care Act (Haw.Rev.Stat. §§ 393- 1 through 393-51).

(B) Nothing in subparagraph (A) shall be construed to exempt from subsection (a)—

(i) any State tax law relating to employee benefit plans, or

(ii) any amendment of the Hawaii Prepaid Health Care Act enacted after September 2, 1974, to the extent it provides for more than the effective administration of such Act as in effect on such date.

(C) Notwithstanding subparagraph (A), parts 1 and 4 of this subtitle, and the preceding sections of this part to the extent they govern matters which are governed by the provisions of such parts 1 and 4, shall supersede the Hawaii Prepaid Health Care Act (as in effect on or after January 14, 1983), but the Secretary may enter into cooperative arrangements under this paragraph and section 506 with officials of the State of Hawaii to assist them in effectuating the policies of provisions of such Act which are superseded by such parts 1 and 4 and the preceding sections of this part.

(6)(A) Notwithstanding any other provision of this section—

(i) in the case of an employee welfare benefit plan which is a multiple employer welfare arrangement and is fully insured (or which is a multiple employer welfare arrangement subject to an exemption under subparagraph (B)), any law of any State which regulates insurance may apply to such arrangement to the extent that such law provides—

(I) standards, requiring the maintenance of specified levels of reserves and specified levels of contributions, which any such plan, or any trust established under such a plan, must meet in order to be considered under such law able to pay benefits in full when due, and

(II) provisions to enforce such standards, and

(ii) in the case of any other employee welfare benefit plan which is a multiple employer welfare arrangement, in addition to this title, any law of any State which regulates insurance may apply to the extent not inconsistent with the preceding sections of this title.

(B) The Secretary may, under regulations which may be prescribed by the Secretary, exempt from subparagraph (A)(ii), individually or by class, multiple employer welfare arrangements which are not fully insured. Any such exemption may be granted with respect to any arrangement or class of arrangements only if such arrangement or each arrangement which is a member of such class meets the requirements of section 3(1) and section 4 necessary to be considered an employee welfare benefit plan to which this title applies.

(C) Nothing in subparagraph (A) shall affect the manner or extent to which the provisions of this title apply to an employee welfare benefit plan which is not a multiple employer welfare arrangement and which is a plan, fund, or program participating in, subscribing to, or otherwise using a multiple employer welfare arrangement to fund or administer benefits to such plan's participants and beneficiaries.

(D) For purposes of this paragraph, a multiple employer welfare arrangement shall be considered fully insured only if the terms of the arrangement provide for benefits the amount of all of which the Secretary determines are guaranteed under a contract, or policy of insurance, issued by an insurance company, insurance service, or insurance organization, qualified to conduct business in a State.

(7) Subsection (a) shall not apply to qualified domestic relations orders (within the meaning of section 206(d)(3)(B)(i)), qualified medical child support orders (within the meaning of section 609(a)(2)(A)), and the provisions of law referred to in section 609(a)(2)(B)(ii) to the extent they apply to qualified medical child support orders.

(8) Subsection (a) shall not be construed to preclude any State cause of action—

(A) with respect to which the State exercises its acquired rights under section 609(b)(3) with respect to a group health plan (as defined in section 607(1)), or

(B) for recoupment of payment with respect to items or services pursuant to a State plan for medical assistance approved under title XIX of the Social Security Act which would not have been payable if such acquired rights had been executed before payment with respect to such items or services by the group health plan.

(9) For additional provisions relating to group health plans, see section 704.

(c) For purposes of this section:

(1) The term "State law" includes all laws, decisions, rules, regulations, or other State action having the effect of law, of any State. A law of the United States applicable only to the District of Columbia shall be treated as a State law rather than a law of the United States.

(2) The term "State" includes a State, any political subdivisions thereof, or any agency or instrumentality of either, which purports to regulate, directly or indirectly, the terms and conditions of employee benefit plans covered by this title.

(d) Nothing in this title shall be construed to alter, amend, modify, invalidate, impair, or supersede any law of the United States (except as provided in sections 111 and 507(c)) or any rule or regulation issued under any such law.

(e)(1) Notwithstanding any other provision of this section, this title shall supersede any law of a State which would directly or indirectly prohibit or restrict the inclusion in any plan of an automatic contribution arrangement. The Secretary may prescribe regulations which would establish minimum standards that such an arrangement would be required to satisfy in order for this subsection to apply in the case of such arrangement.

(2) For purposes of this subsection, the term 'automatic contribution arrangement' means an arrangement—

(A) under which a participant may elect to have the plan sponsor make payments as contributions under the plan on behalf of the participant, or to the participant directly in cash,

(B) under which a participant is treated as having elected to have the plan sponsor make such contributions in an amount equal to a uniform percentage of compensation provided under the plan until the participant specifically elects not to have such contributions made (or specifically elects to have such contributions made at a different percentage), and

(C) under which such contributions are invested in accordance with regulations prescribed by the Secretary under section 404(c)(5).

(3)(A) The plan administrator of an automatic contribution arrangement shall, within a reasonable period before such plan year, provide to each participant to whom the arrangement applies for such plan year notice of the participant's rights and obligations under the arrangement which—

(i) is sufficiently accurate and comprehensive to apprise the participant of such rights and obligations, and

(ii) is written in a manner calculated to be understood by the average participant to whom the arrangement applies.

(B) A notice shall not be treated as meeting the requirements of subparagraph (A) with respect to a participant unless—

(i) the notice includes an explanation of the participant's right under the arrangement not to have elective contributions made on the participant's behalf (or to elect to have such contributions made at a different percentage),

(ii) the participant has a reasonable period of time, after receipt of the notice described in clause (i) and before the first elective contribution is made, to make such election, and

(iii) the notice explains how contributions made under the arrangement will be invested in the absence of any investment election by the participant.

* * *

Part 6—Group Health Plans

§ 601. Plans must provide continuation coverage to certain individuals (§ 1161)

(a) In general—The plan sponsor of each group health plan shall provide, in accordance with this part, that each qualified beneficiary who would lose coverage under the plan as a result of a qualifying event is entitled, under the plan, to elect, within the election period, continuation coverage under the plan.

(b) Exception for certain plans—Subsection (a) shall not apply to any group health plan for any calendar year if all employers maintaining such plan normally employed fewer than 20 employees on a typical business day during the preceding calendar year.

§ 602. Continuation coverage (§ 1162)

For purposes of section 601, the term "continuation coverage" means coverage under the plan which meets the following requirements:

(1) Type of benefit coverage—The coverage must consist of coverage which, as of the time the coverage is being provided, is identical to the coverage provided under the plan to similarly situated beneficiaries under the plan with respect to whom a qualifying event has not occurred. If coverage is modified under the plan for any group of similarly situated beneficiaries, such coverage shall also be modified in the same manner for all individuals who are qualified beneficiaries under the plan pursuant to this part in connection with such group.

(2) Period of coverage—The coverage must extend for at least the period beginning on the date of the qualifying event and ending not earlier than the earliest of the following:

(A) Maximum required period—

(i) General rule for terminations and reduced hours—In the case of a qualifying event described in section 603(2), except as provided in clause (ii), the date which is 18 months after the date of the qualifying event.

(ii) Special rule for multiple qualifying events—If a qualifying event (other than a qualifying event described in section 603(6)) occurs during the 18 months after the date of a qualifying event described in section 603(2), the date which is 36 months after the date of the qualifying event described in section 603(2).

(iii) Special rule for certain bankruptcy proceedings—In the case of a qualifying event described in section 603(6) (relating to bankruptcy proceedings), the date of the death of the covered employee or qualified beneficiary (described in section 607(3)(C)(iii)), or in the case of the surviving spouse or dependent children of the covered employee, 36 months after the date of the death of the covered employee.

(iv) General rule for other qualifying events—In the case of a qualifying event not described in section 603(2) or 603(6), the date which is 36 months after the date of the qualifying event.

(v) **Special rule for PBGC recipients.** In the case of a qualifying event described in section 603(2) with respect to a covered employee who (as of such qualifying event) has a nonforfeitable right to a benefit any portion of which is to be paid by the Pension Benefit Guaranty Corporation under title IV, notwithstanding clause (i) or (ii), the date of the death of the covered employee, or in the case of the surviving spouse or dependent children of the covered employee, 24 months after the date of the death of the covered employee. The preceding sentence shall not require any period of coverage to extend beyond January 1, 2014.

(vi) Special rule for TAA-eligible individuals. In the case of a qualifying event described in section 603(2) with respect to a covered employee who is (as of the date that the period of coverage would, but for this clause or clause (vii), otherwise terminate under clause (i) or (ii)) a TAA-eligible individual (as defined in section 605(b)(4)(B)), the period of coverage shall not terminate by reason of clause (i) or (ii), as the case may be, before the later of the date specified in such clause or the date on which such individual ceases to be such a TAA-eligible individual. The preceding sentence shall not require any period of coverage to extend beyond January 1, 2014.

(vii) Medicare entitlement followed by qualifying event. In the case of a qualifying event described in section 603(2) that occurs less than 18 months after the date the covered employee became entitled to benefits under title XVIII of the Social Security Act, the period of coverage for qualified beneficiaries other than the covered employee shall not terminate under this subparagraph before the close of the 36-month period beginning on the date the covered employee became so entitled.

(viii) Special rule for disability. In the case of a qualified beneficiary who is determined, under title II or XVI of the Social Security Act, to have been disabled at any time during the first 60 days of continuation coverage under this part, any reference in clause (i) or (ii) to 18 months is deemed a reference to 29 months (with respect to all qualified beneficiaries), but only if the qualified beneficiary has provided notice of such determination under section 606(3) before the end of such 18 months.

(B) End of plan—The date on which the employer ceases to provide any group health plan to any employee.

(C) Failure to pay premium—The date on which coverage ceases under the plan by reason of a failure to make timely payment of any premium required under the plan with respect to the qualified beneficiary. The payment of any premium (other than any payment referred to in the last sentence of paragraph (3)) shall be considered to be timely if made within 30 days after the date due or within such longer period as applies to or under the plan.

(D) Group health plan coverage or Medicare entitlement—The date on which the qualified beneficiary first becomes, after the date of the election—

(i) covered under any other group health plan (as an employee or otherwise) which does not contain any exclusion or limitation with respect to any preexisting condition of such beneficiary (other than such an exclusion or limitation which does not apply to (or is satisfied by) such beneficiary by reason of chapter 100 of the Internal Revenue Code of 1986, part 7 of this subtitle, or title XXVII of the Public Health Service Act), or

(ii) in the case of a qualified beneficiary other than a qualified beneficiary described in section 607(3)(C), entitled to benefits under title XVIII of the Social Security Act.

(E) Termination of extended coverage for disability—In the case of a qualified beneficiary who is disabled at any time during the first 60 days of continuation coverage under this part, the month that begins more than 30 days after the date of the final determination under title II or XVI of the Social Security Act that the qualified beneficiary is no longer disabled.

(3) Premium requirements—The plan may require payment of a premium for any period of continuation coverage, except that such premium—

(A) shall not exceed 102 percent of the applicable premium for such period, and

(B) may, at the election of the payor, be made in monthly installments.

In no event may the plan require the payment of any premium before the day which is 45 days after the day on which the qualified beneficiary made the initial election for continuation coverage. In the case of an individual described in the last sentence of paragraph (2)(A), any reference in subparagraph (A) of this paragraph to "102 percent" is deemed a reference to "150 percent" for any month after the 18th month of continuation coverage described in clause (i) or (ii) of paragraph (2)(A).

(4) No requirement of insurability—The coverage may not be conditioned upon, or discriminate on the basis of lack of, evidence of insurability.

(5) Conversion option—In the case of a qualified beneficiary whose period of continuation coverage expires under paragraph (2)(A), the plan must, during the 180-day period ending on such expiration date, provide to the qualified beneficiary the option of enrollment under a conversion health plan otherwise generally available under the plan.

§ 603. Qualifying event (§ 1163)

For purposes of this part, the term "qualifying event" means, with respect to any covered employee, any of the following events which, but for the continuation coverage required under this part, would result in the loss of coverage of a qualified beneficiary:

(1) The death of the covered employee.

(2) The termination (other than by reason of such employee's gross misconduct), or reduction of hours, of the covered employee's employment.

(3) The divorce or legal separation of the covered employee from the employee's spouse.

(4) The covered employee becoming entitled to benefits under title XVIII of the Social Security Act.

(5) A dependent child ceasing to be a dependent child under the generally applicable requirements of the plan.

(6) A proceeding in a case under title 11, United States Code, commencing on or after July 1, 1986, with respect to the employer from whose employment the covered employee retired at any time.

In the case of an event described in paragraph (6), a loss of coverage includes a substantial elimination of coverage with respect to a qualified beneficiary described in section 607(3)(C) within one year before or after the date of commencement of the proceeding.

§ 604. Applicable premium (§ 1164)

For purposes of this part—

(1) In general—The term "applicable premium" means, with respect to any period of continuation coverage of qualified beneficiaries, the cost to the plan for such period of the coverage for similarly situated beneficiaries with respect to whom a qualifying event has not occurred (without regard to whether such cost is paid by the employer or employee).

* * *

§ 605. Election (§ 1165)

For purposes of this part—

(1) Election period—The term "election period" means the period which—

(A) begins not later than the date on which coverage terminates under the plan by reason of a qualifying event,

(B) is of at least 60 days' duration, and

(C) ends not earlier than 60 days after the later of—

(i) the date described in subparagraph (A), or

(ii) in the case of any qualified beneficiary who receives notice under section 606(4), the date of such notice.

* * *

§ 607. Definitions and special rules (§ 1167)

For purposes of this part--

(1) Group health plan—The term "group health plan" means an employee welfare benefit plan providing medical care (as defined in section 213(d) of the Internal Revenue Code of 1986) to participants or beneficiaries directly or through insurance, reimbursement, or otherwise. Such term shall not include any plan substantially all of the coverage under which is for qualified long-term care services (as defined in section 7702B(c) of such Code).

(2) Covered employee—The term "covered employee" means an individual who is (or was) provided coverage under a group health plan by virtue of the performance of services by the individual for 1 or more persons maintaining the plan (including as an employee defined in section 401(c)(1) of the Internal Revenue Code of 1986).

(3) Qualified beneficiary—

(A) In general—The term "qualified beneficiary" means, with respect to a covered employee under a group health plan, any other individual who, on the day before the qualifying event for that employee, is a beneficiary under the plan—

(i) as the spouse of the covered employee, or

(ii) as the dependent child of the employee.

Such term shall also include a child who is born to or placed for adoption with the covered employee during the period of continuation coverage under this part.

(B) Special rule for terminations and reduced employment—In the case of a qualifying event described in section 603(2), the term "qualified beneficiary" includes the covered employee.

(C) Special rule for retirees and widows—In the case of a qualifying event described in section 603(6), the term "qualified beneficiary" includes a covered employee who had retired on or before the date of substantial elimination of coverage and any other individual who, on the day before such qualifying event, is a beneficiary under the plan—

(i) as the spouse of the covered employee,

(ii) as the dependent child of the employee, or

(iii) as the surviving spouse of the covered employee.

(4) Employer—Subsection (n) (relating to leased employees) and subsection (t) (relating to application of controlled group rules to certain employee benefits) of section 414 of the Internal Revenue Code of 1986 shall apply for purposes of this part in the same manner and to the same extent as such subsections apply for purposes of section 106 of such Code. Any regulations prescribed by the Secretary pursuant to the preceding sentence shall be consistent and coextensive with any regulations prescribed for similar purposes by the Secretary of the Treasury (or such Secretary's delegate) under such subsections.

(5) Optional extension of required periods—A group health plan shall not be treated as failing to meet the requirements of this part solely because the plan provides both—

(A) that the period of extended coverage referred to in section 1162(2) of this title commences with the date of the loss of coverage, and

(B) that the applicable notice period provided under section 1166(a)(2) of this title commences with the date of the loss of coverage.

§ 609. Additional standards for group health plans (§ 1169)

(a) Group health plan coverage pursuant to medical child support orders—

(1) In general—Each group health plan shall provide benefits in accordance with the applicable requirements of any qualified medical child support order. A qualified medical child support order with respect to any participant or beneficiary shall be deemed to apply to each group health plan which has received such order, from which the participant or beneficiary is eligible to receive benefits, and with respect to which the requirements of paragraph (4) are met.

(2) Definitions—For purposes of this subsection—

(A) Qualified medical child support order—The term "qualified medical child support order" means a medical child support order—

(i) which creates or recognizes the existence of an alternate recipient's right to, or assigns to an alternate recipient the right to, receive benefits for which a participant or beneficiary is eligible under a group health plan, and

(ii) with respect to which the requirements of paragraphs (3) and (4) are met.

(B) Medical child support order—The term "medical child support order" means any judgment, decree, or order (including approval of a settlement agreement) which—

(i) provides for child support with respect to a child of a participant under a group health plan or provides for health benefit coverage to such a child, is made pursuant to a State domestic relations law (including a community property law), and relates to benefits under such plan, or

(ii) is made pursuant to a law relating to medical child support described in section 1908 of the Social Security Act (as added by section 13822 of the Omnibus Budget Reconciliation Act of 1993) with respect to a group health plan,

if such judgment, decree, or order (I) is issued by a court of competent jurisdiction or (II) is issued through an administrative process established under State law and has the force and effect of law under applicable State law.

For purposes of this subparagraph, an administrative notice which is issued pursuant to an administrative process referred to in subclause (II) of the preceding sentence and which has the effect of an order described in clause (i) or (ii) of the preceding sentence shall be treated as such an order.

(C) Alternate recipient—The term "alternate recipient" means any child of a participant who is recognized under a medical child support order as having a right to enrollment under a group health plan with respect to such participant.

(D) Child—The term "child" includes any child adopted by, or placed for adoption with, a participant of a group health plan.

(3) Information to be included in qualified order—A medical child support order meets the requirements of this paragraph only if such order clearly specifies—

(A) the name and the last known mailing address (if any) of the participant and the name and mailing address of each alternate recipient covered by the order, except that, to the extent provided in the order, the name and mailing address of an official of a State or a political subdivision thereof may be substituted for the mailing address of any such alternate recipient,

(B) a reasonable description of the type of coverage to be provided to each such alternate recipient, or the manner in which such type of coverage is to be determined, and

(C) the period to which such order applies.

(4) Restriction on new types or forms of benefits—A medical child support order meets the requirements of this paragraph only if such order does not require a plan to provide any type or form of benefit, or any option, not otherwise provided under the plan, except to the extent necessary to meet the requirements of a law relating to medical child support described in section 1908 of the Social Security Act (as added by section 13822 of the Omnibus Budget Reconciliation Act of 1993).

(5) Procedural requirements—

(A) Timely notifications and determinations—In the case of any medical child support order received by a group health plan—

(i) the plan administrator shall promptly notify the participant and each alternate recipient of the receipt of such order and the plan's procedures for determining whether medical child support orders are qualified medical child support orders, and

(ii) within a reasonable period after receipt of such order, the plan administrator shall determine whether such order is a qualified medical child support order and notify the participant and each alternate recipient of such determination.

(B) Establishment of procedures for determining qualified status of orders—Each group health plan shall establish reasonable procedures to determine whether medical child support orders are qualified medical child support orders and to administer the provision of benefits under such qualified orders. Such procedures—

(i) shall be in writing,

(ii) shall provide for the notification of each person specified in a medical child support order as eligible to receive benefits under the plan (at the address included in the medical child support order) of such procedures promptly upon receipt by the plan of the medical child support order, and

(iii) shall permit an alternate recipient to designate a representative for receipt of copies of notices that are sent to the alternate recipient with respect to a medical child support order.

(C) National Medical Support Notice deemed to be a qualified medical child support order—

(i) In general—If the plan administrator of a group health plan which is maintained by the employer of a noncustodial parent of a child or to which such an employer contributes receives an appropriately completed National Medical Support Notice promulgated pursuant to section 401(b) of the Child Support Performance and Incentive Act of 1998 in the case of such child, and the Notice meets the requirements of paragraphs (3) and (4), the Notice shall be deemed to be a qualified medical child support order in the case of such child.

(ii) Enrollment of child in plan—In any case in which an appropriately completed National Medical Support Notice is issued in the case of a child of a participant under a group health plan who is a noncustodial parent of the child, and the Notice is deemed under clause (i) to be a qualified medical child support order, the plan administrator, within 40 business days after the date of the Notice, shall—

(I) notify the State agency issuing the Notice with respect to such child whether coverage of the child is available under the terms of the plan and, if so, whether such child is covered under the plan and either the effective date of the coverage or, if necessary, any steps to be taken by the custodial parent (or by the official of a State or political subdivision thereof substituted for the name of such child pursuant to paragraph (3)(A)) to effectuate the coverage; and

(II) provide to the custodial parent (or such substituted official) a description of the coverage available and any forms or documents necessary to effectuate such coverage.

(iii) Rule of construction—Nothing in this subparagraph shall be construed as requiring a group health plan, upon receipt of a National Medical Support Notice, to provide benefits under the plan (or eligibility for such benefits) in addition to benefits (or eligibility for benefits) provided under the terms of the plan as of immediately before receipt of such Notice.

(6) Actions taken by fiduciaries—If a plan fiduciary acts in accordance with part 4 of this subtitle in treating a medical child support order as being (or not being) a qualified medical child support order, then the plan's obligation to the participant and each alternate recipient shall be discharged to the extent of any payment made pursuant to such act of the fiduciary.

(7) Treatment of alternate recipients—

(A) Treatment as beneficiary generally—A person who is an alternate recipient under a qualified medical child support order shall be considered a beneficiary under the plan for purposes of any provision of this Act.

(B) Treatment as participant for purposes of reporting and disclosure requirements—A person who is an alternate recipient under any medical child support order shall be considered a participant under the plan for purposes of the reporting and disclosure requirements of part 1.

(8) Direct provision of benefits provided to alternate recipients—Any payment for benefits made by a group health plan pursuant to a medical child support order in reimbursement for expenses paid by an alternate recipient or an alternate recipient's custodial parent or legal guardian shall be made to the alternate recipient or the alternate recipient's custodial parent or legal guardian.

(9) Payment to State official treated as satisfaction of plan's obligation to make payment to alternate recipient—Payment of benefits by a group health plan to an official of a State or a political subdivision thereof whose name and address have been substituted for the address of an alternate recipient in a qualified medical child support order, pursuant to paragraph (3)(A), shall be treated, for purposes of this subchapter, as payment of benefits to the alternate recipient.

* * *

Part 7—Group Health Plan Requirements

§ 701. Increased portability through limitation on preexisting condition exclusions (§ 1181)

(a) Limitation on preexisting condition exclusion period; crediting for periods of previous coverage—Subject to subsection (d), a group health plan, and a health insurance issuer offering group health insurance coverage, may, with respect to a participant or beneficiary, impose a preexisting condition exclusion only if—

(1) such exclusion relates to a condition (whether physical or mental), regardless of the cause of the condition, for which medical advice, diagnosis, care, or treatment was recommended or received within the 6-month period ending on the enrollment date;

(2) such exclusion extends for a period of not more than 12 months (or 18 months in the case of a late enrollee) after the enrollment date; and

(3) the period of any such preexisting condition exclusion is reduced by the aggregate of the periods of creditable coverage (if any, as defined in subsection (c)(1)) applicable to the participant or beneficiary as of the enrollment date.

(b) Definitions—For purposes of this part—

(1) Preexisting condition exclusion—

(A) In general—The term "preexisting condition exclusion" means, with respect to coverage, a limitation or exclusion of benefits relating to a condition based on the fact that the condition was present before the date of enrollment for such coverage, whether or not any medical advice, diagnosis, care, or treatment was recommended or received before such date.

(B) Treatment of genetic information—Genetic information shall not be treated as a condition described in subsection (a)(1) of this section in the absence of a diagnosis of the condition related to such information.

(2) Enrollment date—The term "enrollment date" means, with respect to an individual covered under a group health plan or health insurance coverage, the date of enrollment of the individual in the plan or coverage or, if earlier, the first day of the waiting period for such enrollment.

(3) Late enrollee—The term "late enrollee" means, with respect to coverage under a group health plan, a participant or beneficiary who enrolls under the plan other than during—

(A) the first period in which the individual is eligible to enroll under the plan, or

(B) a special enrollment period under subsection (f) of this section.

(4) Waiting period—The term "waiting period" means, with respect to a group health plan and an individual who is a potential participant or beneficiary in the plan, the period that must pass with respect to the individual before the individual is eligible to be covered for benefits under the terms of the plan.

(c) Rules relating to crediting previous coverage—

(1) "Creditable coverage" defined—For purposes of this part, the term "creditable coverage" means, with respect to an individual, coverage of the individual under any of the following:

(A) A group health plan.

(B) Health insurance coverage.

(C) Part A or part B of title XVIII of the Social Security Act.

(D) Title XIX of the Social Security Act, other than coverage consisting solely of benefits under section 1928.

(E) Chapter 55 of title 10, United States Code.

(F) A medical care program of the Indian Health Service or of a tribal organization.

(G) A State health benefits risk pool.

(H) A health plan offered under chapter 89 of title 5, United States Code.

(I) A public health plan (as defined in regulations).

(J) A health benefit plan under section 5(e) of the Peace Corps Act (22 U.S.C. 2504(e)).

Such term does not include coverage consisting solely of coverage of excepted benefits (as defined in section 706(c)).

(2) Not counting periods before significant breaks in coverage—

(A) In general—A period of creditable coverage shall not be counted, with respect to enrollment of an individual under a group health plan, if, after such period and before the enrollment date, there was a 63-day period during all of which the individual was not covered under any creditable coverage.

(B) Waiting period not treated as a break in coverage—For purposes of subparagraph (A) and subsection (d)(4) of this section, any period that an individual is in a waiting period for any coverage under a group health plan (or for group health insurance coverage) or is in an affiliation period (as defined in subsection (g)(2) of this section) shall not be taken into account in determining the continuous period under subparagraph (A).

* * *

(3) Method of crediting coverage—

(A) Standard method—Except as otherwise provided under subparagraph (B), for purposes of applying subsection (a)(3) of this section, a group health plan, and a health insurance issuer offering group health insurance coverage, shall count a period of creditable coverage without regard to the specific benefits covered during the period.

(B) Election of alternative method—A group health plan, or a health insurance issuer offering group health insurance coverage, may elect to apply subsection (a)(3) of this section based on coverage of benefits within each of several classes or categories of benefits specified in regulations rather than as provided under subparagraph (A). Such election shall be made on a uniform basis for all participants and beneficiaries. Under such election a group health plan or issuer shall count a period of creditable coverage with respect to any class or category of benefits if any level of benefits is covered within such class or category.

(C) Plan notice—In the case of an election with respect to a group health plan under subparagraph (B) (whether or not health insurance coverage is provided in connection with such plan), the plan shall—

(i) prominently state in any disclosure statements concerning the plan, and state to each enrollee at the time of enrollment under the plan, that the plan has made such election, and

(ii) include in such statements a description of the effect of this election.

(4) Establishment of period—Periods of creditable coverage with respect to an individual shall be established through presentation of certifications described in subsection (e) of this section or in such other manner as may be specified in regulations.

(d) Exceptions—

(1) Exclusion not applicable to certain newborns—Subject to paragraph (4), a group health plan, and a health insurance issuer offering group health insurance coverage, may not impose any preexisting condition exclusion in the case of an individual who, as of the last day of the 30-day period beginning with the date of birth, is covered under creditable coverage.

(2) Exclusion not applicable to certain adopted children—Subject to paragraph (4), a group health plan, and a health insurance issuer offering group health insurance coverage, may not impose any preexisting condition exclusion in the case of a child who is adopted or placed for adoption before attaining 18 years of age and who, as of the last day of the 30-day period beginning on the date of the adoption or placement for adoption, is covered under creditable coverage. The previous sentence shall not apply to coverage before the date of such adoption or placement for adoption.

(3) Exclusion not applicable to pregnancy—A group health plan, and health insurance issuer offering group health insurance coverage, may not impose any preexisting condition exclusion relating to pregnancy as a preexisting condition.

(4) Loss if break in coverage—Paragraphs (1) and (2) shall no longer apply to an individual after the end of the first 63-day period during all of which the individual was not covered under any creditable coverage.

* * *

§ 702. Prohibiting discrimination against individual participants and beneficiaries based on health status (§ 1182)

(a) In eligibility to enroll—

(1) In general—Subject to paragraph (2), a group health plan, and a health insurance issuer offering group health insurance coverage in connection with a group health plan, may not establish rules for eligibility (including continued eligibility) of any individual to enroll under the terms of the plan based on any of the following health status-related factors in relation to the individual or a dependent of the individual:

(A) Health status.

(B) Medical condition (including both physical and mental illnesses).

(C) Claims experience.

(D) Receipt of health care.

(E) Medical history.

(F) Genetic information.

(G) Evidence of insurability (including conditions arising out of acts of domestic violence).

(H) Disability.

(2) No application to benefits or exclusions—To the extent consistent with section 701, paragraph (1) shall not be construed—

(A) to require a group health plan, or group health insurance coverage, to provide particular benefits other than those provided under the terms of such plan or coverage, or

(B) to prevent such a plan or coverage from establishing limitations or restrictions on the amount, level, extent, or nature of the benefits or coverage for similarly situated individuals enrolled in the plan or coverage.

(3) Construction—For purposes of paragraph (1), rules for eligibility to enroll under a plan include rules defining any applicable waiting periods for such enrollment.

(b) In premium contributions—

(1) In general—A group health plan, and a health insurance issuer offering health insurance coverage in connection with a group health plan, may not require any individual (as a condition of enrollment or continued enrollment under the plan) to pay a premium or contribution which is greater than such premium or contribution for a similarly situated individual enrolled in the plan on the basis of any health status-related factor in relation to the individual or to an individual enrolled under the plan as a dependent of the individual.

(2) Construction—Nothing in paragraph (1) shall be construed—

(A) to restrict the amount that an employer may be charged for coverage under a group health plan except as provided in paragraph (3); or

(B) to prevent a group health plan, and a health insurance issuer offering group health insurance coverage, from establishing premium discounts or rebates or modifying otherwise applicable copayments or deductibles in return for adherence to programs of health promotion and disease prevention.

(3) No group-based discrimination on basis of genetic information—

(A) In general— For purposes of this section, a group health plan, and a health insurance issuer offering group health insurance coverage in connection with a group health plan, may not adjust premium or contribution amounts for the group covered under such plan on the basis of genetic information.

(B) Rule of construction—Nothing in subparagraph (A) or in paragraphs (1) and (2) of subsection (d) shall be construed to limit the ability of a health insurance issuer offering health insurance coverage in connection with a group health plan to increase the premium for an employer based on the manifestation of a disease or disorder of an individual who is enrolled in the plan. In such case, the manifestation of a disease or disorder in one individual cannot also be used as genetic information about other group members and to further increase the premium for the employer.

(c) Genetic testing—

(1) Limitation on requesting or requiring genetic testing—A group health plan, and a health insurance issuer offering health insurance coverage in connection with a group health plan, shall not request or require an individual or a family member of such individual to undergo a genetic test.

(2) Rule of construction—Paragraph (1) shall not be construed to limit the authority of a health care professional who is providing health care services to an individual to request that such individual undergo a genetic test.

(3) Rule of construction regarding payment—

(A) In general—Nothing in paragraph (1) shall be construed to preclude a group health plan, or a health insurance issuer offering health insurance coverage in connection with a group health plan, from obtaining and using the results of a genetic test in making a determination regarding payment (as such term is defined for the purposes of applying the regulations promulgated by the Secretary of Health and Human Services under part C of title XI of the Social Security Act and section 264 of the Health Insurance Portability and Accountability Act of 1996, as may be revised from time to time) consistent with subsection (a).

(B) Limitation—For purposes of subparagraph (A), a group health plan, or a health insurance issuer offering health insurance coverage in connection with a group health plan, may request only the minimum amount of information necessary to accomplish the intended purpose.

(4) Research exception—Notwithstanding paragraph (1), a group health plan, or a health insurance issuer offering health insurance coverage in connection with a group health plan, may request, but not require, that a participant or beneficiary undergo a genetic test if each of the following conditions is met:

(A) The request is made, in writing, pursuant to research that complies with part 46 of title 45, Code of Federal Regulations, or equivalent Federal regulations, and any applicable State or local law or regulations for the protection of human subjects in research.

(B) The plan or issuer clearly indicates to each participant or beneficiary, or in the case of a minor child, to the legal guardian of such beneficiary, to whom the request is made that—

(i) compliance with the request is voluntary; and

(ii) non-compliance will have no effect on enrollment status or premium or contribution amounts.

(C) No genetic information collected or acquired under this paragraph shall be used for underwriting purposes.

(D) The plan or issuer notifies the Secretary in writing that the plan or issuer is conducting activities pursuant to the exception provided for under this paragraph, including a description of the activities conducted.

(E) The plan or issuer complies with such other conditions as the Secretary may by regulation require for activities conducted under this paragraph.

(d) Prohibition on collection of genetic information—

(1) In general—A group health plan, and a health insurance issuer offering health insurance coverage in connection with a group health plan, shall not request, require, or purchase genetic information for underwriting purposes (as defined in section 733).

(2) Prohibition on collection of genetic information prior to enrollment—A group health plan, and a health insurance issuer offering health insurance coverage in connection with a group health plan, shall not request, require, or purchase genetic information with respect to any individual prior to such individual's enrollment under the plan or coverage in connection with such enrollment.

(3) Incidental collection—If a group health plan, or a health insurance issuer offering health insurance coverage in connection with a group health plan, obtains genetic information incidental to the requesting, requiring, or purchasing of other information concerning any individual, such request, requirement, or purchase shall not be considered a violation of paragraph (2) if such request, requirement, or purchase is not in violation of paragraph (1).

(e) Application to all plans—The provisions of subsections (a)(1)(F), (b)(3), (c), and (d), and subsection (b)(1) and section 701 with respect to genetic information, shall apply to group health plans and health insurance issuers without regard to section 732(a).

(f) Genetic information of a fetus or embryo—Any reference in this part to genetic information concerning an individual or family member of an individual shall—

(1) with respect to such an individual or family member of an individual who is a pregnant woman, include genetic information of any fetus carried by such pregnant woman; and

(2) with respect to an individual or family member utilizing an assisted reproductive technology, include genetic information of any embryo legally held by the individual or family member.

§ 711. Standards relating to benefits for mothers and newborns (§ 1185)

(a) Requirements for minimum hospital stay following birth—

(1) In general—A group health plan, and a health insurance issuer offering group health insurance coverage, may not—

(A) except as provided in paragraph (2)—

(i) restrict benefits for any hospital length of stay in connection with childbirth for the mother or newborn child, following a normal vaginal delivery, to less than 48 hours, or

(ii) restrict benefits for any hospital length of stay in connection with childbirth for the mother or newborn child, following a cesarean section, to less than 96 hours; or

(B) require that a provider obtain authorization from the plan or the issuer for prescribing any length of stay required under subparagraph (A) (without regard to paragraph (2)).

(2) Exception—Paragraph (1)(A) shall not apply in connection with any group health plan or health insurance issuer in any case in which the decision to discharge the mother or her newborn child prior to the expiration of the minimum length of stay otherwise required under paragraph (1)(A) is made by an attending provider in consultation with the mother.

* * *

§ 712. Parity in mental health and substance use disorder benefits (§ 1185a)

(a) In general—

(1) Aggregate lifetime limits—In the case of a group health plan (or health insurance coverage offered in connection with such a plan) that provides both medical and surgical benefits and mental health or substance use disorder benefits—

(A) No lifetime limit—If the plan or coverage does not include an aggregate lifetime limit on substantially all medical and surgical benefits, the plan or coverage may not impose any aggregate lifetime limit on mental health or substance use disorder benefits.

(B) Lifetime limit—If the plan or coverage includes an aggregate lifetime limit on substantially all medical and surgical benefits (in this paragraph referred to as the "applicable lifetime limit"), the plan or coverage shall either—

(i) apply the applicable lifetime limit both to the medical and surgical benefits to which it otherwise would apply and to mental health and substance use disorder benefits and not distinguish in the application of such limit between such medical and surgical benefits and mental health and substance use disorder benefits; or

(ii) not include any aggregate lifetime limit on mental health or substance use disorder benefits that is less than the applicable lifetime limit.

* * *

(2) Annual limits—In the case of a group health plan (or health insurance coverage offered in connection with such a plan) that provides both medical and surgical benefits and mental health benefits—

(A) No annual limit—If the plan or coverage does not include an annual limit on substantially all medical and surgical benefits, the plan or coverage may not impose any annual limit on mental health or substance use disorder benefits.

(B) Annual limit—If the plan or coverage includes an annual limit on substantially all medical and surgical benefits (in this paragraph referred to as the "applicable annual limit"), the plan or coverage shall either—

(i) apply the applicable annual limit both to medical and surgical benefits to which it otherwise would apply and to mental health and substance use disorder benefits and not distinguish in the application of such limit between such medical and surgical benefits and mental health and substance use disorder benefits; or

(ii) not include any annual limit on mental health or substance use disorder benefits that is less than the applicable annual limit.

* * *

(b) Construction—Nothing in this section shall be construed—

(1) as requiring a group health plan (or health insurance coverage offered in connection with such a plan) to provide any mental health or substance use disorder benefits; or

(2) in the case of a group health plan (or health insurance coverage offered in connection with such a plan) that provides mental health or substance use disorder benefits, as affecting the terms and conditions of the plan or coverage relating to such benefits under the plan or coverage, except as provided in subsection (a).

(c) Exemptions—

(1) Small employer exemption—

(A) In general—This section shall not apply to any group health plan (and group health insurance coverage offered in connection with a group health plan) for any plan year of a small employer.

(B) Small employer— For purposes of subparagraph (A), the term "small employer" means, in connection with a group health plan with respect to a calendar year and a plan year, an employer who employed an average of at least 2 (or 1 in the case of an employer residing in a State that permits small groups to include a single individual) but not more than 50 employees on business days during the preceding calendar year.

* * *

(2) Cost exemption—

(A) In general—With respect to a group health plan (or health insurance coverage offered in connection with such a plan), if the application of this section to such plan (or coverage) results in an increase for the plan year involved of the actual total costs of coverage with respect to medical and surgical benefits and mental health and substance use disorder benefits under the plan (as determined and certified under subparagraph (C)) by an amount that exceeds the applicable percentage described in subparagraph (B) of the actual total plan costs, the provisions of this section shall not apply to such plan (or coverage) during the following plan year, and such exemption shall apply to the plan (or coverage) for 1 plan year. An employer may elect to continue to apply mental health and substance use disorder parity pursuant to this section with respect to the group health plan (or coverage) involved regardless of any increase in total costs.

(B) Applicable percentage—With respect to a plan (or coverage), the applicable percentage described in this subparagraph shall be—

(i) 2 percent in the case of the first plan year in which this section is applied; and

(ii) 1 percent in the case of each subsequent plan year.

* * *

(e) Definitions—For purposes of this section

* * *

(4) Mental health or substance use disorder benefits—The term "mental health or substance use disorder benefits" means benefits with respect to services for mental health conditions, as defined under the terms of the plan and in accordance with applicable Federal and State law.

(5) Substance use disorder benefits—The term "substance use disorder benefits" means benefits with respect to services for substance use disorders, as defined under the terms of the plan and in accordance with applicable Federal and State law.

* * *

§ 713. Required coverage for reconstructive surgery following mastectomies (§ 1185b)

(a) In general—A group health plan, and a health insurance issuer providing health insurance coverage in connection with a group health plan, that provides medical and surgical benefits with respect to a mastectomy shall provide, in a case of a participant or beneficiary who is receiving benefits in connection with a mastectomy and who elects breast reconstruction in connection with such mastectomy, coverage for—

(1) all stages of reconstruction of the breast on which the mastectomy has been performed;

(2) surgery and reconstruction of the other breast to produce a symmetrical appearance; and

(3) prostheses and physical complications of mastectomy, including lymphedemas;

in a manner determined in consultation with the attending physician and the patient. Such coverage may be subject to annual deductibles and coinsurance provisions as may be deemed appropriate and as are consistent with those established for other benefits under the plan or coverage. Written notice of the availability of such coverage shall be delivered to the participant upon enrollment and annually thereafter.

* * *

§ 715. Additional market reforms (§ 1185d)

(a) General rule. Except as provided in subsection (b)—

(1) the provisions of part A of title XXVII of the Public Health Service Act (as amended by the Patient Protection and Affordable Care Act) shall apply to group health plans, and health insurance issuers providing health insurance coverage in connection with group health plans, as if included in this subpart; and

(2) to the extent that any provision of this part conflicts with a provision of such part A with respect to group health plans, or health insurance issuers providing health insurance coverage in connection with group health plans, the provisions of such part A shall apply.

(b) Exception. Notwithstanding subsection (a), the provisions of sections 2716 and 2718 of title XXVII of the Public Health Service Act (as amended by the Patient Protection and Affordable Care Act) shall not apply with respect to self-insured group health plans, and the provisions of this part shall continue to apply to such plans as if such sections of the Public Health Service Act (as so amended) had not been enacted.

§ 731. Preemption; State flexibility; construction (§ 1191)

(a) Continued applicability of State law with respect to health insurance issuers—

(1) In general—Subject to paragraph (2) and except as provided in subsection (b) of this section, this part shall not be construed to supersede any provision of State law which establishes, implements, or continues in effect any standard or requirement solely relating to health insurance issuers in connection with group health insurance coverage except to the extent that such standard or requirement prevents the application of a requirement of this part.

(2) Continued preemption with respect to group health plans—Nothing in this part shall be construed to affect or modify the provisions of section 514 with respect to group health plans.

(b) Special rules in case of portability requirements—

(1) In general—Subject to paragraph (2), the provisions of this part relating to health insurance coverage offered by a health insurance issuer supersede any provision of State law which establishes, implements, or continues in effect a standard or requirement applicable to imposition of a preexisting condition exclusion specifically governed by section 701 which differs from the standards or requirements specified in such section.

(2) Exceptions—Only in relation to health insurance coverage offered by a health insurance issuer, the provisions of this part do not supersede any provision of State law to the extent that such provision—

(A) substitutes for the reference to "6-month period" in section 701(a)(1) a reference to any shorter period of time;

(B) substitutes for the reference to "12 months" and "18 months" in section 701(a)(2) a reference to any shorter period of time;

(C) substitutes for the references to "63 days" in sections 701(c)(2)(A) and (d)(4)(A) a reference to any greater number of days;

(D) substitutes for the reference to "30-day period" in sections 701(b)(2) and (d)(1) a reference to any greater period;

(E) prohibits the imposition of any preexisting condition exclusion in cases not described in section 701(d) or expands the exceptions described in such section;

(F) requires special enrollment periods in addition to those required under section 701(f); or

(G) reduces the maximum period permitted in an affiliation period under section 701(g)(1)(B).

(c) Rules of construction—Except as provided in section 71, nothing in this part shall be construed as requiring a group health plan or health insurance coverage to provide specific benefits under the terms of such plan or coverage.

(d) Definitions—For purposes of this section—

(1) State law—The term "State law" includes all laws, decisions, rules, regulations, or other State action having the effect of law, of any State. A law of the United States applicable only to the District of Columbia shall be treated as a State law rather than a law of the United States.

(2) State—The term "State" includes a State, the Northern Mariana Islands, any political subdivisions of a State or such Islands, or any agency or instrumentality of either.

§ 733. Definitions (§ 1191b)

(a) Group health plan—For purposes of this part—

(1) In general—The term "group health plan" means an employee welfare benefit plan to the extent that the plan provides medical care (as defined in paragraph (2) and including items and services paid for as medical care) to employees or their dependents (as defined under the terms of the plan) directly or through insurance, reimbursement, or otherwise.

(2) Medical care—The term "medical care" means amounts paid for—

(A) the diagnosis, cure, mitigation, treatment, or prevention of disease, or amounts paid for the purpose of affecting any structure or function of the body,

(B) amounts paid for transportation primarily for and essential to medical care referred to in subparagraph (A), and

(C) amounts paid for insurance covering medical care referred to in subparagraphs (A) and (B).

(b) Definitions relating to health insurance—For purposes of this part—

(1) Health insurance coverage—The term "health insurance coverage" means benefits consisting of medical care (provided directly, through insurance or reimbursement, or otherwise and including items and services paid for as medical care) under any hospital or medical service policy or certificate, hospital or medical service plan contract, or health maintenance organization contract offered by a health insurance issuer.

(2) Health insurance issuer—The term "health insurance issuer" means an insurance company, insurance service, or insurance organization (including a health maintenance organization, as defined in paragraph (3)) which is licensed to engage in the business of insurance in a State and which is subject to State law which regulates insurance (within the meaning of section 514(b)(2)). Such term does not include a group health plan.

(3) Health maintenance organization—The term "health maintenance organization" means—

(A) a federally qualified health maintenance organization (as defined in section 1301(a) of the Public Health Service Act (42 U.S.C. 300e(a))),

(B) an organization recognized under State law as a health maintenance organization, or

(C) a similar organization regulated under State law for solvency in the same manner and to the same extent as such a health maintenance organization.

(4) Group health insurance coverage—The term "group health insurance coverage" means, in connection with a group health plan, health insurance coverage offered in connection with such plan.

(c) Excepted benefits—For purposes of this part, the term "excepted benefits" means benefits under one or more (or any combination thereof) of the following:

(1) Benefits not subject to requirements—

(A) Coverage only for accident, or disability income insurance, or any combination thereof.

(B) Coverage issued as a supplement to liability insurance.

(C) Liability insurance, including general liability insurance and automobile liability insurance.

(D) Workers' compensation or similar insurance.

(E) Automobile medical payment insurance.

(F) Credit-only insurance.

(G) Coverage for on-site medical clinics.

(H) Other similar insurance coverage, specified in regulations, under which benefits for medical care are secondary or incidental to other insurance benefits.

(2) Benefits not subject to requirements if offered separately—

(A) Limited scope dental or vision benefits.

(B) Benefits for long-term care, nursing home care, home health care, community-based care, or any combination thereof.

(C) Such other similar, limited benefits as are specified in regulations.

(3) Benefits not subject to requirements if offered as independent, noncoordinated benefits—

(A) Coverage only for a specified disease or illness.

(B) Hospital indemnity or other fixed indemnity insurance.

(4) Benefits not subject to requirements if offered as separate insurance policy—Medicare supplemental health insurance (as defined under section 1882(g)(1) of the Social Security Act), coverage supplemental to the coverage provided under chapter 55 of title 10, United States Code, and similar supplemental coverage provided to coverage under a group health plan.

(d) Other definitions—For purposes of this part—

(1) COBRA continuation provision—The term "COBRA continuation provision" means any of the following:

(A) Part 6 of this subtitle.

(B) Section 4980B of Internal Revenue Code of 1986, other than subsection (f)(1) of such section insofar as it relates to pediatric vaccines.

(C) Title XXII of the Public Health Service Act.

(2) Health status-related factor—The term "health status-related factor" means any of the factors described in section 702(a)(1).

(3) Network plan—The term "network plan" means health insurance coverage offered by a health insurance issuer under which the financing and delivery of medical care (including items and services paid for as medical care) are provided, in whole or in part, through a defined set of providers under contract with the issuer.

(4) Placed for adoption—The term "placement", or being "placed", for adoption, has the meaning given such term in section 609(c)(3)(B).

(5) Family member—The term "family member" means, with respect to an individual—

(A) a dependent (as such term is used for purposes of section 701(f)(2)) of such individual, and

(B) any other individual who is a first-degree, second-degree, third-degree, or fourth-degree relative of such individual or of an individual described in subparagraph (A).

(6) Genetic information—

(A) In general—The term "genetic information" means, with respect to any individual, information about—

(i) such individual's genetic tests,

(ii) the genetic tests of family members of such individual, and

(iii) the manifestation of a disease or disorder in family members of such individual.

(B) Inclusion of genetic services and participation in genetic research—Such term includes, with respect to any individual, any request for, or receipt of, genetic services, or participation in clinical research which includes genetic services, by such individual or any family member of such individual.

(C) Exclusions—The term "genetic information" shall not include information about the sex or age of any individual.

(7) Genetic test—

(A) In general—The term "genetic test" means an analysis of human DNA, RNA, chromosomes, proteins, or metabolites, that detects genotypes, mutations, or chromosomal changes.

(B) Exceptions—The term "genetic test" does not mean—

(i) an analysis of proteins or metabolites that does not detect genotypes, mutations, or chromosomal changes; or

(ii) an analysis of proteins or metabolites that is directly related to a manifested disease, disorder, or pathological condition that could reasonably be detected by a health care professional with appropriate training and expertise in the field of medicine involved.

(8) Genetic services—The term "genetic services" means—

(A) a genetic test;

(B) genetic counseling (including obtaining, interpreting, or assessing genetic information); or

(C) genetic education.

(9) Underwriting purposes—The term "underwriting purposes" means, with respect to any group health plan, or health insurance coverage offered in connection with a group health plan—

(A) rules for, or determination of, eligibility (including enrollment and continued eligibility) for benefits under the plan or coverage;

(B) the computation of premium or contribution amounts under the plan or coverage;

(C) the application of any pre-existing condition exclusion under the plan or coverage; and

(D) other activities related to the creation, renewal, or replacement of a contract of health insurance or health benefits.

Title IV—Plan Termination Insurance

Subtitle A—Pension Benefit Guaranty Corporation

§ 4001. Definitions (§ 1301)

(a) For purposes of this title, the term—

(1) "administrator" means the person or persons described in paragraph (16) of section 3 of this Act;

(2) "substantial employer", for any plan year of a single-employer plan, means one or more persons—

(A) who are contributing sponsors of the plan in such plan year,

(B) who, at any time during such plan year, are members of the same controlled group, and

(C) whose required contributions to the plan for each plan year constituting one of—

(i) the two immediately preceding plan years, or

(ii) the first two of the three immediately preceding plan years,

total an amount greater than or equal to 10 percent of all contributions required to be paid to or under the plan for such plan year;

(3) "multiemployer plan" means a plan—

(A) to which more than one employer is required to contribute,

(B) which is maintained pursuant to one or more collective bargaining agreements between one or more employee organizations and more than one employer, and

(C) which satisfies such other requirements as the Secretary of Labor may prescribe by regulation,

except that, in applying this paragraph—

(i) a plan shall be considered a multiemployer plan on and after its termination date if the plan was a multiemployer plan under this paragraph for the plan year preceding such termination, and

(ii) for any plan year which began before September 26, 1980, the term "multiemployer plan" means a plan described in section 414(f) of the Internal Revenue Code of 1954 as in effect immediately before such date;

(4) "corporation", except where the context clearly requires otherwise, means the Pension Benefit Guaranty Corporation established under section 4002;

(5) "fund" means the appropriate fund established under section 4005;

(6) "basic benefits" means benefits guaranteed under section 4022 (other than under section 4022(c)), or under section 4022A (other than under section 4022A(g));

(7) "non-basic benefits" means benefits guaranteed under section 4022(c) or 4022A(g);

(8) "nonforfeitable benefit" means, with respect to a plan, a benefit for which a participant has satisfied the conditions for entitlement under the plan or the requirements of this Act (other than submission of a formal application, retirement, completion of a required waiting period, or death in the case of a benefit which returns all or a portion of a participant's accumulated mandatory employee contributions upon the participant's death), whether or not the benefit may subsequently be reduced or suspended by a plan amendment, an occurrence of any condition, or operation of this Act or the Internal Revenue Code of 1986;

(9) "reorganization index" means the amount determined under section 4221(b);

(10) "plan sponsor" means, with respect to a multiemployer plan—

(A) the plan's joint board of trustees, or

(B) if the plan has no joint board of trustees, the plan administrator;

(11) "contribution base unit" means a unit with respect to which an employer has an obligation to contribute under a multiemployer plan, as defined in regulations prescribed by the Secretary of the Treasury;

(12) "outstanding claim for withdrawal liability" means a plan's claim for the unpaid balance of the liability determined under part 1 of subtitle E for which demand has been made, valued in accordance with regulations prescribed by the corporation;

(13) "contributing sponsor", of a single-employer plan, means a person described in section 302(b)(1) of this Act (without regard to section 302(b)(2) of this Act) or section 412(b)(1) of the Internal Revenue Code of 1986 (without regard to section 412(b)(2) of such Code).

(14) in the case of a single-employer plan—

(A) "controlled group" means, in connection with any person, a group consisting of such person and all other persons under common control with such person;

(B) the determination of whether two or more persons are under "common control" shall be made under regulations of the corporation which are consistent and coextensive with regulations prescribed for similar purposes by the Secretary of the Treasury under subsections (b) and (c) of section 414 of the Internal Revenue Code of 1986; and

* * *

(15) "single-employer plan" means any defined benefit plan (as defined in section 3(35)) which is not a multiemployer plan;

(16) "benefit liabilities" means the benefits of employees and their beneficiaries under the plan (within the meaning of section 401(a)(2) of the Internal Revenue Code of 1986);

(17) "amount of unfunded guaranteed benefits", of a participant or beneficiary as of any date under a single-employer plan, means an amount equal to the excess of—

(A) the actuarial present value (determined as of such date on the basis of assumptions prescribed by the corporation for purposes of section 4044) of the benefits of the participant or beneficiary under the plan which are guaranteed under section 4022, over

(B) the current value (as of such date) of the assets of the plan which are required to be allocated to those benefits under section 4044;

(18) "amount of unfunded benefit liabilities" means, as of any date, the excess (if any) of—

(A) the value of the benefit liabilities under the plan (determined as of such date on the basis of assumptions prescribed by the corporation for purposes of section 4044), over

(B) the current value (as of such date) of the assets of the plan;

(19) "outstanding amount of benefit liabilities" means, with respect to any plan, the excess (if any) of—

(A) the value of the benefit liabilities under the plan (determined as of the termination date on the basis of assumptions prescribed by the corporation for purposes of section 4044), over

(B) the value of the benefit liabilities which would be so determined by only taking into account benefits which are guaranteed under section 4022 or to which assets of the plan are allocated under section 4044;

(20) "person" has the meaning set forth in section 3(9);

(21) "affected party" means, with respect to a plan—

(A) each participant in the plan,

(B) each beneficiary under the plan who is a beneficiary of a deceased participant or who is an alternate payee (within the meaning of section 206(d)(3)(K)) under an applicable qualified domestic relations order (within the meaning of section 206(d)(3)(B)(i)),

(C) each employee organization representing participants in the plan, and

(D) the corporation,

except that, in connection with any notice required to be provided to the affected party, if an affected party has designated, in writing, a person to receive such notice on behalf of the affected party, any reference to the affected party shall be construed to refer to such person.

(b)(1) An individual who owns the entire interest in an unincorporated trade or business is treated as his own employer, and a partnership is treated as the employer of each partner who is an employee within the meaning of section 401(c)(1) of the Internal Revenue Code of 1986. For purposes of this title, under regulations prescribed by the corporation, all employees of trades or businesses (whether or not incorporated) which are under common control shall be treated as employed by a single employer and all such trades and businesses as a single employer. The regulations prescribed under the preceding sentence shall be consistent and coextensive with regulations prescribed for similar purposes by the Secretary of the Treasury under section 414(c) of the Internal Revenue Code of 1986.

(2) For purposes of subtitle E—

(A) except as otherwise provided in subtitle E, contributions or other payments shall be considered made under a plan for a plan year if they are made within the period prescribed under section 412(c)(10) of the Internal Revenue Code of 1986 (determined, in the case of a terminated plan, as if the plan had continued beyond the termination date), and

(B) the term "Secretary of the Treasury" means the Secretary of the Treasury or such Secretary's delegate.

§ 4002. Pension Benefit Guaranty Corporation (§ 1302)

(a) There is established within the Department of Labor a body corporate to be known as the Pension Benefit Guaranty Corporation. In carrying out its functions under this title, the corporation shall be administered by a Director, who shall be appointed by the President, by and with the advice and consent of the Senate, and who shall act in accordance with the policies established by the board. The purposes of this title, which are to be carried out by the corporation, are—

(1) to encourage the continuation and maintenance of voluntary private pension plans for the benefit of their participants,

(2) to provide for the timely and uninterrupted payment of pension benefits to participants and beneficiaries under plans to which this title applies, and

(3) to maintain premiums established by the corporation under section 4006 at the lowest level consistent with carrying out its obligations under this title.

* * *

§ 4003. Operation of corporation (§ 1303)

(a) Investigatory authority; audit of statistically significant number of terminating plans. The corporation may make such investigations as it deems necessary to enforce any provision of this subchapter or any rule or regulation thereunder, and may require or permit any person to file with it a statement in writing, under oath or otherwise as the corporation shall determine, as to all the facts and circumstances concerning the matter to be investigated. The corporation shall annually audit a statistically significant number of plans terminating under section 4041(b) to determine whether participants and beneficiaries have received their benefit commitments and whether section 4050(a) has been satisfied. Each audit shall include a statistically significant number of participants and beneficiaries.

(b) Discovery powers vested in board members or officers designated by the chairman. For the purpose of any such investigation, or any other proceeding under this title, the Director, any member of the board of directors of the corporation, or any officer designated by the Director or chairman, may administer oaths and affirmations, subpena witnesses, compel their attendance, take evidence, and require the production of any books, papers, correspondence, memoranda, or other records which the corporation deems relevant or material to the inquiry.

(c) Contempt. In case of contumacy by, or refusal to obey a subpena issued to, any person, the corporation may invoke the aid of any court of the United States within the jurisdiction of which such investigation or proceeding is carried on, or where such person resides or carries on business, in requiring the attendance and testimony of witnesses and the production of books, papers, correspondence, memoranda, and other records. The court may issue an order requiring such person to appear before the corporation, or member or officer designated by the corporation, and to produce records or to give testimony related to the matter under investigation or in question. Any failure to obey such order of the court may be punished by the court as a contempt thereof. All process in any such case may be served in the judicial district in which such person is an inhabitant or may be found.

* * *

(e)(1) Civil actions by corporation; jurisdiction; process; expeditious handling of case; costs; limitation on actions. Civil actions may be brought by the corporation for appropriate relief, legal or equitable or both, to enforce (A) the provisions of this title, and (B) in the case of a plan which is covered under this title (other than a multiemployer plan) and for which the conditions for imposition of a lien described in section 303(k)(1)(A) and (B) of this Act or section 430(k)(1)(A) and (B) of the Internal Revenue Code of 1986 have been met, section 302 of this Act and section 412 of such Code.

(2) Except as otherwise provided in this title, where such an action is brought in a district court of the United States, it may be brought in the district where the plan is administered, where the violation took place, or where a defendant resides or may be found, and process may be served in any other district where a defendant resides or may be found.

(3) The district courts of the United States shall have jurisdiction of actions brought by the corporation under this subchapter without regard to the amount in controversy in any such action.

(4) [Repealed]

(5) In any action brought under this title, whether to collect premiums, penalties, and interest under section 4007 or for any other purpose, the court may award to the corporation all or a portion of the costs of litigation incurred by the corporation in connection with such action.

(6)(A) Except as provided in subparagraph (C), an action under this subsection may not be brought after the later of—

(i) 6 years after the date on which the cause of action arose, or

(ii) 3 years after the applicable date specified in subparagraph (B).

(B)(i) Except as provided in clause (ii), the applicable date specified in this subparagraph is the earliest date on which the corporation acquired or should have acquired actual knowledge of the existence of such cause of action.

(ii) If the corporation brings the action as a trustee, the applicable date specified in this subparagraph is the date on which the corporation became a trustee with respect to the plan if such date is later than the date described in clause (i).

(C) In the case of fraud or concealment, the period described in subparagraph (A)(ii) shall be extended to 6 years after the applicable date specified in subparagraph (B).

(f)(1) Civil actions against corporation; appropriate court; award of costs and expenses; limitation on actions; jurisdiction; removal of actions. Except with respect to withdrawal liability disputes under part 1 of subtitle E, any person who is a fiduciary, employer, contributing sponsor, member of a contributing sponsor's controlled group, participant, or beneficiary, and is adversely affected by any action of the corporation with respect to a plan in which such person has an interest, or who is an employee organization representing such a participant or beneficiary so adversely affected for purposes of collective bargaining with respect to such plan, may bring an action against the corporation for appropriate equitable relief in the appropriate court.

(2) For purposes of this subsection, the term "appropriate court" means—

(A) the United States district court before which proceedings under section 4041 or 4042 are being conducted,

(B) if no such proceedings are being conducted, the United States district court for the judicial district in which the plan has its principal office, or

(C) the United States District Court for the District of Columbia.

(3) In any action brought under this subsection, the court may award all or a portion of the costs and expenses incurred in connection with such action to any party who prevails or substantially prevails in such action.

(4) This subsection shall be the exclusive means for bringing actions against the corporation under this title, including actions against the corporation in its capacity as a trustee under section 4042 or 4049.

(5)(A) Except as provided in subparagraph (C), an action under this subsection may not be brought after the later of—

(i) 6 years after the date on which the cause of action arose, or

(ii) 3 years after the applicable date specified in subparagraph (B).

(B)(i) Except as provided in clause (ii), the applicable date specified in this subparagraph is the earliest date on which the plaintiff acquired or should have acquired actual knowledge of the existence of such cause of action.

(ii) In the case of a plaintiff who is a fiduciary bringing the action in the exercise of fiduciary duties, the applicable date specified in this subparagraph is the date on which the plaintiff became a fiduciary with respect to the plan if such date is later than the date specified in clause (i).

(C) In the case of fraud or concealment, the period described in subparagraph (A)(ii) shall be extended to 6 years after the applicable date specified in subparagraph (B).

(6) The district courts of the United States have jurisdiction of actions brought under this subsection without regard to the amount in controversy.

(7) In any suit, action, or proceeding in which the corporation is a party, or intervenes under section 4301, in any State court, the corporation may, without bond or security, remove such suit, action, or proceeding from the State court to the United States district court for the district or division in which such suit, action, or proceeding is pending by following any procedure for removal now or hereafter in effect.

§ 4005. Pension benefit guaranty funds (§ 1305)

(a) There are established on the books of the Treasury of the United States four revolving funds to be used by the corporation in carrying out its duties under this subchapter. One of the funds shall be used with respect to basic benefits guaranteed under section 4022, one of the funds shall be used with respect to basic benefits guaranteed under section 4022A, one of the funds shall be used with respect to nonbasic benefits guaranteed under section 4022 (if any), and the remaining fund shall be used with respect to nonbasic benefits guaranteed under section 4022A (if any), other than subsection (g)(2) thereof (if any). Whenever in this title reference is made to the term "fund" the reference shall be considered to refer to the appropriate fund established under this subsection.

* * *

(b)(3) Whenever the corporation determines that the moneys of any fund are in excess of current needs, it may request the investment of such amounts as it determines advisable by the Secretary of the Treasury in obligations issued or guaranteed by the United States but, until all borrowings under subsection (c) have been repaid, the obligations in which such excess moneys are invested may not yield a rate of return in excess of the rate of interest payable on such borrowings.

(c) The corporation is authorized to issue to the Secretary of the Treasury notes or other obligations in an aggregate amount of not to exceed $100,000,000, in such forms and denominations, bearing such maturities, and subject to such terms and conditions as may be prescribed by the Secretary of the Treasury. Such notes or other obligations shall bear interest at a rate determined by the Secretary of the Treasury, taking into consideration the current average market yield on outstanding marketable obligations of the United States of comparable maturities during the month preceding the issuance of such notes or other obligations of the corporation. The Secretary of the Treasury is authorized and directed to purchase any notes or other obligations issued by the corporation under this subsection, and for that purpose he is authorized to use as a public debt transaction the proceeds from the sale of any securities issued under the Second Liberty Bond Act, and the purposes for which securities may be issued under that Act, are extended to include any purchase of such notes and obligations. The Secretary of the Treasury may at any time sell any of the notes or other obligations acquired by him under this subsection. All redemptions, purchases, and sales by the Secretary of the Treasury of such notes or other obligations shall be treated as public debt transactions of the United States.

* * *

§ 4006. Premium rates (§ 1306)

(a)(1) The corporation shall prescribe such schedules of premium rates and bases for the application of those rates as may be necessary to provide sufficient revenue to the fund for the corporation to carry out its functions under this title. The premium rates charged by the corporation for any period shall be uniform for all plans, other than multiemployer plans, insured by the corporation with respect to basic benefits guaranteed by it under section 4022, and shall be uniform for all multiemployer plans with respect to basic benefits guaranteed by it under section 4022A.

* * *

(3)(A) Except as provided in subparagraph (C), the annual premium rate payable to the corporation by all plans for basic benefits guaranteed under this title is—

(i) in the case of a single-employer plan, for plan years beginning after December 31, 2005, an amount equal to the sum of $30 plus the additional premium (if any) determined under subparagraph (E) for each individual who is a participant in such plan during the plan year;

* * *

(iv) in the case of a multiemployer plan, for plan years beginning after December 31, 2005, $8.00 for each individual who is a participant in such plan during the applicable plan year.

* * *

(E)(i) Except as provided in subparagraph (H), the additional premium determined under this subparagraph with respect to any plan for any plan year shall be an amount equal to the amount determined under clause (ii) divided by the number of participants in such plan as of the close of the preceding plan year.

(ii) The amount determined under this clause for any plan year shall be an amount equal to $9.00 for each $1,000 (or fraction thereof) of unfunded vested benefits under the plan as of the close of the preceding plan year.

* * *

(H)(i) In the case of an employer who has 25 or fewer employees on the first day of the plan year, the additional premium determined under subparagraph (E) for each participant shall not exceed $5 multiplied by the number of participants in the plan as of the close of the preceding plan year.

(ii) For purposes of clause (i), whether an employer has 25 or fewer employees on the first day of the plan year is determined by taking into consideration all of the employees of all members of the contributing sponsor's controlled group. In the case of a plan maintained by two or more contributing sponsors, the employees of all contributing sponsors and their controlled groups shall be aggregated for purposes of determining whether the 25-or-fewer-employees limitation has been satisfied.

* * *

(7) Premium rate for certain terminated single-employer plans—

(A) In general—If there is a termination of a single-employer plan under clause (ii) or (iii) of section 4041(c)(2)(B) or section 4042, there shall be payable to the corporation, with respect to each applicable 12- month period, a premium at a rate equal to $1,250 multiplied by the number of individuals who were participants in the plan immediately before the termination date. Such premium shall be in addition to any other premium under this section.

(B) Special rule for plans terminated in bankruptcy reorganization—In the case of a single-employer plan terminated under section 4041(c)(2)(B)(ii) or under section 4042 during pendency of any bankruptcy reorganization proceeding under chapter 11 of Title 11, United States Code, or under any similar law of a State or a political subdivision of a State (or a case described in section 4041(c)(2)(B)(i) filed by or against such person has been converted, as of such date, to such a case in which reorganization is sought), subparagraph (A) shall not apply to such plan until the date of the discharge or dismissal of such person in such case.

(C) Applicable 12-month period—For purposes of subparagraph (A)—

(i) In general—The term "applicable 12-month period" means—

(I) the 12-month period beginning with the first month following the month in which the termination date occurs, and

(II) each of the first two 12-month periods immediately following the period described in subclause (I).

(ii) Plans terminated in bankruptcy reorganization— In any case in which the requirements of subparagraph (B) are met in connection with the termination of the plan with respect to 1 or more persons described in such subparagraph, the 12-month period described in clause (i)(I) shall be the 12-month period beginning with the first month following the month which includes the earliest date as of which each such person is discharged or dismissed in the case described in such clause in connection with such person.

* * *

Subtitle B—Coverage

§ 4021. Coverage (§ 1321)

(a) Except as provided in subsection (b), this title applies to any plan (including a successor plan) which, for a plan year—

(1) is an employee pension benefit plan (as defined in paragraph (2) of section 3 of this Act) established or maintained—

(A) by an employer engaged in commerce or in any industry or activity affecting commerce, or

(B) by any employee organization, or organization representing employees, engaged in commerce or in any industry or activity affecting commerce, or

(C) by both,

which has, in practice, met the requirements of part I of subchapter D of chapter 1 of the Internal Revenue Code of 1986 (as in effect for the preceding 5 plan years of the plan) applicable to the plans described in paragraph (2) for the preceding 5 plan years; or

(2) is, or has been determined by the Secretary of the Treasury to be, a plan described in section 401(a) of the Internal Revenue Code of 1986, or which meets, or has been determined by the Secretary of the Treasury to meet, the requirements of section 404(a)(2) of such Code.

For purposes of this title, a successor plan is considered to be a continuation of a predecessor plan. For this purpose, unless otherwise specifically indicated in this title, a successor plan is a plan which covers a group of employees which includes substantially the same employees as a previously established plan, and provides substantially the same benefits as that plan provided.

(b) This section does not apply to any plan—

(1) which is an individual account plan, as defined in paragraph (34) of section 3 of this Act,

(2) established and maintained for its employees by the Government of the United States, by the government of any State or political subdivision thereof, or by any agency or instrumentality of any of the foregoing, or to which the Railroad Retirement Act of 1935 or 1937 applies and which is financed by contributions required under that Act, or which is described in the last sentence of section 3(32),

(3) which is a church plan as defined in section 414(e) of the Internal Revenue Code of 1986, unless that plan has made an election under section 410(d) of such Code, and has notified the corporation in accordance with procedures prescribed by the corporation, that it wishes to have the provisions of this part apply to it,

(4)(A) established and maintained by a society, order, or association described in section 501(c)(8) or (9) of the Internal Revenue Code of 1986, if no part of the contributions to or under the plan is made by employers of participants in the plan, or

(B) of which a trust described in section 501(c)(18) of such Code is a part;

(5) which has not at any time after September 2, 1974, provided for employer contributions;

(6) which is unfunded and which is maintained by an employer primarily for the purpose of providing deferred compensation for a select group of management or highly compensated employees;

(7) which is established and maintained outside of the United States primarily for the benefit of individuals substantially all of whom are nonresident aliens;

(8) which is maintained by an employer solely for the purpose of providing benefits for certain employees in excess of the limitations on contributions and benefits imposed by section 415 of the Internal Revenue Code of 1986 on plans to which that section applies, without regard to whether the plan is funded, and, to the extent that a separable part of a plan (as determined by the corporation) maintained by an employer is maintained for such purpose, that part shall be treated for purposes of this title, as a separate plan which is an excess benefit plan;

(9) which is established and maintained exclusively for substantial owners;

(10) of an international organization which is exempt from taxation under the International Organizations Immunities Act;

(11) maintained solely for the purpose of complying with applicable workmen's compensation laws or unemployment compensation or disability insurance laws;

(12) which is a defined benefit plan, to the extent that it is treated as an individual account plan under paragraph (35)(B) of section 3 of this Act; or

(13) established and maintained by a professional service employer which does not at any time after September 2, 1974, have more than 25 active participants in the plan.

(c)(1) For purposes of subsection (b)(1), the term "individual account plan" does not include a plan under which a fixed benefit is promised if the employer or his representative participated in the determination of that benefit.

(2) For purposes of this paragraph and for purposes of subsection (b)(13)—

(A) the term "professional service employer" means any proprietorship, partnership, corporation, or other association or organization (i) owned or controlled by professional individuals or by executors or administrators of professional individuals, (ii) the principal business of which is the performance of professional services, and

(B) the term "professional individuals" includes but is not limited to, physicians, dentists, chiropractors, osteopaths, optometrists, other licensed practitioners of the healing arts, attorneys at law, public accountants, public engineers, architects, draftsmen, actuaries, psychologists, social or physical scientists, and performing artists.

(3) In the case of a plan established and maintained by more than one professional service employer, the plan shall not be treated as a plan described in subsection (b)(13) if, at any time after September 2, 1974, the plan has more than 25 active participants.

(d) For purposes of subsection (b)(9), the term 'substantial owner' means an individual who, at any time during the 60-month period ending on the date the determination is being made—

(1) owns the entire interest in an unincorporated trade or business,

(2) in the case of a partnership, is a partner who owns, directly or indirectly, more than 10 percent of either the capital interest or the profits interest in such partnership, or

(3) in the case of a corporation, owns, directly or indirectly, more than 10 percent in value of either the voting stock of that corporation or all the stock of that corporation.

For purposes of paragraph (3), the constructive ownership rules of section 1563(e) of the Internal Revenue Code of 1986 (other than paragraph (3)(C) thereof) shall apply, including the application of such rules under section 414(c) of such Code.

§ 4022. Single-employer plan benefits guaranteed (§ 1322)

(a) Subject to the limitations contained in subsection (b), the corporation shall guarantee, in accordance with this section, the payment of all nonforfeitable benefits (other than benefits becoming nonforfeitable solely on account of the termination of a plan) under a single-employer plan which terminates at a time when this title applies to it.

(b)(1) Except to the extent provided in paragraph (7)—

(A) no benefits provided by a plan which has been in effect for less than 60 months at the time the plan terminates shall be guaranteed under this section, and

(B) any increase in the amount of benefits under a plan resulting from a plan amendment which was made, or became effective, whichever is later, within 60 months before the date on which the plan terminates shall be disregarded.

(2) For purposes of this subsection, the time a successor plan (within the meaning of section 4021(a)) has been in effect includes the time a previously established plan (within the meaning of section 4021(a)) was in effect. For purposes of determining what benefits are guaranteed under this section in the case of a plan to which section 4021 does not apply on September 3, 1974, the 60-month period referred to in paragraph (1) shall be computed beginning on the first date on which such section does apply to the plan.

(3) The amount of monthly benefits described in subsection (a) provided by a plan, which are guaranteed under this section with respect to a participant, shall not have an actuarial value which exceeds the actuarial value of a monthly benefit in the form of a life annuity commencing at age 65 equal to the lesser of—

(A) his average monthly gross income from his employer during the 5 consecutive calendar year period (or, if less, during the number of calendar years in such period in which he actively participates in the plan) during which his gross income from that employer was greater than during any other such period with that employer determined by dividing 1/12 of the sum of all such gross income by the number of such calendar years in which he had such gross income, or

(B) $750 multiplied by a fraction, the numerator of which is the contribution and benefit base (determined under section 230 of the Social Security Act) in effect at the time the plan terminates and the denominator of which is such contribution and benefit base in effect in calendar year 1974.

The provisions of this paragraph do not apply to non-basic benefits. The maximum guaranteed monthly benefit shall not be reduced solely on account of the age of a participant in the case of a benefit payable by reason of disability that occurred on or before the termination date, if the participant demonstrates to the satisfaction of the corporation that the Social Security Administration has determined that the participant satisfies the definition of disability under title II or XVI of the Social Security Act, and the regulations thereunder. If a benefit payable by reason of disability is converted to an early or normal retirement benefit for reasons other than a change in the health of the participant, such early or normal retirement benefit shall be treated as a continuation of the benefit payable by reason of disability and this subparagraph shall continue to apply.

* * *

(5)(A) For purposes of this paragraph, the term 'majority owner' means an individual who, at any time during the 60-month period ending on the date the determination is being made—

(i) owns the entire interest in an unincorporated trade or business,

(ii) in the case of a partnership, is a partner who owns, directly or indirectly, 50 percent or more of either the capital interest or the profits interest in such partnership, or

(iii) in the case of a corporation, owns, directly or indirectly, 50 percent or more in value of either the voting stock of that corporation or all the stock of that corporation.

For purposes of clause (iii), the constructive ownership rules of section 1563(e) of the Internal Revenue Code of 1986 (other than paragraph (3)(C) thereof) shall apply, including the application of such rules under section 414(c) of such Code.

(B) In the case of a participant who is a majority owner, the amount of benefits guaranteed under this section shall equal the product of—

(i) a fraction (not to exceed 1) the numerator of which is the number of years from the later of the effective date or the adoption date of the plan to the termination date, and the denominator of which is 10, and

(ii) the amount of benefits that would be guaranteed under this section if the participant were not a majority owner.

(6)(A) No benefits accrued under a plan after the date on which the Secretary of the Treasury issues notice that he has determined that any trust which is a part of a plan does not meet the requirements of section 401(a) of the Internal Revenue Code of 1986, or that the plan does not meet the requirements of section 404(a)(2) of such Code, are guaranteed under this section unless such determination is erroneous. This subparagraph does not apply if the Secretary subsequently issues a notice that such trust meets the requirements of section 401(a) of such Code or that the plan meets the requirements of section 404(a)(2) of such Code and if the Secretary determines that the trust or plan has taken action necessary to meet such requirements during the period between the issuance of the notice referred to in the preceding sentence and the issuance of the notice referred to in this sentence.

(B) No benefits accrued under a plan after the date on which an amendment of the plan is adopted which causes the Secretary of the Treasury to determine that any trust under the plan has ceased to meet the requirements of section 401(a) of the Internal Revenue Code of 1986 or that the plan has ceased to meet the requirements of section 404(a)(2) of such Code, are guaranteed under this section unless such determination is erroneous. This subparagraph shall not apply if the amendment is revoked as of the date it was first effective or amended to comply with such requirements.

(7) Benefits described in paragraph (1) are guaranteed only to the extent of the greater of—

(A) 20 percent of the amount which, but for the fact that the plan or amendment has not been in effect for 60 months or more, would be guaranteed under this section, or

(B) $20 per month,

multiplied by the number of years (but not more than 5) the plan or amendment, as the case may be, has been in effect. In determining how many years a plan or amendment has been in effect for purposes of this paragraph, the first 12 months beginning with the date on which the plan or amendment is made or first becomes effective (whichever is later) constitutes one year, and each consecutive period of 12 months thereafter constitutes an additional year. This paragraph does not apply to benefits payable under a plan unless the corporation finds substantial evidence that the plan was terminated for a reasonable business purpose and not for the purpose of obtaining the payment of benefits by the corporation under this title.

(8) If an unpredictable contingent event benefit (as defined in section 206(g)(1)) is payable by reason of the occurrence of any event, this section shall be applied as if a plan amendment had been adopted on the date such event occurred.

(c)(1) In addition to benefits paid under the preceding provisions of this section with respect to a terminated plan, the corporation shall pay the portion of the amount determined under paragraph (2) which is allocated with respect to each participant under section 4044(a). Such payment shall be made to such participant or to such participant's beneficiaries (including alternate payees, within the meaning of section 206(d)(3)(K)).

* * *

(g) Bankruptcy filing substituted for termination date—If a contributing sponsor of a plan has filed or has had filed against such person a petition seeking liquidation or reorganization in a case under title 11, United States Code, or under any similar Federal law or law of a State or political subdivision, and the case has not been dismissed as of the termination date of the plan, then this section shall be applied by treating the date such petition was filed as the termination date of the plan.

Subtitle C—Terminations

§ 4041. Termination of single-employer plans (§ 1341)

(a) General rules governing single-employer plan terminations—

(1) Exclusive means of plan termination—Except in the case of a termination for which proceedings are otherwise instituted by the corporation as provided in section 4042, a single-employer plan may be terminated only in a standard termination under subsection (b) or a distress termination under subsection (c).

(2) 60-day notice of intent to terminate—Not less than 60 days before the proposed termination date of a standard termination under subsection (b) or a distress termination under subsection (c), the plan administrator shall provide to each affected party (other than the corporation in the case of a standard termination) a written notice of intent to terminate stating that such termination is intended and the proposed termination date. The written notice shall include any related additional information required in regulations of the corporation.

(3) Adherence to collective bargaining agreements—The corporation shall not proceed with a termination of a plan under this section if the termination would violate the terms and conditions of an existing collective bargaining agreement. Nothing in the preceding sentence shall be construed as limiting the authority of the corporation to institute proceedings to involuntarily terminate a plan under section 4042.

(b) Standard termination of single-employer plans—

(1) General requirements—A single-employer plan may terminate under a standard termination only if—

(A) the plan administrator provides the 60-day advance notice of intent to terminate to affected parties required under subsection (a)(2),

(B) the requirements of subparagraphs (A) and (B) of paragraph (2) are met,

(C) the corporation does not issue a notice of noncompliance under subparagraph (C) of paragraph (2), and

(D) when the final distribution of assets occurs, the plan is sufficient for benefit liabilities (determined as of the termination date).

* * *

(3) Methods of final distribution of assets—

(A) In general—In connection with any final distribution of assets pursuant to the standard termination of the plan under this subsection, the plan administrator shall distribute the assets in accordance with section 4044. In distributing such assets, the plan administrator shall—

(i) purchase irrevocable commitments from an insurer to provide all benefit liabilities under the plan, or

(ii) in accordance with the provisions of the plan and any applicable regulations, otherwise fully provide all benefit liabilities under the plan. A transfer of assets to the corporation in accordance with section 4050 on behalf of a missing participant shall satisfy this subparagraph with respect to such participant.

* * *

(c) Distress termination of single-employer plans—

(1) In general—A single-employer plan may terminate under a distress termination only if—

(A) the plan administrator provides the 60-day advance notice of intent to terminate to affected parties required under subsection (a)(2),

(B) the requirements of subparagraph (A) of paragraph (2) are met, and

(C) the corporation determines that the requirements of subparagraphs (B) and (D) of paragraph (2) are met.

(2) Termination requirements—

(A) Information submitted to the corporation—As soon as practicable after the date on which the notice of intent to terminate is provided pursuant to subsection (a)(2), the plan administrator shall provide the corporation, in such form as may be prescribed by the corporation in regulations, the following information:

* * *

(B) Determination by the corporation of necessary distress criteria—Upon receipt of the notice of intent to terminate required under subsection (a)(2) and the information required under subparagraph (A), the corporation shall determine whether the requirements of this subparagraph are met as provided in clause (i), (ii), or (iii). The requirements of this subparagraph are met if each person who is (as of the proposed termination date) a contributing sponsor of such plan or a member of such sponsor's controlled group meets the requirements of any of the following clauses:

(i) Liquidation in bankruptcy or insolvency proceedings—The requirements of this clause are met by a person if—

(I) such person has filed or has had filed against such person, as of the proposed termination date, a petition seeking liquidation in a case under Title 11, United States Code, or under any similar Federal law or law of a State or political subdivision of a State (or a case described in clause (ii) filed by or against such person has been converted, as of such date, to a case in which liquidation is sought), and

(II) such case has not, as of the proposed termination date, been dismissed.

(ii) Reorganization in bankruptcy or insolvency proceedings—The requirements of this clause are met by a person if—

(I) such person has filed, or has had filed against such person, as of the proposed termination date, a petition seeking reorganization in a case under

Title 11, United States Code or under any similar law of a State or political subdivision of a State (or a case described in clause (i) filed by or against such person has been converted, as of such date, to such a case in which reorganization is sought),

(II) such case has not, as of the proposed termination date, been dismissed,

(III) such person timely submits to the corporation any request for the approval of the bankruptcy court (or other appropriate court in a case under such similar law of a State or political subdivision) of the plan termination, and

(IV) the bankruptcy court (or such other appropriate court) determines that, unless the plan is terminated, such person will be unable to pay all its debts pursuant to a plan of reorganization and will be unable to continue in business outside the Chapter 11 reorganization process and approves the termination.

(iii) Termination required to enable payment of debts while staying in business or to avoid unreasonably burdensome pension costs caused by declining workforce—The requirements of this clause are met by a person if such person demonstrates to the satisfaction of the corporation that—

(I) unless a distress termination occurs, such person will be unable to pay such person's debts when due and will be unable to continue in business, or

(II) the costs of providing pension coverage have become unreasonably burdensome to such person, solely as a result of a decline of such person's workforce covered as participants under all single-employer plans of which such person is a contributing sponsor.

* * *

(D) Disclosure of termination information—

(i) In general—A plan administrator that has filed a notice of intent to terminate under subparagraph (A) or the regulations under subsection (a)(2) shall provide to an affected party any information provided to the corporation under subparagraph (A) or the regulations under subsection (a)(2) not later than 15 days after—

(I) receipt of a request from the affected party for the information; or

(II) the provision of new information to the corporation relating to a previous request.

* * *

§ 4042. Institution of termination proceedings by the corporation (§ 1342)

(a) The corporation may institute proceedings under this section to terminate a plan whenever it determines that—

(1) the plan has not met the minimum funding standard required under section 412 of the Internal Revenue Code of 1986, or has been notified by the Secretary of the Treasury that a notice of deficiency under section 6212 of such Code has been mailed with respect to the tax imposed under section 4971(a) of such Code,

(2) the plan will be unable to pay benefits when due,

(3) the reportable event described in section 4043(c)(7) has occurred, or

(4) the possible long-run loss of the corporation with respect to the plan may reasonably be expected to increase unreasonably if the plan is not terminated.

The corporation shall as soon as practicable institute proceedings under this section to terminate a single-employer plan whenever the corporation determines that the plan does not have assets available to pay benefits which are currently due under the terms of the plan. The corporation may prescribe a simplified procedure to follow in terminating small plans as long as that procedure includes substantial safeguards for the rights of the participants and beneficiaries under the plans, and for the employers who maintain such plans (including the requirement for a court decree under subsection (c)). Notwithstanding any other provision of this title, the corporation is authorized to pool assets of terminated plans for purposes of administration, investment, payment of liabilities of all such terminated plans, and such other purposes as it determines to be appropriate in the administration of this title.

* * *

§ 4043. Reportable events (§ 1343)

(a) Within 30 days after the plan administrator or the contributing sponsor knows or has reason to know that a reportable event described in subsection (c) has occurred, he shall notify the corporation that such event has occurred, unless a notice otherwise required under this subsection has already been provided with respect to such event. The corporation is authorized to waive the requirement of the preceding sentence with respect to any or all reportable events with respect to any plan, and to require the notification to be made by including the event in the annual report made by the plan.

(b)(1) The requirements of this subsection shall be applicable to a contributing sponsor if, as of the close of the preceding plan year—

(A) the aggregate unfunded vested benefits (as determined under section 4006(a)(3)(E)(iii)) of plans subject to this title which are maintained by such sponsor and members of such sponsor's controlled groups (disregarding plans with no unfunded vested benefits) exceed $50,000,000, and

(B) the funded vested benefit percentage for such plans is less than 90 percent.

For purposes of subparagraph (B), the funded vested benefit percentage means the percentage which the aggregate value of the assets of such plans bears to the aggregate vested benefits of such plans (determined in accordance with section 4006(a)(3)(E)(iii)).

(2) This subsection shall not apply to an event if the contributing sponsor, or the member of the contributing sponsor's controlled group to which the event relates, is—

(A) a person subject to the reporting requirements of section 13 or 15(d) of the Securities Exchange Act of 1934, or

(B) a subsidiary (as defined for purposes of such Act) of a person subject to such reporting requirements.

(3) No later than 30 days prior to the effective date of an event described in paragraph (9), (10), (11), (12), or (13) of subsection (c), a contributing sponsor to which the requirements of this subsection apply shall notify the corporation that the event is about to occur.

(4) The corporation may waive the requirement of this subsection with respect to any or all reportable events with respect to any contributing sponsor.

(c) For purposes of this section a reportable event occurs—

(1) when the Secretary of the Treasury issues notice that a plan has ceased to be a plan described in section 4021(a)(2), or when the Secretary of Labor determines the plan is not in compliance with title I of this Act;

(2) when an amendment of the plan is adopted if, under the amendment, the benefit payable with respect to any participant may be decreased;

(3) when the number of active participants is less than 80 percent of the number of such participants at the beginning of the plan year, or is less than 75 percent of the number of such participants at the beginning of the previous plan year;

(4) when the Secretary of the Treasury determines that there has been a termination or partial termination of the plan within the meaning of section 411(d)(3) of the Internal Revenue Code of 1986, but the occurrence of such a termination or partial termination does not, by itself, constitute or require a termination of a plan under this subchapter;

(5) when the plan fails to meet the minimum funding standards under section 412 of such Code (without regard to whether the plan is a plan described in section 4021(a)(2) of this Act) or under section 302 of this Act;

(6) when the plan is unable to pay benefits thereunder when due;

(7) when there is a distribution under the plan to a participant who is a substantial owner as defined in section 4021(d) if—

(A) such distribution has a value of $10,000 or more;

(B) such distribution is not made by reason of the death of the

participant; and

(C) immediately after the distribution, the plan has nonforfeitable benefits which are not funded;

(8) when a plan merges, consolidates, or transfers its assets under section 208 of this Act, or when an alternative method of compliance is prescribed by the Secretary of Labor under section 110 of this Act;

(9) when, as a result of an event, a person ceases to be a member of the controlled group;

(10) when a contributing sponsor or a member of a contributing sponsor's controlled group liquidates in a case under Title 11, United States Code, or under any similar Federal law or law of a State or political subdivision of a State;

(11) when a contributing sponsor or a member of a contributing sponsor's controlled group declares an extraordinary dividend (as defined in section 1059(c) of the Internal Revenue Code of 1986) or redeems, in any 12-month period, an aggregate of 10 percent or more of the total combined voting power of all classes of stock entitled to vote, or an aggregate of 10 percent or more of the total value of shares of all classes of stock, of a contributing sponsor and all members of its controlled group;

(12) when, in any 12-month period, an aggregate of 3 percent or more of the benefit liabilities of a plan covered by this title and maintained by a contributing sponsor or a member of its controlled group are transferred to a person that is not a member of the controlled group or to a plan or plans maintained by a person or persons that are not such a contributing sponsor or a member of its controlled group; or

(13) when any other event occurs that may be indicative of a need to terminate the plan and that is prescribed by the corporation in regulations.

For purposes of paragraph (7), all distributions to a participant within any 24-month period are treated as a single distribution.

* * *

§ 4044. Allocation of assets (§ 1344)

(a) In the case of the termination of a single-employer plan, the plan administrator shall allocate the assets of the plan (available to provide benefits) among the participants and beneficiaries of the plan in the following order:

(1) First, to that portion of each individual's accrued benefit which is derived from the participant's contributions to the plan which were not mandatory contributions.

(2) Second, to that portion of each individual's accrued benefit which is derived from the participant's mandatory contributions.

(3) Third, in the case of benefits payable as an annuity—

(A) in the case of the benefit of a participant or beneficiary which was in pay status as of the beginning of the 3-year period ending on the termination date of the plan, to each such benefit, based on the provisions of the plan (as in effect during the 5-year period ending on such date) under which such benefit would be the least,

(B) in the case of a participant's or beneficiary's benefit (other than a benefit described in subparagraph (A)) which would have been in pay status as of the beginning of such 3-year period if the participant had retired prior to the beginning of the 3-year period and if his benefits had commenced (in the normal form of annuity under the plan) as of the beginning of such period, to each such benefit based on the provisions of the plan (as in effect during the 5-year period ending on such date) under which such benefit would be the least.

For purposes of subparagraph (A), the lowest benefit in pay status during a 3-year period shall be considered the benefit in pay status for such period.

(4) Fourth—

(A) to all other benefits (if any) of individuals under the plan guaranteed under this title (determined without regard to section 4022B(a)), and

(B) to the additional benefits (if any) which would be determined under subparagraph (A) if section 4022(b)(5)(B) did not apply.

For purposes of this paragraph, section 4021 shall be applied without regard to subsection (c) thereof.

(5) Fifth, to all other nonforfeitable benefits under the plan.

(6) Sixth, to all other benefits under the plan.

* * *

(d)(1) Subject to paragraph (3), any residual assets of a single-employer plan may be distributed to the employer if—

(A) all liabilities of the plan to participants and their beneficiaries have been satisfied,

(B) the distribution does not contravene any provision of law, and

(C) the plan provides for such a distribution in these circumstances.

(2)(A) In determining the extent to which a plan provides for the distribution of plan assets to the employer for purposes of paragraph (1)(C), any such provision, and any amendment increasing the amount which may be distributed to the employer, shall not be treated as effective before the end of the fifth calendar year following the date of the adoption of such provision or amendment.

(B) A distribution to the employer from a plan shall not be treated as failing to satisfy the requirements of this paragraph if the plan has been in effect for fewer than 5 years and the plan has provided for such a distribution since the effective date of the plan.

(C) Except as otherwise provided in regulations of the Secretary of the Treasury, in any case in which a transaction described in section 208 occurs, subparagraph (A) shall continue to apply separately with respect to the amount of any assets transferred in such transaction.

(D) For purposes of this subsection, the term "employer" includes any member of the controlled group of which the employer is a member. For purposes of the preceding sentence, the term "controlled group" means any group treated as a single employer under subsection (b), (c), (m) or (o) of section 414 of the Internal Revenue Code of 1986.

(3)(A) Before any distribution from a plan pursuant to paragraph (1), if any assets of the plan attributable to employee contributions remain after satisfaction of all liabilities described in subsection (a), such remaining assets shall be equitably distributed to the participants who made such contributions or their beneficiaries (including alternate payees, within the meaning of section 206(d)(3)(K)).

(B) For purposes of subparagraph (A), the portion of the remaining assets which are attributable to employee contributions shall be an amount equal to the product derived by multiplying—

(i) the market value of the total remaining assets, by

(ii) a fraction—

(I) the numerator of which is the present value of all portions of the accrued benefits with respect to participants which are derived from participants' mandatory contributions (referred to in subsection (a)(2)), and

(II) the denominator of which is the present value of all benefits with respect to which assets are allocated under paragraphs (2) through (6) of subsection (a).

(C) For purposes of this paragraph, each person who is, as of the termination date—

(i) a participant under the plan, or

(ii) an individual who has received, during the 3-year period ending with the termination date, a distribution from the plan of such individual's entire nonforfeitable benefit in the form of a single sum distribution in accordance with section 203(e) or in the form of irrevocable commitments purchased by the plan from an insurer to provide such nonforfeitable benefit,

shall be treated as a participant with respect to the termination, if all or part of the nonforfeitable benefit with respect to such person is or was attributable to participants' mandatory contributions (referred to in subsection (a)(2)).

(4) Nothing in this subsection shall be construed to limit the requirements of section 4980(d) of the Internal Revenue Code of 1986 (as in effect immediately after the enactment of the Omnibus Budget Reconciliation Act of 1990) or section 404(d) of this Act with respect to any distribution of residual assets of a single-employer plan to the employer.

(e) Bankruptcy filing substituted for termination date—If a contributing sponsor of a plan has filed or has had filed against such person a petition seeking liquidation or reorganization in a case under title 11, United States Code, or under any similar Federal law or law of a State or political subdivision, and the case has not been dismissed as of the termination date of the plan, then subsection (a)(3) shall be applied by treating the date such petition was filed as the termination date of the plan.

(f) Valuation of section 4062(c) liability for determining amounts payable by corporation to participants and beneficiaries—

(1) In general—In the case of a terminated plan, the value of the recovery of liability under section 4062(c) allocable as a plan asset under this section for purposes of determining the amount of benefits payable by the corporation shall be determined by multiplying—

(A) the amount of liability under section 4062(c) as of the termination date of the plan, by

(B) the applicable section 4062(c) recovery ratio.

(2) Section 4062(c) recovery ratio—For purposes of this subsection—

(A) In general—Except as provided in subparagraph (C), the term "section 4062(c) recovery ratio" means the ratio which—

(i) the sum of the values of all recoveries under section 4062(c) determined by the corporation in connection with plan terminations described under subparagraph (B), bears to

(ii) the sum of all the amounts of liability under section 4062(c) with respect to such plans as of the termination date in connection with any such prior termination.

(B) Prior terminations—A plan termination described in this subparagraph is a termination with respect to which—

(i) the value of recoveries under section 4062(c) have been determined by the corporation, and

(ii) notices of intent to terminate were provided (or in the case of a termination by the corporation, a notice of determination under section 4042 was issued) during the 5-Federal fiscal year period ending with the third fiscal year preceding the fiscal year in which occurs the date of the notice of intent to terminate (or the notice of determination under section 4042) with respect to the plan termination for which the recovery ratio is being determined.

(C) Exception—In the case of a terminated plan with respect to which the outstanding amount of benefit liabilities exceeds $20,000,000, the term "section 4062(c) recovery ratio" means, with respect to the termination of such plan, the ratio of—

(i) the value of the recoveries on behalf of the plan under section 4062(c), to

(ii) the amount of the liability owed under section 4062(c) as of the date of plan termination to the trustee appointed under section 4042 (b) or (c).

(3) Subsection not to apply—This subsection shall not apply with respect to the determination of—

(A) whether the amount of outstanding benefit liabilities exceeds $20,000,000, or

(B) the amount of any liability under section 4062 to the corporation or the trustee appointed under section 4042 (b) or (c).

(4) Determinations—Determinations under this subsection shall be made by the corporation. Such determinations shall be binding unless shown by clear and convincing evidence to be unreasonable.

§ 4045. Recapture of payments (§ 1345)

(a) Except as provided in subsection (c), the trustee is authorized to recover for the benefit of a plan from a participant the recoverable amount (as defined in subsection (b)) of all payments from the plan to him which commenced within the 3-year period immediately preceding the time the plan is terminated.

(b) For purposes of subsection (a) the recoverable amount is the excess of the amount determined under paragraph (1) over the amount determined under paragraph (2).

(1) The amount determined under this paragraph is the sum of the amount of the actual payments received by the participant within the 3-year period.

(2) The amount determined under this paragraph is the sum of—

(A) the sum of the amount such participant would have received during each consecutive 12-month period within the 3 years if the participant received the benefit in the form described in paragraph (3),

(B) the sum for each of the consecutive 12-month periods of the lesser of—

(i) the excess, if any, of $10,000 over the benefit in the form described in paragraph (3), or

(ii) the excess of the actual payment, if any, over the benefit in the form described in paragraph (3), and

(C) the present value at the time of termination of the participant's future benefits guaranteed under this subchapter as if the benefits commenced in the form described in paragraph (3).

(3) The form of benefit for purposes of this subsection shall be the monthly benefit the participant would have received during the consecutive 12-month period, if he had elected at the time of the first payment made during the 3- year period, to receive his interest in the plan as a monthly benefit in the form of a life annuity commencing at the time of such first payment.

(c)(1) In the event of a distribution described in section 4043(b)(7) the 3-year period referred to in subsection (b) shall not end sooner than the date on which the corporation is notified of the distribution.

(2) The trustee shall not recover any payment made from a plan after or on account of the death of a participant, or to a participant who is disabled (within the meaning of section 72(m)(7) of the Internal Revenue Code of 1986).

(3) The corporation is authorized to waive, in whole or in part, the recovery of any amount which the trustee is authorized to recover for the benefit of a plan under this section in any case in which it determines that substantial economic hardship would result to the participant or his beneficiaries from whom such amount is recoverable.

* * *

§ 4047. Restoration of plans (§ 1347)

Whenever the corporation determines that a plan which is to be terminated under section 4041 or 4042, or which is in the process of being terminated under section 4041 or 4042, should not be terminated under section 4041 or 4042 as a result of such circumstances as the corporation determines to be relevant, the corporation is authorized to cease any activities undertaken to terminate the plan, and to take whatever action is necessary and within its power to restore the plan to its status prior to the determination that the plan was to be terminated under section 4041 or 4042. In the case of a plan which has been terminated under section 4041 or 4042 the corporation is authorized in any such case in which the corporation determines such action to be appropriate and consistent with its duties under this title, to take such action as may be necessary to restore the plan to its pretermination status, including, but not limited to, the transfer to the employer or a plan administrator of control of part or all of the remaining assets and liabilities of the plan.

§ 4048. Termination date (§ 1348)

(a) For purposes of this title the termination date of a single-employer plan is—

(1) in the case of a plan terminated in a standard termination in accordance with the provisions of section 4041(b), the termination date proposed in the notice provided under section 4041(a)(2),

(2) in the case of a plan terminated in a distress termination in accordance with the provisions of section 4041(c), the date established by the plan administrator and agreed to by the corporation,

(3) in the case of a plan terminated in accordance with the provisions of section 4042, the date established by the corporation and agreed to by the plan administrator, or

(4) in the case of a plan terminated under section 4041(c) or 4042 in any case in which no agreement is reached between the plan administrator and the corporation (or the trustee), the date established by the court.

(b) For purposes of this subchapter, the date of termination of a multiemployer plan is—

(1) in the case of a plan terminated in accordance with the provisions of section 4041A, the date determined under subsection (b) of that section; or

(2) in the case of a plan terminated in accordance with the provisions of section 4042, the date agreed to between the plan administrator and the corporation (or the trustee appointed under section 4042(b)(2), if any), or, if no agreement is reached, the date established by the court.

* * *

Subtitle D—Liability

* * *

§ 4062. Liability for termination of single-employer plans under a distress termination or a termination by corporation (§ 1362)

(a) In general—In any case in which a single-employer plan is terminated in a distress termination under section 4041(c) or a termination otherwise instituted by the corporation under section 4042, any person who is, on the termination date, a contributing sponsor of the plan or a member of such a contributing sponsor's controlled group shall incur liability under this section. The liability under this section of all such persons shall be joint and several. The liability under this section consists of—

(1) liability to the corporation, to the extent provided in subsection (b), and

(2) liability to the trustee appointed under subsection (b) or (c) of section 4042, to the extent provided in subsection (c).

(b) Liability to corporation—

(1) Amount of liability—

(A) In general—Except as provided in subparagraph (B), the liability to the corporation of a person described in subsection (a) of this section shall be the total amount of the unfunded benefit liabilities (as of the termination date) to all participants and beneficiaries under the plan, together with interest (at a reasonable rate) calculated from the termination date in accordance with regulations prescribed by the corporation.

* * *

(c) Liability to section 4042 trustee—A person described in subsection (a) shall be subject to liability under this subsection to the trustee appointed under subsection (b) or (c) of section 4042. The liability of such person under this subsection shall consist of—

(1) the sum of the shortfall amortization charge (within the meaning of section 303(c)(1) of this Act and 430(d)(1) of the Internal Revenue Code of 1986) with respect to the plan (if any) for the plan year in which the termination date occurs, plus the aggregate total of shortfall amortization installments (if any) determined for succeeding plan years under section 303(c)(2) of this Act and section 430(d)(2) of such Code (which, for purposes of this subparagraph, shall include any increase in such sum which would result if all applications for waivers of the minimum funding standard under section 302(c) of this Act and section 412(c) of such Code which are pending with respect to such plan were denied and if no additional contributions (other than those already made by the termination date) were made for the plan year in which the termination date occurs or for any previous plan year), and

(2) the sum of the waiver amortization charge (within the meaning of section 303(e)(1) of this Act and 430(e)(1) of the Internal Revenue Code of 1986) with respect to the plan (if any) for the plan year in which the termination date occurs, plus the aggregate total of waiver amortization installments (if any) determined for succeeding plan years under section 303(e)(2) of this Act and section 430(e)(2) of such Code,

together with interest (at a reasonable rate) calculated from the termination date in accordance with regulations prescribed by the corporation. The liability under this subsection shall be due and payable to such trustee as of the termination date, in cash or securities acceptable to such trustee.

* * *

§ 4068. Lien for liability (§ 1368)

(a) If any person liable to the corporation under section 4062, 4063, or 4064 neglects or refuses to pay, after demand, the amount of such liability (including interest), there shall be a lien in favor of the corporation in the amount of such liability (including interest) upon all property and rights to property, whether real or personal, belonging to such person, except that such lien may not be in an amount in excess of 30 percent of the collective net worth of all persons described in section 4062(a).

(b) The lien imposed by subsection (a) arises on the date of termination of a plan, and continues until the liability imposed under section 4062, 4063, or 4064 is satisfied or becomes unenforceable by reason of lapse of time.

(c)(1) Except as otherwise provided under this section, the priority of a lien imposed under subsection (a) shall be determined in the same manner as under section 6323 of the Internal Revenue Code of 1986 (as in effect on April 7, 1986).

* * *

(2) In a case under title 11 of the United States Code or in insolvency proceedings, the lien imposed under subsection (a) shall be treated in the same manner as a tax due and owing to the United States for purposes of title 11 of the United States Code or section 3713 of title 31 of the United States Code.

* * *

§ 4069. Treatment of transactions to evade liability; effect of corporate reorganization (§ 1369)

(a) Treatment of transactions to evade liability—If a principal purpose of any person in entering into any transaction is to evade liability to which such person would be subject under this subtitle and the transaction becomes effective within five years before the termination date of the termination on which such liability would be based, then such person and the members of such person's controlled group (determined as of the termination date) shall be subject to liability under this subtitle in connection with such termination as if such person were a contributing sponsor of the terminated plan as of the termination date. This subsection shall not cause any person to be liable under this subtitle in connection with such plan termination for any increases or improvements in the benefits provided under the plan which are adopted after the date on which the transaction referred to in the preceding sentence becomes effective.

(b) Effect of corporate reorganization—For purposes of this subtitle, the following rules apply in the case of certain corporate reorganizations:

(1) Change of identity, form, etc—If a person ceases to exist by reason of a reorganization which involves a mere change in identity, form, or place of organization, however effected, a successor corporation resulting from such reorganization shall be treated as the person to whom this subtitle applies.

(2) Liquidation into parent corporation—If a person ceases to exist by reason of liquidation into a parent corporation, the parent corporation shall be treated as the person to whom this subtitle applies.

(3) Merger, consolidation, or division—If a person ceases to exist by reason of a merger, consolidation, or division, the successor corporation or corporations shall be treated as the person to whom this subtitle applies.

AGE DISCRIMINATION IN EMPLOYMENT ACT OF 1967

29 U.S.C. § 621 et seq.

§ 2. Congressional statement of findings and purpose (§ 621)

(a) The Congress hereby finds and declares that—

(1) in the face of rising productivity and affluence, older workers find themselves disadvantaged in their efforts to retain employment, and especially to regain employment when displaced from jobs;

(2) the setting of arbitrary age limits regardless of potential for job performance has become a common practice, and certain otherwise desirable practices may work to the disadvantage of older persons;

(3) the incidence of unemployment, especially long-term unemployment with resultant deterioration of skill, morale, and employer acceptability is, relative to the younger ages, high among older workers; their numbers are great and growing; and their employment problems grave;

(4) the existence in industries affecting commerce, of arbitrary discrimination in employment because of age, burdens commerce and the free flow of goods in commerce.

(b) It is therefore the purpose of this chapter to promote employment of older persons based on their ability rather than age; to prohibit arbitrary age discrimination in employment; to help employers and workers find ways of meeting problems arising from the impact of age on employment.

* * *

§ 4. Prohibition of age discrimination (§ 623)

(a) It shall be unlawful for an employer—

(1) to fail or refuse to hire or to discharge any individual or otherwise discriminate against any individual with respect to his compensation, terms, conditions, or privileges of employment, because of such individual's age;

(2) to limit, segregate, or classify his employees in any way which would deprive or tend to deprive any individual of employment opportunities or otherwise adversely affect his status as an employee, because of such individual's age; or

(3) to reduce the wage rate of any employee in order to comply with this Act.

* * *

(f) It shall not be unlawful for an employer, employment agency, or labor organization—

(1) to take any action otherwise prohibited under subsections (a), (b), (c), or (e) of this section where age is a bona fide occupational qualification reasonably necessary to the normal operation of the particular business, or where the differentiation is based on reasonable factors other than age, or where such practices involve an employee in a workplace in a foreign country, and compliance with such subsections would cause such employer, or a corporation controlled by such employer, to violate the laws of the country in which such workplace is located;

(2) to take any action otherwise prohibited under subsection (a), (b), (c), or (e) of this section—

(A) to observe the terms of a bona fide seniority system that is not intended to evade the purposes of this Act, except that no such seniority system shall require or permit the involuntary retirement of any individual specified by section 12(a) of this Act because of the age of such individual; or

(B) to observe the terms of a bona fide employee benefit plan—

(i) where, for each benefit or benefit package, the actual amount of payment made or cost incurred on behalf of an older worker is no less than that made or incurred on behalf of a younger worker, as permissible under section 1625.10, title 29, Code of Federal Regulations (as in effect on June 22, 1989); or

(ii) that is a voluntary early retirement incentive plan consistent with the relevant purpose or purposes of this Act.

Notwithstanding clause (i) or (ii) of subparagraph (B), no such employee benefit plan or voluntary early retirement incentive plan shall excuse the failure to hire any individual, and no such employee benefit plan shall require or permit the involuntary retirement of any individual specified by section 12(a) of this Act, because of the age of such individual. An employer, employment agency, or labor organization acting under subparagraph (A), or under clause (i) or (ii) of subparagraph (B), shall have the burden of proving that such actions are lawful in any civil enforcement proceeding brought under this Act; or

* * *

(i)(1) Except as otherwise provided in this subsection, it shall be unlawful for an employer, an employment agency, a labor organization, or any combination thereof to establish or maintain an employee pension benefit plan which requires or permits—

(A) in the case of a defined benefit plan, the cessation of an employee's benefit accrual, or the reduction of the rate of an employee's benefit accrual, because of age, or

(B) in the case of a defined contribution plan, the cessation of allocations to an employee's account, or the reduction of the rate at which amounts are allocated to an employee's account, because of age.

(2) Nothing in this section shall be construed to prohibit an employer, employment agency, or labor organization from observing any provision of an employee pension benefit plan to the extent that such provision imposes (without regard to age) a limitation on the amount of benefits that the plan provides or a limitation on the number of years of service or years of participation which are taken into account for purposes of determining benefit accrual under the plan.

(3) In the case of any employee who, as of the end of any plan year under a defined benefit plan, has attained normal retirement age under such plan—

(A) if distribution of benefits under such plan with respect to such employee has commenced as of the end of such plan year, then any requirement of this subsection for continued accrual of benefits under such plan with respect to such employee during such plan year shall be treated as satisfied to the extent of the actuarial equivalent of in-service distribution of benefits, and

(B) if distribution of benefits under such plan with respect to such employee has not commenced as of the end of such year in accordance with section 206(a)(3) of the

Employee Retirement Income Security Act of 1974 and section 401(a)(14)(C) of the Internal Revenue Code of 1986, and the payment of benefits under such plan with respect to such employee is not suspended during such plan year pursuant to section 203(a)(3)(B) of the Employee Retirement Income Security Act of 1974 or section 411(a)(3)(B) of the Internal Revenue Code of 1986, then any requirement of this subsection for continued accrual of benefits under such plan with respect to such employee during such plan year shall be treated as satisfied to the extent of any adjustment in the benefit payable under the plan during such plan year attributable to the delay in the distribution of benefits after the attainment of normal retirement age.

The provisions of this paragraph shall apply in accordance with regulations of the Secretary of the Treasury. Such regulations shall provide for the application of the preceding provisions of this paragraph to all employee pension benefit plans subject to this subsection and may provide for the application of such provisions, in the case of any such employee, with respect to any period of time within a plan year.

(4) Compliance with the requirements of this subsection with respect to an employee pension benefit plan shall constitute compliance with the requirements of this section relating to benefit accrual under such plan.

(5) Paragraph (1) shall not apply with respect to any employee who is a highly compensated employee (within the meaning of section 414(q) of the Internal Revenue Code of 1986) to the extent provided in regulations prescribed by the Secretary of the Treasury for purposes of precluding discrimination in favor of highly compensated employees within the meaning of subchapter D of chapter 1 of such Code.

(6) A plan shall not be treated as failing to meet the requirements of paragraph (1) solely because the subsidized portion of any early retirement benefit is disregarded in determining benefit accruals or it is a plan permitted by subsection (m) of this section..

(7) Any regulations prescribed by the Secretary of the Treasury pursuant to clause (v) of section 411(b)(1)(H) of the Internal Revenue Code of 1986 and subparagraphs (C) and (D) of section 411(b)(2) of such Code shall apply with respect to the requirements of this subsection in the same manner and to the same extent as such regulations apply with respect to the requirements of such sections 411(b)(1)(H) and 411(b)(2).

(8) A plan shall not be treated as failing to meet the requirements of this section solely because such plan provides a normal retirement age described in section 3(24)(B) of the Employee Retirement Income Security Act of 1974 and section 411(a)(8)(B) of the Internal Revenue Code of 1986.

(9) For purposes of this subsection—

(A) The terms "employee pension benefit plan", "defined benefit plan", "defined contribution plan", and "normal retirement age" have the meanings provided such terms in section 3 of the Employee Retirement Income Security Act of 1974.

(B) The term "compensation" has the meaning provided by section 414(s) of the Internal Revenue Code of 1986.

(10) Special rules relating to age—

(A) Comparison to similarly situated younger individual—

(i) In general—A plan shall not be treated as failing to meet the requirements of paragraph (1) if a participant's accrued benefit, as determined as of any date under the terms of the plan, would be equal to or greater than that of any similarly situated, younger individual who is or could be a participant.

(ii) Similarly situated—For purposes of this subparagraph, a participant is similarly situated to any other individual if such participant is identical to such other individual in every respect (including period of service, compensation, position, date of hire, work history, and any other respect) except for age.

(iii) Disregard of subsidized early retirement benefits—In determining the accrued benefit as of any date for purposes of this clause, the subsidized portion of any early retirement benefit or retirement-type subsidy shall be disregarded.

(iv) Accrued benefit—For purposes of this subparagraph, the accrued benefit may, under the terms of the plan, be expressed as an annuity payable at normal retirement age, the balance of a hypothetical account, or the current value of the accumulated percentage of the employee's final average compensation.

(B) Applicable defined benefit plans—

(i) Interest credits—

(I) In general—An applicable defined benefit plan shall be treated as failing to meet the requirements of paragraph (1) unless the terms of the plan provide that any interest credit (or an equivalent amount) for any plan year shall be at a rate which is not greater than a market rate of return. A plan shall not be treated as failing to meet the requirements of this subclause merely because the plan provides for a reasonable minimum guaranteed rate of return or for a rate of return that is equal to the greater of a fixed or variable rate of return.

(II) Preservation of capital—An interest credit (or an equivalent amount) of less than zero shall in no event result in the account balance or similar amount being less than the aggregate amount of contributions credited to the account.

(III) Market rate of return—The Secretary of the Treasury may provide by regulation for rules governing the calculation of a market rate of return for purposes of subclause (I) and for permissible methods of crediting interest to the account (including fixed or variable interest rates) resulting in effective rates of return meeting the requirements of subclause (I). In the case of a governmental plan (as defined in the first sentence of section 414(d) of the Internal Revenue Code of 1986, a rate of return or a method of crediting interest established pursuant to any provision of Federal, State, or local law (including any administrative rule or policy adopted in accordance with any such law) shall be treated as a market rate of return for purposes of subclause (I) and a permissible method of crediting interest for purposes of meeting the requirements of subclause (I), except that this sentence shall only apply to a rate of return or method of crediting interest if such rate or method does not violate any other requirement of this chapter.

(ii) Special rule for plan conversions—If, after June 29, 2005, an applicable plan amendment is adopted, the plan shall be treated as failing to meet the requirements of paragraph (1)(H) unless the requirements of clause (iii) are met with respect to each individual who was a participant in the plan immediately before the adoption of the amendment.

(iii) Rate of benefit accrual—Subject to clause (iv), the requirements of this clause are met with respect to any participant if the accrued benefit of the participant under the terms of the plan as in effect after the amendment is not less than the sum of—

(I) the participant's accrued benefit for years of service before the effective date of the amendment, determined under the terms of the plan as in effect before the amendment, plus

(II) the participant's accrued benefit for years of service after the effective date of the amendment, determined under the terms of the plan as in effect after the amendment.

(iv) Special rules for early retirement subsidies—For purposes of clause (iii)(I), the plan shall credit the accumulation account or similar amount with the amount of any early retirement benefit or retirement-type subsidy for the plan year in which the participant retires if, as of such time, the participant has met the age, years of service, and other requirements under the plan for entitlement to such benefit or subsidy.

(v) Applicable plan amendment—For purposes of this subparagraph—

(I) In general—The term "applicable plan amendment" means an amendment to a defined benefit plan which has the effect of converting the plan to an applicable defined benefit plan.

(II) Special rule for coordinated benefits—If the benefits of 2 or more defined benefit plans established or maintained by an employer are coordinated in such a manner as to have the effect of the adoption of an amendment described in subclause (I), the sponsor of the defined benefit plan or plans providing for such coordination shall be treated as having adopted such a plan amendment as of the date such coordination begins.

(III) Multiple amendments—The Secretary of the Treasury shall issue regulations to prevent the avoidance of the purposes of this subparagraph through the use of 2 or more plan amendments rather than a single amendment.

(IV) Applicable defined benefit plan—For purposes of this subparagraph, the term "applicable defined benefit plan" has the meaning given such term by section 203(f)(3) of the Employee Retirement Income Security Act of 1974.

(vi) Termination requirements—An applicable defined benefit plan shall not be treated as meeting the requirements of clause (i) unless the plan provides that, upon the termination of the plan—

(I) if the interest credit rate (or an equivalent amount) under the plan is a variable rate, the rate of interest used to determine accrued benefits under the plan shall be equal to the average of the rates of interest used under the plan during the 5-year period ending on the termination date, and

(II) the interest rate and mortality table used to determine the amount of any benefit under the plan payable in the form of an annuity payable at normal retirement age shall be the rate and table specified under the plan for such purpose as of the termination date, except that if such interest rate is a variable rate, the interest rate shall be determined under the rules of subclause (I).

(C) Certain offsets permitted—A plan shall not be treated as failing to meet the requirements of paragraph (1) solely because the plan provides offsets against benefits under the plan to the extent such offsets are allowable in applying the requirements of section 401(a) of the Internal Revenue Code of 1986.

(D) Permitted disparities in plan contributions or benefits—A plan shall not be treated as failing to meet the requirements of paragraph (1) solely because the plan provides a disparity in contributions or benefits with respect to which the requirements of section 401(l) of the Internal Revenue Code of 1986 are met.

(E) Indexing permitted—

(i) In general—A plan shall not be treated as failing to meet the requirements of paragraph (1) solely because the plan provides for indexing of accrued benefits under the plan.

(ii) Protection against loss—Except in the case of any benefit provided in the form of a variable annuity, clause (i) shall not apply with respect to any indexing which results in an accrued benefit less than the accrued benefit determined without regard to such indexing.

(iii) Indexing—For purposes of this subparagraph, the term "indexing" means, in connection with an accrued benefit, the periodic adjustment of the accrued benefit by means of the application of a recognized investment index or methodology.

(F) Early retirement benefit or retirement-type subsidy—For purposes of this paragraph, the terms "early retirement benefit" and "retirement-type subsidy" have the meaning given such terms in section 203(g)(2)(A) of the Employee Retirement Income Security Act of 1974.

(G) Benefit accrued to date—For purposes of this paragraph, any reference to the accrued benefit shall be a reference to such benefit accrued to date.

* * *

(*l*) Notwithstanding clause (i) or (ii) of subsection (f)(2)(B) of this section—

(1)(A) It shall not be a violation of subsection (a), (b), (c), or (e) of this section solely because—

(i) an employee pension benefit plan (as defined in section 3(2) of the Employee Retirement Income Security Act of 1974) provides for the attainment of a minimum age as a condition of eligibility for normal or early retirement benefits; or

(ii) a defined benefit plan (as defined in section 3(35) of the Employee Retirement Income Security Act of 1974) provides for—

(I) payments that constitute the subsidized portion of an early retirement benefit; or

(II) social security supplements for plan participants that commence before the age and terminate at the age (specified by the plan) when participants are eligible to receive reduced or unreduced old-age insurance benefits under title II of the Social Security Act (42 U.S.C. 401 et seq.), and that do not exceed such old-age insurance benefits.

(B) A voluntary early retirement incentive plan that—

(i) is maintained by—

(I) a local educational agency (as defined in section 9101 of the Elementary and Secondary Education Act of 1965 (20 U.S.C. 7801), or

(II) an education association which principally represents employees of 1 or more agencies described in subclause (I) and which is described in section 501(c) (5) or (6) of the Internal Revenue Code of 1986 and exempt from taxation under section 501(a) of such Code, and

(ii) makes payments or supplements described in subclauses (I) and (II) of subparagraph (A)(ii) in coordination with a defined benefit plan (as so defined) maintained by an eligible employer described in section 457(e)(1)(A) of such Code or by an education association described in clause (i)(II),

shall be treated solely for purposes of subparagraph (A)(ii) as if it were a part of the defined benefit plan with respect to such payments or supplements. Payments or supplements under such a voluntary early retirement incentive plan shall not constitute severance pay for purposes of paragraph (2).

(2)(A) It shall not be a violation of subsection (a), (b), (c), or (e) of this section solely because following a contingent event unrelated to age—

(i) the value of any retiree health benefits received by an individual eligible for an immediate pension;

(ii) the value of any additional pension benefits that are made available solely as a result of the contingent event unrelated to age and following which the individual is eligible for not less than an immediate and unreduced pension; or

(iii) the values described in both clauses (i) and (ii);

are deducted from severance pay made available as a result of the contingent event unrelated to age.

* * *

(3) It shall not be a violation of subsection (a), (b), (c), or (e) of this section solely because an employer provides a bona fide employee benefit plan or plans under which long-term disability benefits received by an individual are reduced by any pension benefits (other than those attributable to employee contributions)—

(A) paid to the individual that the individual voluntarily elects to receive; or

(B) for which an individual who has attained the later of age 62 or normal retirement age is eligible.

(m) Notwithstanding subsection (f)(2)(b), it shall not be a violation of subsection (a), (b), (c), or (e) solely because a plan of an institution of higher education (as defined in section 1001 of title 20, United States Code) offers employees who are serving under a contract of unlimited tenure (or similar arrangement providing for unlimited tenure) supplemental benefits upon voluntary retirement that are reduced or eliminated on the basis of age, if—

(1) such institution does not implement with respect to such employees any age-based reduction or cessation of benefits that are not such supplemental benefits, except as permitted by other provisions of this Act;

(2) such supplemental benefits are in addition to any retirement or severance benefits which have been offered generally to employees serving under a contract of unlimited tenure (or similar arrangement providing for unlimited tenure), independent of any early retirement or exit-incentive plan, within the preceding 365 days; and

(3) any employee who attains the minimum age and satisfies all non-age-based conditions for receiving a benefit under the plan has an opportunity lasting not less than 180 days to elect to retire and to receive the maximum benefit that could then be elected by a younger but otherwise similarly situated employee, and the plan does not require retirement to occur sooner than 180 days after such election.

* * *

§ 7. Recordkeeping, investigation, and enforcement (§ 626)

* * *

(f)(1) An individual may not waive any right or claim under this Act unless the waiver is knowing and voluntary. Except as provided in paragraph (2), a waiver may not be considered knowing and voluntary unless at a minimum—

(A) the waiver is part of an agreement between the individual and the employer that is written in a manner calculated to be understood by such individual, or by the average individual eligible to participate;

(B) the waiver specifically refers to rights or claims arising under this Act;

(C) the individual does not waive rights or claims that may arise after the date the waiver is executed;

(D) the individual waives rights or claims only in exchange for consideration in addition to anything of value to which the individual already is entitled;

(E) the individual is advised in writing to consult with an attorney prior to executing the agreement;

(F)(i) the individual is given a period of at least 21 days within which to consider the agreement; or

(ii) if a waiver is requested in connection with an exit incentive or other employment termination program offered to a group or class of employees, the individual is given a period of at least 45 days within which to consider the agreement;

(G) the agreement provides that for a period of at least 7 days following the execution of such agreement, the individual may revoke the agreement, and the agreement shall not become effective or enforceable until the revocation period has expired;

(H) if a waiver is requested in connection with an exit incentive or other employment termination program offered to a group or class of employees, the employer (at the commencement of the period specified in subparagraph (F)) informs the individual in writing in a manner calculated to be understood by the average individual eligible to participate, as to—

(i) any class, unit, or group of individuals covered by such program, any eligibility factors for such program, and any time limits applicable to such program; and

(ii) the job titles and ages of all individuals eligible or selected for the program, and the ages of all individuals in the same job classification or organizational unit who are not eligible or selected for the program.

* * *

(3) In any dispute that may arise over whether any of the requirements, conditions, and circumstances set forth in subparagraph (A), (B), (C), (D), (E), (F), (G), or (H) of paragraph (1), or subparagraph (A) or (B) of paragraph (2), have been met, the party asserting the validity of a waiver shall have the burden of proving in a court of competent jurisdiction that a waiver was knowing and voluntary pursuant to paragraph (1) or (2).

(4) No waiver agreement may affect the Commission's rights and responsibilities to enforce this Act. No waiver may be used to justify interfering with the protected right of an employee to file a charge or participate in an investigation or proceeding conducted by the Commission.

§ 12. Age limits (§ 631)

(a) The prohibitions in this Act shall be limited to individuals who are at least 40 years of age.

* * *

(c)(1) Nothing in this Act shall be construed to prohibit compulsory retirement of any employee who has attained 65 years of age and who, for the 2- year period immediately before retirement, is employed in a bona fide executive or a high policymaking position, if such employee is entitled to an immediate nonforfeitable annual retirement benefit from a pension, profit-sharing, savings, or deferred compensation plan, or any combination of such plans, of the employer of such employee, which equals, in the aggregate, at least $44,000.

(2) In applying the retirement benefit test of paragraph (1) of this subsection, if any such retirement benefit is in a form other than a straight life annuity (with no ancillary benefits), or if employees contribute to any such plan or make rollover contributions, such benefit shall be adjusted in accordance with regulations prescribed by the Equal Employment Opportunity Commission, after consultation with the Secretary of the Treasury, so that the benefit is the equivalent of a straight life annuity (with no ancillary benefits) under a plan to which employees do not contribute and under which no rollover contributions are made.

AMERICANS WITH DISABILITIES ACT OF 1990

42 U.S.C. § 12101 et seq.

* * *

§ 3. Definition of disability (§ 12102)

As used in this Act:

(1) Disability—The term "disability" means, with respect to an individual—

(A) a physical or mental impairment that substantially limits one or more major life activities of such individual;

(B) a record of such an impairment; or

(C) being regarded as having such an impairment (as described in paragraph (3)).

(2) Major life activities—

(A) In general—For purposes of paragraph (1), major life activities include, but are not limited to, caring for oneself, performing manual tasks, seeing, hearing, eating, sleeping, walking, standing, lifting, bending, speaking, breathing, learning, reading, concentrating, thinking, communicating, and working.

(B) Major bodily functions—For purposes of paragraph (1), a major life activity also includes the operation of a major bodily function, including but not limited to, functions of the immune system, normal cell growth, digestive, bowel, bladder, neurological, brain, respiratory, circulatory, endocrine, and reproductive functions.

(3) Regarded as having such an impairment—For purposes of paragraph (1)(C):

(A) An individual meets the requirement of "being regarded as having such an impairment" if the individual establishes that he or she has been subjected to an action prohibited under this Act because of an actual or perceived physical or mental impairment whether or not the impairment limits or is perceived to limit a major life activity.

(B) Paragraph (1)(C) shall not apply to impairments that are transitory and minor. A transitory impairment is an impairment with an actual or expected duration of 6 months or less.

(4) Rules of construction regarding the definition of disability—The definition of "disability" in paragraph (1) shall be construed in accordance with the following:

(A) The definition of disability in this Act shall be construed in favor of broad coverage of individuals under this Act, to the maximum extent permitted by the terms of this Act.

(B) The term "substantially limits" shall be interpreted consistently with the findings and purposes of the ADA Amendments Act of 2008.

(C) An impairment that substantially limits one major life activity need not limit other major life activities in order to be considered a disability.

(D) An impairment that is episodic or in remission is a disability if it would substantially limit a major life activity when active.

(E)(i) The determination of whether an impairment substantially limits a major life activity shall be made without regard to the ameliorative effects of mitigating measures such as—

(I) medication, medical supplies, equipment, or appliances, low-vision devices (which do not include ordinary eyeglasses or contact lenses), prosthetics including limbs and devices, hearing aids and cochlear implants or other implantable hearing devices, mobility devices, or oxygen therapy equipment and supplies;

(II) use of assistive technology;

(III) reasonable accommodations or auxiliary aids or services; or

(IV) learned behavioral or adaptive neurological modifications.

(ii) The ameliorative effects of the mitigating measures of ordinary eyeglasses or contact lenses shall be considered in determining whether an impairment substantially limits a major life activity.

(iii) As used in this subparagraph—

(I) the term "ordinary eyeglasses or contact lenses" means lenses that are intended to fully correct visual acuity or eliminate refractive error; and

(II) the term "low-vision devices" means devices that magnify, enhance, or otherwise augment a visual image.

* * *

§ 101. Definitions (§ 12111)

* * *

(8) Qualified individual—The term "qualified individual" means an individual who, with or without reasonable accommodation, can perform the essential functions of the employment position that such individual holds or desires. For the purposes of this subchapter, consideration shall be given to the employer's judgment as to what functions of a job are essential, and if an employer has prepared a written description before advertising or interviewing applicants for the job, this description shall be considered evidence of the essential functions of the job.

* * *

§ 102. Discrimination (§ 12112)

(a) General rule—No covered entity shall discriminate against a qualified individual on the basis of disability in regard to job application procedures, the hiring, advancement, or discharge of employees, employee compensation, job training, and other terms, conditions, and privileges of employment.

* * *

§ 501. Construction (§ 12201)

* * *

(c) Insurance—Titles I through IV of this Act shall not be construed to prohibit or restrict—

(1) an insurer, hospital or medical service company, health maintenance organization, or any agent, or entity that administers benefit plans, or similar organizations from underwriting risks, classifying risks, or administering such risks that are based on or not inconsistent with State law; or

(2) a person or organization covered by this Act from establishing, sponsoring, observing or administering the terms of a bona fide benefit plan that are based on underwriting risks, classifying risks, or administering such risks that are based on or not inconsistent with State law; or

(3) a person or organization covered by this Act from establishing, sponsoring, observing or administering the terms of a bona fide benefit plan that is not subject to State laws that regulate insurance.

Paragraphs (1), (2), and (3) shall not be used as a subterfuge to evade the purposes of title I and III.

* * *

ERISA REORGANIZATION PLAN

REORGANIZATION PLAN NO. 4 OF 1978

5 U.S.C.—Appendix 1.

Prepared by the President and transmitted to the Senate and the House of Representatives in Congress assembled, August 10, 1978, pursuant to the provisions of Chapter 9 of Title 5 of the United States Code.

EMPLOYEE RETIREMENT INCOME SECURITY ACT TRANSFERS

§ 101. Transfer to the Secretary of the Treasury

Except as otherwise provided in Sections 104 and 106 of this Plan, all authority of the Secretary of Labor to issue the following described documents pursuant to the statutes hereinafter specified is hereby transferred to the Secretary of the Treasury:

(a) regulations, rulings, opinions, variances and waivers under Parts 2 and 3 of Subtitle B of Title I and subsection 1012(c) of Title II of the Employee Retirement Income Security Act of 1974 (hereinafter referred to as "ERISA"), *except* for sections and subsections 201, 203(a)(3)(B), 209, and 301(a) of ERISA;

(b) such regulations, rulings, and opinions which are granted to the Secretary of Labor under Sections 404, 410, 411, 412, and 413 of the Internal Revenue Code of 1986, as amended, (hereinafter referred to as the "Code"), *except* for subsection 411(a)(3)(B) of the Code and the definitions of "collectively bargained plan" and "collective bargaining agreement" contained in subsections 404 (a)(1)(B) and (a)(1)(C), 410(b)(2)(A) and (b)(2)(B), and 413(a)(1) of the Code; and

(c) regulations, rulings, and opinions under subsections 3(19), 3(22), 3(23), 3(24), 3(25), 3(27), 3(28), 3(29), 3(30), and 3(31) of Subtitle A of Title I of ERISA.

§ 102. Transfers to the Secretary of Labor

Except as otherwise provided in Section 105 of this Plan, all authority of the Secretary of the Treasury to issue the following described documents pursuant to the statutes hereinafter specified is hereby transferred to the Secretary of Labor:

(a) regulations, rulings, opinions, and exemptions under section 4975 of the Code, except for (i) subsections 4975(a), (b), (c)(3), (d)(3), (e)(1), and (e)(7) of the Code; (ii) to the extent necessary for the continued enforcement of subsections 4975(a) and (b) by the Secretary of the Treasury, subsections 4975(f)(1), (f)(2), (f)(4), (f)(5) and (f)(6) of the Code; and (iii) exemptions with respect to transactions that are exempted by subsection 404(c) of ERISA from the provisions of Part 4 of Subtitle B of Title I of ERISA; and

(b) regulations, rulings, and opinions under subsection 2003(c) of ERISA, except for subsection 2003(c)(1)(B).

§ 103. Coordination Concerning Certain Fiduciary Actions

In the case of fiduciary actions which are subject to Part 4 of Subtitle B of Title I of ERISA, the Secretary of the Treasury shall notify the Secretary of Labor prior to the time of commencing any proceeding to determine whether the action violates the exclusive benefit rule of subsection

401(a) of the Code, but not later than prior to issuing a preliminary notice of intent to disqualify under that rule, and the Secretary of the Treasury shall not issue a determination that a plan or trust does not satisfy the requirements of subsection 401(a) by reason of the exclusive benefit rule of subsection 401(a), unless within 90 days after the date on which the Secretary of the Treasury notifies the Secretary of Labor of pending action, the Secretary of Labor certifies that he has no objection to the disqualification or the Secretary of Labor fails to respond to the Secretary of the Treasury. The requirements of this paragraph do not apply in the case of any termination or jeopardy assessment under sections 6851 or 6861 of the Code that has been approved in advance by the Commissioner of Internal Revenue, or, as delegated, the Assistant Commissioner for Employee Plans and Exempt Organizations.

§ 104. Enforcement by the Secretary of Labor

The transfers provided for in Section 101 of this Plan shall not affect the ability of the Secretary of Labor, subject to the provisions of Title III of ERISA relating to jurisdiction, administration, and enforcement, to engage in enforcement under Section 502 of ERISA or to exercise the authority set forth under Title III of ERISA, including the ability to make interpretations necessary to engage in such enforcement or to exercise such authority. However, in bringing such actions and in exercising such authority with respect to Parts 2 and 3 of Subtitle B of Title I of ERISA and any definitions for which the authority of the Secretary of Labor is transferred to the Secretary of the Treasury as provided in Section 101 of this Plan, the Secretary of Labor shall be bound by the regulations, rulings, opinions, variances, and waivers issued by the Secretary of the Treasury.

§ 105. Enforcement by the Secretary of the Treasury

The transfers provided for in Section 102 of this Plan shall not affect the ability of the Secretary of the Treasury, subject to the provisions of Title III of ERISA relating to jurisdiction, administration, and enforcement, (a) to audit plans and employers and to enforce the excise tax provisions of subsections 4975(a) and 4975(b) of the Code, to exercise the authority set forth in subsections 502(b)(1) and 502(h) of ERISA, or to exercise the authority set forth in Title III of ERISA, including the ability to make interpretations necessary to audit, to enforce such taxes, and to exercise such authority; and (b) consistent with the coordination requirements under Section 103 of this Plan, to disqualify, under section 401 of the Code, a plan subject to Part 4 of Subtitle B of Title I of ERISA, including the ability to make the interpretations necessary to make such disqualification. However, in enforcing such excise taxes and, to the extent applicable, in disqualifying such plans the Secretary of the Treasury shall be bound by the regulations, rulings, opinions, and exemptions issued by the Secretary of Labor pursuant to the authority transferred to the Secretary of Labor as provided in Section 102 of this Plan.

§ 106. Coordination for Section 101 Transfers

(a) The Secretary of the Treasury shall not exercise the functions transferred pursuant to Section 101 of this Plan to issue in proposed or final form any of the documents described in subsection (b) of this Section in any case in which such documents would significantly impact on or substantially affect collectively bargained plans unless, within 100 calendar days after the Secretary of the Treasury notifies the Secretary of Labor of such proposed action, the Secretary of Labor certifies that he has no objection or he fails to respond to the Secretary of the Treasury. The fact of such a notification, except for such notification for documents described in subsection (b)(iv) of this Section, from the Secretary of the Treasury to the Secretary of Labor shall be announced by the Secretary of Labor to the public within ten days following the date of receipt of the notification by the Secretary of Labor.

(b) The documents to which this Section applies are:

(i) amendments to regulations issued pursuant to subsections 202(a)(3), 203(b)(2) and (3)(A), 204(b)(3)(A), (C), and (E), and 210(a)(2) of ERISA, and subsections 410(a)(3) and 411(a)(5), (6)(A), and (b)(3)(A), (C), and (E), 413(b)(4) and (c)(3) and 414(f) of the Code;

(ii) regulations issued pursuant to subsections 204(b)(3)(D), 302(d)(2), and 304(d)(1), (d)(2), and (e)(2)(A) of ERISA, and subsections 411(b)(3)(D), 412(c)(2) and 431(d)(1), (d)(2), and (e)(2)(A)of the Code; and

(iii) revenue rulings (within the meaning of 26 CFR Section 601.201(a)(6)), revenue procedures, and similar publications, if the rulings, procedures and publications are issued under one of the statutory provisions listed in (i) and (ii) of this subsection; and

(iv) rulings (within the meaning of 26 CFR Section 601.201(a)(2)) issued prior to the issuance of a published regulation under one of the statutory provisions listed in (i) and (ii) of this subsection and not issued under a published Revenue Ruling.

(c) For those documents described in subsections (b)(i), (b)(ii) and (b)(iii) of this Section, the Secretary of Labor may request the Secretary of the Treasury to initiate the actions described in this Section 106 of this Plan.

* * *

§ 1.401-1. Qualified pension, profit-sharing, and stock bonus plans.

(a) *Introduction.*

* * *

(2) A qualified pension, profit-sharing, or stock bonus plan is a definite written program and arrangement which is communicated to the employees and which is established and maintained by an employer—

(i) In the case of a pension plan, to provide for the livelihood of the employees or their beneficiaries after the retirement of such employees through the payment of benefits determined without regard to profits (see paragraph (b)(1)(i) of this section);

(ii) In the case of a profit-sharing plan, to enable employees or their beneficiaries to participate in the profits of the employer's trade or business, or in the profits of an affiliated employer who is entitled to deduct his contributions to the plan under section 404(a)(3)(B), pursuant to a definite formula for allocating the contributions and for distributing the funds accumulated under the plan (see paragraph (b)(1)(ii) of this section); and

(iii) In the case of a stock bonus plan, to provide employees or their beneficiaries benefits similar to those of profit-sharing plans, except that such benefits are distributable in stock of the employer, and that the contributions by the employer are not necessarily dependent upon profits. If the employer's contributions are dependent upon profits, the plan may enable employees or their beneficiaries to participate not only in the profits of the employer, but also in the profits of an affiliated employer who is entitled to deduct his contributions to the plan under section 404(a)(3)(B) (see paragraph (b)(1)(iii) of this section).

* * *

(b) *General rules.* (1)(i) A pension plan within the meaning of section 401(a) is a plan established and maintained by an employer primarily to provide systematically for the payment of definitely determinable benefits to his employees over a period of years, usually for life, after retirement. Retirement benefits generally are measured by, and based on, such factors as years of service and compensation received by the employees. The determination of the amount of retirement benefits and the contributions to provide such benefits are not dependent upon profits. Benefits are not definitely determinable if funds arising from forfeitures on termination of service, or other reason, may be used to provide increased benefits for the remaining participants (see § 1.401-7, relating to the treatment of forfeitures under a qualified pension plan). A plan designed to provide benefits for employees or their beneficiaries to be paid upon retirement or over a period of years after retirement will, for the purposes of section 401(a), be considered a pension plan if the employer contributions under the plan can be determined actuarially on the basis of definitely determinable benefits, or, as in the case of money purchase pension plans, such contributions are fixed without being geared to profits. A pension plan may provide for the payment of a pension due to disability and may also provide for the payment of incidental death benefits through insurance or otherwise. However, a plan is not a pension plan if it provides for the payment of benefits not customarily included in a pension plan such as layoff benefits or benefits for sickness, accident, hospitalization, or medical expenses (except medical benefits described in section 401(h) as defined in paragraph (a) of § 1.401-14).

(ii) A profit-sharing plan is a plan established and maintained by an employer to provide for the participation in his profits by his employees or their beneficiaries. The plan must provide a definite predetermined formula for allocating the contributions made to the plan among the participants and for distributing the funds accumulated under the plan after a fixed number of years, the attainment of a stated age, or upon the prior occurrence of some event such as layoff, illness, disability, retirement, death, or severance of employment. A formula for allocating the contributions among the participants is definite if, for example, it provides for an allocation in proportion to the basic compensation of each participant. A plan (whether or not it contains a definite predetermined formula for determining the profits to be shared with the employees) does not qualify under section 401(a) if the contributions to the plan are made at such times or in such amounts that the plan in operation discriminates in favor of officers, shareholders, persons whose principal duties consist in supervising the work of other employees, or highly compensated employees. For the rules with respect to discrimination, see §§ 1.401-3 and 1.401-4. A profit-sharing plan within the meaning of section 401 is primarily a plan of deferred compensation, but the amounts allocated to the account of a participant may be used to provide for him or his family incidental life or accident or health insurance.

(iii) A stock bonus plan is a plan established and maintained by an employer to provide benefits similar to those of a profit-sharing plan, except that the contributions by the employer are not necessarily dependent upon profits and the benefits are distributable in stock of the employer company. For the purpose of allocating and distributing the stock of the employer which is to be shared among his employees or their beneficiaries, such a plan is subject to the same requirements as a profit-sharing plan.

* * *

(2) The term "plan" implies a permanent as distinguished from a temporary program. Thus, although the employer may reserve the right to change or terminate the plan, and to discontinue contributions thereunder, the abandonment of the plan for any reason other than business necessity within a few years after it has taken effect will be evidence that the plan from its inception was not a bona fide program for the exclusive benefit of employees in general. Especially will this be true if, for example, a pension plan is abandoned soon after pensions have been fully funded for persons in favor of whom discrimination is prohibited under section 401(a). The permanency of the plan will be indicated by all of the surrounding facts and circumstances, including the likelihood of the employer's ability to continue contributions as provided under the plan. In the case of a profit-sharing plan, other than a profit-sharing plan which covers employees and owner-employees (see section 401(d)(2)(B)), it is not necessary that the employer contribute every year or that he contribute the same amount or contribute in accordance with the same ratio every year. However, merely making a single or occasional contribution out of profits for employees does not establish a plan of profit-sharing. To be a profit-sharing plan, there must be recurring and substantial contributions out of profits for the employees. In the event a plan is abandoned, the employer should promptly notify the district director, stating the circumstances which led to the discontinuance of the plan.

§ 1.401-2. Impossibility of diversion under the trust instrument.

(a) *In general.* (1) Under section 401(a)(2) a trust is not qualified unless under the trust instrument it is impossible (in the taxable year and at any time thereafter before the satisfaction of all liabilities to employees or their beneficiaries covered by the trust) for any part of the trust corpus or income to be used for, or diverted to, purposes other than for the exclusive benefit of such employees or their beneficiaries.

* * *

(b) *Meaning of "liabilities".* (1) The intent and purpose in section 401(a)(2) of the phrase "prior to the satisfaction of all liabilities with respect to employees and their beneficiaries under the trust" is to permit the employer to reserve the right to recover at the termination of the trust, and only at such termination, any balance remaining in the trust which is due to erroneous actuarial computations during the previous life of the trust. A balance due to an "erroneous actuarial computation" is the surplus arising because actual requirements differ from the expected requirements even though the latter were based upon previous actuarial valuations of liabilities or determinations of costs of providing pension benefits under the plan and were made by a person competent to make such determinations in accordance with reasonable assumptions as to mortality, interest, etc., and correct procedures relating to the method of funding. For example, a trust has accumulated assets of $1,000,000 at the time of liquidation, determined by acceptable actuarial procedures using reasonable assumptions as to interest, mortality, etc., as being necessary to provide the benefits in accordance with the provisions of the plan. Upon such liquidation it is found that $950,000 will satisfy all of the liabilities under the plan. The surplus of $50,000 arises, therefore, because of the difference between the amounts actuarially determined and the amounts actually required to satisfy the liabilities. This $50,000, therefore, is the amount which may be returned to the employer as the result of an erroneous actuarial computation. If, however, the surplus of $50,000 had been accumulated as a result of a change in the benefit provisions or in the eligibility requirements of the plan, the $50,000 could not revert to the employer because such surplus would not be the result of an erroneous actuarial computation.

(2) The term "liabilities" as used in section 401(a)(2) includes both fixed and contingent obligations to employees. For example, if 1,000 employees are covered by a trust forming part of a pension plan, 300 of whom have satisfied all the requirements for a monthly pension, while the remaining 700 employees have not yet completed the required period of service, contingent obligations to such 700 employees have nevertheless arisen which constitute "liabilities" within the meaning of that term.

* * *

§ 1.401(a)-1. Post-ERISA qualified plans and qualified trusts; in general.

(a) *Introduction*—(1) *In general.* This section and the following regulation sections under section 401 reflect the provisions of section 401 after amendment by the Employee Retirement Income Security Act of 1974 (Pub.L. 93- 406) ("ERISA").

(2) [Reserved]

(b) *Requirements for pension plans*—(1) *Definitely determinable benefits.* (i) In order for a pension plan to be a qualified plan under section 401(a), the plan must be established and maintained by an employer primarily to provide systematically for the payment of definitely determinable benefits to its employees over a period of years, usually for life, after retirement or attainment of normal retirement age (subject to paragraph (b)(2) of this section). A plan does not fail to satisfy this paragraph (b)(1)(i) merely because the plan provides, in accordance with section 401(a)(36), that a distribution may be made from the plan to an employee who has attained age 62 and who is not separated from employment at the time of such distribution.

(ii) Section 1.401-1(b)(1)(i), a pre-ERISA regulation, provides rules applicable to this requirement, and that regulation is applicable except as otherwise provided.

(iii) The use of the type of plan provision described in § 1.415(a)-1(d)(1) which automatically freezes or reduces the rate of benefit accrual or the annual addition to insure that the limitations of section 415 will not be exceeded, will not be considered to violate the requirements of this subparagraph provided that the operation of such provision precludes discretion by the employer.

(2) *Normal retirement age*—(i) *General rule.* The normal retirement age under a plan must be an age that is not earlier than the earliest age that is reasonably representative of the typical retirement age for the industry in which the covered workforce is employed.

(ii) *Age 62 safe harbor.* A normal retirement age under a plan that is age 62 or later is deemed to be not earlier than the earliest age that is reasonably representative of the typical retirement age for the industry in which the covered workforce is employed.

(iii) *Age 55 to age 62.* In the case of a normal retirement age that is not earlier than age 55 and is earlier than age 62, whether the age is not earlier than the earliest age that is reasonably representative of the typical retirement age for the industry in which the covered workforce is employed is based on all of the relevant facts and circumstances.

(iv) *Under age 55.* A normal retirement age that is lower than age 55 is presumed to be earlier than the earliest age that is reasonably representative of the typical retirement age for the industry in which the covered workforce is employed, unless the Commissioner determines that under the facts and circumstances the normal retirement age is not earlier than the earliest age that is reasonably representative of the typical retirement age for the industry in which the covered workforce is employed.

(v) *Age 50 safe harbor for qualified public safety employees.* A normal retirement age under a plan that is age 50 or later is deemed to be not earlier than the earliest age that is reasonably representative of the typical retirement age for the industry in which the covered workforce is employed if substantially all of the participants in the plan are qualified public safety employees (within the meaning of section 72(t)(10)(B)).

(3) Benefit distribution prior to retirement. For purposes of paragraph (b)(1)(i) of this section, retirement does not include a mere reduction in the number of hours that an employee works. Accordingly, benefits may not be distributed prior to normal retirement age solely due to a reduction in the number of hours that an employee works.

* * *

§ 1.401(a)-13. Assignment or alienation of benefits.

* * *

(b) *No assignment or alienation*—(1) *General rule.* Under section 401(a)(13), a trust will not be qualified unless the plan of which the trust is a part provides that benefits provided under the plan may not be anticipated, assigned (either at law or in equity), alienated or subject to attachment, garnishment, levy, execution or other legal or equitable process.

(2) Federal tax levies and judgments. A plan provision satisfying the requirements of subparagraph (1) of this paragraph shall not preclude the following:

(i) The enforcement of a Federal tax levy made pursuant to section 6331.

(ii) The collection by the United States on a judgment resulting from an unpaid tax assessment.

(c) *Definition of assignment and alienation*—(1) *In general.* For purposes of this section, the terms "assignment" and "alienation" include—

(i) Any arrangement providing for the payment to the employer of plan benefits which otherwise would be due the participant under the plan, and

(ii) Any direct or indirect arrangement (whether revocable or irrevocable) whereby a party acquires from a participant or beneficiary a right or interest enforceable against the plan in, or to, all or any part of a plan benefit payment which is, or may become, payable to the participant or beneficiary.

(2) *Specific arrangements not considered an assignment or alienation.* The terms "assignment" and "alienation" do not include, and paragraph (e) of this section does not apply to, the following arrangements:

(i) Any arrangement for the recovery of amounts described in section 4045(b) of the Employee Retirement Income Security Act of 1974, 88 Stat. 1027 (relating to the recapture of certain payments),

(ii) Any arrangement for the withholding of Federal, State or local tax from plan benefit payments,

(iii) Any arrangement for the recovery by the plan of overpayments of benefits previously made to a participant,

(iv) Any arrangement for the transfer of benefit rights from the plan to another plan, or

(v) Any arrangement for the direct deposit of benefit payments to an account in a bank, savings and loan association or credit union, provided such arrangement is not part of an arrangement constituting an assignment or alienation. Thus, for example, such an arrangement could provide for the direct deposit of a participant's benefit payments to a bank account held by the participant and the participant's spouse as joint tenants.

(d) *Exceptions to general rule prohibiting assignments or alienations*—(1) *Certain voluntary and revocable assignments or alienations*. Not withstanding paragraph (b)(1) of this section, a plan may provide that once a participant or beneficiary begins receiving benefits under the plan, the participant or beneficiary may assign or alienate the right to future benefit payments provided that the provision is limited to assignments or alienations which—

(i) Are voluntary and revocable;

(ii) Do not in the aggregate exceed 10 percent of any benefit payment; and

(iii) Are neither for the purpose, nor have the effect, of defraying plan administration costs.

For purposes of this subparagraph, an attachment, garnishment, levy, execution, or other legal or equitable process is not considered a voluntary assignment or alienation.

(2) *Benefits assigned or alienated as security for loans*. (i) Notwithstanding paragraph (b)(1) of this section, a plan may provide for loans from the plan to a participant or a beneficiary to be secured (by whatever means) by the participant's accrued nonforfeitable benefit provided that the following conditions are met.

(ii) The plan provision providing for the loans must be limited to loans from the plan. A plan may not provide for the use of benefits accrued or to be accrued under the plan as security for a loan from a party other than the plan, regardless of whether these benefits are nonforfeitable within the meaning of section 411 and the regulations thereunder.

(iii) The loan, if made to a participant or beneficiary who is a disqualified person (within the meaning of section 4975(e)(2)), must be exempt from the tax imposed by section 4975 (relating to the tax imposed on prohibited transactions) by reason of section 4975(d)(1). If the loan is made to a participant or beneficiary who is not a disqualified person, the loan must be one which would be exempt from the tax imposed by section 4975 by reason of section 4975(d)(1) if the loan were made to a disqualified person.

* * *

§ 1.401(a)-20. Requirements of qualified joint and survivor annuity and qualified preretirement survivor annuity.

* * *

Q-28: Does consent contained in an antenuptial agreement or similar contract entered into prior to marriage satisfy the consent requirements of sections 401(a)(11) and 417?

A-28: No. An agreement entered into prior to marriage does not satisfy the applicable consent requirements, even if the agreement is executed within the applicable election period.

* * *

§ 1.401(a)(4)-1. Nondiscrimination requirements of section 401(a)(4).

(a) *In general*. Section 401(a)(4) provides that a plan is a qualified plan only if the contributions or the benefits provided under the plan do not discriminate in favor of HCEs. Whether a plan satisfies this requirement depends on the form of the plan and on its effect in operation. In making this determination, intent is irrelevant. This section sets forth the exclusive rules for determining whether a plan satisfies section 401(a)(4). A plan that complies in form and operation with the rules in this section therefore satisfies section 401(a)(4).

(b) *Requirements a plan must satisfy*—(1) *In general.* In order to satisfy section 401(a)(4), a plan must satisfy each of the requirements of this paragraph (b).

(2) *Nondiscriminatory amount of contributions or benefits*—(i) *General rule.* Either the contributions or the benefits provided under the plan must be nondiscriminatory in amount. It need not be shown that both the contributions and the benefits provided are nondiscriminatory in amount, but only that either the contributions alone or the benefits alone are nondiscriminatory in amount.

(ii) *Defined contribution plans*—(A) *General rule.* A defined contribution plan satisfies this paragraph (b)(2) if the contributions allocated under the plan (including forfeitures) are nondiscriminatory in amount under § 1.401(a)(4)-2. Alternatively, a defined contribution plan (other than an ESOP) satisfies this paragraph (b)(2) if the equivalent benefits provided under the plan are nondiscriminatory in amount under § 1.401(a)(4)-8(b). Section 1.401(a)(4)-8(b) includes a safe-harbor testing method for contributions provided under a target benefit plan.

(B) *Section 401(k) plans and section 401(m) plans.* A section 401(k) plan is deemed to satisfy this paragraph (b)(2) because § 1.410(b)-9 defines a section 401(k) plan as a plan consisting of elective contributions under a qualified cash or deferred arrangement (i.e., one that satisfies section 401(k)(3), the nondiscriminatory amount requirement applicable to qualified cash or deferred arrangements). A section 401(m) plan satisfies this paragraph (b)(2) only if the plan satisfies §§ 1.401(m)-1(b) and 1.401(m)-2. Contributions under a nonqualified cash or deferred arrangement, elective contributions described in § 1.401(k)-1(b)(4)(iv) that fail to satisfy the allocation and compensation requirements of § 1.401(k)-1(b)(4)(i), matching contributions that fail to satisfy § 1.401(m)-1(b)(4)(ii)(A), and qualified nonelective contributions treated as elective or matching contributions for certain purposes under §§ 1.401(k)-1(b)(5) and 1.401(m)-1(b)(5), respectively, are not subject to the special rule in this paragraph (b)(2)(ii)(B), because they are not treated as part of a section 401(k) plan or section 401(m) plan as those terms are defined in § 1.410(b)-9. The contributions described in the preceding sentence must satisfy paragraph (b)(2)(ii)(A) of this section.

(iii) *Defined benefit plans.* A defined benefit plan satisfies this paragraph (b)(2) if the benefits provided under the plan are nondiscriminatory in amount under § 1.401(a)(4)-3. Alternatively, a defined benefit plan satisfies this paragraph (b)(2) if the equivalent allocations provided under the plan are nondiscriminatory in amount under § 1.401(a)(4)-8(c). Section 1.401(a)(4)-8(c) includes a safe-harbor testing method for benefits provided under a cash balance plan. In addition, § 1.401(a)(4)-8(d) provides a safe-harbor testing method for benefits provided under a defined benefit plan that is part of a floor-offset arrangement.

(3) *Nondiscriminatory availability of benefits, rights, and features.* All benefits, rights, and features provided under the plan must be made available in the plan in a nondiscriminatory manner. Rules for determining whether this requirement is satisfied are set forth in § 1.401(a)(4)-4.

(4) *Nondiscriminatory effect of plan amendments and terminations.* The timing of plan amendments must not have the effect of discriminating significantly in favor of HCEs. Rules for determining whether this requirement is satisfied are set forth in § 1.401(a)(4)-5(a). Section 1.401(a)(4)-5(b) provides additional requirements regarding plan terminations.

(c) *Application of requirements*—(1) *In general.* The requirements of paragraph (b) of this section must be applied in accordance with the rules set forth in this paragraph (c).

(2) *Interpretation.* The provisions of §§ 1.401(a)(4)-1 through 1.401(a)(4)-13 must be interpreted in a reasonable manner consis-

tent with the purpose of preventing discrimination in favor of HCEs.

(3) *Plan-year basis of testing.* The requirements of paragraph (b) of this section are generally applied on the basis of the plan year and on the basis of the terms of the plan in effect during the plan year. Thus, unless otherwise provided, the compensation, contributions, benefit accruals, and other items used to apply these requirements must be determined with respect to the plan year being tested. However, § 1.401(a)(4)-11(g) provides rules allowing for corrective amendments made after the close of the plan year to be taken into account in satisfying certain requirements under paragraph (b) of this section.

(4) *Application of section 410(b) rules*—(i) *Relationship between sections 401(a)(4) and 410(b).* To be a qualified plan, a plan must satisfy both sections 410(b) and 401(a)(4). Section 410(b) requires that a plan benefit a nondiscriminatory group of employees, and section 401(a)(4) requires that the contributions or benefits provided to employees benefiting under the plan not discriminate in favor of HCEs. Consistent with this requirement, the definition of a plan subject to testing under section 401(a)(4) is the same as the definition of a plan subject to testing under section 410(b), i.e., the plan determined after applying the mandatory disaggregation rules of § 1.410(b)-7(c) and the permissive aggregation rules of § 1.410(b)-7(d). In addition, whichever testing option is used for the plan year under § 1.410(b)-8(a) (e.g., quarterly testing) must also be used for purposes of determining whether the plan satisfies section 401(a)(4) for the plan year.

(ii) *Special rules for certain aggregated plans.* Special rules are set forth in § 1.401(a)(4)-9(b) for applying the nondiscriminatory amount and availability requirements of paragraphs (b)(2) and (b)(3) of this section to a plan that includes one or more defined benefit plans and one or more defined contribution plans that have been permissively aggregated under § 1.410(b)- 7(d).

(iii) *Restructuring.* In certain circumstances, a plan may be restructured on the basis of employee groups and treated as comprising two or more plans, each of which is treated as a separate plan that must independently satisfy sections 401(a)(4) and 410(b). Rules relating to restructuring plans for purposes of applying the requirements of paragraph (b) of this section are set forth in § 1.401(a)(4)-9(c).

(iv) *References to section 410(b).* Except as otherwise specifically provided, references to satisfying section 410(b) in §§ 1.401(a)(4)-1 through 1.401(a)(4)-13 mean satisfying § 1.410(b)-2 (taking into account any special rules available in satisfying that section, other than the permissive aggregation rules of § 1.410(b)-7(d)). In the case of a plan described in section 410(c)(1) that has not made the election described in section 410(d) and is not subject to section 403(b)(12)(A)(i), references in §§ 1.401(a)(4)-1 through 1.401(a)(4)-13 to satisfying section 410(b) mean satisfying section 410(c)(2).

(5) *Collectively-bargained plans.* The requirements of paragraph (b) of this section are treated as satisfied by a collectively-bargained plan that automatically satisfies section 410(b) under § 1.410(b)-2(b)(7).

(6) *Former employees.* In applying the nondiscriminatory amount and availability requirements of paragraphs (b)(2) and (b)(3) of this section, former employees are tested separately from active employees, unless otherwise provided. Rules for applying paragraphs (b)(2) and (b)(3) of this section to former employees are set forth in § 1.401(a)(4)-10.

(7) *Employee-provided contributions and benefits.* In applying the nondiscriminatory amount requirement of paragraph (b)(2) of this section, employee-provided contributions and benefits are tested separately from employer-provided contributions and benefits, unless otherwise provided. Rules for determining the amount of employer-provided benefits under a defined benefit plan that include employee contributions not allocated to separate accounts are set forth in § 1.401(a)(4)-

6(b), and rules for applying paragraph (b)(2) of this section to employee contributions under such a plan are set forth in § 1.401(a)(4)-6(c). See paragraph (b)(2)(ii)(B) of this section for rules applicable to employee contributions allocated to separate accounts.

(8) *Allocation of earnings.* Notwithstanding any other provision in §§ 1.401(a)(4)-1 through 1.401(a)(4)-13, a defined contribution plan does not satisfy paragraph (b)(2) of this section if the manner in which income, expenses, gains, or losses are allocated to accounts under the plan discriminates in favor of HCEs or former HCEs.

(9) *Rollovers, transfers, and buybacks.* In applying the requirements of paragraph (b) of this section, rollover (including direct rollover) contributions described in section 402(c), 402(e)(6), 403(a)(4), 403(a)(5), or 408(d)(3), elective transfers described in § 1.411(d)-4, Q&A-3(b), transfers of assets and liabilities described in section 414(l), and employee buybacks are treated in accordance with the rules set forth in § 1.401(a)(4)-11(b).

(10) *Vesting.* A plan does not satisfy the nondiscriminatory amount requirement of paragraph (b)(2) of this section unless it satisfies § 1.401(a)(4)-11(c) with respect to the manner in which employees vest in their accrued benefits.

(11) *Crediting service.* A plan does not satisfy paragraphs (b)(2) and (b)(3) of this section unless it satisfies § 1.401(a)(4) 11(d) with respect to the manner in which employees' service is credited under the plan. Service other than actual service with the employer may not be taken into account in determining whether the plan satisfies paragraphs (b)(2) and (b)(3) of this section except as provided in § 1.401(a)(4)-11(d).

* * *

§ 1.401(a)(4)-2. Nondiscrimination in amount of employer contributions under a defined contribution plan.

(a) *Introduction*—(1) *Overview.* This section provides rules for determining whether the employer contributions allocated under a defined contribution plan are nondiscriminatory in amount as required by § 1.401(a)(4)-1(b)(2)(ii)(A). Certain defined contribution plans that provide uniform allocations are permitted to satisfy this requirement by meeting one of the safe harbors in paragraph (b) of this section. Plans that do not provide uniform allocations may satisfy this requirement by satisfying the general test in paragraph (c) of this section. See § 1.401(a)(4)-1(b)(2)(ii)(B) for the exclusive tests applicable to section 401(k) plans and section 401(m) plans.

(2) *Alternative methods of satisfying nondiscriminatory amount requirement.* A defined contribution plan is permitted to satisfy paragraph (b)(2) or (c) of this section on a restructured basis pursuant to § 1.401(a)(4)-9(c). Alternatively, a defined contribution plan (other than an ESOP) is permitted to satisfy the nondiscriminatory amount requirement of § 1.401(a)(4)- 1(b)(2)(ii)(A) on the basis of equivalent benefits pursuant to § 1.401(a)(4)-8(b).

(b) *Safe harbors*—(1) *In general.* The employer contributions allocated under a defined contribution plan are nondiscriminatory in amount for a plan year if the plan satisfies either of the safe harbors in paragraph (b)(2) or (b)(3) of this section. Paragraph (b)(4) of this section provides exceptions for certain plan provisions that do not cause a plan to fail to satisfy this paragraph (b).

(2) *Safe harbor for plans with uniform allocation formula*—(i) *General rule.* A defined contribution plan satisfies the safe harbor in this paragraph (b)(2) for a plan year if the plan allocates all amounts taken into account under paragraph (c)(2)(ii) of this section for the plan year under an allocation formula that allocates to each employee the same percentage of plan year compensation, the same dollar amount, or the same dollar amount for each uniform unit of service (not to exceed one week) performed by the employee during the plan year.

(ii) *Permitted disparity.* If a plan satisfies section 401(l) in form, differences in employees' allocations under the plan attributable to uniform disparities permitted under § 1.401(l)-2 (including differences in disparities that are deemed uniform under § 1.401(l)-2(c)(2)) do not cause the plan to fail to satisfy this paragraph (b)(2).

(3) *Safe harbor for plans with uniform points allocation formula*—(i) *General rule.* A defined contribution plan (other than an ESOP) satisfies the safe harbor in this paragraph (b)(3) for a plan year if it satisfies both of the following requirements:

(A) The plan must allocate amounts under a uniform points allocation formula. A uniform points allocation formula defines each employee's allocation for the plan year as the product of the total of all amounts taken into account under paragraph (c)(2)(ii) of this section and a fraction, the numerator of which is the employee's points for the plan year and the denominator of which is the sum of the points of all employees in the plan for the plan year. For this purpose, an employee's points for a plan year equal the sum of the employee's points for age, service, and units of plan year compensation for the plan year. Under a uniform points allocation formula, each employee must receive the same number of points for each year of age, the same number of points for each year of service, and the same number of points for each unit of plan year compensation. (See § 1.401(a)(4)-11(d)(3) regarding service that may be taken into account as years of service.) A uniform points allocation formula need not grant points for both age and service, but it must grant points for at least one of them. If the allocation formula grants points for years of service, the plan is permitted to limit the number of years of service taken into account to a single maximum number of years of service. A uniform points allocation formula need not grant points for units of plan year compensation, but if it does, the unit used must be a single dollar amount for all employees that does not exceed $200.

(B) For the plan year, the average of the allocation rates for the HCEs in the plan must not exceed the average of the allocation rates for the NHCEs in the plan. For this purpose, allocation rates are determined in accordance with paragraph (c)(2) of this section, without imputing permitted disparity and without grouping allocation rates under paragraphs (c)(2)(iv) and (v) of this section, respectively.

* * *

(c) *General test for nondiscrimination in amount of contributions*—(1) *General rule.* The employer contributions allocated under a defined contribution plan are nondiscriminatory in amount for a plan year if each rate group under the plan satisfies section 410(b). For purposes of this paragraph (c), a rate group exists under a plan for each HCE and consists of the HCE and all other employees in the plan (both HCEs and NHCEs) who have an allocation rate greater than or equal to the HCE's allocation rate. Thus, an employee is in the rate group for each HCE who has an allocation rate less than or equal to the employee's allocation rate.

(2) *Determination of allocation rates*—(i) *General rule.* The allocation rate for an employee for a plan year equals the sum of the allocations to the employee's account for the plan year, expressed either as a percentage of plan year compensation or as a dollar amount.

(ii) *Allocations taken into account.* The amounts taken into account in determining allocation rates for a plan year include all employer contributions and forfeitures that are allocated or treated as allocated to the account of an employee under the plan for the plan year, other than amounts described in paragraph (c)(2)(iii) of this section. For this purpose, employer contributions include annual additions described in § 1.415(c)-1(b)(4) (regarding amounts arising from certain transactions between the plan and the employer). In the case of a defined contribution plan subject to section 412, an employer contribution is taken into account in the plan year for which it is required to be contributed and allocated to employees' accounts under the plan, even if all or part of the required contribution is not actually made.

(iii) *Allocations not taken into account.* Allocations of income, expenses, gains, and losses attributable to the balance in an employee's account are not taken into account in determining allocation rates.

(iv) *Imputation of permitted disparity.* The disparity permitted under section 401(l) may be imputed in accordance with the rules of § 1.401(a)(4)-7.

(v) *Grouping of allocation rates*—(A) *General rule.* An employer may treat all employees who have allocation rates within a specified range above and below a midpoint rate chosen by the employer as having an allocation rate equal to the midpoint rate within that range. Allocation rates within a given range may not be grouped under this paragraph (c)(2)(v) if the allocation rates of HCEs within the range generally are significantly higher than the allocation rates of NHCEs in the range. The specified ranges within which all employees are treated as having the same allocation rate may not overlap and may be no larger than provided in paragraph (c)(2)(v)(B) of this section. Allocation rates of employees that are not within any of these specified ranges are determined without regard to this paragraph (c)(2)(v).

(B) *Size of specified ranges.* The lowest and highest allocation rates in the range must be within five percent (not five percentage points) of the midpoint rate. If allocation rates are determined as a percentage of plan year compensation, the lowest and highest allocation rates need not be within five percent of the midpoint rate, if they are no more than one quarter of a percentage point above or below the midpoint rate.

(vi) *Consistency requirement.* Allocation rates must be determined in a consistent manner for all employees for the plan year.

(3) *Satisfaction of section 410(b) by a rate group*—(i) *General rule.* For purposes of determining whether a rate group satisfies section 410(b), the rate group is treated as if it were a separate plan that benefits only the employees included in the rate group for the plan year. Thus, for example, under § 1.401(a)(4)-1(c)(4)(iv), the ratio percentage of the rate group is determined taking into account all nonexcludable employees regardless of whether they benefit under the plan. Paragraph (c)(3) (ii) and (iii) of this section provide additional special rules for determining whether a rate group satisfies section 410(b).

(ii) *Application of nondiscriminatory classification test.* A rate group satisfies the nondiscriminatory classification test of § 1.410(b)-4 (including the reasonable classification requirement of § 1.410(b)-4(b)) if and only if the ratio percentage of the rate group is greater than or equal to the lesser of—

(A) The midpoint between the safe and the unsafe harbor percentages applicable to the plan; and

(B) The ratio percentage of the plan.

(iii) *Application of average benefit percentage test.* A rate group satisfies the average benefit percentage test of § 1.410(b)-5 if the plan of which it is a part satisfies § 1.410(b)-5 (without regard to § 1.410(b)-5(f)). In the case of a plan that relies on § 1.410(b)-5(f) to satisfy the average benefit percentage test, each rate group under the plan satisfies the average benefit percentage test (if applicable) only if the rate group separately satisfies § 1.410(b)-5(f).

(4) *Examples.* The following examples illustrate the general test in this paragraph (c):

Example 1. Employer X maintains two defined contribution plans, Plan A and Plan B, that are aggregated and treated as a single plan for purposes of sections 410(b) and 401(a)(4) pursuant to § 1.410(b)-7(d). For the 1994 plan year, Employee M has plan year compensation of $10,000 and receives an allocation of $200 under Plan A and an allocation of $800 under Plan B. Employee M's allocation rate under the aggregated plan for the 1994 plan year is 10 percent (i.e., $1,000 divided by $10,000).

* * *

Example 3. (a) Employer Y has only six nonexcludable employees, all of whom benefit under Plan D. The HCEs are H1 and H2, and the NHCEs are N1 through N4. For the 1994 plan year, H1 and N1 through N4 have an allocation rate of 5.0 percent of plan year compensation. For the same plan year, H2 has an allocation rate of 7.5 percent of plan year compensation.

(b) There are two rate groups under Plan D. Rate group 1 consists of H1 and all those employees who have an allocation rate greater than or equal to H1's allocation rate (5.0 percent). Thus, rate group 1 consists of H1, H2, and N1 through N4. Rate group 2 consists only of H2 because no other employee has an allocation rate greater than or equal to H2's allocation rate (7.5 percent).

(c) The ratio percentage for rate group 2 is zero percent—i.e., zero percent (the percentage of all nonhighly compensated nonexcludable employees who are in the rate group) divided by 50 percent (the percentage of all highly compensated nonexcludable employees who are in the rate group). Therefore rate group 2 does not satisfy the ratio percentage test under § 1.410(b)-2(b)(2). Rate group 2 also does not satisfy the nondiscriminatory classification test of § 1.410(b)-4 (as modified by paragraph (c)(3) of this section). Rate group 2 therefore does not satisfy section 410(b) and, as a result, Plan D does not satisfy the general test in paragraph (c)(1) of this section. This is true regardless of whether rate group 1 satisfies § 1.410(b)-2(b)(2).

Example 4. (a) The facts are the same as in Example 3, except that N4 has an allocation rate of 8.0 percent.

(b) There are two rate groups in Plan D. Rate group 1 consists of H1 and all those employees who have an allocation rate greater than or equal to H1's allocation rate (5.0 percent). Thus, rate group 1 consists of H1, H2 and N1 through N4. Rate group 2 consists of H2, and all those employees who have an allocation rate greater than or equal to H2's allocation rate (7.5 percent). Thus, rate group 2 consists of H2 and N4.

(c) Rate group 1 satisfies the ratio percentage test under § 1.410(b)-2(b)(2) because the ratio percentage of the rate group is 100 percent—i.e., 100 percent (the percentage of all nonhighly compensated nonexcludable employees who are in the rate group) divided by 100 percent (the percentage of all highly compensated nonexcludable employees who are in the rate group).

(d) Rate group 2 does not satisfy the ratio percentage test of § 1.410(b)- 2(b)(2) because the ratio percentage of the rate group is 50 percent—i.e., 25 percent (the percentage of all nonhighly compensated nonexcludable employees who are in the rate group) divided by 50 percent (the percentage of all highly compensated nonexcludable employees who are in the rate group).

(e) However, rate group 2 does satisfy the nondiscriminatory classification test of § 1.410(b)-4 because the ratio percentage of the rate group (50 percent) is greater than the safe harbor percentage applicable to the plan under § 1.410(b)-4(c)(4) (45.5 percent).

(f) Under paragraph (c)(3)(iii) of this section, rate group 2 satisfies the average benefit percentage test, if Plan D satisfies the average benefit percentage test. (The requirement that Plan D satisfy the average benefit percentage test applies even though Plan D satisfies the ratio percentage test and would ordinarily not need to run the average benefit percentage test.) If Plan D satisfies the average benefit percentage test, then rate group 2 satisfies section 410(b) and thus, Plan D satisfies the general test in paragraph (c)(1) of this section, because each rate group under the plan satisfies section 410(b).

* * *

§ 1.401(a)(4)-3. Nondiscrimination in amount of employer-provided benefits under a defined benefit plan.

(a) *Introduction*—(1) *Overview*. This section provides rules for determining whether the employer-provided benefits under a defined benefit plan are nondiscriminatory in amount as required by § 1.401(a)(4)-1(b)(2)(iii). Certain defined benefit plans that provide uniform benefits are permitted to satisfy this requirement by meeting one of the safe harbors in paragraph (b) of this section. Plans that do not provide uniform benefits may satisfy this requirement by satisfying the general test in paragraph (c) of this section. Paragraph (d) of this section provides rules for determining the individual benefit accrual rates needed for the general test. Paragraph (e) of this section provides rules for determining compensation for purposes of applying the requirements of this section. Paragraph (f) of this section provides additional rules that apply generally for purposes of both the safe harbors in paragraph (b) of this section and the general test in paragraph (c) of this section. See § 1.401(a)(4)-6 for rules for determining the amount of employer- provided benefits under a contributory DB plan, and for determining whether the employee-provided benefits under such a plan are nondiscriminatory in amount.

(2) *Alternative methods of satisfying nondiscriminatory amount requirement.* A defined benefit plan is permitted to satisfy paragraph (b) or (c) of this section on a restructured basis pursuant to § 1.401(a)(4)-9(c). Alternatively, a defined benefit plan is permitted to satisfy the nondiscriminatory amount requirement of § 1.401(a)(4)-1(b)(2)(iii) on the basis of equivalent allocations pursuant to § 1.401(a)(4)-8(c). In addition, a defined benefit plan that is part of a floor-offset arrangement is permitted to satisfy this section pursuant to § 1.401(a)(4)-8(d).

(b) *Safe harbors*—(1) *In general.* The employer-provided benefits under a defined benefit plan are nondiscriminatory in amount for a plan year if the plan satisfies each of the uniformity requirements of paragraph (b)(2) of this section and any one of the safe harbors in paragraphs (b)(3) (unit credit plans), (b)(4) (fractional accrual plans), and (b)(5) (insurance contract plans) of this section. Paragraph (b)(6) of this section provides exceptions for certain plan provisions that do not cause a plan to fail to satisfy this paragraph (b). Paragraph (f) of this section provides additional rules that apply in determining whether a plan satisfies this paragraph (b).

(2) *Uniformity requirements*—(i) *Uniform normal retirement benefit.* The same benefit formula must apply to all employees. The benefit formula must provide all employees with an annual benefit payable in the same form commencing at the same uniform normal retirement age. The annual benefit must be the same percentage of average annual compensation or the same dollar amount for all employees who will have the same number of years of service at normal retirement age. (See § 1.401(a)(4)-11(d)(3) regarding service that may be taken into account as years of service.) The annual benefit must equal the employee's accrued benefit at normal retirement age (within the meaning of section 411(a)(7)(A)(i)) and must be the normal retirement benefit under the plan (within the meaning of section 411(a)(9)).

(ii) *Uniform post-normal retirement benefit.* With respect to an employee with a given number of years of service at any age after normal retirement age, the annual benefit commencing at that employee's age must be the same percentage of average annual compensation or the same dollar amount that would be payable commencing at normal retirement age to an employee who had that same number of years of service at normal retirement age.

(iii) *Uniform subsidies.* Each subsidized optional form of benefit available under the plan must be currently available (within the meaning of § 1.401(a)(4)-4(b)(2)) to substantially all employees. Whether an optional form of benefit is considered subsidized for this purpose may be determined using any reasonable actuarial assumptions.

(iv) *No employee contributions.* The plan must not be a contributory DB plan.

(v) *Period of accrual.* Each employee's benefit must be accrued over the same years of service that are taken into account in applying the benefit formula under the plan to that employee. For this purpose, any year in which the employee benefits under the plan (within the meaning of § 1.410(b)-3(a)) is included as a year of service in which a benefit accrues. Thus, for example, a plan does not satisfy the safe harbor in paragraph (b)(4) of this section unless the plan uses the same years of service to determine both the normal retirement benefit under the plan's benefit formula and the fraction by which an employee's fractional rule benefit is multiplied to derive the employee's accrued benefit as of any plan year.

(vi) *Examples*. The following examples illustrate the rules in this paragraph (b)(2):

Example 1. Plan A provides a normal retirement benefit equal to two percent of average annual compensation times each year of service commencing at age 65 for all employees. Plan A provides that employees of Division S receive their benefit in the form of a straight life annuity and that employees of Division T receive their benefit in the form of a life annuity with an automatic cost-of- living increase. Plan A does not provide a uniform normal retirement benefit within the meaning of paragraph (b)(2)(i) of this section because the annual benefit is not payable in the same form to all employees.

Example 2. Plan B provides a normal retirement benefit equal to 1.5 percent of average annual compensation times each year of service at normal retirement age for all employees. The normal retirement age under the plan is the earlier of age 65 or the age at which the employee completes 10 years of service, but in no event earlier than age 62. Plan B does not provide a uniform normal retirement benefit within the meaning of paragraph (b)(2)(i) of this section because the same uniform normal retirement age does not apply to all employees.

* * *

(3) *Safe harbor for unit credit plans*—(i) *General rule*. A plan satisfies the safe harbor in this paragraph (b)(3) for a plan year if it satisfies both of the following requirements:

(A) The plan must satisfy the 133 1/3 percent accrual rule of section 411(b)(1)(B).

(B) Each employee's accrued benefit under the plan as of any plan year must be determined by applying the plan's benefit formula to the employee's years of service and (if applicable) average annual compensation, both determined as of that plan year.

(ii) *Example*. The following example illustrates the rules in this paragraph (b)(3):

Example. Plan A provides that the accrued benefit of each employee as of any plan year equals the employee's average annual compensation times a percentage that depends on the employee's years of service determined as of that plan year. The percentage is 2 percent for each of the first 10 years of service, plus 1.5 percent for each of the next 10 years of service, plus 2 percent for all additional years of service. Plan A satisfies this paragraph (b)(3).

(4) *Safe harbor for plans using fractional accrual rule*—(i) *General rule*. A plan satisfies the safe harbor in this paragraph (b)(4) for a plan year if it satisfies each of the following requirements:

(A) The plan must satisfy the fractional accrual rule of section 411(b)(1)(C).

(B) Each employee's accrued benefit under the plan as of any plan year before the employee reaches normal retirement age must be determined by multiplying the employee's fractional rule benefit (within the meaning of § 1.411(b)- 1(b)(3)(ii)(A)) by a fraction, the numerator of which is the employee's years of service determined as of the plan year, and the denominator of which is the employee's projected years of service as of normal retirement age.

(C) The plan must satisfy one of the following requirements:

(*1*) Under the plan, it must be impossible for any employee to accrue in a plan year a portion of the normal retirement benefit described in paragraph (b)(2)(i) of this section that is more than one-third larger than the portion of the same benefit accrued in that or any other plan year by any other employee, when each portion of the benefit is expressed as a percentage of each employee's average annual compensation or as a dollar amount. In making this determination, actual and potential employees in the plan with any amount of service at normal retirement must be taken into account (other than employees with more than 33 years of service at normal retirement age). In addition, in the case of a plan that satisfies section 401(l) in form, an employee is treated as accruing benefits at a rate equal to the excess benefit percentage in the case of a defined benefit excess plan or at a rate equal to the gross benefit percentage in the case of an offset plan.

(2) The normal retirement benefit under the plan must be a flat benefit that requires a minimum of 25 years of service at normal retirement age for an employee to receive the unreduced flat benefit, determined without regard to section 415. For this purpose, a flat benefit is a benefit that is the same percentage of average annual compensation or the same dollar amount for all employees who have a minimum number of years of service at normal retirement age (e.g., 50 percent of average annual compensation), with a pro rata reduction in the flat benefit for employees who have less than the minimum number of years of service at normal retirement age. An employee is permitted to accrue the maximum benefit permitted under section 415 over a period of less than 25 years, provided that the flat benefit under the plan, determined without regard to section 415, can accrue over no less than 25 years.

(3) The plan must satisfy the requirements of paragraph (b)(4)(i)(C)(2) of this section (other than the requirement that the minimum number of years of service for receiving the unreduced flat benefit is at least 25 years), and, for the plan year, the average of the normal accrual rates for all nonhighly compensated nonexcludable employees must be at least 70 percent of the average of the normal accrual rates for all highly compensated nonexcludable employees. The averages in the preceding sentence are determined taking into account all nonexcludable employees (regardless of whether they benefit under the plan). In addition, contributions and benefits under other plans of the employer are disregarded. For purposes of this paragraph (b)(4)(i)(C)(3), normal accrual rates are determined under paragraph (d) of this section.

(ii) *Examples.* The following examples illustrate the rules in this paragraph (b)(4). In each example, it is assumed that the plan has never permitted employee contributions.

Example 1. Plan A provides a normal retirement benefit equal to 1.6 percent of average annual compensation times each year of service up to 25. Plan A further provides that an employee's accrued benefit as of any plan year equals the employee's fractional rule benefit multiplied by a fraction, the numerator of which is the employee's years of service as of the plan year, and the denominator of which is the employee's projected years of service as of normal retirement age. The greatest benefit that an employee could accrue in any plan year is 1.6 percent of average annual compensation (this is the case for an employee with 25 or fewer years of projected service at normal retirement age). Among potential employees with 33 or fewer years of projected service at normal retirement age, the lowest benefit that an employee could accrue in any plan year is 1.212 percent of average annual compensation (this is the case for an employee with 33 years of projected service at normal retirement age). Plan A satisfies paragraph (b)(4)(i)(C)(1) of this section because 1.6 percent is not more than one third larger than 1.212 percent.

* * *

(6) *Use of safe harbors not precluded by certain plan provisions*—(i) *In general.* A plan does not fail to satisfy this paragraph (b) merely because the plan contains one or more of the provisions described in this paragraph (b)(6). Unless otherwise provided, any such provision must apply uniformly to all employees.

(ii) *Section 401(l) permitted disparity.* The plan takes permitted disparity into account in a manner that satisfies section 401(l) in form. Thus, differences in employees' benefits under the plan attributable to uniform disparities permitted under § 1.401(l)-3 (including differences in disparities that are deemed uniform under § 1.401(l)-3(c)(2)) do not cause a plan to fail to satisfy this paragraph (b).

(iii) *Different entry dates.* The plan provides one or more entry dates during the plan year as permitted by section 410(a)(4).

(iv) *Certain conditions on accruals.* The plan provides that an employee's accrual for the plan year is less than a full accrual (including a zero accrual) because of a plan provision permitted by the year-of-participation rules of section 411(b)(4).

(v) *Certain limits on accruals.* The plan limits benefits otherwise provided under the benefit formula or accrual method to a maximum dollar amount or to a maximum percentage of average annual compensation (e.g., by limiting service taken into account in the benefit formula) or in accordance with section 401(a)(5)(D), applies the limits of section 415, or limits the dollar amount of compensation taken into account in determining benefits.

(vi) *Dollar accrual per uniform unit of service.* The plan determines accruals based on the same dollar amount for each uniform unit of service (not to exceed one week) performed by each employee with the same number of years of service under the plan during the plan year. The preceding sentence applies solely for purposes of the unit credit safe harbor in paragraph (b)(3) of this section.

(vii) *Prior benefits accrued under a different formula.* The plan determines benefits for years of service after a fresh-start date for all employees under a benefit formula and accrual method that differ from the benefit formula and accrual method previously used to determine benefit accruals for employees in a fresh-start group for years of service before the fresh-start date. This paragraph (b)(6)(vii) applies solely to plans that satisfy § 1.401(a)(4)-13(c) with respect to the fresh start.

(viii) *Employee contributions.* The plan is a contributory DB plan that would satisfy the requirements of paragraph (b) of this section if the plan's benefit formula provided benefits at employees' employer-provided benefit rates determined under § 1.401(a)(4)-6(b). This paragraph (b)(6)(viii) does not apply to a plan tested under paragraph (b)(4) or (b)(5) of this section unless the plan satisfies one of the methods in § 1.401(a)(4)-6(b)(4) through (b)(6). A minimum benefit added to the plan solely to satisfy § 1.401(a)(4)-6(b)(3) is not taken into account in determining whether this paragraph (b)(6)(viii) is satisfied.

(ix) *Certain subsidized optional forms.* The plan provides a subsidized optional form of benefit that is available to fewer than substantially all employees because the optional form of benefit has been eliminated prospectively as provided in § 1.401(a)(4)-4(b)(3).

(x) *Lower benefits for HCEs*—(A) *General rule.* The benefits (including any subsidized optional form of benefit) provided to one or more HCEs under the plan are inherently less valuable to those HCEs (determined by applying the principles of § 1.401(a)(4)-4(d)(4)) than the benefits that would otherwise be provided to those HCEs if the plan satisfied this paragraph (b) (determined without regard to this paragraph (b)(6)(x)). These inherently less valuable benefits are deemed to satisfy this paragraph (b).

* * *

(c) *General test for nondiscrimination in amount of benefits*—(1) *General rule.* The employer-provided benefits under a defined benefit plan are nondiscriminatory in amount for a plan year if each rate group under the plan satisfies section 410(b). For purposes of this paragraph (c)(1), a rate group exists under a plan for each HCE and consists of the HCE and all other employees (both HCEs and NHCEs) who have a normal accrual rate greater than or equal to the HCE's normal accrual rate, and who also have a most valuable accrual rate greater than or equal to the HCE's most valuable accrual rate. Thus, an employee is in the rate group for each HCE who has a normal accrual rate less than or equal to the employee's normal accrual rate, and who also has a most valuable accrual rate less than or equal to the employee's most valuable accrual rate.

(2) *Satisfaction of section 410(b) by a rate group.* For purposes of determining whether a rate group satisfies section 410(b),

the same rules apply as in § 1.401(a)(4)-2(c)(3). See paragraph (c)(4) of this section and § 1.401(a)(4)-2(c)(4), Example 3 through Example 5, for examples of this rule.

* * *

(d) *Determination of accrual rates*—(1) *Definitions*—(i) *Normal accrual rate.* The normal accrual rate for an employee for a plan year is the increase in the employee's accrued benefit (within the meaning of section 411(a)(7)(A)(i)) during the measurement period, divided by the employee's testing service during the measurement period, and expressed either as a dollar amount or as a percentage of the employee's average annual compensation.

(ii) *Most valuable accrual rate.* The most valuable accrual rate for an employee for a plan year is the increase in the employee's most valuable optional form of payment of the accrued benefit during the measurement period, divided by the employee's testing service during the measurement period, and expressed either as a dollar amount or as a percentage of the employee's average annual compensation. The employee's most valuable optional form of payment of the accrued benefit is determined by calculating for the employee the normalized QJSA associated with the accrued benefit that is potentially payable in the current or any future plan year at any age under the plan and selecting the largest (per year of testing service). If the plan provides a QSUPP, the most valuable accrual rate also takes into account the QSUPP payable in conjunction with the QJSA at each age under the plan. Thus, the most valuable accrual rate reflects the value of all benefits accrued or treated as accrued under section 411(d)(6) that are payable in any form and at any time under the plan, including early retirement benefits, retirement-type subsidies, early retirement window benefits, and QSUPPs. In addition, the most valuable accrual rate must take into account any such benefits that are available during a plan year, even if the benefits cease to be available before the end of the current or any future plan year.

(iii) *Measurement period.* The measurement period can be—

(A) The current plan year;

(B) The current plan year and all prior years; or

(C) The current plan year and all prior and future years.

(iv) *Testing service*—(A) *General rule.* Testing service means an employee's years of service as defined in the plan for purposes of applying the benefit formula under the plan, subject to the requirements of paragraph (d)(1)(iv)(B) of this section. Alternatively, testing service means service determined for all employees in a reasonable manner that satisfies the requirements of paragraph (d)(1)(iv)(B) of this section. For example, the number of plan years that an employee has benefited under the plan within the meaning of § 1.410(b)-3(a) is an acceptable definition of testing service because it determines service in a reasonable manner and satisfies paragraph (d)(1)(iv)(B) of this section. See also § 1.401(a)(4)-11(d)(3) (additional limits on service that may be taken into account as testing service).

(B) *Requirements for testing service*—(*1*) Employees not credited with years of service under the benefit formula. An employee must be credited with testing service for any year in which the employee benefits under the plan (within the meaning of § 1.410(b)-3(a)), unless that year is part of a period of service that may not be taken into account under § 1.401(a)(4)-11(d)(3). This rule applies even if the employee does not receive service credit under the benefit formula for that year (e.g., because of a service cap in the benefit formula or because of a transfer out of the group of employees covered by the plan).

(*2*) *Current year testing service.* In the case of a measurement period that is the current plan year, testing service for the plan year equals one (1).

* * *

§ 1.401(a)(4)-4. Nondiscriminatory availability of benefits, rights, and features.

(a) *Introduction.* This section provides rules for determining whether the benefits, rights, and features provided under a plan (i.e., all optional forms of benefit, ancillary benefits, and other rights and features available to any employee under the plan) are made available in a nondiscriminatory manner. Benefits, rights, and features provided under a plan are made available to employees in a nondiscriminatory manner only if each benefit, right, or feature satisfies the current availability requirement of paragraph (b) of this section and the effective availability requirement of paragraph (c) of this section. Paragraph (d) of this section provides special rules for applying these requirements. Paragraph (e) of this section defines optional form of benefit, ancillary benefit, and other right or feature.

(b) *Current availability*—(1) *General rule.* The current availability requirement of this paragraph (b) is satisfied if the group of employees to whom a benefit, right, or feature is currently available during the plan year satisfies section 410(b) (without regard to the average benefit percentage test of § 1.410(b)-5). In determining whether the group of employees satisfies section 410(b), an employee is treated as benefiting only if the benefit, right, or feature is currently available to the employee.

(2) *Determination of current availability*—(i) *General rule.* Whether a benefit, right, or feature that is subject to specified eligibility conditions is currently available to an employee generally is determined based on the current facts and circumstances with respect to the employee (e.g., current compensation, accrued benefit, position, or net worth).

(ii) *Certain conditions disregarded*—(A) *Certain age and service conditions*— (*1*) *General rule.* Notwithstanding paragraph (b)(2)(i) of this section, any specified age or service condition with respect to an optional form of benefit or a social security supplement is disregarded in determining whether the optional form of benefit or the social security supplement is currently available to an employee. Thus, for example, an optional form of benefit that is available to all employees who terminate employment on or after age 55 with at least 10 years of service is treated as currently available to an employee, without regard to the employee's current age or years of service, and without regard to whether the employee could potentially meet the age and service conditions prior to attaining the plan's normal retirement age.

(*2*) *Time-limited age or service conditions not disregarded.* Notwithstanding paragraph (b)(2)(ii)(A)(*1*) of this section, an age or service condition is not disregarded in determining the current availability of an optional form of benefit or social security supplement if the condition must be satisfied within a limited period of time. However, in determining the current availability of an optional form of benefit or a social security supplement subject to such an age or service condition, the age and service of employees may be projected to the last date by which the age condition or service condition must be satisfied in order to be eligible for the optional form of benefit or social security supplement under the plan. Thus, for example, an optional form of benefit that is available only to employees who terminate employment between July 1, 1995, and December 31, 1995, after attainment of age 55 with at least 10 years of service is treated as currently available to an employee only if the employee could satisfy those age and service conditions by December 31, 1995.

(B) *Certain other conditions.* Specified conditions on the availability of a benefit, right, or feature requiring a specified percentage of the employee's accrued benefit to be nonforfeitable, termination of employment, death, satisfaction of a specified health condition (or failure to meet such condition), disability, hardship, family status, default on a plan loan secured by a participant's account balance, execution of a covenant not to compete, application for benefits or similar ministerial or mechanical acts, election of a benefit form, execution of a waiver of rights under the

Age Discrimination in Employment Act or other federal or state law, or absence from service, are disregarded in determining the employees to whom the benefit, right, or feature is currently available. In addition, if a multiemployer plan includes a reasonable condition that limits eligibility for an ancillary benefit, or other right or feature, to those employees who have recent service under the plan (e.g., a condition on a death benefit that requires an employee to have a minimum number of hours credited during the last two years) and the condition applies to all employees in the multiemployer plan (including the collectively bargained employees) to whom the ancillary benefit, or other right or feature, is otherwise currently available, then the condition is disregarded in determining the employees to whom the ancillary benefit, or other right or feature, is currently available.

(C) *Certain conditions relating to mandatory cash-outs.* In the case of a plan that provides for mandatory cash-outs of all terminated employees who have a vested accrued benefit with an actuarial present value less than or equal to a specified dollar amount (not to exceed the cash-out limit in effect under § 1.411(a)-11(c)(3)(ii)) as permitted by sections 411(a)(11) and 417(e), the implicit condition on any benefit, right, or feature (other than the mandatory cash-out) that requires the employee to have a vested accrued benefit with an actuarial present value in excess of the specified dollar amount is disregarded in determining the employees to whom the benefit, right, or feature is currently available.

(D) *Other dollar limits.* A condition that the amount of an employee's vested accrued benefit or the actuarial present value of that benefit be less than or equal to a specified dollar amount is disregarded in determining the employees to whom the benefit, right, or feature is currently available.

(E) *Certain conditions on plan loans.* In the case of an employee's right to a loan from the plan, the condition that an employee must have an account balance sufficient to be eligible to receive a minimum loan amount specified in the plan (not to exceed $1,000) is disregarded in determining the employees to whom the right is currently available.

(3) *Benefits, rights, and features that are eliminated prospectively*—(i) *Special testing rule.* Notwithstanding paragraph (b)(1) of this section, a benefit, right, or feature that is eliminated with respect to benefits accrued after the later of the eliminating amendment's adoption or effective date (the elimination date), but is retained with respect to benefits accrued as of the elimination date, and that satisfies this paragraph (b) as of the elimination date, is treated as satisfying this paragraph (b) for all subsequent periods. This rule does not apply if the terms of the benefit, right, or feature (including the employees to whom it is available) are changed after the elimination date.

(ii) *Elimination of a benefit, right, or feature*—(A) *General rule.* For purposes of this paragraph (b)(3), a benefit, right, or feature provided to an employee is eliminated with respect to benefits accrued after the elimination date if the amount or value of the benefit, right, or feature depends solely on the amount of the employee's accrued benefit (within the meaning of section 411(a)(7)) as of the elimination date, including subsequent income, expenses, gains, and losses with respect to that benefit in the case of a defined contribution plan.

(B) *Special rule for benefits, rights, and features that are not section 411(d)(6)-protected benefits.* Notwithstanding paragraph (b)(3)(ii)(A) of this section, in the case of a benefit, right, or feature under a defined contribution plan that is not a section 411(d)(6)-protected benefit (within the meaning of § 1.411(d)-4, Q&A-1), e.g., the availability of plan loans, for purposes of this paragraph (b)(3)(ii) each employee's accrued benefit as of the elimination date may be treated, on a uniform basis, as consisting exclusively of the dollar amount of the employee's account balance as of the elimination date.

(C) *Special rule for benefits, rights, and features that depend on adjusted accrued benefits.* For purposes of this paragraph (b)(3), a benefit, right, or feature provided to an employee under a plan that has made a fresh start does not fail to be eliminated as of an elimination date that is the fresh-start date merely because it depends solely on the amount of the employee's adjusted accrued benefit (within the meaning of § 1.401(a)(4)-13(d)(8)).

(c) *Effective availability*—(1) *General rule*. Based on all of the relevant facts and circumstances, the group of employees to whom a benefit, right, or feature is effectively available must not substantially favor HCEs.

(2) *Examples*. The following examples illustrate the rules of this paragraph (c):

Example 1. Employer X maintains Plan A, a defined benefit plan that covers both of its highly compensated nonexcludable employees and nine of its 12 nonhighly compensated nonexcludable employees. Plan A provides for a normal retirement benefit payable as an annuity and based on a normal retirement age of 65, and an early retirement benefit payable upon termination in the form of an annuity to employees who terminate from service with the employer on or after age 55 with 30 or more years of service. Both HCEs of Employer X currently meet the age and service requirement, or will have 30 years of service by the time they reach age 55. All but two of the nine NHCEs of Employer X who are covered by Plan A were hired on or after age 35 and, thus, cannot qualify for the early retirement benefit. Even though the group of employees to whom the early retirement benefit is currently available satisfies the ratio percentage test of § 1.410(b)-2(b)(2) when age and service are disregarded pursuant to paragraph (b)(2)(ii)(A) of this section, absent other facts, the group of employees to whom the early retirement benefit is effectively available substantially favors HCEs.

Example 2. Employer Y maintains Plan B, a defined benefit plan that provides for a normal retirement benefit payable as an annuity and based on a normal retirement age of 65. By a plan amendment first adopted and effective December 1, 1998, Employer Y amends Plan B to provide an early retirement benefit that is available only to employees who terminate employment by December 15, 1998, and who are at least age 55 with 30 or more years of service. Assume that all employees were hired prior to attaining age 25 and that the group of employees who have, or will have, attained age 55 with 30 years of service by December 15, 1998, satisfies the ratio percentage test of § 1.410(b)-2(b)(2). Assume, further, that the employer takes no steps to inform all eligible employees of the early retirement option on a timely basis and that the only employees who terminate from employment with the employer during the two-week period in which the early retirement benefit is available are HCEs. Under these facts, the group of employees to whom this early retirement window benefit is effectively available substantially favors HCEs.

* * *

§ 1.401(a)(4)-5. Plan amendments and plan terminations.

(a) *Introduction*—(1) *Overview*. This paragraph (a) provides rules for determining whether the timing of a plan amendment or series of amendments has the effect of discriminating significantly in favor of HCEs or former HCEs. For purposes of this section, a plan amendment includes, for example, the establishment or termination of the plan, and any change in the benefits, rights, or features, benefit formulas, or allocation formulas under the plan. Paragraph (b) of this section sets forth additional requirements that must be satisfied in the case of a plan termination.

(2) *Facts-and-circumstances determination*. Whether the timing of a plan amendment or series of plan amendments has the effect of discriminating significantly in favor of HCEs or former HCEs is determined at the time the plan amendment first becomes effective for purposes of section 401(a), based on all of the relevant facts and circumstances. These include, for example, the relative numbers of current and former HCEs and NHCEs affected by the plan amendment, the relative length of service of current and former HCEs and NHCEs, the length of time the plan or plan provision being amended has been in effect,

and the turnover of employees prior to the plan amendment. In addition, the relevant facts and circumstances include the relative accrued benefits of current and former HCEs and NHCEs before and after the plan amendment and any additional benefits provided to current and former HCEs and NHCEs under other plans (including plans of other employers, if relevant). In the case of a plan amendment that provides additional benefits based on an employee's service prior to the amendment, the relevant facts and circumstances also include the benefits that employees and former employees who do not benefit under the amendment would have received had the plan, as amended, been in effect throughout the period on which the additional benefits are based.

(3) *Safe harbor for certain grants of benefits for past periods*. The timing of a plan amendment that credits (or increases benefits attributable to) years of service for a period in the past is deemed not to have the effect of discriminating significantly in favor of HCEs or former HCEs if the period for which the service credit (or benefit increase) is granted does not exceed the five years immediately preceding the year in which the amendment first becomes effective, the service credit (or benefit increase) is granted on a reasonably uniform basis to all employees, benefits attributable to the period are determined by applying the current plan formula, and the service credited is service (including pre-participation or imputed service) with the employer or a previous employer that may be taken into account under § 1.401(a)(4)- 11(d)(3) (without regard to § 1.401(a)(4)-11(d)(3)(i)(B)). However, this safe harbor is not available if the plan amendment granting the service credit (or increasing benefits) is part of a pattern of amendments that has the effect of discriminating significantly in favor of HCEs or former HCEs.

(4) *Examples*. The following examples illustrate the rules in this paragraph (a):

Example 1. Plan A is a defined benefit plan that covered both HCEs and NHCEs for most of its existence. The employer decides to wind up its business. In the process of ceasing operations, but at a time when the plan covers only HCEs, Plan A is amended to increase benefits and thereafter is terminated. The timing of this plan amendment has the effect of discriminating significantly in favor of HCEs.

* * *

Example 4. Plan D provides for a benefit of one percent of average annual compensation per year of service. Ten years after Plan D is adopted, it is amended to provide a benefit of two percent of average annual compensation per year of service, including years of service prior to the amendment. The amendment is effective only for employees currently employed at the time of the amendment. The ratio of HCEs to former HCEs is significantly higher than the ratio of NHCEs to former NHCEs. In the absence of any additional factors, the timing of this plan amendment has the effect of discriminating significantly in favor of HCEs.

Example 5. The facts are the same as in *Example 4*, except that, in addition, the years of prior service are equivalent between HCEs and NHCEs who are current employees, and the group of current employees with prior service would satisfy the nondiscriminatory classification test of § 1.410(b)-4 in the current and all prior plan years for which past service credit is granted. The timing of this plan amendment does not have the effect of discriminating significantly in favor of HCEs or former HCEs.

* * *

Example 7. Employer W currently has six nonexcludable employees, two of whom, H1 and H2, are HCEs, and the remaining four of whom, N1 through N4, are NHCEs. The ratio of HCEs to former HCEs is significantly higher than the ratio of NHCEs to former NHCEs. Employer W establishes Plan F, a defined benefit plan providing a benefit of one percent of average annual compensation per year of service, including years of service prior to the establishment of the plan. H1 and H2 each have 15 years of prior service, N1 has nine years of past service, N2 has five years, N3 has three years, and N4 has one year. The timing of this plan establishment has the effect of discriminating significantly in favor of HCEs.

Example 8. Assume the same facts as in *Example 7*, except that N1 through N4 were hired in the current year, and Employer W never employed any NHCEs prior to the current year. Thus, no NHCEs would have received additional benefits had Plan F been in existence during the preceding 15 years. The timing of this plan establishment does not have the effect of discriminating significantly in favor of HCEs or former HCEs.

Example 9. The facts are the same as in *Example 7*, except that Plan F limits the grant of past service credit to five years, and the grant of past service otherwise satisfies the safe harbor in paragraph (a)(3) of this section. The timing of this plan establishment is deemed not to have the effect of discriminating significantly in favor of HCEs or former HCEs.

Example 10. The facts are the same as in *Example 9*, except that, five years after the establishment of Plan F, Employer W amends the plan to provide a benefit equal to two percent of average annual compensation per year of service, taking into account all years of service since the establishment of the plan. The ratio of HCEs to former HCEs who terminated employment during the five-year period since the establishment of the plan is significantly higher than the ratio of NHCEs to former NHCEs who terminated employment during the five-year period since the establishment of the plan. Although the amendment described in this example might separately satisfy the safe harbor in paragraph (a)(3) of this section, the safe harbor is not available with respect to the amendment because, under these facts, the amendment is part of a pattern of amendments that has the effect of discriminating significantly in favor of HCEs.

* * *

(b) *Pre-termination restrictions*—(1) *Required provisions in defined benefit plans*. A defined benefit plan has the effect of discriminating significantly in favor of HCEs or former HCEs unless it incorporates provisions restricting benefits and distributions as described in paragraph (b)(2) and (3) of this section at the time the plan is established or, if later, as of the first plan year to which §§ 1.401(a)(4)-1 through 1.401(a)(4)-13 apply to the plan under § 1.401(a)(4)-13(a) or (b). This paragraph (b) does not apply if the Commissioner determines that such provisions are not necessary to prevent the prohibited discrimination that may occur in the event of an early termination of the plan. The restrictions in this paragraph (b) apply to a plan within the meaning of § 1.410(b)-7(b) (i.e., a section 414(l) plan). Any plan containing a provision described in this paragraph (b) satisfies section 411(d)(2) and does not fail to satisfy section 411(a) or (d)(3) merely because of the provision.

(2) *Restriction of benefits upon plan termination*. A plan must provide that, in the event of plan termination, the benefit of any HCE (and any former HCE) is limited to a benefit that is nondiscriminatory under section 401(a)(4).

(3) *Restrictions on distributions*—(i) *General rule*. A plan must provide that, in any year, the payment of benefits to or on behalf of a restricted employee shall not exceed an amount equal to the payments that would be made to or on behalf of the restricted employee in that year under—

(A) A straight life annuity that is the actuarial equivalent of the accrued benefit and other benefits to which the restricted employee is entitled under the plan (other than a social security supplement); and

(B) A social security supplement, if any, that the restricted employee is entitled to receive.

(ii) *Restricted employee defined*. For purposes of this paragraph (b), the term restricted employee generally means any HCE or former HCE. However, an HCE or former HCE need not be treated as a restricted employee in the current year if the HCE or former HCE is not one of the 25 (or a larger number chosen by the employer) nonexcludable employees and former employees of the employer with the largest amount of compensation in the current or any prior year. Plan provisions defining or altering this group can be amended at any time without violating section 411(d)(6).

(iii) *Benefit defined.* For purposes of this paragraph (b), the term benefit includes, among other benefits, loans in excess of the amounts set forth in section 72(p)(2)(A), any periodic income, any withdrawal values payable to a living employee or former employee, and any death benefits not provided for by insurance on the employee's or former employee's life.

(iv) *Nonapplicability in certain cases.* The restrictions in this paragraph (b)(3) do not apply, however, if any one of the following requirements is satisfied:

(A) After taking into account payment to or on behalf of the restricted employee of all benefits payable to or on behalf of that restricted employee under the plan, the value of plan assets must equal or exceed 110 percent of the value of current liabilities, as defined in section 412(l)(7).

(B) The value of the benefits payable to or on behalf of the restricted employee must be less than one percent of the value of current liabilities before distribution.

(C) The value of the benefits payable to or on behalf of the restricted employee must not exceed the amount described in section 411(a)(11)(A) (restrictions on certain mandatory distributions).

* * *

§ 1.401(a)(4)-7. Imputation of permitted disparity.

(a) *Introduction.* In determining whether a plan satisfies section 401(a)(4) with respect to the amount of contributions or benefits, section 401(a)(5)(C) allows the disparities permitted under section 401(l) to be taken into account. For purposes of satisfying the safe harbors of §§ 1.401(a)(4)-2(b)(2) and 1.401(a)(4)-3(b), permitted disparity may be taken into account only by satisfying section 401(l) in form in accordance with § 1.401(l)-2 or 1.401(l)- 3, respectively. For purposes of the general tests of §§ 1.401(a)(4)-2(c) and 1.401(a)(4)-3(c), permitted disparity may be taken into account only in accordance with the rules of this section. In general, this section allows permitted disparity to be arithmetically imputed with respect to employer- provided contributions or benefits by determining an adjusted allocation or accrual rate that appropriately accounts for the permitted disparity with respect to each employee. Paragraph (b) of this section provides rules for imputing permitted disparity with respect to employer-provided contributions by adjusting each employee's unadjusted allocation rate. Paragraph (c) of this section provides rules for imputing permitted disparity with respect to employer-provided benefits by adjusting each employee's unadjusted accrual rate. Paragraph (d) of this section provides rules of general application.

(b) *Adjusting allocation rates*—(1) *In general.* The rules in this paragraph (b) produce an adjusted allocation rate for each employee by determining the excess contribution percentage under the hypothetical formula that would yield the allocation actually received by the employee, if the plan took into account the full disparity permitted under section 401(l)(2) and used the taxable wage base as the integration level. This adjusted allocation rate is used to determine whether the amount of contributions under the plan satisfies the general test of § 1.401(a)(4)-2(c) and to apply the average benefit percentage test on the basis of contributions under § 1.410(b)-5(d). Paragraphs (b)(2) and (b)(3) of this section apply to employees whose plan year compensation does not exceed and does exceed, respectively, the taxable wage base, and paragraph (b)(4) of this section provides definitions.

(2) *Employees whose plan year compensation does not exceed taxable wage base.* If an employee's plan year compensation does not exceed the taxable wage base, the employee's adjusted allocation rate is the lesser of the A rate and the B rate determined under the formulas below, where the permitted dis-

parity rate and the unadjusted allocation rate are determined under paragraph (b)(4)(ii) and (iv) of this section, respectively.

A Rate = 2 x unadjusted allocation rate

B Rate = unadjusted allocation rate + permitted disparity rate

(3) *Employees whose plan year compensation exceeds taxable wage base.* If an employee's plan year compensation exceeds the taxable wage base, the employee's adjusted allocation rate is the lesser of the C rate and the D rate determined under the formulas below, where allocations and the permitted disparity rate are determined under paragraph (b)(4)(i) and (ii) of this section, respectively.

C Rate =

$$\frac{\text{allocations}}{\text{plan year compensation - 1/2 taxable wage base}}$$

D Rate =

$$\frac{\text{allocations + (permitted disparity rate x taxable wage base)}}{\text{plan year compensation}}$$

(4) *Definitions.* In applying this paragraph (b), the following definitions govern—

(i) *Allocations.* Allocations means the amount determined by multiplying the employee's plan year compensation by the employee's unadjusted allocation rate.

(ii) *Permitted disparity rate*—(A) General rule. Permitted disparity rate means the rate in effect as of the beginning of the plan year under section 401(l)(2)(A)(ii) (e.g., 5.7 percent for plan years beginning in 1990).

* * *

(iii) *Taxable wage base.* Taxable wage base means the taxable wage base, as defined in § 1.401(l)-1(c)(32), in effect as of the beginning of the plan year.

(iv) *Unadjusted allocation rate.* Unadjusted allocation rate means the employee's allocation rate determined under § 1.401(a)(4)-2(c)(2)(i) for the plan year (expressed as a percentage of plan year compensation), without imputing permitted disparity under this section.

(5) *Example.* The following example illustrates the rules in this paragraph (b):

Example. (a) Employees M and N participate in a defined contribution plan maintained by Employer X. Employee M has plan year compensation of $30,000 in the 1990 plan year and has an unadjusted allocation rate of five percent. Employee N has plan year compensation of $100,000 in the 1990 plan year and has an unadjusted allocation rate of eight percent. The taxable wage base in 1990 is $51,300.

(b) Because Employee M's plan year compensation does not exceed the taxable wage base, Employee M's A rate is 10 percent (2 x 5 percent), and Employee M's B rate is 10.7 percent (5 percent + 5.7 percent). Thus, Employee M's adjusted allocation rate is 10 percent, the lesser of the A rate and the B rate.

(c) Employee N's allocations are $8,000 (8 percent x $100,000). Because Employee N's plan year compensation exceeds the taxable wage base, Employee N's C rate is 10.76 percent ($8,000 divided by ($100,000 - (½ x $51,300))), and Employee N's D rate is 10.92 percent (($8,000 + (5.7 percent x $51,300)) divided by $100,000). Thus, Employee N's adjusted allocation rate is 10.76 percent, the lesser of the C rate and the D rate.

(c) *Adjusting accrual rates*—(1) *In general.* The rules in this paragraph (c) produce an adjusted accrual rate for each employee by determining the excess benefit percentage under the hypothetical plan formula that would yield the employer-provided accrual actually received by the employee, if the plan took into account the full permitted disparity under section 401(l)(3)(A) in each of the first 35 years of an employee's testing service under the plan and used the employee's covered compensation as the integration level. This adjusted accrual rate is used to determine whether the amount of employer-provided benefits under the plan satisfies the alternative safe harbor for flat benefit plans under § 1.401(a)(4)-3(b)(4)(i)(C)(3) or the general test of § 1.401(a)(4)-3(c), and to apply the average benefit percentage test on the basis of benefits under § 1.410(b)-5. Paragraphs (c)(2) and (c)(3) of this section apply to employees whose average annual compensation does not exceed and does exceed, respectively, covered compensation, and paragraph (c)(4) of this section provides definitions. Paragraph (c)(5) of this section provides a special rule for employees with negative unadjusted accrual rates.

* * *

§ 1.401(a)(4)-8. Cross-testing.

(a) *Introduction.* This section provides rules for testing defined benefit plans on the basis of equivalent employer-provided contributions and defined contribution plans on the basis of equivalent employer-provided benefits under § 1.401(a)(4)-1(b)(2). Paragraphs (b)(1) and (c)(1) of this section provide general tests for nondiscrimination based on individual equivalent accrual or allocation rates determined under paragraphs (b)(2) and (c)(2) of this section, respectively. Paragraphs (b)(3), (c)(3), and (d) of this section provide additional safe-harbor testing methods for target benefit plans, cash balance plans, and defined benefit plans that are part of floor-offset arrangements, respectively, that generally may be satisfied on a design basis.

(b) *Nondiscrimination in amount of benefits provided under a defined contribution plan*—(1) *General rule and gateway*—(i) *General rule.* Equivalent benefits under a defined contribution plan (other than an ESOP) are nondiscriminatory in amount for a plan year if—

(A) The plan would satisfy § 1.401(a)(4)-2(c)(1) for the plan year if an equivalent accrual rate, as determined under paragraph (b)(2) of this section, were substituted for each employee's allocation rate in the determination of rate groups; and

(B) For plan years beginning on or after January 1, 2002, the plan satisfies one of the following conditions—

(1) The plan has broadly available allocation rates (within the meaning of paragraph (b)(1)(iii) of this section) for the plan year;

(2) The plan has age-based allocation rates that are based on either a gradual age or service schedule (within the meaning of paragraph (b)(1)(iv) of this section) or a uniform target benefit allocation (within the meaning of paragraph (b)(1)(v) of this section) for the plan year; or

(3) The plan satisfies the minimum allocation gateway of paragraph (b)(1)(vi) of this section for the plan year.

(ii) *Allocations after testing age.* A plan does not fail to satisfy paragraph (b)(1)(i)(A) of this section merely because allocations are made at the same rate for employees who are older than their testing age (determined without regard to the current-age rule in paragraph (4) of the definition of testing age in § 1.401(a)(4)-12) as they are made for employees who are at that age.

(iii) *Broadly available allocation rates*—(A) *In general.* A plan has broadly available allocation rates for the plan year if each allocation rate under the plan is currently available during the plan year (within the meaning of § 1.401(a)(4)-4(b)(2)), to a group of employees that satisfies section 410(b) (without regard to the average benefit percentage test of § 1.410(b)- 5). For this purpose, if two allocation rates could be permissively aggregated under § 1.401(a)(4)-4(d)(4), assuming the allocation rates were treated as benefits, rights or features, they may be aggregated and treated as a single allocation rate. In addition, the disregard of age and service conditions described in § 1.401(a)(4)-4(b)(2)(ii)(A) does not apply for purposes of this paragraph (b)(1)(iii)(A).

* * *

(iv) *Gradual age or service schedule*—(A) *In general.* A plan has a gradual age or service schedule for the plan year if the allocation formula for all employees under the plan provides for a single schedule of allocation rates under which—

(1) The schedule defines a series of bands based solely on age, years of service, or the number of points representing the sum of age and years of service (age and service points), under which the same allocation rate applies to all employees whose age, years of service, or age and service points are within each band; and

(2) The allocation rates under the schedule increase smoothly at regular intervals, within the meaning of paragraphs (b)(1)(iv)(B) and (C) of this section.

(B) *Smoothly increasing schedule of allocation rates.* A schedule of allocation rates increases smoothly if the allocation rate for each band within the schedule is greater than the allocation rate for the immediately preceding band (i.e., the band with the next lower number of years of age, years of service, or age and service points) but by no more than 5 percentage points. However, a schedule of allocation rates will not be treated as increasing smoothly if the ratio of the allocation rate for any band to the rate for the immediately preceding band is more than 2.0 or if it exceeds the ratio of allocation rates between the two immediately preceding bands.

(C) *Regular intervals.* A schedule of allocation rates has regular intervals of age, years of service or age and service points, if each band, other than the band associated with the highest age, years of service, or age and service points, is the same length. For this purpose, if the schedule is based on age, the first band is deemed to be of the same length as the other bands if it ends at or before age 25. If the first age band ends after age 25, then, in determining whether the length of the first band is the same as the length of other bands, the starting age for the first age band is permitted to be treated as age 25 or any age earlier than 25. For a schedule of allocation rates based on age and service points, the rules of the preceding two sentences are applied by substituting 25 age and service points for age 25. For a schedule of allocation rates based on service, the starting service for the first service band is permitted to be treated as one year of service or any lesser amount of service.

(D) *Minimum allocation rates permitted.* A schedule of allocation rates under a plan does not fail to increase smoothly at regular intervals, within the meaning of paragraphs (b)(1)(iv)(B) and (C) of this section, merely because a minimum uniform allocation rate is provided for all employees or the minimum benefit described in section 416(c)(2) is provided for all non-key employees (either because the plan is top heavy or without regard to whether the plan is top heavy) if the schedule satisfies one of the following conditions—

(1) The allocation rates under the plan that are greater than the minimum allocation rate can be included in a hypothetical schedule of allocation rates that increases smoothly at regular intervals, within the meaning of paragraphs (b)(1)(iv)(B) and (C) of this section, where the hypothetical schedule has a lowest allocation rate no lower than 1% of plan year compensation; or

(2) For a plan using a schedule of allocation rates based on age, for each age band in the schedule that provides an allocation rate greater than the minimum allocation rate, there could be an employee in that age band with an equivalent accrual rate that is less than or equal to the equivalent accrual rate that would apply to an employee whose age is the highest age for which the allocation rate equals the minimum allocation rate.

(v) *Uniform target benefit allocations.* A plan has allocation rates that are based on a uniform target benefit allocation for the plan year if the plan fails to satisfy the requirements for the safe harbor testing method in paragraph (b)(3) of this section merely because the determination of the allocations under the plan differs from the allocations determined under that safe harbor testing method for any of the following reasons—

(A) The interest rate used for determining the actuarial present value of the stated plan benefit and the theoretical reserve is lower than a standard interest rate;

(B) The stated benefit is calculated assuming compensation increases at a specified rate; or

(C) The plan computes the current year contribution using the actual account balance instead of the theoretical reserve.

(vi) *Minimum allocation gateway*—(A) *General rule.* A plan satisfies the minimum allocation gateway of this paragraph (b)(1)(vi) if each NHCE has an allocation rate that is at least one third of the allocation rate of the HCE with the highest allocation rate.

(B) *Deemed satisfaction.* A plan is deemed to satisfy the minimum allocation gateway of this paragraph (b)(1)(vi) if each NHCE receives an allocation of at least 5% of the NHCE's compensation within the meaning of section 415(c)(3), measured over a period of time permitted under the definition of plan year compensation.

(vii) *Determination of allocation rate.* For purposes of paragraph (b)(1)(i)(B) of this section, allocations and allocation rates are determined under § 1.401(a)(4)-2(c)(2), but without taking into account the imputation of permitted disparity under § 1.401(a)(4)-7. However, in determining whether the plan has broadly available allocation rates as provided in paragraph (b)(1)(iii) of this section, differences in allocation rates attributable solely to the use of permitted disparity described in § 1.401(l)-2 are disregarded.

* * *

(2) *Determination of equivalent accrual rates*—(i) *Basic definition.* An employee's equivalent accrual rate for a plan year is the annual benefit that is the result of normalizing the increase in the employee's account balance during the measurement period, divided by the number of years in which the employee benefited under the plan during the measurement period, and expressed either as a dollar amount or as a percentage of the employee's average annual compensation. A measurement period that includes future years may not be used for this purpose.

* * *

(c) *Nondiscrimination in amount of contributions under a defined benefit plan*—(1) *General rule.* Equivalent allocations under a defined benefit plan are nondiscriminatory in amount for a plan year if the plan would satisfy § 1.401(a)(4)-3(c)(1) (taking into account § 1.401(a)(4)-3(c)(3)) for the plan year if an equivalent normal and most valuable allocation rate, as determined under paragraph (c)(2) of this section, were substituted for each employee's normal and most valuable accrual rate, respectively, in the determination of rate groups.

(2) *Determination of equivalent allocation rates*—(i) *Basic definitions.* An employee's equivalent normal and most valuable allocation rates for a plan year are, respectively, the actuarial present value of the increase over the plan year in the benefit that would be taken into account in determining the employee's normal and most valuable accrual rates for the plan year, expressed either as a dollar amount or as a percentage of the employee's plan year compensation. In the case of a contributory DB plan, the rules in § 1.401(a)(4)-6(b)(1), (b)(5), or (b)(6) must be used to determine the amount of each employee's employer-provided benefit that would be taken into account for this purpose.

* * *

§ 1.401(a)(4)-9. Plan aggregation and restructuring.

(a) *Introduction.* Two or more plans that are permissively aggregated and treated as a single plan under §§ 1.410(b)-7(d) must also be treated as a single plan for purposes of section 401(a)(4). See § 1.401(a)(4)-12 (definition of plan). An aggregated plan is generally tested under the same rules applicable to single plans. Paragraph (b) of this section, however, provides special rules for determining whether a plan that consists of one or more defined contribution plans and one or more defined benefit plans (a DB/DC plan) satisfies section 401(a)(4) with respect to the amount of employer- provided benefits and the availability of benefits, rights, and features. Paragraph (c) of this section provides rules allowing a plan to be treated as consisting of separate component plans and allowing the component plans to be tested separately under section 401(a)(4).

(b) *Application of nondiscrimination requirements to DB/DC plans*—(1) *General rule*. Except as provided in paragraph (b)(2) of this section, whether a DB/DC plan satisfies section 401(a)(4) is determined using the same rules applicable to a single plan. In addition, paragraph (b)(3) of this section provides an optional rule for demonstrating nondiscrimination in availability of benefits, rights, and features provided under a DB/DC plan.

* * *

(c) *Plan restructuring*—(1) *General rule*. A plan may be treated, in accordance with this paragraph (c), as consisting of two or more component plans for purposes of determining whether the plan satisfies section 401(a)(4). If each of the component plans of a plan satisfies all of the requirements of sections 401(a)(4) and 410(b) as if it were a separate plan, then the plan is treated as satisfying section 401(a)(4).

(2) *Identification of component plans*. A plan may be restructured into component plans, each consisting of all the allocations, accruals, and other benefits, rights, and features provided to a selected group of employees. The employer may select the group of employees used for this purpose in any manner, and the composition of the groups may be changed from plan year to plan year. Every employee must be included in one and only one component plan under the same plan for a plan year.

(3) *Satisfaction of section 401(a)(4) by a component plan*—(i) *General rule*. The rules applicable in determining whether a component plan satisfies section 401(a)(4) are the same as those applicable to a plan. Thus, for this purpose, any reference to a plan in section 401(a)(4) and the regulations thereunder (other than this paragraph (c)) is interpreted as a reference to a component plan. As is true for a plan, whether a component plan satisfies the uniformity and other requirements applicable to safe harbor plans under §§ 1.401(a)(4)- 2(b) and 1.401(a)(4)-3(b) is determined on a design basis. Thus, for example, plan provisions are not disregarded merely because they do not currently apply to employees in the component plan if they will apply to those employees as a result of the mere passage of time.

(ii) *Restructuring not available for certain testing purposes*. The safe harbor in § 1.401(a)(4)-2(b)(3) for plans with uniform points allocation formulas is not available in testing (and thus cannot be satisfied by) contributions under a component plan. Similarly, component plans cannot be used for purposes of determining whether a plan provides broadly available allocation rates (as defined in § 1.401(a)(4)-8(b)(1)(iii)), determining whether a plan has a gradual age or service schedule (as defined in § 1.401(a)(4)-8(b)(1)(iv)), determining whether a plan has allocation rates that are based on a uniform target benefit allocation (as defined in § 1.401(a)(4)-8(b)(1)(v)), or determining whether a plan is primarily defined benefit in character or consists of broadly available separate plans (as defined in paragraphs (b)(2)(v)(B) and (C) of this section). In addition, the minimum allocation gateway of § 1.401(a)(4)-8(b)(1)(vi) and the minimum aggregate allocation gateway of paragraph (b)(2)(v)(D) of this section cannot be satisfied on the basis of component plans. See §§ 1.401(k)-1(b)(3)(iii) and 1.401(m)-1(b)(3)(iii) for rules regarding the inapplicability of restructuring to section 401(k) plans and section 401(m) plans.

(4) *Satisfaction of section 410(b) by a component plan*—(i) *General rule*. The rules applicable in determining whether a component plan satisfies section 410(b) are generally the same as those applicable to a plan. However, a component plan is deemed to satisfy the average benefit percentage test of § 1.410(b)-5 if the plan of which it is a part satisfies § 1.410(b)-5 (without regard to § 1.410(b)-5(f)). In the case of a component plan that is part of a plan that relies on § 1.410(b)-5(f) to satisfy the average benefit percentage test, the component plan is deemed to satisfy the average benefit percentage test

only if the component plan separately satisfies § 1.410(b)-5(f). In addition, all component plans of a plan are deemed to satisfy the average benefit percentage test if the plan makes an early retirement window benefit (within the meaning of § 1.401(a)(4)-3(f)(4)(iii)) currently available (within the meaning of § 1.401(a)(4)-3(f)(4)(ii)(A)) to a group of employees that satisfies section 410(b) (without regard to the average benefit percentage test), and if it would not be necessary for the plan or any rate group or component plan of the plan to satisfy that test in order for the plan to satisfy sections 401(a)(4) and 410(b) in the absence of the early retirement window benefit.

(ii) *Relationship to satisfaction of section 410(b) by the plan.* Satisfaction of section 410(b) by a component plan is relevant solely for purposes of determining whether the plan of which it is a part satisfies section 401(a)(4), and not for purposes of determining whether the plan satisfies section 410(b) itself. The plan must still independently satisfy section 410(b) in order to be a qualified plan. Similarly, satisfaction of section 410(b) by a plan is relevant solely for purposes of determining whether the plan, and not the component plan, satisfies section 410(b). Thus, for example, a component plan that does not satisfy the ratio percentage test of § 1.410(b)-2(b)(2) must still satisfy the average benefit test of § 1.410(b)-2(b)(3), even though the plan of which it is a part satisfies the ratio percentage test.

(5) *Effect of restructuring under other sections.* The restructuring rules provided in this paragraph (c) apply solely for purposes of sections 401(a)(4) and 401(l), and those portions of sections 410(b), 414(s), and any other provisions that are specifically applicable in determining whether the requirements of section 401(a)(4) are satisfied. Thus, for example, a component plan is not treated as a separate plan under section 401(a)(26).

(6) *Examples.* The following examples illustrate the rules in this paragraph (c):

Example 1. Employer X maintains a defined benefit plan. The plan provides a normal retirement benefit equal to 1.0 percent of average annual compensation times years of service to employees at Plant S, and 1.5 percent of average annual compensation times years of service to employees at Plant T. Under paragraph (c)(2) of this section, the plan may be treated as consisting of two component defined benefit plans, one providing retirement benefits equal to 1.0 percent of average annual compensation times years of service to the employees at Plant S, and another providing benefits equal to 1.5 percent of average annual compensation times years of service to employees at Plant T. If each component plan satisfies sections 401(a)(4) and 410(b) as if it were a separate plan under the rules of this paragraph (c), then the entire plan satisfies section 401(a)(4).

Example 2. (a) Employer Y maintains Plan A, a defined benefit plan, for its Employees M, N, O, P, Q, and R. Plan A provides benefits under a uniform formula that satisfies the requirements of § 1.401(a)(4)-3(b)(2) and (b)(3) before it is amended on February 14, 1994. The amendment provides an early retirement window benefit that is a subsidized optional form of benefit under § 1.401(a)(4)-3(b)(2)(iii) and that is available on the same terms to all employees who satisfy the eligibility requirements for the window. The early retirement window benefit is available only to employees who retire between June 1, 1994, and November 30, 1994.

(b) Assume that Employees M, N, and O will be eligible to receive the window benefit by the end of the window period and Employees P, Q, and R will not. Because substantially all employees will not satisfy the eligibility requirements for the early retirement window benefit by the close of the early retirement window benefit period, Plan A fails to satisfy the uniform subsidies requirement of § 1.401(a)(4)-3(b)(2)(iii). See § 1.401(a)(4)-3(b)(2)(vi), Example 6.

(c) Under paragraph (c)(2) of this section, Employees M, N, O, P, Q, and R may be grouped into two component plans, one consisting of Employees M, N, and O, and all their accruals and other benefits, rights, and features under the plan (including the early retirement window benefit), and another consisting of Employees P, Q, and R, and all their accruals and other benefits, rights, and features under the plan. Each of the component plans identified in this manner satisfies the uniform subsidies requirement of § 1.401(a)(4)-3(b)(2)(iii), and thus satisfies § 1.401(a)(4)-3(b). The entire plan satisfies section 401(a)(4) under the rules of this paragraph (c), if each of these component plans also satisfies section 410(b) as if it were a separate plan (including, if applicable, the reasonable classification requirement of § 1.410(b)-4(b), and taking into account the special rule of paragraph (c)(4)(i) of this section that forgives the average benefit percentage test in certain situations in which the average benefit percentage test would be required solely as a result of the early retirement window benefit).

* * *

§ 1.401(a)(4)-13. Effective dates and fresh-start rules.

* * *

(c) *Fresh-start rules for defined benefit plans*—(1) *Introduction.* This paragraph (c) provides rules that must be satisfied in order to use the fresh- start testing options for defined benefit plans in § 1.401(a)(4)-3(b)(6)(vii) and (d)(3)(iii), relating to the safe harbors and the general test, respectively. Those fresh-start options are designed to allow a plan to be tested without regard to benefits accrued before a selected fresh-start date. To the extent provided in paragraph (d) of this section, those options also may be used to disregard certain increases in benefits attributable to compensation increases after a fresh-start date. Although this paragraph (c) generally requires a plan to be amended to freeze employees' accrued benefits as of a fresh-start date and to provide any additional accrued benefits after the fresh-start date solely in accordance with certain specified formulas, certain of these requirements do not apply to a plan that is tested under the general test of § 1.401(a)(4)-3(c). See § 1.401(a)(4)-3(b)(6)(vii) and (d)(3)(iii).

(2) *General rule.* A defined benefit plan satisfies this paragraph (c) if—

(i) Accrued benefits of employees in the fresh-start group are frozen as of the fresh-start date in accordance with paragraph (c)(3) of this section;

(ii) Accrued benefits after the fresh-start date for employees in the fresh- start group are determined under one of the fresh-start formulas in paragraph (c)(4) of this section; and

(iii) Paragraph (c)(5) of this section is satisfied.

(3) *Definition of frozen*—(i) *General rule.* An employee's accrued benefit under a plan is frozen as of the fresh-start date if it is determined as if the employee terminated employment with the employer as of the fresh-start date (or the date the employee actually terminated employment with the employer, if earlier), and without regard to any amendment to the plan adopted after that date, other than amendments recognized as effective as of or before that date under section 401(b) or § 1.401(a)(4)-11(g). The assumption that an employee has terminated employment applies solely for purposes of this paragraph (c)(3). Thus, for example, the fresh start has no effect on the service taken into account for purposes of determining vesting and eligibility for benefits, rights, and features under the plan.

* * *

(4) *Fresh-start formulas*—(i) *Formula without wear-away.* An employee's accrued benefit under the plan is equal to the sum of—

(A) The employee's frozen accrued benefit; and

(B) The employee's accrued benefit determined under the formula applicable to benefit accruals in the current plan year (current formula) as applied to the employee's years of service after the fresh-start date.

(ii) *Formula with wear-away.* An employee's accrued benefit under the plan is equal to the greater of—

(A) The employee's frozen accrued benefit; or

(B) The employee's accrued benefit determined under the current formula as applied to the employee's total years of service (before and after the fresh-start date) taken into account under the current formula.

(iii) *Formula with extended wear-away.* An employee's accrued benefit under the plan is equal to the greater of—

(A) The amount determined under paragraph (c)(4)(i) of this section; or

(B) The amount determined under paragraph (c)(4)(ii)(B) of this section.

§ 1.401(a)(9)-2. Distributions commencing during an employee's lifetime.

Q-1. In the case of distributions commencing during an employee's lifetime, how must the employee's entire interest be distributed in order to satisfy section 401(a)(9)(A)?

A-1. (a) In order to satisfy section 401(a)(9)(A), the entire interest of each employee must be distributed to such employee not later than the required beginning date, or must be distributed, beginning not later than the required beginning date, over the life of the employee or joint lives of the employee and a designated beneficiary or over a period not extending beyond the life expectancy of the employee or the joint life and last survivor expectancy of the employee and the designated beneficiary.

(b) Section 401(a)(9)(G) provides that lifetime distributions must satisfy the incidental death benefit requirements.

(c) The amount required to be distributed for each calendar year in order to satisfy section 401(a)(9)(A) and (G) generally depends on whether a distribution is in the form of distributions under a defined contribution plan or annuity payments under a defined benefit plan or under an annuity contract. For the method of determining the required minimum distribution in accordance with section 401(a)(9)(A) and (G) from an individual account under a defined contribution plan, see § 1.401(a)(9)-5. For the method of determining the required minimum distribution in accordance with section 401(a)(9)(A) and (G) in the case of annuity payments from a defined benefit plan or an annuity contract, see § 1.401(a)(9)-6.

Q-2. For purposes of section 401(a)(9)(C), what does the term required beginning date mean?

A-2. (a) Except as provided in paragraph (b) of this A-2 with respect to a 5- percent owner, as defined in paragraph (c) of this A-2, the term required beginning date means April 1 of the calendar year following the later of the calendar year in which the employee attains age 70½ or the calendar year in which the employee retires from employment with the employer maintaining the plan.

(b) In the case of an employee who is a 5-percent owner, the term required beginning date means April 1 of the calendar year following the calendar year in which the employee attains age 70½.

(c) For purposes of section 401(a)(9), a 5-percent owner is an employee who is a 5-percent owner (as defined in section 416) with respect to the plan year ending in the calendar year in which the employee attains age 70½.

(d) Paragraph (b) of this A-2 does not apply in the case of a governmental plan (within the meaning of section 414(d)) or a church plan. For purposes of this paragraph, the term church plan means a plan maintained by a church for church employees, and the term church means any church (as defined in section 3121(w)(3)(A)) or qualified church-controlled organization (as defined in section 3121(w)(3)(B)).

(e) A plan is permitted to provide that the required beginning date for purposes of section 401(a)(9) for all employees is April 1 of the calendar year following the calendar year in which an employee attains age 70½ regardless of whether the employee is a 5-percent owner.

Q-3. When does an employee attain age 70½?

A-3. An employee attains age 70½ as of the date six calendar months after the 70th anniversary of the employee's birth. For example, if an employee's date of birth was June 30, 1933, the 70th anniversary of such employee's birth is June 30, 2003. Such employee attains age 70½ on December 30, 2003. Consequently, if the employee is a 5-percent owner or retired, such employee's required beginning date is April 1, 2004. However, if the employee's date of birth was July 1, 1933, the 70th anniversary of such employee's birth would be July 1, 2003. Such employee would then attain age 70½ on January 1, 2004 and such employee's required beginning date would be April 1, 2005.

Q-4. Must distributions made before the employee's required beginning date satisfy section 401(a)(9)?

A-4. Lifetime distributions made before the employee's required beginning date for calendar years before the employee's first distribution calendar year, as defined in A-1(b) of § 1.401(a)(9)-5, need not be made in accordance with section 401(a)(9). However, if distributions commence before the employee's required beginning date under a particular distribution option, such as in the form of an annuity, the distribution option fails to satisfy section 401(a)(9) at the time distributions commence if, under terms of the particular distribution option, distributions to be made for the employee's first distribution calendar year or any subsequent distribution calendar year will fail to satisfy section 401(a)(9).

Q-5. If distributions have begun to an employee during the employee's lifetime (in accordance with section 401(a)(9)(A)(ii)), how must distributions be made after an employee's death?

A-5. Section 401(a)(9)(B)(i) provides that if the distribution of the employee's interest has begun in accordance with section 401(a)(9)(A)(ii) and the employee dies before his entire interest has been distributed to him, the remaining portion of such interest must be distributed at least as rapidly as under the distribution method being used under section 401(a)(9)(A)(ii) as of the date of his death. The amount required to be distributed for each distribution calendar year following the calendar year of death generally depends on whether a distribution is in the form of distributions from an individual account under a defined contribution plan or annuity payments under a defined benefit plan. For the method of determining the required minimum distribution in accordance with section 401(a)(9)(B)(i) from an individual account, see § 1.401(a)(9)-5. In the case of annuity payments from a defined benefit plan or an annuity contract, see § 1.401(a)(9)-6.

Q-6. For purposes of section 401(a)(9)(B), when are distributions considered to have begun to the employee in accordance with section 401(a)(9)(A)(ii)?

A-6. (a) General rule. Except as otherwise provided in A-10 of § 1.401(a)(9)-6, distributions are not treated as having begun to the employee in accordance with section 401(a)(9)(A)(ii) until the employee's required beginning date, without regard to whether payments have been made before that date. Thus, section 401(a)(9)(B)(i) only applies if an employee dies on or after the employee's required beginning date. For example, if employee A retires in 2003, the calendar year A attains age 65½, and begins receiving installment distributions from a profit-sharing plan over a period not exceeding the joint life and last survivor expectancy of A and A's spouse, benefits are not treated as having begun in accordance with section 401(a)(9)(A)(ii) until April 1, 2009 (the April 1 following the calendar year in which A attains age 70½). Consequently, if A dies before April 1, 2009 (A's required beginning date), distributions after A's death must be made in accordance with section 401(a)(9)(B)(ii) or (iii) and (iv) and § 1.401(a)(9)-3, and not section 401(a)(9)(B)(i). This is the case without regard to whether the plan has distributed the minimum distribution for the first distribution calendar year (as defined in A-1(b) of § 1.401(a)(9)-5) before A's death.

(b) If a plan provides, in accordance with A-2(e) of this section, that the required beginning date for purposes of section 401(a)(9) for all employees is April 1 of the calendar year following the calendar year in which an employee attains age 70½, an employee who dies on or after the required beginning date determined under the plan terms is treated as dying after the employee's distributions have begun for purposes of this A-6 even though the employee dies before the April 1 following the calendar year in which the employee retires.

§ 1.401(a)(9)-3. Death before required beginning date.

Q-1. If an employee dies before the employee's required beginning date, how must the employee's entire interest be distributed in order to satisfy section 401(a)(9)?

A-1. (a) Except as otherwise provided in A-10 of § 1.401(a)(9)-6, if an employee dies before the employee's required beginning date (and, thus, before distributions are treated as having begun in accordance with section 401(a)(9)(A)(ii)), distribution of the employee's entire interest must be made in accordance with one of the methods described in section 401(a)(9)(B)(ii) or (iii) and (iv). One method (the 5-year rule in section 401(a)(9)(B)(ii)) requires that the entire interest of the employee be distributed within 5 years of the employee's death regardless of who or what entity receives the distribution. Another method (the life expectancy rule in section 401(a)(9)(B)(iii) and (iv)) requires that any portion of an employee's interest payable to (or for the benefit of) a designated beneficiary be distributed, commencing within one year of the employee's death, over the life of such beneficiary (or over a period not extending beyond the life expectancy of such beneficiary). Section 401(a)(9)(B)(iv) provides special rules where the designated beneficiary is the surviving spouse of the employee, including a special commencement date for distributions under section 401(a)(9)(B)(iii) to the surviving spouse.

(b) See A-4 of this section for the rules for determining which of the methods described in paragraph (a) of this A-1 applies. See A-3 of this section to determine when distributions under the exception to the 5-year rule in section 401(a)(9)(B)(iii) and (iv) must commence. See A-2 of this section to determine when the 5-year period in section 401(a)(9)(B)(ii) ends. For distributions using the life expectancy rule in section 401(a)(9)(B)(iii) and (iv), see §1.401(a)(9)-4 in order to determine the designated beneficiary under section 401(a)(9)(B)(iii) and (iv), see § 1.401(a)(9)-5 for the rules for determining the required minimum distribution under a defined contribution plan, and see § 1.401(a)(9)-6 for required minimum distributions under defined benefit plans.

Q-2. By when must the employee's entire interest be distributed in order to satisfy the 5-year rule in section 401(a)(9)(B)(ii)?

A-2. In order to satisfy the 5-year rule in section 401(a)(9)(B)(ii), the employee's entire interest must be distributed by the end of the calendar year which contains the fifth anniversary of the date of the employee's death. For example, if an employee dies on January 1, 2003, the entire interest must be distributed by the end of 2008, in order to satisfy the 5-year rule in section 401(a)(9)(B)(ii).

Q-3. When are distributions required to commence in order to satisfy the life expectancy rule in section 401(a)(9)(B)(iii) and (iv)?

A-3. (a) *Nonspouse beneficiary*. In order to satisfy the life expectancy rule in section 401(a)(9)(B)(iii), if the designated beneficiary is not the employee's surviving spouse, distributions must commence on or before the end of the calendar year immediately following the calendar year in which the employee died. This rule also applies to the distribution of the entire remaining benefit if another individual is a designated beneficiary in addition to the employee's surviving spouse. See A-2 and A-3 of §1.401(a)(9)-8, however, if the employee's benefit is divided into separate accounts.

(b) *Spousal beneficiary*. In order to satisfy the rule in section 401(a)(9)(B)(iii) and (iv), if the sole designated beneficiary is the employee's surviving spouse, distributions must commence on or before the later of—

(1) The end of the calendar year immediately following the calendar year in which the employee died; and

(2) The end of the calendar year in which the employee would have attained age 70½.

Q-4. How is it determined whether the 5-year rule in section 401(a)(9)(B)(ii) or the life expectancy rule in section 401(a)(9)(B)(iii) and (iv) applies to a distribution?

A-4. (a) *No plan provision.* If a plan does not adopt an optional provision described in paragraph (b) or (c) of this A-4 specifying the method of distribution after the death of an employee, distribution must be made as follows:

(1) If the employee has a designated beneficiary, as determined under §1.401(a)(9)-4, distributions are to be made in accordance with the life expectancy rule in section 401(a)(9)(B)(iii) and (iv).

(2) If the employee has no designated beneficiary, distributions are to be made in accordance with the 5-year rule in section 401(a)(9)(B)(ii).

(b) *Optional plan provisions.* A plan may adopt a provision specifying either that the 5-year rule in section 401(a)(9)(B)(ii) will apply to certain distributions after the death of an employee even if the employee has a designated beneficiary or that distribution in every case will be made in accordance with the 5-year rule in section 401(a)(9)(B)(ii). Further, a plan need not have the same method of distribution for the benefits of all employees in order to satisfy section 401(a)(9).

(c) *Elections.* A plan may adopt a provision that permits employees (or beneficiaries) to elect on an individual basis whether the 5-year rule in section 401(a)(9)(B)(ii) or the life expectancy rule in section 401(a)(9)(B)(iii) and (iv) applies to distributions after the death of an employee who has a designated beneficiary. Such an election must be made no later than the earlier of the end of the calendar year in which distribution would be required to commence in order to satisfy the requirements for the life expectancy rule in section 401(a)(9)(B)(iii) and (iv) (see A-3 of this section for the determination of such calendar year) or the end of the calendar year which contains the fifth anniversary of the date of death of the employee. As of the last date the election may be made, the election must be irrevocable with respect to the beneficiary (and all subsequent beneficiaries) and must apply to all subsequent calendar years. If a plan provides for the election, the plan may also specify the method of distribution that applies if neither the employee nor the beneficiary makes the election. If neither the employee nor the beneficiary elects a method and the plan does not specify which method applies, distribution must be made in accordance with paragraph (a) of this A-4.

Q-5. If the employee's surviving spouse is the employee's sole designated beneficiary and such spouse dies after the employee, but before distributions have begun to the surviving spouse under section 401(a)(9)(B)(iii) and (iv), how is the employee's interest to be distributed?

A-5. Pursuant to section 401(a)(9)(B)(iv)(II), if the surviving spouse is the employee's sole designated beneficiary and dies after the employee, but before distributions to such spouse have begun under section 401(a)(9)(B)(iii) and (iv), the 5-year rule in section 401(a)(9)(B)(ii) and the life expectancy rule in section 401(a)(9)(B)(iii) are to be applied as if the surviving spouse were the employee. In applying this rule, the date of death of the surviving spouse shall be substituted for the date of death of the employee. However, in such case, the rules in section 401(a)(9)(B)(iv) are not available to the surviving spouse of the deceased employee's surviving spouse.

Q-6. For purposes of section 401(a)(9)(B)(iv)(II), when are distributions considered to have begun to the surviving spouse?

A-6. Distributions are considered to have begun to the surviving spouse of an employee, for purposes of section 401(a)(9)(B)(iv)(II), on the date, determined in accordance with A-3 of this section, on which distributions are required to commence to the surviving spouse, even though payments have actually been made before that date. See A-11 of §1.401(a)(9)-6 for a special rule for annuities.

§ 1.401(a)(9)-4. Determination of the designated beneficiary.

Q-1. Who is a designated beneficiary under section 401(a)(9)(E)?

A-1. A designated beneficiary is an individual who is designated as a beneficiary under the plan. An individual may be designated as a beneficiary under the plan either by the terms of the plan or, if the plan so provides, by an affirmative election by the employee (or the employee's surviving spouse) specifying the beneficiary. A beneficiary designated as such under the plan is an individual who is entitled to a portion of an employee's benefit, contingent on the employee's death or another specified event. For example, if a distribution is in the form of a joint and survivor annuity over the life of the employee and another individual, the plan does not satisfy section 401(a)(9) unless such other individual is a designated beneficiary under the plan. A designated beneficiary need not be specified by name in the plan or by the employee to the plan in order to be a designated beneficiary so long as the individual who is to be the beneficiary is identifiable under the plan. The members of a class of beneficiaries capable of expansion or contraction will be treated as being identifiable if it is possible, to identify the class member with the shortest life expectancy. The fact that an employee's interest under the plan passes to a certain individual under a will or otherwise under applicable state law does not make that individual a designated beneficiary unless the individual is designated as a beneficiary under the plan. See A-6 of § 1.401(a)(9)-8 for rules which apply to qualified domestic relation orders.

Q-2. Must an employee (or the employee's spouse) make an affirmative election specifying a beneficiary for a person to be a designated beneficiary under section 401(a)(9)(E)?

A-2. No, a designated beneficiary is an individual who is designated as a beneficiary under the plan whether or not the designation under the plan was made by the employee. The choice of beneficiary is subject to the requirements of sections 401(a)(11), 414(p), and 417.

Q-3. May a person other than an individual be considered to be a designated beneficiary for purposes of section 401(a)(9)?

A-3. No, only individuals may be designated beneficiaries for purposes of section 401(a)(9). A person that is not an individual, such as the employee's estate, may not be a designated beneficiary. If a person other than an individual is designated as a beneficiary of an employee's benefit, the employee will be treated as having no designated beneficiary for purposes of section 401(a)(9), even if there are also individuals designated as beneficiaries. However, see A-5 of this section for special rules that apply to trusts and A-2 and A-3 of § 1.401(a)(9)-8 for rules that apply to separate accounts.

Q-4. When is the designated beneficiary determined?

A-4. (a) General rule. In order to be a designated beneficiary, an individual must be a beneficiary as of the date of death. Except as provided in paragraph (b) and §1.401(a)(9)-6, the employee's designated beneficiary will be determined based on the beneficiaries designated as of the date of death who remain beneficiaries as of September 30 of the calendar year following the calendar year of the employee's death. Consequently, except as provided in § 1.401(a)(9)-6, any person who was a beneficiary as of the date of the employee's death, but is not a beneficiary as of that September 30 (e.g., because the person receives the entire benefit to which the person is entitled before that September 30), is not taken into account in determining the employee's designated beneficiary for purposes of determining the distribution period for required minimum distributions after the employee's death. Accordingly, if a person disclaims entitlement to the employee's benefit, pursuant to a disclaimer that satisfies section 2518 by that September 30 thereby allowing other beneficiaries to receive the benefit in lieu of that person, the disclaiming person is not taken into account in determining the employee's designated beneficiary.

(b) *Surviving spouse.* As provided in A-5 of § 1.401(a)(9)-3, if the employee's spouse is the sole designated beneficiary as of September 30 of the calendar year following the calendar year of the employee's death, and the surviving spouse dies after the employee and before the date on which distributions have begun to the surviving spouse under section 401(a)(9)(B)(iii) and (iv), the rule in section 401(a)(9)(B)(iv)(II) will apply. Thus, for example, the relevant designated beneficiary for determining the distribution period after the death of the surviving spouse is the designated beneficiary of the surviving spouse. Similarly, such designated beneficiary will be determined based on the beneficiaries designated as of the date of the surviving spouse's death and who remain beneficiaries as of September 30 of the calendar year following the calendar year of the surviving spouse's death. Further, if, as of that September 30, there is no designated beneficiary under the plan with respect to that surviving spouse, distribution must be made in accordance with the 5-year rule in section 401(a)(9)(B)(ii) and A-2 of § 1.401(a)(9)-3.

(c) *Deceased beneficiary.* For purposes of this A-4, an individual who is a beneficiary as of the date of the employee's death and dies prior to September 30 of the calendar year following the calendar year of the employee's death without disclaiming continues to be treated as a beneficiary as of the September 30 of the calendar year following the calendar year of the employee's death in determining the employee's designated beneficiary for purposes of determining the distribution period for required minimum distributions after the employee's death, without regard to the identity of the successor beneficiary who is entitled to distributions as the beneficiary of the deceased beneficiary. The same rule applies in the case of distributions to which A-5 of § 1.401(a)(9)-3 applies so that, if an individual is designated as a beneficiary of an employee's surviving spouse as of the spouse's date of death and dies prior to September 30 of the year following the year of the surviving spouse's death, that individual will continue to be treated as a designated beneficiary.

Q-5. If a trust is named as a beneficiary of an employee, will the beneficiaries of the trust with respect to the trust's interest in the employee's benefit be treated as having been designated as beneficiaries of the employee under the plan for purposes of determining the distribution period under section 401(a)(9)?

A-5. (a) If the requirements of paragraph (b) of this A-5 are met with respect to a trust that is named as the beneficiary of an employee under the plan, the beneficiaries of the trust (and not the trust itself) will be treated as having been designated as beneficiaries of the employee under the plan for purposes of determining the distribution period under section 401(a)(9).

(b) The requirements of this paragraph (b) are met if, during any period during which required minimum distributions are being determined by treating the beneficiaries of the trust as designated beneficiaries of the employee, the following requirements are met—

(1) The trust is a valid trust under state law, or would be but for the fact that there is no corpus.

(2) The trust is irrevocable or will, by its terms, become irrevocable upon the death of the employee.

(3) The beneficiaries of the trust who are beneficiaries with respect to the trust's interest in the employee's benefit are identifiable within the meaning of A-1 of this section from the trust instrument.

(4) The documentation described in A-6 of this section has been provided to the plan administrator.

(c) In the case of payments to a trust having more than one beneficiary, see A-7 of § 1.401(a)(9)-5 for the rules for determining the designated beneficiary whose life expectancy will be used to determine the distribution period and A-3 of this section for the rules that apply if a person other than an individual is designated as a beneficiary of an employee's benefit. However, the separate account rules under A-2 of § 1.401(a)(9)-8 are not available to beneficiaries of a trust with respect to the trust's interest in the employee's benefit.

(d) If the beneficiary of the trust named as beneficiary of the employee's interest is another trust, the beneficiaries of the other trust will be treated as being designated as beneficiaries of the first trust, and thus, having been designated by the employee under the plan for purposes of determining the distribution period under section 401(a)(9)(A)(ii), provided that the requirements of paragraph (b) of this A-5 are satisfied with respect to such other trust in addition to the trust named as beneficiary.

Q-6. If a trust is named as a beneficiary of an employee, what documentation must be provided to the plan administrator?

A-6. (a) *Required minimum distributions before death.* If an employee designates a trust as the beneficiary of his or her entire benefit and the employee's spouse is the sole beneficiary of the trust, in order to satisfy the documentation requirements of this A-6 so that the spouse can be treated as the sole designated beneficiary of the employee's benefits (if the other requirements of paragraph (b) of A-5 of this section are satisfied), the employee must either—

(1) Provide to the plan administrator a copy of the trust instrument and agree that if the trust instrument is amended at any time in the future, the employee will, within a reasonable time, provide to the plan administrator a copy of each such amendment; or

(2) Provide to the plan administrator a list of all of the beneficiaries of the trust (including contingent and remaindermen beneficiaries with a description of the conditions on their entitlement sufficient to establish that the spouse is the sole beneficiary) for purposes of section 401(a)(9); certify that, to the best of the employee's knowledge, this list is correct and complete and that the requirements of paragraph (b)(1), (2), and (3) of A-5 of this section are satisfied; agree that, if the trust instrument is amended at any time in the future, the employee will, within a reasonable time, provide to the plan administrator corrected certifications to the extent that the amendment changes any information previously certified; and agree to provide a copy of the trust instrument to the plan administrator upon demand.

(b) *Required minimum distributions after death.* In order to satisfy the documentation requirement of this A-6 for required minimum distributions after the death of the employee (or spouse in a case to which A-5 of § 1.401(a)(9)-3 applies), by October 31 of the calendar year immediately following the calendar year in which the employee died, the trustee of the trust must either—

(1) Provide the plan administrator with a final list of all beneficiaries of the trust (including contingent and remaindermen beneficiaries with a description of the conditions on their entitlement) as of September 30 of the calendar year following the calendar year of the employee's death; certify that, to the best of the trustee's knowledge, this list is correct and complete and that the requirements of paragraph (b)(1), (2), and (3) of A-5 of this section are satisfied; and agree to provide a copy of the trust instrument to the plan administrator upon demand; or

(2) Provide the plan administrator with a copy of the actual trust document for the trust that is named as a beneficiary of the employee under the plan as of the employee's date of death.

* * *

§ 1.401(a)(9)-5. Required minimum distributions from defined contribution plans.

Q-1. If an employee's benefit is in the form of an individual account under a defined contribution plan, what is the amount required to be distributed for each calendar year?

A-1. (a) *General rule.* If an employee's accrued benefit is in the form of an individual account under a defined contribution plan, the minimum amount required to be distributed for each distribution calendar year, as defined in paragraph (b) of this A-1, is equal to the quotient obtained by dividing the account (determined under A-3 of this section) by the applicable distribution period (determined under A-4 or A-5 of this section, whichever is applicable). However, the required minimum distribution amount will never exceed the entire account balance on the date of the distribution. See A-8 of this section for rules that apply if a portion of the employee's account is not vested. Further, the minimum distribution required to be distributed on or before an employee's required beginning date is always determined under section 401(a)(9)(A)(ii) and this A-1 and not section 401(a)(9)(A)(i).

(b) *Distribution calendar year.* A calendar year for which a minimum distribution is required is a distribution calendar year. If an employee's required beginning date is April 1 of the calendar year following the calendar year in which the employee attains age 70½, the employee's first distribution calendar year is the year the employee attains age 70½. If an employee's required beginning date is April 1 of the calendar year following the calendar year in which the employee retires, the employee's first distribution calendar year is the calendar year in which the employee retires. In the case of distributions to be made in accordance with the life expectancy rule in § 1.401(a)(9)-3 and in section 401(a)(9)(B)(iii) and (iv), the first distribution calendar year is the calendar year containing the date described in A-3(a) or A-3(b) of § 1.401(a)(9)-3, whichever is applicable.

(c) *Time for distributions.* The distribution required to be made on or before the employee's required beginning date shall be treated as the distribution required for the employee's first distribution calendar year (as defined in paragraph (b) of this A-1). The required minimum distribution for other distribution calendar years, including the required minimum distribution for the distribution calendar year in which the employee's required beginning date occurs, must be made on or before the end of that distribution calendar year.

(d) *Minimum distribution incidental benefit requirement.* If distributions of an employee's account balance under a defined contribution plan are made in accordance with this section, the minimum distribution incidental benefit requirement of section 401(a)(9)(G) is satisfied. Further, with respect to the retirement benefits provided by that account balance, to the extent the incidental benefit requirement of § 1.401-1(b)(1)(i) requires a distribution, that requirement is deemed to be satisfied if distributions satisfy the minimum distribution incidental benefit requirement of section 401(a)(9)(G) and this section.

(e) *Annuity contracts.* Instead of satisfying this A-1, the minimum distribution requirement may be satisfied by the purchase of an annuity contract from an insurance company in accordance with A-4 of § 1.401(a)(9)-6 with the employee's entire individual account. If such an annuity is purchased after distributions are required to commence (the required beginning date, in the case of distributions commencing before death, or the date determined under A-3 of § 1.401(a)(9)-3, in the case of distributions commencing after death), payments under the annuity contract purchased will satisfy section 401(a)(9) for distribution calendar years after the calendar year of the purchase if payments under the annuity contract are made in accordance with § 1.401(a)(9)-6. In such a case, payments under the annuity contract will be treated as distributions from the individual account for purposes of determining if the individual account satisfies section 401(a)(9) for the calendar year of the purchase. An employee may also purchase an annuity contract with a portion of the employee's account under the rules of A-2(a)(3) of § 1.401(a)(9)-8.

Q-2. If an employee's benefit is in the form of an individual account and, in any calendar year, the amount distributed exceeds the minimum required, will credit be given in subsequent calendar years for such excess distribution?

A-2. If, for any distribution calendar year, the amount distributed exceeds the minimum required, no credit will be given in subsequent calendar years for such excess distribution.

Q-3. What is the amount of the account of an employee used for determining the employee's required minimum distribution in the case of an individual account?

A-3. (a) In the case of an individual account, the benefit used in determining the required minimum distribution for a distribution calendar year is the account balance as of the last valuation date in the calendar year immediately preceding that distribution calendar year (valuation calendar year) adjusted in accordance with paragraphs (b) and (c) of this A-3.

(b) The account balance is increased by the amount of any contributions or forfeitures allocated to the account balance as of dates in the valuation calendar year after the valuation date. For this purpose, contributions that are allocated to the account balance as of dates in the valuation calendar year after the valuation date, but that are not actually made during the valuation calendar year, are permitted to be excluded.

(c) The account balance is decreased by distributions made in the valuation calendar year after the valuation date.

(d) If an amount is distributed by one plan and rolled over to another plan (receiving plan), A-2 of § 1.401(a)(9)-7 provides additional rules for determining the benefit and required minimum distribution under the receiving plan. If an amount is transferred from one plan (transferor plan) to another plan (transferee plan), A-3 and A-4 of § 1.401(a)(9)-7 provide additional rules for determining the amount of the required minimum distribution and the benefit under both the transferor and transferee plans.

Q-4. For required minimum distributions during an employee's lifetime, what is the applicable distribution period?

A-4. (a) *General rule.* Except as provided in paragraph (b) of this A-4, the applicable distribution period for required minimum distributions for distribution calendar years up to and including the distribution calendar year that includes the employee's date of death is determined using the Uniform Lifetime Table in A-2 of § 1.401(a)(9)-9 for the employee's age as of the employee's birthday in the relevant distribution calendar year. If an employee dies on or after the required beginning date, the distribution period applicable for calculating the amount that must be distributed during the distribution calendar year that includes the employee's death is determined as if the employee had lived throughout that year. Thus, a minimum required distribution, determined as if the employee had lived throughout that year, is required for the year of the employee's death and that amount must be distributed to a beneficiary to the extent it has not already been distributed to the employee.

(b) *Spouse is sole beneficiary*—(1) *General rule.* Except as otherwise provided in paragraph (b)(2) of this A-4, if the sole designated beneficiary of an employee is the employee's surviving spouse, for required minimum distributions during the employee's lifetime, the applicable distribution period is the longer of the distribution period determined in accordance with paragraph (a) of this A-4 or the joint life expectancy of the employee and spouse using the employee's and spouse's attained ages as of the employee's and the spouse's birthdays in the distribution calendar year. The spouse is sole designated beneficiary for purposes of determining the applicable distribution period for a distribution calendar year during the employee's lifetime only if the spouse is the sole beneficiary of the employee's entire interest at all times during the distribution calendar year.

(2) *Change in marital status.* If the employee and the employee's spouse are married on January 1 of a distribution calendar year, but do not remain married throughout that year (i.e., the employee or the employee's spouse die or they become divorced during that year), the employee will not fail to have a spouse as the employee's sole beneficiary for that year merely because they are not married throughout that year. If an employee's spouse predeceases the employee, the spouse will not fail to be the employee's sole beneficiary for the distribution calendar year that includes the date of the spouse's death solely because, for the period remaining in that year after the spouse's death, someone other than the spouse is named as beneficiary. However, the change in beneficiary due to the death or divorce of the spouse will be effective for purposes of determining the applicable distribution period under section 401(a)(9) in the distribution calendar year following the distribution calendar year that includes the date of the spouse's death or divorce.

Q-5. For required minimum distributions after an employee's death, what is the applicable distribution period?

A-5. (a) *Death on or after the employee's required beginning date.* If an employee dies after distribution has begun as determined under A-6 of § 1.401(a)(9)-2 (generally on or after the employee's required beginning date), in order to satisfy section 401(a)(9)(B)(i), the applicable distribution period for distribution calendar years after the distribution calendar year containing the employee's date of death is either—

(1) If the employee has a designated beneficiary as of the date determined under A-4 of § 1.401(a)(9)-4, the longer of—

(i) The remaining life expectancy of the employee's designated beneficiary determined in accordance with paragraph (c)(1) or (2) of this A-5; and

(ii) The remaining life expectancy of the employee determined in accordance with paragraph (c)(3) of this A-5; or

(2) If the employee does not have a designated beneficiary as of the date determined under A-4 of § 1.401(a)(9)-4, the remaining life expectancy of the employee determined in accordance with paragraph (c)(3) of this A-5.

(b) *Death before an employee's required beginning date.* If an employee dies before distribution has begun, as determined under A-5 of § 1.401(a)(9)-2 (generally before the employee's required beginning date), in order to satisfy section 401(a)(9)(B)(iii) or (iv) and the life expectancy rule described in A-1 of § 1.401(a)(9)-3, the applicable distribution period for distribution calendar years after the distribution calendar year containing the employee's date of death is determined in accordance with paragraph (c) of this A-5. See A-4 of § 1.401(a)(9)-3 to determine when the 5-year rule of in section 401(a)(9)(B)(ii) applies (e.g., there is no designated beneficiary or the 5-year rule is elected or specified by plan provision).

(c) *Life expectancy*—(1) *Nonspouse designated beneficiary.* Except as otherwise provided in paragraph (c)(2), the applicable distribution period measured by the beneficiary's remaining life expectancy is determined using the beneficiary's age as of the beneficiary's birthday in the calendar year immediately following the calendar year of the employee's death. In subsequent calendar years, the applicable distribution period is reduced by one for each calendar year that has elapsed after the calendar year immediately following the calendar year of the employee's death.

(2) *Spouse designated beneficiary.* If the surviving spouse of the employee is the employee's sole beneficiary, the applicable distribution period is measured by the surviving spouse's life expectancy using the surviving spouse's birthday for each distribution calendar year after the calendar year of the employee's death up through the calendar year of the spouse's death. For calendar years after the calendar year of the spouse's death, the appli-

cable distribution period is the life expectancy of the spouse using the age of the spouse as of the spouse's birthday in the calendar year of the spouse's death, reduced by one for each calendar year that has elapsed after the calendar year of the spouse's death.

(3) *No designated beneficiary.* If the employee does not have a designated beneficiary, the applicable distribution period measured by the employee's remaining life expectancy is the life expectancy of the employee using the age of the employee as of the employee's birthday in the calendar year of the employee's death. In subsequent calendar years the applicable distribution period is reduced by one for each calendar year that has elapsed after the calendar year of the employee's death.

Q-6. What life expectancies must be used for purposes of determining required minimum distributions under section 401(a)(9)?

A-6. Life expectancies for purposes of determining required minimum distributions under section 401(a)(9) must be computed using the Single Life Table in A-1 of § 1.401(a)(9)-9 and the Joint and Last Survivor Table in A-3 of § 1.401(a)(9)-9.

Q-7. If an employee has more than one designated beneficiary, which designated beneficiary's life expectancy will be used to determine the applicable distribution period?

A-7. (a) *General rule*—(1) Except as otherwise provided in paragraph (c) of this A-7, if more than one individual is designated as a beneficiary with respect to an employee as of the applicable date for determining the designated beneficiary under A-4 of § 1.401(a)(9)-4, the designated beneficiary with the shortest life expectancy will be the designated beneficiary for purposes of determining the applicable distribution period.

(2) See A-3 of § 1.401(a)(9)-4 for rules that apply if a person other than an individual is designated as a beneficiary and see A-2 and A-3 of § 1.401(a)(9)-8 for special rules that apply if an employee's benefit under a plan is divided into separate accounts and the beneficiaries with respect to a separate account differ from the beneficiaries of another separate account.

(b) *Contingent beneficiary.* Except as provided in paragraph (c)(1) of this A-7, if a beneficiary's entitlement to an employee's benefit after the employee's death is a contingent right, such contingent beneficiary is nevertheless considered to be a beneficiary for purposes of determining whether a person other than an individual is designated as a beneficiary (resulting in the employee being treated as having no designated beneficiary under the rules of A-3 of § 1.401(a)(9)-4) and which designated beneficiary has the shortest life expectancy under paragraph (a) of this A-7.

(c) *Successor beneficiary*—(1) A person will not be considered a beneficiary for purposes of determining who is the beneficiary with the shortest life expectancy under paragraph (a) of this A-7, or whether a person who is not an individual is a beneficiary, merely because the person could become the successor to the interest of one of the employee's beneficiaries after that beneficiary's death. However, the preceding sentence does not apply to a person who has any right (including a contingent right) to an employee's benefit beyond being a mere potential successor to the interest of one of the employee's beneficiaries upon that beneficiary's death. Thus, for example, if the first beneficiary has a right to all income with respect to an employee's individual account during that beneficiary's life and a second beneficiary has a right to the principal but only after the death of the first income beneficiary (any portion of the principal distributed during the life of the first income beneficiary to be held in trust until that first beneficiary's death), both beneficiaries must be taken into account in determining the beneficiary with the shortest life expectancy and whether only individuals are beneficiaries.

(2) If the individual beneficiary whose life expectancy is being used to calculate the distribution period dies after September 30 of the calendar year following the calendar year of the employee's death, such beneficiary's remaining life expectancy will be used to de-

termine the distribution period without regard to the life expectancy of the subsequent beneficiary.

(3) This paragraph (c) is illustrated by the following examples:

Example 1. (i) Employer M maintains a defined contribution plan, Plan X. Employee A, an employee of M, died in 2005 at the age of 55, survived by spouse, B, who was 50 years old. Prior to A's death, M had established an account balance for A in Plan X. A's account balance is invested only in productive assets. A named a testamentary trust (Trust P) established under A's will as the beneficiary of all amounts payable from A's account in Plan X after A's death. A copy of the Trust P and a list of the trust beneficiaries were provided to the plan administrator of Plan X by October 31 of the calendar year following the calendar year of A's death. As of the date of A's death, the Trust P was irrevocable and was a valid trust under the laws of the state of A's domicile. A's account balance in Plan X was includible in A's gross estate under § 2039.

(ii) Under the terms of Trust P, all trust income is payable annually to B, and no one has the power to appoint Trust P principal to any person other than B. A's children, who are all younger than B, are the sole remainder beneficiaries of the Trust P. No other person has a beneficial interest in Trust P. Under the terms of the Trust P, B has the power, exercisable annually, to compel the trustee to withdraw from A's account balance in Plan X an amount equal to the income earned on the assets held in A's account in Plan X during the calendar year and to distribute that amount through Trust P to B. Plan X contains no prohibition on withdrawal from A's account of amounts in excess of the annual required minimum distributions under section 401(a)(9). In accordance with the terms of Plan X, the trustee of Trust P elects, in order to satisfy section 401(a)(9), to receive annual required minimum distributions using the life expectancy rule in section 401(a)(9)(B)(iii) for distributions over a distribution period equal to B's life expectancy. If B exercises the withdrawal power, the trustee must withdraw from A's account under Plan X the greater of the amount of income earned in the account during the calendar year or the required minimum distribution. However, under the terms of Trust P, and applicable state law, only the portion of the Plan X distribution received by the trustee equal to the income earned by A's account in Plan X is required to be distributed to B (along with any other trust income.)

(iii) Because some amounts distributed from A's account in Plan X to Trust P may be accumulated in Trust P during B's lifetime for the benefit of A's children, as remaindermen beneficiaries of Trust P, even though access to those amounts are delayed until after B's death, A's children are beneficiaries of A's account in Plan X in addition to B and B is not the sole designated beneficiary of A's account. Thus the designated beneficiary used to determine the distribution period from A's account in Plan X is the beneficiary with the shortest life expectancy. B's life expectancy is the shortest of all the potential beneficiaries of the testamentary trust's interest in A's account in Plan X (including remainder beneficiaries). Thus, the distribution period for purposes of section 401(a)(9)(B)(iii) is B's life expectancy. Because B is not the sole designated beneficiary of the testamentary trust's interest in A's account in Plan X, the special rule in 401(a)(9)(B)(iv) is not available and the annual required minimum distributions from the account to Trust M must begin no later than the end of the calendar year immediately following the calendar year of A's death.

Example 2. (i) The facts are the same as Example 1 except that the testamentary trust instrument provides that all amounts distributed from A's account in Plan X to the trustee while B is alive will be paid directly to B upon receipt by the trustee of Trust P.

(ii) In this case, B is the sole designated beneficiary of A's account in Plan X for purposes of determining the designated beneficiary under section 401(a)(9)(B)(iii) and (iv). No amounts distributed from A's account in Plan X to Trust P are accumulated in Trust P during B's lifetime for the benefit of any other beneficiary. Therefore, the residuary beneficiaries of Trust P are mere potential successors to B's interest in Plan X. Because B is the sole beneficiary of the testamentary trust's interest in A's account in Plan X, the annual required minimum distributions from A's account to Trust P must begin no later than the end of the calendar year in which A would have attained age 70½, rather than the calendar year immediately following the calendar year of A's death.

Q-8. If a portion of an employee's individual account is not vested as of the employee's required beginning date, how is the determination of the required minimum distribution affected?

A-8. If the employee's benefit is in the form of an individual account, the benefit used to determine the required minimum distribution for any distribution calendar year will be determined in accordance with A-1 of this section without regard to whether or not all of the employee's benefit is vested. If any portion of the employee's benefit is not vested, distributions will be treated as being paid from the vested portion of the benefit first. If, as of the end of a distribution calendar year (or as of the employee's required beginning date, in the case of the employee's first distribution calendar year), the total amount of the employee's vested benefit is less than the required minimum distribution for the calendar year, only the vested portion, if any, of the employee's benefit is required to be distributed by the end of the calendar year (or, if applicable, by the employee's required beginning date). However, the required minimum distribution for the subsequent distribution calendar year must be increased by the sum of amounts not distributed in prior calendar years because the employee's vested benefit was less than the required minimum distribution.

Q-9. Which amounts distributed from an individual account are taken into account in determining whether section 401(a)(9) is satisfied and which amounts are not taken into account in determining whether section 401(a)(9) is satisfied?

A-9. (a) *General rule.* Except as provided in paragraph (b), all amounts distributed from an individual account are distributions that are taken into account in determining whether section 401(a)(9) is satisfied, regardless of whether the amount is includible in income. Thus, for example, amounts that are excluded from income as recovery of investment in the contract under section 72 are taken into account for purposes of determining whether section 401(a)(9) is satisfied for a distribution calendar year. Similarly, amounts excluded from income as net unrealized appreciation on employer securities also are amounts distributed for purposes of determining if section 401(a)(9) is satisfied.

(b) *Exceptions.* The following amounts are not taken into account in determining whether the required minimum amount has been distributed for a calendar year:

(1) Elective deferrals and employee contributions that, pursuant to § 1.415-6(b)(6)(iv), are returned (together with the income allocable to these corrective distributions) as a result of the application of the section 415 limitations.

(2) Corrective distributions of excess deferrals as described in § 1.402(g)-1(e)(3), together with the income allocable to these distributions.

(3) Corrective distributions of excess contributions under a qualified cash or deferred arrangement under section 401(k)(8) and excess aggregate contributions under section 401(m)(6), together with the income allocable to these distributions.

(4) Loans that are treated as deemed distributions pursuant to section 72(p).

(5) Dividends described in section 404(k) that are paid on employer securities. (Amounts paid to the plan that, pursuant to section 404(k)(2)(A)(iii)(II), are included in the account balance and subsequently distributed from the account lose their character as dividends.)

(6) The costs of life insurance coverage (P.S. 58 costs).

(7) Similar items designated by the Commissioner in revenue rulings, notices, and other guidance published in the Internal Revenue Bulletin. See § 601.601(d)(2)(ii)(b) of this chapter.

§ 1.401(a)(9)-6. Required minimum distributions for defined benefit plans and annuity contracts.

Q-1. How must distributions under a defined benefit plan be paid in order to satisfy section 401(a)(9)?

A-1. (a) *General rules.* In order to satisfy section 401(a)(9), except as otherwise provided in this section, distributions of the employee's entire interest under a defined benefit plan must be paid in the form of periodic annuity payments for the employee's life (or the joint lives of the employee and beneficiary) or over a period certain that does not exceed the maximum length of the period certain determined in accordance with A-3 of this section. The interval between payments for the annuity must be uniform over the entire distribution period and must not exceed one year. Once payments have commenced over a period, the period may only be changed in accordance with A-13 of this section. Life (or joint and survivor) annuity payments must satisfy the minimum distribution incidental benefit requirements of A-2 of this section. Except as otherwise provided in this section (such as permitted increases described in A-14 of this section), all payments (whether paid over an employee's life, joint lives, or a period certain) also must be nonincreasing.

(b) *Life annuity with period certain.* The annuity may be a life annuity (or joint and survivor annuity) with a period certain if the life (or lives, if applicable) and period certain each meet the requirements of paragraph (a) of this A-1. For purposes of this section, if distributions are permitted to be made over the lives of the employee and the designated beneficiary, references to a life annuity include a joint and survivor annuity.

(c) *Annuity commencement.* (1) Annuity payments must commence on or before the employee's required beginning date (within the meaning of A-2 of § 1.401(a)(9)- 2). The first payment, which must be made on or before the employee's required beginning date, must be the payment which is required for one payment interval. The second payment need not be made until the end of the next payment interval even if that payment interval ends in the next calendar year. Similarly, in the case of distributions commencing after death in accordance with section 401(a)(9)(B)(iii) and (iv), the first payment, which must be made on or before the date determined under A-3(a) or (b) (whichever is applicable) of § 1.401(a)(9)-3, must be the payment which is required for one payment interval. Payment intervals are the periods for which payments are received, e.g., bimonthly, monthly, semi-annually, or annually. All benefit accruals as of the last day of the first distribution calendar year must be included in the calculation of the amount of annuity payments for payment intervals ending on or after the employee's required beginning date.

(2) This paragraph (c) is illustrated by the following example:

Example. A defined benefit plan (Plan X) provides monthly annuity payments of $500 for the life of unmarried participants with a 10-year period certain. An unmarried, retired participant (A) in Plan X attains age 70½ in 2005. In order to meet the requirements of this paragraph, the first monthly payment of $500 must be made on behalf of A on or before April 1, 2006, and the payments must continue to be made in monthly payments of $500 thereafter for the life and 10-year period certain.

(d) *Single sum distributions.* In the case of a single sum distribution of an employee's entire accrued benefit during a distribution calendar year, the amount that is the required minimum distribution for the distribution calendar year (and thus not eligible for rollover under section 402(c)) is determined using either the rule in paragraph (d)(1) or the rule in paragraph (d)(2) of this A-1.

(1) The portion of the single sum distribution that is a required minimum distribution is determined by treating the single sum distribution as a distribution from an individual account plan and treating the amount of the single sum distribution as the employee's account balance as of the end of the relevant valuation calendar year. If the single sum distribution is being made in the calendar year containing the required beginning date and the required minimum distribution for the employee's first distribution calendar year has not been distributed, the portion of the single sum distribution that represents the required minimum distribution for the employee's first and second distribution calendar years is not eligible for rollover.

(2) The portion of the single sum distribution that is a required minimum distribution is permitted to be determined by expressing the employee's benefit as an annuity that would satisfy this section with an annuity starting date as of the first day of the distribution calendar year for which the required minimum distribution is being determined, and treating one year of annuity payments as the required minimum distribution for that year, and not eligible for rollover. If the single sum distribution is being made in the calendar year containing the required beginning date and the required minimum distribution for the employee's first distribution calendar year has not been made, the benefit must be expressed as an annuity with an annuity starting date as of the first day of the first distribution calendar year and the payments for the first two distribution calendar years would be treated as required minimum distributions, and not eligible for rollover.

(e) *Death benefits.* The rule in paragraph (a) of this A-1, prohibiting increasing payments under an annuity applies to payments made upon the death of an employee. However, for purposes of this section, an ancillary death benefit described in this paragraph (e) may be disregarded in applying that rule. Such an ancillary death benefit is excluded in determining an employee's entire interest and the rules prohibiting increasing payments do not apply to such an ancillary death benefit. A death benefit with respect to an employee's benefit is an ancillary death benefit for purposes of this A-1 if—

(1) It is not paid as part of the employee's accrued benefit or under any optional form of the employee's benefit; and

(2) The death benefit, together with any other potential payments with respect to the employee's benefit that may be provided to a survivor, satisfy the incidental benefit requirement of § 1.401-1(b)(1)(i).

(f) *Additional guidance.* Additional guidance regarding how distributions under a defined benefit plan must be paid in order to satisfy section 401(a)(9) may be issued by the Commissioner in revenue rulings, notices, or other guidance published in the Internal Revenue Bulletin. See § 601.601(d)(2)(ii)(b) of this chapter.

Q-2. How must distributions in the form of a life (or joint and survivor) annuity be made in order to satisfy the minimum distribution incidental benefit (MDIB) requirement of section 401(a)(9)(G) and the distribution component of the incidental benefit requirement of § 1.401-1(b)(1)(i)?

A-2. (a) *Life annuity for employee.* If the employee's benefit is payable in the form of a life annuity for the life of the employee satisfying section 401(a)(9) without regard to the MDIB requirement, the MDIB requirement of section 401(a)(9)(G) will be satisfied.

(b) *Joint and survivor annuity, spouse beneficiary.* If the employee's sole beneficiary, as of the annuity starting date for annuity payments, is the employee's spouse and the distributions satisfy section 401(a)(9) without regard to the MDIB requirement, the distributions to the employee will be deemed to satisfy the MDIB requirement of section 401(a)(9)(G). For example, if an employee's benefit is being distributed in the form of a joint and survivor annuity for the lives of the employee and the employee's spouse and the spouse is the sole beneficiary of the employee, the amount of the periodic payment payable to the spouse would not violate the MDIB requirement if it was 100 percent of the annuity payment payable to the employee, regardless of the difference in the ages between the employee and the employee's spouse.

(c) *Joint and survivor annuity, nonspouse beneficiary*—(1) *Explanation of rule.* If distributions commence under a distribution option that is in the form of a joint and survivor annuity for the joint lives of the employee and a beneficiary other than the employee's spouse, the minimum distribution incidental benefit requirement will not be satisfied as of the date distributions commence unless under the distribution option, the annuity payments to be made on and after the employee's required beginning date will satisfy the conditions of this paragraph (c). The periodic annuity payment payable to the survivor must not at any time on and after the employee's required beginning date exceed the applicable percentage of the annuity payment payable to the employee using the table in paragraph (c)(2) of this A-2. The applicable percentage is based on the adjusted employee/beneficiary age difference. The adjusted employee/beneficiary age difference is determined by first calculating the excess of the age of the employee over the age of the beneficiary based on their ages on their birthdays in a calendar year. Then, if the employee is younger than age 70, the age difference determined in the previous sentence is reduced by the number of years that the employee is younger than age 70 on the employee's birthday in the calendar year that contains the annuity starting date. In the case of an annuity that provides for increasing payments, the requirement of this paragraph (c) will not be violated merely because benefit payments to the beneficiary increase, provided the increase is determined in the same manner for the employee and the beneficiary.

(2) *Table.*

Excess of age of employee over age of beneficiary	*Applicable percentage*
10 years or less	100%
11	96%
12	93%
13	90%
14	87%
15	84%
16	82%
17	79%
18	77%
19	75%
20	73%
21	72%
22	70%
23	68%
24	67%
25	66%
26	64%
27	63%
28	62%
29	61%
30	60%
31	59%
32	59%
33	58%
34	57%
35	56%
36	56%
37	55%
38	55%
39	54%
40	54%
41	53%
42	53%
43	53%
44 and greater	52%

(3) *Example.* This paragraph (c) is illustrated by the following example:

Example. Distributions commence on January 1, 2003 to an employee (Z), born March 1, 1937, after retirement at age 65. Z's daughter (Y), born February 5, 1967, is Z's beneficiary. The distributions are in the form of a joint and survivor annuity for the lives of Z and Y with payments of $500 a month to Z and upon Z's death of $500 a month to Y, i.e., the projected monthly payment to Y is 100 percent of the monthly amount payable to Z. Accordingly, under A-10 of this section, compliance with the rules of this section is determined as of the annuity starting date. The adjusted employee/beneficiary age difference is calculated by taking the excess of the employee's age over the beneficiary's age and subtracting the number of years the employee is younger than age 70. In this case, Z is 30 years older than Y and is commencing benefit 4 years before attaining age 70 so the adjusted employee/beneficiary age difference is 26 years. Under the table in paragraph (c)(2) of this A-2, the applicable percentage for a 26-year adjusted employee/beneficiary age difference is 64 percent. As of January 1, 2003 (the annuity starting date) the plan does not satisfy the MDIB requirement because, as of such date, the distribution option provides that, as of Z's required beginning date, the monthly payment to Y upon Z's death will exceed 66 percent of Z's monthly payment.

(d) *Period certain and annuity features.* If a distribution form includes a period certain, the amount of the annuity payments payable to the beneficiary need not be reduced during the period certain, but in the case of a joint and survivor annuity with a period certain, the amount of the annuity payments payable to the beneficiary must satisfy paragraph (c) of this A-2 after the expiration of the period certain.

(e) *Deemed satisfaction of incidental benefit rule.* Except in the case of distributions with respect to an employee's benefit that include an ancillary death benefit described in paragraph A-1(e) of this section, to the extent the incidental benefit requirement of § 1.401-1(b)(1)(i) requires a distribution, that requirement is deemed to be satisfied if distributions satisfy the minimum distribution incidental benefit requirement of this A-2. If the employee's benefits include an ancillary death benefit described in paragraph A-1(e) of this section, the benefits (including the ancillary death benefit) must be distributed in accordance with the incidental benefit requirement described in § 1.401-1(b)(1)(i) and the benefits (excluding the ancillary death benefit) must also satisfy the minimum distribution incidental benefit requirement of this A-2.

* * *

Q-14. Are annuity payments permitted to increase?

A-14. (a) *General rules.* Except as otherwise provided in this section, all annuity payments (whether paid over an employee's life, joint lives, or a period certain) must be nonincreasing or increase only in accordance with one or more of the following—

(1) With an annual percentage increase that does not exceed the percentage increase in an eligible cost-of-living index as defined in paragraph (b) of this A-14 for a 12-month period ending in the year during which the increase occurs or the prior year;

(2) With a percentage increase that occurs at specified times (e.g., at specified ages) and does not exceed the cumulative total of annual percentage increases in an eligible cost-of-living index as defined in paragraph (b) of this A-14 since the annuity starting date, or if later, the date of the most recent percentage increase. However, in cases providing such a cumulative increase, an actuarial increase may not be provided to reflect the fact that increases were not provided in the interim years;

(3) To the extent of the reduction in the amount of the employee's payments to provide for a survivor benefit, but only if there is no longer a survivor benefit because the beneficiary whose life was being used to determine the period described in section 401(a)(9)(A)(ii) over which payments were being made dies or is no longer the employee's beneficiary pursuant to a qualified domestic relations order within the meaning of section 414(p);

(4) To pay increased benefits that result from a plan amendment;

(5) To allow a beneficiary to convert the survivor portion of a joint and survivor annuity into a single sum distribution upon the employee's death; or

(6) To the extent increases are permitted in accordance with paragraph (c) or (d) of this A-14.

(b)(1) For purposes of this A-14, an eligible cost-of-living index means an index described in paragraphs (b)(2), (b)(3), or (b)(4) of this A-14.

(2) A consumer price index that is based on prices of all items (or all items excluding food and energy) and issued by the Bureau of Labor Statistics, including an index for a specific population (such as urban consumers or urban wage earners and clerical workers) and an index for a geographic area or areas (such as a given metropolitan area or state).

(3) A percentage adjustment based on a cost-of-living index described in paragraph (b)(2) of this A-14, or a fixed percentage if less. In any year when the cost-of-living index is lower than the fixed percentage, the fixed percentage may be treated as an increase in an eligible cost-of-living index, provided it does not exceed the sum of:

(i) The cost-of-living index for that year, and

(ii) The accumulated excess of the annual cost-of-living index from each prior year over the fixed annual percentage used in that year (reduced by any amount previously utilized under this paragraph (b)(3)(ii)).

(4) A percentage adjustment based on the increase in compensation for the position held by the employee at the time of retirement, and provided under either the terms of a governmental plan within the meaning of section 414(d) or under the terms of a nongovernmental plan as in effect on April 17, 2002.

(c) *Additional permitted increases for annuity payments under annuity contracts purchased from insurance companies.* In the case of annuity payments paid from an annuity contract purchased from an insurance company, if the total future expected payments (determined in accordance with paragraph (e)(3) of this A-14) exceed the total value being annuitized (within the meaning of paragraph (e)(1) of this A-14), the payments under the annuity will not fail to satisfy the nonincreasing payment requirement in A-1(a) of this section merely because the payments are increased in accordance with one or more of the following—

(1) By a constant percentage, applied not less frequently than annually;

(2) To provide a final payment upon the death of the employee that does not exceed the excess of the total value being annuitized (within the meaning of paragraph (e)(1) of this A-14) over the total of payments before the death of the employee;

(3) As a result of dividend payments or other payments that result from actuarial gains (within the meaning of paragraph (e)(2) of this A-14), but only if actuarial gain is measured no less frequently than annually and the resulting dividend payments or other payments are either paid no later than the year following the year for which the actuarial experience is measured or paid in the same form as the payment of the annuity over the remaining period of the annuity (beginning no later than the year following the year for which the actuarial experience is measured); and

(4) An acceleration of payments under the annuity (within the meaning of paragraph (e)(4) of this A-14).

(d) *Additional permitted increases for annuity payments from a qualified trust.* In the case of annuity payments paid under a defined benefit plan qualified under section 401(a) (other than annuity payments under an annuity contract purchased from an insurance company that satisfy paragraph (c) of this section), the payments under the annuity will not fail to satisfy the nonincreasing payment requirement in A-1(a) of this section merely because the payments are increased in accordance with one of the following—

(1) By a constant percentage, applied not less frequently than annually, at a rate that is less than 5 percent per year;

(2) To provide a final payment upon the death of the employee that does not exceed the excess of the actuarial present value of the employee's accrued benefit (within the meaning of section 411(a)(7)) calculated as the annuity starting date using the applicable interest

rate and the applicable mortality table under section 417(e) (or, if greater, the total amount of employee contributions) over the total of payments before the death of the employee; or

(3) As a result of dividend payments or other payments that result from actuarial gains (within the meaning of paragraph (e)(2) of this A-14), but only if—

(i) Actuarial gain is measured no less frequently than annually;

(ii) The resulting dividend payments or other payments are either paid no later than the year following the year for which the actuarial experience is measured or paid in the same form as the payment of the annuity over the remaining period of the annuity (beginning no later than the year following the year for which the actuarial experience is measured);

(iii) The actuarial gain taken into account is limited to actuarial gain from investment experience;

(iv) The assumed interest used to calculate such actuarial gains is not less than 3 percent; and

(v) The payments are not increasing by a constant percentage as described in paragraph (d)(1) of this A-14.

* * *

§ 1.401(a)(9)-7. Rollovers and Transfers.

Q-1. If an amount is distributed by one plan (distributing plan) and is rolled over to another plan, is the required minimum distribution under the distributing plan affected by the rollover?

A-1. No, if an amount is distributed by one plan and is rolled over to another plan, the amount distributed is still treated as a distribution by the distributing plan for purposes of section 401(a)(9), notwithstanding the rollover. See A-1 of § 1.402(c)-2 for the definition of a rollover and A-7 of § 1.402(c)-2 for rules for determining the portion of any distribution that is not eligible for rollover because it is a required minimum distribution.

Q-2. If an amount is distributed by one plan (distributing plan) and is rolled over to another plan (receiving plan), how are the benefit and the required minimum distribution under the receiving plan affected?

A-2. If an amount is distributed by one plan (distributing plan) and is rolled over to another plan (receiving plan), the benefit of the employee under the receiving plan is increased by the amount rolled over for purposes of determining the required minimum distribution for the calendar year immediately following the calendar year in which the amount rolled over is distributed. If the amount rolled over is received after the last valuation date in the calendar year under the receiving plan, the benefit of the employee as of such valuation date, adjusted in accordance with A-3 of § 1.401(a)(9)-5, will be increased by the rollover amount valued as of the date of receipt. In addition, if the amount rolled over is received in a different calendar year from the calendar year in which it is distributed, the amount rolled over is deemed to have been received by the receiving plan in the calendar year in which it was distributed.

Q-3. In the case of a transfer of an amount of an employee's benefit from one plan (transferor plan) to another plan (transferee plan), are there any special rules for satisfying section 401(a)(9) or determining the employee's benefit under the transferor plan?

A-3. (a) In the case of a transfer of an amount of an employee's benefit from one plan (transferor plan) to another (transferee plan), the transfer is not treated as a distribution by the transferor plan for purposes of section 401(a)(9). Instead, the benefit of the employee under the transferor plan is decreased by the amount transferred. However, if any portion of an employee's benefit is transferred in a distribution calendar year with respect to that employee, in order to satisfy section 401(a)(9), the transferor plan must determine the amount of the required minimum distribution with respect to that employee for the calendar year of the transfer using the employee's benefit under the transferor plan before the transfer. Additionally, if any portion of an employee's benefit is transferred in the employee's second distribution calendar year but on or before the employee's required beginning date, in order to satisfy section 401(a)(9), the transferor plan must determine the amount of the minimum distribution requirement for the employee's first distribution calendar year based on the employee's benefit under the transferor plan before the transfer. The transferor plan may satisfy the minimum distribution requirement for the calendar year of the transfer (and the prior year if applicable) by segregating the amount which must be distributed from the employee's benefit and not transferring that amount. Such amount may be retained by the transferor plan and must be distributed on or before the date required under section 401(a)(9).

(b) For purposes of determining any required minimum distribution for the calendar year immediately following the calendar year in which the transfer occurs, in the case of a transfer after the last valuation date for the calendar year of the transfer under the transferor plan, the benefit of the employee as of such valuation date, adjusted in accordance with A-3 of § 1.401(a)(9)-5, will be decreased by the amount transferred, valued as of the date of the transfer.

Q-4. If an amount of an employee's benefit is transferred from one plan (transferor plan) to another plan (transferee plan), how are the benefit and the required minimum distribution under the transferee plan affected?

A-4. In the case of a transfer from one plan (transferor plan) to another (transferee plan), the benefit of the employee under the transferee plan is increased by the amount transferred in the same manner as if it were a plan receiving a rollover contribution under A-2 of this section.

Q-5. How is a spinoff, merger or consolidation (as defined in § 1.414(l)-1) treated for purposes of determining an employee's benefit and required minimum distribution under section 401(a)(9)?

A-5. For purposes of determining an employee's benefit and required minimum distribution under section 401(a)(9), a spinoff, a merger, or a consolidation (as defined in § 1.414(l)-1) will be treated as a transfer of the benefits of the employees involved. Consequently, the benefit and required minimum distribution of each employee involved under the transferor and transferee plans will be determined in accordance with A-3 and A-4 of this section.

§ 1.401(a)(9)-9. Life expectancy and distribution period tables.

Q-1. What is the life expectancy for an individual for purposes of determining required minimum distributions under section 401(a)(9)?

A-1. The following table, referred to as the Single Life Table, is used for determining the life expectancy of an individual:

Single Life Table

Age	*Life Expectancy*	*Age*	*Life Expectancy*	*Age*	*Life Expectancy*	*Age*	*Life Expectancy*
0	82.4	29	54.3	58	27.0	87	6.7
1	81.6	30	53.3	59	26.1	88	6.3
2	80.6	31	52.4	60	25.2	89	5.9
3	79.7	32	51.4	61	24.4	90	5.5
4	78.7	33	50.4	62	23.5	91	5.2
5	77.7	34	49.4	63	22.7	92	4.9
6	76.7	35	48.5	64	21.8	93	4.6
7	75.8	36	47.5	65	21.0	94	4.3
8	74.8	37	46.5	66	20.2	95	4.1
9	73.8	38	45.6	67	19.4	96	3.8
10	72.8	39	44.6	68	18.6	97	3.6
11	71.8	40	43.6	69	17.8	98	3.4
12	70.8	41	42.7	70	17.0	99	3.1
13	69.9	42	41.7	71	16.3	100	2.9
14	68.9	43	40.7	72	15.5	101	2.7
15	67.9	44	39.8	73	14.8	102	2.5
16	66.9	45	38.8	74	14.1	103	2.3
17	66.0	46	37.9	75	13.4	104	2.1
18	65.0	47	37.0	76	12.7	105	1.9
19	64.0	48	36.0	77	12.1	106	1.7
20	63.0	49	35.1	78	11.4	107	1.5
21	62.1	50	34.2	79	10.8	108	1.4
22	61.1	51	33.3	80	10.2	109	1.2
23	60.1	52	32.3	81	9.7	110	1.1
24	59.1	53	31.4	82	9.1	111+	1.0
25	58.2	54	30.5	83	8.6		
26	57.2	55	29.6	84	8.1		
27	56.2	56	28.7	85	7.6		
28	55.3	57	27.9	86	7.1		

Q-2. What is the applicable distribution period for an individual account for purposes of determining required minimum distributions during an employee's lifetime under section 401(a)(9)?

A-2. Table for determining distribution period. The following table, referred to as the Uniform Lifetime Table, is used for determining the distribution period for lifetime distributions to an employee in situations in which the employee's spouse is either not the sole designated beneficiary or is the sole designated beneficiary but is not more than 10 years younger than the employee.

Uniform Lifetime Table

Age of the employee	*Distribution period*
70	27.4
71	26.5
72	25.6
73	24.7
74	23.8
75	22.9
76	22.0
77	21.2
78	20.3
79	19.5
80	18.7
81	17.9
82	17.1
83	16.3
84	15.5
85	14.8
86	14.1
87	13.4
88	12.7
89	12.0
90	11.4
91	10.8
92	10.2
93	9.6
94	9.1
95	8.6
96	8.1
97	7.6
98	7.1
99	6.7
100	6.3
101	5.9
102	5.5
103	5.2
104	4.9
105	4.5
106	4.2
107	3.9
108	3.7
109	3.4
110	3.1
111	2.9
112	2.6
113	2.4
114	2.1
115 and older	1.9

Q-3. What is the joint life and last survivor expectancy of an individual and beneficiary for purposes of determining required minimum distributions under section 401(a)(9)?

A-3. The following table, referred to as the Joint and Last Survivor Table, is used for determining the joint and last survivor life expectancy of two individuals:

Joint and Last Survivor Table

* * *

§ 1.401(a)(17)-1. Limitation on annual compensation.

* * *

(c) *Limit on compensation for nondiscrimination rules*—(1) *General rule*. The annual compensation limit applies for purposes of applying the nondiscrimination rules under sections 401(a)(4), 401(a)(5), 401(l), 401(k)(3), 401(m)(2), 403(b)(12), 404(a)(2) and 410(b)(2). The annual compensation limit also applies in determining whether an alternative method of determining compensation impermissibly discriminates under section 414(s)(3). Thus, for example, the annual compensation limit applies when determining a self-employed individual's total earned income that is used to determine the equivalent alternative compensation amount under § 1.414(s)-1(g)(1). This paragraph (c) provides rules for applying the annual compensation limit for these purposes. For purposes of this paragraph (c), compensation means the compensation used in applying the applicable nondiscrimination rule.

* * *

§ 1.401(a)(26)-1. Minimum participation requirements.

* * *

(b) *Exceptions to section 401(a)(26)*—(1) Plans that do not benefit any highly compensated employees. A plan, other than a frozen defined benefit plan as defined in § 1.401(a)(26)-2(b), satisfies section 401(a)(26) for a plan year if the plan is not a top-heavy plan under section 416 and the plan meets the following requirements:

(i) The plan benefits no highly compensated employee or highly compensated former employee of the employer; and

(ii) The plan is not aggregated with any other plan of the employer to enable the other plan to satisfy section 401(a)(4) or 410(b). The plan may, however, be aggregated with the employer's other plans for purposes of the average benefit percentage test in section 410(b)(2)(A)(ii).

* * *

§ 1.401(a)(31)-1. Requirement to offer direct rollover of eligible rollover distributions; questions and answers.

* * *

Q-3: What is a direct rollover that satisfies section 401(a)(31), and how is it accomplished?

A-3: A direct rollover that satisfies section 401(a)(31) is an eligible rollover distribution that is paid directly to an eligible retirement plan for the benefit of the distributee. A direct rollover may be accomplished by any reasonable means of direct payment to an eligible retirement plan. Reasonable means of direct payment include, for example, a wire transfer or the mailing of a check to the eligible retirement plan. If payment is made by check, the check must be negotiable only by the trustee of the eligible retirement plan. If the payment is made by wire transfer, the wire transfer must be directed only to the trustee of the eligible retirement plan. In the case of an eligible retirement plan that does not have a trustee (such as a custodial individual retirement account or an individual retirement annuity), the custodian of the plan or issuer of the contract under the plan, as appropriate, should be substituted for the trustee for purposes of this Q&A-3, and Q&A-4 of this section.

Q-4: Is providing a distributee with a check for delivery to an eligible retirement plan a reasonable means of accomplishing a direct rollover?

A-4: Providing the distributee with a check and instructing the distributee to deliver the check to the eligible retirement plan is a reasonable means of direct payment, provided that the check is made payable as follows: [Name of the trustee] as trustee of [name of the eligible retirement plan]. For example, if the name of the eligible retirement plan is "Individual Retirement Account of John Q. Smith," and the name of the trustee is "ABC Bank," the payee line of a check would read "ABC Bank as trustee of Individual Retirement Account of John Q. Smith." Unless the name of the distributee is included in the name of the eligible retirement plan, the check also must indicate that it is for the benefit of the distributee. If the eligible retirement plan is not an individual retirement account or an individual retirement annuity, the payee line of the check need not identify the trustee by name. For example, the payee line of a check for the benefit of distributee Jane Doe might read, "Trustee of XYZ Corporation Savings Plan FBO Jane Doe."

* * *

§ 1.401(b)-1. Certain retroactive changes in plan.

(a) *General rule*. Under section 401(b) a stock bonus, pension, profit- sharing, annuity, or bond purchase plan which does not satisfy the requirements of section 401(a) on any day solely as a result of a disqualifying provision (as defined in paragraph (b) of this section) shall be considered to have satisfied such requirements on such date if, on or before the last day of the remedial amendment period (as determined under paragraphs (d), (e) and (f) of this section) with respect to such disqualifying provision, all provisions of the plan which are necessary to satisfy all requirements of sections 401(a), 403(a), or 405(a) are in effect and have been made effective for all purposes for the whole of such period. Under some facts and circumstances, it may not be possible to amend a plan retroactively so that all provisions of the plan which are necessary to satisfy the requirements of section 401(a) are in fact made effective for the whole remedial amendment period. If it is not possible, the requirements of this section will not be satisfied even if the employer adopts a retroactive plan amendment which, in form, appears to satisfy such requirements. Section 401(b) does not permit a plan to be made retroactively effective, for qualification purposes, for a taxable year prior to the taxable year of the employer in which the plan was adopted by such employer.

(b) *Disqualifying provisions*. For purposes of this section, with respect to a plan described in paragraph (a) of this section, the term "disqualifying provision" means:

(1) A provision of a new plan, the absence of a provision from a new plan, or an amendment to an existing plan, which causes such plan to fail to satisfy the requirements of the Code applicable to qualification of such plan as of the date such plan or amendment is first made effective

* * *

(3) A plan provision designated by the Commissioner, at the Commissioner's discretion, as a disqualifying provision that either—

(i) Results in the failure of the plan to satisfy the qualification requirements of the Internal Revenue Code by reason of a change in those requirements; or

(ii) Is integral to a qualification requirement of the Internal Revenue Code that has been changed.

(c) *Special rules applicable to disqualifying provisions*—(1) *Absence of plan provision*. For purposes of paragraphs (b)(2) and (3) of this section, a disqualifying provision includes the absence from a plan of a provision required by, or, if applicable, integral to the applicable change to the qualification requirements of the Internal Revenue Code, if the plan was in effect on the date the change became effective with respect to the plan.

(2) *Method of designating disqualifying provisions*. The Commissioner may designate a plan provision as a disqualifying provision pursuant to paragraph (b)(3) of this section only in revenue rulings, notices, and other guidance published in the Internal Revenue Bulletin. See § 601.601(d)(2) of this chapter.

(3) *Authority to impose limitations*. In the case of a provision that has been designated as a disqualifying provision by the Commissioner pursuant to paragraph (b)(3) of this section, the Commissioner may impose limits and provide additional rules regarding the amendments that may be made with respect to that disqualifying provision during the remedial amendment period. The Commissioner may provide guidance in revenue rulings, notices, and other guidance published in the Internal Revenue Bulletin. See § 601.601(d)(2) of this chapter.

(d) *Remedial amendment period*. (1) The remedial amendment period with respect to a disqualifying provision begins:

(i) In the case of a provision of, or absence of a provision from, a new plan, described in paragraph (b)(1) of this section, the date the plan is put into effect,

(ii) In the case of an amendment to an existing plan, described in paragraph (b)(1) of this section, the date the plan amendment is adopted or put into effect (whichever is earlier),

* * *

(iv) In the case of a disqualifying provision described in paragraph (b)(3)(i) of this section, the date on which the change effected by an amendment to the Internal Revenue Code became effective with respect to the plan; or

(v) In the case of a disqualifying provision described in paragraph (b)(3)(ii) of this section, the first day on which the plan was operated in accordance with such provision, as amended, unless another time is specified by the Commissioner in revenue rulings, notices, and other guidance published in the Internal Revenue Bulletin. See § 601.601(d)(2) of this chapter.

(2) Unless further extended as provided by paragraph (e) of this section, the remedial amendment period ends with the latest of:

(i) In the case of a plan maintained by one employer, the time prescribed by law, including extensions, for filing the income tax return (or partnership return of income) of the employer for the employer's taxable year in which falls the latest of:

(A) The date on which the remedial amendment period begins.

(B) The date on which a plan amendment described in paragraph (b)(1) of this section is adopted, or

(C) The date on which a plan amendment described in paragraph (b)(1) of this section is made effective,

(ii) In the case of a plan maintained by one employer, the last day of the plan year within which falls the latest of:

(A) The date on which the remedial amendment period begins,

(B) The date on which a plan amendment described in paragraph (b)(1) of this section is adopted, or

(C) The date on which a plan amendment described in paragraph (b)(1) of this section is made effective,

* * *

(f) *Discretionary extensions.* At his discretion, the Commissioner may extend the remedial amendment period or may allow a particular plan to be amended after the expiration of its remedial amendment period and any applicable extension of such period. In determining whether such an extension will be granted, the Commissioner shall consider, among other factors, whether substantial hardship to the employer would result if such an extension were not granted, whether such an extension is in the best interest of plan participants, and whether the granting of the extension is adverse to the interests of the Government.

* * *

§ 1.401(k)-1. Certain cash or deferred arrangements.

(a) *General rules*—(1) *Certain plans permitted to include cash or deferred arrangements.* A plan, other than a profit-sharing, stock bonus, pre-ERISA money purchase pension, or rural cooperative plan, does not satisfy the requirements of section 401(a) if the plan includes a cash or deferred arrangement. A profit-sharing, stock bonus, pre-ERISA money purchase pension, or rural cooperative plan does not fail to satisfy the requirements of section 401(a) merely because the plan includes a cash or deferred arrangement. A cash or deferred arrangement is part of a plan for purposes of this section if any contributions to the plan, or accruals or other benefits under the plan, are made or provided pursuant to the cash or deferred arrangement.

(2) Rules applicable to cash or deferred arrangements generally—(i) *Definition of cash or deferred arrangement.* Except as provided in paragraphs (a)(2)(ii) and (iii) of this section, a cash or deferred arrangement is an arrangement under which an eligible employee may make a cash or deferred election with respect to contributions to, or accruals or other benefits under, a plan that is intended to satisfy the requirements of section 401(a) (including a contract that is intended to satisfy the requirements of section 403(a)).

(ii) *Treatment of after-tax employee contributions.* A cash or deferred arrangement does not include an arrangement under which amounts contributed under a plan at an employee's election are designated or treated at the time of contribution as after-tax employee contributions (e.g., by treating the contributions as taxable income subject to applicable withholding requirements). See also section 414(h)(1). A designated Roth contribution, however, is not treated as an after-tax contribution for purposes of this section, § 1.401(k)-2 through § 1.401(k)-6 and § 1.401(m)-1 through § 1.401(m)- 5. A contribution can be an after-tax employee contribution under the rule of this paragraph (a)(2)(ii) even if the employee's election to make after-tax employee contributions is made before the amounts subject to the election are currently available to the employee.

(iii) *Treatment of ESOP dividend election.* A cash or deferred arrangement does not include an arrangement under an ESOP under which dividends are either distributed or invested pursuant to an election made by participants or their beneficiaries in accordance with section 404(k)(2)(A)(iii).

(iv) *Treatment of elective contributions as plan assets.* The extent to which elective contributions constitute plan assets for purposes of the prohibited transaction provisions of section 4975 and Title I of the Employee Retirement Income Security Act of 1974 is determined in accordance with regulations and rulings issued by the Department of Labor. See 29 CFR 2510.3-102.

(3) *Rules applicable to cash or deferred elections generally*—(i) *Definition of cash or deferred election.* A cash or deferred election is any direct or indirect election (or modification of an earlier election) by an employee to have the employer either—

(A) Provide an amount to the employee in the form of cash (or some other taxable benefit) that is not currently available; or

(B) Contribute an amount to a trust, or provide an accrual or other benefit, under a plan deferring the receipt of compensation.

(ii) *Automatic enrollment.* For purposes of determining whether an election is a cash or deferred election, it is irrelevant whether the default that applies in the absence of an affirmative election is described in paragraph (a)(3)(i)(A) of this section (i.e., the employee receives an amount in cash or some other taxable benefit) or in paragraph (a)(3)(i)(B) of this section (i.e., the employer contributes an amount to a trust or provides an accrual or other benefit under a plan deferring the receipt of compensation).

(iii) *Rules related to timing*—(A) *Requirement that amounts not be currently available.* A cash or deferred election can only be made with respect to an amount that is not currently available to the employee on the date of the election. Further, a cash or deferred election can only be made with respect to amounts that would (but for the cash or deferred election) become currently available after the later of the date on which the employer adopts the cash or deferred arrangement or the date on which the arrangement first becomes effective.

(B) *Contribution may not precede election.* A contribution is made pursuant to a cash or deferred election only if the contribution is made after the election is made.

(C) *Contribution may not precede services*—(*1*) *General rule.* Contributions are made pursuant to a cash or deferred election only if the contributions are made after the employee's performance of service with respect to which the contributions are made (or when the cash or other taxable benefit would be currently available, if earlier).

(*2*) *Exception for bona fide administrative considerations.* The timing of contributions will not be treated as failing to satisfy the requirements of this paragraph (a)(3)(iii)(C) merely because contributions for a pay period are occasionally made before the services with respect to that pay period are performed, provided the contributions are made early in order to accommodate bona fide administrative considerations (for example, the temporary absence of the bookkeeper with responsibility to transmit contributions to the plan) and are not paid early with a principal purpose of accelerating deductions.

(iv) *Current availability defined.* Cash or another taxable benefit is currently available to the employee if it has been paid to the employee or if the employee is able currently to receive the cash or other taxable benefit at the employee's discretion. An amount is not currently available to an employee if there is a significant limitation or restriction on the employee's right to receive the amount currently. Similarly, an amount is not currently available as of a date if the employee may under no circumstances receive the amount before a particular time in the future. The determination of whether an amount is currently available to an employee does not depend on whether it has been constructively received by the employee for purposes of section 451.

(v) *Certain one-time elections not treated as cash or deferred elections.* A cash or deferred election does not include a one-time irrevocable election made no later than the employee's first becoming eligible under the plan or any other plan or arrangement of the employer that is described in section 219(g)(5)(A) (whether or not such other plan or arrangement has terminated), to have contributions equal to a specified amount or percentage of the employee's compensation (including no amount of compensation) made by the employer on the employee's behalf to the plan and a specified amount or percentage of the employee's compensation (including no amount of compensation) divided among all other plans or arrangements of the employer (including plans or arrangements not yet established) for the duration of the employee's employment with the employer, or in the case of a defined benefit plan to receive accruals or other benefits (including no benefits) under such plans. Thus, for example, employer contributions made pursuant to a one-time irrevocable election described in this paragraph are not treated as having been made pursuant to a cash or deferred election and are not includible in an employee's gross income by reason of § 1.402(a)-1(d).

* * *

(vi) *Tax treatment of employees.* An amount generally is includible in an employee's gross income for the taxable year in which the employee actually or constructively receives the amount. But for section 402(e)(3), an employee is treated as having received an amount that is contributed to an exempt trust or plan described in section 401(a) or 403(a) pursuant to the employee's cash or deferred election. This is the case even if the election to defer is made before the year in which the amount is earned, or before the amount is currently available. See § 1.402(a)-1(d).

(vii) *Examples.* The following examples illustrate the application of this paragraph (a)(3):

Example 1. (i) An employer maintains a profit-sharing plan under which each eligible employee has an election to defer an annual bonus payable on January 30 each year. The bonus equals 10% of compensation during the previous calendar year. Deferred amounts are not treated as after-tax employee contributions. The bonus is currently available on January 30.

(ii) An election made prior to January 30 to defer all or part of the bonus is a cash or deferred election, and the bonus deferral arrangement is a cash or deferred arrangement.

Example 2. (i) An employer maintains a profit-sharing plan which provides for discretionary profit sharing contributions and under which each eligible employee may elect to reduce his compensation by up to 10% and to have the employer contribute such amount to the plan. The employer pays each employee every two weeks for services during the immediately preceding two weeks. The employee's election to defer compensation for a payroll period must be made prior to the date the amount would otherwise be paid. The employer contributes to the plan the amount of compensation that each employee elected to defer, at the time it would otherwise be paid to the employee, and does not treat the contribution as an after-tax employee contribution.

(ii) The election is a cash or deferred election and the contributions are elective contributions.

Example 3. (i) The facts are the same as in Example 2, except that the employer makes a $10,000 contribution on January 31 of the plan year that is in addition to the contributions that satisfy the employer's obligation to make contributions with respect to cash or deferred elections for prior payroll periods. Employee A makes an election on February 15 to defer $2,000 from compensation that is not currently available and the employer reduces the employee's compensation to reflect the election.

(ii) None of the additional $10,000 contributed January 31 is a contribution made pursuant to Employee A's cash or deferred election, because the contribution was made before the election was made. Accordingly, the employer must make an additional contribution of $2,000 in order to satisfy its obligation to contribute an amount to the plan pursuant to Employee A's election. The $10,000 contribution may be allocated under the plan terms providing for discretionary profit sharing contributions.

Example 4. (i) The facts are the same as in Example 3, except that Employee A had an outstanding election to defer $500 from each payroll period's compensation. The $10,000 additional payment that is contributed early is not made early in order to accommodate bona fide administrative considerations.

(ii) None of the additional $10,000 contributed January 31 is a contribution made pursuant to Employee A's cash or deferred election for future payroll periods, because the contribution was made before the earlier of Employee A's performance of services to which the contribution is attributable or when the compensation would be currently available. Furthermore, the exception for early contributions in paragraph (a)(3)(iii)(C)(2) of this section does not apply. Accordingly, the employer must make an additional contribution of $500 per payroll period in order to satisfy its obligation to contribute an amount to the plan pursuant to Employee A's election. The $10,000 contribution may be allocated under the plan terms providing for discretionary profit sharing contributions.

Example 5. (i) Employer B establishes a money purchase pension plan in 1986. This is the first qualified plan established by Employer B. All salaried employees are eligible to participate under the plan. Hourly-paid employees are not eligible to participate under the plan. In 2000, Employer B establishes a profit-sharing plan under which all employees (both salaried and hourly) are eligible. Employer B permits all employees on the effective date of the profit-sharing plan to make a one-time irrevocable election to have Employer B contribute 5% of compensation on their behalf to the plan and make no other contribution to any other plan of Employer B (including plans not yet established) for the duration of the employee's employment with Employer B, and have their salaries reduced by 5%.

(ii) The election provided under the profit-sharing plan is not a one-time irrevocable election within the meaning of paragraph (a)(3)(v) of this section with respect to the salaried employees of Employer B who, before becoming eligible to participate under the profit-sharing plan, became eligible to participate under the money purchase pension plan. The election under the profit-sharing plan is a one-time irrevocable election within the meaning of paragraph (a)(3)(v) of this section with respect to the hourly employees, because they were not previously eligible to participate under another plan of the employer.

(4) *Rules applicable to qualified cash or deferred arrangements*—(i) *Definition of qualified cash or deferred arrangement.* A qualified cash or deferred arrangement is a cash or deferred arrangement that satisfies the requirements of paragraphs (b), (c), (d), and (e) of this section.

(ii) *Treatment of elective contributions as employer contributions.* Except as otherwise provided in § 1.401(k)-2(b)(3), elective contributions under a qualified cash or deferred arrangement (including designated Roth contributions) are treated as employer contributions. Thus, for example, elective contributions under such an arrangement are treated as employer contributions for purposes of sections 401(a), 401(k), 402, 404, 409, 411, 412, 415, 416, and 417.

(iii) *Tax treatment of employees.* Except as provided in section 402(g), 402A (effective for taxable years beginning after December 31, 2005), or § 1.401(k)- 2(b)(3), elective contributions under a qualified cash or deferred arrangement are neither includible in an employee's gross income at the time the cash would have been includible in the employee's gross income (but for the cash or deferred election), nor at the time the elective contributions are contributed to the plan. See § 1.402(a)-1(d)(2)(i).

(iv) *Application of nondiscrimination requirements to plan that includes a qualified cash or deferred arrangement*—(A) *Exclusive means of amounts testing.* Elective contributions (including elective contributions that are designated Roth contributions) under a qualified cash or deferred arrangement satisfy the requirements of section 401(a)(4) with respect to amounts if and only if the amount of elective contributions satisfies the nondiscrimination test of section 401(k) under paragraph (b)(1) of this section. See § 1.401(a)(4)-1(b)(2)(ii)(B).

(B) *Testing benefits, rights and features.* A plan that includes a qualified cash or deferred arrangement must satisfy the requirements of section 401(a)(4) with respect to benefits, rights and features in addition to the requirements regarding amounts described in paragraph (a)(4)(iv)(A) of this section. For example, the right to make each level of elective contributions under a cash or deferred arrangement and the right to make designated Roth contributions are rights or features subject to the requirements of section 401(a)(4). See § 1.401(a)(4)-4(e)(3)(i) and (iii)(D). Thus, for example, if all employees are eligible to make a stated level of elective contributions under a cash or deferred arrangement, but that level of contributions can only be made from compensation in excess of a stated amount, such as the Social Security taxable wage base, the arrangement will generally favor HCEs with respect to the availability of elective contributions and thus will generally not satisfy the requirements of section 401(a)(4).

(C) *Minimum coverage requirement.* A qualified cash or deferred arrangement is treated as a separate plan that must satisfy the requirements of section 410(b). See § 1.410(b)-7(c)(1) for special rules. The determination of whether a cash or deferred arrangement satisfies the requirements of section 410(b) must be made without regard to the modifications to the disaggregation rules set forth in paragraph (b)(4)(v) of this section. See also § 1.401(a)(4)-11(g)(3)(vii)(A), relating to corrective amendments that may be made to satisfy the minimum coverage requirements of section 410(b).

(5) *Rules applicable to nonqualified cash or deferred arrangements*—(i) *Definition of nonqualified cash or deferred arrangement.* A nonqualified cash or deferred arrangement is a cash or deferred arrangement that fails to satisfy one or more of the requirements in paragraph (b), (c), (d) or (e) of this section.

(ii) *Treatment of elective contributions as nonelective contributions.* Except as specifically provided otherwise, elective contributions under a nonqualified cash or deferred arrangement are treated as nonelective employer contributions. Thus, for example, the elective contributions under such an arrangement are treated as nonelective employer contributions for purposes of sections 401(a) (including section 401(a)(4)) and 401(k), 404, 409, 411, 412, 415, 416, and 417 and are not subject to the requirements of section 401(m).

(iii) *Tax treatment of employees.* Elective contributions under a nonqualified cash or deferred arrangement are includible in an employee's gross income at the time the cash or other taxable amount that the employee would have received (but for the cash or deferred election) would have been includible in the employee's gross income. See § 1.402(a)-1(d)(1).

(iv) *Qualification of plan that includes a nonqualified cash or deferred arrangement*—(A) *In general.* A profit-sharing, stock bonus, pre-ERISA money purchase pension, or rural cooperative plan does not fail to satisfy the requirements of section 401(a) merely because the plan includes a nonqualified cash or deferred arrangement. In determining whether the plan satisfies the requirements of section 401(a)(4), the nondiscrimination tests of sections 401(k), paragraph (b)(1) of this section, section 401(m)(2) and § 1.401(m)-1(b) may not be used. See §§ 1.401(a)(4)-1(b)(2)(ii)(B) and 1.410(b)-9 (definition of section 401(k) plan).

(B) *Application of section 401(a)(4) to certain plans.* The amount of employer contributions under a nonqualified cash or deferred arrangement is treated as satisfying section 401(a)(4) if the arrangement is part of a collectively bargained plan that automatically satisfies the requirements of section 410(b). See §§ 1.401(a)(4)-(c)(5) and 1.410(b)-2(b)(7). Additionally, the requirements of sections 401(a)(4) and 410(b) do not apply to a governmental plan (within the meaning of section 414(d)) maintained by a State or local government or political subdivision thereof (or agency or instrumentality thereof). See sections 401(a)(5) and 410(c)(1)(A).

(v) *Example.* The following example illustrates the application of this paragraph (a)(5):

Example. (i) For the 2006 plan year, Employer A maintains a collectively bargained plan that includes a cash or deferred arrangement. Employer contributions under the cash or deferred arrangement do not satisfy the nondiscrimination test of section 401(k) and paragraph (b) of this section.

(ii) The arrangement is a nonqualified cash or deferred arrangement. The employer contributions under the cash or deferred arrangement are considered to be nondiscriminatory under section 401(a)(4), and the elective contributions are generally treated as employer contributions under paragraph (a)(5)(ii) of this section. Under paragraph (a)(5)(iii) of this section and under § 1.402(a)-1(d)(1), however, the elective contributions are includible in each employee's gross income.

(6) *Rules applicable to cash or deferred arrangements of self-employed individuals*—(i) *Application of general rules.* Generally, a partnership or sole proprietorship is permitted to maintain a cash or deferred arrangement, and individual partners or owners are permitted to make cash or deferred elections with respect to compensation attributable to services rendered to the entity, under the same rules that apply to other cash or deferred arrangements. For example, any contributions made on behalf of an individual partner or owner pursuant to a cash or deferred arrangement of a partnership or sole proprietorship are elective contributions unless they are designated or treated as after-tax employee contributions. In the case of a partnership, a cash or deferred arrangement includes any arrangement that directly or indirectly permits individual partners to vary the amount of contributions made on their behalf. Consistent with § 1.402(a)-1(d), the elective contributions under such an arrangement are includible in income and are not deductible under section 404(a) unless the arrangement is a qualified cash or deferred arrangement (i.e., the requirements of section 401(k) and this section are satisfied). Also, even if the arrangement is a qualified cash or deferred arrangement, the elective contributions are includible in gross income and are not deductible under section 404(a) to the extent they exceed the applicable limit under section 402(g). See also § 1.401(a)-30.

(ii) *Treatment of matching contributions made on behalf of self-employed individuals.* Under section 402(g)(8), matching contributions made on behalf of a self-employed individual are not treated as elective contributions made pursuant to a cash or deferred election, without regard to whether such matching contributions indirectly permit individual partners to vary the amount of contributions made on their behalf.

(iii) *Timing of self-employed individual's cash or deferred election.* For purposes of paragraph (a)(3)(iv) of this section, a partner's compensation is deemed currently available on the last day of the partnership taxable year and a sole proprietor's compensation is deemed currently available on the last day of the individual's taxable year. Accordingly, a self-employed individual may not make a cash or deferred election with respect to compensation for a partnership or sole proprietorship taxable year after the last day of that year. See § 1.401(k)-2(a)(4)(ii) for the rules regarding when these contributions are treated as allocated.

(iv) *Special rule for certain payments to self-employed individuals.* For purposes of sections 401(k) and 401(m), the earned income of a self-employed individual for a taxable year constitutes payment for services during that year. Thus, for example, if a partnership provides for cash advance payments during the taxable year to be made to a partner based on the value of the partner's services prior to the date of payment (and which do not exceed a reasonable estimate of the partner's earned income for the taxable year), a contribution of a portion of these payments to a profit sharing plan in accordance with an election to defer the portion of the advance payments does not fail to be made pursuant to a cash or deferred election within the meaning of paragraph (a)(3)(iii) of this section merely because the contribution is made before the amount of the partner's earned income is finally determined and reported. However, see § 1.401(k)-2(a)(4)(ii) for rules on when earned income is treated as received.

* * *

(d) *Distribution limitation*—(1) *General rule.* A cash or deferred arrangement satisfies this paragraph (d) only if amounts attributable to elective contributions may not be distributed before one of the following events, and any distributions so permitted also satisfy the additional requirements of paragraphs (d)(2) through (5) of this section (to the extent applicable)—

(i) The employee's death, disability, or severance from employment;

(ii) In the case of a profit-sharing, stock bonus or rural cooperative plan, the employee's attainment of age 59 1/2 , or the employee's hardship; or

(iii) The termination of the plan.

(2) *Rules applicable to distributions upon severance from employment.* An employee has a severance from employment when the employee ceases to be an employee of the employer maintaining the plan. An employee does not have a severance from employment if, in connection with a change of employment, the employee's new employer maintains such plan with respect to the employee. For example, a new employer maintains a plan with respect to an employee by continuing or assuming sponsorship of the plan or by accepting a transfer of plan assets and liabilities (within the meaning of section 414(l)) with respect to the employee.

(3) *Rules applicable to hardship distributions*—(i) *Distribution must be on account of hardship.* A distribution is treated as made after an employee's hardship for purposes of paragraph (d)(1)(ii) of this section if and only if it is made on account of the hardship. For purposes of this rule, a distribution is made on account of hardship only if the distribution both is made on account of an immediate and heavy financial need of the employee and is necessary to satisfy the financial need. The determination of the existence of an immediate and heavy financial need and of the amount necessary to meet the need must be made in accordance with nondiscriminatory and objective standards set forth in the plan.

(ii) *Limit on maximum distributable amount*—(A) *General rule.* A distribution on account of hardship must be limited to the maximum distributable amount. The maximum distributable amount is equal to the employee's total elective contributions as of the date of distribution, reduced by the amount of previous distributions of elective contributions. Thus, the maximum distributable amount does not include earnings, QNECs or QMACs, unless grandfathered under paragraph (d)(3)(ii)(B) of this section.

* * *

(iii) *Immediate and heavy financial need*—(A) *In general.* Whether an employee has an immediate and heavy financial need is to be determined based on all the relevant facts and circumstances. Generally, for example, the need to pay the funeral expenses of a family member would constitute an immediate and heavy financial need. A distribution made to an employee for the purchase of a boat or television would generally not constitute a distribution made on account of an immediate and heavy financial need. A financial need may be immediate and heavy even if it was reasonably foreseeable or voluntarily incurred by the employee.

(B) *Deemed immediate and heavy financial need.* A distribution is deemed to be on account of an immediate and heavy financial need of the employee if the distribution is for—

(1) Expenses for (or necessary to obtain) medical care that would be deductible under section 213(d) (determined without regard to whether the expenses exceed 7.5% of adjusted gross income);

(2) Costs directly related to the purchase of a principal residence for the employee (excluding mortgage payments);

(3) Payment of tuition, related educational fees, and room and board expenses, for up to the next 12 months of post-secondary education for the employee, or the employee's spouse, children, or dependents (as defined in section 152, and, for taxable years beginning on or after January 1, 2005, without regard to section 152(b)(1), (b)(2) and (d)(1)(B));

(4) Payments necessary to prevent the eviction of the employee from the employee's principal residence or foreclosure on the mortgage on that residence;

(5) Payments for burial or funeral expenses for the employee's deceased parent, spouse, children or dependents (as defined in section 152, and, for taxable years beginning on or after January 1, 2005, without regard to section 152(d)(1)(B)); or

(6) Expenses for the repair of damage to the employee's principal residence that would qualify for the casualty deduction under section 165 (determined without regard to whether the loss exceeds 10% of adjusted gross income).

(iv) *Distribution necessary to satisfy financial need*—(A) *Distribution may not exceed amount of need.* A distribution is treated as necessary to satisfy an immediate and heavy financial need of an employee only to the extent the amount of the distribution is not in excess of the amount required to satisfy the financial need. For this purpose, the amount required to satisfy the financial need may include any amounts necessary to pay any federal, state, or local income taxes or penalties reasonably anticipated to result from the distribution.

(B) *No alternative means available.* A distribution is not treated as necessary to satisfy an immediate and heavy financial need of an employee to the extent the need may be relieved from other resources that are reasonably available to the employee. This determination generally is to be made on the basis of all the relevant facts and circumstances. For purposes of this paragraph (d)(3)(iv), the employee's resources are deemed to include those assets of the employee's spouse and minor children that are reasonably available to the employee. Thus, for example, a vacation home owned by the employee and the employee's spouse, whether as community property, joint tenants, tenants by the entirety, or tenants in common, generally will be deemed a resource of the employee. However, property held for the employee's child under an irrevocable trust or under the Uniform Gifts to Minors Act (or comparable State law) is not treated as a resource of the employee.

(C) *Employer reliance on employee representation.* For purposes of paragraph (d)(3)(iv)(B) of this section, an immediate and heavy financial need generally may be treated as not capable of being relieved from other resources that are reasonably available to the employee, if the employer relies upon the employee's representation (made in writing or such other form as may be prescribed by the Commissioner), unless the employer has actual knowledge to the contrary, that the need cannot reasonably be relieved— (1) Through reimbursement or compensation by insurance or otherwise;

(2) By liquidation of the employee's assets;

(3) By cessation of elective contributions or employee contributions under the plan;

(4) By other currently available distributions (including distribution of ESOP dividends under section 404(k)) and nontaxable (at the time of the loan) loans, under plans maintained by the employer or by any other employer; or

(5) By borrowing from commercial sources on reasonable commercial terms in an amount sufficient to satisfy the need.

(D) *Employee need not take counterproductive actions.* For purposes of this paragraph (d)(3)(iv), a need cannot reasonably be relieved by one of the actions described in paragraph (d)(3)(iv)(C) of this section if the effect would be to increase the amount of the need. For example, the need for funds to purchase a principal residence cannot reasonably be relieved by a plan loan if the loan would disqualify the employee from obtaining other necessary financing.

(E) *Distribution deemed necessary to satisfy immediate and heavy financial need.* A distribution is deemed necessary to satisfy an immediate and heavy financial need of an employee if each of the following requirements are satisfied—

(1) The employee has obtained all other currently available distributions (including distribution of ESOP dividends under section 404(k), but not hardship distributions) and nontaxable (at the time of the loan) loans, under the plan and all other plans maintained by the employer; and

(2) The employee is prohibited, under the terms of the plan or an otherwise legally enforceable agreement, from making elective contributions and employee contributions to the plan and all other plans maintained by the employer for at least 6 months after receipt of the hardship distribution.

(F) *Definition of other plans.* For purposes of paragraph (d)(3)(iv)(C)(4) and (E)(1) of this section, the phrase plans maintained by the employer means all qualified and nonqualified plans of deferred compensation maintained by the employer, including a cash or deferred arrangement that is part of a cafeteria plan within the meaning of section 125. However, it does not include the mandatory employee contribution portion of a defined benefit plan or a health or welfare benefit plan (including one that is part of a cafeteria plan). In addition, for purposes of paragraph (d)(3)(iv)(E)(2) of this section, the phrase plans maintained by the employer also includes a stock option, stock purchase, or similar plan maintained by the employer. See § 1.401(k)-6 for the continued treatment of suspended employees as eligible employees.

(v) *Commissioner may expand standards.* The Commissioner may prescribe additional guidance of general applicability, published in the Internal Revenue Bulletin (see § 601.601(d)(2) of this chapter), expanding the list of deemed immediate and heavy financial needs and prescribing additional methods for distributions to be deemed necessary to satisfy an immediate and heavy financial need.

* * *

(e) *Additional requirements for qualified cash or deferred arrangements*—(1) *Qualified plan requirement.* A cash or deferred arrangement satisfies this paragraph (e) only if the plan of which it is a part is a profit-sharing, stock bonus, pre-ERISA money purchase or rural cooperative plan that otherwise satisfies the requirements of section 401(a) (taking into account the cash or deferred arrangement). A plan that includes a cash or deferred arrangement may provide for other contributions, including employer contributions (other than elective contributions), employee contributions, or both. However, except as expressly permitted under section

401(m), 410(b)(2)(A)(ii) or 416(c)(2)(A), elective contributions and matching contributions taken into account under § 1.401(k)-2(a) may not be taken into account for purposes of determining whether any other contributions under any plan (including the plan to which the contributions are made) satisfy the requirements of section 401(a).

(2) *Election requirements*—(i) *Cash must be available.* A cash or deferred arrangement satisfies this paragraph (e) only if the arrangement provides that the amount that each eligible employee may defer as an elective contribution is available to the employee in cash. Thus, for example, if an eligible employee is provided the option to receive a taxable benefit (other than cash) or to have the employer contribute on the employee's behalf to a profit-sharing plan an amount equal to the value of the taxable benefit, the arrangement is not a qualified cash or deferred arrangement. Similarly, if an employee has the option to receive a specified amount in cash or to have the employer contribute an amount in excess of the specified cash amount to a profit-sharing plan on the employee's behalf, any contribution made by the employer on the employee's behalf in excess of the specified cash amount is not treated as made pursuant to a qualified cash or deferred arrangement, but would be treated as a matching contribution. This cash availability requirement applies even if the cash or deferred arrangement is part of a cafeteria plan within the meaning of section 125.

(ii) *Frequency of elections.* A cash or deferred arrangement satisfies this paragraph (e) only if the arrangement provides an employee with an effective opportunity to make (or change) a cash or deferred election at least once during each plan year. Whether an employee has an effective opportunity is determined based on all the relevant facts and circumstances, including the adequacy of notice of the availability of the election, the period of time during which an election may be made, and any other conditions on elections.

(3) *Separate accounting requirement*—(i) *General rule.* A cash or deferred arrangement satisfies this paragraph (e) only if the portion of an employee's benefit subject to the requirements of paragraphs (c) and (d) of this section is determined by an acceptable separate accounting between that portion and any other benefits. Separate accounting is not acceptable unless contributions and withdrawals are attributed to the separate accounts and gains, losses, and other credits or charges are separately allocated on a reasonable and consistent basis to the accounts subject to the requirements of paragraphs (c) and (d) of this section and to other accounts. Subject to section 401(a)(4), forfeitures are not required to be allocated to the accounts in which benefits are subject to paragraphs (c) and (d) of this section. The separate accounting requirement of this paragraph (e)(3)(i) applies at the time the elective contribution is contributed to the plan and continues to apply until the contribution is distributed under the plan.

(ii) *Satisfaction of separate accounting requirement.* The requirements of paragraph (e)(3)(i) of this section are treated as satisfied if all amounts held under a plan that includes a qualified cash or deferred arrangement (and, if applicable, under another plan to which QNECs and QMACs are made) are subject to the requirements of paragraphs (c) and (d) of this section.

* * *

(6) *Other benefits not contingent upon elective contributions*—(i) *General rule.* A cash or deferred arrangement satisfies this paragraph (e) only if no other benefit is conditioned (directly or indirectly) upon the employee's electing to make or not to make elective contributions under the arrangement. The preceding sentence does not apply to—

(A) Any matching contribution (as defined in § 1.401(m)-1(a)(2)) made by reason of such an election;

(B) Any benefit, right or feature (such as a plan loan) that requires, or results in, an amount to be withheld from an employee's pay (e.g. to pay for the benefit or to repay the loan), to the extent the cash or deferred arrangement restricts elective contributions to amounts available after such withholding from the employee's pay (after deduction of all applicable income and employment taxes);

(C) Any reduction in the employer's top-heavy contributions under section 416(c)(2) because of matching contributions that resulted from the elective contributions; or

(D) Any benefit that is provided at the employee's election under a plan described in section 125(d) in lieu of an elective contribution under a qualified cash or deferred arrangement.

(ii) *Definition of other benefits.* For purposes of this paragraph (e)(6), other benefits include, but are not limited to, benefits under a defined benefit plan; nonelective contributions under a defined contribution plan; the availability, cost, or amount of health benefits; vacations or vacation pay; life insurance; dental plans; legal services plans; loans (including plan loans); financial planning services; subsidized retirement benefits; stock options; property subject to section 83; and dependent care assistance. Also, increases in salary, bonuses or other cash remuneration (other than the amount that would be contributed under the cash or deferred election) are benefits for purposes of this paragraph (e)(6). The ability to make after-tax employee contributions is a benefit, but that benefit is not contingent upon an employee's electing to make or not make elective contributions under the arrangement merely because the amount of elective contributions reduces dollar-for-dollar the amount of after-tax employee contributions that may be made. Additionally, benefits under any other plan or arrangement (whether or not qualified) are not contingent upon an employee's electing to make or not to make elective contributions under a cash or deferred arrangement merely because the elective contributions are or are not taken into account as compensation under the other plan or arrangement for purposes of determining benefits.

(iii) *Effect of certain statutory limits.* Any benefit under an excess benefit plan described in section 3(36) of the Employee Retirement Income Security Act of 1974 that is dependent on the employee's electing to make or not to make elective contributions is not treated as contingent. Deferred compensation under a nonqualified plan of deferred compensation that is dependent on an employee's having made the maximum elective deferrals under section 402(g) or the maximum elective contributions permitted under the terms of the plan also is not treated as contingent.

(iv) *Nonqualified deferred compensation.* Except as otherwise provided in paragraph (e)(6)(iii) of this section, participation in a nonqualified deferred compensation plan is treated as contingent for purposes of this paragraph (e)(6) to the extent that an employee may receive additional deferred compensation under the nonqualified plan to the extent the employee makes or does not make elective contributions.

(v) *Plan loans and distributions.* A loan or distribution of elective contributions is not a benefit conditioned on an employee's electing to make or not make elective contributions under the arrangement merely because the amount of the loan or distribution is based on the amount of the employee's account balance.

* * *

(7) *Plan provision requirement.* A plan that includes a cash or deferred arrangement satisfies this paragraph (e) only if it provides that the nondiscrimination requirements of section 401(k) will be met. Thus, the plan must provide for satisfaction of one of the specific alternatives described in paragraph (b)(1)(ii) of this section and, if with respect to that alternative there are optional choices, which of the optional choices will apply. For example, a plan that uses the ADP test of section 401(k)(3), as described in paragraph (b)(1)(ii)(A) of this section, must specify whether it is using the current year testing method or prior year testing method. Additionally, a plan that uses the prior year testing method must specify whether the ADP for eligible NHCEs for the first plan year is 3% or the ADP for the eligible NHCEs for the first plan year. Similarly, a plan that uses the safe

harbor method of section 401(k)(12), as described in paragraph (b)(1)(ii)(B) of this section, must specify whether the safe harbor contribution will be the nonelective safe harbor contribution or the matching safe harbor contribution and is not permitted to provide that ADP testing will be used if the requirements for the safe harbor are not satisfied. In addition, a plan that uses the safe harbor method of section 401(k)(13), as described in paragraph (b)(1)(ii)(C) of this section, must specify the default percentages that apply for the plan year and whether the safe harbor contribution will be the nonelective safe harbor contribution or the matching safe harbor contribution, and is not permitted to provide that ADP testing will be used if the requirements for the safe harbor are not satisfied. For purposes of this paragraph (e)(7), a plan may incorporate by reference the provisions of section 401(k)(3) and § 1.401(k)-2 if that is the nondiscrimination test being applied. The Commissioner may, in guidance of general applicability, published in the Internal Revenue Bulletin (see § 601.601(d)(2) of this chapter), specify the options that will apply under the plan if the nondiscrimination test is incorporated by reference in accordance with the preceding sentence.

(8) *Section 415 compensation required.* With respect to compensation that is paid (or would have been paid but for a cash or deferred election) in plan years beginning on or after July 1, 2007, a cash or deferred arrangement satisfies this paragraph (e) only if cash or deferred elections can only be made with respect to amounts that are compensation within the meaning of section 415(c)(3) and § 1.415(c)-2. Thus, for example, the arrangement is not a qualified cash or deferred arrangement if an eligible employee who is not in qualified military service (as that term is defined in section 414(u)) and who is not permanently and totally disabled (as defined in section 22(e)(3)) can make a cash or deferred election with respect to an amount paid after severance from employment, unless the amount is paid by the later of 2 1/2 months after severance from employment or the end of the year that includes the date of severance from employment and is described in § 1.415(c)-2(e)(3)(ii) or (iii).

(f) *Special rules for designated Roth contributions*—(1) *In general.* The term designated Roth contribution means an elective contribution under a qualified cash or deferred arrangement that, to the extent permitted under the plan, is—

(i) Designated irrevocably by the employee at the time of the cash or deferred election as a designated Roth contribution that is being made in lieu of all or a portion of the pre-tax elective contributions the employee is otherwise eligible to make under the plan;

(ii) Treated by the employer as not excludible from the employee's gross income (in accordance with paragraph (f)(2) of this section);

(iii) Maintained by the plan in a separate account (in accordance with paragraph (f)(3) of this section).

(2) *Inclusion treatment.* An elective contribution is generally treated as not excludible from gross income if it is treated as includible in gross income by the employer (e.g., by treating the contribution as wages subject to applicable income tax withholding). However, in the case of a self-employed individual, an elective contribution is treated as not excludible from gross income only if the individual does not claim a deduction for such amount. If an elective contribution would not have been includible in gross income if the amount had been paid directly to the employee (rather than being subject to a cash or deferral election), the elective contribution is nevertheless permitted to be a designated Roth contribution, provided the employee is entitled to treat the amount as an investment in the contract pursuant to section 72(f)(2).

(3) *Separate accounting required.* Under the separate accounting requirement of this paragraph (f)(3), contributions and withdrawals of designated Roth contributions must be credited and debited to a designated Roth account maintained for the employee and the plan must maintain a record of the employee's

investment in the contract (that is, designated Roth contributions that have not been distributed) with respect to the employee's designated Roth account. In addition, gains, losses, and other credits or charges must be separately allocated on a reasonable and consistent basis to the designated Roth account and other accounts under the plan. However, forfeitures may not be allocated to the designated Roth account and no contributions other than designated Roth contributions and rollover contributions described in section 402A(c)(3)(B) may be allocated to such account. The separate accounting requirement applies at the time the designated Roth contribution is contributed to the plan and must continue to apply until the designated Roth account is completely distributed. See A-13 of § 1.402A-1 for additional requirements for separate accounting.

(4) *Designated Roth contributions must satisfy rules applicable to elective contributions*—(i) *In general.* A designated Roth contribution must satisfy the requirements applicable to elective contributions made under a qualified cash or deferred arrangement. Thus, for example, a designated Roth contribution must satisfy the requirements of paragraphs (c) and (d) of this section and is treated as an employer contribution for purposes of sections 401(a), 401(k), 402, 404, 409, 411, 412, 415, 416 and 417. In addition, the designated Roth contributions are treated as elective contributions for purposes of the ADP test. Similarly, the designated Roth account under the plan is subject to the rules of section 401(a)(9)(A) and (B) in the same manner as an account that contains pre-tax elective contributions.

(ii) *Special rules for direct rollovers.* A direct rollover from a designated Roth account under a qualified cash or deferred arrangement may only be made to another designated Roth account under an applicable retirement plan described in section 402A(e)(1) or to a Roth IRA described in section 408A, and only to the extent the rollover is permitted under the rules of section 402(c). Moreover, a participant's designated Roth account and the participant's other accounts under a plan are treated as accounts held under two separate plans (within the meaning of section 414(l)) for purposes of applying the automatic rollover rules for mandatory distributions under section 401(a)(31)(B)(i)(I) and the special rules in A-9 through A-11 of § 1.401(a)(31)-1.

(5) *Rules regarding designated Roth contribution elections*—(i) *Frequency of elections.* The rules under paragraph (e)(2)(ii) of this section regarding frequency of elections apply in the same manner to both pre-tax elective contributions and designated Roth contributions. Thus, an employee must have an effective opportunity to make (or change) an election to make designated Roth contributions at least once during each plan year.

(ii) *Default elections*—(A) In the case of a plan that provides for both pre-tax elective contributions and designated Roth contributions and in which, under paragraph (a)(3)(ii) of this section, the default in the absence of an affirmative election is to make a contribution under the cash or deferred arrangement, the plan terms must provide the extent to which the default contributions are pre-tax elective contributions and the extent to which the default contributions are designated Roth contributions.

(B) If the default contributions under the plan are designated Roth contributions, then an employee who has not made an affirmative election is deemed to have irrevocably designated the contributions (in accordance with section 402A(c)(1)(B)) as designated Roth contributions.

* * *

§ 1.401(k)-2. ADP test.

(a) *Actual deferral percentage (ADP) test*—(1) *In general*—(i) *ADP test formula.* A cash or deferred arrangement satisfies the ADP test for a plan year only if—

(A) The ADP for the eligible HCEs for the plan year is not more than the ADP for the eligible NHCEs for the applicable year multiplied by 1.25; or

(B) The excess of the ADP for the eligible HCEs for the plan year over the ADP for the eligible NHCEs for the applicable year is not more than 2 percentage points, and the ADP for the eligible HCEs for the plan year is not more than the ADP for the eligible NHCEs for the applicable year multiplied by 2.

(ii) *HCEs as sole eligible employees.* If, for the applicable year for determining the ADP of the NHCEs for a plan year, there are no eligible NHCEs (i.e., all of the eligible employees under the cash or deferred arrangement for the applicable year are HCEs), the arrangement is deemed to satisfy the ADP test for the plan year.

* * *

(2) *Determination of ADP*—(i) *General rule.* The ADP for a group of eligible employees (either eligible HCEs or eligible NHCEs) for a plan year or applicable year is the average of the ADRs of the eligible employees in that group for that year. The ADP for a group of eligible employees is calculated to the nearest hundredth of a percentage point.

(ii) *Determination of applicable year under current year and prior year testing method.* The ADP test is applied using the prior year testing method or the current year testing method. Under the prior year testing method, the applicable year for determining the ADP for the eligible NHCEs is the plan year immediately preceding the plan year for which the ADP test is being performed. Under the prior year testing method, the ADP for the eligible NHCEs is determined using the ADRs for the eligible employees who were NHCEs in that preceding plan year, regardless of whether those NHCEs are eligible employees or NHCEs in the plan year for which the ADP test is being calculated. Under the current year testing method, the applicable year for determining the ADP for the eligible NHCEs is the same plan year as the plan year for which the ADP test is being performed. Under either method, the ADP for eligible HCEs is the average of the ADRs of the eligible HCEs for the plan year for which the ADP test is being performed. See paragraph (c) of this section for additional rules for the prior year testing method.

(3) *Determination of ADR*—(i) *General rule.* The ADR of an eligible employee for a plan year or applicable year is the sum of the employee's elective contributions taken into account with respect to such employee for the year, determined under the rules of paragraphs (a)(4) and (5) of this section, and the qualified nonelective contributions and qualified matching contributions taken into account with respect to such employee under paragraph (a)(6) of this section for the year, divided by the employee's compensation taken into account for the year. The ADR is calculated to the nearest hundredth of a percentage point. If no elective contributions, qualified nonelective contributions, or qualified matching contributions are taken into account under this section with respect to an eligible employee for the year, the ADR of the employee is zero.

* * *

(4) *Elective contributions taken into account under the ADP test*—(i) *General rule.* An elective contribution is taken into account in determining the ADR for an eligible employee for a plan year or applicable year only if each of the following requirements is satisfied—

(A) The elective contribution is allocated to the eligible employee's account under the plan as of a date within that year. For purposes of this rule, an elective contribution is considered allocated as of a date within a year only if—

(*1*) The allocation is not contingent on the employee's participation in the plan or performance of services on any date subsequent to that date; and

(*2*) The elective contribution is actually paid to the trust no later than the end of the 12-month period immediately following the year to which the contribution relates.

(B) The elective contribution relates to compensation that either—

(1) Would have been received by the employee in the year but for the employee's election to defer under the arrangement; or

(2) Is attributable to services performed by the employee in the year and, but for the employee's election to defer, would have been received by the employee within 2 1/2 months after the close of the year, but only if the plan provides for elective contributions that relate to compensation that would have been received after the close of a year to be allocated to such prior year rather than the year in which the compensation would have been received.

(ii) *Elective contributions for partners and self-employed individuals.* For purposes of this paragraph (a)(4), a partner's distributive share of partnership income is treated as received on the last day of the partnership taxable year and a sole proprietor's compensation is treated as received on the last day of the individual's taxable year. Thus, an elective contribution made on behalf of a partner or sole proprietor is treated as allocated to the partner's account for the plan year that includes the last day of the partnership taxable year, provided the requirements of paragraph (a)(4)(i) of this section are met.

(iii) *Elective contributions for HCEs.* Elective contributions of an HCE must include any excess deferrals, as described in § 1.402(g)-1(a), even if those excess deferrals are distributed, pursuant to § 1.402(g)-1(e).

(5) *Elective contributions not taken into account under the ADP test*—(i) *General rule.* Elective contributions that do not satisfy the requirements of paragraph (a)(4)(i) of this section may not be taken into account in determining the ADR of an eligible employee for the plan year or applicable year with respect to which the contributions were made, or for any other plan year. Instead, the amount of the elective contributions must satisfy the requirements of section 401(a)(4) (without regard to the ADP test) for the plan year for which they are allocated under the plan as if they were nonelective contributions and were the only nonelective contributions for that year. See §§ 1.401(a)(4)-1(b)(2)(ii)(B) and 1.410(b)-7(c)(1).

(ii) *Elective contributions for NHCEs.* Elective contributions of an NHCE shall not include any excess deferrals, as described in § 1.402(g)-1(a), to the extent the excess deferrals are prohibited under section 401(a)(30). However, to the extent that the excess deferrals are not prohibited under section 401(a)(30), they are included in elective contributions even if distributed pursuant to § 1.402(g)-1(e).

(iii) *Elective contributions treated as catch-up contributions.* Elective contributions that are treated as catch-up contributions under section 414(v) because they exceed a statutory limit or employer-provided limit (within the meaning of § 1.414(v)-1(b)(1)) are not taken into account under paragraph (a)(4) of this section for the plan year for which the contributions were made, or for any other plan year.

(iv) *Elective contributions used to satisfy the ACP test.* Except to the extent necessary to demonstrate satisfaction of the requirement of § 1.401(m)- 2(a)(6)(ii), elective contributions taken into account for the ACP test under § 1.401(m)-2(a)(6) are not taken into account under paragraph (a)(4) of this section.

(v) *Additional elective contributions pursuant to section 414(u).* Additional elective contributions made pursuant to section 414(u) by reason of an eligible employee's qualified military service are not taken into account under paragraph (a)(4) of this section for the plan year for which the contributions are made, or for any other plan year.

(vi) *Default elective contributions pursuant to section 414(w).* Default elective contributions made under an eligible automatic contribution arrangement (within the meaning of § 1.414(w)-1(b)) that are distributed pursuant to § 1.414(w)-1(c) for plan years beginning on or after January 1, 2008, are not taken into account under paragraph (a)(4) of this section for the plan year for which the contributions are made, or for any other plan year.

(6) *Qualified nonelective contributions and qualified matching contributions that may be taken into account under the ADP test.* Qualified nonelective contributions and qualified matching contributions may be taken into account in determining the ADR for an eligible employee for a plan year or applicable year but only to the extent the contributions satisfy the following requirements—

(i) *Timing of allocation.* The qualified nonelective contribution or qualified matching contribution is allocated to the employee's account as of a date within that year within the meaning of paragraph (a)(4)(i)(A) of this section. Consequently, under the prior year testing method, in order to be taken into account in calculating the ADP for the eligible NHCEs for the applicable year, a qualified nonelective contribution or qualified matching contribution must be contributed no later than the end of the 12-month period immediately following the applicable year even though the applicable year is different than the plan year being tested.

* * *

(iv) *Disproportionate contributions not taken into account*—(A) *General rule.* Qualified nonelective contributions cannot be taken into account for a plan year for an NHCE to the extent such contributions exceed the product of that NHCE's compensation and the greater of 5% or two times the plan's representative contribution rate. Any qualified nonelective contribution taken into account under an ACP test under § 1.401(m)-2(a)(6) (including the determination of the representative contribution rate for purposes of § 1.401(m)-2(a)(6)(v)(B)), is not permitted to be taken into account for purposes of this paragraph (a)(6) (including the determination of the representative contribution rate under paragraph (a)(6)(iv)(B) of this section).

(B) *Definition of representative contribution rate.* For purposes of this paragraph (a)(6)(iv), the plan's representative contribution rate is the lowest applicable contribution rate of any eligible NHCE among a group of eligible NHCEs that consists of half of all eligible NHCEs for the plan year (or, if greater, the lowest applicable contribution rate of any eligible NHCE in the group of all eligible NHCEs for the plan year and who is employed by the employer on the last day of the plan year).

(C) *Definition of applicable contribution rate.* For purposes of this paragraph (a)(6)(iv), the applicable contribution rate for an eligible NHCE is the sum of the qualified matching contributions taken into account under this paragraph (a)(6) for the eligible NHCE for the plan year and the qualified nonelective contributions made for the eligible NHCE for the plan year, divided by the eligible NHCE's compensation for the same period.

* * *

(b) *Correction of excess contributions*—(1) *Permissible correction methods*—(i) *In general.* A cash or deferred arrangement does not fail to satisfy the requirements of section 401(k)(3) and paragraph (a)(1) of this section if the employer, in accordance with the terms of the plan that includes the cash or deferred arrangement, uses any of the following correction methods—

(A) *Qualified nonelective contributions or qualified matching contributions.* The employer makes qualified nonelective contributions or qualified matching contributions that are taken into account under this section and, in combination with other amounts taken into account under paragraph (a) of this section, allow the cash or deferred arrangement to satisfy the requirements of paragraph (a)(1) of this section.

(B) *Excess contributions distributed.* Excess contributions are distributed in accordance with paragraph (b)(2) of this section.

(C) *Excess contributions recharacterized.* Excess contributions are recharacterized in accordance with paragraph (b)(3) of this section.

(ii) *Combination of correction methods.* A plan may provide for the use of any of the correction methods described in paragraph (b)(1)(i) of this section, may limit elective contributions in a manner designed to prevent excess contributions from being made, or may use a combination of these methods, to avoid or correct excess contributions. A plan may permit an HCE to elect whether any excess contributions are to be recharacterized or distributed. Similarly, a plan may permit an HCE with elective contributions for a year that includes both pre-tax elective contributions and designated Roth contributions to elect whether the excess contributions are to be attributed to pre-tax elective contributions or designated Roth contributions. If the plan uses a combination of correction methods, any contribution made under paragraph (b)(1)(i)(A) of this section must be taken into account before application of the correction methods in paragraph (b)(1)(i)(B) or (C) of this section.

(iii) *Exclusive means of correction.* A failure to satisfy the requirements of paragraph (a)(1) of this section may not be corrected using any method other than the ones described in paragraphs (b)(1)(i) and (ii) of this section. Thus, excess contributions for a plan year may not remain unallocated or be allocated to a suspense account for allocation to one or more employees in any future year. In addition, excess contributions may not be corrected using the retroactive correction rules of § 1.401(a)(4)-11(g). See § 1.401(a)(4)-11(g)(3)(vii) and (5).

(2) *Corrections through distribution*—(i) *General rule.* This paragraph (b)(2) contains the rules for correction of excess contributions through a distribution from the plan. Correction through a distribution generally involves a 4-step process. First, the plan must determine, in accordance with paragraph (b)(2)(ii) of this section, the total amount of excess contributions that must be distributed under the plan. Second, the plan must apportion the total amount of excess contributions among HCEs in accordance with paragraph (b)(2)(iii) of this section. Third, the plan must determine the income allocable to excess contributions in accordance with paragraph (b)(2)(iv) of this section. Finally, the plan must distribute the apportioned excess contributions and allocable income in accordance with paragraph (b)(2)(v) of this section. Paragraph (b)(2)(vi) of this section provides rules relating to the tax treatment of these distributions. Paragraph (b)(2)(vii) provides other rules relating to these distributions.

(ii) *Calculation of total amount to be distributed.* The following procedures must be used to determine the total amount of the excess contributions to be distributed—

(A) *Calculate the dollar amount of excess contributions for each HCE.* The amount of excess contributions attributable to a given HCE for a plan year is the amount (if any) by which the HCE's contributions taken into account under this section must be reduced for the HCE's ADR to equal the highest permitted ADR under the plan. To calculate the highest permitted ADR under a plan, the ADR of the HCE with the highest ADR is reduced by the amount required to cause that HCE's ADR to equal the ADR of the HCE with the next highest ADR. If a lesser reduction would enable the arrangement to satisfy the requirements of paragraph (b)(2)(ii)(C) of this section, only this lesser reduction is used in determining the highest permitted ADR.

(B) *Determination of the total amount of excess contributions.* The process described in paragraph (b)(2)(ii)(A) of this section must be repeated until the arrangement would satisfy the requirements of paragraph (b)(2)(ii)(C) of this section. The sum of all reductions for all HCEs determined under paragraph (b)(2)(ii)(A) of this section is the total amount of excess contributions for the plan year.

(C) *Satisfaction of ADP.* A cash or deferred arrangement satisfies this paragraph (b)(2)(ii)(C) if the arrangement would satisfy the requirements of paragraph (a)(1)(ii) of this section if the ADR for each HCE were determined after the reductions described in paragraph (b)(2)(ii)(A) of this section.

(iii) *Apportionment of total amount of excess contributions among the HCEs.* The following procedures must be used in apportioning the total amount of excess contributions determined under paragraph (b)(2)(ii) of this section among the HCEs:

(A) *Calculate the dollar amount of excess contributions for each HCE.* The contributions of the HCE with the highest dollar amount of contributions taken into account under this section are reduced by the amount required to cause that HCE's contributions to equal the dollar amount of the contributions taken into account under this section for the HCE with the next highest dollar amount of contributions taken into account under this section. If a lesser apportionment to the HCE would enable the plan to apportion the total amount of excess contributions, only the lesser apportionment would apply.

(B) *Limit on amount apportioned to any individual.* For purposes of this paragraph (b)(2)(iii), the amount of contributions taken into account under this section with respect to an HCE who is an eligible employee in more than one plan of an employer is determined by taking into account all contributions otherwise taken into account with respect to such HCE under any plan of the employer during the plan year of the plan being tested as being made under the plan being tested. However, the amount of excess contributions apportioned for a plan year with respect to any HCE must not exceed the amount of contributions actually contributed to the plan for the HCE for the plan year. Thus, in the case of an HCE who is an eligible employee in more than one plan of the same employer to which elective contributions are made and whose ADR is calculated in accordance with paragraph (a)(3)(ii) of this section, the amount required to be distributed under this paragraph (b)(2)(iii) shall not exceed the contributions actually contributed to the plan and taken into account under this section for the plan year.

(C) *Apportionment to additional HCEs.* The procedure in paragraph (b)(2)(iii)(A) of this section must be repeated until the total amount of excess contributions determined under paragraph (b)(2)(ii) of this section has been apportioned.

(iv) *Income allocable to excess contributions*—(A) *General rule.* For plan years beginning on or after January 1, 2008, the income allocable to excess contributions is equal to the allocable gain or loss through the end of the plan year. See paragraph (b)(2)(iv)(D) of this section for rules that apply to plan years beginning before January 1, 2008.

(B) *Method of allocating income.* A plan may use any reasonable method for computing the income allocable to excess contributions, provided that the method does not violate section 401(a)(4), is used consistently for all participants and for all corrective distributions under the plan for the plan year, and is used by the plan for allocating income to participant's accounts. See § 1.401(a)(4)-1(c)(8). A plan will not fail to use a reasonable method for computing the income allocable to excess contributions merely because the income allocable to excess contributions is determined on a date that is no more than 7 days before the distribution.

(C) *Alternative method of allocating plan year income.* A plan may allocate income to excess contributions for the plan year by multiplying the income for the plan year allocable to the elective contributions and other amounts taken into account under this section (including contributions made for the plan year), by a fraction, the numerator of which is the excess contributions for the employee for the plan year, and the denominator of which is the sum of the—

(*1*) Account balance attributable to elective contributions and other contributions taken into account under this section as of the beginning of the plan year, and

(*2*) Any additional amount of such contributions made for the plan year.

* * *

(v) *Distribution.* Within 12 months after the close of the plan year in which the excess contribution arose, the plan must distribute to each HCE the excess contributions apportioned to such HCE under paragraph (b)(2)(iii) of this section and the allocable income. Except as otherwise provided in this paragraph (b)(2)(v) and paragraph (b)(4)(i) of this section, a distribution of excess contributions must be in addition to any other distributions made during the year and must be designated as a corrective distribution by the employer. In the event of a complete termination of the plan during the plan year in which an excess contribution arose, the corrective distribution must be made as soon as administratively feasible after the date of termination of the plan, but in no event later than 12 months after the date of termination. If the entire account balance of an HCE is distributed prior to when the plan makes a distribution of excess contributions in accordance with this paragraph (b)(2), the distribution is deemed to have been a corrective distribution of excess contributions (and income) to the extent that a corrective distribution would otherwise have been required.

(vi) *Tax treatment of corrective distributions*—(A) *Corrective distributions for plan years beginning on or after January 1, 2008.* Except as provided in this paragraph (b)(2)(vi), for plan years beginning on or after January 1, 2008, a corrective distribution of excess contributions (and allocable income) is includible in the employee's gross income for the employee's taxable year in which distributed. In addition, the corrective distribution is not subject to the early distribution tax of section 72(t). See paragraph (b)(5) of this section for additional rules relating to the employer excise tax on amounts distributed more than 2 1/2 months (6 months in the case of certain plans that include an eligible automatic contribution arrangement within the meaning of section 414(w)) after the end of the plan year. See also § 1.402(c)-2, A-4 for restrictions on rolling over distributions that are excess contributions.

* * *

(C) *Corrective distributions attributable to designated Roth contributions.* Notwithstanding paragraphs (b)(2)(vi)(A) and (B) of this section, a distribution of excess contributions is not includible in gross income to the extent it represents a distribution of designated Roth contributions. However, the income allocable to a corrective distribution of excess contributions that are designated Roth contributions is included in gross income in accordance with paragraph (b)(2)(vi)(A) or (B) of this section (i.e., in the same manner as income allocable to a corrective distribution of excess contributions that are pre-tax elective contributions).

(vii) *Other rules*—(A) *No employee or spousal consent required.* A corrective distribution of excess contributions (and income) may be made under the terms of the plan without regard to any notice or consent otherwise required under sections 411(a)(11) and 417.

(B) *Treatment of corrective distributions as elective contributions.* Excess contributions are treated as employer contributions for purposes of sections 404 and 415 even if distributed from the plan.

(C) *No reduction of required minimum distribution.* A distribution of excess contributions (and income) is not treated as a distribution for purposes of determining whether the plan satisfies the minimum distribution requirements of section 401(a)(9). See § 1.401(a)(9)-5, A-9(b).

(D) *Partial distributions.* Any distribution of less than the entire amount of excess contributions (and allocable income) with respect to any HCE is treated as a pro rata distribution of excess contributions and allocable income.

* * *

(3) *Recharacterization of excess contributions*—(i) *General rule.* Excess contributions are recharacterized in accordance with this paragraph (b)(3) only if the excess contributions that would have to be distributed under (b)(2) of this section if the plan was correcting through distribution of excess contributions are recharacterized as described in paragraph (b)(3)(ii) of this section, and all of the conditions set forth in paragraph (b)(3)(iii) of this section are satisfied.

(ii) *Treatment of recharacterized excess contributions.* Recharacterized excess contributions are includible in the employee's gross income as if such amounts were distributed under paragraph (b)(2) of this section. The recharacterized excess contributions are treated as employee contributions for purposes of section 72, sections 401(a)(4), 401(m), § 1.401(k)-1(d) and § 1.401(k)-2. This requirement is not treated as satisfied unless the payor or plan administrator reports the recharacterized excess contributions as employee contributions to the Internal Revenue Service and the employee by timely providing such Federal tax forms and accompanying instructions and timely taking such other action as is prescribed by the Commissioner in revenue rulings, notices and other guidance published in the Internal Revenue Bulletin (see § 601.601(d)(2) of this chapter) as well as the applicable Federal tax forms and accompanying instructions.

(iii) *Additional rules*—(A) *Time of recharacterization.* Excess contributions may not be recharacterized under this paragraph (b)(3) after 2 1/2 months after the close of the plan year to which the recharacterization relates. Recharacterization is deemed to have occurred on the date on which the last of those HCEs with excess contributions to be recharacterized is notified in accordance with paragraph (b)(3)(ii) of this section.

(B) *Employee contributions must be permitted under plan.* The amount of recharacterized excess contributions, in combination with the employee contributions actually made by the HCE, may not exceed the maximum amount of employee contributions (determined without regard to the ACP test of section 401(m)(2)) permitted under the provisions of the plan as in effect on the first day of the plan year.

(C) *Treatment of recharacterized excess contributions.* Recharacterized excess contributions continue to be treated as employer contributions for all purposes under the Internal Revenue Code (other than those specified in paragraph (b)(3)(ii) of this section), including section 401(a) and sections 404, 409, 411, 412, 415, 416, and 417. Thus, for example, recharacterized excess contributions remain subject to the requirements of § 1.401(k)-1(c); must be deducted under section 404; and are treated as employer contributions described in section 415(c)(2)(A).

(4) *Rules applicable to all corrections*—(i) *Coordination with distribution of excess deferrals*—(A) *Treatment of excess deferrals that reduce excess contributions.* The amount of excess contributions (and allocable income) to be distributed under paragraph (b)(2) of this section or the amount of excess contributions recharacterized under paragraph (b)(3) of this section with respect to an employee for a plan year, is reduced by any amounts previously distributed to the employee from the plan to correct excess deferrals for the employee's taxable year ending with or within the plan year in accordance with section 402(g)(2).

(B) *Treatment of excess contributions that reduce excess deferrals.* Under § 1.402(g)-1(e), the amount required to be distributed to correct an excess deferral to an employee for a taxable year is reduced by any excess contributions (and allocable income) previously distributed or excess contributions recharacterized with respect to the employee for the plan year beginning with or within the taxable year. The amount of excess contributions includible in the gross income of the employee, and the amount of excess contributions reported by the payer or plan administrator as includible in the gross income of the employee, does not include the amount of any reduction under § 1.402(g)-1(e)(6).

(ii) *Forfeiture of match on distributed excess contributions.* A matching contribution is taken into account under section 401(a)(4) even if the match is with respect to an elective contribution that is distributed or recharacterized under this paragraph (b). This requires that, after correction of excess contributions, each level of matching contributions be currently and effectively available to a group of employees that satisfies section 410(b). See § 1.401(a)(4)-4(e)(3)(iii)(G). Thus, a plan that provides the same rate of matching contributions to all employees will not meet the requirements of section 401(a)(4) if elective contributions are distributed under this paragraph (b) to HCEs to the extent needed to meet the requirements of section 401(k)(3), while matching contributions attributable to those elective contributions remain allocated to the HCEs' accounts. Under section 411(a)(3)(G) and § 1.411(a)-4(b)(7), a plan may forfeit matching contributions attributable to excess contributions, excess aggregate contributions or excess deferrals to avoid a violation of section 401(a)(4). See also § 1.401(a)(4)- 11(g)(3)(vii)(B) regarding the use of additional allocations to the accounts of NHCEs for the purpose of correcting a discriminatory rate of matching contributions.

(iii) *Permitted forfeiture of QMAC.* Pursuant to section 401(k)(8)(E), a qualified matching contribution is not treated as forfeitable under § 1.401(k)- 1(c) merely because under the plan it is forfeited in accordance with paragraph (b)(4)(ii) of this section or § 1.414(w)-1(d)(2).

(iv) *No requirement for recalculation.* If excess contributions are distributed or recharacterized in accordance with paragraphs (b)(2) and (3) of this section, the cash or deferred arrangement is treated as meeting the nondiscrimination test of section 401(k)(3) regardless of whether the ADP for the HCEs, if recalculated after the distributions or recharacterizations, would satisfy section 401(k)(3).

(v) *Treatment of excess contributions that are catch-up contributions.* A cash or deferred arrangement does not fail to meet the requirements of section 401(k)(3) and paragraph (a)(1) of this section merely because excess contributions that are catch-up contributions because they exceed the ADP limit, as described in § 1.414(v)-1(b)(1)(iii), are not corrected in accordance with this paragraph (b).

(5) *Failure to timely correct*—(i) *Failure to correct within 2 1/2 months after end of plan year.* If a plan does not correct excess contributions within 2 1/2 months after the close of the plan year for which the excess contributions are made, the employer will be liable for a 10% excise tax on the amount of the excess contributions. See section 4979 and § 54.4979-1 of this chapter. Qualified nonelective contributions and qualified matching contributions properly taken into account under paragraph (a)(6) of this section for a plan year may enable a plan to avoid having excess contributions, even if the contributions are made after the close of the 2 1/2 month period.

(ii) *Failure to correct within 12 months after end of plan year.* If excess contributions are not corrected within 12 months after the close of the plan year for which they were made, the cash or deferred arrangement will fail to satisfy the requirements of section 401(k)(3) for the plan year for which the excess contributions are made and all subsequent plan years during which the excess contributions remain in the trust.

(iii) Special rule for eligible automatic contribution arrangements. In the case of excess contributions under a plan that includes an eligible automatic contribution arrangement within the meaning of section 414(w), 6 months is substituted for 2 1/2 months in paragraph (b)(5)(i) of this section. The additional time described in this paragraph (b)(5)(iii) applies to a distribution of excess contributions for a plan year beginning on or after January 1, 2010 only where all the eligible NHCEs and eligible HCEs are covered employees under the eligible automatic contribution arrangement (within the meaning of § 1.414(w)-1(e)(3)) for the entire plan year (or for the portion of the plan year that the eligible NHCEs and eligible HCEs are eligible employees).

* * *

§ 1.402(a)-1. Taxability of beneficiary under a trust which meets the requirements of section 401(a).

* * *

(d) *Salary reduction, cash or deferred arrangements*—(1) *Inclusion in income.* Whether a contribution to an exempt trust or plan described in section 401(a) or 403(a) is made by the employer or the employee is determined on the basis of the particular facts and circumstances of each case. Nevertheless, an amount contributed to a plan or trust will, except as otherwise provided under paragraph (d)(2) of this section, be treated as contributed by the employee if it was contributed at the employee's election, even though the election was made before the year in which the amount was earned by the employee or before the year in which the amount became currently available to the employee. Any amount treated as contributed by the employee is includible in the gross income of the employee for the year in which the amount would have been received by the employee but for the election. Thus, for example, amounts contributed to an exempt trust or plan by reason of a salary reduction agreement under a cash or deferred arrangement are treated as received by the employee when they would have been received by the employee but for the election to defer. Accordingly, they are includible in the gross income of the employee for that year (except as provided under paragraph (d)(2) of this section). See § 1.401(k)- 1(a)(3)(iii) and (2)(i) for the meaning of currently available and cash or deferred arrangement, respectively.

(2) *Amounts not included in income*—(i) *Qualified cash or deferred arrangement.* Elective contributions as defined in § 1.401(k)-1(g)(3) for a plan year made by an employer on behalf of an employee pursuant to a cash or deferred election under a qualified cash or deferred arrangement, as defined in § 1.401(k)-1(a)(4)(i), are not treated as received by or distributed to the employee or as employee contributions. For plan years beginning after December 31, 1992, whether a cash or deferred election is made under a qualified cash or deferred arrangement is determined without regard to the special rules for certain collectively bargained plans contained in § 1.401(k)-1(a)(7). As a result, elective contributions under these plans are treated as employee contributions for purposes of this section if the cash or deferred arrangement does not satisfy the actual deferral percentage test of section 401(k)(3) or otherwise fails to be a qualified cash or deferred arrangement.

(ii) *Matching contributions.* Matching contributions described in § 1.401(m)-1(f)(12) and section 401(m)(4) are not treated as contributed by an employee merely because they are made by the employer as a result of an employee's election.

(iii) *Effect of certain one-time elections.* Amounts contributed to an exempt plan or trust described in section 401(a) or 403(a) pursuant to the one-time irrevocable employee election to participate in a plan described in § 1.401(k)-1(a)(3)(iv) are not treated as contributed by an employee. Similarly, amounts contributed to an exempt plan or trust described in section 401(a) or 403(a) in which self-employed individuals may participate pursuant to the one-time irrevocable election described in § 1.401(k)-1(a)(6)(ii)(C) are not treated as contributed by an employee.

* * *

§ 1.402(c)-2. Eligible rollover distributions; questions and answers.

* * *

Q-4: Are there other amounts that are not eligible rollover distributions?

A-4: Yes. The following amounts are not eligible rollover distributions:

(a) Elective deferrals, as defined in section 402(g)(3), and employee contributions that, pursuant to rules prescribed by the Commissioner in revenue rulings, notices, or other guidance published in the Internal Revenue Bulletin (see § 601.601(d)(2) of this chapter), are returned to the employee (together with the income allocable thereto) in order to comply with the section 415 limitations.

(b) Corrective distributions of excess deferrals as described in § 1.402(g)-1(e)(3), together with the income allocable to these corrective distributions.

(c) Corrective distributions of excess contributions under a qualified cash or deferred arrangement described in § 1.401(k)-1(f)(4) and excess aggregate contributions described in § 1.401(m)-1(e)(3), together with the income allocable to these distributions.

(d) Loans that are treated as deemed distributions pursuant to section 72(p).

(e) Dividends paid on employer securities as described in section 404(k).

(f) The costs of life insurance coverage (P.S. 58 costs).

(g) Prohibited allocations that are treated as deemed distributions pursuant to section 409(p).

(h) A distribution that is a permissible withdrawal from an eligible automatic contribution arrangement within the meaning of section 414(w).

(i) [Reserved]

(j) Similar items designated by the Commissioner in revenue rulings, notices, and other guidance published in the Internal Revenue Bulletin. See § 601.601(d)(2)(ii)(b) of this chapter.

* * *

Q-7: When is a distribution from a plan a required minimum distribution under section 401(a)(9)?

A-7: (a) *General rule*. Except as provided in paragraphs (b) and (c) of this Q&A, if a minimum distribution is required for a calendar year, the amounts distributed during that calendar year are treated as required minimum distributions under section 401(a)(9), to the extent that the total required minimum distribution under section 401(a)(9) for the calendar year has not been satisfied. Accordingly, these amounts are not eligible rollover distributions. For example, if an employee is required under section 401(a)(9) to receive a required minimum distribution for a calendar year of $5,000 and the employee receives a total of $7,200 in that year, the first $5,000 distributed will be treated as the required minimum distribution and will not be an eligible rollover distribution and the remaining $2,200 will be an eligible rollover distribution if it otherwise qualifies. If the total section 401(a)(9) required minimum distribution for a calendar year is not distributed in that calendar year (e.g., when the distribution for the calendar year in which the employee reaches age 70 1/2 is made on the following April 1), the amount that was required but not distributed is added to the amount required to be distributed for the next calendar year in determining the portion of any distribution in the next calendar year that is a required minimum distribution.

(b) *Distribution before age 70 1/2*. Any amount that is paid before January 1 of the year in which the employee attains (or would have attained) age 70 1/2 will not be treated as required under section 401(a)(9) and, thus, is an eligible rollover distribution if it otherwise qualifies.

(c) *Special rule for annuities*. In the case of annuity payments from a defined benefit plan, or under an annuity contract purchased from an insurance company (including a qualified plan distributed annuity contract (as defined in Q&A-10 of this section)), the entire amount of any such annuity payment made on or after January 1 of the year in which an employee attains (or would have attained) age 70 1/2 will be treated as an amount required under section 401(a)(9) and, thus, will not be an eligible rollover distribution.

Q-8: How are amounts that are not includible in gross income allocated for purposes of determining the required minimum distribution?

A-8: If section 401(a)(9) has not yet been satisfied by the plan for the year with respect to an employee, a distribution is made to the employee that exceeds the amount required to satisfy section 401(a)(9) for the year for the employee, and a portion of that distribution is excludible from gross income, the following rule applies for purposes of determining the amount of the distribution that is an eligible rollover distribution. The portion of the distribution that is excludible from gross income is first allocated toward satisfaction of section 401(a)(9) and then the remaining portion of the required minimum distribution, if any, is satisfied from the portion of the distribution that is includible in gross income. For example, assume an employee is required under section 401(a)(9) to receive a minimum distribution for a calendar year of $4,000 and the employee receives a $4,800 distribution, of which $1,000 is excludible from income as a return of basis. First, the $1,000 return of basis is allocated toward satisfying the required minimum distribution. Then, the remaining $3,000 of the required minimum distribution is satisfied from the $3,800 of the distribution that is includible in gross income, so that the remaining balance of the distribution, $800, is an eligible rollover distribution if it otherwise qualifies.

Q-9: What is a distribution of a plan loan offset amount, and is it an eligible rollover distribution?

A-9: (a) *General rule.* A distribution of a plan loan offset amount, as defined in paragraph (b) of this Q&A, is an eligible rollover distribution if it satisfies Q&A-3 of this section. Thus, an amount equal to the plan loan offset amount can be rolled over by the employee (or spousal distributee) to an eligible retirement plan within the 60-day period under section 402(c)(3), unless the plan loan offset amount fails to be an eligible rollover distribution for another reason. See § 1.401(a)(31)-1, Q&A-16 for guidance concerning the offering of a direct rollover of a plan loan offset amount. See § 31.3405(c)-1, Q&A-11 of this chapter for guidance concerning special withholding rules with respect to plan loan offset amounts.

(b) *Definition of plan loan offset amount.* For purposes of section 402(c), a distribution of a plan loan offset amount is a distribution that occurs when, under the plan terms governing a plan loan, the participant's accrued benefit is reduced (offset) in order to repay the loan (including the enforcement of the plan's security interest in a participant's accrued benefit). A distribution of a plan loan offset amount can occur in a variety of circumstances, e.g., where the terms governing a plan loan require that, in the event of the employee's termination of employment or request for a distribution, the loan be repaid immediately or treated as in default. A distribution of a plan loan offset amount also occurs when, under the terms governing the plan loan, the loan is cancelled, accelerated, or treated as if it were in default (e.g., where the plan treats a loan as in default upon an employee's termination of employment or within a specified period thereafter). A distribution of a plan loan offset amount is an actual distribution, not a deemed distribution under section 72(p).

(c) *Examples.* The rules with respect to a plan loan offset amount in this Q&A-9, § 1.401(a)(31)-1, Q&A-16 and § 31.3405(c)-1, Q&A-11 of this chapter are illustrated by the following examples:

Example 1. (a) In 1996, Employee A has an account balance of $10,000 in Plan Y, of which $3,000 is invested in a plan loan to Employee A that is secured by Employee A's account balance in Plan Y. Employee A has made no after-tax employee contributions to Plan Y. Plan Y does not provide any direct rollover option with respect to plan loans. Upon termination of employment in 1996, Employee A, who is under age 70½, elects a distribution of Employee A's entire account balance in Plan Y, and Employee A's outstanding loan is offset against the account balance on distribution. Employee A elects a direct rollover of the distribution.

(b) In order to satisfy section 401(a)(31), Plan Y must pay $7,000 directly to the eligible retirement plan chosen by Employee A in a direct rollover. When Employee A's account balance was offset by the amount of the $3,000 unpaid loan balance, Employee A received a plan loan offset amount (equivalent to $3,000) that is an eligible rollover distribution. However, under § 1.401(a)(31)-1, Q&A-16 Plan Y satisfies section 401(a)(31), even though a direct rollover option was not provided with respect to the $3,000 plan loan offset amount.

(c) No withholding is required under section 3405(c) on account of the distribution of the $3,000 plan loan offset amount because no cash or other property (other than the plan loan offset amount) is received by Employee A from which to satisfy the withholding. Employee A may roll over $3,000 to an eligible retirement plan within the 60 day period provided in section 402(c)(3).

Example 2. (a) The facts are the same as in Example 1, except that the terms governing the plan loan to Employee A provide that, upon termination of employment, Employee A's account balance is automatically offset by the amount of any unpaid loan balance to repay the loan. Employee A terminates employment but does not request a distribution from Plan Y. Nevertheless, pursuant to the terms governing the plan loan, Employee A's account balance is automatically offset by the amount of the $3,000 unpaid loan balance.

(b) The $3,000 plan loan offset amount attributable to the plan loan in this example is treated in the same manner as the $3,000 plan loan offset amount in Example 1.

Example 3. (a) The facts are the same as in Example 2, except that, instead of providing for an automatic offset upon termination of employment to repay the plan loan, the terms governing the plan loan require full repayment of the loan by Employee A within 30 days of termination of employment. Employee A terminates employment, does not elect a distribution from Plan Y, and also fails to repay the plan loan within 30 days. The plan administrator of Plan Y declares the plan loan to Employee A in default and executes on the loan by offsetting Employee A's account balance by the amount of the $3,000 unpaid loan balance.

(b) The $3,000 plan loan offset amount attributable to the plan loan in this example is treated in the same manner as the $3,000 plan loan offset amount in Example 1 and in Example 2. The result in this Example 3 is the same even though the plan administrator treats the loan as in default before offsetting Employee A's accrued benefit by the amount of the unpaid loan.

Example 4. (a) The facts are the same as in Example 1, except that Employee A elects to receive the distribution of the account balance that remains after the $3,000 offset to repay the plan loan, instead of electing a direct rollover of the remaining account balance.

(b) In this case, the amount of the distribution received by Employee A is $10,000, not $3,000. Because the amount of the $3,000 offset attributable to the loan is included in determining the amount that equals 20 percent of the eligible rollover distribution received by Employee A, withholding in the amount of $2,000 (20 percent of $10,000) is required under section 3405(c). The $2,000 is required to be withheld from the $7,000 to be distributed to Employee A in cash, so that Employee A actually receives a check for $5,000.

Example 5. The facts are the same as in Example 4, except that the $7,000 distribution to Employee A after the offset to repay the loan consists solely of employer securities within the meaning of section 402(e)(4)(E). In this case, no withholding is required under section 3405(c) because the distribution consists solely of the $3,000 plan loan offset amount and the $7,000 distribution of employer securities. This is the result because the total amount required to be withheld does not exceed the sum of the cash and the fair market value of other property distributed, excluding plan loan offset amounts and employer securities. Employee A may roll over the employer securities and $3,000 to an eligible retirement plan within the 60-day period provided in section 402(c)(3).

Example 6. Employee B, who is age 40, has an account balance in Plan Z, a profit sharing plan qualified under section 401(a) that includes a qualified cash or deferred arrangement described in section 401(k). Plan Z provides for no after-tax employee contributions. In 1990, Employee B receives a loan from Plan Z, the terms of which satisfy section 72(p)(2), and which is secured by elective contributions subject to the distribution restrictions in section 401(k)(2)(B). In 1996, the loan fails to satisfy section 72(p)(2) because Employee B stops repayment. In that year, pursuant to section 72(p), Employee B is taxed on a deemed distribution equal to the amount of the unpaid loan balance. Under Q&A-4 of this section, the deemed distribution is not an eligible rollover distribution. Because Employee B has not separated from service or experienced any other event that permits the distribution under section

401(k)(2)(B) of the elective contributions that secure the loan, Plan Z is prohibited from executing on the loan. Accordingly, Employee B's account balance is not offset by the amount of the unpaid loan balance at the time Employee B stops repayment on the loan. Thus, there is no distribution of an offset amount that is an eligible rollover distribution in 1996.

* * *

Q-12: How does section 402(c) apply to a distributee who is not the employee?

A-12: (a) *Spousal distributee.* If any distribution attributable to an employee is paid to the employee's surviving spouse, section 402(c) applies to the distribution in the same manner as if the spouse were the employee. The same rule applies if any distribution attributable to an employee is paid in accordance with a qualified domestic relations order (as defined in section 414(p)) to the employee's spouse or former spouse who is an alternate payee. Therefore, a distribution to the surviving spouse of an employee (or to a spouse or former spouse who is an alternate payee under a qualified domestic relations order), including a distribution of ancillary death benefits attributable to the employee, is an eligible rollover distribution if it meets the requirements of section 402(c)(2) and (4) and Q&A-3 through Q&A-10 and Q&A-14 of this section. However, a qualified plan (as defined in Q&A-2 of this section) is not treated as an eligible retirement plan with respect to a surviving spouse. Only an individual retirement plan is treated as an eligible retirement plan with respect to an eligible rollover distribution to a surviving spouse.

(b) *Non-spousal distributee.* A distributee other than the employee or the employee's surviving spouse (or a spouse or former spouse who is an alternate payee under a qualified domestic relations order) is not permitted to roll over distributions from a qualified plan. Therefore, those distributions do not constitute eligible rollover distributions under section 402(c)(4) and are not subject to the 20-percent income tax withholding under section 3405(c).

* * *

§ 1.404(a)-12. Contributions of an employer under a plan that does not meet the requirements of section 401(a); application of section 404(a)(5).

(a) *In general.* Section 404(a)(5) covers all cases for which deductions are allowable under section 404(a) (for contributions paid by an employer under a stock bonus, pension, profit sharing, or annuity plan or for any compensation paid on account of any employee under a plan deferring the receipt of such compensation) but not allowable under paragraph (1), (2), (3), (4), or (7) of such section. For the rules with respect to the taxability of an employee when rights under a nonexempt trust become substantially vested, see section 402(b) and the regulations thereunder.

(b) *Contributions made after August 1, 1969*—(1) *In general.* A deduction is allowable for a contribution paid after August 1, 1969, under section 404(a)(5) only in the taxable year of the employer in which or with which ends the taxable year of an employee in which an amount attributable to such contribution is includible in his gross income as compensation, and then only to the extent allowable under section 404(a). See § 1.404(a)-1. For example, if an employer A contributes $1,000 to the account of its employee E for its taxable (calendar) year 1977, but the amount in the account attributable to that contribution is not includible in E's gross income until his taxable (calendar) year 1980 (at which time the includible amount is $1,150), A's deduction for that contribution is $1,000 in 1980 (if allowable under section 404(a)). For purposes of this (1), a contribution is considered to be so includible where the employee or his beneficiary excludes it from his gross income under section 101(b) or subchapter N. To the extent that property of the employer is transferred in connection with such a contribution, such transfer will constitute a disposition of such property by the employer upon which gain or loss is recognized, except as provided in section 1032 and the regulations thereunder. The amount of gain or loss recognized from such disposition shall be the difference between the value of such property used to measure the deduction allowable under this section and the employer's adjusted basis in such property.

(2) *Special rule for unfunded pensions and certain death benefits.* If unfunded pensions are paid directly to former employees, such payments are includible in their gross income when paid, and accordingly, such amounts are deductible under section 404(a)(5) when paid. Similarly, if amounts are paid as a death benefit to the beneficiaries of an employee (for example, by continuing his salary for a reasonable period), and if such amounts meet the requirements of section 162 or 212, such amounts are deductible under section 404(a)(5) in any case when they are not includible under the other paragraphs of section 404(a).

(3) *Separate accounts for funded plans with more than one employee.* In the case of a funded plan under which more than one employee participates, no deduction is allowable under section 404(a)(5) for any contribution unless separate accounts are maintained for each employee. The requirement of separate accounts does not require that a separate trust be maintained for each employee. However, a separate account must be maintained for each employee to which employer contributions under the plan are allocated, along with any income earned thereon. In addition, such accounts must be sufficiently separate and independent to qualify as separate shares under section 663(c). Nothing shall preclude a trust which loses its exemption under section 501(a) from setting up such accounts and meeting the separate account requirement of section 404(a)(5) with respect to the taxable years in which such accounts are set up and maintained.

§ 1.408-4 Treatment of distributions from individual retirement arrangements.

(a) *General rule*—(1) *Inclusion in income.* Except as otherwise provided in this section, any amount actually paid or distributed or deemed paid or distributed from an individual retirement account or individual retirement annuity shall be included in the gross income of the payee or distributee for the taxable year in which the payment or distribution is received.

(2) *Zero basis.* Notwithstanding section 1015(d) or any other provision of the Code, the basis (or investment in the contract) of any person in such an account or annuity is zero. For purposes of this section, an assignment of an individual's rights under an individual retirement account or an individual retirement annuity shall, except as provided in § 1.408-4(g) (relating to transfer incident to divorce), be deemed a distribution to such individual from such account or annuity of the amount assigned.

* * *

(g) *Transfer incident to divorce*—(1) *General rule.* The transfer of an individual's interest, in whole or in part, in an individual retirement account, individual retirement annuity, or a retirement bond, to his former spouse under a valid divorce decree or a written instrument incident to such divorce shall not be considered to be a distribution from such an account or annuity to such individual or his former spouse; nor shall it be considered a taxable transfer by such individual to his former spouse notwithstanding any other provision of Subtitle A of the Code.

(2) *Spousal account.* The interest described in this paragraph (g) which is transferred to the former spouse shall be treated as an individual retirement account of such spouse if the interest is an individual retirement account; an individual retirement annuity of such spouse if such interest is an individual retirement annuity; and a retirement bond of such spouse if such interest is a retirement bond.

§ 1.408-8. Distribution requirements for individual retirement plans.

The following questions and answers relate to the distribution rules for IRAs provided in sections 408(a)(6) and 408(b)(3).

Q-1. Is an IRA subject to the distribution rules provided in section 401(a)(9) for qualified plans?

A-1. (a) Yes, an IRA is subject to the required minimum distribution rules provided in section 401(a)(9). In order to satisfy section 401(a)(9) for purposes of determining required minimum distributions for calendar years beginning on or after January 1, 2003, the rules of §§ 1.401(a)(9)-1 through 1.401(a)(9)-9 and 1.401(a)(9)-6T for defined contribution plans must be applied, except as otherwise provided in this section. For example, whether the 5-year rule or the life expectancy rule applies to distributions after death occurring before the IRA owner's required beginning date is determined in accordance with § 1.401(a)(9)-3 and the rules of § 1.401(a)(9)-4 apply for purposes of determining an IRA owner's designated beneficiary. Similarly, the amount of the minimum distribution required for each calendar year from an individual account is determined in accordance with § 1.401(a)(9)-5. For purposes of this section, the term IRA means an individual retirement account or annuity described in section 408(a) or (b). The IRA owner is the individual for whom an IRA is originally established by contributions for the benefit of that individual and that individual's beneficiaries.

(b) For purposes of applying the required minimum distribution rules in §§ 1.401(a)(9)-1 through 1.401(a)(9)-9 and 1.401(a)(9)-6 for qualified plans, the IRA trustee, custodian, or issuer is treated as the plan administrator, and the IRA owner is substituted for the employee.

(c) See A-14 and A-15 of § 1.408A-6 for rules under section 401(a)(9) that apply to a Roth IRA.

Q-2. Are IRAs that receive employer contributions under a simplified employee pension (defined in section 408(k)) or a SIMPLE IRA (defined in section 408(p)) treated as IRAs for purposes of section 401(a)(9)?

A-2. Yes, IRAs that receive employer contributions under a simplified employee pension (defined in section 408(k)) or a SIMPLE plan (defined in section 408(p)) are treated as IRAs, rather than employer plans, for purposes of section 401(a)(9) and are, therefore, subject to the distribution rules in this section.

Q-3. In the case of distributions from an IRA, what does the term required beginning date mean?

A-3. In the case of distributions from an IRA, the term required beginning date means April 1 of the calendar year following the calendar year in which the individual attains age 70½.

Q-4. What portion of a distribution from an IRA is not eligible for rollover because the amount is a required minimum distribution?

A-4. The portion of a distribution that is a required minimum distribution from an IRA and thus not eligible for rollover is determined in the same manner as provided in A-7 of § 1.402(c)-2 for distributions from qualified plans. For example, if a minimum distribution is required under section 401(a)(9) for a calendar year, an amount distributed during a calendar year from an IRA is treated as a required minimum distribution under section 401(a)(9) to the extent that the total required minimum distribution for the year under section 401(a)(9) for that IRA has not been satisfied. This requirement may be satisfied by a distribution from the IRA or, as permitted under A-9 of this section, from another IRA.

Q-5. May an individual's surviving spouse elect to treat such spouse's entire interest as a beneficiary in an individual's IRA upon the death of the individual (or the remaining part of such interest if distribution to the spouse has commenced) as the spouse's own account?

A-5. (a) The surviving spouse of an individual may elect, in the manner described in paragraph (b) of this A-5, to treat the spouse's entire interest as a beneficiary in an individual's IRA (or the remaining part of such interest if distribution thereof has commenced to the spouse) as the spouse's own IRA. This election is permitted to be made at any time after the individual's date of death. In order to make this election, the spouse must be the sole beneficiary of the IRA and have an unlimited right to withdraw amounts from the IRA. If a trust is named as beneficiary of the IRA, this requirement is not satisfied even if the spouse is the sole beneficiary of the trust. If the surviving spouse makes the election, the required minimum distribution for the calendar year of the election and each subsequent calendar year is determined under section 401(a)(9)(A) with the spouse as IRA owner and not section 401(a)(9)(B) with the surviving spouse as the deceased IRA owner's beneficiary. However, if the election is made in the calendar year containing the IRA owner's death, the spouse is not required to take a required minimum distribution as the IRA owner for that calendar year. Instead, the spouse is required to take a required minimum distribution for that year, determined with respect to the deceased IRA owner under the rules of A-4(a) of § 1.401(a)(9)-5, to the extent such a distribution was not made to the IRA owner before death.

(b) The election described in paragraph (a) of this A-5 is made by the surviving spouse redesignating the account as an account in the name of the surviving spouse as IRA owner rather than as beneficiary. Alternatively, a surviving spouse eligible to make the election is deemed to have made the election if, at any time, either of the following occurs—

(1) Any amount in the IRA that would be required to be distributed to the surviving spouse as beneficiary under section 401(a)(9)(B) is not distributed within the time period required under section 401(a)(9)(B); or

(2) Any additional amount is contributed to the IRA which is subject, or deemed to be subject, to the lifetime distribution requirements of section 401(a)(9)(A).

(c) The result of an election described in paragraph (b) of this A-5 is that the surviving spouse shall then be considered the IRA owner for whose benefit the trust is maintained for all purposes under the Internal Revenue Code (e.g., section 72(t)).

Q-6. How is the benefit determined for purposes of calculating the required minimum distribution from an IRA?

A-6. For purposes of determining the minimum distribution required to be made from an IRA in any calendar year, the account balance of the IRA as of December 31 of the calendar year immediately preceding the calendar year for which distributions are required to be made is substituted in A-3 of § 1.401(a)(9)-5 for the account balance of the employee. Except as provided in A-7 and A-8 of this section, no adjustments are made for contributions or distributions after that date.

Q-7. What rules apply in the case of a rollover to an IRA of an amount distributed by a qualified plan or another IRA?

A-7. If the surviving spouse of an employee rolls over a distribution from a qualified plan, such surviving spouse may elect to treat the IRA as the spouse's own IRA in accordance with the provisions in A-5 of this section. In the event of any other rollover to an IRA of an amount distributed by a qualified plan or another IRA, the rules in § 1.401(a)(9)-7 will apply for purposes of determining the account balance for the receiving IRA and the required minimum distribution from the receiving IRA. However, because the value of the account balance is determined as of December 31 of the year preceding the year for which the required minimum distribution is being determined and not as of a valuation date in the preceding year, the account balance of the receiving IRA is only adjusted if the amount is not received in the calendar year in which the amount rolled over is distributed. In that case, for purposes of determining the required minimum distribution for the calendar year in which such amount is actually received, the account balance of the receiving IRA as of December 31 of the preceding year must be adjusted by the amount received in accordance with A-2 of § 1.401(a)(9)-7.

Q-8. What rules apply in the case of a transfer (including a recharacterization) from one IRA to another?

A-8. (a) *General rule*. In the case of a trustee-to-trustee transfer from one IRA to another IRA that is not a distribution and rollover, the transfer is not treated as a distribution by the transferor IRA for purposes of section 401(a)(9). Accordingly, the minimum distribution requirement with respect to the transferor IRA must still be satisfied. Except as provided in paragraph (b) of this A-8 for recharacterizations, after the transfer the employee's account balance and the required minimum distribution under the transferee IRA are determined in the same manner as an account balance and required minimum distribution are determined under an IRA receiving a rollover contribution under A-7 of this section.

(b) *Recharacterizations*. If an amount is contributed to a Roth IRA that is a conversion contribution or failed conversion contribution and that amount (plus net income allocable to that amount) is transferred to another IRA (transferee IRA) in a subsequent year as a recharacterized contribution, the recharacterized contribution (plus allocable net income) must be added to the December 31 account balance of the transferee IRA for the year in which the conversion or failed conversion occurred.

Q-9. Is the required minimum distribution from one IRA of an owner permitted to be distributed from another IRA in order to satisfy section 401(a)(9)?

A-9. Yes, the required minimum distribution must be calculated separately for each IRA. The separately calculated amounts may then be totaled and the total distribution taken from any one or more of the individual's IRAs under the rules set forth in this A-9. Generally, only amounts in IRAs that an individual holds as the IRA owner may be aggregated. However, amounts in IRAs that an individual holds as a beneficiary of the same decedent and which are being distributed under the life expectancy rule in section 401(a)(9)(B)(iii) or (iv) may be aggregated, but such amounts may not be aggregated with amounts held in IRAs that the individual holds as the IRA owner or as the beneficiary of another decedent. Distributions from section 403(b) contracts or accounts will not satisfy the distribution requirements from IRAs, nor will distributions from IRAs satisfy the distribution requirements from section 403(b) contracts or accounts. Distributions from Roth IRAs (defined in section 408A) will not satisfy the distribution requirements applicable to IRAs or section 403(b) accounts or contracts and distributions from IRAs or section 403(b) contracts or accounts will not satisfy the distribution requirements from Roth IRAs.

Q-10. Is any reporting required by the trustee, custodian, or issuer of an IRA with respect to the minimum amount that is required to be distributed from that IRA?

A-10. Yes, the trustee, custodian, or issuer of an IRA is required to report information with respect to the minimum amount required to be distributed from the IRA for each calendar year to individuals or entities, at the time, and in the manner, prescribed by the Commissioner in revenue rulings, notices, and other guidance published in the Internal Revenue Bulletin (see § 601.601(d)(2)(ii)(b) of this chapter) as well as the applicable Federal tax forms and accompanying instructions.

Q-11. Which amounts distributed from an IRA are taken into account in determining whether section 401(a)(9) is satisfied?

A-11. (a) *General rule*. Except as provided in paragraph (b) of this A-11, all amounts distributed from an IRA are taken into account in determining whether section 401(a)(9) is satisfied, regardless of whether the amount is includible in income.

(b) *Amounts not taken into account*. The following amounts are not taken into account in determining whether the required minimum amount with respect to an IRA for a calendar year has been distributed—

(1) Contributions returned pursuant to section 408(d)(4), together with the income allocable to these contributions;

(2) Contributions returned pursuant to section 408(d)(5);

(3) Corrective distributions of excess simplified employee pension contributions under section 408(k)(6)(C), together with the income allocable to these distributions; and

(4) Similar items designated by the Commissioner in revenue rulings, notices, and other guidance published in the Internal Revenue Bulletin. See § 601.601(d)(2)(ii)(b) of this chapter.

§ 1.410(a)-3. Minimum age and service conditions.

* * *

(d) *Other conditions.* Section 410(a), § 1.410(a)-4, and this section relate solely to age and service conditions and do not preclude a plan from establishing conditions, other than conditions relating to age or service, which must be satisfied by plan participants. For example, such provisions would not preclude a qualified plan from requiring, as a condition of participation, that an employee be employed within a specified job classification. See section 410(b) and the regulations thereunder for rules with respect to coverage of employees under qualified plans.

(e) *Age and service requirements*—(1) *General rule.* For purposes of applying the rules of this section, plan provisions may be treated as imposing age or service requirements even though the provisions do not specifically refer to age or service. Plan provisions which have the effect of requiring an age or service requirement with the employer or employers maintaining the plan will be treated as if they imposed an age or service requirement. In general, a plan under which an employee cannot participate unless he retires will impose an age and service requirement. However, a plan may provide benefits which supplement benefits provided for employees covered under a pension plan, as defined in section 3(2) of the Employee Retirement Income Security Act of 1974, satisfying the requirements of section 410(a)(1) without violating the age and service rules.

(2) *Examples.* The rules of this paragraph are illustrated by the following examples:

Example (1). Corporation A is divided into two divisions. In order to work in division 2 an employee must first have been employed in division 1 for 5 years. A plan provision which required division 2 employment for participation will be treated as a service requirement because such a provision has the effect of requiring 5 years of service.

Example (2). Plan B requires as a condition of participation that each employee have had a driver's license for 15 years or more. This provision will be treated as an age requirement because such a provision has the effect of requiring an employee to attain a specified age.

* * *

§ 1.410(b)-2. Minimum coverage requirements (after 1993).

(a) *In general.* A plan is a qualified plan for a plan year only if the plan satisfies section 410(b) for the plan year. A plan satisfies section 410(b) for a plan year if and only if it satisfies paragraph (b) of this section with respect to employees for the plan year and paragraph (c) of this section with respect to former employees for the plan year. The rules in paragraphs (a), (b), and (c) of this section apply to all plans as a condition of qualification, including plans under which no employee is able to accrue any additional benefits (for example, frozen plans).

* * *

(b) *Requirements with respect to employees*—(1) *In general.* A plan satisfies this paragraph (b) for a plan year if and only if it satisfies at least one of the tests in paragraphs (b)(2) through (b)(7) of this section for the plan year.

(2) *Ratio percentage test*—(i) *In general.* A plan satisfies this paragraph (b)(2) for a plan year if and only if the plan's ratio percentage for the plan year is at least 70 percent. This test incorporates both the percentage test of section 410(b)(1)(A) and the ratio test of section 410(b)(1)(B). See § 1.410(b)-9 for the definition of ratio percentage.

(ii) *Examples.* The following examples illustrate the ratio percentage test of this paragraph (b)(2).

Example 1. For a plan year, Plan A benefits 70 percent of an employer's nonhighly compensated employees and 100 percent of the employer's highly compensated employees. The plan's ratio percentage for the year is 70 percent (70 percent/100 percent), and thus the plan satisfies the ratio percentage test.

Example 2. For a plan year, Plan B benefits 40 percent of the employer's nonhighly compensated employees and 60 percent of the employer's highly compensated employees. Plan B fails to satisfy the ratio percentage test because the plan's ratio percentage is only 66.67 percent (40 percent/60 percent).

(3) *Average benefit test.* A plan satisfies this paragraph (b)(3) for a plan year if and only if the plan satisfies both the nondiscriminatory classification test of § 1.410(b)-4 and the average benefit percentage test of § 1.410(b)-5 for the plan year.

* * *

(5) *Employers with no nonhighly compensated employees.* A plan satisfies this paragraph (b)(5) for a plan year if and only if the plan is maintained by an employer that has no nonhighly compensated employees at any time during the plan year.

(6) *Plans benefiting no highly compensated employees.* A plan satisfies this paragraph (b)(6) for a plan year if and only if the plan benefits no highly compensated employees for the plan year.

(7) *Plans benefiting collectively bargained employees.* A plan that benefits solely collectively bargained employees for a plan year satisfies this paragraph (b)(7) for the plan year. If a plan (within the meaning of § 1.410(b)-7(b)) benefits both collectively bargained employees and noncollectively bargained employees for a plan year, § 1.410(b)-7(c)(4) provides that the portion of the plan that benefits collectively bargained employees is treated as a separate plan from the portion of the plan that benefits noncollectively bargained employees. Thus, the mandatorily disaggregated portion of the plan that benefits the collectively bargained employees automatically satisfies this paragraph (b)(7) for the plan year and hence section 410(b). See § 1.410(b)-9 for the definitions of collectively bargained employee and noncollectively bargained employee.

* * *

§ 1.410(b)-4. Nondiscriminatory classification test.

(a) *In general.* A plan satisfies the nondiscriminatory classification test of this section for a plan year if and only if, for the plan year, the plan benefits the employees who qualify under a classification established by the employer in accordance with paragraph (b) of this section, and the classification of employees is nondiscriminatory under paragraph (c) of this section.

(b) *Reasonable classification* established by the employer. A classification is established by the employer in accordance with this paragraph (b) if and only if, based on all the facts and circumstances, the classification is reasonable and is established under objective business criteria that identify the category of employees who benefit under the plan. Reasonable classifications generally include specified job categories, nature of compensation (i.e., salaried or hourly), geographic location, and similar bona fide business criteria. An enumeration of employees by name or other specific criteria having substantially the same effect as an enumeration by name is not considered a reasonable classification.

(c) *Nondiscriminatory classification*—(1) *General rule.* A classification is nondiscriminatory under this paragraph (c) for a plan year if and only if the group of employees included in the classification benefiting under the plan satisfies the requirements of either paragraph (c)(2) or (c)(3) of this section for the plan year.

(2) *Safe harbor.* A plan satisfies the requirement of this paragraph (c)(2) for a plan

year if and only if the plan's ratio percentage is greater than or equal to the employer's safe harbor percentage, as defined in paragraph (c)(4)(i) of this section. See § 1.410(b)-9 for the definition of a plan's ratio percentage.

(3) *Facts and circumstances*—(i) *General rule*. A plan satisfies the requirements of this paragraph (c)(3) if and only if—

(A) The plan's ratio percentage is greater than or equal to the unsafe harbor percentage, as defined in paragraph (c)(4)(ii) of this section, and

(B) The classification satisfies the factual determination of paragraph (c)(3)(ii) of this section.

(ii) *Factual determination*. A classification satisfies this paragraph (c)(3)(ii) if and only if, based on all the relevant facts and circumstances, the Commissioner finds that the classification is nondiscriminatory. No one particular fact is determinative. Included among the facts and circumstances relevant in determining whether a classification is nondiscriminatory are the following—

(A) The underlying business reason for the classification. The greater the business reason for the classification, the more likely the classification is to be nondiscriminatory. Reducing the employer's cost of providing retirement benefits is not a relevant business reason.

(B) The percentage of the employer's employees benefiting under the plan. The higher the percentage, the more likely the classification is to be nondiscriminatory.

(C) Whether the number of employees benefiting under the plan in each salary range is representative of the number of employees in each salary range of the employer's workforce. In general, the more representative the percentages of employees benefiting under the plan in each salary range, the more likely the classification is to be nondiscriminatory.

(D) The difference between the plan's ratio percentage and the employer's safe harbor percentage. The smaller the difference, the more likely the classification is to be nondiscriminatory.

(E) The extent to which the plan's average benefit percentage (determined under § 1.410(b)-5) exceeds 70 percent.

(4) *Definitions*—(i) *Safe harbor percentage*. The safe harbor percentage of an employer is 50 percent, reduced by 3/4 of a percentage point for each whole percentage point by which the nonhighly compensated employee concentration percentage exceeds 60 percent. See paragraph (c)(4)(iv) for a table that illustrates the safe harbor percentage and unsafe harbor percentage.

(ii) *Unsafe harbor percentage*. The unsafe harbor percentage of an employer is 40 percent, reduced by 3/4 of a percentage point for each whole percentage point by which the nonhighly compensated employee concentration percentage exceeds 60 percent. However, in no case is the unsafe harbor percentage less than 20 percent.

(iii) *Nonhighly compensated employee concentration percentage*. The nonhighly compensated employee concentration percentage of an employer is the percentage of all the employees of the employer who are nonhighly compensated employees. Employees who are excludable employees for purposes of the average benefit test are not taken into account.

(iv) *Table*. The following table sets forth the safe harbor and unsafe harbor percentages at each nonhighly compensated employee concentration percentage:

Nonhighly compensated employee concentration percentage	*Safe harbor percentage*	*Unsafe harbor percentage*
0-60	50.00	40.00
61	49.25	39.25
62	48.50	38.50
63	47.75	37.75

64	47.00	37.00
65	46.25	36.25
66	45.50	35.50
67	44.75	34.75
68	44.00	34.00
69	43.25	33.25
70	42.50	32.50
71	41.75	31.75
72	41.00	31.00
73	40.25	30.25
74	39.50	29.50
75	38.75	28.75
76	38.00	28.00
77	37.25	27.25
78	36.50	26.50
79	35.75	25.75
80	35.00	25.00
81	34.25	24.25
82	33.50	23.50
83	32.75	22.75
84	32.00	22.00
85	31.25	21.25
86	30.50	20.50
87	29.75	20.00
88	29.00	20.00
89	28.25	20.00
90	27.50	20.00
91	26.75	20.00
92	26.00	20.00
93	25.25	20.00
94	24.50	20.00
95	23.75	20.00
96	23.00	20.00
97	22.25	20.00
98	21.50	20.00
99	20.75	20.00

(5) *Examples.* The following examples illustrate the rules in this paragraph (c).

Example 1. Employer A has 200 nonexcludable employees, of whom 120 are nonhighly compensated employees and 80 are highly compensated employees. Employer A maintains a plan that benefits 60 nonhighly compensated employees and 72 highly compensated employees. Thus, the plan's ratio percentage is 55.56 percent ([60/120]/[72/80]=50%/90%=0.5556), which is below the percentage necessary to satisfy the ratio percentage test of § 1.410(b)-2(b)(2). The employer's nonhighly compensated employee concentration percentage is 60 percent (120/200); thus, Employer A's safe harbor percentage is 50 percent and its unsafe harbor percentage is 40 percent. Because the plan's ratio percentage is greater than the safe harbor percentage, the plan's classification satisfies the safe harbor of paragraph (c)(2) of this section.

Example 2. The facts are the same as in *Example 1*, except that the plan benefits only

40 nonhighly compensated employees. The plan's ratio percentage is thus 37.03 percent ([40/120]/[72/80]=33.33%/90%=0.3703). Under these facts, the plan's classification is below the unsafe harbor percentage and is thus considered discriminatory.

Example 3. The facts are the same as in *Example 1,* except that the plan benefits 45 nonhighly compensated employees. The plan's ratio percentage is thus 41.67 percent ([45/120]/[72/80]=37.50%/90%=0.4167), above the unsafe harbor percentage (40 percent) and below the safe harbor percentage (50 percent). The Commissioner may determine that the classification is nondiscriminatory after considering all the relevant facts and circumstances.

* * *

§ 1.411(a)-4. Forfeitures, suspensions, etc.

(a) *Nonforfeitability.* Certain rights in an accrued benefit must be nonforfeitable to satisfy the requirements of section 411(a). This section defines the term "nonforfeitable" for purposes of these requirements. For purposes of section 411 and the regulations thereunder, a right to an accrued benefit is considered to be nonforfeitable at a particular time if, at that time and thereafter, it is an unconditional right. Except as provided by paragraph (b) of this section, a right which, at a particular time, is conditioned under the plan upon a subsequent event, subsequent performance, or subsequent forbearance which will cause the loss of such right is a forfeitable right at that time. Certain adjustments to plan benefits such as adjustments in excess of reasonable actuarial reductions, can result in rights being forfeitable. Rights which are conditioned upon a sufficiency of plan assets in the event of a termination or partial termination are considered to be forfeitable because of such condition. However, a plan does not violate the nonforfeitability requirements merely because in the event of a termination an employee does not have any recourse toward satisfaction of his nonforfeitable benefits from other than the plan assets or the Pension Benefit Guaranty Corporation. Furthermore, nonforfeitable rights are not considered to be forfeitable by reason of the fact that they may be reduced to take into account benefits which are provided under the Social Security Act or under any other Federal or State law and which are taken into account in determining plan benefits. To the extent that rights are not required to be nonforfeitable to satisfy the minimum vesting standards, or the nondiscrimination requirements of section 401(a)(4), they may be forfeited without regard to the limitations on forfeitability required by this section.

* * *

§ 1.411(a)-11. Restriction and valuation of distributions.

(a) *Scope*—(1) *In general.* Section 411(a)(11) restricts the ability of a plan to distribute any portion of a participant's accrued benefit without the participant's consent. Section 411(a)(11) also restricts the ability of defined benefit plans to distribute any portion of a participant's accrued benefit in optional forms of benefit without complying with specified valuation rules for determining the amount of the distribution. If the consent requirements or the valuation rules of this section are not satisfied, the plan fails to satisfy the requirements of section 411(a).

(2) *Accrued benefit.* For purposes of this section, an accrued benefit is valued taking into consideration the particular optional form in which the benefit is to be distributed. The value of an accrued benefit is the present value of the benefit in the distribution form determined under the plan. For example, a plan that provides a subsidized early retirement annuity benefit may specify that the optional single sum distribution form of benefit available at early retirement age is the present value of the subsidized early retirement annuity benefit. In this case, the subsidized early retirement annuity benefit must be used to apply the valuation requirements of this section and the resulting amount of the single sum distribution. However, if a plan that provides a subsidized early retirement annuity benefit specifies that the single sum distribution benefit

available at early retirement age is the present value of the normal retirement annuity benefit, then the normal retirement annuity benefit is used to apply the valuation requirements of this section and the resulting amount of the single sum distribution available at early retirement age.

* * *

(d) *Distribution valuation requirements.* In determining the present value of any distribution of any accrued benefit from a defined benefit plan, the plan must take into account specified valuation rules. For this purpose, the valuation rules are the same valuation rules for valuing distributions as set forth in section 417(e); see § 1.417(e)-1(d). This paragraph (d) applies both before and after the participant's death regardless of whether the accrued benefit is immediately distributable. This paragraph also applies whether or not the participant's consent is required under paragraphs (b) and (c) of this section.

* * *

§ 1.411(d)-2. Termination or partial termination; discontinuance of contributions.

* * *

(b) *Partial termination*—(1) *General rule.* Whether or not a partial termination of a qualified plan occurs (and the time of such event) shall be determined by the Commissioner with regard to all the facts and circumstances in a particular case. Such facts and circumstances include: the exclusion, by reason of a plan amendment or severance by the employer, of a group of employees who have previously been covered by the plan; and plan amendments which adversely affect the rights of employees to vest in benefits under the plan.

(2) *Special rule.* If a defined benefit plan ceases or decreases future benefit accruals under the plan, a partial termination shall be deemed to occur if, as a result of such cessation or decrease, a potential reversion to the employer, or employers, maintaining the plan (determined as of the date such cessation or decrease is adopted) is created or increased. If no such reversion is created or increased, a partial termination shall be deemed not to occur by reason of such cessation or decrease. However, the Commissioner may determine that a partial termination of such a plan occurs pursuant to subparagraph (1) of this paragraph for reasons other than such cessation or decrease.

(3) *Effect of partial termination.* If a termination of a qualified plan occurs, the provisions of section 411(d)(3) apply only to the part of the plan that is terminated.

* * *

§ 1.411(d)-3. Section 411(d)(6) protected benefits.

(a) *Protection of accrued benefits*—(1) *General rule.* Under section 411(d)(6)(A), a plan is not a qualified plan (and a trust forming a part of such plan is not a qualified trust) if a plan amendment decreases the accrued benefit of any plan participant, except as provided in section 412(d)(2) (section 412(c)(8) for plan years beginning before January 1, 2008), section 4281 of the Employee Retirement Income Security Act of 1974 as amended (ERISA), or other applicable law (see, for example, sections 418D and 418E of the Internal Revenue Code, and section 1107 of the Pension Protection Act of 2006, Public Law 109-280 (120 Stat. 780, 1063)). However, such an amendment does not violate section 411(d)(6) to the extent it applies with respect to benefits that accrue after the applicable amendment date. The protection of section 411(d)(6) applies to a participant's entire accrued benefit under the plan as of the applicable amendment date, without regard to whether the entire accrued benefit was accrued before a participant's severance from employment or whether any portion was the result of an increase in the accrued benefit of the participant pursuant to a plan amendment adopted after the participant's severance from employment.

(2) *Plan provisions taken into account*—(i) *Direct or indirect reduction in accrued benefit.* For purposes of determining whether a participant's accrued benefit is decreased, all of the amendments to the provisions of a plan affecting, directly or indirectly, the computation of accrued benefits are taken into account. Plan provisions indirectly affecting the computation of accrued benefits include, for example, provisions relating to years of service and compensation.

(ii) *Amendments effective with the same applicable amendment date.* In determining whether a reduction in a participant's accrued benefit has occurred, all plan amendments with the same applicable amendment date are treated as one amendment. Thus, if two amendments have the same applicable amendment date and one amendment, standing alone, increases participants' accrued benefits and the other amendment, standing alone, decreases participants' accrued benefits, the amendments are treated as one amendment and will only violate section 411(d)(6) if, for any participant, the net effect is to decrease participants' accrued benefit as of that applicable amendment date.

(iii) *Multiple amendments*—(A) *General rule.* A plan amendment violates the requirements of section 411(d)(6) if it is one of a series of plan amendments that, when taken together, have the effect of reducing or eliminating a section 411(d)(6) protected benefit in a manner that would be prohibited by section 411(d)(6) if accomplished through a single amendment.

(B) *Determination of the time period for combining plan amendments.* For purposes of applying the rule in paragraph (a)(2)(iii)(A) of this section, generally only plan amendments adopted within a 3-year period are taken into account.

* * *

(g) *Definitions and use of terms.* The definitions in this paragraph (g) apply for purposes of this section.

* * *

(6) *Definitions of types of section 411(d)(6)(B) protected benefits*—(i) *Early retirement benefit.* The term early retirement benefit means the right, under the terms of a plan, to commence distribution of a retirement-type benefit at a particular date after severance from employment with the employer and before normal retirement age. Different early retirement benefits result from differences in terms relating to timing.

(ii) *Optional form of benefit*—(A) *In general.* The term optional form of benefit means a distribution alternative (including the normal form of benefit) that is available under the plan with respect to an accrued benefit or a distribution alternative with respect to a retirement-type benefit. Different optional forms of benefit exist if a distribution alternative is not payable on substantially the same terms as another distribution alternative. The relevant terms include all terms affecting the value of the optional form, such as the method of benefit calculation and the actuarial factors or assumptions used to determine the amount distributed. Thus, for example, different optional forms of benefit may result from differences in terms relating to the payment schedule, timing, commencement, medium of distribution (e.g., in cash or in kind), election rights, differences in eligibility requirements, or the portion of the benefit to which the distribution alternative applies. Likewise, differences in the normal retirement ages of employees or in the form in which the accrued benefit of employees is payable at normal retirement age under a plan are taken into account in determining whether a distribution alternative constitutes one or more optional forms of benefit.

(B) *Death benefits.* If a death benefit is payable after the annuity starting date for a specific optional form of benefit and the same death benefit would not be provided if another optional form of benefit were elected by a participant, then that death benefit is part of the specific optional form of benefit and is thus protected under section 411(d)(6). A death benefit is not treated as part of a specific optional form of benefit merely because the same benefit is not provided to a participant who has received his or her entire accrued benefit prior to death. For example, a $5,000 death benefit that is payable to all participants except any participant who has received his or her accrued benefit in a single-sum distribution is not part of a specific optional form of benefit.

(iii) *Retirement-type benefit.* The term retirement-type benefit means—

(A) The payment of a distribution alternative with respect to an accrued benefit; or

(B) The payment of any other benefit under a defined benefit plan (including a QSUPP as defined in § 1.401(a)(4)-12) that is permitted to be in a qualified pension plan, continues after retirement, and is not an ancillary benefit.

(iv) *Retirement-type subsidy.* The term retirement-type subsidy means the excess, if any, of the actuarial present value of a retirement-type benefit over the actuarial present value of the accrued benefit commencing at normal retirement age or at actual commencement date, if later, with both such actuarial present values determined as of the date the retirement-type benefit commences. Examples of retirement-type subsidies include a subsidized early retirement benefit and a subsidized qualified joint and survivor annuity.

(v) *Subsidized early retirement benefit or early retirement subsidy.* The terms subsidized early retirement benefit or early retirement subsidy mean the right, under the terms of a plan, to commence distribution of a retirement-type benefit at a particular date after severance from employment with the employer and before normal retirement age where the actuarial present value of the optional forms of benefit available to the participant under the plan at that annuity starting date exceeds the actuarial present value of the accrued benefit commencing at normal retirement age (with such actuarial present values determined as of the annuity starting date). Thus, an early retirement subsidy is an early retirement benefit that provides a retirement-type subsidy.

* * *

§ 1.411(d)-4. Section 411(d)(6) protected benefits.

Q-1: What are "section 411(d)(6) protected benefits"?

A-1: (a) *In general.* The term "section 411(d)(6) protected benefit" includes any benefit that is described in one or more of the following categories—

(1) Benefits described in section 411(d)(6)(A),

(2) Early retirement benefits (as defined in § 1.411(d)-3(g)(6)(i)) and retirement-type subsidies (as defined in § 1.411(d)-3(g)(6)(iv)), and

(3) Optional forms of benefit described in section 411(d)(6)(B)(ii).

Such benefits, to the extent they have accrued, are subject to the protection of section 411(d)(6) and, where applicable, the definitely determinable requirement of section 401(a) (including section 401(a)(25)) and cannot, therefore, be reduced, eliminated, or made subject to employer discretion except to the extent permitted by regulations.

(b) *Optional forms of benefit*— (1) *In general.* The term optional form of benefit has the same meaning as in § 1.411(d)-3(g)(6)(ii). Under this definition, different optional forms of benefit exist if a distribution alternative is not payable on substantially the same terms as another distribution alternative. Thus, for example, different optional forms of benefit may result from differences in terms relating to the payment schedule, timing, commencement, medium of distribution (e.g., in cash or in kind), election rights, differences in eligibility requirements, or the portion of the benefit to which the distribution alternative applies.

* * *

(c) *Plan terms*—(1) *General rule.* Generally, benefits described in section 411(d)(6)(A), early retirement benefits, retirement-type subsidies, and optional forms of benefit are section 411(d)(6) protected benefits only if they are provided under the terms of a plan. However, if an employer establishes a pattern of repeated plan amendments providing for similar benefits in similar situations for substantially consecutive, limited periods of time, such benefits will be treated as provided under the terms of the plan, without regard to the limited periods of time, to the extent necessary to carry out the purposes of section 411(d)(6) and, where applicable, the definitely determinable requirement of section 401(a), including section 401(a)(25). A pattern of repeated plan amendments providing that a particular optional form of benefit is available to certain named employees for a limited period of time is within the scope of this rule and may result in such optional form of benefit being treated as provided under the terms of the plan to all employees covered under the plan without regard to the limited period of time and the limited group of named employees.

* * *

(d) *Benefits that are not section 411(d)(6) protected benefits.* The following benefits are examples of items that are not section 411(d)(6) protected benefits:

(1) Ancillary life insurance protection;

(2) Accident or health insurance benefits;

(3) Social security supplements described in section 411(a)(9), except qualified social security supplements as defined in § 1.401(a)(4)-12;

(4) The availability of loans (other than the distribution of an employee's accrued benefit upon default under a loan);

(5) The right to make after-tax employee contributions or elective deferrals described in section 402(g)(3);

(6) The right to direct investments;

(7) The right to a particular form of investment (e.g., investment in employer stock or securities or investment in certain types of securities, commercial paper, or other investment media);

(8) The allocation dates for contributions, forfeitures, and earnings, the time for making contributions (but not the conditions for receiving an allocation of contributions or forfeitures for a plan year after such conditions have been satisfied), and the valuation dates for account balances;

(9) Administrative procedures for distributing benefits, such as provisions relating to the particular dates on which notices are given and by which elections must be made; and

(10) Rights that derive from administrative and operational provisions, such as mechanical procedures for allocating investment experience among accounts in defined contribution plans.

Q-2: To what extent may section 411(d)(6) protected benefits under a plan be reduced or eliminated?

A-2: (a) *Reduction or elimination of section 411(d)(6) protected benefits*—(1) *In general.* A plan is not permitted to be amended to eliminate or reduce a section 411(d)(6) protected benefit that has already accrued, except as provided in § 1.411(d)-3 or this section. This is generally the case even if such elimination or reduction is contingent upon the employee's consent. However, a plan may be amended to eliminate or reduce section 411(d)(6) protected benefits with respect to benefits not yet accrued as of the later of the amendment's adoption date or effective date without violating section 411(d)(6).

(2) *Selection of optional forms of benefit*—(i) *General rule.* A plan may treat a participant as receiving his entire nonforfeitable accrued benefit under the plan if the participant receives his benefit in an optional form of benefit in an amount determined under the plan that is at least the actuarial equivalent of the employee's nonforfeitable accrued benefit payable at normal retirement age under the plan. This is true even though the participant could have elected to receive an optional form of benefit with a greater actuarial value than the value of the optional form received, such as an optional form including retirement-type subsidies, and without regard to whether such other, more valuable optional form could have commenced immediately or could have be-

come available only upon the employee's future satisfaction of specified eligibility conditions.

* * *

(e) *Permitted plan amendments affecting alternative forms of payment under defined contribution plans*—(1) *General rule.* A defined contribution plan does not violate the requirements of section 411(d)(6) merely because the plan is amended to eliminate or restrict the ability of a participant to receive payment of accrued benefits under a particular optional form of benefit for distributions with annuity starting dates after the date the amendment is adopted if, after the plan amendment is effective with respect to the participant, the alternative forms of payment available to the participant include payment in a single-sum distribution form that is otherwise identical to the optional form of benefit that is being eliminated or restricted.

(2) *Otherwise identical single-sum distribution.* For purposes of this paragraph (e), a single-sum distribution form is otherwise identical to an optional form of benefit that is eliminated or restricted pursuant to paragraph (e)(1) of this Q&A-2 only if the single-sum distribution form is identical in all respects to the eliminated or restricted optional form of benefit (or would be identical except that it provides greater rights to the participant) except with respect to the timing of payments after commencement. For example, a single-sum distribution form is not otherwise identical to a specified installment form of benefit if the single-sum distribution form is not available for distribution on the date on which the installment form would have been available for commencement, is not available in the same medium of distribution as the installment form, or imposes any condition of eligibility that did not apply to the installment form. However, an otherwise identical distribution form need not retain rights or features of the optional form of benefit that is eliminated or restricted to the extent that those rights or features would not be protected from elimination or restriction under section 411(d)(6) or this section.

(3) *Example.* The following example illustrates the application of this paragraph (e):

Example. (i) P is a participant in Plan M, a qualified profit-sharing plan with a calendar plan year that is invested in mutual funds. The distribution forms available to P under Plan M include a distribution of P's vested account balance under Plan M in the form of distribution of various annuity contract forms (including a single life annuity and a joint and survivor annuity). The annuity payments under the annuity contract forms begin as of the first day of the month following P's severance from employment (or as of the first day of any subsequent month, subject to the requirements of section 401(a)(9)). P has not previously elected payment of benefits in the form of a life annuity, and Plan M is not a direct or indirect transferee of any plan that is a defined benefit plan or a defined contribution plan that is subject to section 412. Distributions on the death of a participant are made in accordance with plan provisions that comply with section 401(a)(11)(B)(iii)(I). On September 2, 2005, Plan M is amended so that, effective for payments that begin on or after November 1, 2005, P is no longer entitled to any distribution in the form of the distribution of an annuity contract. However, after the amendment is effective, P is entitled to receive a single-sum cash distribution of P's vested account balance under Plan M payable as of the first day of the month following P's severance from employment (or as of the first day of any subsequent month, subject to the requirements of section 401(a)(9)).

(ii) Plan M does not violate the requirements of section 411(d)(6) (or section 401(a)(11)) merely because, as of November 1, 2005, the plan amendment has eliminated P's option to receive a distribution in any of the various annuity contract forms previously available.

* * *

Q-4: May a plan provide that the employer may, through the exercise of discretion, deny a participant a section 411(d)(6) protected benefit for which the participant is otherwise eligible?

A-4: (a) *In general.* Except as provided in paragraph (d) of Q&A-2 of this section with respect to certain employee stock ownership plans, a plan that permits the employer, either directly or indirectly, through the exercise of discretion, to deny a participant a section 411(d)(6) protected benefit provided under the plan for which the participant is otherwise eligible (but for the employer's exercise of discretion) violates the requirements of section 411(d)(6). A plan provision that makes a section 411(d)(6) protected benefit available only to those employees as the employer may designate is within the scope of this prohibition. Thus, for example, a plan provision under which only employees who are designated by the employer are eligible to receive a subsidized early retirement benefit constitutes an impermissible provision under section 411(d)(6). In addition, a pension plan that permits employer discretion to deny the availability of a section 411(d)(6) protected benefit violates the definitely determinable requirement of section 401(a), including section 401(a)(25). See § 1.401-1(b)(1)(i). This is the result even if the plan specifically limits the employer's discretion to choosing among section 411(d)(6) protected benefits, including optional forms of benefit, that are actuarially equivalent. In addition, the provisions of sections 411(a)(11) and 417(e) that allow a plan to make involuntary distributions of certain amounts are not excepted from this limitation on employer discretion. Thus, for example, a plan may not permit employer discretion with respect to whether benefits will be distributed involuntarily in the event that the present value of the employee's benefit is not more than the cash-out limit in effect under § 1.411(a)-11(c)(3)(ii) within the meaning of sections 411(a)(11) and 417(e). (An exception is provided for such provisions with respect to the nondiscrimination requirements of section 401(a)(4). See § 1.401(a)(4)- 4(b)(2)(ii)(C).)

(b) *Exception for administrative discretion.* A plan may permit limited discretion with respect to the ministerial or mechanical administration of the plan, including the application of objective plan criteria specifically set forth in the plan. Such plan provisions do not violate the requirements of section 411(d)(6) or the definitely determinable requirement of section 401(a), including section 401(a)(25). For example, these requirements are not violated by the following provisions that permit limited administrative discretion:

(1) Commencement of benefit payments as soon as administratively feasible after a stated date or event;

(2) Employer authority to determine whether objective criteria specified in the plan (e.g., objective criteria designed to identify those employees with a heavy and immediate financial need or objective criteria designed to determine whether an employee has a permanent and total disability) have been satisfied; and

(3) Employer authority to determine, pursuant to specific guidelines set forth in the plan, whether the participant or spouse is dead or cannot be located.

* * *

Q-6: May a plan condition the availability of a section 411(d)(6) protected benefit on the satisfaction of objective conditions that are specifically set forth in the plan?

A-6: (a) *Certain objective conditions permissible*—(1) *In general.* The availability of a section 411(d)(6) protected benefit may be limited to employees who satisfy certain objective conditions provided the conditions are ascertainable, clearly set forth in the plan and not subject to the employer's discretion except to the extent reasonably necessary to determine whether the objective conditions have been met. Also, the availability of the section 411(d)(6) protected benefit must meet the nondiscrimination requirements of section 401(a)(4). See § 1.401(a)-4.

(2) *Examples of permissible conditions.* The following examples illustrate of permissible objective conditions: a plan may deny a single sum distribution form to employees for whom life insurance is not available at stan-

dard rates as defined under the terms of the plan at the time the single sum distribution would otherwise be payable; a plan may provide that a single sum distribution is available only if the employee is in extreme financial need as defined under the terms of the plan at the time the single sum distribution would otherwise be payable; a plan may condition the availability of a single sum distribution on the execution of a covenant not to compete, provided that objective conditions with respect to the terms of such covenant and the employees and circumstances requiring execution of such covenant are set forth in the plan.

(b) *Conditions based on factors within employer's discretion generally impermissible.* A plan may not limit the availability of section 411(d)(6) protected benefits permitted under the plan on objective conditions that are within the employer's discretion. For example, the availability of section 411(d)(6) protected benefits in a plan may not be conditioned on a determination with respect to the level of the plan's funded status, because the amount of plan funding is within the employer's discretion. However, for example, although conditions based on the plan's funded status are impermissible, a plan may limit the availability of a section 411(d)(6) protected benefit (e.g., a single sum distribution) in an objective manner, such as the following:

(1) Single sum distributions of $25,000 and less are available without limit; and

(2) Single sum distributions in excess of $25,000 are available for a year only to the extent that the total amount of such single sum distributions for the year is not greater than $5,000,000; and

(3) An objective and nondiscriminatory method for determining which particular single sum distributions will not be available during a year in order for the $5,000,000 limit to be satisfied is set forth in the plan.

* * *

§ 1.414(c)-2. Two or more trades or businesses under common control.

(a) *In general.* For purposes of this section, the term "two or more trades or businesses under common control" means any group of trades or businesses which is either a "parent-subsidiary group of trades or businesses under common control" as defined in paragraph (b) of this section, a "brother-sister group of trades or businesses under common control" as defined in paragraph (c) of this section, or a "combined group of trades or businesses under common control" as defined in paragraph (d) of this section. For purposes of this section and §§ 1.414(c)-3 and 1.414(c)-4, the term "organization" means a sole proprietorship, a partnership (as defined in section 7701(a)(2)), a trust, an estate, or a corporation.

(b) *Parent-subsidiary group of trades or businesses under common control*—(1) *In general.* The term "parent-subsidiary group of trades or businesses under common control" means one or more chains of organizations conducting trades or businesses connected through ownership of a controlling interest with a common parent organization if—

(i) A controlling interest in each of the organizations, except the common parent organization, is owned (directly and with the application of § 1.414(c)- 4(b)(1), relating to options) by one or more of the other organizations; and

(ii) The common parent organization owns (directly and with the application of § 1.414(c)-4(b)(1), relating to options) a controlling interest in at least one of the other organizations, excluding, in computing such controlling interest, any direct ownership interest by such other organizations.

(2) *Controlling interest defined*—(i) *Controlling interest.* For purposes of paragraphs (b) and (c) of this section, the phrase "controlling interest" means:

(A) In the case of an organization which is a corporation, ownership of stock possessing at least 80 percent of total combined voting power of all classes of stock entitled to vote of such corporation or at least 80 percent of the total value of shares of all classes of stock of such corporation;

(B) In the case of an organization which is a trust or estate, ownership of an actuarial interest of at least 80 percent of such trust or estate;

(C) In the case of an organization which is a partnership, ownership of at least 80 percent of the profits interest or capital interest of such partnership; and

(D) In the case of an organization which is a sole proprietorship, ownership of such sole proprietorship.

(ii) *Actuarial interest.* For purposes of this section, the actuarial interest of each beneficiary of trust or estate shall be determined by assuming the maximum exercise of discretion by the fiduciary in favor of such beneficiary. The factors and methods prescribed in § 20.2031-7 or, for certain prior periods, § 20.2031-7A (Estate Tax Regulations), for use in ascertaining the value of an interest in property for estate tax purposes shall be used for purposes of this subdivision in determining a beneficiary's actuarial interest.

(c) *Brother-sister group of trades or businesses under common control*—(1) *In general.* The term "brother-sister group of trades or businesses under common control" means two or more organizations conducting trades or businesses if (i) the same five or fewer persons who are individuals, estates, or trusts own (directly and with the application of § 1.414(c)-4) a controlling interest in each organization, and (ii) taking into account the ownership of each such person only to the extent such ownership is identical with respect to each such organization, such persons are in effective control of each organization. The five or fewer persons whose ownership is considered for purposes of the controlling interest requirement for each organization must be the same persons whose ownership is considered for purposes of the effective control requirement.

(2) Effective control defined. For purposes of this paragraph, persons are in "effective control" of an organization if—

(i) In the case of an organization which is a corporation, such persons own stock possessing more than 50 percent of the total combined voting power of all classes of stock entitled to vote or more than 50 percent of the total value of shares of all classes of stock of such corporation;

(ii) In the case of an organization which is a trust or estate, such persons own an aggregate actuarial interest of more than 50 percent of such trust or estate;

(iii) In the case of an organization which is a partnership, such persons own an aggregate of more than 50 percent of the profits interest or capital interest of such partnership; and

(iv) In the case of an organization which is a sole proprietorship, one of such persons owns such sole proprietorship.

(d) *Combined group of trades or businesses under common control.* The term "combined group of trades or businesses under common control" means any group of three or more organizations, if (1) each such organization is a member of either a parent-subsidiary group of trades or businesses under common control or a brother-sister group of trades or businesses under common control, and (2) at least one such organization is the common parent organization of a parent- subsidiary group of trades or businesses under common control and is also a member of a brother-sister group of trades or businesses under common control.

(e) *Examples.* The definitions of parent-subsidiary group of trades or businesses under common control, brother-sister group of trades or businesses under common control, and combined group of trades or businesses under common control may be illustrated by the following examples.

Example (1). (a) The ABC partnership owns stock possessing 80 percent of the total combined voting power of all classes of stock entitled to voting of S corporation. ABC partnership is the common parent of a parent-subsidiary group of trades or businesses under common control consisting of the ABC partnership and S Corporation.

(b) Assume the same facts as in (a) and assume further that S owns 80 percent of the profits interest in the DEF Partnership. The ABC Partnership is the common parent of a parent-subsidiary group of trades or businesses under common control consisting of the ABC Partnership, S Corporation, and the DEF Partnership. The result would be the same if the ABC Partnership, rather than S, owned 80 percent of the profits interest in the DEF Partnership.

Example (2). L Corporation owns 80 percent of the only class of stock of T Corporation, and T, in turn, owns 40 percent of the capital interest in the GHI Partnership. L also owns 80 percent of the only class of stock of N Corporation and N, in turn, owns 40 percent of the capital interest in the GHI Partnership. L is the common parent of a parent-subsidiary group of trades or businesses under common control consisting of L Corporation, T Corporation, N Corporation, and the GHI Partnership.

Example (3). ABC Partnership owns 75 percent of the only class of stock of X and Y Corporations; X owns all the remaining stock of Y, and Y owns all the remaining stock of X. Since interorganization ownership is excluded (that is, treated as not outstanding) for purposes of determining whether ABC owns a controlling interest of at least one of the other organizations, ABC is treated as the owner of stock possessing 100 percent of the voting power and value of all classes of stock of X and of Y for purposes of paragraph (b)(1)(ii) of this section. Therefore, ABC is the common parent of a parent-subsidiary group of trades or businesses under common control consisting of the ABC Partnership, X Corporation, and Y Corporation.

Example (4). Unrelated individuals A, B, C, D, E, and F own an interest in sole proprietorship A, a capital interest in the GHI Partnership, and stock of corporations M, W, X, Y, and Z (each of which has only one class of stock outstanding) in the following proportions:

ORGANIZATIONS

Individuals	*A*	*GHI*	*M*	*W*	*X*	*Y*	*Z*
A	100%	50%	100%	60%	40%	20%	60%
B	—	40%	—	15%	40%	50%	30%
C	—	—	—	—	10%	10%	10%
D	—	—	—	25%	—	20%	—
E	—	10%	—	—	10%	—	—
	100%	100%	100%	100%	100%	100%	100%

Under these facts the following four brother-sister groups of trades or businesses under common control exist: GHI, X and Z; X, Y and Z; W and Y; A and M. In the case of GHI, X, and Z, for example, A and B together have effective control of each organization because their combined identical ownership of GHI, X and Z is greater than 50%. (A's identical ownership of GHI, X and Z is 40% because A owns at least a 40% interest in each organization. B's identical ownership of GHI, X and Z is 30% because B owns at least a 30% interest in each organization.) A and B (the persons whose ownership is considered for purposes of the effective control requirement) together own a controlling interest in each organization because they own at least 80% of the capital interest of partnership GHI and at least 80% of the total combined voting power of corporations X and Z. Therefore, GHI, X and Z comprise a brother-sister group of trades or businesses under common control. Y is not a member of this group because neither the effective control requirement nor the 80% controlling interest requirement are met. (The effective control requirement is not met because A's and B's combined identical ownership in GHI, X, Y and Z (20% for A and 30% for B) does not exceed 50%. The 80% controlling interest test is not met because A and B together only own 70% of the total combined voting power of the stock of Y.) A and M are not members of this group because B owns no interest in either organization and A's ownership of GHI, X and Z, considered alone, is less than 80%.

* * *

§ 1.414(c)-4. Rules for determining ownership.

(a) *In general.* In determining the ownership of an interest in an organization for purposes of § 1.414(c)-2 and § 1.414(c)-3, the constructive ownership rules of paragraph (b) of this section shall apply, subject to the operating rules contained in paragraph (c). For purposes of this section the term "interest" means: in the case of a corporation, stock; in the case of a trust or estate, an actuarial interest; in the case of a partnership, an interest in the profits or capital; and in the case of a sole proprietorship, the proprietorship.

(b) *Constructive ownership*—(1) *Options.* If a person has an option to acquire any outstanding interest in an organization, such interest shall be considered as owned by such person. For this purpose, an option to acquire an option, and each one of a series of such options shall be considered as an option to acquire such interest.

(2) *Attribution from partnerships*—(i) General. An interest owned, directly or indirectly, by or for a partnership shall be considered as owned by any partner having an interest of 5 percent or more in either the profits or capital of the partnership in proportion to such partner's interest in the profits or capital, whichever such proportion is greater.

* * *

(3) *Attribution from estates and trusts*—(i) *In general.* An interest in an organization (hereinafter called an "organization interest") owned, directly or indirectly, by or for an estate or trust shall be considered as owned by any beneficiary of such estate or trust who has an actuarial interest of 5 percent or more in such organization interest, to the extent of such actuarial interest. For purposes of this subparagraph, the actuarial interest of each beneficiary shall be determined by assuming the maximum exercise of discretion by the fiduciary in favor of such beneficiary and the maximum use of the organization interest to satisfy the beneficiary's rights. A beneficiary of an estate or trust who cannot under any circumstances receive any part of an organization interest held by the estate or trust, including the proceeds from the disposition thereof, or the income therefrom, does not have an actuarial interest in such organization interest. Thus, where stock owned by a decedent's estate has been specifically bequeathed to certain beneficiaries and the remainder of the estate has been specifically bequeathed to other beneficiaries, the stock is attributable only to the beneficiaries to whom it is specifically bequeathed. Similarly a remainderman of a trust who cannot under any circumstances receive any interest in the stock of a corporation which is a part of the corpus of the trust (including any accumulated income therefrom or the proceeds from a disposition thereof) does not have an actuarial interest in such stock. However, an income beneficiary of a trust does have an actuarial interest in stock if he has any right to the income from such stock even though under the terms of the trust instrument such stock can never be distributed to him. The factors and methods prescribed in § 20.2031-7 or, for certain prior periods, § 20.2031-7A (Estate Tax Regulations) for use in ascertaining the value of an interest in property for estate tax purposes shall be used for purposes of this subdivision in determining a beneficiary's actuarial interest in an organization interest owned directly or indirectly by or for an estate or trust.

(ii) *Special rules for estates.* (A) For purposes of this paragraph (b)(3) with respect to an estate, property of a decedent shall be considered as owned by his or her estate if such property is subject to administration by the executor or administrator for the purposes of paying claims against the estate and expenses of administration notwithstanding that, under local law, legal title to such property vests in the decedent's heirs, legatees or devisees immediately upon death.

(B) For purposes of this paragraph (b)(3) with respect to an estate, the term "beneficiary" includes any person entitled to receive property of a decedent pursuant to a will or pursuant to laws of descent and distribution.

(C) For purposes of this paragraph (b)(3) with respect to an estate, a person shall no longer be considered a beneficiary of an estate when all the property to which he or she is entitled has been received by him or her, when he or she no longer has a claim against the estate arising out of having been a beneficiary, and when there is only a remote possibility that it will be necessary for the estate to seek the return of property from him or her or to seek payment from him or her by contribution or otherwise to satisfy claims against the estate or expenses of administration.

(iii) *Grantor trusts, etc.* An interest owned, directly or indirectly, by or for any portion of a trust of which a person is considered the owner under subpart E, part I, subchapter J of the Code (relating to grantors and others treated as substantial owners) is considered as owned by such person.

(4) *Attribution from corporations*—(i) *General.* An interest owned, directly or indirectly, by or for a corporation shall be considered as owned by any person who owns (directly and, in the case of a parent-subsidiary group of trades or businesses under common control, with the application of paragraph (b)(1) of this section, or in the case of a brother-sister group of trades or business under common control, with the application of this section), 5 percent or more in value of the stock in that proportion which the value of the stock which such person so owns bears to the total value of all the stock in such corporation.

(ii) *Example.* The provisions of paragraph (b)(4)(i) of this section may be illustrated by the following example:

Example. B, an individual, owns 60 of the 100 shares of the only class of outstanding stock of corporation P. C, an individual, owns 4 shares of the P stock, and corporation X owns 36 shares of the P stock. Corporation P owns, directly and indirectly, 50 shares of the stock of corporation S. Under this subparagraph, B is considered to own 30 shares of the S stock (60/100 x 50), and X is considered to own 18 shares of S stock (36/100 x 50). Since C does not own 5 percent or more in the value of P stock, he is not considered as owning any of the S stock owned by P. If in this example, C's wife had owned directly 1 share of the P stock, C and his wife would each be considered as owning 5 shares of the P stock, and therefore C and his wife would be considered as owning 2.5 shares of the S stock (5/100 x 50).

(5) *Spouse*—(i) *General rule.* Except as provided in paragraph (b)(5)(ii) of this section, an individual shall be considered to own an interest owned, directly or indirectly, by or for his or her spouse, other than a spouse who is legally separated from the individual under a decree of divorce, whether interlocutory or final, or a decree of separate maintenance.

(ii) *Exception.* An individual shall not be considered to own an interest in an organization owned, directly or indirectly, by or for his or her spouse on any day of a taxable year of such organization, provided that each of the following conditions are satisfied with respect to such taxable year:

(A) Such individual does not, at any time during such taxable year, own directly any interest in such organization;

(B) Such individual is not a member of the board of directors, a fiduciary, or an employee of such organization and does not participate in the management of such organization at any time during such taxable year;

(C) Not more than 50 percent of such organization's gross income for such taxable year was derived from royalties, rents, dividends, interest, and annuities; and

(D) Such interest in such organization is not, at any time during such taxable year, subject to conditions which substantially restrict or limit the spouse's right to dispose of such interest and which run in favor of the individual or the individual's children who have not attained the age of 21 years. The principles of § 1.414(c)-3(d)(6)(i) shall apply in determining whether a condition is a condition described in the preceding sentence.

(iii) *Definitions*. For purposes of paragraph (b)(5)(ii)(C) of this section, the gross income of an organization shall be determined under section 61 and the regulations thereunder. The terms "interest", "royalties", "rents", "dividends", and "annuities" shall have the same meaning such terms are given for purposes of section 1244(c) and § 1.1244(c)-1(e)(1).

(6) *Children, grandchildren, parents, and grandparents*—(i) *Children and parents*. An individual shall be considered to own an interest owned, directly or indirectly, by or for the individual's children who have not attained the age of 21 years, and if the individual has not attained the age of 21 years, an interest owned, directly or indirectly, by or for the individual's parents.

(ii) *Children, grandchildren, parents, and grandparents*. If an individual is in effective control (within the meaning of § 1.414(c)-2(c)(2)), directly and with the application of the rules of this paragraph without regard to this subdivision, of an organization, then such individual shall be considered to own an interest in such organization owned, directly or indirectly, by or for the individual's parents, grandparents, grandchildren, and children who have attained the age of 21 years.

(iii) *Adopted children*. For purposes of this section, a legally adopted child of an individual shall be treated as a child of such individual.

(iv) *Example*. The provisions of this subparagraph (6) may be illustrated by the following example:

Example—(A) *Facts*. Individual F owns directly 40 percent of the profits interest of the DEF Partnership. His son, M, 20 years of age, owns directly 30 percent of the profits interest of DEF, and his son, A, 30 years of age, owns directly 20 percent of the profits interest of DEF. The 10 percent remaining of the profits interest and 100 percent of the capital interest of DEF is owned by an unrelated person.

(B) *F's ownership*. F owns 40 percent of the profits interest in DEF directly and is considered to own the 30 percent profits interest owned directly by M. Since, for purposes of the effective control test contained in paragraph (b)(6)(ii) of this section, F is treated as owning 70 percent of the profits interest of DEF, F is also considered as owning the 20 percent profits interest of DEF owned by his adult son, A. Accordingly, F is considered as owning a total of 90 percent of the profits interest in DEF.

(C) *M's ownership*. Minor son, M. owns 30 percent of the profits interest in DEF directly, and is considered to own the 40 percent profits interest owned directly by his father, F. However, M is not considered to own the 20 percent profits interest of DEF owned directly by his brother, A, and constructively by F, because an interest constructively owned by F by reason of family attribution is not considered as owned by him for purposes of making another member of his family the constructive owner of such interest. (See paragraph (c)(2) of this section.) Accordingly, M is considered as owning a total of 70 percent of the profits interest of the DEF Partnership.

(D) *A's ownership*. Adult son, A, owns 20 percent of the profits interest in DEF directly. Since, for purposes of determining whether A effectively controls DEF under paragraph (b)(6)(ii) of this section, A is treated as owning only the percentage of profits interest he owns directly, he does not satisfy the condition precedent for the attribution of the DEF profits interest from his father. Accordingly, A is considered as owning only the 20 percent profits interest in DEF which he owns directly.

(c) *Operating rules*—(1) *In general.* Except as provided in paragraph (c)(2) of this section, an interest constructively owned by a person by reason of the application of paragraph (b) (1), (2), (3), (4), (5), or (6) of this section shall, for the purposes of applying such paragraph, be treated as actually owned by such person.

(2) *Members of family.* An interest constructively owned by an individual by reason of the application of paragraph (b) (5) or (6) of this section shall not be treated as owned by such individual for purposes of again applying such subparagraphs in order to make another the constructive owner of such interest.

(3) *Precedence of option attribution.* For purposes of this section, if an interest may be considered as owned under paragraph (b)(1) of this section (relating to option attribution) and under any other subparagraph of paragraph (b) of this section, such interest shall be considered as owned by such person under paragraph (b)(1) of this section.

(4) *Examples.* The provisions of this paragraph may be illustrated by the following examples:

Example (1). A, 30 years of age, has a 90 percent interest in the capital and profits of DEF Partnership. DEF owns all the outstanding stock of corporation X and X owns 60 shares of the 100 outstanding shares of corporation Y. Under paragraph (c)(1) of this section, the 60 shares of Y constructively owned by DEF by reason of paragraph (b)(4) of this section are treated as actually owned by DEF for purposes of applying paragraph (b)(2) of this section. Therefore, A is considered as owning 54 shares of the Y stock (90 percent of 60 shares).

Example (2). Assume the same facts as in example (1). Assume further that B, who is 20 years of age and the brother of A, directly owns 40 shares of Y stock. Although the stock of Y owned by B is considered as owned by C (the father of A and B) under paragraph (b)(6)(i) of this section, under paragraph (c)(2) of this section such stock may not be treated as owned by C for purposes of applying paragraph (b)(6)(ii) of this section in order to make A the constructive owner of such stock.

Example (3). Assume the same facts as in example (2), and further assume that C has an option to acquire the 40 shares of Y stock owned by his son, B. The rule contained in paragraph (c)(2) of this section does not prevent the reattribution of such 40 shares to A because, under paragraph (c)(3) of this section, C is considered as owning the 40 shares by reason of option attribution and not by reason of family attribution. Therefore, since A is in effective control of Y under paragraph (b)(6)(ii) of this section, the 40 shares of Y stock constructively owned by C are reattributed to A. A is considered as owning a total of 94 shares of Y stock.

§ 1.414(s)-1. Definition of compensation.

(a) *Introduction*—(1) *In general.* Section 414(s) and this section provide rules for defining compensation for purposes of applying any provision that specifically refers to section 414(s) or this section. For example, section 414(s) is referred to in many of the nondiscrimination provisions applicable to pension, profit-sharing, and stock bonus plans qualified under section 401(a). In accordance with section 414(s)(1), this section defines compensation as compensation within the meaning of section 415(c)(3). It also implements the election provided in section 414(s)(2) to treat certain deferrals as compensation and exercises the authority granted to the Secretary in section 414(s)(3) to prescribe alternative nondiscriminatory definitions of compensation.

(2) *Limitations on scope of section 414(s).* Section 414(s) and this section do not apply unless a provision specifically refers to section 414(s) or this section. For example, even though a definition of compensation permitted under section 414(s) must be used in determining whether the contributions or benefits under a pension, profit-sharing, or stock bonus

plan satisfy a certain applicable provision (such as section 401(a)(4)), except as otherwise specified, the plan is not required to use a definition of compensation that satisfies section 414(s) in calculating the amount of contributions or benefits actually provided under the plan.

(3) *Overview.* Paragraph (b) of this section provides rules of general application that govern a definition of compensation that satisfies section 414(s). Paragraph (c) of this section contains specific definitions of compensation that satisfy section 414(s) without satisfying any additional nondiscrimination requirement under section 414(s). Paragraph (d) of this section provides rules permitting the use of alternative definitions of compensation that satisfy section 414(s) as long as the nondiscrimination requirement and other requirements described in paragraph (d) of this section are satisfied. Paragraphs (e) and (f) of this section provide special rules permitting the use of rate of compensation, or prior-employer compensation or imputed compensation, rather than actual compensation, under a definition of compensation that satisfies section 414(s). Paragraph (g) of this section provides other special rules, including a special rule for determining the compensation of a self-employed individual under an alternate definition of compensation. Paragraph (h) of this section provides definitions for certain terms used in this section.

(b) *Rules of general application*—(1) *Use of a definition.* Any definition of compensation that satisfies section 414(s) may be used when a provision explicitly refers to section 414(s) unless the reference or this section specifically indicates otherwise.

(2) *Consistency rule*—(i) *General rule.* A definition of compensation selected by an employer for use in satisfying an applicable provision must be used consistently to define the compensation of all employees taken into account in satisfying the requirements of the applicable provision for the determination period. For example, although any definition of compensation that satisfies section 414(s) may be used for section 401(a)(4) purposes, the same definition of compensation generally must be used consistently to define the compensation of all employees taken into account in determining whether a plan satisfies section 401(a)(4). Furthermore, a different definition of compensation that satisfies section 414(s) is permitted to be used to determine whether another plan maintained by the same employer separately satisfies the requirements of section 401(a)(4). Although a definition of compensation must be used consistently, an employer may change its definition of compensation for a subsequent determination period with respect to the applicable provision. Rules provided under any applicable provision may modify the consistency requirements of this paragraph (b)(2).

* * *

(c) *Specific definitions of compensation that satisfy section 414(s)*—(1) *General rules.* The definitions of compensation provided in paragraphs (c)(2) and (c)(3) of this section satisfy section 414(s) and need not satisfy any additional requirements under section 414(s). Paragraph (c)(2) of this section describes definitions of compensation within the meaning of section 415(c)(3). Paragraph (c)(3) of this section provides a safe harbor alternative definition that excludes certain additional items of compensation. Paragraph (c)(4) of this section permits any definition provided in paragraph (c)(2) or (c)(3) of this section to include certain types of elective contributions and deferred compensation. Paragraph (c)(5) of this section permits certain modifications to a definition otherwise provided under this paragraph (c).

(2) *Compensation within the meaning of section 415(c)(3).* A definition of compensation that includes all compensation within the meaning of section 415(c)(3) and excludes all other compensation satisfies section 414(s). Sections 1.415(c)-2(b) and (c) provide rules for determining items of compensation included in and excluded from compensation within the meaning of section 415(c)(3). In addition, section 414(s) is satisfied by the safe harbor definitions provided in § 1.415(c)-2(d)(2) , (d)(3) and (d)(4) and any additional

definitions of compensation prescribed by the Commissioner under the authority provided in § 1.415(c)-2(d)(1) that are treated as satisfying section 415(c)(3).

(3) *Safe harbor alternative definition.* Under the safe harbor alternative definition in this paragraph (c)(3), compensation is compensation as defined in paragraph (c)(2) of this section, reduced by all of the following items (even if includible in gross income): reimbursements or other expense allowances, fringe benefits (cash and noncash), moving expenses, deferred compensation, and welfare benefits.

(4) *Inclusion of certain deferrals in compensation.* Any definition of compensation provided in paragraph (c)(2) or (c)(3) of this section satisfies section 414(s) even though it is modified to include all of the following types of elective contributions and all of the following types of deferred compensation—

(i) Elective contributions that are made by the employer on behalf of its employees that are not includible in gross income under section 125, section 402(e)(3), section 402(h), and section 403(b);

(ii) Compensation deferred under an eligible deferred compensation plan within the meaning of section 457(b) (deferred compensation plans of state and local governments and tax-exempt organizations); and

(iii) Employee contributions (under governmental plans) described in section 414(h)(2) that are picked up by the employing unit and thus are treated as employer contributions.

(5) *Exclusions applicable solely to highly compensated employees.* Any definition of compensation that satisfies paragraph (c)(2) or (c)(3) of this section, with or without the modification permitted by paragraph (c)(4) of this section, may be modified to exclude any portion of the compensation of some or all of the employer's highly compensated employees (including, for example, any one or more of the types of elective contributions or deferred compensation described in paragraph (c)(4) of this section).

(d) *Alternative definitions of compensation that satisfy section 414(s)*—(1) *General rule.* In addition to the definitions provided in paragraph (c) of this section, any definition of compensation satisfies section 414(s) with respect to employees (other than self-employed individuals treated as employees under section 401(c)(1)) if the definition of compensation does not by design favor highly compensated employees, is reasonable within the meaning of paragraph (d)(2) of this section, and satisfies the nondiscrimination requirement in paragraph (d)(3) of this section.

(2) *Reasonable definition of compensation*—(i) *General rule.* An alternative definition of compensation under this paragraph (d) is reasonable under section 414(s) if it is a definition of compensation provided in paragraph (c) of this section, modified to exclude all or any portion of one or more of the types of compensation described in paragraph (d)(2)(ii) of this section. See paragraph (e) of this section, however, for special rules that permit definitions of compensation based on employees' rates of compensation and paragraph (f) of this section for special rules that permit definitions of compensation that include prior-employer compensation or imputed compensation.

(ii) *Items that may be excluded.* A reasonable definition of compensation is permitted to exclude, on a consistent basis, all or any portion of irregular or additional compensation, including (but not limited to) one or more of the following: Any type of additional compensation for employees working outside their regularly scheduled tour of duty (such as overtime pay, premiums for shift differential, and call-in premiums), bonuses, or any one or more of the types of compensation excluded under the safe harbor alternative definition in paragraph (c)(3) of this section. Whether a type of compensation is irregular or additional is determined based on all the relevant facts and circumstances. A reasonable definition is also permitted to include, on a consistent basis, all or any portion of the types of elective contributions or deferred compensation described in paragraph (c)(4) of this section and, thus, need not include all those types of elective contributions or deferred compensation as otherwise required under paragraph (c)(4) of this section.

(iii) *Limits on the amount excluded from compensation.* A definition of compensation is not reasonable if it provides that each employee's compensation is a specified portion of the employee's compensation measured for the otherwise applicable determination period under another definition. For example, a definition of compensation that specifically limits each employee's compensation for a determination period to 95 percent of the employee's compensation using a definition provided in paragraph (c) of this section is not reasonable. Similarly, a definition of compensation that limits each employee's compensation used to satisfy an applicable provision with a 12-month determination period to compensation under a definition provided in paragraph (c) of this section for one month is not a reasonable definition of compensation. However, a definition of compensation is not unreasonable merely because it excludes all compensation in excess of a specified dollar amount.

(3) *Nondiscrimination requirement*—(i) *In general.* An alternative definition of compensation under this paragraph (d) is nondiscriminatory under section 414(s) for a determination period if the average percentage of total compensation included under the alternative definition of compensation for an employer's highly compensated employees, as a group for the determination period does not exceed by more than a de minimis amount the average percentage of total compensation included under the alternative definition for the employer's nonhighly compensated employees as a group.

(ii) *Total compensation*—(A) *General rule.* For purposes of this paragraph (d)(3), total compensation must be determined using a definition of compensation provided in paragraph (c)(2) of this section, either with or without the modification permitted by paragraph (c)(4) of this section. Thus, total compensation does not include prior-employer compensation or imputed compensation described in paragraph (f)(1) of this section (including imputed compensation for a period during which an employee performs services for another employer). Total compensation taken into account for each employee (including, if added, the elective contributions and deferred compensation described in paragraph (c)(4) of this section) may not exceed the annual compensation limit of section 401(a)(17).

(B) *Alternative definitions with exclusions applicable solely to highly compensated employees.* If an alternative definition of compensation contains a provision that excludes amounts from compensation and, as described in paragraph (c)(5) of this section, the provision only applies in defining the compensation of some highly compensated employees, then, for purposes of this paragraph (d)(3), the total compensation of any highly compensated employee subject to the provision must be reduced by any amount excluded from the employee's compensation as a result of the provision. However, if the provision applies consistently in defining the compensation of all highly compensated employees, this adjustment to total compensation is not required.

* * *

§ 1.415(c)-2. Compensation.

(a) *General definition.* Except as otherwise provided in this section, compensation from the employer within the meaning of section 415(c)(3), which is used for purposes of section 415 and regulations promulgated under section 415, means all items of remuneration described in paragraph (b) of this section, but excludes the items of remuneration described in paragraph (c) of this section. Paragraph (d) of this section provides safe harbor definitions of compensation that are permitted to be provided in a plan in lieu of the generally applicable definition of compensation. Paragraph (e) of this section provides timing rules relating to compensation. Paragraph (f) of this section provides rules regarding the application of the rules of section 401(a)(17) to the definition of compensation for purposes of section 415. Paragraph (g) of this section provides special rules relating to the determination of compensation, including rules for determining compensation for a section 403(b) annuity contract, rules for determining the compensation of employees of controlled groups or affiliated service groups, rules for disabled employees, rules relating to foreign compensation, rules regarding deemed section 125 compensation, rules for employees in qualified military service, and rules relating to back pay.

(b) *Items includible as compensation.* For purposes of applying the limitations of section 415, except as otherwise provided in this section, the term compensation means remuneration for services of the following types—

(1) The employee's wages, salaries, fees for professional services, and other amounts received (without regard to whether or not an amount is paid in cash) for personal services actually rendered in the course of employment with the employer maintaining the plan, to the extent that the amounts are includible in gross income (or to the extent amounts would have been received and includible in gross income but for an election under section 125(a), 132(f)(4), 402(e)(3), 402(h)(1)(B), 402(k), or 457(b)). These amounts include, but are not limited to, commissions paid to salespersons, compensation for services on the basis of a percentage of profits, commissions on insurance premiums, tips, bonuses, fringe benefits, and reimbursements or other expense allowances under a nonaccountable plan as described in § 1.62-2(c).

(2) In the case of an employee who is an employee within the meaning of section 401(c)(1) and regulations promulgated under section 401(c)(1), the employee's earned income (as described in section 401(c)(2) and regulations promulgated under section 401(c)(2)), plus amounts deferred at the election of the employee that would be includible in gross income but for the rules of section 402(e)(3), 402(h)(1)(B), 402(k), or 457(b).

(3) Amounts described in section 104(a)(3), 105(a), or 105(h), but only to the extent that these amounts are includible in the gross income of the employee.

(4) Amounts paid or reimbursed by the employer for moving expenses incurred by an employee, but only to the extent that at the time of the payment it is reasonable to believe that these amounts are not deductible by the employee under section 217.

(5) The value of a nonstatutory option (which is an option other than a statutory option as defined in § 1.421-1(b)) granted to an employee by the employer, but only to the extent that the value of the option is includible in the gross income of the employee for the taxable year in which granted.

(6) The amount includible in the gross income of an employee upon making the election described in section 83(b).

(7) Amounts that are includible in the gross income of an employee under the rules of section 409A or section 457(f)(1)(A) or because the amounts are constructively received by the employee.

(c) *Items not includible as compensation.* The term compensation does not include—

(1) Contributions (other than elective contributions described in section 402(e)(3), section 408(k)(6), section 408(p)(2)(A)(i), or section 457(b)) made by the employer to a plan of deferred compensation (including a simplified employee pension described in section 408(k) or a simple retirement account described in section 408(p), and whether or not qualified) to the extent that the contributions are not includible in the gross income of the employee for the taxable year in which contributed. In addition, any distributions from a plan of deferred compensation (whether or not qualified) are not considered as compensation for section 415 purposes, regardless of whether such amounts are includible in the gross income of the employee when distributed. However, if the plan so provides, any amounts received by an employee pursuant to a nonqualified unfunded deferred compensation plan are permitted to be considered as compensation for section 415 purposes in the

year the amounts are actually received, but only to the extent such amounts are includible in the employee's gross income.

(2) Amounts realized from the exercise of a nonstatutory option (which is an option other than a statutory option as defined in § 1.421-1(b)), or when restricted stock or other property held by an employee either becomes freely transferable or is no longer subject to a substantial risk of forfeiture (see section 83 and regulations promulgated under section 83).

(3) Amounts realized from the sale, exchange, or other disposition of stock acquired under a statutory stock option (as defined in § 1.421-1(b)).

(4) Other amounts that receive special tax benefits, such as premiums for group-term life insurance (but only to the extent that the premiums are not includible in the gross income of the employee and are not salary reduction amounts that are described in section 125).

(5) Other items of remuneration that are similar to any of the items listed in paragraphs (c)(1) through (c)(4) of this section.

(d) *Safe harbor rules with respect to plan's definition of compensation*—(1) *In general.* Paragraphs (d)(2) through (4) of this section contain safe harbor definitions of compensation that are automatically considered to satisfy section 415(c)(3) if specified in the plan. The Commissioner may, in revenue rulings, notices, and other guidance of general applicability published in the Internal Revenue Bulletin (see § 601.601(d)(2) of this chapter), provide additional definitions of compensation that are treated as satisfying section 415(c)(3).

(2) *Simplified compensation.* The safe harbor definition of compensation under this paragraph (d)(2) includes only those items specified in paragraph (b)(1) or (2) of this section and excludes all those items listed in paragraph (c) of this section.

(3) *Section 3401(a) wages.* The safe harbor definition of compensation under this paragraph (d)(3) includes wages within the meaning of section 3401(a) (for purposes of income tax withholding at the source), plus amounts that would be included in wages but for an election under section 125(a), 132(f)(4), 402(e)(3), 402(h)(1)(B), 402(k), or 457(b). However, any rules that limit the remuneration included in wages based on the nature or location of the employment or the services performed (such as the exception for agricultural labor in section 3401(a)(2)) are disregarded for this purpose.

(4) *Information required to be reported under sections 6041, 6051 and 6052.* The safe harbor definition of compensation under this paragraph (d)(4) includes amounts that are compensation under the safe harbor definition of paragraph (d)(3) of this section, plus all other payments of compensation to an employee by his employer (in the course of the employer's trade or business) for which the employer is required to furnish the employee a written statement under sections 6041(d), 6051(a)(3), and 6052. See §§ 1.6041-1(a), 1.6041-2(a)(1), 1.6052-1, and 1.6052-2, and also see § 31.6051- 1(a)(1)(i)(C) of this chapter. This safe harbor definition of compensation may be modified to exclude amounts paid or reimbursed by the employer for moving expenses incurred by an employee, but only to the extent that, at the time of the payment, it is reasonable to believe that these amounts are deductible by the employee under section 217.

(e) *Timing rules*—(1) *In general*—(i) *Payment during the limitation year.* Except as otherwise provided in this paragraph (e), in order to be taken into account for a limitation year, compensation within the meaning of section 415(c)(3) must be actually paid or made available to an employee (or, if earlier, includible in the gross income of the employee) within the limitation year. For this purpose, compensation is treated as paid on a date if it is actually paid on that date or it would have been paid on that date but for an election under section 125, 132(f)(4), 401(k), 403(b), 408(k), 408(p)(2)(A)(i), or 457(b).

(ii) *Payment prior to severance from employment.* Except as otherwise provided in this paragraph (e), in order to be taken into account for a limitation year, compensation within the meaning of section 415(c)(3) must be paid or treated as paid to the employee (in accordance with the rules of paragraph (e)(1)(i) of this section) prior to the employee's severance from employment with the employer maintaining the plan. See § 1.415(a)-1(f)(5) for the definition of severance from employment.

(2) *Certain minor timing differences.* Notwithstanding the provisions of paragraph (e)(1)(i) of this section, a plan may provide that compensation for a limitation year includes amounts earned during that limitation year but not paid during that limitation year solely because of the timing of pay periods and pay dates if—

(i) These amounts are paid during the first few weeks of the next limitation year;

(ii) The amounts are included on a uniform and consistent basis with respect to all similarly situated employees; and

(iii) No compensation is included in more than one limitation year.

(3) *Compensation paid after severance from employment*—(i) *In general.* Any compensation described in paragraph (e)(3)(ii) of this section does not fail to be compensation (within the meaning of section 415(c)(3)) pursuant to the rule of paragraph (e)(1)(ii) of this section merely because it is paid after the employee's severance from employment with the employer maintaining the plan, provided the compensation is paid by the later of 2 1/2 months after severance from employment with the employer maintaining the plan or the end of the limitation year that includes the date of severance from employment with the employer maintaining the plan. In addition, the plan may provide that amounts described in paragraph (e)(3)(iii) of this section are included in compensation (within the meaning of section 415(c)(3)) if—

(A) Those amounts are paid by the later of 2 1/2 months after severance from employment with the employer maintaining the plan or the end of the limitation year that includes the date of severance from employment with the employer maintaining the plan; and

(B) Those amounts would have been included in the definition of compensation if they were paid prior to the employee's severance from employment with the employer maintaining the plan.

(ii) *Regular pay after severance from employment.* An amount is described in this paragraph (e)(3)(ii) if—

(A) The payment is regular compensation for services during the employee's regular working hours, or compensation for services outside the employee's regular working hours (such as overtime or shift differential), commissions, bonuses, or other similar payments; and

(B) The payment would have been paid to the employee prior to a severance from employment if the employee had continued in employment with the employer.

(iii) *Leave cashouts and deferred compensation.* An amount is described in this paragraph (e)(3)(iii) if the amount is either—

(A) Payment for unused accrued bona fide sick, vacation, or other leave, but only if the employee would have been able to use the leave if employment had continued; or

(B) Received by an employee pursuant to a nonqualified unfunded deferred compensation plan, but only if the payment would have been paid to the employee at the same time if the employee had continued in employment with the employer and only to the extent that the payment is includible in the employee's gross income.

(iv) *Other post-severance payments.* Any payment that is not described in paragraph (e)(3)(ii) or (iii) of this section is not considered compensation under paragraph (e)(3)(i) of this section if paid after severance from employment with the employer maintaining the plan, even if it is paid within the time period described in paragraph (e)(3)(i) of this section. Thus, compensation does not include severance pay, or parachute payments within the meaning of section 280G(b)(2), if they are paid after severance from employment with the employer maintaining the plan, and does not include post-severance payments under a nonqualified unfunded deferred compensation plan unless the payments would have been paid at that time without regard to the severance from employment.

(4) *Salary continuation payments for military service and disabled participants.* The rule of paragraph (e)(1)(ii) of this section does not apply to payments to an individual who does not currently perform services for the employer by reason of qualified military service (as that term is used in section 414(u)(1)) to the extent those payments do not exceed the amounts the individual would have received if the individual had continued to perform services for the employer rather than entering qualified military service, but only if the plan so provides. In addition, the rule of paragraph (e)(1)(ii) of this section does not apply to compensation paid to a participant who is permanently and totally disabled (as defined in section 22(e)(3)) if the conditions set forth in paragraph (g)(4)(ii)(A) of this section are satisfied (applied by substituting a continuation of compensation for the continuation of contributions), but only if the plan so provides.

(5) *Special rule for governmental plans.* For purposes of applying the rules of paragraph (e)(3) of this section, a governmental plan (as defined in section 414(d)) may provide for the substitution of the calendar year in which the severance from employment with the employer maintaining the plan occurs for the limitation year in which the severance from employment with the employer maintaining the plan occurs.

(6) *Examples.* The provisions of this paragraph (e) are illustrated by the following examples:

Example 1. (i) *Facts.* Participant A was a common law employee of Employer X, performing services as a script writer for Employer X from January 1, 2005 to December 31, 2005. Pursuant to a collective bargaining agreement, Employer X, Employer Y and Employer Z maintain and contribute to Plan T, a multiemployer plan (as defined in section 414(f)) in which Participant A participates. Under the collective bargaining agreement, Participant A is entitled to residual payments whenever television shows that Participant A wrote are re-used commercially (These residual payments constitute compensation described in paragraph (b) of this section and do not constitute compensation described in paragraph (c) of this section.). In the year 2008, Participant A receives residual payments from Employer X for television programs using the scripts that Participant A wrote in the year 2005 that were rebroadcast in the year 2008. In the years 2006, 2007, and 2008, Participant A was a common law employee of Employer Y, and did not perform any services for Employer X.

(ii) *Conclusion.* The residual payments received from Employer X by Participant A in the year 2008 are compensation for purposes of section 415(c)(3). The payments are not treated as made after severance from employment because Plan T is a multiemployer plan (as defined in section 414(f)) and Participant A continues to be employed by an employer maintaining Plan T.

Example 2. (i) *Facts.* The facts are the same as in Example 1, except that Participant A: ceased employment with Employer Y in the year 2006; subsequently moved away from the area in which A formerly worked; performs no services as an employee for any employer; and commenced receiving distributions under Plan T in March, 2006.

(ii) *Conclusion.* Based on the facts and circumstances, A has ceased employment with any employer maintaining Plan T. Pursuant to paragraph (e)(1)(ii) of this section, compensation must be paid prior to an employee's severance from employment with the employer maintaining the plan. Accordingly, the residual payments received by Participant A in the year 2008 are not compensation for purposes of section 415(c)(3).

(f) *Interaction with section 401(a)(17).* Because a plan may not base allocations (in the case of a defined contribution plan) or benefits (in the case of a defined benefit plan) on compensation in excess of the limitation under section 401(a)(17), a plan's definition of compensation for a year that is used for purposes of applying the limitations of section 415 is not permitted to reflect compensation for a year that is in excess of the limitation under section 401(a)(17) that applies to that year. See §§ 1.401(a)(17)-1(a)(3)(i) and 1.401(a)(17)-1(b)(3)(ii) for rules regarding the effective date of increases in the section 401(a)(17) compensation limitation for a plan year and for a 12-month period other than the plan year.

(g) Special rules—(1) Compensation for section 403(b) annuity contract. In the case of an annuity contract described in section 403(b), the term participant's compensation means the participant's includible compensation determined under section 403(b)(3). Accordingly, the rules for determining a participant's compensation pursuant to section 415(c)(3) (other than section 415(c)(3)(E)) and this section do not apply to a section 403(b) annuity contract.

(2) *Employees of controlled groups of corporations, etc.* In the case of an employee of two or more corporations which are members of a controlled group of corporations (as defined in section 414(b) as modified by section 415(h)), the term compensation for such employee includes compensation from all employers that are members of the group, regardless of whether the employee's particular employer has a qualified plan. This special rule is also applicable to an employee of two or more trades or businesses (whether or not incorporated) that are under common control (as defined in section 414(c) as modified by section 415(h)), to an employee of two or more members of an affiliated service group as defined in section 414(m), and to an employee of two or more members of any group of employers who must be aggregated and treated as one employer pursuant to section 414(o).

(3) *Aggregation of section 403(b) annuity with qualified plan of controlled employer.* If a section 403(b) annuity contract is aggregated with a qualified plan of a controlled employer in accordance with § 1.415(f)-1(f)(2), then, in applying the limitations of section 415(c) in connection with the aggregation of the section 403(b) annuity with a qualified plan, the total compensation from both employers is permitted to be taken into account.

(4) *Permanent and total disability of defined contribution plan participant*—(i) *In general.* Pursuant to section 415(c)(3)(C), if the conditions set forth in paragraph (g)(4)(ii) of this section are satisfied, then, in the case of a participant in any defined contribution plan who is permanently and totally disabled (as defined in section 22(e)(3)), the participant's compensation means the compensation the participant would have received for the year if the participant was paid at the rate of compensation paid immediately before becoming permanently and totally disabled, if such compensation is greater than the participant's compensation determined without regard to this paragraph (g)(4).

(ii) *Conditions for deemed disability compensation.* The rule of paragraph (g)(4)(i) of this section applies only if the following conditions are satisfied—

(A) Either the participant is not a highly compensated employee (as defined in section 414(q)) immediately before becoming disabled, or the plan provides for the continuation of contributions on behalf of all participants who are permanently and totally disabled for a fixed or determinable period;

(B) The plan provides that the rule of this paragraph (g)(4) (treating certain amounts as compensation for a disabled participant) applies with respect to the participant; and

(C) Contributions made with respect to amounts treated as compensation under this paragraph (g)(4) are nonforfeitable when made.

* * *

(8) *Back pay.* Payments awarded by an administrative agency or court or pursuant to a bona fide agreement by an employer to compensate an employee for lost wages are compensation within the meaning of section

415(c)(3) for the limitation year to which the back pay relates, but only to the extent such payments represent wages and compensation that would otherwise be included in compensation under this section.

§ 1.415(d)-1. Cost-of-living adjustments.

(a) *Defined benefit plans*—(1) *Dollar limitation*—(i) *Determination of adjusted limit.* Under section 415(d)(1)(A), the dollar limitation described in section 415(b)(1)(A) applicable to defined benefit plans is adjusted annually to take into account increases in the cost of living. The adjustment of the dollar limitation is made by multiplying the adjustment factor for the year, as described in paragraph (a)(1)(ii)(A) of this section, by $160,000, and rounding the result in accordance with paragraph (a)(1)(iii) of this section. The adjusted dollar limitation is prescribed by the Commissioner and published in the Internal Revenue Bulletin. See § 601.601(d)(2) of this chapter.

(ii) *Determination of adjustment factor*—(A) *Adjustment factor.* The adjustment factor for a calendar year is equal to a fraction, the numerator of which is the value of the applicable index for the calendar quarter ending September 30 of the preceding calendar year, and the denominator of which is the value of such index for the base period. The applicable index is determined consistent with the procedures used to adjust benefit amounts under section 215(i)(2)(A) of the Social Security Act, Public Law 92-336 (86 Stat. 406), as amended. If, however, the value of that fraction is less than one for a calendar year, then the adjustment factor for the calendar year is equal to one.

(B) *Base period.* For the purpose of adjusting the dollar limitation pursuant to paragraph (a)(1)(ii)(A) of this section, the base period is the calendar quarter beginning July 1, 2001.

(iii) *Rounding.* Any increase in the $160,000 amount specified in section 415(b)(1)(A) which is not a multiple of $5,000 is rounded to the next lowest multiple of $5,000.

(2) *Average compensation for high-3 years of service limitation*—(i) *Determination of adjusted limit.* Under section 415(d)(1)(B), with regard to participants who have had a severance from employment with the employer maintaining the plan, the compensation limitation described in section 415(b)(1)(B) is permitted to be adjusted annually to take into account increases in the cost of living. For any limitation year beginning after the severance occurs, the adjustment of the compensation limitation is made by multiplying the annual adjustment factor (as defined in paragraph (a)(2)(ii) of this section) by the compensation limitation applicable to the participant in the prior limitation year. The annual adjustment factor is prescribed by the Commissioner and published in the Internal Revenue Bulletin. See § 601.601(d)(2) of this chapter.

(ii) *Annual adjustment factor.* The annual adjustment factor for a calendar year is equal to a fraction, the numerator of which is the value of the applicable index for the calendar quarter ending September 30 of the preceding calendar year, and the denominator of which is the value of such index for the calendar quarter ending September 30 of the calendar year prior to that preceding calendar year. The applicable index is determined consistent with the procedures used to adjust benefit amounts under section 215(i)(2)(A) of the Social Security Act. If the value of the fraction described in the first sentence of this paragraph (a)(2)(ii) is less than one for a calendar year, then the adjustment factor for the calendar year is equal to one. In such a case, the annual adjustment factor for future calendar years will be determined in accordance with revenue rulings, notices, or other published guidance prescribed by the Commissioner and published in the Internal Revenue Bulletin. See § 601.601(d)(2) of this chapter.

(iii) *Special rule for rehired employees.* If, after having a severance from employment with the employer maintaining the plan, an employee is rehired by the employer maintaining the plan, the employee's compensation limit under section 415(b)(1)(B) is the greater of—

(A) 100 percent of the participant's average compensation for the period of the participant's high-3 years of service, as determined prior to the employee's severance from employment with the employer maintaining the plan, as adjusted pursuant to paragraph (a)(2)(i) of this section (if the plan so provides); or

(B) 100 percent of the participant's average compensation for the period of the participant's high-3 years of service, with the period of the participant's high-3 years of service determined pursuant to § 1.415(b)-1(a)(5)(iii).

(3) *Effective date of adjustment.* The adjusted dollar limitation applicable to defined benefit plans and the adjusted compensation limit applicable to a participant are effective as of January 1 of each calendar year and apply with respect to limitation years ending with or within that calendar year. However, benefit payments (and, in the case of plans that are subject to the requirements of section 411, accrued benefits for a limitation year) cannot exceed the currently applicable dollar limitation or compensation limitation (as in effect before the January 1 adjustment) prior to January 1. Thus, where there is an increase in the limitation under section 415(b)(1), any increase in a participant's benefits associated with the limitation increase is permitted to occur as of a date no earlier than January 1 of the calendar year for which the increase in the limitation is effective, and can only be applied for payments due on or after January 1 of such calendar year. For example, assume that a participant in a defined benefit plan is currently receiving a benefit in the form of a straight life annuity, payable monthly, in an amount equal to the section 415(b)(1)(A) dollar limit, and the defined benefit plan has a limitation year that runs from July 1 to June 30. If the plan is amended to reflect the section 415(d) increase to the section 415(b)(1)(A) dollar limit that is effective as of January 1, 2009, the associated increase in the participant's monthly benefit payments is only effective for payments due on or after January 1, 2009, and the participant's benefit cannot be increased to reflect the section 415(d) increase that is effective January 1, 2009, with respect to any monthly payment due prior to January 1, 2009.

(4) *Application of adjusted figure*—(i) *In general.* If the dollar limitation of section 415(b)(1)(A) or the compensation limitation of section 415(b)(1)(B) is adjusted pursuant to section 415(d) for a limitation year, the adjustment is applied as provided in this paragraph (a)(4).

(ii) *Application of adjusted limitations to benefits that have not commenced.* An adjustment to the dollar limitation of section 415(b)(1)(A) is permitted to be applied to a participant who has not commenced benefits before the date on which the adjustment is effective. Annual adjustments to the compensation limit of section 415(b)(1)(B) as described in paragraph (a)(2) of this section are permitted to be made for all limitation years that begin after the participant's severance from employment, and apply to distributions that commence after the effective dates of such adjustments. However, no adjustment to the compensation limit of section 415(b)(1)(B) is made for any limitation year that begins on or before the date of the participant's severance from employment with the employer maintaining the plan.

(iii) *Application of adjusted dollar limitation to remaining payments under benefits that have commenced.* With respect to a distribution of accrued benefits that commenced before the date on which an adjustment to the section 415(b)(1)(A) dollar limitation is effective, a plan is permitted to apply the adjusted limitations to that distribution, but only to the extent that benefits have not been paid. Thus, for example, a plan cannot provide that the adjusted dollar limitation applies to a participant who has previously received the entire plan benefit in a single-sum distribution. However, a plan can provide for an increase in benefits to a participant who accrues additional benefits under the plan that could have been accrued without regard to the adjustment of the dollar limitation (including benefits that accrue as a result of a plan amendment) on or after the effective date of the adjusted limitation.

(iv) *Manner of adjustment for benefits that have commenced.* If a plan is amended to increase benefits payable under the plan in accordance with paragraphs (a)(5) or (a)(6) of this section (or the plan is treated as applying paragraph (a)(5) of this section because the plan incorporates the section 415(d) cost-of-living adjustments automatically by reference pursuant to § 1.415(a)-1(d)(3)(v)), or if benefits payable under the plan are increased pursuant to a form of benefit that is described in § 1.415(b)-1(c)(5), then the distribution as increased will be treated as continuing to satisfy the requirements of section 415(b). If benefits payable under a plan are increased in a manner other than as described in the preceding sentence, the plan must satisfy the requirements of § 1.415(b)-1(b)(1)(iii), treating the commencement of the additional benefit as the commencement of a new distribution that gives rise to a new annuity starting date.

(5) *Safe harbor for annual adjustments to distributions.* An amendment to a plan to incorporate adjustments to the section 415(b) limits that increases a distribution that has previously commenced is described in this paragraph (a)(5) if—

(i) The employee has received one or more distributions that satisfy the requirements of section 415(b) before the date the adjustment to the applicable limits is effective (as determined under paragraph (a)(3) of this section);

(ii) The increased distribution is solely as a result of the amendment of the plan to reflect the adjustment to the applicable limits pursuant to section 415(d); and

(iii) The amounts payable to the employee on and after the effective date of the adjustment (as determined under paragraph (a)(3) of this section) are not greater than the amounts that would otherwise be payable without regard to the adjustment, multiplied by a fraction determined for the limitation year, the numerator of which is the limitation under section 415(b) (which is the lesser of the applicable dollar limitation under section 415(b)(1)(A), as adjusted for age at commencement, and the applicable compensation-based limitation under section 415(b)(1)(B)) in effect with respect to the distribution taking into account the section 415(d) adjustment, and the denominator of which is the limitation under section 415(b) in effect for the distribution immediately before the adjustment.

(6) *Safe harbor for periodic adjustments to distributions*—(i) *General rule.* An amendment to a plan that increases a distribution that has previously commenced is made using the safe harbor methodology of this paragraph (a)(6) if—

(A) The employee has received one or more distributions that satisfy the requirements of section 415(b) before the date on which the increase is effective; and

(B) The amounts payable to the employee on and after the effective date of the increase are not greater than the amounts that would otherwise be payable without regard to the increase, multiplied by the cumulative adjustment fraction.

(ii) *Cumulative adjustment fraction.* The cumulative adjustment fraction for purposes of this paragraph (a)(6) is equal to the product of all of the fractions described in paragraph (a)(5)(iii) of this section that would have applied after benefits commence if the plan had been amended each year to incorporate the section 415(d) adjustments to the applicable section 415(b) limits and had otherwise satisfied the safe harbor methodology described in paragraph (a)(5) of this section. For purposes of the preceding sentence, if for the limitation year for which the increase to the section 415(b)(1)(A) dollar limitation pursuant to section 611(a)(1)(A) of the Economic Growth and Tax Relief Reconciliation Act of 2001 (115 Stat. 38), Public Law 107-16 (EGTRRA), is first effective (generally, the first limitation year beginning after December 31, 2001), the section 415(b)(1)(A) dollar limit applicable to a participant is less than the section 415(b)(1)(B) compensation limit for the participant, then the fraction described in paragraph (a)(5)(iii) of this section for that limitation year is 1.0.

(7) *Examples.* The following examples illustrate the application of this paragraph (a):

Example 1. (i) X is a participant in a qualified defined benefit plan maintained by X's employer. The plan has a calendar year limitation year. Under the terms of the plan, X is entitled to a benefit consisting of a straight life annuity equal to 100 percent of X's average compensation for the period of X's high-3 years of service. X's average compensation for the period of X's high-3 years of service is $50,000. X incurs a severance from employment with the employer maintaining the plan on October 3, 2007, at age 65 with a nonforfeitable right to the accrued benefit after more than 10 years of participation in the plan. X begins to receive annual benefit payments (payable monthly) of $50,000, commencing on November 1, 2007. The dollar limitation for the 2007 limitation year (as adjusted pursuant to section 415(d)) is $180,000. Assume that the dollar limitation for the 2008 limitation year (as adjusted pursuant to section 415(d)) is $185,000 and the annual adjustment factor for adjusting the compensation limitation of section 415(b)(1)(B) for the 2008 limitation year is 1.0334. Effective January 1, 2008, the plan is amended to incorporate these adjustments to the dollar and compensation limitations, and accordingly, X's annual benefit payment is increased, effective for payments due on or after January 1, 2008. Prior to the plan amendment incorporating the application of the adjusted dollar and compensation limitations, X has received one or more distributions that satisfy the requirements of section 415(b). In addition, the adjustment to X's annual benefit payments is solely on account of the plan amendment incorporating the adjusted limitations.

(ii) For the limitation year beginning January 1, 2008, the dollar limit applicable to X under section 415(b)(1)(A) is $185,000, and the compensation limit applicable to X under section 415(b)(1)(B) is $51,670 ($50,000 multiplied by the annual adjustment factor of 1.0334). Accordingly, the adjustment to X's benefit satisfies the safe harbor for cost-of-living adjustments under paragraph (a)(5) of this section if, after the adjustment, X's benefit payable in the 2008 limitation year is no greater than $50,000 multiplied by $51,670 (X's section 415(b) limitation for 2008)/$50,000 (X's section 415(b) limitation for 2007).

Example 2. (i) The facts are the same as in Example 1, except that X's average compensation for the period of X's high-3 consecutive years of service is $200,000. Consequently, X's annual benefit payments commencing on November 1, 2007, are limited to $180,000.

(ii) For the limitation year beginning January 1, 2008, the dollar limit applicable to X under section 415(b)(1)(A) is $185,000, and the compensation limit applicable to X under section 415(b)(1)(B) is $206,680 ($200,000 multiplied by the annual adjustment factor of 1.0334). Accordingly, the adjustment to X's benefit satisfies the safe harbor for cost-of-living adjustments under paragraph (a)(5) of this section if, after the adjustment, X's benefit payable in 2008 is no greater than $180,000 multiplied by $185,000 (X's section 415(b) limitation for 2008)/$180,000 (X's section 415(b) limitation for 2007).

Example 3. (i) X is a participant in Plan T, a qualified defined benefit plan maintained by X's employer. In the year 2008, X receives a single-sum distribution of X's entire accrued benefit under the plan. At the time that X receives the single-sum distribution, X's accrued benefit under Plan T is limited by the section 415(b)(1)(A) age-adjusted dollar limit. X accrues no further benefits under Plan T after X receives the single-sum distribution. In the 2009 limitation year, pursuant to section 415(d) and § 1.415(d)-1, the section 415(b)(1)(A) dollar limit is increased.

(ii) In the 2009 limitation year, Plan T may not provide additional benefits to X on account of the increase in the section 415(b)(1)(A) dollar limit pursuant to section 415(d) and § 1.415(d)-1.

Example 4. (i) X is a participant in Plan T, a qualified defined benefit plan maintained by X's employer, Employer S. Plan T has a calendar limitation year. In 2008, X incurs a severance from employment with Employer S and X commences receiving distributions from Plan T in the form of a single life annuity in an annual amount of $30,000. At the time that X commences receiving distributions from Plan T, X's accrued benefit under Plan T is limited by the section 415(b)(1)(B) compensation limit. In 2009, the annual adjustment factor described in paragraph (a)(2) of this section (which is the factor for adjusting the compensation limit described in section 415(b)(1)(B)) is 1.03. Employer S amends Plan T, effective as of January 1, 2009, to increase the annual benefit of all participants who, prior to January 1, 2009, incurred a severance from employment with Employer S and who have commenced receiving benefits from Plan T by a factor of 1.015. Assume that for limitation years prior to 2009, X's distributions from Plan T satisfy the requirements of section 415(b).

(ii) The increase in X's annual benefit pursuant to the amendment effective January 1, 2009, is within the safe harbor described in paragraph (a)(6) of this section. This is because the amount payable to X under Plan T for the 2009 limitation year and limitation years thereafter (as increased by the amendment effective January 1, 2009) is not greater than the product of the amount payable to X under Plan T for such limitation years (as determined without regard to the amendment increasing X's benefit effective January 1, 2009) and the cumulative adjustment fraction (which, in X's case, is 1.03). Thus, X's annual benefit, as increased by the amendment, is not determined pursuant to the rules of § 1.415(b)-1(b)(1)(iii).

Example 5. (i) Participant P participated in Plan A, maintained by Employer M, for more than 10 years. Plan A uses a calendar year limitation year and Plan A automatically adjusts a participant's section 415(b)(1)(B) compensation limit for limitation years after the limitation year in which the participant incurs a severance from employment as described in § 1.415(a)-1(d)(3)(v). Prior to separating from employment with M in 2010, P's average compensation for P's period of high-3 years while a participant in Plan A is $50,000, based on P's compensation for 2007, 2008, and 2009, which was $50,000 for each year. P's compensation for year 2010 was $45,000. In year 2012, P is rehired by M and resumes participation in Plan A. P's compensation in year 2012 is $45,000, and is $70,000 in year 2013. Assume that the annual adjustment factor described in § 1.415(d)-1(a)(2)(ii) for the limitation years 2011 through 2013 is 1.03 for each year. Thus, disregarding P's rehire by M, P's average compensation for P's period of high-3 years while a participant in Plan A for the 2013 limitation year would be equal to $54,636 (or 1.03 * 1.03 * 1.03 * $50,000). See § 1.415(b)-1(a)(5)(iii).

(ii) Under § 1.415(d)-1(a)(2)(iii), P's average compensation for P's period of high-3 years while a participant in Plan A for the 2013 limitation year is $54,636.

§ 54.4980F-1. Notice requirements for certain pension plan amendments significantly reducing the rate of future benefit accrual.

* * *

Q-1. What are the notice requirements of section 4980F(e) of the Internal Revenue Code and section 204(h) of ERISA?

A-1. (a) *Requirements of Internal Revenue Code section 4980F(e) and ERISA section 204(h).* Section 4980F of the Internal Revenue Code (section 4980F) and section 204(h) of the Employee Retirement Income Security Act of 1974, as amended (ERISA), 29 U.S.C. 1054(h) (section 204(h)) each generally requires notice of an amendment to an applicable pension plan that either provides for a significant reduction in the rate of future benefit accrual or that eliminates or significantly reduces an early retirement benefit or retirement-type subsidy. The notice is required to be provided to plan participants and alternate payees who are applicable individuals (as defined in Q&A-10 of this section), to certain employee organizations, and to contributing employers under a multiemployer plan (as described in Q&A-10(a) of this section). The plan administrator must generally provide the notice before the effective date of the plan amendment. Q&A-9 of this section sets forth the time frames for providing notice, Q&A-11 of this section sets forth the content requirements for the notice, and Q&A-12 of this section contains special rules for cases in which participants can choose between the old and new benefit formulas.

(b) *Other notice requirements*. Other provisions of law may require that certain parties be notified of a plan amendment. See, for example, sections 102 and 104 of ERISA, and the regulations thereunder, for requirements relating to summary plan descriptions and summaries of material modifications.

Q-2. What are the differences between section 4980F and section 204(h)?

A-2. The notice requirements of section 4980F generally are parallel to the notice requirements of section 204(h), as amended by the Economic Growth and Tax Relief Reconciliation Act of 2001, Public Law 107-16 (115 Stat. 38) (2001) (EGTRRA). However, the consequences of the failure to satisfy the requirements of the two provisions differ: Section 4980F imposes an excise tax on a failure to satisfy the notice requirements, while section 204(h)(6), as amended by EGTRRA, contains a special rule with respect to an egregious failure to satisfy the notice requirements. See Q&A-14 and Q&A-15 of this section. Except to the extent specifically indicated, these regulations apply both to section 4980F and to section 204(h).

* * *

Q-9. When must section 204(h) notice be provided?

A-9. (a) 45-day general rule. Except as otherwise provided in this Q&A-9, section 204(h) notice must be provided at least 45 days before the effective date of any section 204(h) amendment. See paragraph (e) of this Q&A-9 for special rules for amendments permitting participant choice.

(b) 15-day rule for small plans. Except for amendments described in paragraphs (d)(2) and (g) of this Q&A-9, section 204(h) notice must be provided at least 15 days before the effective date of any section 204(h) amendment in the case of a small plan. For purposes of this section, a small plan is a plan that the plan administrator reasonably expects to have, on the effective date of the section 204(h) amendment, fewer than 100 participants who have an accrued benefit under the plan.

(c) 15-day rule for multiemployer plans. Except for amendments described in paragraphs (d)(2) and (g) of this Q&A-9, section 204(h) notice must be provided at least 15 days before the effective date of any section 204(h) amendment in the case of a multiemployer plan. For purposes of this section, a multiemployer plan means a multiemployer plan as defined in section 414(f) of the Internal Revenue Code.

(d) Special timing rule for business transactions—(1) 15-day rule for section 204(h) amendment in connection with an acquisition or disposition. Except for amendments described in paragraphs (d)(2) and (g) of this Q&A-9, if a section 204(h) amendment is adopted in connection with an acquisition or disposition, section 204(h) notice must be provided at least 15 days before the effective date of the section 204(h) amendment.

(2) Later notice permitted for a section 204(h) amendment significantly reducing early retirement benefit or retirement-type subsidies in connection with certain plan transfers, mergers, or consolidations. If a section 204(h) amendment is adopted with respect to liabilities that are transferred to another plan in connection with a transfer, merger, or consolidation of assets or liabilities as described in section 414(l) of the Internal Revenue Code and § 1.414(l)-1 of this chapter, the amendment is adopted in connection with an acquisition or disposition, and the amendment significantly reduces an early retirement benefit or retirement-type subsidy, but does not significantly

reduce the rate of future benefit accrual, then section 204(h) notice must be provided no later than 30 days after the effective date of the section 204(h) amendment.

(3) *Definition of acquisition or disposition.* For purposes of this paragraph (d), see § 1.410(b)-2(f) of this chapter for the definition of acquisition or disposition.

(e) *Timing rule for amendments permitting participant choice.* In general, section 204(h) notice of a section 204(h) amendment that provides applicable individuals with a choice between the old and the new benefit formulas (as described in Q&A-12 of this section) must be provided in accordance with the time period applicable under paragraphs (a) through (d) of this Q&A-9. See Q&A-12 of this section for additional guidance regarding section 204(h) notice in connection with participant choice.

(f) *Special timing rule for certain plans maintained by commercial airlines. See* section 402 of PPA '06 for a special rule that applies to certain plans maintained by an employer that is a commercial passenger airline or the principal business of which is providing catering services to a commercial passenger airline. Under this special rule, section 204(h) notice must be provided at least 15 days before the effective date of the amendment.

(g) *Special timing rules relating to certain section 204(h) amendments that reduce section 411(d)(6) protected benefits* --(1) *Plan amendments permitted to reduce prior accruals.* This paragraph (g) generally provides special rules with respect to a plan amendment that would not violate section 411(d)(6) even if the amendment were to reduce section 411(d)(6) protected benefits, which are limited to accrued benefits that are attributable to service before the applicable amendment date. For example, this paragraph (g) applies to amendments that are permitted to be effective retroactively under section 412(d)(2) of the Code (section 412(c)(8) for plan years beginning before January 1, 2008), section 418D of the Code, section 418E of the Code, section 4281 of ERISA, or section 1107 of PPA '06. *See,* generally, § 1.411(d)-3(a)(1).

(2) *General timing rule for amendments to which this paragraph (g) applies.* For an amendment to which this paragraph (g) applies, the amendment is effective on the first date on which the plan is operated as if the amendment were in effect. Thus, except as otherwise provided in this paragraph (g), a section 204(h) notice for an amendment to which paragraph (a) of this section applies that is adopted after the effective date of the amendment must be provided, with respect to any applicable individual, at least 45 days before (or such other date as may apply under paragraph (b), (c), (d), or (f) of this Q&A-9) the date the amendment is put into operational effect.

(3) *Special rules for section 204(h) notices provided in connection with other disclosure requirements* --(i) *In general.* Notwithstanding the requirements in this Q&A-9 and Q&A-11 of this section, if a plan provides one of the notices in paragraph (g)(3)(ii) of this Q&A-9, in accordance with the applicable timing and content rules for such notice, the plan is treated as timely providing a section 204(h) notice with respect to a section 204(h) amendment.

(ii) *Notice requirements.* The notices in this paragraph (g)(3)(ii) are--

(A) A notice required under any revenue ruling, notice, or other guidance published under the authority of the Commissioner in the Internal Revenue Bulletin to affected parties in connection with a retroactive plan amendment described in section 412(d)(2) (section 412(c)(8) for plan years beginning before January 1, 2008);

(B) A notice required under section 101(j) of ERISA if an amendment is adopted to comply with the benefit limitation requirements of section 206(g) of ERISA (section 436 of the Code);

(C) A notice required under section

432(b)(3)(D) of the Code for an amendment adopted to comply with the benefit restrictions under section 432(f)(2);

(D) A notice required under section 418D, or section 4244A(b) of ERISA, for an amendment that reduces or eliminates accrued benefits attributable to employer contributions with respect to a multiemployer plan in reorganization;

(E) A notice required under section 418E, or section 4245(e) of ERISA, relating to the effects of the insolvency status for a multiemployer plan; and

(F) A notice required under section 4281 of ERISA for an amendment of a multiemployer plan reducing benefits pursuant to section 4281(c) of ERISA.

(4) *Delegation of authority to Commissioner.* The Commissioner may provide special rules under section 4980F, in revenue rulings, notices, or other guidance published in the Internal Revenue Bulletin (*See* § 601.601(d)(2)(ii)(*b*) of this chapter), that the Commissioner determines to be necessary or appropriate with respect to a section 204(h) amendment--

(A) That applies to benefits accrued before the applicable amendment date but that does not violate section 411(d)(6); or

(B) For which there is a required notice relating to a reduction in benefits and such notice has timing and content requirements similar to a section 204(h) notice with respect to a significant reduction in the rate of future benefit accruals.

* * *

Q-14. What are the consequences if a plan administrator fails to provide section 204(h) notice?

A-14. (a) Egregious failures—(1) Effect of egregious failure to provide section 204(h) notice. Section 204(h)(6)(A) of ERISA provides that, in the case of any egregious failure to meet the notice requirements with respect to any plan amendment, the plan provisions are applied so that all applicable individuals are entitled to the greater of the benefit to which they would have been entitled without regard to the amendment, or the benefit under the plan with regard to the amendment. For a special rule applicable in the case of a plan termination, see Q&A-17(b) of this section.

(2) Definition of egregious failure. For purposes of section 204(h) of ERISA and this Q&A-14, there is an egregious failure to meet the notice requirements if a failure to provide required notice is within the control of the plan sponsor and is either an intentional failure or a failure, whether or not intentional, to provide most of the individuals with most of the information they are entitled to receive. For this purpose, an intentional failure includes any failure to promptly provide the required notice or information after the plan administrator discovers an unintentional failure to meet the requirements. A failure to give section 204(h) notice is deemed not to be egregious if the plan administrator reasonably determines, taking into account section 4980F, section 204(h), these regulations, other administrative pronouncements, and relevant facts and circumstances, that the reduction in the rate of future benefit accrual resulting from an amendment is not significant (as described in Q&A-8 of this section), or that an amendment does not significantly reduce an early retirement benefit or retirement-type subsidy.

(3) Example. The following example illustrates the provisions of this paragraph (a):

Example. (i) Facts. Plan A is amended to reduce significantly the rate of future benefit accrual effective January 1, 2003. Section 204(h) notice is required to be provided 45 days before January 1, 2003. Timely section 204(h) notice is provided to all applicable individuals (and to each employee organization representing participants who are applicable individuals), except that the employer intentionally fails to provide section 204(h) notice to certain participants until May 16, 2003.

(ii) Conclusion. The failure to provide section 204(h) notice is egregious. Accordingly, for the period from January 1, 2003 through June 30, 2003 (which is the date that is 45 days after May 16, 2003), all participants and alternate payees are entitled to the greater of the benefit to which they would have been entitled under Plan A as in effect before the amendment or the benefit under the plan as amended.

(b) Effect of non-egregious failure to provide section 204(h) notice. If an egregious failure has not occurred, the amendment with respect to which section 204(h) notice is required may become effective with respect to all applicable individuals. However, see section 502 of ERISA for civil enforcement remedies. Thus, where there is a failure, whether or not egregious, to provide section 204(h) notice in accordance with this section, individuals may have recourse under section 502 of ERISA.

(c) Excise taxes. See section 4980F and Q&A-15 of this section for excise taxes that may apply to a failure to notify applicable individuals of a pension plan amendment that provides for a significant reduction in the rate of future benefit accrual or eliminates or significantly reduces an early retirement benefit or retirement-type subsidy, regardless of whether or not the failure is egregious.

Q-15. What are some of the rules that apply with respect to the excise tax under section 4980F?

A-15. (a) Person responsible for excise tax. In the case of a plan other than a multiemployer plan, the employer is responsible for reporting and paying the excise tax. In the case of a multiemployer plan, the plan is responsible for reporting and paying the excise tax.

(b) Excise tax inapplicable in certain cases. Under section 4980F(c)(1) of the Internal Revenue Code, no excise tax is imposed on a failure for any period during which it is established to the satisfaction of the Commissioner that the employer (or other person responsible for the tax) exercised reasonable diligence, but did not know that the failure existed. Under section 4980F(c)(2) of the Internal Revenue Code, no excise tax applies to a failure to provide section 204(h) notice if the employer (or other person responsible for the tax) exercised reasonable diligence and corrects the failure within 30 days after the employer (or other person responsible for the tax) first knew, or exercising reasonable diligence would have known, that such failure existed. For purposes of section 4980F(c)(1) of the Internal Revenue Code, a person has exercised reasonable diligence, but did not know that the failure existed if and only if—

(1) The person exercised reasonable diligence in attempting to deliver section 204(h) notice to applicable individuals by the latest date permitted under this section; and

(2) At the latest date permitted for delivery of section 204(h) notice, the person reasonably believes that section 204(h) notice was actually delivered to each applicable individual by that date.

(c) Example. The following example illustrates the provisions of paragraph (b) of this Q&A-15:

Example. (i) Facts. Plan A is amended to reduce significantly the rate of future benefit accrual. The employer sends out a section 204(h) notice to all affected participants and other applicable individuals and to any employee organization representing applicable individuals, including actual delivery by hand to employees at worksites and by first-class mail for any other applicable individual and to any employee organization representing applicable individuals. However, although the employer exercises reasonable diligence in seeking to deliver the notice, the notice is not delivered to any participants at one worksite due to a failure of an overnight delivery service to provide the notice to appropriate personnel at that site for them to timely hand deliver the notice to affected employees. The error is discovered when the employer subsequently calls to confirm delivery. Appropriate section 204(h) notice is then promptly delivered to all affected participants at the worksite.

(ii) Conclusion. Because the employer exercised reasonable diligence, but did not know that a failure existed, no excise tax applies, assuming that participants at the worksite receive section 204(h) notice within 30 days after the employer first knew, or exercising reasonable diligence would have known, that the failure occurred.

Code of Federal Regulations, Title 29

§ 1625.6. Bona fide occupational qualifications.

(a) Whether occupational qualifications will be deemed to be "bona fide" to a specific job and "reasonably necessary to the normal operation of the particular business," will be determined on the basis of all the pertinent facts surrounding each particular situation. It is anticipated that this concept of a bona fide occupational qualification will have limited scope and application. Further, as this is an exception to the Act it must be narrowly construed.

(b) An employer asserting a BFOQ defense has the burden of proving that (1) the age limit is reasonably necessary to the essence of the business, and either (2) that all or substantially all individuals excluded from the job involved are in fact disqualified, or (3) that some of the individuals so excluded possess a disqualifying trait that cannot be ascertained except by reference to age. If the employer's objective in asserting a BFOQ is the goal of public safety, the employer must prove that the challenged practice does indeed effectuate that goal and that there is no acceptable alternative which would better advance it or equally advance it with less discriminatory impact.

(c) Many State and local governments have enacted laws or administrative regulations which limit employment opportunities based on age. Unless these laws meet the standards for the establishment of a valid bona fide occupational qualification under section 4(f)(1) of the Act, they will be considered in conflict with and effectively superseded by the ADEA.

§ 1625.7. Differentiations based on reasonable factors other than age.

(a) Section 4(f) (1) of the Act provides that * * * it shall not be unlawful for an employer, employment agency, or labor organization * * * to take any action otherwise prohibited under paragraphs (a), (b), (c), or (e) of this section * * * where the differentiation is based on reasonable factors other than age * * *.

(b) No precise and unequivocal determination can be made as to the scope of the phrase "differentiation based on reasonable factors other than age." Whether such differentiations exist must be decided on the basis of all the particular facts and circumstances surrounding each individual situation.

(c) When an employment practice uses age as a limiting criterion, the defense that the practice is justified by a reasonable factor other than age is unavailable.

(d) When an employment practice, including a test, is claimed as a basis for different treatment of employees or applicants for employment on the grounds that it is a "factor other than" age, and such a practice has an adverse impact on individuals within the protected age group, it can only be justified as a business necessity. Tests which are asserted as "reasonable factors other than age" will be scrutinized in accordance with the standards set forth at Part 1607 of this Title.

(e) When the exception of "a reasonable factor other than age" is raised against an individual claim of discriminatory treatment, the employer bears the burden of showing that the "reasonable factor other than age" exists factually.

(f) A differentiation based on the average cost of employing older employees as a group is unlawful except with respect to employee benefit plans which qualify for the section 4(f)(2) exception to the Act.

§ 1625.10. Costs and benefits under employee benefit plans.

(a)(1) *General.* Section 4(f)(2) of the Act provides that it is not unlawful for an employer, employment agency, or labor organization to observe the terms of any bona fide employee benefit plan such as a retirement, pension, or insurance plan, which is not a subterfuge to evade the purposes of this Act, except that no such employee benefit plan shall excuse the failure to hire any individual, and no such * * * employee benefit plan shall require or permit the involuntary retirement of any individual specified by section 12(a) of this Act because of the age of such individuals.

The legislative history of this provision indicates that its purpose is to permit age based reductions in employee benefit plans where such reductions are justified by significant cost considerations. Accordingly, section 4(f)(2) does not apply, for example, to paid vacations and uninsured paid sick leave, since reductions in these benefits would not be justified by significant cost considerations. Where employee benefit plans do meet the criteria in section 4(f)(2), benefit levels for older workers may be reduced to the extent necessary to achieve approximate equivalency in cost for older and younger workers. A benefit plan will be considered in compliance with the statute where the actual amount of payment made, or cost incurred, in behalf of an older worker is equal to that made or incurred in behalf of a younger worker, even though the older worker may thereby receive a lesser amount of benefits or insurance coverage. Since section 4(f)(2) is an exception from the general non-discrimination provisions of the Act, the burden is on the one seeking to invoke the exception to show that every element has been clearly and unmistakably met. The exception must be narrowly construed. The following sections explain three key elements of the exception:

(i) What a "bona fide employee benefit plan" is;

(ii) what it means to "observe the terms" of such a plan; and

(iii) what kind of plan, or plan provision, would be considered "a subterfuge to evade the purposes of [the] Act."

There is also a discussion of the application of the general rules governing all plans with respect to specific kinds of employee benefit plans.

(2) *Relation of section 4(f)(2) to sections 4(a), 4(b) and 4(c)*. Sections 4(a), 4(b) and 4(c) prohibit specified acts of discrimination on the basis of age. Section 4(a) in particular makes it unlawful for an employer to "discriminate against any individual with respect to his compensation, terms, conditions, or privileges of employment, because of such individual's age * * *." Section 4(f)(2) is an exception to this general prohibition. Where an employer under an employee benefit plan provides the same level of benefits to older workers as to younger workers, there is no violation of section 4(a), and accordingly the practice does not have to be justified under section 4(f)(2).

(b) *"Bona fide employee benefit plan."* Section 4(f)(2) applies only to bona fide employee benefit plans. A plan is considered "bona fide" if its terms (including cessation of contributions or accruals in the case of retirement income plans) have been accurately described in writing to all employees and if it actually provides the benefits in accordance with the terms of the plan. Notifying employees promptly of provisions and changes in an employee benefit plan is essential if they are to know how the plan affects them. For these purposes, it would be sufficient under the ADEA for employers to follow the disclosure requirements of ERISA and the regulations thereunder. The plan must actually provide the benefits its provisions describe, since otherwise the notification of the provisions to employees is misleading and inaccurate. An "employee benefit plan" is a plan, such as a retirement, pension, or insurance plan, which provides employees with what are frequently referred to as "fringe benefits." The term does not refer to wages or salary in cash; neither section 4(f)(2) nor any other section of the Act excuses the payment of lower wages or salary to older employees on account of age. Whether or not any particular employee benefit plan may lawfully provide lower benefits to older employees on account of age depends on whether all of the elements of the exception have been met. An "employee-pay-all" employee benefit plan is one of the "terms, conditions, or privileges of employment" with respect to which discrimination on the basis of age is forbidden under section 4(a)(1). In such a plan, benefits for older workers may be reduced only to the extent and according to the same principles as apply to other plans under section 4(f)(2).

(c) *"To observe the terms" of a plan.* In order for a bona fide employee benefit plan which provides lower benefits to older employees on account of age to be within the section 4(f)(2) exception, the lower benefits must be provided in "observ[ance of] the terms of" the plan. As this statutory text makes clear, the section 4(f)(2) exception is limited to otherwise discriminatory actions which are actually prescribed by the terms of a bona fide employee benefit plan. Where the employer, employment agency, or labor organization is not required by the express provisions of the plan to provide lesser benefits to older workers, section 4(f)(2) does not apply. Important purposes are served by this requirement. Where a discriminatory policy is an express term of a benefit plan, employees presumably have some opportunity to know of the policy and to plan (or protest) accordingly. Moreover, the requirement that the discrimination actually be prescribed by a plan assures that the particular plan provision will be actually applied to all employees of the same age. Where a discriminatory provision is an optional term of the plan, it permits individual, discretionary acts of discrimination, which do not fall within the section 4(f)(2) exception.

(d) *"Subterfuge."* In order for a bona fide employee benefit plan which prescribes lower benefits for older employees on account of age to be within the section 4(f)(2) exception, it must not be "a subterfuge to evade the purposes of [the] Act." In general, a plan or plan provision which prescribes lower benefits for older employees on account of age is not a "subterfuge" within the meaning of section 4(f)(2), provided that the lower level of benefits is justified by age-related cost considerations. (The only exception to this general rule is with respect to certain retirement plans. See paragraph (f)(4) of this section.) There are certain other requirements that must be met in order for a plan not to be a subterfuge. These requirements are set forth below.

(1) *Cost data—General.* Cost data used in justification of a benefit plan which provides lower benefits to older employees on account of age must be valid and reasonable. This standard is met where an employer has cost data which show the actual cost to it of providing the particular benefit (or benefits) in question over a representative period of years. An employer may rely in cost data for its own employees over such a period, or on cost data for a larger group of similarly situated employees. Sometimes, as a result of experience rating or other causes, an employer incurs costs that differ significantly from costs for a group of similarly situated employees. Such an employer may not rely on cost data for the similarly situated employees where such reliance would result in significantly lower benefits for its own older employees. Where reliable cost information is not available, reasonable projections made from existing cost data meeting the standards set forth above will be considered acceptable.

(2) *Cost data—Individual benefit basis and "benefit package" basis.* Cost comparisons and adjustments under section 4(f)(2) must be made on a benefit-by- benefit basis or on a "benefit package" basis, as described below.

(i) *Benefit-by-benefit basis.* Adjustments made on a benefit-by-benefit basis must be made in the amount or level of a specific form of benefit for a specific event or contingency. For example, higher group term life insurance costs for older workers would justify a corresponding reduction in the amount of group term life insurance coverage for older workers, on the basis of age. However, a benefit-by-benefit approach would not justify the substitution of one form of benefit for another, even though both forms of benefit are designed for the same contingency, such as death. See paragraph (f)(1) of this section.

(ii) *"Benefit package" basis*. As an alternative to the benefit-by-benefit basis, cost comparisons and adjustments under section 4(f)(2) may be made on a limited "benefit package" basis. Under this approach, subject to the limitations described below, cost comparisons and adjustments can be made with respect to section 4(f)(2) plans in the aggregate. This alternative basis provides greater flexibility than a benefit-by-benefit basis in order to carry out the declared statutory purpose "to help employers and workers find ways of meeting problems arising from the impact of age on employment." A "benefit package" approach is an alternative approach consistent with this purpose and with the general purpose of section 4(f)(2) only if it is not used to reduce the cost to the employer or the favorability to the employees of overall employee benefits for older employees. A "benefit package" approach used for either of these purposes would be a subterfuge to evade the purposes of the Act. In order to assure that such a "benefit package" approach is not abused and is consistent with the legislative intent, it is subject to the limitations described in paragraph (f) of this section, which also includes a general example.

(3) *Cost data—Five year maximum basis*. Cost comparisons and adjustments under section 4(f)(2) may be made on the basis of age brackets of up to 5 years. Thus a particular benefit may be reduced for employees of any age within the protected age group by an amount no greater than that which could be justified by the additional cost to provide them with the same level of the benefit as younger employees within a specified five-year age group immediately preceding theirs. For example, where an employer chooses to provide unreduced group term life insurance benefits until age 60, benefits for employees who are between 60 and 65 years of age may be reduced only to the extent necessary to achieve approximate equivalency in costs with employees who are 55 to 60 years old. Similarly, any reductions in benefit levels for 65 to 70 year old employees cannot exceed an amount which is proportional to the additional costs for their coverage over 60 to 65 year old employees.

(4) *Employee contributions in support of employee benefit plans—*

(i) *As a condition of employment*. An older employee within the protected age group may not be required as a condition of employment to make greater contributions than a younger employee in support of an employee benefit plan. Such a requirement would be in effect a mandatory reduction in take-home pay, which is never authorized by section 4(f)(2), and would impose an impediment to employment in violation of the specific restrictions in section 4(f)(2).

(ii) *As a condition of participation in a voluntary employee benefit plan*. An older employee within the protected age group may be required as a condition of participation in a voluntary employee benefit plan to make a greater contribution that a younger employee only if the older employee is not thereby required to bear a greater proportion of the total premium cost (employer-paid and employee-paid) than the younger employee. Otherwise the requirement would discriminate against the older employee by making compensation in the form of an employer contribution available on less favorable terms than for the younger employee and denying that compensation altogether to an older employee unwilling or unable to meet the less favorable terms. Such discrimination is not authorized by section 4(f)(2). This principle applies to three different contribution arrangements as follows:

(A) *Employee-pay-all plans*. Older employees, like younger employees, may be required to contribute as a condition of participation up to the full premium cost for their age.

(B) *Non-contributory ("employer-pay-all") plans*. Where younger employees are not required to contribute any portion of the total premium cost, older employees may not be required to contribute any portion.

(C) *Contributory plans.* In these plans employers and participating employees share the premium cost. The required contributions of participants may increase with age so long as the proportion of the total premium required to be paid by the participants does not increase with age.

(iii) *As an option in order to receive an unreduced benefit.* An older employee may be given the option, as an individual, to make the additional contribution necessary to receive the same level of benefits as a younger employee (provided that the contemplated reduction in benefits is otherwise justified by section 4(f)(2).

(5) *Forfeiture clauses.* Clauses in employee benefit plans which state that litigation or participation in any manner in a formal proceeding by an employee will result in the forfeiture of his rights are unlawful insofar as they may be applied to those who seek redress under the Act. This is by reason of section 4(d) which provides that it is unlawful for an employer, employment agency, or labor organization to discriminate against any individual because such individual "has made a charge, testified, assisted, or participated in an investigation, proceeding, or litigation under this Act."

(6) *Refusal to hire clauses.* Any provision of an employee benefit plan which requires or permits the refusal to hire an individual specified in section 12(a) of the Act on the basis of age is a subterfuge to evade the purposes of the Act and cannot be excused under section 4(f)(2).

(7) *Involuntary retirement clauses.* Any provision of an employee benefit plan which requires or permits the involuntary retirement of any individual specified in section 12(a) of the Act on the basis of age is a subterfuge to evade the purpose of the Act and cannot be excused under section 4(f)(2).

(e) *Benefits provided by the Government.* An employer does not violate the Act by permitting certain benefits to be provided by the Government, even though the availability of such benefits may be based on age. For example, it is not necessary for an employer to provide health benefits which are otherwise provided to certain employees by Medicare. However, the availability of benefits from the Government will not justify a reduction in employer-provided benefits if the result is that, taking the employer-provided and Government- provided benefits together, an older employee is entitled to a lesser benefit of any type (including coverage for family and/or dependents) than a similarly situated younger employee. For example, the availability of certain benefits to an older employee under Medicare will not justify denying an older employee a benefit which is provided to younger employees and is not provided to the older employee by Medicare.

(f) *Application of section 4(f)(2) to various employees benefit plans.* (1) *Benefit-by-benefit approach.* This portion of the interpretation discusses how a benefit-by-benefit approach would apply to four of the most common types of employee benefit plans.

(i) *Life insurance.* It is not uncommon for life insurance coverage to remain constant until a specified age, frequently 65, and then be reduced. This practice will not violate the Act (even if reductions start before age 65), provided that the reduction for an employee of a particular age is no greater than is justified by the increased cost of coverage for that employee's specific age bracket encompassing no more than five years. It should be noted that a total denial of life insurance, on the basis of age, would not be justified under a benefit-by-benefit analysis. However, it is not unlawful for life insurance coverage to cease upon separation from service.

(ii) *Long-term disability.* Under a benefit-by-benefit approach, where employees who are disabled at younger ages are entitled to long-term disability benefits, there is no cost—based justification for denying such benefits altogether, on the basis of age, to employees who are disabled at older ages. It is not unlawful to cut off long-term disability benefits and coverage on the basis of some non-age factor, such as recovery from disability. Reductions on the basis of age in the level or duration of benefits available for disability are justifiable only on the basis of age-related cost considerations as set forth elsewhere in this section. An employer which provides long-term disability coverage to all employees may avoid any increases in the cost to it that such coverage for older employees would entail by reducing the level of benefits available to older employees. An employer may also avoid such cost increases by reducing the duration of benefits available to employees who become disabled at older ages, without reducing the level of benefits. In this connection, the Department would not assert a violation where the level of benefits is not reduced and the duration of benefits is reduced in the following manner:

(A) With respect to disabilities which occur at age 60 or less, benefits cease at age 65.

(B) With respect to disabilities which occur after age 60, benefits cease 5 years after disablement. Cost data may be produced to support other patterns of reduction as well.

(iii) *Retirement plans.* (A) *Participation.* No employee hired prior to normal retirement age may be excluded from a defined contribution plan. With respect to defined benefit plans not subject to the Employee Retirement Income Security Act (ERISA), Pub.L. 93-406, 29 U.S.C. 1001, 1003(a) and (b), an employee hired at an age more than 5 years prior to normal retirement age may not be excluded from such a plan unless the exclusion is justifiable on the basis of cost considerations as set forth elsewhere in this section. With respect to defined benefit plans subject to ERISA, such an exclusion would be unlawful in any case. An employee hired less than 5 years prior to normal retirement age may be excluded from a defined benefit plan, regardless of whether or not the plan is covered by ERISA. Similarly, any employee hired after normal retirement age may be excluded from a defined benefit plan.

(2) *"Benefit Package" Approach.* A "benefit package" approach to compliance under section 4(f)(2) offers greater flexibility than a benefit-by-benefit approach by permitting deviations from a benefit-by-benefit approach so long as the overall result is no lesser cost to the employer and no less favorable benefits for employees. As previously noted, in order to assure that such an approach is used for the benefit of older workers and not to their detriment, and is otherwise consistent with the legislative intent, it is subject to limitations as set forth below:

(i) A benefit package approach shall apply only to employee benefit plans which fall within section 4(f)(2).

(ii) A benefit package approach shall not apply to a retirement or pension plan. The 1978 legislative history sets forth specific and comprehensive rules governing such plans, which have been adopted above. These rules are not tied to actuarially significant cost considerations but are intended to deal with the special funding arrangements of retirement or pension plans. Variations from these special rules are therefore not justified by variations from the cost-based benefit-by-benefit approach in other benefit plans, nor may variations from the special rules governing pension and retirement plans justify variations from the benefit-by-benefit approach in other benefit plans.

(iii) A benefit package approach shall not be used to justify reductions in health benefits greater than would be justified under a benefit-by-benefit approach. Such benefits appear to be of particular importance to older workers in meeting "problems arising from the impact of age" and were of particular concern to Congress. Therefore, the "benefit package" approach may not be used to reduce health insurance benefits by more than is warranted by the increase in the cost to the employer of those benefits alone. Any greater reduction would be a subterfuge to evade the purpose of the Act.

(iv) A benefit reduction greater than would be justified under a benefit-by- benefit approach must be offset by another benefit available to the same employees. No employees may be deprived because of age of one benefit without an offsetting benefit being made available to them.

(v) Employers who wish to justify benefit reductions under a benefit package approach must be prepared to produce data to show that those reductions are fully justified. Thus employers must be able to show that deviations from a benefit-by-benefit approach do not result in lesser cost to them or less favorable benefits to their employees. A general example consistent with these limitations may be given. Assume two employee benefit plans, providing Benefit "A" and Benefit "B." Both plans fall within section 4(f)(2), and neither is a retirement or pension plan subject to special rules. Both benefits are available to all employees. Age-based cost increases would justify a 10% decrease in both benefits on a benefit-by-benefit basis. The affected employees would, however, find it more favorable—that is, more consistent with meeting their needs—for no reduction to be made in Benefit "A" and a greater reduction to be made in Benefit "B." This "trade-off" would not result in a reduction in health benefits. The "trade-off" may therefore be made. The details of the "trade-off" depend on data on the relative cost to the employer of the two benefits. If the data show that Benefit "A" and Benefit "B" cost the same, Benefit "B" may be reduced up to 20% if Benefit "A" is unreduced . If the data show that Benefit "A" costs only half as much as Benefit "B", however, Benefit "B" may be reduced up to only 15% if Benefit "A" is unreduced, since a greater reduction in Benefit "B" would result in an impermissible reduction in total benefit costs.

(g) *Relation of ADEA to State laws.* The ADEA does not preempt State age discrimination in employment laws. However, the failure of the ADEA to preempt such laws does not affect the issue of whether section 514 of the Employee Retirement Income Security Act (ERISA) preempts State laws which related to employee benefit plans.

ERISA REGULATIONS

Code of Federal Regulations, Title 29

§ 2509.08-1 Supplemental guidance relating to fiduciary responsibility in considering economically targeted investments.

This Interpretive Bulletin sets forth the Department of Labor's interpretation of sections 403 and 404 of the Employee Retirement Income Security Act of 1974 (ERISA), as applied to employee benefit plan investments in "economically targeted investments," that is, investments selected for the economic benefits they create apart from their investment return to the employee benefit plan. The guidance set forth in this interpretive bulletin modifies and supersedes the guidance set forth in interpretive bulletin 94-1 (29 CFR 2509.94-1).

ERISA requires that a fiduciary act solely in the interest of the plan's participants and beneficiaries and for the exclusive purpose of providing benefits to their participants and beneficiaries. The Act specifically states, in relevant part, that:

• "[A]ssets of a plan shall never inure to the benefit of any employer and shall be held for the exclusive purposes of providing benefits to participants in the plan and their beneficiaries.* * *" [Sec. 403(c)(1)]

• "[A] fiduciary shall discharge his duties with respect to a plan solely in the interest of the participants and beneficiaries and for the exclusive purpose of providing benefits to participants and their beneficiaries." [Sec. 404(a)(1)(A)(i)]

ERISA's plain text thus establishes a clear rule that in the course of discharging their duties, fiduciaries may never subordinate the economic interests of the plan to unrelated objectives, and may not select investments on the basis of any factor outside the economic interest of the plan except in very limited circumstances enumerated below.

With regard to investing plan assets, the Department has issued a regulation, at 29 CFR 2550.404a-1, interpreting the prudence requirements of ERISA as they apply to the investment duties of fiduciaries of employee benefit plans. The regulation provides that the prudence requirements of section 404(a)(1)(B) are satisfied if (1) the fiduciary making an investment or engaging in an investment course of action has given appropriate consideration to those facts and circumstances that, given the scope of the fiduciary's investment duties, the fiduciary knows or should know are relevant, and (2) the fiduciary acts accordingly. This includes giving appropriate consideration to the role that the investment or investment course of action plays (in terms of such factors as diversification, liquidity and risk/return characteristics) with respect to that portion of the plan's investment portfolio within the scope of the fiduciary's responsibility.

Other facts and circumstances relevant to an investment or investment course of action would, in the view of the Department, include consideration of the expected return on alternative investments with similar risks available to the plan. It follows that, because every investment necessarily causes a plan to forgo other investment opportunities, an investment will not be prudent if it would be expected to provide a plan with a lower rate of return than available alternative investments with commensurate degrees of risk or is riskier than alternative available investments with commensurate rates of return.

ERISA's plain text does not permit fiduciaries to make investment decisions on the basis of any factor other than the economic interest of the plan. Situations may arise, however, in which two or more investment alternatives are of equal economic value to a plan. The Department has recognized in past guidance that under these limited circumstances, fiduciaries can choose between the investment alternatives on the basis of a factor other than the economic interest of the plan. The Department has interpreted the statute to permit this selection because (1) ERISA requires fiduciaries to invest plan assets and to make choices between investment alternatives, (2) ERISA does not itself specifically provide a basis for making the investment choice in this circumstance, and (3) the economic interests of the plan are fully protected by the fact that the available investment alternatives are, from the plan's perspective, economically indistinguishable.

Given the significance of ERISA's requirement that fiduciaries act "solely in the interest of participants and beneficiaries," the Department believes that, before selecting an economically targeted investment, fiduciaries must have first concluded that the alternative options are truly equal, taking into account a quantitative and qualitative analysis of the economic impact on the plan. ERISA's fiduciary standards expressed in sections 403 and 404 do not permit fiduciaries to select investments based on factors outside the economic interests of the plan until they have concluded, based on economic factors, that alternative investments are equal. A less rigid rule would allow fiduciaries to act on the basis of factors outside the economic interest of the plan in situations where reliance on those factors might compromise or subordinate the interests of plan participants and their beneficiaries. The Department rejects a construction of ERISA that would render the Act's tight limits on the use of plan assets illusory, and that would permit plan fiduciaries to expend ERISA trust assets to promote myriad public policy preferences.

A plan fiduciary's analysis is required to comply with, but is not necessarily limited to, the requirements set forth in 29 CFR 2550.404a-1(b). In evaluating the plan portfolio, as well as portions of the portfolio, the fiduciary is required to examine the level of diversification, degree of liquidity, and the potential risk/return in comparison with available alternative investments. The same type of analysis must also be applied when choosing between investment alternatives. Potential investments should be compared to other investments that would fill a similar role in the portfolio with regard to diversification, liquidity, and risk/return.

In light of the rigorous requirements established by ERISA, the Department believes that fiduciaries who rely on factors outside the economic interests of the plan in making investment choices and subsequently find their decision challenged will rarely be able to demonstrate compliance with ERISA absent a written record demonstrating that a contemporaneous economic analysis showed that the investment alternatives were of equal value.

Examples:

A plan owns an interest in a limited partnership that is considering investing in a company that competes with the plan sponsor. The fiduciaries may not replace the limited partnership investment with another investment based on this fact unless they prudently determine that a replacement investment is economically equal or superior to the limited partnership investment and would not adversely affect the plan's investment portfolio, taking into account factors including diversification, liquidity, risk and expected return. The competition of the limited partnership with the plan sponsor is a factor outside the economic interests of the plan, and thus cannot be considered unless an alternative investment is equal or superior to the limited partnership.

A multiemployer plan covering employees in a metropolitan area's construction industry wants to invest in a large loan for a construction project located in the same area because it will create local jobs. The plan has taken steps to ensure that the loan poses no prohibited transaction issues. The loan carries a return fully commensurate with the risk of nonpayment. Moreover, the loan's expected return is equal to or greater than construction loans of similar quality that are available to the plan. However, the plan has already made several other loans for construction projects in the same metropolitan area, and this loan could create a risk of large losses to the plan's portfolio due to lack of diversification. The fiduciaries may not choose this investment on the basis of the local job creation factor because, due to lack of diversification, the investment is not of equal economic value to the plan.

A plan is considering an investment in a bond to finance affordable housing for people in the local community. The bond provides a return at least as favorable to the plan as other bonds with the same risk rating. However, the bond's size and lengthy duration raises a potential risk regarding the plan's ability to meet its predicted liquidity needs. Other available bonds under consideration by the plan do not pose this same risk. The return on the bond, although equal to or greater than the alternatives, would not be sufficient to offset the additional risk for the plan created by the role that this bond would play in the plan's portfolio. The plan's fiduciaries may not make this investment based on factors outside the economic interest of the plan because it is not of equal or greater economic value to other investment alternatives.

A plan sponsor adopts an investment policy that favors plan investment in companies meeting certain environmental criteria (so-called "green" companies). In carrying out the policy, the plan's fiduciaries may not simply consider investments only in green companies. They must consider all investments that meet the plan's prudent financial criteria. The fiduciaries may apply the investment policy to eliminate a company from consideration only if they appropriately determine that other available investments provide equal or better returns at the same or lower risks, and would play the same role in the plan's portfolio.

A collective investment fund, which holds assets of several plans, is designed to invest in commercial real estate constructed or renovated with union labor. Fiduciaries of plans that invest in the fund must determine that the fund's overall risk and return characteristics are as favorable, or more favorable, to the plans as other available investment alternatives that would play a similar role in their plans' portfolios. The fund's managers may select investments constructed or improved with union labor, after an economic analysis indicates that these investment options are equal or superior to their alternatives. The managers will best be able to justify their investment choice by recording their analysis in writing. However, if real estate investments that satisfy both ERISA's fiduciary requirements and the union labor criterion are unavailable, the fund managers may have to select investments without regard to the union labor criterion.

§ 2509.08-2 Interpretive bulletin relating to the exercise of shareholder rights and written statements of investment policy, including proxy voting policies or guidelines.

This interpretive bulletin sets forth the Department of Labor's (the Department) interpretation of sections 402, 403 and 404 of the Employee Retirement Income Security Act of 1974 (ERISA) as those sections apply to voting of proxies on securities held in employee benefit plan investment portfolios and the maintenance of and compliance with statements of investment policy, including proxy voting policy. In addition, this interpretive bulletin provides guidance on the appropriateness under ERISA of active monitoring of corporate management by plan fiduciaries. The guidance set forth in this interpretive bulletin modifies and supersedes the guidance set forth in interpretive bulletin 94-2 (29 CFR 2509.94-2).

(1) Proxy Voting

The fiduciary act of managing plan assets that are shares of corporate stock includes the management of voting rights appurtenant to those shares of stock. As a result, the responsibility for voting or deciding not to vote proxies lies exclusively with the plan trustee except to the extent that either (1) the trustee is subject to the direction of a named fiduciary pursuant to ERISA Sec. 403(a)(1); or (2) the power to manage, acquire or dispose of the relevant assets has been delegated by a named fiduciary to one or more investment managers pursuant to ERISA Sec. 403(a)(2). Where the authority to manage plan assets has been delegated to an investment manager pursuant to

Sec. 403(a)(2), no person other than the investment manager has authority to make voting decisions for proxies appurtenant to such plan assets except to the extent that the named fiduciary has reserved to itself (or to another named fiduciary so authorized by the plan document) the right to direct a plan trustee regarding the voting of proxies. In this regard, a named fiduciary, in delegating investment management authority to an investment manager, could reserve to itself the right to direct a trustee with respect to the voting of all proxies or reserve to itself the right to direct a trustee as to the voting of only those proxies relating to specified assets or issues.

If the plan document or investment management agreement provides that the investment manager is not required to vote proxies, but does not expressly preclude the investment manager from voting proxies, the investment manager would have exclusive responsibility for proxy voting decisions. Moreover, an investment manager would not be relieved of its own fiduciary responsibilities by following directions of some other person regarding the voting of proxies, or by delegating such responsibility to another person. If, however, the plan document or the investment management contract expressly precludes the investment manager from voting proxies, the responsibility for voting proxies would lie exclusively with the trustee. The trustee, however, consistent with the requirements of ERISA Sec. 403(a)(1), may be subject to the directions of a named fiduciary if the plan so provides.

The fiduciary duties described at ERISA Sec. 404(a)(1)(A) and (B), require that, in voting proxies, regardless of whether the vote is made pursuant to a statement of investment policy, the responsible fiduciary shall consider only those factors that relate to the economic value of the plan's investment and shall not subordinate the interests of the participants and beneficiaries in their retirement income to unrelated objectives. Votes shall only be cast in accordance with a plan's economic interests. If the responsible fiduciary reasonably determines that the cost of voting (including the cost of research, if necessary, to determine how to vote) is likely to exceed the expected economic benefits of voting, or if the exercise of voting results in the imposition of unwarranted trading or other restrictions, the fiduciary has an obligation to refrain from voting. In making this determination, objectives, considerations, and economic effects unrelated to the plan's economic interests cannot be considered. The fiduciary's duties under ERISA Sec. 404(a)(1)(A) and (B) also require that the named fiduciary appointing an investment manager periodically monitor the activities of the investment manager with respect to the management of plan assets, including decisions made and actions taken by the investment manager with regard to proxy voting decisions. The named fiduciary must carry out this responsibility solely in the participants' and beneficiaries' interest in the economic value of the plan assets and without regard to the fiduciary's relationship to the plan sponsor.

It is the view of the Department that compliance with the duty to monitor necessitates proper documentation of the activities that are subject to monitoring. Thus, the investment manager or other responsible fiduciary would be required to maintain accurate records as to proxy voting decisions, including, where appropriate, cost-benefit analyses. Moreover, if the named fiduciary is to be able to carry out its responsibilities under ERISA Sec. 404(a) in determining whether the investment manager is fulfilling its fiduciary obligations in investing plans assets in a manner that justifies the continuation of the management appointment, the proxy voting records must enable the named fiduciary to review not only the investment manager's voting procedure with respect to plan-owned stock, but also to review the actions taken in individual proxy voting situations.

The fiduciary obligations of prudence and loyalty to plan participants and beneficiaries require the responsible fiduciary to vote proxies on issues that may affect the economic value of the plan's investment. However, fiduciaries also need to take into account costs when deciding whether and how to exercise their shareholder rights, including the voting of shares. Such costs include, but are not limited to, expenditures related to developing proxy resolutions, proxy voting services and the analysis of the likely net effect of a particular issue on the economic value of the plan's investment. Fiduciaries must take all of these factors into account in determining whether the exercise of such rights (e.g., the voting of a proxy), independently or in conjunction with other shareholders, is expected to have an effect on the economic value of the plan's investment that will outweigh the cost of exercising such rights. With respect to proxies appurtenant to shares of foreign corporations, a fiduciary, in deciding whether to purchase shares of a foreign corporation, should consider whether any additional difficulty and expense in voting such shares is reflected in their market price.

(2) Statements of Investment Policy

The maintenance by an employee benefit plan of a statement of investment policy designed to further the purposes of the plan and its funding policy is consistent with the fiduciary obligations set forth in ERISA section 404(a)(1)(A) and (B). Because the fiduciary act of managing plan assets that are shares of corporate stock includes the voting, where appropriate, of proxies appurtenant to those shares of stock, a statement of proxy voting policy would be an important part of any comprehensive statement of investment policy. For purposes of this document, the term "statement of investment policy" means a written statement that provides the fiduciaries who are responsible for plan investments with guidelines or general instructions concerning various types or categories of investment management decisions, which may include proxy voting decisions. A statement of investment policy is distinguished from directions as to the purchase or sale of a specific investment at a specific time or as to voting specific plan proxies.

In plans where investment management responsibility is delegated to one or more investment managers appointed by the named fiduciary pursuant to ERISA Sec. 402(c)(3), inherent in the authority to appoint an investment manager, the named fiduciary responsible for appointment of investment managers has the authority to condition the appointment on acceptance of a statement of investment policy. Thus, such a named fiduciary may expressly require, as a condition of the investment management agreement, that an investment manager comply with the terms of a statement of investment policy that sets forth guidelines concerning investments and investment courses of action that the investment manager is authorized or is not authorized to make. Such investment policy may include a policy or guidelines on the voting of proxies on shares of stock for which the investment manager is responsible. Such guidelines must be consistent with the fiduciary obligations set forth in ERISA Sec. 404(a)(1)(A) and (B) and this Interpretive Bulletin, and may not subordinate the economic interests of the plan participants to unrelated objectives. In the absence of such an express requirement to comply with an investment policy, the authority to manage the plan assets placed under the control of the investment manager would lie exclusively with the investment manager. Although a trustee may be subject to the direction of a named fiduciary pursuant to ERISA Sec. 403(a)(1), an investment manager who has authority to make investment decisions, including proxy voting decisions, would never be relieved of its fiduciary responsibility if it followed the direction as to specific investment decisions from the named fiduciary or any other person.

Statements of investment policy issued by a named fiduciary authorized to appoint investment managers would be part of the "documents and instruments governing the plan" within the meaning of ERISA Sec. 404(a)(1)(D). An investment manager to whom such investment policy applies would be required to comply with such policy, pursuant to ERISA Sec. 404(a)(1)(D) insofar as the policy directives or guidelines are consistent with titles I and IV of ERISA. Therefore, if, for example, compliance with the guidelines in a given instance would be imprudent, then the investment manager's failure to follow the guidelines would not violate ERISA

Sec. 404(a)(1)(D). Moreover, ERISA Sec. 404(a)(1)(D) does not shield the investment manager from liability for imprudent actions taken in compliance with a statement of investment policy.

The plan document or trust agreement may expressly provide a statement of investment policy to guide the trustee or may authorize a named fiduciary to issue a statement of investment policy applicable to a trustee. Where a plan trustee is subject to an investment policy, the trustee's duty to comply with such investment policy would also be analyzed under ERISA Sec. 404(a)(1)(D). Thus, the trustee would be required to comply with the statement of investment policy unless, for example, it would be imprudent to do so in a given instance.

Maintenance of a statement of investment policy by a named fiduciary does not relieve the named fiduciary of its obligations under ERISA Sec. 404(a) with respect to the appointment and monitoring of an investment manager or trustee. In this regard, the named fiduciary appointing an investment manager must periodically monitor the investment manager's activities with respect to management of the plan assets. Moreover, compliance with ERISA Sec. 404(a)(1)(B) would require maintenance of proper documentation of the activities of the investment manager and of the named fiduciary of the plan in monitoring the activities of the investment manager. In addition, in the view of the Department, a named fiduciary's determination of the terms of a statement of investment policy is an exercise of fiduciary responsibility and, as such, statements may need to take into account factors such as the plan's funding policy and its liquidity needs as well as issues of prudence, diversification and other fiduciary requirements of ERISA.

An investment manager of a pooled investment vehicle that holds assets of more than one employee benefit plan may be subject to a proxy voting policy of one plan that conflicts with the proxy voting policy of another plan. If the investment manager determines that compliance with one of the conflicting voting policies would violate ERISA Sec. 404(a)(1), for example, by being imprudent or not solely in the economic interest of plan participants, the investment manager would be required to ignore the policy and vote in accordance with ERISA's obligations. If, however, the investment manager reasonably concludes that application of each plan's voting policy is consistent with ERISA's obligations, such as when the policies reflect different but reasonable judgments or when the plans have different economic interests, ERISA Sec. 404(a)(1)(D) would generally require the manager, to the extent permitted by applicable law, to vote the proxies in proportion to each plan's interest in the pooled investment vehicle. An investment manager may also require participating investors to accept the investment manager's own investment policy statement, including any statement of proxy voting policy, before they are allowed to invest, which may help to avoid such potential conflicts. As with investment policies originating from named fiduciaries, a policy initiated by an investment manager and adopted by the participating plans would be regarded as an instrument governing the participating plans, and the investment manager's compliance with such a policy would be governed by ERISA Sec. 404(a)(1)(D).

(3) Shareholder Activism

An investment policy that contemplates activities intended to monitor or influence the management of corporations in which the plan owns stock is consistent with a fiduciary's obligations under ERISA where the responsible fiduciary concludes that there is a reasonable expectation that such monitoring or communication with management, by the plan alone or together with other shareholders, will enhance the economic value of the plan's investment in the corporation, after taking into account the costs involved. Such a reasonable expectation may exist in various circumstances, for example, where plan investments in corporate stock are held as long-term investments or where a plan may not be able to easily dispose such an investment. Active monitoring and communication activities would generally concern such issues as the independence and expertise of candidates for the corporation's board of directors and assuring that the board has sufficient information to carry out its responsibility to monitor management. Other issues may include such matters as consideration of the appropriateness of executive compensation, the corporation's policy regarding mergers and acquisitions, the extent of debt financing and capitalization, the nature of long-term business plans, the corporation's investment in training to develop its work force, other workplace practices and financial and non-financial measures of corporate performance that are reasonably likely to affect the economic value of the plan. Active monitoring and communication may be carried out through a variety of methods including by means of correspondence and meetings with corporate management as well as by exercising the legal rights of a shareholder. In creating an investment policy, a fiduciary shall consider only factors that relate to the economic interest of participants and their beneficiaries in plan assets, and shall not use an investment policy to promote myriad public policy preferences.

(4) Socially-Directed Proxy Voting, Investment Policies and Shareholder Activism.

Plan fiduciaries risk violating the exclusive purpose rule when they exercise their fiduciary authority in an attempt to further legislative, regulatory or public policy issues through the proxy process. In such cases, the Department would expect fiduciaries to be able to demonstrate in enforcement actions their compliance with the requirements of section 404(a)(1)(A) and (B). The mere fact that plans are shareholders in the corporations in which they invest does not itself provide a rationale for a fiduciary to spend plan assets to pursue, support, or oppose such proxy proposals. Because of the heightened potential for abuse in such cases, the fiduciaries must be prepared to articulate a clear basis for concluding that the proxy vote, the investment policy, or the activity intended to monitor or influence the management of the corporation is more likely than not to enhance the economic value of the plan's investment before expending plan assets.

The use of pension plan assets by plan fiduciaries to further policy or political issues through proxy resolutions that have no connection to enhancing the economic value of the plan's investment in a corporation would, in the view of the Department, violate the prudence and exclusive purpose requirements of section 404(a)(1)(A) and (B). For example, the likelihood that the adoption of a proxy resolution or proposal requiring corporate directors and officers to disclose their personal political contributions would enhance the economic value of a plan's investment in the corporation appears sufficiently remote that the expenditure of plan assets to further such a resolution or proposal clearly raises compliance issues under section 404(a)(1)(A) and (B).

§ 2509.75-5. Questions and answers relating to fiduciary responsibility.

* * *

D-1 Q: Is an attorney, accountant, actuary or consultant who renders legal, accounting, actuarial or consulting services to an employee benefit plan (other than an investment adviser to the plan) a fiduciary to the plan solely by virtue of the rendering of such services, absent a showing that such consultant (a) exercises discretionary authority or discretionary control respecting the management of the plan, (b) exercises authority or control respecting management or disposition of the plan's assets, (c) renders investment advice for a fee, direct or indirect, with respect to the assets of the plan, or has any authority or responsibility to do so, or (d) has any discretionary authority or discretionary responsibility in the administration of the plan?

A: No. However, while attorneys, accountants, actuaries and consultants performing their usual professional functions will ordinarily not be considered fiduciaries, if the factual situation in a particular case falls within one of the categories described in clauses (a) through (d) of this question, such persons would be considered to be fiduciaries within the meaning of section 3(21) of the Act. The Internal Revenue Service notes that such persons would also be considered to be fiduciaries within the meaning of section 4975(e)(3) of the Internal Revenue Code of 1954.

* * *

§ 2509.75-8. Questions and answers relating to fiduciary responsibility under the Employee Retirement Income Security Act of 1974.

* * *

D-2 Q: Are persons who have no power to make any decisions as to plan policy, interpretations, practices or procedures, but who perform the following administrative functions for an employee benefit plan, within a framework of policies, interpretations, rules, practices and procedures made by other persons, fiduciaries with respect to the plan:

(1) Application of rules determining eligibility for participation or benefits;

(2) Calculation of services and compensation credits for benefits;

(3) Preparation of employee communications material;

(4) Maintenance of participants' service and employment records;

(5) Preparation of reports required by government agencies;

(6) Calculation of benefits;

(7) Orientation of new participants and advising participants of their rights and options under the plan;

(8) Collection of contributions and application of contributions as provided in the plan;

(9) Preparation of reports concerning participants' benefits;

(10) Processing of claims; and

(11) Making recommendations to others for decisions with respect to plan administration?

A: No. Only persons who perform one or more of the functions described in section 3(21)(A) of the Act with respect to an employee benefit plan are fiduciaries. Therefore, a person who performs purely ministerial functions such as the types described above for an employee benefit plan within a framework of policies, interpretations, rules, practices and procedures made by other persons is not a fiduciary because such person does not have discretionary authority or discretionary control respecting management of the plan, does not exercise any authority or control respecting management or disposition of the assets of the plan, and does not render investment advice with respect to any money or other property of the plan and has no authority or responsibility to do so.

However, although such a person may not be a plan fiduciary, he may be subject to the bonding requirements contained in section 412 of the Act if he handles funds or other property of the plan within the meaning of applicable regulations.

The Internal Revenue Service notes that such persons would not be considered plan fiduciaries within the meaning of section 4975(e)(3) of the Internal Revenue Code of 1954.

* * *

D-4 Q: In the case of a plan established and maintained by an employer, are members of the board of directors of the employer fiduciaries with respect to the plan?

A: Members of the board of directors of an employer which maintains an employee benefit plan will be fiduciaries only to the extent that they have responsibility for the functions described in section 3(21)(A) of the Act. For example, the board of directors may be responsible for the selection and retention of plan fiduciaries. In such a case, members of the board of directors exercise "discretionary authority or discretionary control respecting management of such plan" and are, therefore, fiduciaries with respect to the plan. However, their responsibility, and, consequently, their liability, is limited to the selection and retention of fiduciaries (apart from co-fiduciary liability arising under circumstances described in section 405(a) of the Act). In addition, if the directors are made named fiduciaries of the plan, their liability may be limited pursuant to a procedure provided for in the plan instrument for the allocation of fiduciary responsibilities among named fiduciaries or for the designation of persons other than named fiduciaries to carry out fiduciary responsibilities, as provided in section 405(c)(2).

* * *

FR-11 Q: In discharging fiduciary responsibilities, may a fiduciary with respect to a plan rely on information, data, statistics or analyses provided by other persons who perform purely ministerial functions for such plan, such as those persons described in D-2 above?

A: A plan fiduciary may rely on information, data, statistics or analyses furnished by persons performing ministerial functions for the plan, provided that he has exercised prudence in the selection and retention of such persons. The plan fiduciary will be deemed to have acted prudently in such selection and retention if, in the exercise of ordinary care in such situation, he has no reason to doubt the competence, integrity or responsibility of such persons.

* * *

FR-17 Q: What are the ongoing responsibilities of a fiduciary who has appointed trustees or other fiduciaries with respect to these appointments?

A: At reasonable intervals the performance of trustees and other fiduciaries should be reviewed by the appointing fiduciary in such manner as may be reasonably expected to ensure that their performance has been in compliance with the terms of the plan and statutory standards, and satisfies the needs of the plan. No single procedure will be appropriate in all cases; the procedure adopted may vary in accordance with the nature of the plan and other facts and circumstances relevant to the choice of the procedure.

§ 2510.3-1. Employee welfare benefit plan.

(a) *General.* (1) The purpose of this section is to clarify the definition of the terms "employee welfare benefit plan" and "welfare plan" for purposes of Title I of the Act and this chapter by identifying certain practices which do not constitute employee welfare benefit plans for those purposes. In addition, the practices listed in this section do not constitute employee pension benefit plans within the meaning of section 3(2) of the Act, and, therefore, do not constitute employee benefit plans within the meaning of section 3(3). Since under section 4(a) of the Act, only employee benefit plans within the meaning of section 3(3) are subject to Title I of the Act, the practices listed in this section are not subject to Title I.

(2) The terms "employee welfare benefit plan" and "welfare plan" are defined in section 3(1) of the Act to include plans providing "(i) medical, surgical, or hospital care or benefits, or benefits in the event of sickness, accident, disability, death or unemployment, or vacation benefits, apprenticeship or other training programs, or day care centers, scholarship funds, or prepaid legal services, or (ii) any benefit described in section 302(c) of the Labor Management Relations Act, 1947 (other than pensions on retirement or death, and insurance to provide such pensions)." Under this definition, only plans which provide benefits described in section 3(1)(A) of the Act or in section 302(c) of the Labor-Management Relations Act, 1947 (hereinafter "the LMRA")(other than pensions on retirement or death) constitute welfare plans. For example, a system of payroll deductions by an employer for deposit in savings accounts owned by its employees is not an employee welfare benefit plan within the meaning of section 3(1) of the Act because it does not provide benefits described in section 3(1)(A) of the Act or section 302(c) of the LMRA. (In addition, if each employee has the right to withdraw the balance in his or her account at any time, such a payroll savings plan does not meet the requirements for a pension plan set forth in section 3(2) of

the Act and, therefore, is not an employee benefit plan within the meaning of section 3(3) of the Act).

(3) Section 302(c) of the LMRA lists exceptions to the restrictions contained in subsections (a) and (b) of that section on payments and loans made by an employer to individuals and groups representing employees of the employer. Of these exceptions, only those contained in paragraphs (5), (6), (7) and (8) describe benefits provided through employee benefit plans. Moreover, only paragraph (6) describes benefits not described in section 3(1)(A) of the Act. The benefits described in section 302(c)(6) of the LMRA but not in section 3(1)(A) of the Act are " * * * holiday, severance or similar benefits". Thus, the effect of section 3(1)(B) of the Act is to include within the definition of "welfare plan" those plans which provide holiday and severance benefits, and benefits which are similar (for example, benefits which are in substance severance benefits, although not so characterized).

(4) Some of the practices listed in this section as excluded from the definition of "welfare plan" or mentioned as examples of general categories of excluded practices are inserted in response to questions received by the Department of Labor and, in the Department's judgment, do not represent borderline cases under the definition in section 3(1) of the Act. Therefore, this section should not be read as implicitly indicating the Department's views on the possible scope of section 3(1).

(b) *Payroll practices.* For purposes of Title I of the Act and this chapter, the terms "employee welfare benefit plan" and "welfare plan" shall not include—

(1) Payment by an employer of compensation on account of work performed by an employee, including compensation at a rate in excess of the normal rate of compensation on account of performance of duties under other than ordinary circumstances, such as—

(i) Overtime pay,

(ii) Shift premiums,

(iii) Holiday premiums,

(iv) Weekend premiums;

(2) Payment of an employee's normal compensation, out of the employer's general assets, on account of periods of time during which the employee is physically or mentally unable to perform his or her duties, or is otherwise absent for medical reasons (such as pregnancy, a physical examination or psychiatric treatment); and

(3) Payment of compensation, out of the employer's general assets, on account of periods of time during which the employee, although physically and mentally able to perform his or her duties and not absent for medical reasons (such as pregnancy, a physical examination or psychiatric treatment) performs no duties; for example—

(i) Payment of compensation while an employee is on vacation or absent on a holiday, including payment of premiums to induce employees to take vacations at a time favorable to the employer for business reasons,

(ii) Payment of compensation to an employee who is absent while on active military duty,

(iii) Payment of compensation while an employee is absent for the purpose of serving as a juror or testifying in official proceedings,

(iv) Payment of compensation on account of periods of time during which an employee performs little or no productive work while engaged in training (whether or not subsidized in whole or in part by Federal, State or local government funds), and

(v) Payment of compensation to an employee who is relieved of duties while on sabbatical leave or while pursuing further education.

(c) *On-premises facilities.* For purposes of Title I of the Act and this chapter, the terms "employee welfare benefit plan" and "welfare plan" shall not include—

(1) The maintenance on the premises of an employer or of an employee organization

of recreation, dining or other facilities (other than day care centers) for use by employees or members; and

(2) The maintenance on the premises of an employer of facilities for the treatment of minor injuries or illness or rendering first aid in case of accidents occurring during working hours.

(d) *Holiday gifts*. For purposes of Title I of the Act and this chapter the terms "employee welfare benefit plan" and "welfare plan" shall not include the distribution of gifts such as turkeys or hams by an employer to employees at Christmas and other holiday seasons.

(e) *Sales to employees*. For purposes of Title I of the Act and this chapter, the terms "employee welfare benefit plan" and "welfare plan" shall not include the sale by an employer to employees of an employer, whether or not at prevailing market prices, of articles or commodities of the kind which the employer offers for sale in the regular course of business.

(f) *Hiring halls*. For purposes of Title I of the Act and this chapter, the terms "employee welfare benefit plan" and "welfare plan" shall not include the maintenance by one or more employers, employee organizations, or both, of a hiring hall facility.

(g) *Remembrance funds*. For purposes of Title I of the Act and this chapter, the terms "employee welfare benefit plan" and "welfare plan" shall not include a program under which contributions are made to provide remembrances such as flowers, an obituary notice in a newspaper or a small gift on occasions such as the sickness, hospitalization, death or termination of employment of employees, or members of an employee organization, or members of their families.

(h) *Strike funds*. For purposes of Title I of the Act and this chapter, the terms "employee welfare benefit plan" and "welfare plan" shall not include a fund maintained by an employee organization to provide payments to its members during strikes and for related purposes.

(i) *Industry advancement programs*. For purposes of Title I of the Act and this chapter, the terms "employee welfare benefit plan" and "welfare plan" shall not include a program maintained by an employer or group or association of employers, which has no employee participants and does not provide benefits to employees or their dependents, regardless of whether the program serves as a conduit through which funds or other assets are channeled to employee benefit plans covered under Title I of the Act.

(j) *Certain group or group-type insurance programs*. For purposes of Title I of the Act and this chapter, the terms "employee welfare benefit plan" and "welfare plan" shall not include a group or group-type insurance program offered by an insurer to employees or members of an employee organization, under which

(1) No contributions are made by an employer or employee organization;

(2) Participation the program is completely voluntary for employees or members;

(3) The sole functions of the employer or employee organization with respect to the program are, without endorsing the program, to permit the insurer to publicize the program to employees or members, to collect premiums through payroll deductions or dues checkoffs and to remit them to the insurer; and

(4) The employer or employee organization receives no consideration in the form of cash or otherwise in connection with the program, other than reasonable compensation, excluding any profit, for administrative services actually rendered in connection with payroll deductions or dues checkoffs.

(k) *Unfunded scholarship programs*. For purposes of Title I of the Act and this chapter, the terms "employee welfare benefit plan" and "welfare plan" shall not include a scholarship program, including a tuition and education expense refund program, under which payments are made solely from the general assets of an employer or employee organization.

§ 2510.3-2. Employee pension benefit plan.

(a) *General.* This section clarifies the limits of the defined terms "employee pension benefit plan" and "pension plan" for purposes of Title I of the Act and this chapter by identifying certain specific plans, funds and programs which do not constitute employee pension benefit plans for those purposes. To the extent that these plans, funds and programs constitute employee welfare benefit plans within the meaning of section 3(1) of the Act and § 2510.3-1 of this part, they will be covered under Title I; however, they will not be subject to parts 2 and 3 of Title I of the Act.

(b) *Severance pay plans.* (1) For purposes of Title I of the Act and this chapter, an arrangement shall not be deemed to constitute an employee pension benefit plan or pension plan solely by reason of the payment of severance benefits on account of the termination of an employee's service, provided that:

(i) Such payments are not contingent, directly or indirectly, upon the employee's retiring;

(ii) The total amount of such payments does not exceed the equivalent of twice the employee's annual compensation during the year immediately preceding the termination of his service; and

(iii) All such payments to any employee are completed,

(A) In the case of an employee whose service is terminated in connection with a limited program of terminations, within the later of 24 months after the termination of the employee's service, or 24 months after the employee reaches normal retirement age; and

(B) In the case of all other employees, within 24 months after the termination of the employee's service.

(2) For purposes of this paragraph (b),

(i) "Annual compensation" means the total of all compensation, including wages, salary, and any other benefit of monetary value, whether paid in the form of cash or otherwise, which was paid as consideration for the employee's service during the year, or which would have been so paid at the employee's usual rate of compensation if the employee had worked a full year.

(ii) "Limited program of terminations" means a program of terminations:

(A) Which, when begun, was scheduled to be completed upon a date certain or upon the occurrence of one or more specified events;

(B) Under which the number, percentage or class or classes of employees whose services are to be terminated is specified in advance; and

(C) Which is described in a written document which is available to the Secretary upon request, and which contains information sufficient to demonstrate that the conditions set forth in paragraphs (b)(2)(ii)(A) and (B) of this section have been met.

(c) *Bonus program.* For purposes of Title I of the Act and this chapter, the terms "employee pension benefit plan" and "pension plan" shall not include payments made by an employer to some or all of its employees as bonuses for work performed, unless such payments are systematically deferred to the termination of covered employment or beyond, or so as to provide retirement income to employees.

(d) *Individual Retirement Accounts.* (1) For purposes of Title I of the Act and this chapter, the terms "employee pension benefit plan" and "pension plan" shall not include an individual retirement account described in section 408(a) of the Code, an individual retirement annuity described in section 408(b) of the Internal Revenue Code of 1954 (hereinafter "the Code") and an individual retirement bond described in section 409 of the Code, provided that—

(i) No contributions are made by the employer or employee association;

(ii) Participation is completely voluntary for employees or members;

(iii) The sole involvement of the employer or employee organization is without endorsement to permit the sponsor to publicize the program to employees or members, to collect contributions through payroll deductions or dues checkoffs and to remit them to the sponsor; and

(iv) The employer or employee organization receives no consideration in the form of cash or otherwise, other than reasonable compensation for services actually rendered in connection with payroll deductions or dues checkoffs.

* * *

§ 2510.3-3. Employee benefit plan.

(a) *General.* This section clarifies the definition in section 3(3) of the term "employee benefit plan" for purposes of Title I of the Act and this chapter. It states a general principle which can be applied to a large class of plans to determine whether they constitute employee benefit plans within the meaning of section 3(3) of the Act. Under section 4(a) of the Act, only employee benefit plans within the meaning of section 3(3) are subject to Title I.

(b) *Plans without employees.* For purposes of Title I of the Act and this chapter, the term "employee benefit plan" shall not include any plan, fund or program, other than an apprenticeship or other training program, under which no employees are participants covered under the plan, as defined in paragraph (d) of this section. For example, a so-called "Keogh" or "H.R. 10" plan under which only partners or only a sole proprietor are participants covered under the plan will not be covered under Title I. However, a Keogh plan under which one or more common law employees, in addition to the self-employed individuals, are participants covered under the plan, will be covered under Title I. Similarly, partnership buyout agreements described in section 736 of the Internal Revenue Code of 1954 will not be subject to Title I.

(c) *Employees.* For purposes of this section:

(1) An individual and his or her spouse shall not be deemed to be employees with respect to a trade or business, whether incorporated or unincorporated, which is wholly owned by the individual or by the individual and his or her spouse, and

(2) A partner in a partnership and his or her spouse shall not be deemed to be employees with respect to the partnership.

* * *

§ 2510.3-21. Definition of "Fiduciary."

(a), (b) [Reserved]

(c) *Investment Advice.* (1) A person shall be deemed to be rendering "investment advice" to an employee benefit plan, within the meaning of section 3(21)(A)(ii) of the Employee Retirement Income Security Act of 1974 (the Act) and this paragraph, only if:

(i) Such person renders advice to the plan as to the value of securities or other property, or makes recommendation as to the advisability of investing in, purchasing, or selling securities or other property; and

(ii) Such person either directly or indirectly (e.g., through or together with any affiliate)—

(A) Has discretionary authority or control, whether or not pursuant to agreement, arrangement or understanding, with respect to purchasing or selling securities or other property for the plan; or

(B) Renders any advice described in paragraph (c)(1)(i) of this section on a regular basis to the plan pursuant to a mutual agreement, arrangement or understanding, written or otherwise, between such person and the plan or a fiduciary with respect to the plan, that such services will serve as a primary basis for investment decisions with respect to plan assets, and that such person will render individualized investment advice to the plan based on the particular needs of the plan regarding such matters as, among other things, investment policies or strategy, overall portfolio composition, or diversification of plan investments.

(2) A person who is a fiduciary with respect to a plan by reason of rendering investment advice (as defined in paragraph (c)(1) of this section) for a fee or other compensation, direct or indirect, with respect to any moneys or other property of such plan, or having any authority or responsibility to do so, shall not be deemed to be a fiduciary regarding any assets of the plan with respect to which such person does not have any discretionary authority, discretionary control or discretionary responsibility, does not exercise any authority or control, does not render investment advice (as defined in paragraph (c)(1) of this section) for a fee or other compensation, and does not have any authority or responsibility to render such investment advice, provided that nothing in this paragraph shall be deemed to:

(i) Exempt such person from the provisions of section 405(a) of the Act concerning liability for fiduciary breaches by other fiduciaries with respect to any assets of the plan; or

(ii) Exclude such person from the definition of the term "party in interest" (as set forth in section 3(14)(B) of the Act) with respect to any assets of the plan.

(d) *Execution of securities transactions.* (1) A person who is a broker or dealer registered under the Securities Exchange Act of 1934, a reporting dealer who makes primary markets in securities of the United States Government or of an agency of the United States Government and reports daily to the Federal Reserve Bank of New York its positions with respect to such securities and borrowings thereon, or a bank supervised by the United States or a State, shall not be deemed to be a fiduciary, within the meaning of section 3(21)(A) of the Act, with respect to an employee benefit plan solely because such person executes transactions for the purchase or sale of securities on behalf of such plan in the ordinary course of its business as a broker, dealer, or bank, pursuant to instructions of a fiduciary with respect to such plan, if:

(i) Neither the fiduciary nor any affiliate of such fiduciary is such broker, dealer, or bank; and

(ii) The instructions specify (A) the security to be purchased or sold, (B) a price range within which such security is to be purchased or sold, or, if such security is issued by an open-end investment company registered under the Investment Company Act of 1940 (15 U.S.C. 80a-1, et seq.), a price which is determined in accordance with Rule 22c-1 under the Investment Company Act of 1940 (17 CFR 270.22c-1), (C) a time span during which such security may be purchased or sold (not to exceed five business days), and (D) the minimum or maximum quantity of such security which may be purchased or sold within such price range, or, in the case of a security issued by an open-end investment company registered under the Investment Company Act of 1940, the minimum or maximum quantity of such security which may be purchased or sold, or the value of such security in dollar amount which may be purchased or sold, at the price referred to in paragraph (d)(1)(ii)(B) of this section.

(2) A person who is a broker-dealer, reporting dealer, or bank which is a fiduciary with respect to an employee benefit plan solely by reason of the possession or exercise of discretionary authority or discretionary control in the management of the plan or the management or disposition of plan assets in connection with the execution of a transaction or transactions for the purchase or sale of securities on behalf of such plan which fails to comply with the provisions of paragraph (d)(1) of this section, shall not be deemed to be a fiduciary regarding any assets of the plan with respect to which such broker- dealer, reporting dealer or bank does not have any discretionary authority, discretionary control or discretionary responsibility, does not exercise any authority or control, does not render investment advice (as defined in paragraph (c)(1) of this section) for a fee or other compensation, and does not have any authority or responsibility to render such investment ad-

vice, provided that nothing in this paragraph shall be deemed to:

(i) Exempt such broker-dealer, reporting dealer, or bank from the provisions of section 405(a) of the Act concerning liability for fiduciary breaches by other fiduciaries with respect to any assets of the plan; or

(ii) Exclude such broker-dealer, reporting dealer, or bank from the definition, of the term "party in interest" (as set forth in section 3(14)(B) of the Act) with respect to any assets of the plan.

(c) *Affiliate and control.* (1) For purposes of paragraphs (c) and (d) of this section, an "affiliate" of a person shall include:

(i) Any person directly or indirectly, through one or more intermediaries, controlling, controlled by, or under common control with such person;

(ii) Any officer, director, partner, employee or relative (as defined is section 3(15) of the Act) of such person; and

(iii) Any corporation or partnership of which such person is an officer, director or partner.

(2) For purposes of this paragraph, the term "control" means the power to exercise a controlling influence over the management or policies of a person other than an individual.

§ 2530.206 Time and order of issuance of domestic relations orders.

(a) *Scope.* This section implements section 1001 of the Pension Protection Act of 2006 by clarifying certain timing issues with respect to domestic relations orders and qualified domestic relations orders under the Employee Retirement Income Security Act of 1974, as amended (ERISA), 29 U.S.C. 1001 et seq. The examples herein illustrate the application of this section in certain circumstances. This section also applies in circumstances not described in the examples.

(b) *Subsequent domestic relations orders.*

(1) Subject to paragraph (d)(1) of this section, a domestic relations order shall not fail to be treated as a qualified domestic relations order solely because the order is issued after, or revises, another domestic relations order or qualified domestic relations order.

(2) The rule described in paragraph (b)(1) of this section is illustrated by the following examples:

Example (1). Subsequent domestic relations order between the same parties. Participant and Spouse divorce, and the administrator of Participant's 401(k) plan receives a domestic relations order. The administrator determines that the order is a QDRO. The QDRO allocates a portion of Participant's benefits to Spouse as the alternate payee. Subsequently, before benefit payments have commenced, Participant and Spouse seek and receive a second domestic relations order. The second order reduces the portion of Participant's benefits that Spouse was to receive under the QDRO. The second order does not fail to be treated as a QDRO solely because the second order is issued after, and reduces the prior assignment contained in, the first order.

Example (2). Subsequent domestic relations order between different parties. Participant and Spouse divorce, and the administrator of Participant's 401(k) plan receives a domestic relations order. The administrator determines that the order is a QDRO. The QDRO allocates a portion of Participant's benefits to Spouse as the alternate payee. Participant marries Spouse 2, and then they divorce. Participant's 401(k) plan administrator subsequently receives a domestic relations order pertaining to Spouse 2. The order assigns to Spouse 2 a portion of Participant's 401(k) benefits not already allocated to Spouse 1. The second order does not fail to be a QDRO solely because the second order is issued after the plan administrator has determined that an earlier order pertaining to Spouse 1 is a QDRO.

(c) *Timing.*

(1) Subject to paragraph (d)(1) of this section, a domestic relations order shall not fail to

be treated as a qualified domestic relations order solely because of the time at which it is issued.

(2) The rule described in paragraph (c)(1) of this section is illustrated by the following examples:

Example (1). Orders issued after death. Participant and Spouse divorce, and the administrator of Participant's plan receives a domestic relations order, but the administrator finds the order deficient and determines that it is not a QDRO. Shortly thereafter, Participant dies while actively employed. A second domestic relations order correcting the defects in the first order is subsequently submitted to the plan. The second order does not fail to be treated as a QDRO solely because it is issued after the death of the Participant.

Example (2). Orders issued after divorce. Participant and Spouse divorce. As a result, Spouse no longer meets the definition of "surviving spouse" under the terms of the plan. Subsequently, the plan administrator receives a domestic relations order requiring that Spouse be treated as the Participant's surviving spouse for purposes of receiving a death benefit payable under the terms of the plan only to a participant's surviving spouse. The order does not fail to be treated as a QDRO solely because, at the time it is issued, Spouse no longer meets the definition of a "surviving spouse" under the terms of the plan.

Example (3). Orders issued after annuity starting date. Participant retires and commences benefit payments in the form of a straight life annuity, with respect to which Spouse waives the surviving spousal rights provided under the plan and section 205 of ERISA. Participant and Spouse divorce after Participant's annuity starting date and present the plan with a domestic relations order providing for Spouse, as alternate payee, to receive half of the benefit payments that are made to Participant after a specified future date. Pursuant to paragraph (c)(1) of this section, the order does not fail to be a QDRO solely because it is issued after the annuity starting date.

(d) *Requirements and protections.*

(1) Any domestic relations order described in this section shall be subject to the same requirements and protections that apply to qualified domestic relations orders under section 206(d)(3) of ERISA.

(2) The rule described in paragraph (d)(1) of this section is illustrated by the following examples:

Example (1). Type or form of benefit. Participant and Spouse divorce, and their divorce decree provides that the parties will prepare a domestic relations order assigning 50 percent of Participant's benefits under a 401(k) plan to Spouse to be paid in monthly installments over a ten-year period. Shortly thereafter, Participant dies while actively employed. A domestic relations order consistent with the decree is subsequently submitted to the 401(k) plan; however, the plan does not provide for ten-year installment payments of the type described in the order. Pursuant to paragraph (c)(1) of this section, the order does not fail to be treated as a QDRO solely because it is issued after the death of Participant, but the order would fail to be a QDRO under section 206(d)(3)(D)(i) and paragraph (d)(1) of this section because the order requires the plan to provide a type or form of benefit, or any option, not otherwise provided under the plan.

Example (2). Segregation of payable benefits. Participant and Spouse divorce, and the administrator of Participant's plan receives a domestic relations order under which Spouse would begin to receive benefits immediately if the order is determined to be a QDRO. The plan administrator separately accounts for the amounts covered by the domestic relations order as is required under section 206(d)(3)(H)(v) of ERISA. The plan administrator finds the order deficient and determines that it is not a QDRO. Subsequently, after the expiration of the segregation period pertaining to that order, the plan administrator receives a second domestic relations order relating to the same parties under which Spouse would begin to receive benefits immediately if the second order is determined to be a QDRO. Notwithstanding the expiration of the first segregation period, the amounts covered by the second order must be separately accounted for by the plan administrator for an 18-month period, in accordance with section 206(d)(3)(H) of ERISA and paragraph (d)(1) of this section.

Example (3). Previously assigned benefits. Participant and Spouse divorce, and the administrator of Participant's 401(k) plan receives a domestic relations order. The administrator determines that the order is a QDRO. The QDRO assigns a portion of Participant's benefits to Spouse as the alternate payee. Participant marries Spouse 2, and then they divorce. Participant's 401(k) plan administrator subsequently receives a domestic relations order pertaining to Spouse 2. The order assigns to Spouse 2 a portion of Participant's 401(k) benefits already assigned to Spouse 1. The second order does not fail to be treated as a QDRO solely because the second order is issued after the plan administrator has determined that an earlier order pertaining to Spouse 1 is a QDRO. The second order, however, would fail to be a QDRO under section 206(d)(3)(D)(iii) and paragraph (d)(1) of this section because it assigns all or a portion of Participant's benefits that are already assigned to Spouse 1 by the prior QDRO.

§ 2550.404a-1. Investment duties.

(a) *In general.* Section 404(a)(1)(B) of the Employee Retirement Income Security Act of 1974 (the Act) provides, in part, that a fiduciary shall discharge his duties with respect to a plan with the care, skill, prudence, and diligence under the circumstances then prevailing that a prudent man acting in a like capacity and familiar with such matters would use in the conduct of an enterprise of a like character and with like aims.

(b) *Investment duties.* (1) With regard to an investment or investment course of action taken by a fiduciary of an employee benefit plan pursuant to his investment duties, the requirements of section 404(a)(1)(B) of the Act set forth in subsection (a) of this section are satisfied if the fiduciary:

(i) Has given appropriate consideration to those facts and circumstances that, given the scope of such fiduciary's investment duties, the fiduciary knows or should know are relevant to the particular investment or investment course of action involved, including the role the investment or investment course of action plays in that portion of the plan's investment portfolio with respect to which the fiduciary has investment duties; and

(ii) Has acted accordingly.

(2) For purposes of paragraph (b)(1) of this section, "appropriate consideration" shall include, but is not necessarily limited to,

(i) A determination by the fiduciary that the particular investment or investment course of action is reasonably designed, as part of the portfolio (or, where applicable, that portion of the plan portfolio with respect to which the fiduciary has investment duties), to further the purposes of the plan, taking into consideration the risk of loss and the opportunity for gain (or other return) associated with the investment or investment course of action, and

(ii) Consideration of the following factors as they relate to such portion of the portfolio:

(A) The composition of the portfolio with regard to diversification;

(B) The liquidity and current return of the portfolio relative to the anticipated cash flow requirements of the plan; and

(C) The projected return of the portfolio relative to the funding objectives of the plan.

(3) An investment manager appointed, pursuant to the provisions of section 402(c)(3) of the Act, to manage all or part of the assets of a plan, may, for purposes of compliance with the provisions of paragraphs (b)(1) and (2) of this section, rely on, and act upon the basis of, information pertaining to the plan provided by or at the direction of the appointing fiduciary, if—

(i) Such information is provided for the stated purpose of assisting the manager in the performance of his investment duties, and

(ii) The manager does not know and has no reason to know that the information is incorrect.

(c) *Definitions*. For purposes of this section:

(1) The term "investment duties" means any duties imposed upon, or assumed or undertaken by, a person in connection with the investment of plan assets which make or will make such person a fiduciary of an employee benefit plan or which are performed by such person as a fiduciary of an employee benefit plan as defined in section 3(21)(A)(i) or (ii) of the Act.

(2) The term "investment course of action" means any series or program of investments or actions related to a fiduciary's performance of his investment duties.

(3) The term "plan" means an employee benefit plan to which title I of the Act applies.

§ 2550.404a-2. Safe harbor for automatic rollovers to individual retirement plans.

(a) *In general.* (1) Pursuant to section 657(c) of the Economic Growth and Tax Relief Reconciliation Act of 2001, Public Law 107–16, June 7, 2001, 115 Stat. 38, this section provides a safe harbor under which a fiduciary of an employee pension benefit plan subject to Title I of the Employee Retirement Income Security Act of 1974, as amended (the Act), 29 U.S.C. 1001 et seq., will be deemed to have satisfied his or her fiduciary duties under section 404(a) of the Act in connection with an automatic rollover of a mandatory distribution described in section 401(a)(31)(B) of the Internal Revenue Code of 1986, as amended (the Code). This section also provides a safe harbor for certain other mandatory distributions not described in section 401(a)(31)(B) of the Code.

(2) The standards set forth in this section apply solely for purposes of determining whether a fiduciary meets the requirements of this safe harbor. Such standards are not intended to be the exclusive means by which a fiduciary might satisfy his or her responsibilities under the Act with respect to rollovers of mandatory distributions described in paragraphs (c) and (d) of this section.

(b) *Safe harbor.* A fiduciary that meets the conditions of paragraph (c) or paragraph (d) of this section is deemed to have satisfied his or her duties under section 404(a) of the Act with respect to both the selection of an individual retirement plan provider and the investment of funds in connection with the rollover of mandatory distributions described in those paragraphs to an individual retirement plan, within the meaning of section 7701(a)(37) of the Code.

(c) *Conditions*. With respect to an automatic rollover of a mandatory distribution described in section 401(a)(31)(B) of the Code, a fiduciary shall qualify for the safe harbor described in paragraph (b) of this section if:

(1) The present value of the nonforfeitable accrued benefit, as determined under section 411(a)(11) of the Code, does not exceed the maximum amount under section 401(a)(31)(B) of the Code;

(2) The mandatory distribution is to an individual retirement plan within the meaning of section 7701(a)(37) of the Code;

(3) In connection with the distribution of rolled-over funds to an individual retirement plan, the fiduciary enters into a written agreement with an individual retirement plan provider that provides:

(i) The rolled-over funds shall be invested in an investment product designed to preserve principal and provide a reasonable rate of return, whether or not such return is guaranteed, consistent with liquidity;

(ii) For purposes of paragraph (c)(3)(i) of this section, the investment product selected for the rolled-over funds shall seek to maintain, over the term of the investment, the dollar value that is equal to the amount invested in the product by the individual retirement plan;

(iii) The investment product selected for the rolled-over funds shall be offered by a state or federally regulated financial institution, which shall be: A bank or savings association, the deposits of which are insured by the Federal Deposit Insurance Corporation; a credit union, the member accounts of which are insured within the meaning of section 101(7) of the Federal Credit Union Act; an insurance company, the products of which are protected by State guaranty associations; or an investment company registered under the Investment Company Act of 1940;

(iv) All fees and expenses attendant to an individual retirement plan, including investments of such plan, (e.g., establishment charges, maintenance fees, investment expenses, termination costs and surrender charges) shall not exceed the fees and expenses charged by the individual retirement plan provider for comparable individual retirement plans established for reasons other than the receipt of a rollover distribution subject to the provisions of section 401(a)(31)(B) of the Code; and

(v) The participant on whose behalf the fiduciary makes an automatic rollover shall have the right to enforce the terms of the contractual agreement establishing the individual retirement plan, with regard to his or her rolled-over funds, against the individual retirement plan provider.

(4) Participants have been furnished a summary plan description, or a summary of material modifications, that describes the plan's automatic rollover provisions effectuating the requirements of section 401(a)(31)(B) of the Code, including an explanation that the mandatory distribution will be invested in an investment product designed to preserve principal and provide a reasonable rate of return and liquidity, a statement indicating how fees and expenses attendant to the individual retirement plan will be allocated (i.e., the extent to which expenses will be borne by the account holder alone or shared with the distributing plan or plan sponsor), and the name, address and phone number of a plan contact (to the extent not otherwise provided in the summary plan description or summary of material modifications) for further information concerning the plan's automatic rollover provisions, the individual retirement plan provider and the fees and expenses attendant to the individual retirement plan; and

(5) Both the fiduciary's selection of an individual retirement plan and the investment of funds would not result in a prohibited transaction under section 406 of the Act, unless such actions are exempted from the prohibited transaction provisions by a prohibited transaction exemption issued pursuant to section 408(a) of the Act.

(d) *Mandatory distributions of $1,000 or less.* A fiduciary shall qualify for the protection afforded by the safe harbor described in paragraph (b) of this section with respect to a mandatory distribution of one thousand dollars ($1,000) or less described in section 411(a)(11) of the Code, provided there is no affirmative distribution election by the participant and the fiduciary makes a rollover distribution of such amount into an individual retirement plan on behalf of such participant in accordance with the conditions described in paragraph (c) of this section, without regard to the fact that such rollover is not described in section 401(a)(31)(B) of the Code.

(e) *Effective date.* This section shall be effective and shall apply to any rollover of a mandatory distribution made on or after March 28, 2005.

§ 2550.404c-1. ERISA section 404(c) plans.

(a) *In general.* (1) Section 404(c) of the Employee Retirement Income Security Act of 1974 (ERISA or the Act) provides that if a pension plan that provides for individual accounts permits a participant or beneficiary to exercise control over assets in his account and that participant or beneficiary in fact exercises control over assets in his account, then the participant or beneficiary shall not be deemed to be a fiduciary by reason of his exercise of control and no person who is otherwise a fiduciary shall be liable for any loss, or by reason of any breach, which results from such exercise of control. This section describes the kinds of plans that are "ERISA section 404(c) plans," the circumstances in which a participant or beneficiary is considered to have exercised independent control over the assets in his account as contemplated by section 404(c), and the consequences of a participant's or beneficiary's exercise of control.

(2) The standards set forth in this section are applicable solely for the purpose of determining whether a plan is an ERISA section 404(c) plan and whether a particular transaction engaged in by a participant or beneficiary of such plan is afforded relief by section 404(c). Such standards, therefore, are not intended to be applied in determining whether, or to what extent, a plan which does not meet the requirements for an ERISA section 404(c) plan or a fiduciary with respect to such a plan satisfies the fiduciary responsibility or other provisions of Title I of the Act.

(b) *ERISA section 404(c) plans.* (1) *In general.* An "ERISA section 404(c) Plan" is an individual account plan described in section 3(34) of the Act that:

(i) Provides an opportunity for a participant or beneficiary to exercise control over assets in his individual account (see paragraph (b)(2) of this section); and

(ii) Provides a participant or beneficiary an opportunity to choose, from a broad range of investment alternatives, the manner in which some or all of the assets in his account are invested (see paragraph (b)(3) of this section).

(2) *Opportunity to exercise control.* (i) A plan provides a participant or beneficiary an opportunity to exercise control over assets in his account only if:

(A) Under the terms of the plan, the participant or beneficiary has a reasonable opportunity to give investment instructions (in writing or otherwise, with opportunity to obtain written confirmation of such instructions) to an identified plan fiduciary who is obligated to comply with such instructions except as otherwise provided in paragraph (b)(2)(ii)(B) and (d)(2)(ii) of this section; and

(B) The participant or beneficiary is provided or has the opportunity to obtain sufficient information to make informed decisions with regard to investment alternatives available under the plan, and incidents of ownership appurtenant to such investments. For purposes of this subparagraph, a participant or beneficiary will not be considered to have sufficient investment information unless—

(1) The participant or beneficiary is provided by an identified plan fiduciary (or a person or persons designated by the plan fiduciary to act on his behalf):

(i) An explanation that the plan is intended to constitute a plan described in section 404(c) of the Employee Retirement Income Security Act, and title 29 of the Code of Federal Regulations Section 2550.440c-1, and that the fiduciaries of the plan may be relieved of liability for any losses which are the direct and necessary result of investment instructions given by such participant or beneficiary;

(ii) A description of the investment alternatives available under the plan and, with respect to each designated investment alternative, a general description of the investment objectives and risk and return characteristics of each such alternative, including information relating to the type and diversification of assets comprising the portfolio of the designed investment alternative;

(iii) Identification of any designated investment managers;

(iv) An explanation of the circumstances under which participants and beneficiaries may give investment instructions and explanation of any specified limitations on such instructions under the terms of the plan, including any restrictions on transfer to or from a designated investment alternative, and any restrictions on the exercise of voting, tender and similar rights appurtenant to a participant's or beneficiary's investment in an investment alternative;

(v) A description of any transaction fees and expenses which affect the participant's or beneficiary's account balance in connection with purchases or sales of interests in investment alternatives (e.g., commissions, sales load, deferred sales charges, redemption or exchange fees);

(vi) The name, address, and phone number of the plan fiduciary (and, if applicable, the person or persons designated by the plan fiduciary to act on his behalf) responsible for providing the information described in paragraph (b)(2)(i)(B)(2) upon request of a participant or beneficiary and a description of the information described in paragraph (b)(2)(i)(B)(2) which may be obtained on request;

(vii) In the case of plans which offer an investment alternative which is designed to permit a participant or beneficiary to directly or indirectly acquire or sell any employer security (employer security alternative), a description of the procedures established to provide for the confidentiality of information relating to the purchase, holding and sale of employer securities, and the exercise of voting, tender and similar rights, by participants and beneficiaries, and the name, address and phone number of the plan fiduciary responsible for monitoring compliance with the procedures (see paragraphs (d)(2)(ii)(E)(4)(vii), (viii) and (ix) of this section); and

(viii) In the case of an investment alternative which is subject to the Securities Act of 1933, and in which the participant or beneficiary has no assets invested, immediately following the participant's or beneficiary's initial investment, a copy of the most recent prospectus provided to the plan. This condition will be deemed satisfied if the participant or beneficiary has been provided with a copy of such most recent prospectus immediately prior to the participant's or beneficiary's initial investment in such alternative;

(ix) Subsequent to an investment in a investment alternative, any materials provided to the plan relating to the exercise of voting, tender or similar rights which are incidental to the holding in the account of the participant or beneficiary of an ownership interest in such alternative to the extent that such rights are passed through to participants and beneficiaries under the terms of the plan, as well as a description of or reference to plan provisions relating to the exercise of voting, tender or similar rights.

(2) The participants or beneficiary is provided by the identified plan fiduciary (or a person or persons designated by the plan fiduciary to act on his behalf), either directly or upon request, the following information, which shall be based on the latest information available to the plan:

(i) A description of the annual operating expenses of each designated investment alternative (e.g., investment management fees, administrative fees, transaction costs) which reduce the rate of return to participants and beneficiaries, and the aggregate amount of such expenses expressed as a percentage of average net assets of the designated investment alternative;

(ii) Copies of any prospectuses, financial statements and reports, and of any other materials relating to the investment alternatives available under the plan, to the extent such information is provided to the plan;

(iii) A list of the assets comprising the portfolio of each designated investment alternative which constitute plan assets within the meaning of 29 CFR 2510.3-101, the value of each such asset (or the proportion of the investment alternative which it comprises), and, with respect to each such asset which is a fixed rate investment contract issued by a bank, savings and loan association or insurance company, the name of the issuer of the contract, the term of the contract and the rate of return on the contract;

(iv) Information concerning the value of shares or units in designated investment alternatives available to participants and beneficiaries under the plan, as well as the past and current investment performance of such alternatives, determined, net of expenses, on a reasonable and consistent basis; and

(v) Information concerning the value of shares or units in designated investment alternatives held in the account of the participant or beneficiary.

(ii) A plan does not fail to provide an opportunity for a participant or beneficiary to exercise control over his individual account merely because it—

(A) Imposes charges for reasonable expenses. A plan may charge participants' and beneficiaries' accounts for the reasonable expenses of carrying out investment instructions, provided that procedures are established under the plan to periodically inform such participants and beneficiaries of actual expenses incurred with respect to their respective individual accounts;

(B) Permits a fiduciary to decline to implement investment instructions by participants and beneficiaries. A fiduciary may decline to implement participant and beneficiary instructions which are described at paragraph (d)(2)(ii) of this section, as well as instructions specified in the plan, including instructions—

(1) Which would result in a prohibited transaction described in ERISA section 406 or section 4975 of the Internal Revenue Code, and

(2) Which would generate income that would be taxable to the plan;

(C) Imposes reasonable restrictions on frequency of investment instructions. A plan may impose reasonable restrictions on the frequency with which participants and beneficiaries may give investment instructions. In no event, however, is such a restriction reasonable unless, with respect to each investment alternative made available by the plan, it permits participants and beneficiaries to give investment instructions with a frequency which is appropriate in light of the market volatility to which the investment alternative may reasonably be expected to be subject, provided that—

(1) At least three of the investment alternatives made available pursuant to the requirements of paragraph (b)(3)(i)(B) of this section, which constitute a broad range of investment alternatives, Permit participants and beneficiaries to give investment instructions no less frequently than once within any three month period; and

(2)(i) At least one of the investment alternatives meeting the requirements of paragraph (b)(2)(ii)(C)(1) of this section permits participants and beneficiaries to give investment instructions with regard to transfers into the investment alternative as frequently as participants and beneficiaries are permitted to give investment instructions with respect to any investment alternative made available by the plan which permits participants and beneficiaries to give investment instructions more frequently than once within any three month period; or

(ii) With respect to each investment alternative which permits participants and beneficiaries to give investment instructions more frequently than once within any three month period, participants and beneficiaries are permitted to direct their investments from such alternative into an income producing, low risk, liquid fund, subfund, or account as frequently as they are permitted to give investment instructions with respect to each such alternative and, with respect to such fund, subfund or account, participants and beneficiaries are permitted to direct investments from the fund, subfund or account to an investment alternative meeting the requirements of paragraph (b)(2)(ii)(C)(1) as frequently as they are permitted to give investment instructions with respect to that investment alternative; and

(3) With respect to transfers from an investment alternative which is designed to permit a participant or beneficiary to directly or indirectly acquire or sell any employer security (employer security alternative) either:

(i) All of the investment alternatives meeting the requirements of paragraph (b)(2)(ii)(C)(1) of this section must permit participants and beneficiaries to give investment instructions with regard to transfers into each of the investment alternatives as frequently as participants and beneficiaries are permitted to give investment instructions with respect to the employer security alternative; or

(ii) Participants and beneficiaries are permitted to direct their investments from each employer security alternative into an income producing, low risk, liquid fund, subfund, or account as frequently as they are permitted to give investment instructions with respect to such employer security alternative and, with respect to such fund, subfund, or account, participants and beneficiaries are permitted to direct investments from the fund, subfund or account to each investment alternative meeting the requirements of paragraph (b)(2)(ii)(C)(1) as frequently as they are permitted to give investment instructions with respect to each such investment alternative.

(iii) Paragraph (c) of this section describes the circumstances under which a participant or beneficiary will be considered to have exercised independent control with respect to a particular transaction.

(3) *Broad range of investment alternatives.* (i) A plan offers a broad range of investment alternatives only if the available investment alternatives are sufficient to provide the participant or beneficiary with a reasonable opportunity to:

(A) Materially affect the potential return on amounts in his individual account with respect to which he is permitted to exercise control and the degree of risk to which such amounts are subject;

(B) Choose from at least three investment alternatives:

(1) Each of which is diversified;

(2) Each of which has materially different risk and return characteristics;

(3) Which in the aggregate enable the participant or beneficiary by choosing among them to achieve a portfolio with aggregate risk and return characteristics at any point within the range normally appropriate for the participant or beneficiary; and

(4) Each of which when combined with investments in the other alternatives tends to minimize through diversification the overall risk of a participant's or beneficiary's portfolio;

(C) Diversify the investment of that portion of his individual account with respect to which he is permitted to exercise control so as to minimize the risk of large losses, taking into account the nature of the plan and the size of participants' or beneficiaries' accounts. In determining whether a plan provides the participant or beneficiary with a reasonable opportunity to diversify his investments, the nature of the investment alternatives offered by the plan and the size of the portion of the individual's account over which he is permitted to exercise control must be considered. Where such portion of the account of any participant or beneficiary is so limited in size that the opportunity to invest in look-through investment vehicles is the only prudent means to assure an opportunity to achieve appropriate diversification, a plan may satisfy the requirements of this paragraph only by offering look-through investment vehicles.

(ii) *Diversification and look-through investment vehicles.* Where look-through investment vehicles are available as investment alternatives to participants and beneficiaries, the underlying investments of the look-through investment vehicles shall be considered in determining whether the plan satisfies the requirements of subparagraphs (b)(3)(i)(B) and (b)(3)(i)(C).

(c) *Exercise of control.* (1) *In general.* (i) Sections 404(c)(1) and 404(c)(2) of the Act and paragraphs (a) and (d) of this section apply only with respect to a transaction where a participant or beneficiary has exercised independent control in fact with respect to the investment of assets in his individual account under an ERISA section 404(c) plan.

(ii) For purposes of sections 404(c)(1) and 4040(c)(2) of the Act and paragraphs (a) and (d) of this section, a participant or beneficiary will be deemed to have exercised control with respect to the exercise of voting, tender and similar rights appurtenant to the participant's or beneficiary's ownership interest in an investment alternative, provided that the participant's or beneficiary's investment in the investment alternative was itself the result of an exercise of control, the participant or beneficiary was provided a reasonable opportunity to give instruction with respect to such incidents of ownership, including the provision of the information described in paragraph (b)(2)(i)(B)(1)(ix) of this section, and the participant or beneficiary has not failed to exercise control by reason of the circumstances described in paragraph (c)(2) with respect to such incidents of ownership.

(2) *Independent control.* Whether a participant or beneficiary has exercised independent control in fact with respect to a transaction depends on the facts and circumstances of the particular case. However, a participant's or beneficiary's exercise of control is not independent in fact if:

(i) The participant or beneficiary is subjected to improper influence by a plan fiduciary or the plan sponsor with respect to the transaction;

(ii) A plan fiduciary has concealed material non-public facts regarding the investment from the participant or beneficiary, unless the disclosure of such information by the plan fiduciary to the participant or beneficiary would violate any provision of federal law or any provision of state law which is not preempted by the Act; or

(iii) The participant or beneficiary is legally incompetent and the responsible plan fiduciary accepts the instructions of the participant or beneficiary knowing him to be legally incompetent.

(3) *Transactions involving a fiduciary.* In the case of a sale, exchange or leasing of property (other than a transaction described in paragraph (d)(2)(ii)(E) of this section) between an ERISA section 404(c) plan and a plan fiduciary or an affiliate of such a fiduciary, or a loan to a plan fiduciary or an affiliate of such a fiduciary, the participant or beneficiary will not be deemed to have exercised independent control unless the transaction is fair and reasonable to him. For purposes of this paragraph (c)(3), a transaction will be deemed to be fair and reasonable to a participant or beneficiary if he pays no more than, or receives no less than, adequate consideration (as defined in section 3(18) of the Act) in connection with the transaction.

(4) *No obligation to advise.* A fiduciary has no obligation under part 4 of Title I of the Act to provide investment advice to a participant or beneficiary under an ERISA section 404(c) plan.

(d) *Effect of independent exercise of control—*

(1) *Participant or beneficiary not a fiduciary.* If a participant or beneficiary of an ERISA section 404(c) plan exercises independent control over assets in his individual account in the manner described in paragraph (c), then such participant or beneficiary is not a fiduciary of the plan by reason of such exercise of control.

(2) *Limitation on liability of plan fiduciaries.* (i) If a participant or beneficiary of an ERISA section 404(c) plan exercises independent control over assets in his individual account in the manner described in paragraph (c), then no other person who is a fiduciary with respect to such plan shall be liable for any loss, or with respect to any breach of part 4 of Title I of the Act, that is the direct and necessary result of that participant's or beneficiary's exercise of control.

(ii) Paragraph (d)(2)(i) does not apply with respect to any instruction, which if implemented—

(A) Would not be in accordance with the documents and instruments governing the plan insofar as such documents and instruments are consistent with the provisions of Title I of ERISA;

(B) Would cause a fiduciary to maintain the indicia of ownership of any assets of the plan outside the jurisdiction of the district courts of the United States other than as permitted by section 404(b) of the Act and 29 CFR 2550.404b-1;

(C) Would jeopardize the plan's tax qualified status under the Internal Revenue Code;

(D) Could result in a loss in excess of a participant's or beneficiary's account balance; or

(E) Would result in a direct or indirect:

(1) Sale, exchange, or lease of property between a plan sponsor or any affiliate of the sponsor and the plan except for the acquisition or disposition of any interest in a fund, subfund or portfolio managed by a plan sponsor or an affiliate of the sponsor, or the purchase or sale of any qualifying employer security (as defined in section 407(d)(5) of the Act) which meets the conditions of section 408(e) of ERISA and section (d)(2)(ii)(E)(4) below;

(2) Loan to a plan sponsor or any affiliate of the sponsor;

(3) Acquisition or sale of any employer real property (as defined in section 407(d)(2) of the Act); or

(4) Acquisition or sale of any employer security except to the extent that:

(*i*) Such securities are qualifying employer securities (as defined in section 407(d)(5) of the Act);

(*ii*) Such securities are stock or an equity interest in a publicly traded partnership (as defined in section 7704(b) of the Internal Revenue Code of 1986), but only if such partnership is an existing partnership as defined in section 10211(c)(2)(A) of the Revenue Act of 1987 (Public Law 100-203);

(*iii*) Such securities are publicly traded on a national exchange or other generally recognized market;

(*iv*) Such securities are traded with sufficient frequency and in sufficient volume to assure that participant and beneficiary directions to buy or sell the security may be acted upon promptly and efficiently;

(*v*) Information provided to shareholders of such securities is provided to participants and beneficiaries with accounts holding such securities;

(*vi*) Voting, tender and similar rights with respect to such securities are passed through to participants and beneficiaries with accounts holding such securities;

(*vii*) Information relating to the purchase, holding, and sale of securities, and the exercise of voting, tender and similar rights with respect to such securities by participants and beneficiaries, is maintained in accordance with procedures which are designed to safeguard the confidentiality of such information, except to the extent necessary to comply with Federal laws or state laws not preempted by the Act;

(*viii*) The plan designates a fiduciary who is responsible for ensuring that: The procedures required under subparagraph (d)(2)(ii)(E)(4) (vii) are sufficient to safeguard the confidentiality of the information described in that subparagraph, such procedures are being followed, and the independent fiduciary required by subparagraph (d)(2)(ii)(E)(4)(ix) is appointed; and

(*ix*) An independent fiduciary is appointed to carry out activities relating to any situations which the fiduciary designated by the plan for purposes of subparagraph (d)(2)(ii)(E)(4)(viii) determines involve a potential for undue employer influence upon participants and beneficiaries with regard to the direct or indirect exercise of shareholder rights. For purposes of this subparagraph, a fiduciary is not independent if the fiduciary is affiliated with any sponsor of the plan.

(iii) The individual investment decisions of an investment manager who is designated directly by a participant or beneficiary or who manages a look- through investment vehicle in which a participant or beneficiary has invested are not direct and necessary results of the designation of the investment manager or of investment in the look-through investment vehicle. However, this paragraph (d)(2)(iii) shall not be construed to result in liability under section 405 of ERISA with respect to a fiduciary (other than the investment manager) who would otherwise be relieved of liability by reason of section 404(c)(2) of the Act and paragraph (d) of this section.

(3) *Prohibited Transactions*. The relief provided by section 404(c) of the Act and this section applies only to the provisions of part 4 of title I of the Act. Therefore, nothing in this section relieves a disqualified person from the taxes imposed by sections 4975 (a) and (b) of the Internal Revenue Code with respect to the transactions prohibited by section 4975(c)(1) of the Code.

(e) *Definitions*. For purposes of this section:

(1) Look-through investment vehicle means:

(i) An investment company described in section 3(a) of the Investment Company Act of 1940, or a series investment company described in section 18(f) of the 1940 Act or any of the segregated portfolios of such company;

(ii) A common or collective trust fund or a pooled investment fund maintained by a bank or similar institution, a deposit in a bank or similar institution, or a fixed rate investment contract of a bank or similar institution;

(iii) A pooled separate account or a fixed rate investment contract of an insurance company qualified to do business in a State; or

(iv) Any entity whose assets include plan assets by reason of a plan's investment in the entity;

(2) Adequate consideration has the meaning given it in section 3(18) of the Act and in any regulations under this title;

(3) An affiliate of a person includes the following:

(i) Any person directly or indirectly controlling, controlled by, or under common control with the person;

(ii) Any officer, director, partner, employee, an employee of an affiliated employer, relative (as defined in section 3(15) of ERISA), brother, sister, or spouse of a brother or sister, of the person; and

(iii) Any corporation or partnership of which the person is an officer director or partner.

For purposes of this paragraph (e)(3), the term "control" means, with respect to a person other than an individual, the power to exercise a controlling influence over the management or policies of such person.

(4) A designated investment alternative is a specific investment identified by a plan fiduciary as an available investment alternative under the plan.

(f) *Examples*. The provisions of this section are illustrated by the following examples. Examples (5) through (11) assume that the participant has exercised independent control with respect to his individual account under an ERISA section 404(c) plan described in paragraph (b) and has not directed a transaction described in paragraph (d)(2)(ii).

(1) Plan A is an individual account plan described in section 3(34) of the Act. The plan states that a plan participant or beneficiary may direct the plan administrator to invest any portion of his individual account in a particular diversified equity fund managed by an entity which is not affiliated with the plan sponsor, or any other asset administratively feasible for the plan to hold. However, the plan provides that the plan administrator will not implement certain listed instructions for which plan fiduciaries would not be relieved of liability under section 404(c) (see paragraph (d)(2)(ii)). Plan participants and beneficiaries are permitted to give investment instructions during the first week of each month with respect to the equity fund and at any time with respect to other investments. The plan provides for the pass-through of voting, tender and similar rights incidental to the holding in the account of a participant or beneficiary of an ownership interest in the equity fund or any other investment alternative available under the plan. The plan administrator of plan A provides each participant and beneficiary with the information described in subparagraphs (*i*), (*ii*), (*iii*), (*iv*), (*v*), (*vi*) and (*vii*) of paragraph (b)(2)(i)(B)(*1*) upon their entry into the

plan, and provides updated information in the event of any material change in the information provided. Immediately following an investment by a participant or beneficiary in the equity fund, the plan administrator provides a copy of the most recent prospectus received from the fund to the investing participant or beneficiary. Immediately following any investment by a participant or beneficiary in any other investment alternative which is subject to the Securities Act of 1933, the plan administrator provides the participant or beneficiary with the most recent prospectus received from that investment alternative (see paragraph (b)(2)(i)(B)(*1*)(*viii*)). Finally, subsequent to any investment by a participant or beneficiary, the plan administrator forwards to the investing participant or beneficiary any materials provided to the plan relating to the exercise of voting, tender or similar rights attendant to ownership of an interest in such investment (see paragraph (b)(2)(i)(B)(*1*)(*ix*)). Upon request, the plan administrator provides each participant or beneficiary with copies of any prospectuses, financial statements and reports, and any other materials relating to the investment alternatives available under the plan which are received by the plan (see paragraph (b)(2)(i)(B)(*2*)(*ii*)). Also upon request, the plan administrator provides each participant and beneficiary with the other information required by paragraph (b)(2)(i)(B)(*2*) with respect to the equity fund, which is a designated investment alternative, including information concerning the latest available value of the participant's or beneficiary's interest in the equity fund (see paragraph (b)(2)(i)(B)(*2*)(*v*)). Plan A meets the requirements of paragraphs (b)(2)(i)(B)(*1*) and (*2*) of this section regarding the provision of investment information. Note: The regulation imposes no additional obligation on the administrator to furnish or make available materials relating to the companies in which the equity fund invests (e.g., prospectuses, proxies, etc.).

(2) Plan C is an individual account plan described in section 3(34) of the Act under which participants and beneficiaries may choose among three investment alternatives which otherwise meet the requirements of paragraph (b) of this section. The plan permits investment instruction with respect to each investment alternative only on the first 10 days of each calendar quarter, i.e. January 1-10, April 1-10, July 1-10 and October 1-10. Plan C satisfies the condition of paragraph (b)(2)(ii)(C)(*1*) that instruction be permitted not less frequently than once within any three month period, since there is not any three month period during which control could not be exercised.

(3) Assume the same facts as in paragraph (f)(2), except that investment instruction may only be given on January 1, April 4, July 1 and October 1. Plan C is not an ERISA section 404(c) plan because it does not satisfy the condition of paragraph (b)(2)(ii)(C)(*1*) that instruction be permitted not less frequently than once within any three month period. Under these facts, there is a three month period, e.g., January 2 through April 1, during which control could not be exercised by participants and beneficiaries.

(4) Plan D is an individual account plan described in section 3(34) of the Act under which participants and beneficiaries may choose among three diversified investment alternatives which constitute a broad range of investment alternatives. The plan also permits investment instruction with respect to an employer securities alternative but provides that a participant or beneficiary can invest no more than 25% of his account balance in this alternative. This restriction does not affect the availability of relief under section 404(c) inasmuch as it does not relate to the three diversified investment alternatives and, therefore, does not cause the plan to fail to provide an opportunity to choose from a broad range of investment alternatives.

(5) A participant, P, independently exercises control over assets in his individual account plan by directing a plan fiduciary, F, to invest 100% of his account balance in a single stock. P is not a fiduciary with respect to the plan by reason of his exercise of control and F will not be liable for any losses that necessarily result form P's investment instruction.

(6) Assume the same facts as in paragraph (f)(5), except that P directs F to purchase the stock from B, who is a party in interest with respect to the plan. Neither P nor F has engaged in a transaction prohibited under section 406 of the Act: P because he is not a fiduciary with respect to the plan by reason of his exercise of control and F because he is not liable for any breach of part 4 of Title I that is the direct and necessary consequence of P's exercise of control. However, a prohibited transaction under section 4975(c) of the Internal Revenue Code may have occurred, and, in the absence of an exemption, tax liability may be imposed pursuant to sections 495 (a) and (b) of the Code.

(7) Assume the same facts as in paragraph (f)(5), except that P does not specify that the stock be purchased from B, and F chooses to purchase the stock from B. In the absence of an exemption, F has engaged in a prohibited transaction described in 406(a) of ERISA because the decision to purchase the stock from B is not a direct or necessary result of P's exercise of control.

(8) Pursuant to the terms of the plan, plan fiduciary F designates three reputable investment managers whom participants may appoint to manage assets in their individual accounts. Participant P selects M, one of the designated managers, to manage the assets in his account. M prudently manages P's account for 6 months after which he incurs losses in managing the account through his imprudence. M has engaged in a breach of fiduciary duty because M's imprudent management of P's account is not a direct or necessary result of P's exercise of control (the choice of M as manager). F has no fiduciary liability for M's imprudence because he has no affirmative duty to advise P (see paragraph (c)(4)) and because F is relieved of co-fiduciary liability by reason of section 404(c)(2) (see paragraph (d)(2)(iii)). F does have a duty to monitor M's performance to determine the suitability of continuing M as an investment manager, however, and M's imprudence would be a factor which F must consider in periodically reevaluating its decision to designate M.

(9) Participant P instructs plan fiduciary F to appoint G as his investment manager pursuant to the terms of the plan which provide P total discretion in choosing an investment manager. Through G's imprudence, G incurs losses in managing P's account. G has engaged in a breach of fiduciary duty because G's imprudent management of P's account is not a direct or necessary result of P's exercise of control (the choice of G as manager). Plan fiduciary F has no fiduciary liability for G's imprudence because F has no obligation to advise P (see paragraph (c)(4)) and because F is relieved of co-fiduciary liability for G's actions by reason of section 404(c)(2) (see paragraph (d)(2)(iii)). In addition, F also has no duty to determine the suitability of G as an investment manager because the plan does not designate G as an investment manager.

(10) Participant P directs a plan fiduciary, F, a bank, to invest all of the assets in his individual account in a collective trust fund managed by F that is designed to be invested solely in a diversified portfolio of common stocks. Due to economic conditions, the value of the common stocks in the bank collective trust fund declines while the value of publicly-offered fixed income obligations remains relatively stable. F is not liable for any losses incurred by P solely because his individual account was not diversified to include fixed income obligations. Such losses are the direct result of P's exercise of control; moreover, under paragraph (c)(4) of this section F has no obligation to advise P regarding his investment decisions.

(11) Assume the same facts as in paragraph (f)(10) except that F, in managing the collective trust fund, invests the assets of the fund solely in a few highly speculative stocks. F is liable for losses resulting from its imprudent investment in the speculative stocks and for its failure to diversify the assets of the account. This conduct involves a separate breach of F's fiduciary duty that is not a direct or necessary result of P's exercise of control (see paragraph (d)(2)(iii)).

* * *

§ 2550.404c-5. Fiduciary relief for investments in qualified default investment alternatives.

(a) *In general.* (1) This section implements the fiduciary relief provided under section 404(c)(5) of the Employee Retirement Income Security Act of 1974, as amended (ERISA or the Act), 29 U.S.C. 1001 et seq., under which a participant or beneficiary in an individual account plan will be treated as exercising control over the assets in his or her account for purposes of ERISA section 404(c)(1) with respect to the amount of contributions and earnings that, in the absence of an investment election by the participant, are invested by the plan in accordance with this regulation. If a participant or beneficiary is treated as exercising control over the assets in his or her account in accordance with ERISA section 404(c)(1) no person who is otherwise a fiduciary shall be liable under part 4 of title I of ERISA for any loss or by reason of any breach which results from such participant's or beneficiary's exercise of control. Except as specifically provided in paragraph (c)(6) of this section, a plan need not meet the requirements for an ERISA section 404(c) plan under 29 CFR 2550.404c-1 in order for a plan fiduciary to obtain the relief under this section.

(2) The standards set forth in this section apply solely for purposes of determining whether a fiduciary meets the requirements of this regulation. Such standards are not intended to be the exclusive means by which a fiduciary might satisfy his or her responsibilities under the Act with respect to the investment of assets in the individual account of a participant or beneficiary.

(b) *Fiduciary relief.* (1) Except as provided in paragraphs (b)(2), (3), and (4) of this section, a fiduciary of an individual account plan that permits participants or beneficiaries to direct the investment of assets in their accounts and that meets the conditions of paragraph (c) of this section shall not be liable for any loss, or by reason of any breach under part 4 of title I of ERISA, that is the direct and necessary result of (i) investing all or part of a participant's or beneficiary's account in any qualified default investment alternative within the meaning of paragraph (e) of this section, or (ii) investment decisions made by the entity described in paragraph (e)(3) of this section in connection with the management of a qualified default investment alternative.

(2) Nothing in this section shall relieve a fiduciary from his or her duties under part 4 of title I of ERISA to prudently select and monitor any qualified default investment alternative under the plan or from any liability that results from a failure to satisfy these duties, including liability for any resulting losses.

(3) Nothing in this section shall relieve any fiduciary described in paragraph (e)(3)(i) of this section from its fiduciary duties under part 4 of title I of ERISA or from any liability that results from a failure to satisfy these duties, including liability for any resulting losses.

(4) Nothing in this section shall provide relief from the prohibited transaction provisions of section 406 of ERISA, or from any liability that results from a violation of those provisions, including liability for any resulting losses.

(c) *Conditions.* With respect to the investment of assets in the individual account of a participant or beneficiary, a fiduciary shall qualify for the relief described in paragraph (b)(1) of this section if:

(1) Assets are invested in a qualified default investment alternative within the meaning of paragraph (e) of this section;

(2) The participant or beneficiary on whose behalf the investment is made had the opportunity to direct the investment of the assets in his or her account but did not direct the investment of the assets;

(3) The participant or beneficiary on whose behalf an investment in a qualified default investment alternative may be made is furnished a notice that meets the requirements of paragraph (d) of this section:

(i)(A) At least 30 days in advance of the date of plan eligibility, or at least 30 days in advance of the date of any first investment in a qualified default investment alternative on behalf of a participant or beneficiary described in paragraph (c)(2) of this section; or

(B) On or before the date of plan eligibility provided the participant has the opportunity to make a permissible withdrawal (as determined under section 414(w) of the Internal Revenue Code of 1986, as amended (Code)); and

(ii) Within a reasonable period of time of at least 30 days in advance of each subsequent plan year;

(4) A fiduciary provides to a participant or beneficiary the material set forth in 29 CFR 2550.404c-1(b)(2)(i)(B)(1)(viii) and (ix) and 29 CFR 404c-1(b)(2)(i)(B)(2) relating to a participant's or beneficiary's investment in a qualified default investment alternative;

(5)(i) Any participant or beneficiary on whose behalf assets are invested in a qualified default investment alternative may transfer, in whole or in part, such assets to any other investment alternative available under the plan with a frequency consistent with that afforded to a participant or beneficiary who elected to invest in the qualified default investment alternative, but not less frequently than once within any three month period;

(ii)(A) Except as provided in paragraph (c)(5)(ii)(B) of this section, any transfer described in paragraph (c)(5)(i), or any permissible withdrawal as determined under section 414(w)(2) of the Code, by a participant or beneficiary of assets invested in a qualified default investment alternative, in whole or in part, resulting from the participant's or beneficiary's election to make such a transfer or withdrawal during the 90-day period beginning on the date of the participant's first elective contribution as determined under section 414(w)(2)(B) of the Code, or other first investment in a qualified default investment alternative on behalf of a participant or beneficiary described in paragraph (c)(2) of this section, shall not be subject to any restrictions, fees or expenses (including surrender charges, liquidation or exchange fees, redemption fees and similar expenses charged in connection with the liquidation of, or transfer from, the investment);

(B) Paragraph (c)(5)(ii)(A) of this section shall not apply to fees and expenses that are charged on an ongoing basis for the operation of the investment itself (such as investment management fees, distribution and/or service fees, "12b-1" fees, or legal, accounting, transfer agent and similar administrative expenses), and are not imposed, or do not vary, based on a participant's or beneficiary's decision to withdraw, sell or transfer assets out of the qualified default investment alternative; and

(iii) Following the end of the 90-day period described in paragraph (c)(5)(ii)(A) of this section, any transfer or permissible withdrawal described in this paragraph (c)(5) of this section shall not be subject to any restrictions, fees or expenses not otherwise applicable to a participant or beneficiary who elected to invest in that qualified default investment alternative; and

(6) The plan offers a "broad range of investment alternatives" within the meaning of 29 CFR 2550.404c-1(b)(3).

(d) *Notice.* The notice required by paragraph (c)(3) of this section shall be written in a manner calculated to be understood by the average plan participant and shall contain the following:

(1) A description of the circumstances under which assets in the individual account of a participant or beneficiary may be invested on behalf of the participant or beneficiary in a qualified default investment alternative; and, if applicable, an explanation of the circumstances under which elective contributions will be made on behalf of a participant, the percentage of such contributions, and the right of the participant to elect not to have such contributions made on the participant's behalf (or to elect to have such contributions made at a different percentage);

(2) An explanation of the right of participants and beneficiaries to direct the investment of assets in their individual accounts;

(3) A description of the qualified default investment alternative, including a description of the investment objectives, risk and return characteristics (if applicable), and fees and expenses attendant to the investment alternative;

(4) A description of the right of the participants and beneficiaries on whose behalf assets are invested in a qualified default investment alternative to direct the investment of those assets to any other investment alternative under the plan, including a description of any applicable restrictions, fees or expenses in connection with such transfer; and

(5) An explanation of where the participants and beneficiaries can obtain investment information concerning the other investment alternatives available under the plan.

(e) *Qualified default investment alternative*. For purposes of this section, a qualified default investment alternative means an investment alternative available to participants and beneficiaries that:

(1)(i) Does not hold or permit the acquisition of employer securities, except as provided in paragraph (ii).

(ii) Paragraph (e)(1)(i) of this section shall not apply to: (A) Employer securities held or acquired by an investment company registered under the Investment Company Act of 1940 or a similar pooled investment vehicle regulated and subject to periodic examination by a State or Federal agency and with respect to which investment in such securities is made in accordance with the stated investment objectives of the investment vehicle and independent of the plan sponsor or an affiliate thereof; or (B) with respect to a qualified default investment alternative described in paragraph (e)(4)(iii) of this section, employer securities acquired as a matching contribution from the employer/plan sponsor, or employer securities acquired prior to management by the investment management service to the extent the investment management service has discretionary authority over the disposition of such employer securities;

(2) Satisfies the requirements of paragraph (c)(5) of this section regarding the ability of a participant or beneficiary to transfer, in whole or in part, his or her investment from the qualified default investment alternative to any other investment alternative available under the plan;

(3) Is:

(i) Managed by: (A) an investment manager, within the meaning of section 3(38) of the Act; (B) a trustee of the plan that meets the requirements of section 3(38)(A), (B) and (C) of the Act; or (C) the plan sponsor, or a committee comprised primarily of employees of the plan sponsor, which is a named fiduciary within the meaning of section 402(a)(2) of the Act;

(ii) An investment company registered under the Investment Company Act of 1940; or

(iii) An investment product or fund described in paragraph (e)(4)(iv) or (v) of this section; and

(4) Constitutes one of the following:

(i) An investment fund product or model portfolio that applies generally accepted investment theories, is diversified so as to minimize the risk of large losses and that is designed to provide varying degrees of long-term appreciation and capital preservation through a mix of equity and fixed income exposures based on the participant's age, target retirement date (such as normal retirement age under the plan) or life expectancy. Such products and portfolios change their asset allocations and associated risk levels over time with the objective of becoming more conservative (i.e., decreasing risk of losses) with increasing age. For purposes of this paragraph (e)(4)(i), asset allocation decisions for such products and portfolios are not required to take into account risk tolerances, investments or other preferences of an individual participant. An example of such a fund or portfolio may be a "life-cycle" or "targeted-retirement-date" fund or account.

(ii) An investment fund product or model portfolio that applies generally accepted investment theories, is diversified so as to minimize the risk of large losses and that is designed to provide long-term appreciation and capital preservation through a mix of equity and fixed income exposures consistent with a target level of risk appropriate for participants of the plan as a whole. For purposes of this paragraph (e)(4)(ii), asset allocation decisions for such products and portfolios are not required to take into account the age, risk tolerances, investments or other preferences of an individual participant. An example of such a fund or portfolio may be a "balanced" fund.

(iii) An investment management service with respect to which a fiduciary, within the meaning of paragraph (e)(3)(i) of this section, applying generally accepted investment theories, allocates the assets of a participant's individual account to achieve varying degrees of long-term appreciation and capital preservation through a mix of equity and fixed income exposures, offered through investment alternatives available under the plan, based on the participant's age, target retirement date (such as normal retirement age under the plan) or life expectancy. Such portfolios are diversified so as to minimize the risk of large losses and change their asset allocations and associated risk levels for an individual account over time with the objective of becoming more conservative (i.e., decreasing risk of losses) with increasing age. For purposes of this paragraph (e)(4)(iii), asset allocation decisions are not required to take into account risk tolerances, investments or other preferences of an individual participant. An example of such a service may be a "managed account."

(iv)(A) Subject to paragraph (e)(4)(iv)(B) of this section, an investment product or fund designed to preserve principal and provide a reasonable rate of return, whether or not such return is guaranteed, consistent with liquidity. Such investment product shall for purposes of this paragraph (e)(4)(iv):

(1) Seek to maintain, over the term of the investment, the dollar value that is equal to the amount invested in the product; and

(2) Be offered by a State or federally regulated financial institution.

(B) An investment product described in this paragraph (e)(4)(iv) shall constitute a qualified default investment alternative for purposes of paragraph (e) of this section for not more than 120 days after the date of the participant's first elective contribution (as determined under section 414(w)(2)(B) of the Code).

(v)(A) Subject to paragraph (e)(4)(v)(B) of this section, an investment product or fund designed to preserve principal; provide a rate of return generally consistent with that earned on intermediate investment grade bonds; and provide liquidity for withdrawals by participants and beneficiaries, including transfers to other investment alternatives. Such investment product or fund shall, for purposes of this paragraph (e)(4)(v), meet the following requirements:

(1) There are no fees or surrender charges imposed in connection with withdrawals initiated by a participant or beneficiary; and

(2) Such investment product or fund invests primarily in investment products that are backed by State or federally regulated financial institutions.

(B) An investment product or fund described in this paragraph (c)(4)(v) shall constitute a qualified default investment alternative for purposes of paragraph (e) of this section solely for purposes of assets invested in such product or fund before December 24, 2007.

(vi) An investment fund product or model portfolio that otherwise meets the requirements of this section shall not fail to constitute a product or portfolio for purposes of paragraph (e)(4)(i) or (ii) of this section solely because the product or portfolio is offered through variable annuity or similar contracts or through common or collective trust funds or pooled investment funds and without regard to whether such contracts or funds provide annuity purchase rights, investment guarantees, death benefit guarantees or other features ancillary to the investment fund product or model portfolio.

(f) *Preemption of State laws.*

(1) Section 514(e)(1) of the Act provides that title I of the Act supersedes any State law that would directly or indirectly prohibit or restrict the inclusion in any plan of an automatic contribution arrangement. For purposes of section 514(e) of the Act and this paragraph (f), an automatic contribution arrangement is an arrangement (or the provisions of a plan) under which:

(i) A participant may elect to have the plan sponsor make payments as contributions under the plan on his or her behalf or receive such payments directly in cash;

(ii) A participant is treated as having elected to have the plan sponsor make such contributions in an amount equal to a uniform percentage of compensation provided under the plan until the participant specifically elects not to have such contributions made (or specifically elects to have such contributions made at a different percentage); and

(iii) Contributions are invested in accordance with paragraphs (a) through (e) of this section.

(2) A State law that would directly or indirectly prohibit or restrict the inclusion in any pension plan of an automatic contribution arrangement is superseded as to any pension plan, regardless of whether such plan includes an automatic contribution arrangement as defined in paragraph (f)(1) of this section.

(3) The administrator of an automatic contribution arrangement within the meaning of paragraph (f)(1) of this section shall be considered to have satisfied the notice requirements of section 514(e)(3) of the Act if notices are furnished in accordance with paragraphs (c)(3) and (d) of this section.

(4) Nothing in this paragraph (f) precludes a pension plan from including an automatic contribution arrangement that does not meet the conditions of paragraphs (a) through (e) of this section.

§ 2550.408b-1. General statutory exemption for loans to plan participants and beneficiaries who are parties in interest with respect to the plan.

* * *

(f) *Adequate Security.* (1) A loan will be considered to be adequately secured if the security posted for such loan is something in addition to and supporting a promise to pay, which is so pledged to the plan that it may be sold, foreclosed upon, or otherwise disposed of upon default of repayment of the loan, the value and liquidity of which security is such that it may reasonably be anticipated that loss of principal or interest will not result from the loan. The adequacy of such security will be determined in light of the type and amount of security which would be required in the case of an otherwise identical transaction in a normal commercial setting between unrelated parties on arm's-length terms. A participant's vested accrued benefit under a plan may be used as security for a participant loan to the extent of the plan's ability to satisfy the participant's outstanding obligation in the event of default.

(2) For purposes of this paragraph, (i) no more than 50% of the present value of a participant's vested accrued benefit may be considered by a plan as security for the outstanding balance of all plan loans made to that participant; (ii) a plan will be in compliance with paragraph (f)(2)(i) of this section if, with respect to any participant, it meets the provisions of paragraph (f)(2)(i) of this section immediately after the origination of each participant loan secured in whole or in part by that participant's vested accrued benefit; and (iii) any loan secured in whole or in part by a portion of a participant's vested accrued benefit must also meet the requirements of paragraph (f)(1) of this section.